# TRAVELLERS' INDIA
## An Anthology

'Native Travelling in India'. *Illustrated London News*, 30 Nov. 1872

# TRAVELLERS' INDIA
## An Anthology

Chosen and edited by

H. K. KAUL

DELHI

OXFORD UNIVERSITY PRESS

BOMBAY CALCUTTA MADRAS

1979

*Oxford University Press*

OXFORD  LONDON  GLASGOW
NEW YORK  TORONTO  MELBOURNE  WELLINGTON
NAIROBI  DAR ES SALAAM  CAPE TOWN
KUALA LUMPUR  SINGAPORE  HONG KONG  TOKYO
DELHI  BOMBAY  CALCUTTA  MADRAS  KARACHI

Filmset by Tej Press, New Delhi 110002
Printed by Rajbandhu Industrial Co. New Delhi 1100027
and published by R. Dayal, Oxford University Press
2/11 Ansari Road, Daryaganj, New Delhi 110002

# Preface

This anthology deals with published travel accounts from ancient times to the early twentieth-century. Much travel literature has been produced during the last 2500 years in almost all the major languages of the world. Much has also been published, but a great deal still remains inaccessible to an English-reading public, thanks to the lack of translations. As a result, considerable material is still stacked in manuscript form in various archives and libraries in different parts of the world. However, no doubt because of their special association with India, the accounts of English writers and travellers far outnumber those from any other area and are comparatively easily available to readers of the language.

This volume is based on the compiler's judgement of the importance and liveliness of passages, and, in some cases, on the criticisms a traveller made of India in his travel account. Within the limitations of space, an effort has also been made to give a comprehensive and detailed picture of India from as many travellers as possible. As a result, some very worthwhile accounts have had to be left out of this selection. However, the compiler hopes to fill such a gap in separate volumes which will deal more specifically with themes contained in each chapter of this book.

I am grateful to the librarians of the National Archives of India, Central Secretariat Library, Archaeological Survey of India and Hardinge Public Library for providing access to travel collections in their libraries. The British Council's 'India Collection' housed at the India International Centre has been a great source of help. I should like to thank my friend J. L. Ferreira, whose suggestions were of great help. My thanks are due to Ellen Vollebaek, S.A.I. Tirmizi, Hira Kapasi, Premilla Dixit, J. C. Reignier, Nadia Bogoslovskay and G. Manica for their useful suggestions. Lastly, I should thank my wife, Kamal, and my daughter, Manu, for allowing me to devote evenings and holidays over a number of years to the preparation of this book.

H. K. Kaul

# Contents

CONTENTS ix

# Plates

# Introduction

The home of an ancient civilization, India has been much written of until recently as the land of luxury and exotic beauty, of pearls and jewels, of the banian and the palm, of mystic religions and the centre of the choicest condiments. It has had a fluourishing image overseas from times immemorial, even with the remotest nations of the world. This image did not grow out of deliberate self-promotion, nor has India usually wished to expand her frontiers beyond the lofty Himalayas or beyond its coastal boundaries. Although splintered and welded from time to time by political upheavals, the subcontinent's overall geographical dimensions have remained mostly unchanged in historical times.

India's classical image was established by travellers from outside—those remarkable people who ventured to remote lands in the garb of merchants, ambassadors, conquerors, rulers, chaplains, pioneers, administrators, soldiers, artists, writers, poets, seekers of philosophical or religious teachings, or missionaries—many conveyed back impressions to their countrymen through lively tales, anecdotes and travel journals. These travellers came from far and near. They were from China, Russia, Persia, the Arab countries, Turkey, the Slavic countries, Italy, Tibet, Germany, Holland, France, Portugal, England, America, and many other lands.

## Ancient travellers

Apart from the prehistoric movements of tribes, the earliest documented accounts of travel concerning India are traced back to 975 B.C. when the Phoenicians imported Indian products. In order to decorate the palaces and the temples of King Solomon, Hiram, the king of Tyre, sent his fleet from Ezion Geber, at the head of the Gulf of Akaba in the Red Sea, to obtain 'ivory, apes and peacocks' from the port of Ophir; these are considered to have been Indian products. Besides Indian products, Indian philosophy and religion have been of interest to travellers throughout the ages. There appears to have been close contact between Indian and Greek philosophers, and through their respective centres, the philosophies and the religions of the East spread in all directions. The credit for the outflow must go to travellers. It is said that Pythagoras (c. 580 B.C.) and Histaspis, the father of Darius the Persian king, visited India and studied Indian philosphy.The Greek historian Herodotus (489-425 B.C.), wrote about the dress of Indians, their implements of warfare and the various products of the area. Another Greek chronicler, Ctesias (c. 416-398 B.C.), was a physician at the court of the Persian emperor Darius I and was therefore well placed to collect all the known facts about India. He wrote *Persica*, a history of Persia from Persian sources, and his account confirms and reinforces Herodotus' record of Indian merchandise, merchants and envoys, thus indicating a regular movement of travellers on land and by sea routes.

The first actual account by a traveller is that by Scylax of Caryanda, the Greek historian and geographer of the sixth century B.C. who was sent by Darius I, the King of Persia, to explore the course of the Indus. He sailed down it to the sea and westward through the Indian Ocean to the Red Sea. Next, Nearchus, the Macedonian officer who accompanied Alexander in 326 B.C., recorded events when Alexander invaded India. Nearchus commanded the fleet in his journey from the mouth of the Indus to the Persian Gulf. The accounts of his voyage from the Indus to the Euphrates were collected by Arrian, the Greek historian of the second century A.D. The second book of the journal deals with the geography of the Punjab, the wealth and population of the area, besides other details of the journey to the delta of the Indus.

Alexander travelled along the Kabul river through the Kuner and Swat valleys. Besides Nearchus, Onesicritus, the master pilot of Nearchus, Aristobulus, a geographer, and Kleitarchus accompanied Alexander. Onesicritus' account contained much exaggeration, but that of Aristobulus was used by Arrian. Arrian probably found the account of Kleitarchus unreliable, perhaps because it was written when he was over eighty years of age.

In 302 B.C. arrived Megasthenese, the Greek ambassador sent by Seleucus to the court of Chandragupta Maurya at Pataliputra. He wrote after travelling from north India to Pataliputra and his is the first dated account of the times. During that period India had a brisk sea-trade with the Persian Gulf ports of Mesopotamia and the Red

Sea ports of Egypt. One of the main trade routes was the caravan route from Taxila to Balkh. Slightly later, Ashoka, the grandson of Chandragupta, dispatched missionaries to Greece and Egypt to spread Buddhism. Sponsored by Ashoka, monks also carried Buddhism to Sri Lanka, Southeast Asia, China, Japan, Korea, Tibet and Mongolia, resulting in an increased exchange of travellers with those countries, so much so that later rulers had to keep special watch on the movements of foreigners.[1] But Megasthenese had a special status and managed to investigate the customs of the day closely.

From 302 B.C. to A.D. 535 no important travel account appeared, although secondary historical accounts did. The Greek ruler of Egypt, Ptolemy Philadelphus (285-247 B.C. ) sent Dionysius to the court of the Maurya King, Bindusara, as his envoy. As a result of the frequent visits of Greeks from Egypt in the third century B.C., Greek names for certain items of common use are found to resemble their equivalents in Tamil. We have already mentioned that Arrian, Alexander's historian, based his accounts on the travels of Nearchus and provided useful information. Claudius Ptolemaeus, an Alexandrian astronomer, mathematician and geographer, produced a map of India, which was later published in 1475.

By the beginning of the Christian era, Jews and Christians had started landing on the Indian shores. Some scholars believe that the influx of Christians might have begun around A.D. 47 when Hippalus, a sea captain discovered the south-west monsoon. St. Thomas is reputed to have preached Christianity in India from A.D. 21-52. Around A.D. 68 a number of Jews, apparently under the threat of Roman persecution, seem to have reached the South and settled in Malabar. After the destruction of Jerusalem in A.D. 70 Jewish merchants sailed towards the Indian Ocean and settled along the Malabar coast. Pliny (A.D. 23–79) has observed that the demand in Rome for pepper and ginger from India was such that they were bought by weight, like gold and silver. Large sums were spent by the Roman Empire for the purchase of oriental products.

Some eight centuries after Megasthanese an important travel account was that of Indicoplentes, a merchant who later became a Christian monk. He was in western India and Sri Lanka from A.D. 535 to A.D. 547 and wrote *Topographia Christiana*. This contains valuable information on India's trade relations with Sri Lanka and

[1] R. K. Mookerji's, *Indian Shipping*. Allahabad: Kitab Mahal, 1962, pp. 78-9.

countries in touch with its southern coasts. The Tamils were famous for their trade in pepper, pearls and beryls, which attracted travellers from east and west.

From the first century B.C., the Kushans, a section of the Yueh-chi tribe who had settled in Bactria, started making raids into India, and later established a vast empire in the country. They were followed by the Huns from Central Asia who invaded India a number of times in the fifth century A.D. until A.D. 500 when Toramana, their leader, established himself as an independent ruler in Malwa.

It was during Kushan times that Indian missionaries developed ties with China, but the maritime contacts of China with India date from about 680 B.C.,[1] when sea traders of the Indian Ocean, mainly Hindus, moved eastward selling Indian products such as rubies, pearls, sugar, etc. They were pushed back by the gradual advance of the Chinese, which made many Indians settle in Cambodia and other eastern countries and islands. This resulted in the establishing of Indian colonies in Pegu, Cambodia, Java, Sumatra and Borneo and trading settlements in southern China and the Malayan peninsula.

The first important Chinese traveller was the Buddhist priest Fah-Hien. He started his journey by land to India in A.D. 399 via the south of the Gobi Desert and Yarkand. Entering India through the Indus valley he spent about ten years (A.D. 401?-412?) in the area during the reign of Chandragupta II. He travelled all over northern India and was in Pataliputra for about three years. Fa-Hien's main interest was the study of Buddhism, which he fulfilled at Pataliputra, but he described many cities and rulers and other details in his account.

In ancient times maritime traders faced difficulties in landing on Indian shores, as the eastern coast was harbourless from Cape Comorin to Balasore and dangerous serf had to be contended with. The western coasts were cut off from the interior by the forest-clad barriers of the Western Ghats. With the rapid development of shipping and India's increasing maritime relations with the east and the west, the coastlines were greatly improved for trade.

## Land routes

Land routes to India covered the north-eastern and north-

[1] G. Phillips, in *Journal of the Royal Asiatic Society*, 1895, p. 525.

western boundaries of the subcontinent. Iran, Afghanistan, Russia, Tibet, China and Burma were the areas through which travellers passed before arriving. To the north-east, travellers coming from China could take numerous routes. Starting from Burma, they could cross northern Burma and reach Assam. To do so three routes could be used. From upper Burma through the Patkoi range and its passes they would cross into the Brahmaputra valley and Assam; from the Chindwin valley they could reach Manipur; and through the Irrawadi valley they could reach the Arrakans. From Tibet they could cross into Sikkim through passes such as the Chorten Nyima La, Kangra La, and Gora La, or they could cross into western Nepal via the Kagmara Pass. The Jesuit Fathers, Johann Grueber and Albert d' Orville journeyed from Lhasa to Kathmandu on their way from China: leaving Peking in April 1661, they reached Kathmandu in March 1662. Again, travellers coming through Tibet could cross the Lipu Lekh Pass and reach the Kumaon and Garhwal areas; via the Nela Pass they could reach Gangotri and via the Mana and Niti Passes they could reach Badrinath. Also from Tibet, the Lahul and Spiti area could be reached through the Baralacha Pass, and Manali and Kulu through the Kanzan, Rohtang and Pin Parbati Passes. In the extreme north, travellers from Tibet could reach Leh through the Khardunga La and Karakoram Passes. These north-eastern routes were frequently used to diffuse Buddhism and Buddhist art from India into Central Asia, China and the eastern lands, and are historic trade-routes.

The routes of the north-west have remained alive for traders, adventurers and invaders from ancient times. The main routes on this side were again through numerous passes and valleys: travellers crossing northern Iran and the Oxus region would proceed to Kabul and through the Khyber Pass to the Indus. Those crossing central and south Iran would go to Kandhar, then to the extreme southerly regions of the Indus or Makran and then to the Indus delta. Besides these, many other Passes were used to cross into India, such as the Dorah, Shandur, Karambar, Chillinji, Mintaka and Mustang Passes. An important and frequently used ancient route was via the Hindu Kush, south-east of ancient Bactria, following the northerly line of the Kabul river to Charsada, a historic town north-east of Peshawar. Other important routes were through the Kurram Valley, the Peiwar Pass, the Tochi Valley, the Gumal Valley, Kalat, Las **Bela** and the Zhob Valley. From Quetta, a south-eastern route entered the plains of Sibi and a western camel route entered Kirman and southern and western Iran. In 1857 Adolphe Schlagentweit started from Sultanpur in Kulu for Yarkand and Kashgar by the Chhangchhinmo Pass over the Karakoram range and Aksai Chin. Caravan routes operated from Shikarpur to Kandahar through the Bolan Pass and from Dera Ismail Khan to Ghazni via the Ghuleri Pass, and goods were also exported through the Abkhana and Tatra Passes to Afghanistan and Turkestan.

During the closing centuries of the first millenium B.C. the connection between India and West Asia, Africa, Central Asia, and East Europe was mostly through overland north-western routes. Invasions, commerce and human migration occurred via the Iranian plateau and the Oxus valley through these routes; and well known travellers, like the Chinese monk Fah-Hien came to India via Yarkand and the Indus, and Hiuen Tsiang via the Hindu Kush.

## Sea routes

The Indian Ocean (known to Greeks as the Erythraean Sea) naturally provided routes to India. The route through the Persian Gulf and Arabian Sea is probably the most ancient and the maritime commerce of the Indus Valley civilization was likely to have been linked with West Asia through this route. A later sea-route connecting India with South Arabia at the junction of the Red Sea and the Arabian Sea seems to have been opened up in c. 1000 B.C., when South Arabians — Sabaens or Himgarites — founded cities in Southern Hijaz and Hadramaut. In the seventh century B.C. the Phoenicians seems to have been the first Europeans to explore the Indian Ocean and Herodotus reports that Necho, an Egyptian monarch who flourished about 610 B.C. sent some vessels manned by Phoenicians into the Indian Ocean through the Persian Gulf. Again, in the sixth century B.C., Hanno, a Phoenician admiral of Carthage sailed to India. Nearchus, whose voyages were reported by the Greek historian Arrian, sailed from the Indus to the mouth of the Tigris and Euphrates with the help of the monsoon winds. It was Hippalus the Egyptian navigator who observed the regularity of the monsoon in A.D. 47 and used this knowledge to sail into the Indian Ocean, avoiding the attacks of pirates along the coasts. The Arabs had been making voyages along the Indian Ocean from ancient times, but after the ninth century A.D. these became frequent. The merchandise from Malabar and Cambay was first conveyed to Ormus on the Persian Gulf and then transported to Bassora on the Euphrates. From Bassora it sailed up the Tigris to Baghdad and then to Antioch and Licia, from where it was distributed to other countries. From the two ports on the Egyptian coast, Berenica and Myos Hormos, ships sailed to India along the coasts of Arabia and Persia. Strabo, Alexander's contemporary, describes seeing 120 ships sailing from Myos Hormos to India.[1]

In 1486 the Portuguese discovered the route through the Cape of Good Hope and Vasco da Gama established it when he sailed from Lisbon on 8 July 1497 and arrived at Calicut on 19 May 1498. With this development a new interest grew for Indian curiosities and commodities in European markets. The opening of the Suez Canal some four centuries later gradually replaced the Cape route, but before that a journey had to be performed by caravan from Alexandria to the Isthmus of Suez in order to reach the Arabian Sea from Europe.

To the east of the Indian Ocean, travellers from Austronesia, the Pacific Islands, Indonesia, China, Indo-China, Java, Sumatra and other small and big islands undertook major voyages at great personal risk either for commerce or in search of a better home. One important route, sometimes known as the 'Outrigger route', was used from Tahiti and other islands: people would move westward across the equitorial Pacific and reach the Indian Ocean south of Indonesia via the Coral Sea or the northern coasts of New Guinea. From there they would reach the Nicobars and then the Coromandel Coast, or Ceylon or Madagascar. The next route into the Indian Ocean was through the Malacca Straits. Being safer and nearer India, this route was much used for trade between the Austronesian countries and India. There seems to have been constant contact between Indian merchants and those of Insular Asia; Indians introduced not only Buddhism and Hinduism to Insular Asia, but also the methods of irrigation, new strains of rice, etc. and many settled in these islands. In return, travellers from the Pacific Islands and Insular Asia emigrated to India. Being from coastal and riverine areas they settled mostly on islands and the coasts of India. Their movement was in fact helped by different types of ships produced in India and elsewhere. Chinese ships, probably the largest in ancient and medieval times, had made voyages beyond their seas from Sung

[1] Mookerji, op. cit., p. 84

times (*c.* fifth century A.D.). They moved through the Indian Ocean up to the Persian Gulf and the Red Sea and maintained strong trade links until the Arabs, and later the Europeans, dominated maritime trade with India.

Whether they came by sea or overland routes, travellers had to face a number of hardships. On the overland routes dacoity and murder were common and, moreover, travelling on horses and camels was cumbersome. The hardships of travel by sea were equally great. With fears of Indian food, shopkeepers, dacoits and servants, Europeans travelling by sea after Vasco da Gama discovered the Cape route were kept both alert and biased. Their fears would haunt them along the journey. Hurricanes, gales, winds and months of travel introduced sea sickness which reduced some to skeletons. But, whatever the difficulties and perhaps because of them, the prospect of nearing the destination was greeted with untold relief. In his preliminary discourse to the Asiatic Society of Bengal Sir William Jones[1] described this pleasure:

When I was at sea last August on my voyage to this country which I had long and ardently desired to visit, I found one evening, on inspecting the observations of the day, that India lay before us, and Persia on our left; whilst a breeze from Arabia, blew nearly on our stern. A situation so pleasing in itself, and to me so new, could not fail to awaken a train of reflections in a mind, which had early been accustomed to contemplate with delight, the eventful histories and agreeable fictions of the eastern world. It gave me inexpressible pleasure to find myself in the midst of so noble an amphitheatre, almost encircled by the vast regions of Asia, which has ever been esteemed the nurse of sciences, the investress of delightful and useful arts, the scene of glorious actions, fertile in the productions of human genius, abounding in natural wonders, and infinitely diversified in the forms of religion and government, in the laws, manners, customs and languages, as well as in the features and complexions of men.

## Medieval and Modern travellers

During medieval and modern times travellers to India came in large numbers from Islamic and Christian countries. Their voyages and accounts can usefully be classified under four main groups: Arab and African; Asian; European; and American and Canadian. The chronology given at the end of this Introduction (see p. xxxvii) provides a select list of the travellers concerned.

[1] James Forbes, *Oriental Memoirs,* 4 Vols. London, 1813, V.2, p. 212.

Travellers have played an important role in bringing about social and cultural changes in India. With the invasion and conquest of Sind by the Arabs under Muhammad-bin-Qasim in A.D. 712 an era of Muslim conquest and influence in India began. The decline of the Byzantine Empire in the West and the rise of the Arabs resulted in their making repeated inroads into India and opening several trading centres and cities to their merchants and travellers. Some important Arab travellers, like Sulaiman who visited India in A.D. 851, have left behind valuable accounts. Although Arab merchants had commercial contacts with India from ancient times, their trade with the area increased spectacularly during this period.

## Iranian and Afghan travellers

Iran had travel links with India long before its conquest by Alexander in 326 B.C. They can be traced as far back as the Aryan invasions or even to the Indus Valley civilization, but documented travels can only be traced to the times of the early Greek historians and travellers of Alexander's age, discussed earlier. A new beginning in Indo-Iranian relations was made in the seventh century when the Arabs rose to power and conquered Iran. This resulted in a major exodus of Zoroastrians to India. Their number increased through the centuries and we find numerous references to Parsis in the accounts of Alberuni (11th century A.D.), in the memoirs of Timur (fourteenth century) and in accounts left by early European travellers. Through the centuries, the Parsis have joined the cultural stream of the country and became more Indian than Iranian.

Abu Ishaq Ibrahim bin Muhammad Istakhri of Persepolis, the ancient capital of Persia, was the first important Persian traveller to visit India in the latter half of the tenth century. Thereafter, with the conquest of India by the Turks and a series of dynasties from Central Asia, the Iranian impact in India spread and, as is well known, proved over the centuries a major cultural influence in the country.

India's contacts with Russia were few, but some interesting visitors did come form this region. Athanasius Nikitin, who arrived in 1470, was the first important Russian traveller to India; some three centuries later, he was followed by Hirasim Lebedeff, the Indologist who also founded the first European theatre in India (in 1795). In 1880 Ivan Pavlovich Minayeff, another Indologist, arrived.

## Travellers from the West

With the spread of Arab power, Indian products reached European markets at exorbitant prices, for European traders and travellers found it difficult to reach India through Arab lands and the goods were routed through Arab merchants. The only European traveller of repute during this period was the celebrated Marco Polo who, in the late thirteenth-century, travelled to China through the Gobi Desert, and later visited India by way of Sumatra. Medieval Europeans wrote of India as a fairyland of infinite riches and, since this conviction was based on mythical reports and concocted tales, such as those of Sir John Mandeville, India remained as exotic as remote for Europeans of the time.

After the Cape route was discovered, European travellers to India rapidly grew in number. Their tales and travelogues attracted attention in their own lands and not only provided useful imagery for poets and dramatists but also aroused a passion for a knowledge of unknown lands. With Vasco da Gama's opening of the Cape route in 1498, European contacts with India became more regular; numerous travel accounts and scholarly works were produced and, by the eighteenth and nineteenth centuries the proliferation of guidebooks on India reflects the existence of much travelling from Europe.

Whatever the reason for interest in India, whether the traveller came from East or West, he had to steel himself for separation from those he loved before leaving home. Thus J.W. Massie wrote in 1822:

I received a laconic, but summary direction to join the ship's party next day at Gravesend. As a matter almost of course, affection's tear trickled from the eyes, and many farewells were mingled with these warm gushings of the heart, while the more sacred and hallowed relations were bound the firmer by expressions of devotional sympathy and Christian converse. We were yet able to embrace the cheerful anticipation, that if no more again permitted to join each other's society on earth, we should meet in a better and in an immutable state. When the parting hour came, the lines of Brethren's poet had more than once been recited, written, repeated and felt . . .

This is a nineteenth century account, when transport facilities were comparatively good and there was reasonable hope of a traveller's return. In ancient times a traveller, whether alone or with a band of colleagues, had to face genuine threats en route and departures must have involved greater emotional and psychological traumas.

During the heyday of the Roman Empire and up to the middle of the thirteenth century, travellers from Italy were mainly traders who did not leave behind any important accounts. The accounts of Italian travellers to India begin with the visit of Marco Polo and he was followed by many others. A number of Jesuit missionaries also visited India towards the end of the sixteenth century, but the Franciscan Friar, Odorico da Pordenone, was the first Italian missionary to reach the shores of India, in 1321. He left behind a narrative that highlights the unusual customs of India, such as Sati, and even wrote notes on the country's flora and fauna.

Czech travellers also joined the Jesuit missionaries in spreading Christianity in India and intensified their activities after the arrival of Francis Xavier in 1542, when there existed more than thirty Jesuit missionary stations, mainly along the western coast of India and in the South. At the end of the sixteenth century a number of Czech missionaries joined the Jesuit Fathers, and W.P. Kirwitzer reached Goa in 1616. From other Central European areas, such as Poland, Austria and Hungary, some travellers also visited India, and, indeed, a few left accounts of their travels and appear to have devoted themselves to a study of the local languages.

Vasco da Gama's voyage to India was a great success and he returned to Portugal after two years with a rich cargo of spices and pepper. But da Gama's success may have been based on the information unobtrusively dispatched to the King of Portugal by the first Portuguese adventurer in India, Pedro de Covilha, who, disguised as an Arab merchant, arrived at Cannanore in 1488, aboard an Arab trading ship, and collected information about the sea-routes to India after visits to Goa, Calicut and other coastal cities. However, da Gama had made history; he revisited India with 20 ships in 1502, and soon, with the arrival of Afonso de Albuquerque in 1503, the Portuguese became more involved in trade and occupation. Before long, many Portuguese travellers were on their way to India, to consolidate their power and spread Christianity. The Jesuits reached Akbar's court in 1580. Important among them were Father Antonio Monserrate, a distinguished scholar who wrote his account in Latin, and Father Jerome Xavier who was received by Akbar in 1595.

The first known German traveller to India was the minnesinger,

Heinrich von Morungen who arrived in 1197; but few Germans followed him until the Portuguese opened the Cape route. The Germans then appear to have closely studied the voyages of the Portuguese, perhaps because two Germans, Martın Behaim and Johannes Muller, actually accompanied Vasco da Gama to India. No doubt in recognition of the knowledge of the Germans about Portuguese pursuits in the Indies, King Manuel of Portugal licensed the Germans in 1503 to participate in the Portuguese trade with India. Three ships, the *Hieronymus,* the *Raphael* and the *Leonhard* were set apart by German merchants for the purpose, and, in 1505 Hans Mayr and Balthasar Sprenger accompanied Dom Francisco D' Almeida, the first Portuguese Viceroy, to India.

Given her imperial interests, from the sixteenth to the mid-twentieth centuries travellers from Britain to India naturally far outnumbered those from any other country. They explored the farthest corners of the subcontinent and produced works on innumerable topics. In the sixteenth century their number was insignificant when compared to that of the Portuguese, but with the expansion of British power it gradually increased during the seventeenth and the eighteenth centuries, and by the nineteenth century, when Britain had come to dominate India, the English came in far greater numbers. Some found time for sport and enjoyment, and the scholars were free to study India in depth. It is not possible or necessary to name all the visitors and their works here, but some mention of the earlier travellers might be interesting.

The first Englishman alleged to have visited India was Sighelmus, around A.D. 883 (See *Anglo-Saxon Chronicle.* An. DCC. LXXX III: DCCC. L XXXXIV). Perhaps sent by King Alfred to the shrine of St. Thomas in South India, he did not however leave an account of his journey. The first account in English is that of Father Thomas Stephens, who arrived in 1579 and remained in India until his death in 1619. Starting as a rector of a college at Rachol in Salsette, he later devoted himself to missionary activities. He produced several works including *The Christian Purana,* in Marathi. Another missionary, Henry Lord, who was appointed as a preacher by the East India Company around 1630, devoted his energies to the study of the Hindus and the Parsis. The author of *A discoverie of the sect of the banians,* his second work, *The religion of the Parsees,* was dedicated to the Archbishop of Canterbury. There were naturally a number of other important missionaries, but William Carey, who established the Serampur Mission, Joshua Marshman, of the Baptist Missionary Society and Claudius Buchanan, are major names in the history of Christianity and scholarship in modern India.

Irrespective of their vocation, the British produced a wealth of literature on India in comparison to that produced by travellers from other countries. This trend began with Ralph Fitch, the first English merchant traveller to India who arrived in 1583, and we soon receive lively accounts like those by Thomas Coryat and Thomas Roe about Mughal rule in India. Before long, the English were writing on every aspect of life in India and, in the process of governing it, naturally influenced through their ideas and activities the pattern of life in the entire subcontinent. This anthology contains selections from a wide range of their writings: it excludes, however, the writings of those born in India, such as the great Rudyard Kipling and many other worthwhile names like Robert Grant, Charles D'Oyly and James Kyd.

The Dutch interest began about a century after the Portuguese discovered the new route to India. In 1592 a group of merchants in Amsterdam formed a company to trade directly with India, instead of doing so through Portuguese or Spanish merchants, and in 1595 Cornelis de Houtman led the first Dutch expedition intended to reach India: but, crossing the Cape of Good Hope, he reached Sumatra and Bantam, and not India. However, soon more Dutch companies were formed, to be amalgamated in 1602 into the United East India Company of the Netherlands. The Dutch gradually established factories at Pulicat (1610), Surat (1616), Bimlipatam (1641), Chinsura (1653) and, within the next decade, Dutch factories were also established in Balasore, Baranagore, Kasim Bazar, Patna, Nagapatam and Cochin.

Towards the close of the sixteenth century, Jan Huyghen van Linschoten became the first important Dutch traveller to visit the coast between Goa and Cochin. He stayed at Goa from September 1583 to January 1589 and wrote an eye-witness account of his visits to the coastal areas. In the seventeenth century, the important Dutch travellers include Abraham Regornis, Philip Baldaeus and Daniel Havart. All described Hindu customs, the people, places, commercial products, religion, the languages, etc. of South India. During the eighteenth and nineteenth centuries some of the important Dutch travellers produced chronicles and documents, and the

*Dagh Register,* maintained in Batavia from 1624 onwards, also contained records of Dutch activities in India.

There were relatively few Belgian travellers, but mention should be made of Count Eugene Goblet d' Alviella of Brussels, who accompanied the Prince of Wales to India in 1875 as a special correspondent of *Independence Belge.*

The French seem to have reached the Indian Ocean around the fifteen-twenties. Roger Galchant describes in his *Hisoire de l'Inde des Francais* that G. de Virgile of Languedoc arrived in Diu on the ship *Marie du Bon Secours* in 1526. The ship was seized, Virgile returned to France, and he is supposed to have written of his experiences. The Portuguese traveller Joao de Barros reports that a Norman ship belonging to some merchants appeared at Diu in July 1527. In 1529, two brothers from Dieppe, Jean and Raoul Parmentier, visited the Maldives. In 1531 they published an account of their travels in the Indian Ocean. The seventeenth century saw the start of the more important French travels to India, however. Francois Martin de Vitre and Francois Pyrard de Laval sailed from St. Malo in May 1601 in two separate ships, the *Croissant* and *Corbin* and reached the Maldives in 1602 where the *Corbin* sank and Pyrard de Laval was taken captive. Martin de Vitre' returned to France and wrote an account of his voyage in 1603; Pyrard de Laval after his release in 1607 visited Chittagong, Calicut and Goa and wrote *Discours du voyage de Francois aux Indes orientales,* which was published in 1611.

Between 1604 and 1652 six French companies were formed to trade with the Indies, and in 1664 the French East India Company was established at the instance of Colbert. Soon after its establishment it founded factories at Surat (1668), Masulipatam (1669), and secured a site at Pondicherry in 1673. Thus began the involvement of the French with the Dutch, English and Indians.

Jean Baptiste Tavernier was amongst the first important French travellers to India; he made six voyages to the East from 1631 to 1657. The Capuchin missionaries headed by Father Raphael due Mans arrived in 1643 and later disseminated information about India in France. So also did the French Jesuit missionaries who arrived from Siam in 1689 and established a mission in Pondicherry and later at Chandranagare, Jingee, Vellore, and Golkunda. In the seventeenth century Francois Bernier, a French physician who visited India from 1656 to 1668, and the Abbé' Carre, who arrived in 1672, made useful contributions. Of the eighteenth-century travellers, mention must be made of the Abbé' J. A. Dubois, whose study of Hindu customs and ceremonies has become a classic on the subject and is still widely read.

The Danes had close contacts with the Dutch and established an East India Company in 1616. Around 1620, the Danes leased some territory in Tranquebar from the Governor of Tanjore and retained possession of it until 1845 when the Danish possessions were sold to the English. Like other Europeans, the Danes also established factories and developed trade links as best they could. Soon after the establishment of the Company, brief accounts of Admiral Ove Gjedde's expedition to India in 1618 and Jon Olafsson's expedition to Tranquebar in 1622 were published. About half a century later, in 1678, Frederik Bolling published an account of his Indian experiences. Benjamin Schulze, a Dane by birth, went as a Lutheran Missionary to Tranquebar in 1719. He founded the S.P.C.K. Mission at Vepery in Madras in 1728, was a vigorous missionary and published a number of works including a *Hindustani grammar* (1745).

The Americans did not have direct contacts with India until 1776, when the United States became an independent nation. In 1787 the first American ship *The Grand Turk* reached Calcutta, and soon after, in 1793, an American consular office was opened in Calcutta. Trade was the major interest, and soon exports from India to America increased. More Americans came to India, but few produced scholarly works or travel literature. American missionary work in India began in the nineteenth century on a modest scale: a number of missionaries worked in South India, and reference must be made of Adoniram Judson and Samuel Kellogg. Judson was sent to India in 1812 by the American Board of Commissioners for Foreign Missions. He was ordered by the Bengal Government to leave Calcutta and later settled in Rangoon, where he preached to the Burmese. Kellogg, on the other hand, remained longer in India. Sent to India by the American Presbyterian Board in 1864, he became Instructor in the Theological Training School at Allahabad. Fitz-Edward Hall was the first American to publish a text in Sanskrit. He arrived in India in 1850 and became Anglo-Sanskrit Professor at Banaras in 1851. Amongst the other Americans who arrived in the nineteenth- and early twentieth-centuries were Colonel Olcott, who organized the Theosophical Society, and Mark Twain, whose account of his visit to India contains the wit and sparkle characteristic of his writings.

The Select Chronology (see pp. xxxvii-lvii) provides a select list of travellers to India from the different parts of the world. It is not comprehensive, for, naturally, a great many more visited the land. Their travel accounts exist in many languages and are scattered in different archives and libraries all over the world. This vast literature needs to be brought together and it is to be hoped that at least one library, perhaps in India, will be entirely devoted to the literature produced by travellers and scholars on the country. It should not be difficult to collect the relevant documents and literature scattered in libraries and archives in India and different parts of the world, process them, arrange translations, and disseminate the available information in classified form to facilitate researches on India.

# Select Chronology

915     Al-Masudi. Author of *Muruju-l Zahab*

c.A.D. 951     Abu Ishak Al Istakhri. Author of *Kitabu-l Akalim*

c.A.D. 951     Ibn Hawqal. Author of *Ashkalu-l Bilad*

c.A.D. 1000     Abu Dulaf Mis'ar bin Muhalhil. Poet. His original account in Arabic has been translated into French by G. Ferrand and into German by A. von Rohr-Sauer.

c.A.D. 1017     Alberuni. Author of *Tarikh-i-Hind*

c.A.D. 1150     Al-Idrisi. Geographer. Author of *Muzhat-al-Mushtaq*

1724/25     Abbas bin Ali al-Musawi. Author of *Nuzhat-ul-Jalis wa Munyat-ul-Anis*

## Austria

1774     Johann Philipp Wesdin. Carmelite monk. Author of *Viaggio alle Indie orientali*, pub. under pseudonym of Fra Paolino da S. Bartolomeo

1843     Aloys Sprenger (from Tyrol). Author of *English-Hindustani grammar*; etc.

## Belgium

1875     Count Eugene Goblet d' Alviella (of Brussels). Correspondent of *Independence Belge*. Author of *Inde et Himalaya*; etc.

1878     Archbishop Geothals. Came to India as a Bishop.

## Canada

c. 1890     Sarah Jeannette Duncan. Correspondent of *Toronto Globe and Montreal Star*. Author of *The simple adventures of a memsahib*; etc.

## China

c.A.D. 401     Fah-Hien. Buddhist monk. Author of *Fo-koue-ki*

518     Sung Yun. Narrative published in fifth section of Honann Fu's *History of the temples of Lo-Yang*

518     Sung Yun. Narrative published in fifth section of Honan Fu's *History of the temples of Lo-Yang*

630     Hiuen Tsang. Buddhist monk. Author of *Hsi-Yu-shi*

675     I-tsing. Buddhist monk. Author of *A record of the Buddhist religion as practised in India and Malay archipelago*. Tr. by J. Takakusu

727     Hui-Chao

13th cent.     Chao Ju-kua. Author of *Chu-fan-Chih*

c. 1330-49     Wang Ta-Yuan. Author of *Tao-i-Chi-Pio*

15th cent.     Cheng Ho

15th cent.     Fei Hsin. Author of *Hsing-cha-Sheng-lan*

15th cent.     Ma Huan. Author of *Ying-yai-Sheng-lan*

## Czechoslovakia

1338     Giovanni de Marignolli. Bishop. Author of **Cronica Boemorum**

1616     W. P. Kirwitzer. Mathematician. Author of *Observationes cometarum auni 1618 factae a Nostris in India Orientali*

1749     Karel Prikryl (from Prague). Theologian. Author of *Epistolae, quibus civitas, collegium et portus Goani, mores Orientalium describuntur et errores plurium, qui in bac materia versati sunt, deteguntur;* etc.

1753     Vaclav Prutky-Remedius. Franciscan monk. Author of *Itinerary*

19th cent.     Jan Vilem Helfer. Naturalist. Diaries were published in 1873

1863     Ferdinand Stoliczka. Geologist. Wrote on the fauna of South India and on the geology of the route to Kashgar

"     Otakar Feistmantel. Geologist. Published observations on culture, history, agriculture, etc. and organized the first exhibition on India in Prague in 1884

1909     Otakar Pertold. Author of *Cesty po Hindustanu*

### Denmark

1618     Ove Gjedde. Admiral

1622     Jon Olafsson. Author of *The life of the Icelander Jon Olafsson*

c. 1670     Frederik Bolling. Published in 1678 a report of his experiences. Author of *Friderici Bollingii Oost-Indiske Reise-bog, hvor udi befattis hans Reise til Oost-Indien;* etc.

1719     Benjamin Schulze. Lutheran missionary. Author of *Hindustani grammar;* etc.

1821     Rasmus Christian Rask. Philologist. Author of *Frisische Sprachlehre, bearb nach dem namlichen Plane wie die Islandische und Angelsachsische* ...

c. 1841     Niel Ludwig Westergaad. Orientalist. Author of *Zendavesta;* etc.

### England

A.D. 883     Sighelmus. Believed to have been sent to India by Alfred

1579     Thomas Stephens. Missionary. Author of *The Christian Purana,* etc.

1583     Ralph Fitch. Travelled with Levant merchants. see: *Ralph Fitch—England's pioneer to India and Burma*

1603     John Mildenhall. Visited the Court of Jahangir. Author of a letter written on October 3, 1606 from Persia

1608     William Finch. Merchant. Agent to an expedition

which obtained trading previleges from the East
India Co.

Wrote letters from Lahore. Published in *Purchas
his pilgrims*

1608  William Hawkins. Sea Captain and merchant.
Author of *Hawkins' Voyages*

1611  Henry Middleton. Merchant and sea Captain.
Wrote letters
Published in *Purchas his pilgrims.*

1612  Nicholas Withington. Factor. Accompanied
Captain Thomas Best. His observations are
published in *Purchas his pilgrims.*

1615  Thomas Roe. Diplomat. Author of *The embassy
of Sir Thomas Roe to the Court of the Great
Mogul*

1616  Thomas Coryat. Traveller. Reached Agra in
October, 1616. Author of *Coryat's crudities;
with letters from India*

1628  Peter Mundy. Worked as a cabin-boy on a merchant ship. Author of *The travels of Peter Mundy
in Europe and Asia*

1630  Henry Lord. Missionary. Author of *A discoverie
of the sect of the banians;* etc.

1655  John Burnell. Factor. Author of *Bombay in the
days of Queen Anne.*

1668  John Marshall. Perhaps the first Englishman to
study Indian antiquities. Author of *Notes and
observations on East India*

1670's  John Fryer. Travelled in the East. Author of *A
new account of East India and Persia*

1689  John Ovington. Chaplain at Surat. Author of *A
Vogage to Surat in the year 1689*

1732  John Zephaniah Holwell. Surgeon to the East
India Co. Author of *Narrative of the black hole;*
etc.

1742  Robert Orme. Accountant General. Author of
*A history of the military transactions of the British
nation in Indostan*

1750  John Henry Grose. A writer in the E.I. Co.'s
service. Author of *A voyage to the East Indies*

1755  Edward Ives. Naval surgeon and traveller. Author
of *A voyage from England to India*

1758  William Nicholson. Sailed to the East Indies on
board the *Elizabeth.* Author of *Sundry remarks
and observations made in a voyage*

1760  James Rennell. Surveyor. Author of the **Bengal**
*atlas;* etc.

1765 James Forbes. Member of the I.C.S., an artist and a scholar. Author of *Oriental memoirs;* etc.

1769 William Hickey. Law officer with East India Co. Author of *Memoirs*

1770 Charles Wilkins. Orientalist and Sanskrit scholar Writer in the East India Co.'s service. Translated *Histopadesa*; etc.

1773 Nathaniel Brassey Halhed. Orientalist and linguist. Author of *A code of gentoo laws*; etc.

1776 William Roxburgh. Botanist. Supdt., Calcutta Botanical Garden. Author of *Plants of the coast of Coromandel*; etc. Left Mss on Indian botany

1778 William Hodges. Landscape painter. Author of *Travels in India during the years 1780–83*; etc.

1779 Eliza Fay. Wife of Anthony Fay, who practiced in the courts of Calcutta. Author of *Original letters from India*

1780 Innes Munro. Lieut.-Col. Fought against Hyder Ali. Author of *A narrative of the military operations on the Coromandel coast*

1781 Donald Campbell. Captain in the service of the Nawab of the Carnatic. Author of *A narrative of the extra-ordinary adventures* ...

,, David Price. Worked in the army; Judge-advocate, Bombay Army. Author of *A chronological retrospect of Muhammadan history*; etc.

,, Patrick Russell. Physician and naturalist; botanist to the East India Co. in the Carnatic. Author of *The poisonous snakes on the Coromandel coast*; etc.

1782 H. T. Colebrooke. Orientalist and Professor, Fort William College. Author of *A digest of Hindu law*; etc.

,, George Forster. E. I. Co.'s civil service. Author of *A journey from Bengal to England* ...; etc.

,, John Malcolm. Administrator and diplomat. Author of *Political history of India*; etc.

,, Edward Moor. Served with the Maharatta army; member, Asiatic Society of Calcutta; wrote on Hindu mythology. Author of *Hindu pantheon*; etc.

1783 William Jones. Orientalist and jurist; founded Bengal Asiatic Society; judge, High Court, Calcutta. Wrote on Hindu religion and law. Translated *Hitopadesa*; etc.

1784 Thomas Daniell. Artist. Author of *Oriental scenery*.

| | |
|---|---|
| 1784 | William Daniell. Artist. Author of *A picturesque voyage to India;* etc. |
| 1788 | Mathew Ainslie. Doctor. Author of *Materia medica of Hindustan* |
| 1790 | Robet Home. Artist. Author of *The Select views in Mysore* |
| 1791 | Charles Gold. Artist. Author of *Oriental drawings* |
| 1792 | Thomas Twining. Visited India and the United States. Author of *Travels in India.* |
| 1794 | N. E. Kindersley. Civil Servant. Author of *A letter . . . on the propagation of Christianity in India*, etc. |
| *c.* 1794 | Joshua Marshman. Linguist. Edited *Samachar Darpan*, the first Bengali weekly in 1818 |
| 1795 | Thomas Duer Broughton. Worked with the Bengal and Madras establishments. Author of *Letters from a Maratha camp*; etc. |
| 1797 | Claudius Buchanan. Missionary. Author of *Christian researches in Asia* |
| 1799 | John Clark Marshman. Educationist. Accompanied his father Joshua Marshman to Serampur. Edited *Friend of India*. Author of *History of Bengal*; etc. |
| ,, | James Tod. Attached to the Resident at Gwalior; surveyed and mapped Rajasthan. Author of *Annals and antiquities of Rajasthan*; etc. |
| 1804 | Robert Melville Grindlay. Artist and Captain, Bombay Native Infantry. Author of *Scenery, costumes and architecture* . . . . |
| ,, | Mary Martha Sherwood. Wife of Captain Henry Sherwood of the 53rd regt. Author of *The Indian pilgrim*; etc. |
| ,, | William Taylor. Bengal civil service. Artist. Author of *Sketches illustrating the manners and customs of the Indians and Anglo-Indians* |
| 1805 | Daniel Johnson. Surgeon. Author of *Sketches of Indian field sports* |
| 1808 | Maria Graham. Married in India to Thomas Graham and later to Sir A. W. Callcott and travelled in Bengal and southern India. Author of *Journal of a residence in India*; etc. |
| ,, | William Moorcraft. Veterinary surgeon. Author of *Travels in the Himalayan provinces of Hindustan and the Punjab* |
| ,, | Horace Hayman Wilson. Orientalist. Translated *Meghaduta*; etc. |
| 1809 | William Henry Sleeman. Govt. official and major-general. Superintendent, suppression |

of Thaggi and dacoity Author of *Rambles and recollections of an Indian official*; etc.

1810 Sydney Cottcn. Commanded the N. W. frontier in 1853. Anthor of *Nine years on the N. W. Frontier, 1854–63*

1814 Francis Buchanan-Hamilton. Doctor. Author of *Fishes of the Ganges*

1815 James Baillie Fraser. Author of *Journal of a tour through parts of the snowy range of the Himalayan mountains* ...

1817 G. Fitzclarence, Lt.-Col. in the service of the East India Company. Author of *Journal of a route across India*

1818 Moyle Sherer. 34th regt. Author of *Sketches of India*; etc

1819 Thomas Williamson. Captain in Bengal Army. Author of *Oriental field sports*

1822 Reginald Heber. Missionary traveller. Author of *Narrative of a journey* ...

,, John William Massie. Missionary. Author of *Continental India*

,, Fanny Parkes. Accompanied her husband to India; visited India three times. Author of *Wanderings of a pilgrim*

,, G. A. Prinsep. Studied for three months the external commerce of Bengal. Author of *Remarks on the external commerce and exchanges of Bengal*

1823 Alexender Burnes. Political Officer in the Bombay Native infantry. Author of *Travels into Bokhara*

,, Philip Meadows Taylor. Nizam's military service. Author of *Confessions of a thug;* etc.

1825 Alexander Gibson. Botanist. Author of *The Bombay flora*

1826 Henry Miers Elliot. Civil servant. Author of *The history of India as told by its own historians*

1827 Edward C. Archer. Aid-De-Camp to Lord Combermere. Author of *Tours in upper India* ...

,, James Burnes. Physician. Author of *Narrative of a visit to Sind*

,, Godfrey Charles Mundy. Aid-De-Camp to Lord Combermere. Author of *Pen and pencil sketches, being a journal of a tour in India*

1829 Francis George White. 31st regt. Artist. Author of *Views in India*

1830's John Hobart Caunter. Writer and cadet. Author of *Oriental annual*

1830     Robert Elliot. Draughtsman. Author of *Views in the East*

"          Henry Lawrence. Soldier and distinguished administrator. Author of *Adventures of an officer in the service of Ranjeet Singh*; etc.

1831     Thomas Bacon. Bengal Horse Artillery. Author of *First impressions and studies from nature in Hindustan*

1832     John William Kaye. Military historian. Author of *History of the Sepoy war in India*; etc.

"          Godfrey Charles Vigne. Barrister. Author of *Travels in Kashmir*; etc.

1833     Harriette Ashmore. Author of *Narrative of a three months' march in India* ...

"          Alexander Cunningham. Executive Engineer and well known scholar. Author of *Corpus inscriptionum indicarum*; etc.

"          Albert Hervey. Captain, Madras Infantry. Author of *Ten years in India*

1835     James Fergusson. Architect and distinguished art historian. Author of *The rock-cut temples of India*; etc.

"          Thomas C. Jerdon. Madras medical service. Author of *Birds of India*; etc.

1836     Emily Eden. Novelist and artist. Author of *Up the Country*; etc.

"          Henry Edward Fane. Author of *Five years in India* ...

"          Julia Charlotte Maitland. Wife of Jas Thomas (died at Madras in 1840). Author of *The letters from Madras*

"          John Frederick Shore. Judge. Author of *Notes on Indian affairs*

1840's   H. A. Leveson. Hyderabad Subsidiary Force. Author of *The hunting grounds of the old world*

1840     Henry Yule. Linguist. Co-author of *Hobson-Jobson*

1841     John Butler. Major, Bengal Native Infantry. Author of *A sketch of Assam*

"          Thomas Erskine Perry. Judge, Supreme Court of Bombay. Author of *A bird's eye view of India*; etc.

1842     T. Acland. Clergyman. Author of *A popular account of the manners and customs of India*

"          George Cambell. Administrator. Author of *The capital of India*; etc.

"          Robert Gill. Artist and sportsman. Author of *The rock-cut temples of India*; etc.

1844    George Bruce Malleson. Colonel and military
        writer. Author of *The mutiny of the Bengal
        army*; etc.

1845    James Robert Ballantyne. Linguist. Author of
        *Elements of Hindi and Braj Bakha grammar*;
        etc.

,,      W. W. W. Humbley. Captain, Queen's Royal
        Lancers; joined Sikh campaign. Author of
        *Journal of a cavalry officer*

1846    Henry George Briggs. Served in the Bombay
        secretariat. Author of *Cities of Gujarashtra*

1847    Edward Braddon. Commissioner, Bhagalpur
        and Oudh. Author of *Thirty years of shikar*

,,      Joseph Dalton Hooker. Botanist. Author of
        *Himalayan journals*; etc.

,,      Henry George Keene. Civil servant and scholar.
        Author of *Fall of the Mughal empire*; etc.

c. 1847 Henry Martin Scudder. Missionary. Author of
        *The bazaar book*; etc.

1848    Charles Richard Francis. Doctor. Author of
        *Sketches of native life in India*

,,      Frederick Markhan. Lt. General. Author of
        *Shooting in the Himalayas*

,,      Henry Morris. Madras civil service. Author of
        *Anglo-Indian worthies*; etc.

1849    Andrew Leith Adams. Naturalist. Author of
        *Wanderings of a naturalist in India*

,,      Allan O. Hume. Civil servant, ornithologist, and
        founder of the Indian National Congress. Author
        of *Nest and eggs of Indian birds*; etc.

1850    Joseph Fayrer. Surgeon-general. Author of *The
        thanatophidia of India*; etc.

,,      Donald Macintyre. Commanded 2nd Gurkhas.
        Author of *Wanderings and wild sport on and
        beyond the Himalaya*

,,      William Rice. Lieut.; 25th regt., Bombay. Author
        of *Tiger shooting in India*

1852    Francis Egerton. Author of *Journal of a winter's
        tour in India*

,,      Mathew Atmore Sherring. Missionary. Author
        of *The Indian church during the rebellion;* etc.

1854    Ralph Thomas Hotchkin Griffith. Orientalist.
        Translated *Ramayana*; etc.

1855    James Burgess. Archaeologist. Author of *The
        rock temples of Elephanta*; etc.

,,      William Knighton. Professor of History and
        Logic, Hindu College, Calcutta University.

Author of *Private life of an Eastern king*; etc.

1855    Alfred C. Lyall. Civil servant and scholar. Author of *Verses written in India*; etc.

1856    Edwin Arnold. Orientalist and poet. Author of *The light of Asia*; etc.

1857    George Francklin Atkinson. Captain, Bengal Engineers. Author of *Curry and rice on 40 plates; or, the ingredients of social life at our station in India*; etc.

1859    Clements Robert Markham. Introduced cinchona trees from Peru into India. Author of *Memoirs of the Indian surveys.*

c. 1860    T.G. Fraser. Lieut.-Col., Bombay Fusiliers. Author of *Record of sport and military life in Western India*

1860    Lepel Henry Griffin. Civil servant. Author of *The Panjab chiefs*; etc.

1860's    Monier-Williams. Distinguished Sanskristist. Author of the major Sanskrit dictonary and *Life and thought in India*; etc.

c. 1860    George Otto Trevelyan. Distinguished civil servant. Author of *The competition wallah*; etc.

1861    Baden Henry Baden-Powell. Civil servant and scholar. Author of *Land systems of British India:* etc.

c. 1862    James Forsyth. Conservator of Forests. Author of *The highlands of central India;* etc.

1862    William Wilson Hunter. Scholar, educationalist and civil servant. Editor of *Imperial gazetteer of India*; etc.

1864    Charles E. Gover. Principal, Madras Orphan Male Asylum. Author of *The folk-songs of southern India*; etc.

"    G.P. Sanderson, Officer-in-Charge, Govt. Elephant-Catching Establishment, Mysore. Author of *Thirteen years among the wild beasts of India*

1865    F. F. Wyman. Author of *From Calcutta to the snowy range.*

1866    Mary Carpenter. Educationalist and reformer; Author of *Six months in India.*

1867    John Faithful Fleet. Epigraphist. Author of *Epigraphia Indica*; etc.

1868    J.H. Baldwin. Captain, Bengal Staff Corps. Author of *The large and small game of Bengal and the N.W. Provinces of India*

1868   Mountstuart Elphinstone Grant-Duff. Governor
       of Madras. Author of *Notes of an Indian
       journey*; etc.
1869   William Lee-Warner. Civil servant. Author of
       *The citizen of India*; etc.
1870   George Robert Aberigh-Mackay. Principal of
       Rajkumar College, Indore and other
       institutions. Author of *Twenty-one days in
       India* .....; etc.
  ,,   Edward Braddon. Commissioner of Bhagalpur
       and member of Oudh Commission. Author of
       *Thirty years of shikar*; etc.
  ,,   M. G. Gerard. Brig.-Major in the Afghan war.
       Author of *Leaves from the diaries of a soldier
       and sportsman* ....
  ,,   Denzil Charles Ibbetson. Scholar the civil servant.
       Editor of *Gazetteer of the Punjab*; etc.
1871   William Crooke. Scholar, magistrate and
       collector. Author of *The popular religion and
       folklore of northern India*; etc.
  ,,   Andrew H. L. Fraser. Civil servant. Author of
       *Among Indian rajahs and ryots*
  ,,   John Garrett. Director of Public Instruction.
       Author of *A classical dictionary of India*
1872   George William Forrest. Director, Govt. of
       India Records. Author of *Cities of India*; etc.
  ,,   T. W. Holderness. Civil servant. Author of
       *Peoples and problems of India*
1873   G. A. Grierson. Linguist. Author of *The langu-
       ages of India*
  ,,   Edward Lear. Artist. Author of *Edward Lear's
       Indian journal*
  ,,   Robert H. Risley. Scholar and civil servant.
       Author of *Primitive marriage in Bengal*; etc.
1875   John David Rees. Madras civil servant. Author
       of *The Muhammadans*
1877   A. H. Arden. Linguist. Author of *The Pancha-
       tantra in Tamil*; etc.
  ,,   Samuel John Thomson. Indian medical service.
       Author of *The silent India*; etc.
1879   J. C. Murray-Aynsley. Visited India twice.
       Author of *Our tour in southern India*; etc.
1880   E. H. Aitkin. Missionary. Author of *Behind the
       bungalow*; etc.
1882   E. F. Burton. Major-Gen., Madras Staff Corps.
       Author of *Reminiscences of sport in India*; etc.
1884   Cecil Bendal. Orientalist. Author of *A journey*

*of literary and archaeological research in Nipal and northern India*

1887    Charles Robert Wilson. Bombay Education Department. Author of *Inscriptions on tombs and monuments in Bengal*

1891    Charistina S. Bremner. Travelled in northern India. Author of *A month in a Dandi*

1891    Ethel St. Clair Grimwood. Wife of the English political agent in Manipur. Author of *My three years in Manipur*; etc.

,,    E. F. Knight. Barrister and journalist. Author of *Where three empires meet*; etc.

1892    Edward Carpenter. Author of *Adams Peak to Elephants*; etc.

*c.* 1900    Edward F. Elwin. Missionary. Author of *India jottings*; etc.

1904    Walter Del Mar. Author of *India of today*; etc.

1905    Flora Annie Steel. Married a Bengal civilian. Author of *From the five rivers*; etc.

1906    William H. Hart. Lived in Calcutta. Author of *Everyday life in Bengal* ......

1911    John Fortesque. Author of *Narrative of a visit to India*

1912    E. M. Forster. Celebrated novelist. Author of *A passage to India*; etc.

1913    G. C. Dyson. Author of *From a Punjab pomegranate grove*

,,    Frank Elias. Author of *The gorgeous East*; etc.

1922    John McKenzie. Taught at Wilson College, Bombay. Author of *Hindu ethics*; etc.

*France*

1529    Jean and Raoul Parmentier. Visited Maldives. Author of *Journal du voyage de Jean Parmentier* ...

1602    Francois Martin de Vitre and Francois Pyrard de Laval. Visited Maldives. Martin wrote *Description du premier voyage facit aux Indes orientales par les Francois en l'an 1603*

1607    Francois Pyrard de Laval. Author of *Discours du voyage de Francois aux Indes oreintales*

*c.* 1615    Jean Mocquet. Author of *Voyages en Afrique, Asie, Indes, orientales et occidentales*

1631    Jean Baptiste Tavernier. Made six voyages to India. Author of *Les six voyages de Jean-Baptiste Tavernier*

*c.* 1650    La Boullaye le Gouz. Author of *La Boullaye Le Gouz sa vie et ses voyages*

1956    Francois Bernier. Physician. Author of *Historie de la derniere revolution des etats du gran Mogol*

1665    Jean Chardin. Businessman. Wrote on Suleman III of Persia. Author of *Journal du voyage du chevalier Chardin en Perse et Indes orientales*

1666    Jean de Thevenot. Author of *Voyages de Mr. de Thevenot, contenant la relation de l' Hindostan, des nouveaux Mogols et des autres peuples et pays des Indes*

1672    Abbe Carre. Author of *Voyage des Indes orientales, male de plusieurs histories curieuses*

c. 1690    Francois Martin. Author of *Memoirs*

1690    Abraham Duquesne. Captain. Author of *Journal d'un voyage fait aux Indes orientales* . . . . .

c. 1700    Luillier-Lagaudiers. Author of *Voyage du sieur Luillier aux grandes Indes*

1752    Jean Baptiste Joseph Gentil. Author of *Memoirs sur l'Indoustan: Historie de Radjahs de l'indoustan*

c. 1770    Comte Duprat. Author of *Voyage du Comte Duprat dans l'Inde, ecrit par lui-meme*

1789    Louis Marie Joseph O'hier comte de Grandpre. Author of *Voyage dans l'Inde et au Bengale, fait dans les annees 1789 et 1790*

1792    Abbe J. A. Dubois. Author of *Moeurs, institutions et ceremonies des peuples de l'Inde*; etc.

c. 1795    Joseph Francois Carpentier de Cossigny. Author of *Voyage au Bengale* . . . .

c. 1799    Francois Balthazar Solvyns (from Antwerp) Artist. Author of *Les Hindous*

1802    Charles Franacois Tombe. Author of *Voyage-aux Indes orientales pendant les annees* . . . .

1803    Guy de Courson. Author of *Une mission aux Indes, 1803–04* . . . .

,,    Jules Damian. Author of *Prospectus: Un pelerinage dans l'Inde*

1828    Victor Jacquemont. Botanist. Author of *Correspondance* . . . .

1830    Cyrille Pierre Theodore Laplace. Author of *Voyage autour du monde par les mers de l'Inde et de Chine*

1838    Saint-Hubert Theroulde. Author of *Voyage dans l'Inde*

1864    Louis Rousselet. Studied art and architecture. Author of *India and its princes*

1886    James Darmesteter. Orientalist. Author of *Lettres sur l'Inde*

1897    Sylvain Levi. Sanskritist. Author of *Le theatre Indien*; etc.

| | |
|---|---|
| 19th cent. | Michel Perrin. Author of *Voyage dans l'Indoustan* |
| | Victor Fontanier. Author of *Voyage dans l'Inde* .... |
| | Francois Devay. Author of *Journal d'un voyage dans l'Inde anglaise* .... |
| | Alfred Grandidier. Author of *Voyage dans les provinces meridionales de l'Inde* |
| | Emile Charles Marie Senart. Sanskrit scholar. Author of *Kaccyana et la litterature grammaticale du Pali;* etc. |
| | A. Thenon. Author of *A travers l'Inde* |
| | Eugene Felicien Albert Goblet d'Alviella. Author of *Inde et Himalaya* .... |
| | Louis Jacolliot. Author of *Voyage au pays des Brahmes;* etc. |
| | Henry Bohan. Author of *Voyage aux Indes orientales* |
| | Emile Guimet. Musician. Author of *Huit jours aux Indes* |
| | Leon Clery. Author of *De Paris a Lahore, lettres familieres* |
| 20th cent. | Prince d'Orleans et Bragance Louis. Author of *A travers l'Hindo-kush* |
| | Maurice George Rene Maindron. Author of *Dans l'Inde du Sud* |

**Germany**

| | |
|---|---|
| 1197 | Heinrich von Morungen. Minnesinger. |
| 1498 | Martin Behaim and Johannes Muller; accompanied Vasco da Gama. |
| 1505 | Hans Mayr and Balthasar Sprenger; accompanied Dom Francisco d'Almeida. |
| 1607 | Johann Verken (of Meissen). Soldier in Dutch service. |
| 1638 | Albrecht von Mandelslo. Author of *Albrechts von Mandelslo morgenlandische reise-beschreibung* |
| c. 1670 | Martin Wintergeist. His account of India was published in *Reisebeschreibungen* ....; edited by S.P.L'N honore Naber (The Hague, 1930–32). |
| 1675 | Christoph Schweitzer (of Swabia). Author of *Reise nach Java und Ceylon*, ed. by S. P. L'Nhonore Naber |
| 1682 | Bartholomaus Ziegenbalg. Lutheran theologian. Author of *Genealogie der Malabarishen Gotter;* etc. |
| c. 1700 | Johann Earnst Haxleden. Catholic missionary. Malayalam and Sanskrit scholar. Author of *Puthenpana; or, the life of Christ;* etc. |

c. 1757  Walter Balthasar Reinhardt, nicknamed
'Sombre'. Served Shah Alam II in 1772 civil
war; husband of Begum Samru

c. 1770  Johann Philipp Fabricius and Christian
Breithaupt. Co-authors of *A Malabar and English dictionary*

1776  Johann Peter Rottler (of Strassburg). Produced
a report on botanical researches on his journey from Tranquebar to Madras. Also, author
of *Tamil-English dictionary*; etc.

c. 1788  Johann Gottfried Haensel. Missionary in
Nicobar. Author of *Letters on the Nicobar Islands*

1832  Joseph Wolff. Missionary. Author of *Travels
and adventures of Dr. Wolff*

1842  Herman Beythan. Tamil scholar. Author of
*Praktische grammatik der Tamil sprache*

„     J. C. F. Heyer. Telugu scholar. Author of
religious songs in Telugu

c. 1850  Hermann Gundert. Malyalam scholar.
Author of *Grammar of the Malyalam language*;
etc.

1859  Martin H. Haug (of Wurtemburg). Orientalist.
Author of *The Aitareya Brahmana*; etc.

1866  **William Schpich (of Hesse-Darmstadt).** Author-
of *A manual of forestry*; etc.

1870  Augusts Rudolf Frederic Hoernle. Celebrated linguist. Author of *Comparative grammar of
the North Indian languages*

1873  Herman Georg Jacobi. Celebrated Sanskritist. Author of *Das Ramayana*; etc.

1882  Julius E. Jolly (of Heidlberg). Physicist and
celebrated philologist. Translated into
English *The institutes of Narada*; etc.

1884  Eugen Hultzsch (of Dresden). Celebrated
philologist. Author of *Prolegomena zu
Vasantaraja Sakuna*; etc.

1892  Paul Deussen. Orientalist. Author of *Das system
des Vedanta*; etc.

1894  F. Kittel. Kannada scholar. Author of *Kannada-
English dictionary*

*Greece*

326 B.C.  Nearchus. Author of *The voyage of Nearchus
from the Indus to the Euphrates, collected from
the original journal preserved by Arrian* ...

302 B.C.  Megasthenese. Ambassador. Author of *Indica*

3rd cent B.C.  Dionysius. Envoy.

A.D. 535–547  Cosmas Indicopleustes. Merchant. Author of
*Typographia Christiana*

*Holland*

|  |  |
|---|---|
| 1583 | Jan Hyghen van Linschoten. Author of *Reysgeschrift and Itinerario*. |
| c. 1650 | Abraham Rojernis. Calvinist clergyman. Author of *De open-deure tot de verborgen heydendom* |
| c. 1660 | Philippus Baldaeus. Clergyman. Author of *Ausfuhrliche Beschreibung der beruhmten ostindischen Kusten Malabàr, Coromandel und Ceylon* |
| c. 1680 | Daniel Havart. Author of *Op-en Ondergang van Choromandel* |
| c. 1720 | Francois Valentyn, Author of *Oud en nieuw Oost-Indien* |

*Hungary*

|  |  |
|---|---|
| 1847 | Edward Rehatsek. Latin scholar and mathematician. Contributed to *Calcutta Review* and published works on Islam, Christianity; etc. |
| 1864 | Gottlieb Wilhelm Leitner. Principal, Govt. College, Lahore. Author of several works. Edited *Asiatic Quarterly Review* |
| 1888 | Mark Aurel Stein. Archaeologist. Principal of the Oriental College and Registrar of Punjab University, Lahore. Produced many works and catalogues including *Memoirs of the ancient geography of Kashmir* |

*Iran*

|  |  |
|---|---|
| 10th cent | Abu Ishaq Ibrahim bin Muhammad Istakhari (of Persepolis). Author of *Kitab-al-aqalim* |
| 13th cent | Shaikh Sadi (of Shiraz). Poet. Author of *Bustan* |
| 14th cent | Hafiz (of Shiraz). Poet. d. 1389. Wrote a *Dewan* |
| 1432 | Shaikh Azuri (of Khurasan). Poet. Author of *Jawahir-ul-Asrar*; etc. |
| 16th cent | Mir Sayyad Ali Tabrizi. Painter; accompanied Humayun to India. |
| ,, | Khwaja Abd-us-Samad Shirazi. Painter; accompanied Humayun to India. |
| ,, | Shahpur Khorasani. Painter. Urfi (of Shiraz) Poet. d. 1590. |
| c. 1560 | Muhammad Kasim Farishta (from Astrabad). Historian. Author of *Tarikhi-i-Firishta* |
| 1577 | Asaf Khan (of Qazwin), also called Mirza Jafar Beg Poet. |
| 17th cent | Muhammad Hussain Naziri. Poet. d. 1612. |
| ,, | Mulla Zuhuri (of Khursan) Poet; Works include *Mina Bazar*; *Saqi-nama* |
| c. 1610 | Abu Talib 'Kalim' (of Hamdan). Poet. Author of *Zafar-nama-i-Shah Jahan* |

1649    Mirza Muhammad Muqim Fauji (of Shiraz). Poet, but was also a soldier in Bengal.

1734    Shaikh Muhammad Ali Hazim. Author of *Tazkarat-ul-Ahwal*

1809    Mirza Abul-Hasan Khan. Ambassador. Author of *Hirat-nama*

*Ireland*

1787    George Thomas. Commanded the army of Begum Samru.

1802    George Annesley Valentia. Succeeded to the Irish peerage as second Earl of Mountnorres. Author of *Voyages and travels in India, the Red Sea, Abyssinia and Egypt from 1802 to 1806*

*Italy*

1295    Marco Polo. Author of *Il Milione*. Originally written in French, and lost. Later reconstructed from various manuscripts copied from the original. Translated into Latin, Italian, English, etc.

1321    Odorico da Pordenone. Missionary. Author of *Itinerarius orientalis*

*c.* 1419   Nicolo dei Conti (from Venice). Author of *India recognita* forming Book IV of *De varietate fortunae* by Poggio Bracciolini

*c.* 1499   Gerolamo di Santo Stefano. His account is contained in a letter published in *Viaggi in Persia, India e Giava di Nicolo De Conti, Girolamo Adorno e Girolamo da Santo Stefano,* ed. M. Longhena

1503    Giovanni da Empoli. A Florentine merchant. Author of *Lettera di G. da Empoli*, ed. A. Bausani

1505    Ludovico de Varthema. Author of *Itinerario*

1515    Andrea Corsali (from Florence). Wrote letters.

1565    Cesare Federici (Venecian jeweller). An account of his travels was written by Fra Barto lomeo Dionigi

1578    Rodolfo Acquaviva, Jesuit in the court of Akbar. Wrote letters, published in J. Wicki's *Monumenta missionum*, vols. 28–30; *Documenta Indica* (vol. 11, 1577–80, Rome 1970); (vol. 12, 1580–83, Rome, 1972)

1579    Gasparo Balbi (Venecian jeweller). Author of *Viaggi di C. Federici e G. Balbi all Indie orientali*, ed. O. Pinto

1582    Filippo Sassetti (from Florence) Wrote letters.

1584    Jacobo Fenicio. Missionary. Author of *Livro primeiro da Seita dos Indios orientalis*

1599    Francesco Carletti. Florentine merchant.
        of *Ragionamenti*

1605    Roberto de Nobili. Missionary. His works
        include *Apologia*

1622    Pietro Della Valle. Author of *De'Viaggi di
        Pietro Della Valle il Pellegrino*

1656    Nicolo Manucci (From Venece). Author of
        *Storia do Mogor*

,,      Giuseppe di S. Maria. A missionary. Author of
        *Prima speditione all' Indie orientali;* etc.

,,      Vincenzo Maria di S. Caterina da Siena.
        Missionary. Author of *II viaggio all' Indie
        orientali*

*c.* 1693   Giovanni Francesco Gemelli Careri. Author of
        *Giro del mondo*

1756    Maro della Tomba. Missionary. His accounts
        in *Gli Scritti del Pandre Marco Della Tomba* by
        Angelo de Gubernatis

1776    **Paolino** di S. Bartolomeo. Missionary. Author
        of *Viaggio alle Indie orientali*

1781    Eustachio Delfini. Captain. Author of *Raggua-
        lic della spedizione della flotta francese all' Indie
        orientali, seguita negli anni 1781–1782–1783
        sotto la condotta del Generale De Suffren*

1792    Lazzaro Papi (of Tuscany). Missionary. Author
        of *Storia dell' Indostan*

1810    Angelo de Gubernatis (of Turin). Sanskrit
        scholar. Founded *Rivista Orientale*, and Wrote
        *Piccola enciclopedia Indiana*; etc.

*Poland*

*c.* 1490   Gaspar de Gama (from Poznan) Worked as Port
        Manager

*c.* 1596   Krzysztof Pawlowski. Author of *Les Indes
        Portugaises a la fin du XVIme siecle*

*c.* 1610   Pawel Palczewksi. Pub. his accounts in
        1610

1625    Andrzej Rudomina. A Jesuit, whose departure
        for India was commemorated by the Polish poet
        Maciej Sarbiewski in an ode

1736    Mikolaj Szostak. Missionary.

18th cent   Maksymilian Wiklinski. Recorded everyday life
        in Pondicherry and Calcutta in his diary.

1814    Rhenius. A missionary from Gradudenz. Author
        of the *The essence of the true Veda*

1830    Count Wladyslaw Malachowski. His account is
        available in MS form in the University of War-
        saw: registered under no.9708

**Portugal**

| | |
|---|---|
| 1488 | Pedro de Covilha. Adventurer. Reached Cannanore, disguised as an Arab |
| 1498 | Vasco da Gama. Renowned navigator. Author of *Navigatione di V. di Gaman* ...; etc. |
| 1500 | Pedro Alvares Cabral. Author of *Nauigation del Capitano Pedro Aluares scritta per vn pilotto portoghese* |
| 1503 | Afonso de Albuquerque. Author of *Commentarios de Afonso Dalboquerque* ... |
| 1520 | Domingo Paes. Wrote on Vijayanagar. Account pub. in *A forgotten empire by* Sewell |
| 1528 | Fernao Lopez de Castanheda. Wrote *Historiaa do descobrimento e Conquesto da India polos Portuguese* |
| 1535 | Fernao Nuniz. A horse dealer. Wrote on Vijayanagar. Atcount pub. in *A forgotten empire* by Sewell |
| 1541/42 | Francis Xavier. Renouned Jesuit missionary, and canonized a saint. Author of *Lettres de S. Francois Xavier* |
| 1553 | Camoens. Epic poet. Composed most of *Lusiads* in India |
| c. 1559 | Diogo do Couto. Keeper of Goa Records. Author of *Da Asia (1602–45),* 12 vols. |
| 1560 | Edoardo Barbosa. Jesuit missionary |
| 1573 | Antonio Cabral. Envoy of the Portuguese Viceroy at Goa to Akbar's court |
| 1580 | Antonio Monserrate. Jesuit; spent several years in Akbar's court. Author of *Mongolicæ legationis commentarius*; etc. |
| 1584 | Don Duart de Menezes. Viceroy. Author of *Chronica do Condo D. Duarte de Menezes* |
| 1590 | Pedro Teixeira. A soldier. Author of *Relaciones ...de'el origen descendencia y svccession de los reyes de Persia ...dende la India Oriental hasta Italia portierra* |
| 1595 | Jerome Xavier. Jesuit Father. Wrote letters from Akbar's court along with his colleague Emanuel Pinheiro |
| 1604 | Sebastian Manrique. Member of Augustinian order. Wrote *Itinerario* in Spanish |
| c. 1616 | Manuel Barradas. Jesuit missionary. Wrote on Vijayanagar. Author of *Discricao da cidade de Columbo*; etc. |
| 1631 | Antonio Bocarro. Historian and Keeper of Goa Records. Author of *Decada* ...; etc. |

**Russia**

| | |
|---|---|
| A.D. 13th cent. | Minhaj-al-Siraj Jurjani. Poet. Wrote an historical account, *Tabaqat-i-Nasiri* |

A.D. 13th cent.   Muhammad 'Anji (of Bukhara). Author of
                  *Lubab-al-Albab*

1442              Kamaluddin Abdur Razzaq Samarqandi.
                  Remained in Vijayanagar. Author of *Malta-us-
                  Sadain*

1470              Athanasius Nikitin. Merchant traveller. Author
                  of *Khodzenie za tri morya*

1698              S. Malenkov. Merchant traveller

1785              Herasim Lebedeff. Indologist. Author of *A
                  grammar of the pure and mixed East Indian
                  dialects*

1855              Helena Petrovna Blavatsky. Theosophist

1880              Ivan Pavlovitch Minayeff. Indologist. Author
                  of *Dnevniki puteshestvii v Indiu i Birmu, 1880
                  1885–1886;* etc.

**Scandinavia**

1863              Lars Olsen Skrefsrud. Missionary from
                  Faaberg. Author of *Santali grammar*; etc.

1894              Theo Sorensen and Edvard Amundsen. Studied
                  Tibetan religion and customs in India

**Scotland**

1763              John Stewart. Wrote *Travels to discover the
                  source of moral motion*; etc.

1789              James Moffat. Portrait artist

1823              John Stevenson. Missionary. Founded *Bombay
                  Gazette* and wrote *Principles of Mahratti
                  grammar*; etc.

1829              John Wilson. Missionary and orientalist.
                  Founded *Oriental Christian Spectator.*
                  Wrote a *History of the suppression of infanticide
                  in western India*

„                 Alexander Duff. Missionary. Edited *Calcutta
                  Review* and wrote *India and Indian missions*

1839              Thomas Smith. Missionary. Wrote *Modern
                  missions and culture*; etc.

1859              John Watson McCrindle. Author of *Ancient
                  India as described by Ktesias the Knidian*; etc.

c. 1880           Edward Hamilton Aitkin. Missionary. Author
                  of *Tribes on my frontier*; etc.

**Switzerland**

1803              DeCaselli. Army officer from Basle. Specia-
                  lized in portrait painting.

**Tibet**

A.D. 7th cent 2nd decade   Thomni Sambhota. A scholar.
8th cent          Salnang. A scholar.
8/9th cent.       Namnang. A scholar.
11th cent.        Rinchhen Sangpo. A monk.
„                 Legs pahi S'erab. A monk.
„                 Nag-Tcho. A Scholar.
„                 Brogmi. A scholar. Translated *Hevajra tantra* into
                  Tibetan.
„                 Mar-pa. A scholar.

*Turkey*

1535    Bairam Khan. Accompanied Humayun from
        Persia. A distinguished officer in the Mughal
        court. Author of a *Diwan*
1554    Sidi Ali Reis. Admiral in the navy. Author of
        *Mirat ul memalik*

# 1. General Impressions

## 1. Of the firme Land of the Greater India

From Zeilan sayling sixtie miles to the West is the great Province of Malabar, which is not an Iland, but firme Continent, called India the greater, the richest Province in the World. There are in it foure Kings, the chiefe of which is Senderbandi, in whose Kingdome they fish for Pearles, to wit, betwixt Malabar and Zeilan, in a Bay where the Sea is not above ten or twelve fathome, in which divers descend, and in bags of nets tyed to their bodies bring up the Oysters in which they are. And because there are great fishes which kill the Fishermen, they hire certaine Bramines to charme them (being skilfull to charme all sorts of beasts also and birds) and these have the twentieth, the King the tenth. These Oysters are found all Aprill, and till the midst of May, and not else: in September they finde them in a place above three hundred miles off, and till the midst of October. The King goeth as naked as the rest, save that he weareth some honorable Ensignes, as a Coller of precious stones about his necke, and a threed of Silke to his breast with one hundred and four faire Pearles (as Beads) to number his Prayers, of which he must daily say so many to his Idols: like Bracelets he weareth on three places of his armes, and likewise on his legs; and on his fingers also and toes. The prayers which he sayth are Pacauca, pacauca, pacauca, one hundred and four times. This King hath one thousand women and if any please his sense he takes her; as one he did from his brother, whence warres had followed, but the mother threatening to cut off her breasts which had nourished them, if they proceeded, stayed the broyle. He hath many Horsemen for his Guard which alway accompanie him, who when the King dies, throw themselves voluntarily into the fire wherein he is burned to doe him service in the next World. This and his brethren the Kings of Malabar buy their Horses from Ormus, and other parts. The Country breeds none, and of it happens sometimes, yet are they there bred ill-favoured and naught. Condemned persons will offer themselves to die in honour of such an Idoll, which is performed with twelve Knives, and twelve wounds in divers parts of the bodie, at every blow, saying, I kill my selfe in honour of that Idol, and the last he thrusts in his heart; and then is burned by his kindred. The wives also cast themselves into the fire with their husbands; they being disreputed which refuse it. (1320)

MARCO POLO[1]

## 2. Vasco Da Gama welcomed by Brahmins in India

At the Temple doore foure men met them naked to the navill, thence clothed with silke to the knees, having three threads from the right shoulder crossed to the left side (the habit of Bramenes) which sprinkled holy water on them, and gave them sweet poulders. The walls of the Temple had many Images painted on them. In the midst was a round high Chappell, with a brazen narrow doore, having many steps to it, and within, an Image which the darkenesse would not suffer them to discerne, neyther might any enter but the Priests, who approaching to the Image with their finger pointing to it, twice called Maria, whereat the Catual and his companie falling flat on the Earth, presently arose and sayd their prayers. The Portugals think-ing it to be some Service of the Blessed Virgin, worshipped her after their wonted manner. Thence they passed to another Temple of like magnificence, and after that, to the Kings Palace, Trumpets and Pipes sounding all the while: and the people so thronged, that had not the Nairos made way with their Swords, they could not have passed. At the Gate they were met by certaine Nobles, called Caimaes, and approaching to the roome where the King was, an aged man clothed in silke from the shoulders to the anckles, com-ming forth, embraced Gama. This was the chiefe of the Bramenes. The others being first permitted entrance, he last of all holding Gama by the hand, followed. It was a large Hall, with many Benches artificially wrought one above another, in forme of a Theatre. The Floore was covered with Silke, the Walls hanged with Curtaines of Silke, embroydered with Gold. The King lay in a rich Bed, with a Tyre on his head set with Stones and wrought with Gold, clothed with Silke, having many golden Claspes on the Brest. On his Eares hung Jewels of great value: his Toes and Fingers, with Rings and Gemmes made a glorious splendour: His personage was comely, tall, majesticall. Gama saluted him as the use here is to the King, and was then placed in a Seat next him; the other Portugals also sate downe. Water was brought to wash and coole their hands, and divers Fruits to refresh them. (1498)

VASCO DA GAMA[2]

## 3. First reception of a stranger

From the ship a stranger is conveyed on shore in a boat of the country, called a Massoolah boat: a work of curious construction, and well calculated to elude the violent shocks of the surf, that breaks here with great violence: they are formed without a keel, flat bottomed, with the sides raised high, and sewed together with the fibres of the cocoa-nut tree, and caulked with the same material: they are remarkably light, and are managed with great dexterity by the natives: they are usually attended by two kattamarans (rafts), paddled by one man each, the intention of which is, that, should the boat be overset by the violence of the surf, the persons in it may be preserved. The boat is driven, as the sailors say, high and dry; and the passengers are landed on a fine, sandy beach: and immediately enter the fort of Madras.

The appearance of the natives is exceedingly varied, some are wholly naked, and others so clothed, that nothing but the face and neck is to be discovered; besides this, the European is struck at first with many other objects, such as women carried on men's shoulders on pallankeens, and men riding on horseback clothed in linen dresses like women: which, united with the very different face of the country from all he had ever seen or conceived of, excite the strongest emotions of surprise! (1780)

WILLIAM HODGES[3]

## 4. Under the name of India

Under the name of India is comprehended an extensive portion of the globe, no less remarkable for its riches and fertility, than for having, in all ages, attracted the attention of other nations. The character of its inhabitants, the peculiarity of their manners, and the singular institutions by which the stability of their customs has been preserved for so long a period, have engaged the researches of the philosopher, by presenting an ample and curious field of his specula-tions. The wealth of many of its provinces has rendered it an object, no less suited to encourage the enterprise of the soldier; and,

unhappily entailed upon it all those miseries, which never fail to
mark his progress: whilst the variety and excellence of its natural
and artificial productions, have bestowed upon it an importance, in
the eyes of the mercantile adventurer, which has led him to sur-
mount every obstacle that nature or art has thrown in the way of
their acquisition.

From the most authentic accounts which we possess, regarding
the progress of civilized manners, we learn, that India was one of the
first countries in which the human race made any considerable
advances in the career of improvement. Its inhabitants are said, by
some writers, to have borrowed their knowledge of the arts and
sciences from the natives of Egypt; but there now appears little
wanting, in the evidence adduced by others, to prove that the
reverse of this was the case. But although it may not be allowed, that
the Egyptians preceded the Hindus in civilization, there is reason to
believe, that they were the first people with whom any communication betwixt the eastern and western quarters of the ancient world
existed. (1810)

JAMES BRYCE[4]

## 5. The favoured country of Hindostan

Nature seems to have taken pleasure in embellishing and enriching
the favoured country of Hindostan with every choicest gift. Under a
pure sky and brilliant sun the soil produces the most exquisite fruits,
and the most abundant harvests; the rocks are rich in gems, the
mountains teem with gold, and the fleecy pod of the cotton furnishes
in profusion the light garment fitted to the climate. In travelling in
the interior your eyes will often be enchanted with the most delicious landscapes. Amidst stupendous forests you will not unfrequently be charmed with a cultivated spot, where, if ever, you might
realize the dreams of the poets, and indulge in that impassioned
indolence which is the parent of poetry and of the fine arts.

One would imagine Milton had mused in oriental groves when he
describes

> Insuperable heights of loftiest shade,
> Cedar and pine, and fir, and branching palm,
> A sylvan scene—

• • • • •

Groves whose rich trees wept odorous gums and balm.

> Others whose fruit burnished with golden rind
> Hung amiable, Hesperian fables true,
> If true, here only, and of delicious taste:
> Betwixt them lawns, or level downs, and flocks
> Grazing the tender herb were interposed
> On palmy hillock; or the flowery lap
> Of some irriguous valley spread her store,
> Flow'rs of all hues, and without thorn the rose.

I might go on to quote all his descriptions of Paradise and all its bowers, before I could exhaust the resemblances.

But, alas! it is not the natural riches of the country, nor the exquisite beauty of its sylvan scenery, that will most attract your attention. Vast cities now too large for their diminished inhabitants, towns embellished with temples and with tombs now falling to decay, and absolutely unpeopled, and stupendous monuments of art, which have not served to transmit even the names of their founders down to our times, will frequently arrest your steps; but while these are hastening to decay, the customs and habits of the natives seem immortal, and present us now with the same traits under which they are painted by the Greeks who visited them two thousand years ago. (1814)

MARIA GRAHAM[5]

## 6. First impressions

Soon after daylight on the morning of the 20th of July, we made the coast of Coromandel, and about noon four of the natives came out to us on *katamarans*, a species of raft used along this coast for riding through the surf: it is constructed of two large pieces of timber, lashed together at some little distance from each other, so as to admit the action of the water between them. These black fellows brought fruit and fish for sale; but, oh, how the ladies, both old, middle-aged, and young, did blush when they saw four hairy rascals jump on board in a constume to which, in comparison, Achilles in Hyde Park is liberally clad; some turned their heads and placed a thin veil between their organs of vision and the eysore; some screened their eyes with their open fingers or lattice-worked ivory fans, while others again—but come, I will spare them and the modest reader further blushes.

We gave the fellows some small copper coins and a bottle of brandy, with which they disappeared over the ship's side highly delighted with their speculation. We saw them tap the spirits by breaking a round hole in the shoulder of the bottle, and the scramble for the contents which ensued was highly amusing. Some after dark the Madras light-house hove in sight, and a spanking breeze carried us into the roads, where we cast anchor at ten o'clock P.M. (1831)

THOMAS BACON[6]

## 7. First reactions

I hope we shall soon have a respite from uninvited company, and be able to ask young Ch——, whom we are both longing to see; but our house is a complete hotel for people we do not care to see, and I know not a greater bore than 'Indian hospitality,' as it is called by travellers. Some time ago there was an order given to build a public bungalow at this place; but the Government changed their minds, and desired that none should be built at the *stations*, 'as the residents can always receive travellers.' This is mean enough, but all of a piece with the rest of their proceedings. In order to save money, Lord W. Bentinck reduced the army and sold the stores; and now there is a war beginning, and not soldiers enough to carry it on. They are trying to raise regiments in a hurry, and find that all the able-bodied men who ought to be soldiers, have been shipped off as slaves to the Mauritius. The Commanders-in-Chief at the three Presidencies are all going home, and the Governors can do nothing without them: so India is in fact governed by the private secretaries, who are not responsible for the mischief they do, and are often intent only on feathering their own nests and promoting their young relations. Half the experienced men in the service who really understand matters are kept in subordinate situations, and young raw snips placed over their heads, to ride races and try fancies, whilst the country is in the most dangerous condition. (1836–9)

JULIA CHARLOTTE MAITLAND[7]

## 8. The aspect of the country

The increase and extension of geographical knowledge is as much a feature of modern improvement as any recent discovery in the arts, or in the circle of sciences. When Columbus went forth to explore the farther Indies by a western route, the region now denominated

'Katamarans Crossing the **Surf** on the Coromandel Coast', drawn by Charles Gold

British India was a *terra incognita,* as much as the laws which now regulate chemical affinities were unknown to the alchemist, or the fanatic enthusiast, who wildly groped in search of the philosopher's stone. The land of the banian and the palm, of the spice-cane and the pepper, where the choicest condiments and most valuable articles of commerce are in abundance produced, lay upon the map an unexplored region; since its paths had for ages been untrodden, and its many tribes had been despised as a people of a strange speech. The rays of science and the light of literature have now shone on the lofty mountains, and penetrated the valleys and trackless wilds; the energies of commerce and the daring of ambition have stemmed the majestic rivers, and circumnavigated the outstretched coast of Hindostan. The historian and the painter have recently described her inhabitants and her scenery. Industry and talent, enterprise, and perseverance, have explored regions and tribes which were long hidden, or but partially known. What was scattered in many and inaccessible repertories has been condensed; and the information which was shut up or monopolized in the libraries of the wealthy or the learned is now widely and cheaply diffused, and brought to our fire-sides and tea-tables. Hindostan is better known to-day than the Hebrides were in the time of Johnson, or than the Shetland Isles were at the beginning of the present century; while the aggressions and acquisitions of our English nabobs in oriental countries, the subversion of Asiatic despotism, and the substitution of British rule among the nations of the East, are the records of our cabinet libraries, and form the *vade mecums* of every inquirer after knowledge. (1839)

J.W. MASSIE[8]

## 9. *The land of wonders*

So far as I am able to judge, nothing has been left undone, either by man or Nature, to make India the most extraordinary country that the sun visits on his round. Nothing seems to have been forgotten, nothing overlooked. Always, when you think you have come to the end of her tremendous specialties and have finished hanging tags upon her as the Land of the Thug, the Land of the Plague, the Land of Famine, the Land of Giant Illusions, the Land of Stupendous Mountains, and so forth, another specialty crops up and another tag is required. I have been overlooking the fact that India is by an

unapproachable supremacy—the Land of Murderous Wild Creatures. Perhaps it will be simplest to throw away the tags and
generalize her with one all-comprehensive name, as the Land of
Wonders. (1896)

MARK TWAIN[9]

## 10. The problem of India

India is full of problems, the first and greatest of all being to the
Englishman how to get through each successive hot weather; for
hidden away in this mere question of personal discomfort lies a very
large question.

How long can we—a race who, owing to the climate, cannot bring
up our children in India—remain lords paramount of the soil; for we
are the Government, and the Government is absolute owner of
every inch of land? It is true that what with permanently assessed
land-tax here, and the rights of hereditary tenants there, we have
frittered away much of our sovereign power uselessly, idly; but the
land from time immemorial was the Crown's, and only the Crown's.

But it is evident we cannot colonise it. Nature has decreed that we
remain in India on sufferance.

Are we to remain so always, spending our best years, giving our
best lives to India, or are we by and by to take off our hats and say
politely, 'That is enough, you can fend for yourselves'?

That is a great problem; and the second is like unto it. In what
condition ought we in this case to leave India? Shall she be attired in
the latest Paris fashion, or should she be dressed in a manner more
suitable to the climate?

So far the answer has been unhesitatingly 'the Paris frock.' For
the last fifty years we have done our best by every means in our
power to 'raise' the standard of personal comfort in India. To a
certain extent we have succeeded. It is not nearly so easy for the
very poor to live as it used to be. There is a greater variation
between their status and the status of the rich. In the old days, from
one end to the other of India, the people, rich or poor, lived mostly
on the food staple of their particular country—wheat where it was
wheat, rice where it was rice. A little more clarified butter and sugar
for the rich, a little less for the poor—therein lay the chief difference
between them. They were housed in much the same fashion. The
palace was larger than the hovel, more decorated, but both alike

were devoid of luxury. Even now in conservative palaces there is no furniture,—a table, a chair or two for the convenience of Europeans or Europeanised natives; for the rest, often tattered carpets and string beds. Some years ago when the chief of perhaps the richest State in India lay sick of typhoid fever, the English doctor asked for a teaspoon. There was not one. Salt, sugar, everything was laid before His Highness in a leaf, and he helped himself with his fingers.

Only the other day some philanthropical ladies were shocked at their horrified complaints that the poor plague patients actually had no sheets to their beds being met by a hearty laugh. There are no sheets or towels in India.

Fine clothes, rich jewels, and a redundancy of fat differentiated the Raja from his ryots; little-else.

Are we to change this simplicity of life if we can, by our shibboleth of raising the standard of personal comfort? Are we to preach our Gospel of Ease for the few, and inoculate India with all its resulting discomfort for the many? There is no poor law in India: none is necessary. The patriarchal system and religious charity supply its place.

Are we to discourage this, levy a poors' rate, and build work-houses? Is it necessary for the due mental progress of India that her sons should be educated to admire the *Spectator*, and translate Tennyson's 'Lotos-Eaters' into Urdu doggerel?

Not long ago all these minor evils were considered to be inevitably bound up in all true progress. Pauperism was its lineal descendant. Some one must be left behind in the race. The conflict of classes, the over specialisation of the individual both in work and play, the Trades-Union doctrine of labour limited by the lowest and not by the highest,—these, and many another palpably immoral position had to be borne with for the sake of civilisation. (1905)

FLORA ANNIE STEEL[10]

## 11. Impressions

The tourist who credits unfavourable accounts of the country about to be visited starts with the advantage of avoiding many disappointments and of being prepared for many shortcomings. The pleasures of anticipation may not be so keen; but, on the other hand, there will be fewer cherished illusions to be dispelled, and a spirit of tolerance and sweet reasonableness will take the place of

the too usual feeling of annoyance. Every defect such a tourist
discovers will confirm his prejudices and flatter his judgment; while
any excellence met with will come as an unexpected pleasure. If full
credit had been given to all the critics of India and the Indians, we
should have concluded that to thoroughly enjoy touring in India one
must have the digestion of an ostrich, the patience of Job, the
temper of an angel, the nerves of a veteran and a sailor's capacity for
sleep. We were told that the food was of bad quality, ill-cooked, and
unclean; that the hotels were abominable, and the dak bungalows
worse: that the shopkeepers were cheats and swindlers; that servants were liars and rogues; that railway night travelling was most
uncomfortable, and the turmoil around the hotels unbearable; and
that cholera, dysentery, and enteric lurked in the water, plague and
tetanus in the earth beneath, and small pox and fever in the air
above. Lastly, we were warned that Northern India is always cold in
winter, and sometimes very cold indeed, so we were prepared to
meet the rigours of what turned out to be the coldest Indian winter
'in the memory of the oldest inhabitants,' and enjoyed the comforts
of our warmest clothes and heaviest wraps instead of shivering in
the barn-like rooms constructed to keep out the sun and let in the
penetrating winds.

Although there is some foundation for much of what is said about
the discomforts and even hardships of travelling in India, yet most
of the dangers can be avoided by taking proper precautions, and
most of the discomforts minimised by the experienced traveller. It is
true that most of the hotels are poor; but as long as the resident
sahibs insist on getting full board and lodgings at six rupees (say
eight shillings), or less, a day, they are not likely to be very good; but
in the centres where tourists congregate, and higher prices are
willingly paid, the hotels are in many cases improving in their details
of management, and more modern buildings are springing up to
meet the increased demand. (1905)

WALTER DEL MAR[11]

## 12.  'Why India interests us'

It is sometimes a little surprising to find how many people at home
take a keen interest in matters which concern our great empire in
the East. It is not always one which appears to lead to any very exact
acquaintance with either its geography or its history, but it is

genuine, so far as it goes. It will be found that this interest is very generally one with personal considerations behind it; for our national connexion with India has, during the last two hundred years, affected more or less closely a very large number of families at home. It will be at once seen that we stand in a very different position towards India from that which we occupy in relation to our great colonial possessions. We never cease to be exiles in the East. Large numbers of people go out to our colonies and become presently lost to English life and almost to English memory. They become absorbed in the growing population of the new country, and settle permanently there. It is not so with India. There we do not and cannot colonize. We send out a steadily increasing stream of people, bent on the affairs of commerce, of government, or of religion, but they all come back again. The exceptions to the rule consist almost wholly of those who have gone to that bourne from which no traveller returns. Hence one finds everywhere people who are interested in anything which concerns life and work in India.

And it is indeed a country, or rather a continent, worthy of our attention and concern. It has a wonderful and stirring history. It was the home of ancient civilizations which go back to the dim dawn of history. There, six hundred years before Christ, one of the most influential systems of religion the world has ever known, still powerful to-day, had its birth. Three hundred years later Alexander the Great crossed its borders in his conquering career. Long before the Buddha taught, Hinduism, in the days of its comparative purity, ruled the minds and consciences of men; and long before Alexander came, Hindu monarchs reigned in pomp and power. In later days, still ancient as our newer races count antiquity, Mohammedan and other empires have reared themselves on the ruins of the old, and at last we, first represented by little bands of merchant adventurers, are become the heirs of all.

There is no story written that is more thrilling than that of the toils and triumphs of the British in India, but it is not our purpose even to attempt to tell it here. There are pages in the story, of course, that we might well wish to have expunged; but, on the whole, it is a worthy record, and one of which we have no reason to be ashamed. The position of to-day has been gained, not by craft and fraud, but by sacrifice and suffering. We never set out to win an empire, though it has come. But the great possession has cost a great price; and many a life-story in India, whether of the obscure or well-known man, might well be summed up in the words of that noble line on the tomb of Henry Lawrence in the Residency garden at Lucknow: 'He tried to do his duty.'

To-day the statesman finds in India some of the most absorbing problems that can occupy his attention, and to many of these British rule is affording a remarkable solution. It displays a great variety of method and a great power of adaptation to the needs of the many races of the continent. The British Government has gone to a length not often realized at home in placing matters of internal administration in capable native hands, as in the outstanding case of the Mysore State, which has long been restored to its Indian rulers.

The merchant knows that here is one of the great markets of the world, the imports and exports of which together amount to over a hundred and fifty millions sterling per annum. He knows, too, that it is a market that calls for the closest attention, if Great Britain is to retain its predominant importance there. (1906)

WILLIAM H. HART[12]

## 13. The country

A country makes its inhabitants in more senses than one. This is true of India.

In the first place a country must be able to sustain inhabitants, or they will not exist. There is a natural limit to its population. At one extreme is the Sahara desert, at the other the Nile valley. In India both extremes are found. The native state of Jaisalmir in western Rajputana can barely support a population of under five persons to the square mile. In the Gangetic plain 500 to the square mile is of common occurrence. We are speaking of course of purely agricultural tracts. Where manufactures exist which can be exchanged for food, the case is different.

Again, a country may be said to make its inhabitants in that their faculties and dispositions are largely influenced by its physical and climatic conditions. The statement that man is the product of his surroundings is qualified by the fact that race has a great resisting power. The qualities of race will often persist in the face of adverse circumstances. The many races that make up the population of India maintain their distinctive characters, though for centuries they have lived side by side. None the less India has stamped them with a common seal, and has wrought out a recognizable type amid a great profusion of species.

Lastly, a country makes its inhabitants so far as it determines their political history. The fertility of a country may prove its ruin, if accompanied by a soft and languid climate which saps the energies and weakens the combative instincts of the inhabitants. Of this Egypt is an instructive example. It has passed from one conqueror to another until it has lost the consciousness of national life. India, like Egypt, has been the coveted prize of the strong. But unlike Egypt it has in the long run absorbed its invaders and maintained its own civilization. It has been able to do this because its natural frontiers have protected it from invasion except at one or two points. These points are so distant from the centre that invasions of India always lost something of their first impetus before they could be pressed home. (1911)

T.W. HOLDERNESS[13]

## 14. The greatness of India

India. What does this name signify to ninety-nine out of a hundred of us beyond a triangle, coloured red, upon the map of Asia? We are told that the said triangle measures nineteen hundred miles in length from its widest point, from east to west; and that it contains an area rather larger than that of Europe west of the Vistula. The statement conveys little to us. We accept it as undoubtedly true, and, if we look at a map ot India superimposed upon one of Europe on the same scale, we are perhaps a little staggered. But we in our little island are accustomed to reckon by acres, not by thousands of square miles; and, strive as we may against the tendency, we find ourselves always attempting to apply our own puny standards to things Asiatic. We hear of great rivers, and instinctively recall the Thames at London Bridge, forgetting that a great Indian river in flood would fill the space from Westminster Abbey to the Crystal Palace. We are told of mighty mountains, and commit to memory the bald fact that some of them soar to twice the height of Mount Blanc; we are aware, perhaps, that they form a barrier practically impassable by man along the immense northern frontier of India; possibly we may even realise with awe that they make the vast reservoir of water, in the form of snow, which feeds the gigantic rivers already mentioned. So much we may gather, with moderate intelligence, from our maps. But there is one thing more, the most important thing of all, and of all the most impossible to grasp. This red-coloured triangle contains three hundred and twenty million people, six times the population of France, thrice the population of the United States, one-fifth, as it is reckoned, of the men, women and children living upon this planet. (1911)

JOHN FORTESCUE[14]

## 15 *The two Indias*

There are indeed two Indias: the India of the large towns from which the casual visitor draws his impressions, and which with considerable clamour voices the aspirations of perhaps a tenth of the total population of the country; and the India—the real India—of the silent millions who lead a simple rural life, contented with the thoughts and occupations of their fore-fathers, inherited from the distant past. This is the population of which only the experienced Anglo-Indian has any real cognisance, and it is from long contact with this that he principally derives those feelings of kindliness and sympathy which make for friendship and esteem between the races. (1913)

SAMUEL JOHN THOMSON[15]

# 2. Philosophy

## 1. No freewill with Hindoos

Serenaut [Srinath], the Bamin [Brahman] Doctor at Pottana, saith tis writ in their Bookes That man hath no Freewill, and saith that mans heart may be compared to God as a Spider web is to a Spider, for which way soever the Spider draws, the Webb follows; or as a man that holds the Sail of a Ship, and as he turnes the saile, so the ship goes. So as God turnes the heart of man, so it acts, for they are one. And so hee saith That there is no such thing as Sinn in the world; and as for murders, thefts, etc.—these are but sports to God and the persons instruments wherwith hee playes. And as for the Bamins not killing any living creature or not eating flesh, etc., these are only to keep in awe the ignorant etc., least should rebell.

Hee also saith that the Soule of man may be compared to the flame of a candle which when once is extinct, is no more; so our soule when leaves this body is annihilated as to (?) us. That tis like water which sometimes retains one colour, sometimes another. So God puts out our Soules from this body, [and] sometimes puts it into another body and at sometimes useth it no more. That all the Actions in the world are but sports to God, whereby hee pleaseth himselfe with changing them, and causeth some men to act one way, others another, and all their actions proceed from their heart or will, which is all one with God. So that man is but an instrument wherewith God sports and pleaseth himselfe, and the Soule which is the same with God, if God enlightens it in another body, it remembers not that it ever acted here before.

That God and mans Soule may be compared to the Sea and other water, for all water at first was in the Sea, yet knows not that it was so. Sometimes tis tinctured with one colour, sometimes with another, yet tis but all one water. So all is but one Soule, though in severall parts of the world and acting distinctly as to us, but as to God all one; as a Net that hath many turnings and winding, yet is but one thred and is for one use. So that the severall Soules of men are but as sparkes of God kindling severall parts of the matter in the world in severall bodies or clays, where resides so long as the fewell is capable of giveing nourishment to it, after which it extinguisheth and becomes what it was before it had kindled that clay. (1668–72)

JOHN MARSHALL[16]

## 2.  The philosophical schools

The *six* philosophical schools, whose principles are explained in *Dersana Sastra*, comprise all the metaphysicks of the old *Academy*, the *Stoa*, the *Lyceum;* nor is it possible to read the *Vedanta*, or the many fine composition in illustrations of it, without believing PYTHAGORAS and PLATO derived their sublime theories from the same fountain with the sages of *India*. (1786)

WILLIAM JONES[17]

## 3.  Hindu systems of philosophy

The Hindus have six systems of philosophy, named the *Nyaya, Vaiseshika, Sankhya, Yoga, Vedanta,* and *Mimansa.* The *Vaiseshika* being in some sort supplementary to the *Nyaya,* the two are familiarly spoken of as one collective system, under the name of the *Nyaya*; and as the case is somewhat similar with the two other pairs, it is customary to speak of Hindu philosophy as being divisible into the *Nyaya,* the *Sankhya,* and the *Vedanta.*

These three systems, if we follow the commentators, differ more in appearance than in reality; and hence they are, each in its degree, viewed with a certain amount of favour by orthodox Hindus. The partisans of one system may and do impugn the dogmas of another; but, although every one in such a contest nerves his arms to the uttermost, and fights as if his character were staked upon the issue, yet the lances are lances of courtesy, and the blows are loving ones. It is a very different affair when the *denier of the Vedas* is dealt with. With Buddhist. for example—though his notion of the chief end of man differs in no respect from that of the others—the battle is *a l'outrance.* The common bond of the others is their implicit acceptance of the Vedas, *which they explain differently.* According to the epigrammatic remark, that theological dislikes vary inversely as the amount of disagreement, some might expect that these dissentient accepters of the Veda should be more bitter against one another than against the common enemy. But epigrams are not always to be

trusted. As Dominican and Franciscan are brothers in asserting the
infallibility of Rome; so are the *Nyaya*, the *Sankhya*, and the
*Vedanta*, in asserting the infallibility of the Veda against the Buddhist.

Assuming, each of them implicitly, the truth of the Vedas, and
proceeding to give, on that foundation, a comprehensive view of the
totality of things, the three systems differ in their *point of view*. To
illustrate this, suppose that three men in succession take up a
cylindrical ruler: the one, viewing it with its end towards his eye,
sees a circle; the second, viewing it upright before his eye, sees a
parallelogram; the third, viewing it in a direction slanting away in
front of his eye, sees a frustum of a cone. These three views are
different, but nowise irreconcileable. So far are they from being
irreconcileable, that it might be argued that *all* of them must be
accepted in succession, before any adequate conception of the form
of the ruler can be arrived at. Now, in somewhat such a way the
three Hindu systems differ mainly in their severally regarding the
universe from different points of view,—viz., as it stands in relation
severally to *sensation*, *emotion*, and *intellection*.

The *Naiyayika*, founding on the fact that we have various
*sensations*, enquires what and how many are the channels through
which such varied knowledge flows in. Finding that there are five
very different channels, he imagines five different externals adapted
to these. Hence his theory of the five elements, the aggregate of
what the *Nyaya* regards as the causes of affliction.

The *Sankhya*, struck with the fact that we have *emotions*— with
an eye to the question *whence* our impressions come,—enquires
their *quality*. Are they pleasing, displeasing, or indifferent? These
three qualities constitute, for him, the external; and to their aggregate he gives the name of Nature. With the *Naiyayika* he agrees in
wishing that he were well rid of all three; holding that things
pleasing, and things indifferent, are not less incompatible with
man's chief end than things positively displeasing.

Thus while the *Nyaya* allows to the external a substantial existence, the *Sankhya* admits its existence only as an aggregate of
qualities; while both allow that it really (eternally and necessarily)
exists.

The *Vedantin*, rising above the question as to what is pleasing,
displeasing, or indifferent, asks simply, what *is*, and what is *not*. The
categories are here reduced to two—the Real and the Unreal. The

categories of the *Nyaya* and the *Sankhya* were merely scaffolding for reaching this pinnacle of philosophy. The implied foundation was everywhere the same—viz., the **Veda**; and this, therefore, we shall find is the field on which the battle with Hindu philosophy must ultimately be fought.

The *Nyaya,* it may be gathered from what has been said, is conveniently introductory to the *Sankhya,* and the *Sankhya* to the *Vedanta.* Accordingly in Hindu schools, where all three are taught, it is in this order that the learner, who learns all three, takes them up. The *Nyaya* is the exoteric doctrine, the *Sankhya* a step nearer what is held as the truth, and the *Vedanta* the esoteric doctrine, or the naked truth. (1859)

JAMES R. BALLANTYNE[18]

## 4. *The Yoga*

The Yoga, commonly regarded as a branch of the Sankhya, is scarcely worthy of the name of a system of philosophy, though it has undoubted charms for the naturally contemplative and ascetical Hindu, and lays claim to greater orthodoxy than the Sankhya proper by directly acknowledging the existence of Isvara or a supreme Being. In fact, the aim of the Yoga is to teach the means by which the human soul may attain complete union with the supreme soul. This fusion (*laya*) or union of individual with universal spirit may be effected even in the body. According to Patanjali, the author of the system, the very word *Yoga* is interpreted to mean the act of 'fixing or concentrating the mind in abstract meditation,' and this is said to be effected by preventing the modifications of *Citta* or the thinking principle (which modifications arise through the three *Pramanas,* perception, inference, and verbal testimony, as well as through incorrect ascertainment, fancy, sleep, and recollection), by the constant habit (*abhyasa*) of keeping the mind in its unmodified state — a state clear as crystal when uncoloured by contact with other substances—and by the practice of *Vairagya*—that is, complete suppression of the passions. This *Vairagya* is only to be obtained by *Isvarapranidhana* or the contemplation of the supreme Being, who is defined to be a particular *Purusha* or Spirit unaffected by works, afflictions, etc., and having the appellation *Pranava* or *Om.* The repetition of this monosyllable is supposed to be attended with marvellous results, and the muttering of it with reflection on its meaning is said to be conducive to a knowledge of the Supreme and to a prevention of all the obstacles to Yoga. The eight means of mental concetration are—1, *Yama,* 'forbearance', 'restraint'. 2. *Niyama,* 'religious observances'. 3. *Asana,* 'postures'. 4. *Pranayama,* 'suppression of the breath' or 'breathing in a peculiar way'. 5. *Pratyahara,* 'restraint of the senses'. 6. *Dharana,* 'profound meditation', or rather a state of religious trance, which, according to the Bhagvad-gita (VI. 13), is most effectually attained by such practices as fixing the eyes intently and incessantly on the tip of the nose, etc. The system of Yoga appears, in fact, to be a mere contrivance for getting rid of all thought, or at least for concentrating the mind with the utmost intensity upon nothing in particular. It is a strange compound of mental and bodily exercises, consisting in unnatural restraint, forced and painful postures, twistings and contrortions of the limbs, suppressions of the breath, and utter absence of mind. But although the Yoga of Patanjali professes to effect union with the universal Spirit by means such as these, it should be ovserved that farmore severe austerities and self-imposed physical mortifications are popularly connected with the Yoga system. All Hindu devotees and ascetics, especially those who, as forming a division of the Saiva sect, identify the terrific god Siva with the supreme Being, are commonly called Yogins or Yogis, and indeed properly so called, in so far as the professed object of their austerities is union with the Deity. (1875)

MONIER WILLIAMS[19]

## 5. *Meditations of a Hindu prince*

All the world over, I wonder, in lands that I never have trod,
Are the people eternally seeking for the signs and steps of a
    God?
Westward across the ocean, and Northward ayont the snow,
Do they all stand gazing, as ever, and what do the wisest
    know?

Here, in this mystical India, the deities hover and swarm
Like the wild bees heard in the tree-tops, or the gusts of a
    gathering storm;
In the air men hear their voices, their feet on the rocks are
    seen,

Yet we all say, 'Whence is the message, and what may the
  wonders mean?'

A million shrines stand open, and ever the censer swings,
As they bow to a mystic symbol, or the figures of ancient kings;
And the incense rises ever, and rises the endless cry
Of those who are heavy laden, and of cowards, loth to die.

For the Destiny drives us together, like deer in a pass of the
  hills,
Above is the sky, and around us the sound of the shot that
  kills;
Pushed by a Power we see not, and struck by a hard unknown,
We pray to the trees for shelter, and press our lips to a stone.

The trees wave a shadowy answer, and the rock frowns hollow
  and grim,
And the form and the nod of the demon are caught in the
  twilight dim;
And we look to the sunlight falling afar on the mountain crest,
Is there never a path runs upward to a refuge there and a rest?

The path, ah! who has shown it, and which is the faithful
  guide?
The haven ah! who has known it? for steep is the mountain
  side,
For ever the shot strikes surely, and ever the wasted breath
Of the praying multitude rises, whose answer is only death.

Here are the tombs of my kinsfolk, the fruit of an ancient
  name,
Chiefs who were slain on the war-field, and women who died
  in flame;
They are gods, these kings of the foretime, they are spirits who
  guard our race;
Ever, I watch and worship; they sit with a marble face.

And the myriad idols around me, and the legion of muttering
  priests,
The revels and rites unholy, the dark unspeakable feasts!
What have they wrung from the Silence? Hath ever a whisper
  come
Of the secret, Whence and Whither? Alas! for the gods are
  dumb.

Shall I list to the word of the English, who come from the
   uttermost sea?
"The Secret, hath it been told you, and what is your message
   to me?"
It is nought but the wide-world story how the earth and the
   heavens began,
How the gods are glad and angry, and a Diety once
   was man.

I had thought, 'Perchance in the cities where the rulers of
   India dwell,
Whose orders flash from the far land, who girdle the earth with
   a spell,
They have fathomed the depths we float on, or measured the
   unknown main—'
Sadly they turn from the venture, and say that the quest is
   vain.

Is life, then, a dream and delusion, and where shall the
   dreamer awake?
Is the world seen like shadows on water, and what if the mirror
   break?
Shall it pass as a camp that is struck, as a tent that is gathered
   and gone
From the sands that were lamp-lit at eve, and at morning are
   level and lone?

Is there nought in the heaven above, whence the hail and the
   levin are hurled,
But the wind that is swept around us by the rush of the rolling
   world?
The wind that shall scatter my ashes, and bear me to silence
   and sleep
With the dirge, and the sounds of lamenting, and voices of
   women who weep. (1889)

ALFRED COMYN LYALL[20]

## 6. *A visit to a Gnani*

Everything in the East is different from the West, and so are the
methods of teaching. Teaching in the East is mainly authoritative
and traditional. That is its strong point and also its defect. The pupil

is not expected to ask questions of a sceptical nature or expressive of doubt; the teacher does not go about to 'prove' his thesis to the pupil, or support it with arguments drawn from the plane of the pupil's intelligence; he simply redelivers to the pupil, in a certain order and sequence, the doctrines which were delivered to him in his time, which have been since verified by his own experience, and which he can illustrate by phrases and metaphors and citations drawn from the sacred books. He has, of course, his own way of presenting the whole, but the body of knowledge which he thus hands down is purely traditional, and may have come along for thousands of years with little or no change. Originality plays no part in the teaching of the Indian Sages. The knowledge which they have to impart is of a kind in which invention is not required. It purports to be a knowledge of the original fact of the universe itself—something behind which no man can go. The West may originate, the West may present new views of the prime fact—the East only seeks to give to a man that fact itself, the supreme consciousness, undifferentiated, the key to all that exists.

The Indian teachers, therefore, say there are as a rule three conditions of the attainment of Divine knowledge or *gnanam*—(1) the study of the sacred books; (2) the help of a Guru; and (3) the verification of the tradition by one's own experience. Without this last the others are, of course, of no use; and the chief aid of the Guru is directed to the instruction of the pupil in the methods by which he may attain to personal experience. The sacred books give the philosophy and some of the experiences of the *gnani* or illuminated person, but they do not, except in scattered hints, give instruction as to how this illumination is to be obtained. The truth is, it is a question of evolution; and it would neither be right that such instruction should be given to everybody, nor indeed possible, since even in the case of those prepared for it the methods must differ, according to the idiosyncrasy and character of the pupil.

There are apparently isolated cases in which individuals attain to *gnanam* through their own spontaneous development, and without instruction from a Guru, but these are rare. As a rule, every man who is received into the body of Adepts receives his initiation through another Adept who himself received it from a forerunner, and the whole constitutes a kind of church or brotherhood with genealogical branches so to speak—the line of Adepts from which a man descends being imparted to him on his admission into the fraternity. I need not say that this resembles the methods of the ancient mysteries and initiation of classic times; and, indeed, the Indian teachers claim that the Greek and Egyptian and other Western schools of arcane lore were merely branches, more or less degenerate, of their own.

The course of preparation for *gnanam* is called *yogam*, and the person who is going through this stage is called a *yogi*—from the root *yog*, to join—one who is seeking union with the universal spirit. Yogis are common all over India, and exist among all classes and in various forms. Some emaciate themselves and torture their bodies, others seek only control over their minds, some retire into the jungles and mountains, others frequent the cities and exhibit themselves in the crowded fairs, others again carry on the avocations of daily life with but little change of outward habit. Some are humbugs, led on by vanity or greed of gain (for to give to a holy man is highly meritorious); others are genuine students or philosophers; some are profoundly imbued with the religious sense; others by mere distaste for the world. The majority probably take to a wandering life of the body, some become wandering in mind; a great many attain to phases of clairvoyance and abnormal power of some kind or other, and a very few become Adepts of a high order. (1892)

EDWARD CARPENTER[21]

## 7. Of Hindu ethical thought

... Hindu ethical thought and practice have rested on presuppositions of a different kind from those on which the ethical thought and practice of the West have rested. All down through the history of Hindu thought it has been almost taken for granted that individuality is a limitation, and that as such it is something that must be transcended. In the great systems of philosophy this is taken as almost axiomatic, though there are differences in the explanations given of the illusion of individuality and the methods by which it is to be dispelled. We are not unmindful of Ramanuja, or of other thinkers and religious leaders who have taught the doctrine of the reality of the soul not as essentially one with God, but as distinct from God and capable of entering into union with Him. The significance of such doctrines has already been discussed, and nothing that we have seen of them in their theoretical formulation or their practical expression serves to modify the general impression which we receive of the practical tendencies of Hindu thought. Without committing ourselves to any sweeping generalization, we may say that even with thinkers who have denied the illusoriness of personal existence, the end of man has been thought of as being in the silence. It has been characteristic of Hindu thought generally that the world of ordinary experience has been thought of as a barrier blocking the way to Reality. It is not conceived as in any way revealing the Real, which is to be found through negation of the phenomenal.

The reply is sometimes made that these conceptions are not distinctive of Hindu thought. Deussen in particular has sought to maintain the essential similarity of the solution of the philosophical problem given by the great thinkers of India and of the West. But in spite of all that may be said, the great thinkers of the West have held that there is a pathway to the Real through the phenomenal, and that there is a pathway to the goal of human attainment through the performance of the duties of 'the good neighbour and the honest citizen.' Hindu philosophy has its *Karma-kanda,* its system of works propaideutic to the *Jnana-kanda,* but none of the great systems of thought contains anything that can properly be called a system of ethics. They represent the end as a form of being in which the ethical is simply transcended, and, what is more important, as standing in no vital relation to any discipline of a strictly ethical kind.

Let the case be stated bluntly. Those ideas which bulk so largely in the Vedanta, and which find expression in other systems of philosophy, when logically applied, leave no room for ethics. Nevertheless, as has been already shown, if human life is to go on at all there are certain principles in accordance with which it must be carried on. This practical need is met by the system of *dharma,* in which guidance is given for human conduct in almost infinite detail. These details are to a large extent connected with ritual obser-vance, and only to a limited extent are they of the nature of moral precepts. In so far as moral duties are inculcated, the details of the moral law are partly drawn from sources common to primitive morality generally, as in the case of the duties of hospitality to strangers, liberality, and such like; partly they are the outcome of the peculiar philosophical notions which had grown up, as in the case of the various ascetic disciplines. We cannot draw a sharp line of distinction between these two sources, for disciplines which later came to have a more strictly moral appearance were in some cases practised originally in the belief that they had magical efficacy. But the important thing for us to consider now is the fact that *dharma* has to do with a lower sphere of experience. It serves as a sort of platform over which one may climb to a position from which it becomes easier to reach the higher, but when this position has been reached it is no longer needed. (1922)

JOHN McKENZIE[22]

# 3. Religion

## A. HINDUISM

### 1. A form of Worship

The Hindus honour their idols on account of those who erected
them, not on account of the material of which they are made. We
have already mentioned that the idol of Multan was of wood, *e.g.*
the *linga* which Rama erected when he had finished the war with the
demons was of sand, which he had heaped up with his own hand.
But then it became petrified all at once, since the astrologically
correct moment for the erecting of the monument fell before the
moment when the workmen had finished the cutting of the stone
monument which Rama originally had ordered. Regarding the
building of the temple and its peristyle, the cutting of the trees of
four different kinds, the astrological determination of the favourable moment for the erection, the celebration of the rites due on such
an occasion, regarding all this Rama gave very long and tedious
instructions. Further, he ordered that servants and priests to minister to the idols should be nominated from different classes of the
people. 'To the idol of Vishnu are devoted the class called
Bhagavata; to the idol of the Sun, the Maga, i.e. the Magians; to the
idol of Mahadeva, a class of saints, anchorites with long hair, who
cover their skin with ashes, hang on their persons the bones of dead
people, and swim in the pools. The Brahmana are devoted to the
Eight Mothers, the Shamanians to Buddha, to Arhant the class
called *Nagna*. On the whole, to each idol certain people are devoted
who constructed it, for those know best how to serve it.' (c. A.D.
1000)

ALBERUNI[23]

### 2. Manner of worshipping

... They pray facing eastwards, in the Russian manner; they raise
high both hands and put them on their crown, and lie face downwards on the ground and stretch out on it—that is how they worship.

And when they sit down to take a meal, some wash their hands and feet, and also rinse their mouths. Their *butkhanahs* have no doors, and face eastwards; the *buts,* too, stand facing eastwards. And when someone dies, they burn him and scatter the ashes over water. And when a woman gives birth to a child, it is her husband who receives it; a son is named by the father, and daughter by the mother. In coming or going, they bow after the fashion of monks, touching the ground with both hands and saying nothing.

They go to Parvat at Lent to worship their *but*; that is their Jerusalem, or Mecca in the Moslem tongue. And they all arrive naked, too, save for a dhoti about their buttocks; some wear dhotis and pearl necklaces and many sapphires, and also gold bracelets and rings, in faith they do. And they go to the *butkhanah* astride on oxen, and each ox has its horns encased in brass, and wears about 300 bells round its neck, and has its hoofs shod. And those oxen are called 'fathers'. The Indians call the ox 'father' and the cow, 'mother'; they use the dung as fuel to bake bread and cook their food, and smear their faces, foreheads, and bodies with the ashes. That is their sign. On Sundays and Mondays, they have one meal, by day. (1466–72)

AFANASY NIKITIN[24]

## 3. The delusive pictures

Blue crystal vault, and elemental fires,
   That in the ethereal fluid blaze and breathe,
   Thou tossing main, whose snaky branches wreathe
   This pensile orb with intertwisted gyres;
     Mountains whose radiant spires

Presumptuous rear their summits to the skies,
   And blend their emerald hue with sapphire light;
   Smooth meads and lawns, that glow with varying dyes
   Of dew-bespangled leaves and blossoms bright,
     Hence vanish from my sight:

Delusive pictures, unsubstantial shows!
   My soul absorbed One only being knows,
   Of all perceptions One abundant source,
   Whence every object every moment flows,
     Suns hence derive their force,

Hence planets learn their course;
But suns and fading worlds I view no more:
God only I perceive; God only I adore. (1783-94)

WILLIAM JONES[25]

## 4. The Hindu religion

The Hindoo religion admits of no proselytes; and is therefore a principal means of preserving the castes pure and distinct: neither have the Mahomedan conquests and oppressions, nor the intercourse of Europeans with the Hindoos, been able to subvert a system of theology and jurisprudence, founded on a firm basis, and interdicted from all change by the most rigid laws.

This religious and moral system is no doubt of great antiquity; but those who have deeply investigated the ancient and pleasing fictions in the Hindoo mythology, which bears a great resemblance to that of the Greeks, and may perhaps be traced to the same origin, are of opinion, that the religious and civil laws of the Hindoos, called the Institutes of Menu, were compiled about eight hundred and eighty years before the birth of our Saviour; that the Vedas, or sacred volumes, were written three hundred years prior to the Institutes; and that preceding this period, every thing being handed down by oral tradition, the account was obscure and fabulous.

But divested of extraneous matter, there appears to be a great degree of purity and sublimity in the genuine principles of the Hindoo religion, though now obscured by superstitious rites and ceremonies, and blended with gross idolatry: in their original simplicity, they teach that there is one supreme ruler of the universe; who is styled Brahma, or the Great One: they inculcate also, that his supreme intelligence consists of a triad, or triple divinity, expressed by the mystic word Om; and distinguished by the names of Vishnu, Brahma, and Sheva; or the creating, preserving, and destructive power of the Almighty. Images of these attributes are placed in their temples; and worship and sacrifices are daily performed before them, and a variety of other statues, representing the different qualities of the Supreme Being: so that it is a complete system of polytheism, and a source of a thousand fables subversive of truth and simplicity. (1812)

JAMES FORBES[26]

## 5. *A hymn to Comdeo*

Sir William Jones has translated a hymn to Camdeo (a deity), which
is replete with beauty and oriental imagery, from which I shall only
select these stanzas, as a most elegant illustration of the character of
this powerful deity, and especially of his bow and arrows.

What potent god from *Agra's* orient bow'rs
Floats thro'the lucid air, whilst living flow'rs
With sunny twine the vocal arbours wreathe,
And gales enamour'd heav'nly fragrance breathe?
  Hail, pow'r unknown, for at thy beck
  Vales and groves their bosoms deck;
  And ev'ry laughing blossom dresses
  With gems of dew his musky tresses.
I feel, I feel thy genial flame divine,
And hallow thee, and kiss thy shrine.

God of the flow'ry shafts and flow'ry bow,
Delight of all above and all below!
Thy lov'd companion, constant from his birth,
In heav'n clep'd *Bessent,* and gay *Spring* on earth,
  Weaves thy green robe and flaunting bow'rs,
  And from thy clouds draws balmy show'rs;
  He with fresh arrows fills thy quiver,
  (Sweet the gift, and sweet the giver!)
And bids the many-plum'd warbling throng
Burst the pent blossoms with their song.

He bends the luscious cane, and twists the string,
With bees how sweet! but ah, how keen their sting!
He with five flow'rets tips thy ruthless darts
Which thro' five senses pierce enraptur'd hearts:
  Strong *Champa,* rich in od'rous gold,
  Warm *Amer,* nurs'd in heav'nly mould.
  Dry *Nagkeser,* in silver smiling,
  Hot *Kiticum* our sense beguiling
And last, to kindle fierce the scorching flame
*Loveshaft,* which gods bright *Bela* name

Thy mildest influence to thy bard impart,
To warm, but not consume, his heart. (1812)

JAMES FORBES[27]

## 6. *The religion of Brahminism*

The character of a people is not always easily discriminated, and the
theme becomes almost boundless, when it embraces the nations
spread over the wide surface of continental India. For though the
Hindoo race inhabit the whole of Hindostan, the varied tribes are
not less diversified than are the distinct branches of the elder
Scythian family now scattered over the continent of Europe; it
would, therefore, be no less indiscriminate to hold up the Gentoo as
an exemplification or model of the whole Indian community, than it
would be to denominate the Italians the representatives of every
European nation. It is true that the religion of Brahminism possesses sway in the principal seats of commerce and of population
throughout British India, and religion is the general modeller of
human character. But the unity is a name rather than a reality, and
that which is prevalent is susceptible of shades as varying as are the
changes of colour. A glaring discrepancy and source of diversity, if
not also of division, are visible in the objects selected for male and
female partiality and devout adoration. While Brahmins celebrate
their licentious and midnight orgies before the goddess Kalee, or
the males of another caste adorn themselves with gross representations of sensual pleasure, and render the homage of their passions to
the emblematic lingam, which in a silver casket is suspended upon
their bosom, and exposed to the view of all, the Indian women
embrace Krishna (an eighth incarnation of Vishnu) as the darling
god of their affections, and hymn his praise in strains of amorous
delight, some of which are far from being inoffensive by their
indelicacy, and prohibit our transcription. A specimen, the least
objectionable, will suffice to exhibit whether their worship has any
claim to devotion or spirituality: 'With a garland of wild flowers,
descending even to the yellow mantle that girds his azure limbs,'
these are the words of their divine song, 'distinguished by smiling
cheeks, and earings that sparkle as he plays, Heri exults in the
assemblies of amorous damsels, of whom, one presses him to
her heaving bosom, while she warbles with exquisite melody;

another, affected by the glance of his eye, stands meditating on the lotos of his face; a third, on pretence of whispering a secret into his ear, approaches his temples, and kisses them with ardour. One seizes his mantle, and draws him toward her, pointing to the bower on the banks of the Yamuna, where elegant Vanjulas interweave their branches. He applauds another who dances in the sportive circle, while her bracelets ring as she beats time with her palms.' (1839)

J.W. MASSIE[28]

## 7. *Hindu system of religion*

The Hindu system is this. A great divine spirit or essence *Brimh* pervades the whole universe; and the soul of every human being is a drop from this great ocean, to which, when it becomes perfectly purified, it is reunited. The reunion is the eternal beatitude to which all look forward with hope; and the soul of the Brahman is nearest to it. If he has been a good man, his soul becomes absorbed in the *Brimh;* and if a bad man, it goes to *Naruk,* hell; and after the expiration of its period there of *limited imprisonment,* it returns to earth, and occupies the body of some other animal. It again advances by degrees to the body of the Brahman; and thence, when fitted for it, into the great Brimh. From this great eternal essence emanate Brimha, the creator, whose consort is Saraswatee; Vishnoo, the preserver, whose consort is Lukshmee; and Sewa, alias Mahadeo, the destroyer, whose consort is Parbuttee. According to popular belief, *Jumraj* is the judicial deity who has been appointed by the greater powers to pass the final judgment on the tenor of men's lives, according to proceedings drawn up by his secretary *Chuttergopat.* If men's actions have been good, their souls are, at the next stage, advanced a step towards the great essence Brimh; and if bad, they are thrown back, and obliged to occupy the bodies of brutes or of people of inferior caste, as the balance against them may be great or small. There is an intermediate stage, a *Naruk* or hell, for bad men, and a Bykout, or paradise, for the good, in which they find their felicity in serving that god of the three to which they have specially devoted themselves while on earth. But from this stage after the period of their sentence is expired, men go back to their pilgrimage on earth again.

There are numerous Deos, or good spirits, of whom Indur is the

chief; and Dyts, or bad spirits; and there have also been a great
number of incarnations from the three great gods and their con-
sorts, who have made their appearance upon the earth when required for particular purposes. All these incarnations are called
Outars, or descents. Vishnoo has been eleven times on the globe, in
different shapes, and Sewa seven times. The outars of Vishnoo are
celebrated in many popular poems, such as the Rumaen, or history
of the rape of Seeta, the wife of Ram, the seventh incarnation, the
Mahabhurut, and the Bhagiout, which describe the wars and
amours of this god in his last human shape. All these books are
believed to have been written either by the hand or by the inspiration of the god himself thousands of years before the events they
describe actually took place. 'It was, they say, as easy for the deity to
write or dictate a battle, an *amour,* or any other important event ten
thousand years before, as the day after it took place'; and I believe
nine-tenths, perhaps ninety-nine in a hundred, of the Hindoo population believe implicitly, that these accounts were all so written. It is
now pretty clear that all these works are of comparatively recent
date—that the great poem of the Mahabhurut could not have been
written before the year 786 of the Christian era, and was probably
written so late as A.D. 1157—that Krishna, *if born at all,* must have
been born on the 7th of August A.D. 600, but was most likely a
mere creation of the imagination to serve the purpose of the
Brahmans of Ojeyn, in whom the fiction originated—that the other
incarnations were invented about the same time, and for the same
object, though other persons described as incarnations were real
princes, Pursaram before Christ 1176, and Rama born before
Christ 961. In the Mahabhurut Krishna is described as fighting in
the same army with Judishter and his four brothers. Judishter was a
real person who ascended the throne at Dehlie 575 B.C., or 1175
years before the birth of Krishna. (1844)

WILLIAM HENRY SLEEMAN[20]

## 8. *Well of Fate*

For certain reasons you will next go and do homage at this well. You
will find it in the Dandpan Temple, in the city [Benares]. The
sunlight falls into it from a square hole in the masonry above. You
will approach it with awe, for your life is now at stake. You will
bend over and look. If the fates are propitious, you will see your face

pictured in the water far down in the well. If matters have been otherwise ordered, a sudden cloud will mask the sun and you will see nothing. This means that you have not six months to live. If you are already at the point of death, your circumstances are now serious. There is no time to lose. Let this world go, arrange for the next one. Handily situated, at your very elbow, is opportunity for this. You turn and worship the image of Maha Kal, the Great Fate, and happiness in the life to come is secured. If there is breath in your body yet, you should now make an effort to get a further lease of the present life. You have a chance. There is a chance for everything in this admirably stocked and wonderfully systemized Spiritual and Temporal Army and Navy Store. (1896)

MARK TWAIN[30]

## 9. *Hinduism*

Benares still holds Hinduism past and present. In one of its wide old gardens, set thick, not so much with flowers as with flowering trees, there lived till lately a survival of the most ancient days of Hinduism; for Swami Baskeranund claimed to be a Vedic man—that is, a man whose spiritual life, based on the teaching of the Vedas, knew nothing of priests or castes, or ceremonials. Certainly, he was a striking figure, and the very human vanity which led to his childish delight in his own marble statue, the very human perspicacity which made him invariably pick out those of the highest rank amongst his visitors for special favour, only emphasised the extraordinary expression of clear calm content upon his face. Almost naked, thin as an anatomy, hairless, toothless, there was such a dignity about him as doth hedge a king, and the look in his eyes was exactly that of the Child in the Madonna di San Sisto, a look of wearied yet unwearied wisdom.

What then was the creed of this man? Taking him as an example of what Hinduism teaches in the highest to its most apt pupils, it was the creed of Aristotle, of Plato, Socrates, Buddha, the Christ—the creed, that is, which comes again and again to the world robed in a new white robe of salvation for the sinner. He had already gone beyond the veil of the flesh; he had found unity behind it in the Holy-of-Holies. This sense of unity lies at the bottom of all philosophies, all religions; they do but voice man's eternal conviction of some higher life in which his puny, futile one can be merged.

It is not a conception which appeals much to the multitude, and so in India this fundamental belief is to be found overlaid with such a supercargo of superstition and crazy creeds that it is sometimes difficult to see that it exists.

But it does. The veriest coolie, if hard pressed, will tell you that even your Honour's anger is all '*Maya*' or illusion, and that the reality lies elsewhere; where, being a matter which scarcely concerns him, poor creature of a day. For all that, his mortal life is a perfect prey to such illusions, and the number of sanctions and limitations which he has to consider before he can get through a single day of it decently is perfectly appalling. These took possession of him long ere he was born, when his father and mother, in honour of his expected arrival, performed various ceremonies, the Uncooked-Food ceremony, the Cooked-Food ceremony, and finally the Feast-of-the-Five-Gifts, when milk, clarified butter, curds, honey, and cow dung are worshipped as the food of the gods.

There is a belief prevalent amongst Europeans that every Hindu has to be born in a cow-house. If this were so, it would still be no more hardship than the birth of the Christ in a stable; but it is not the case. The mother, being ceremonially unclean, cannot remain in the house, and therefore finds refuge in some building or lumber room, where she stays until the days of her purification are over. The seventh night after birth, Brahma, in his Wisdom-form, is supposed to come and write its fate upon the child's forehead. The following ceremonials vary with every caste, every race; but the name-giving, in which the father writes the name with a golden ring in unhusked rice, is curiously persistent; its persistency pointing to some now-forgotten symbolism. The ceremony of giving the child its first grain of rice when it is six months old is also a great festival; and so is the shaving of its head into the orthodox scalp lock, and the beginning of its education. For the latter, on some auspicious day agreed upon by the family priest, friends and relatives are called together, and with varying customs and rites the child, if it be a boy, is handed over to a teacher, who, invoking the aid of the gods, teaches his pupil the form of the first vowel by drawing it once more in unhusked rice.

Amongst Brahmans, however, the great festival of a boy's life is the day on which he is invested with the *zonar,* or sacred thread of second birth. Worn over the left shoulder, it is twisted of cotton wool and silk, and is the dearest possession of the priestly race. With it goes the right of repeating the sacred text, which is always whispered so that no other can hear it:

'Om! O! Earth, O! Air, O! Heaven Om! Let us meditate on the supreme splendour of the Divine Sun, and may His Light lighten us.'

This ceremony over, and child starts fair on its life as an orthodox Hindu, and for the most part leads the life of an apprentice to learning until the age of sixteen is reached. For Hinduism divides the life of man into four divisions or ages—Discipleship, Husbandhood, Parenthood, Saintship. In the first age you learn, in the second love and the world claim you, in the third your children, in the fourth the world beyond. So you pass out of one life into the next.

To a Hindu man or woman marriage is a solemn religious duty. It is an absolutely inviolable sacrament, and divorce is unknown; the underlying theory being that before God the male and the female form together the perfect human being. Therefore neither can really worship apart from the other. Before such a belief as this, it is idle to talk of the woman's position being degraded. It is not so in theory, whatever it may be in practice. Indeed, to any one who really thinks upon the vexed question of the relationship between the sexes, the Hindu standpoint is the only one that affords a stable foothold. For, once we allow personal passion its right on marriage, the difficulty of finding any point on which to cry 'Halt' becomes apparent.

Once married, a Hindu almost invariably becomes a perfect prey to his women folk, at any rate for some years. So many things are lucky, so many unlucky, that life tends to be one long propitiation or praise, festival or fast. It is astonishing to what lengths the woman's influence may go, and many an accurately dressed Europeanized native may carry about with him, carefully concealed, some ludicrous or even horrible talisman against evil spirits in which, were you to ask him, he would deny belief. He might also deny the efficacy of pilgrimages, but he goes on them, and the thirty and odd big festivals which raise his whole household to a pitch of pleasurable excitement during the year, find him quite ready to take his part in them. It is a quaint background to his self-contained semi-European life as clerk or merchant, lawyer or doctor. Yet it exists, and the man who has pled his case in court with a legal etiquette acquired in England, or spent his day over the commerce of many continents, may end it by wreathing the Goddess of Smallpox with strung flowers, or even by bathing in some dreadful admixture of the Five Gifts.

And yet under all the turmoil of almost senseless worship, behind all the thirty thousand and odd deities which are so worshipped in India, there is not one Hindu from Cape Cormorin to the Himalayas who would not scout the idea of there being more Gods than one, and that One Unknowable, Mysterious, Absolute Holiness. The rest are but Ideas founded by man in the vain effort to bring the Incomprehensible into comprehension.

Beyond this unalterable belief, and the belief in *Maya* or Illusion, there is no dogma in Hinduism. And *Maya* is the illusion of personality, of individualism. The whole universe is God, all things are forms of Him, yet men claim individual life, think of themselves as apart from Him. This is *Maya*. To escape from it is to realise Unity, to find oneself in all things, and all things in God. This is *Nirvana*.

So we come back to the philosophers of all ages, to the secret of all religions, to the merging of a puny individual life in the Greater one of Greater Dimensions. That this view of ourselves, our life, should necessarily lead to quietism, is the belief of the Western nations, to whom deadly doing and the gospel of personal comfort are a religion in themselves; but it is an erroneous belief, for once beyond the galling limitations of merely individual life the whole activities of the world are yours, and the blossoming of a flower, the glad song of the bird, the hammering on an ironclad's side, and the great cry for freedom which goes up from mankind are all equal harmonies in the symphony of existence.

It is a boundless horizon, but it is one which the Hindu has ever before his eyes, despite the multiplicity of his gods, and the endless tale of ceremony which compass him about on every side.

A Brahman, if he desires to perform his religious rites properly, should spend at least five hours a day over them, so complex have become the rules for ablution, expiation, and purification; and yet his aim is, as a great missionary writes almost contemptuously, 'to obtain knowledge which will ensure his reunion with God.'

The belief in life after death is general amongst Hindus. Heaven for a longer or shorter period awaits the soul which has striven towards the light, hell the soul which has chosen darkness. Then once more comes another chance, another reincarnation. So the wheel with its two pivots of birth and death turns, until the soul, escaping from the illusion, the limitations of personality, finds rest in the perfection of the Supreme. The process may last

for millions of years, but, in the end, as all things have emanated
from God, to Him they will return. (1912)

FLORA ANNIE STEEL[31]

## 10. *Pilgrims to Banaras*

From thence [Allahabad] wee went to Bannaras which is a great
towne, and great store of cloth is made there of cotton, and Shashes
for the Moores. In this place they be all Gentiles, and be the greatest
idolaters that euer I sawe. To this towne come the Gentiles on
Pilgrimage out of farre countreys. Here alongst the waters side bee
very many faire houses, and in all of them, or for the most part they
haue their images standing, which be euill fauoured, made of stone
and wood, some like lions, leopards, and monkeis, some like men
and women, and pecocks, and some like the deuil with foure armes
and 4. hands. They sit crosse legged, some with one thing in their
hands, & some another, and by breake of day and before, there are
men and women which come out of the towne and wash themselues
in Ganges. And there are diuers old men which upon places of earth
made for the purpose, sit praying, and they giue the people three or
fource strawes, which they take and hold them betweene their
fingers when they wash themselues: and some sit to marke them in
the foreheads, and they haue in a cloth a little Rice, Barlie, or
money, which, when they haue washed themselues, they giue to the
old men which sit there praying. Afterwards they go to diuers of
their images, & giue them of their sacrifices. And when they giue,
the old men say certaine prayers, and then is all holy. And in diuers
places there standeth a kind of image which in their language they
call Ada. And they haue diuers great stones carued, whereon they
poure water, and throw thereupon some rice, wheate, barlie, and
some other things. This Ada hath foure hands with clawes.
Moreouer, they haue a great place made of stone like to a well with
steppes to goe down; wherein the water standeth very foule and
stinketh: for the great quantitie of flowers, which continually they
throwe into it, doe make it stinke. There be alwayes many people in
it: for they say when they wash themselues in it, that their sinnes be
forgiuen them, because God, as they say, did wash himselfe in that
place. They gather up the sand in the bottome of it, and say it is holy.
They neuer pray but in the water, and they wash themselues ouer-
head, and lade up water with both their handes, and turne them-

selues about, and then they drinke a little of the water three times, and so goe to their gods which stand in those houses. Some of them will wash a place which is their length, and then will pray upon the earth with their armes and legs at length out, and will rise up and lie downe, and kisse the ground twentie or thirtie times but they will not stirre their right foote. And some of them will make their ceremonies with fifteene or sixteene pots litle and great, and ring a litle bel when they make their mixtures tenne or twelue times: and they make a circle of water round about their pots and pray, and diuers sit by them, and one that reacheth them their pots: and they say diuers things ouer their pots many times, and when they haue done, they goe to their gods, and strowe their sacrifices which they thinke are very holy, and marke many of them which sit by, in the foreheads, which they take as a great gift. There come fiftie and sometime an hundred together, to wash them in this well, and to offer to these idols. (1583)

RALPH FITCH[32]

## 11. Pilgrims at Puri

The great temple of Juggernauth—although, at some distance, and particularly from the sea view, it presents an imposing appearance—is, on a closer inspection, neither remarkable for its architecture, nor the materials of which it is composed; the latter being rough stone overlaid with a coating of course chunam. The khetr, chief tower, and other minor buildings connected with it, are comprised within a wall surrounding a platform raised high above the ground and no less than six hundred and fifty feet in length. The height of the tower is two hundred feet. According to ancient Brahmanical records preserved in the building, the temple of Sri Jeo or Juggernauth, existed many centuries before Christ; was destroyed and rebuilt sundry times, and was lastly restored, in A.D. 1198 by Rajah Bhim Deo, of Orissa, who is said to have expended nearly five hundred thousand pounds on the work. Within its holy precincts many inferior deities are provided with lodgings and attendants: but the most revered of the divine occupants are Juggernauth (the Lord of the World), an *alias* of the many-named Vishnu; Buldeo his brother, and their sister, the saffron-coloured Subhadra.

These personages are only twice a year indulged in an airing, which is fortunate, as a team of fifteen hundred men is required to

'A Hindoo Mendicant Pilgrim', *Illustrated London News,* 12 Feb. 1876.

drag each of their carriages. The grand ceremony of the installation
of the idol on his triumphal car, styled the Rath Jatra, will take place
next month. The usual influx of pilgrims at this epoch is immense:
crowds of votaries are already assembled in the town, or are wearily
plodding their way towards this Mecca of their hopes. But their
numbers decrease yearly, and the sanctity of Juggernauth wanes in
proportion to the progress of civilization in India. The mad fanaticism which formerly led hundreds of voluntary victims to immolate
themselves beneath the wheels of the idol's car—an offering which
is said to extract a ghastly smile of delight from the blood-loving
Dagon—is now much sobered down. Sterling mentions that, during
the four years in which he witnessed the ceremony, Juggernauth was
only propitiated with three sacrifices; and that these wretches, being
afflicted with some grievous bodily complaints, merely embraced
that method of ridding themselves of a miserable existence, as
preferable to the more common-place suicide of hanging or drowning.

The average number of pilgrims annually resorting to Pooree is
said to be about one hundred and twenty thousand, many of whom
are destined never to return. Thousands of these poor wretches die
from famine, over fatigue during the journey, or from the pernici-
ous climate of the rainy season; and their corpses, thrown on the
sands near the English station, are either burnt, or left to be devoured by the troops of Pariah dogs, jackals and vultures, with
which this place, so rich in food for them, swarms. The chaplain of
the district assured me that he had himself seen, on the space of half
an acre of ground, as many as one hundred and fifty bodies, with
twice as many of the above-named scavengers fighting over their
horrid feast,

'As they lazily mumbled the bones of the dead,

When they scarcely could rise from the spot where they fed!'
(1829)

GODFREY CHARLES MUNDY[33]


## 12. Carriers of holy water

Pilgrims, carriers of the holy water, come in gangs from great
distances to the Triveni; the processions are most picturesque, and
they are very remarkable people. They carry two baskets, suspended by a bamboo over their shoulders, with a canopy above

them, gaily decorated with bells and flags; these baskets contain small stumpy bottles of the thinnest green glass, having long necks; they are filled with Ganges water at the junction, and sealed with the seal of a Brahman at the Bene (bathing-place). These people travel all over the country, selling the sacred water at a high price at the distant stations. Some of the bottles are not above two inches high, others contain a quart; they are of all sizes, and the price varies accordingly. The salutation of these people on passing is, 'Ram ram,' or 'Bom bom mahadeo;' a pilgrim of this class is called a Kanwar Wala. The men come for this water to place it in their houses for religious and medicinal uses. and sometimes perform a journey on the occasion of five or six months; it is also used in the English courts of justice_ in administering an oath to an Hindoo. (1850)

FANNY PARKES[34]

## 13. Indian ascetics

One of the strangest sights in India is that of the ascetics who make pilgrimages from one part of the country to another. English travellers sometimes, while far away from the great cities on the plains or the coast, will meet a lonely man, his body covered only in a rag, his feet worn by rough roads, his step slow, and will be told that the man is a pilgrim who believes that by thus making a journey to some holy river or sacred mountain or city he is preparing for himself some great happiness in another world. Perhaps he has lived in the hot plains, yet here he is upon the mountains where the snows never melt. He is not allowed to starve or to go by without receiving offerings of money from the people who see him, for they believe him to be holy. But they do not give him coverings for his body. He still wears only the rag. Nevertheless he is often able to bear the bite of cold, and he is able to endure the rough roads. For his mind is set upon a single idea, and that single idea is to carry out the promise he has made to himself to perform the long journey to the source of the great and holy river, the Ganges.

They are unpleasant men to quarrel with, and for the most part they are ignorant. Yet some of them know a great deal about the workings of the mind. The people look at them in awe and even terror. Being terribly superstitious, they easily believe that these wild creatures, with their uncovered bodies, their glaring eyes, and their faces smeared with ashes, have powers that are denied to ordinary people. These holy men, the people think, can look into the future as into a book, and can read a man's life whom they have never seen before. But, worse than that, they think that the ascetic has power not only to read their future, but even to shape it. If they ill-use him, he can so arrange things, they say, that they will have nothing but misery for the rest of their lives. It is true that only ignorant people are afraid of a fakir, yet, should it so happen that a man who has been cursed by one of these terrible 'magicians' experiences some misfortune, however plainly the unhappy event is due to ordinary causes, the people believe that the man has received the punishment which he was promised.

And these men are very clever in keeping up the native belief in their powers. The Hindu is easily influenced by a powerful mind, and the minds of these ascetics are most of them very powerful. They tell the native that he must believe this and that about them, and simply because he cannot help it the native believes. It is because their minds are so powerful that they are able to endure the roads over which they walk, the winds that blow upon them in the high hills, and the sun that beats down upon them in the plains. They care nothing for any of these things. They have learnt to bear all that may meet them. And so, wherever we may wander in the wide streets of Bombay, among the temples and beside the river at Benares, on lonely mountain-roads and on village greens, we see some of this company of 'holy' men, dirty, stained with ashes, their feet hard with walking, their bodies thin with fasting and hard travelling, their eyes glaring with defiance of all weathers and roads and people who would hold them back. And as we watch them we cannot but think to ourselves what a waste do we see of energy and of strength and of hope! (1913)

FRANK ELIAS[35]

## B. BUDDHISM

### 1. The land of Buddha

This country is exceedingly prosperous; the people are very wealthy, and all of them, without exception, reverence the Law of Buddha, and take delight in attending to their religious duties. The

body of priests may, perhaps, amount to ten thousand men, and
principally belong to the system of the Great Vehicle. They all
partake of their meals in common. The people of the country build
their houses in clusters. Before the doors of their houses they erect
small towers. The smallest are about twenty-two feet high. They
also construct apartments for foreign priests, where they entertain
them as guests, and provide them with all they require. The ruler of
the country located Fah Hian and his companions in a Sangharama,
which was called Gomati. The priests of this temple belong to the
system known as the Great Vehicle. At the sound of the gong, three
thousand priests assemble together to take their meal. Whilst entering the dining hall they observe the greatest decorum and propriety
of conduct; one after another they take their seats. Silence is observed amongst them all; they make no noise with their rice-bowls,
and when they require more food there is no chattering one with the
other. but they simply make a sign with their fingers (and so are
supplied).

Hwui King, Tao Ching, and Hwui Ta, set out in advance towards
Ki'a-Cha (Kartchou), whilst Fah Hian and the rest, wishing to
witness the ceremony of the procession of images, halted here for a
period of three months and some days. In this country there are
fourteen large Sangharamas, without reckoning the smaller ones.
On the first day of the fourth month, they begin within the city to
sweep and water the roads, and to decorate the streets. Above the
chief gate of the city they stretch out a large cloth screen, and
ornament the covered space in every possible way, then the King
and the court ladies, with their attendants, take their places there.
The priests of the Gomati temple belonging to the Greater Vehicle,
being chiefly honoured by the King, first take their images in procession. They construct a four-wheeled image-car about three or four li
from the city, its height is about thirty-five feet, and in appearance like a moving royal pavilion. It is adorned with seven precious
substances, and adorned with silken streamers and flags and curtains. The chief image is then placed upright in the centre of the
carriage, with two Bodhisatwas in attendance, and surrounded by
all the Devas. All are made of gold and silver, whilst glittering gems
are hung suspended in the air. When the image is about one hundred
paces from the city gate, the King removes his royal head-dress, and
putting on new garments, with bare feet he proceeds from the city to
meet the procession, holding flowers and incense in his hand, and

followed by his suite. On meeting the car he bows down with his face to the ground in adoration, whilst he scatters the flowers and burns the incense. At the time when the image enters the city, the court ladies and their attendants throw down from the pavilion above the gate flowers in endless variety. Thus everything is sumptuously arranged. Each Sangharama has its own car, and its own day, for the procession. Beginning on the first day of the fourth month, they continue till the fourteenth day, after which they conclude, and the King and the ladies return to the palace. Seven or eight li to the west of this city is a Sangharama, called the Royal New Temple. During the last eighty years three kings have contributed towards its completion. It is about two hundred and ninety feet high. There are many inscribed plates of gold and silver within it. Jewels of every description combine to give a perfect finish (to the pinnacle) above the roof. There is a hall of Buddha behind the main tower, which is perfectly adorned and very magnificent. The beams, pillars, doors, and windows are covered with gold plates. Besides this, there are priests, chambers elegantly finished and adorned, so that no words can adequately describe them. All the kings of the six kingdoms to the east of the great mountain range called (Tsung) Ling send as religious offerings to this temple whatever most costly gems they have, and in such abundance that but few of them can be used. (A.D. 401–12)

FAH-HIAN[36]

## 2. The Indian fig

Its branches shoot to heaven and sink to earth,
Even as the deeds of men, which take their birth
    From qualities: its silver sprays and blooms,
And all the eager verdure of its girth,

Leap to quick life at kiss of sun and air,
As men's lives quicken to the temptings fair
    Of wooing sense: its hanging rootlets seek
The soil beneath, helping to hold it there,

As actions wrought amid this world of men
Bind them by ever-tightening bonds again.
    If ye knew well the teaching of the Tree,
What its shape saith; and whence its springs; and then

How it must end, and all the ills of it,
The axe of sharp Detachment ye would whet,
    And cleave the clinging snaky roots, and lay
This Aswattha of sense-life low,—to set

New growths upspringing to that happier sky,—
Which they who reach shall have no day to die,
    Nor fade away, nor fall—to Him, I mean,
FATHER and FIRST, who made the mystery

Of old Creation; for to Him come they
From passion and from dreams who break away;
    Who part the bonds constraining them to flesh,
And,—Him, the Highest, worshipping alway—

No longer grow at mercy of what breeze
Of summer pleasure stirs the sleeping trees,
    What blast of tempest tears them, bough and stem:
To the eternal world pass such as these!

Another Sun gleams there! another Moon!
Another Light,—not Dusk, nor Dawn, nor Noon—
    Which they who once behold return no more;
They have attained My rest, My utmost boon.
(1886)

EDWIN ARNOLD[37]

## 3. *The mystery-play*

At an early hour of the morning of June 16 we were awoke to a realisation of where we were by the sounding of the priestly shawms in different quarters of the great monastery. We arose, and found it had been snowing in the night, and the distant mountains were white almost down to the level of the Indus—an unfavourable circumstance for Bower's start on the morrow.

After breakfast we repaired with the Naib Wazir, the Treasurer, and other notables to the gallery overlooking the quadrangle, where seats had been prepared for us. The jovial Treasurer, finding that I appreciated the national beverage, produced at intervals flowing bowls of chung to cheer us as we gazed at the successive whirling troops of devils and monsters that passed before us.

The great crowd had already collected—men and women of Ladak and Chinese Tibet, lamas and nuns red and yellow, and a sprinkling of Hindoos and scornful Mussulmans, filling the galleries, covering the roofs, and squatting on the floor all round the quadrangle. Several sepoys of the irregular Ladaki levy—in the Ladaki dress, and not in the least like soldiers—and lamas with scourges in their hands, kept the spectators in order, and prevented them from pressing on to the space reserved for the performers. In a state-box of the gallery opposite to us, hung with silken draperies, sat the Gialpo, or deposed Rajah of Ladak, with his suite and attendant lamas. Though of the same Mongolian stock as his people, he was of much fairer complexion; his features were highly refined, having much of the pure beauty of asceticism, contrasting strangely with the ignoble faces around. One could distinguish at once that he was of an ancient and well-bred race. He quite looked the Buddhist mystic and devotee absorbed in the contemplation of Nirvana. His expression was sad, resigned, and dreamy. He never smiled, and seldom spoke to those by him. His young son, equally conspicuous among his companions for his refined look and bearing, had been devoted by the Gialpo to the Church, and was one of the singing-boys who took part in the ceremony.

It is difficult to give an account of the ever-changing and very interesting mummery which was carried on for the whole of this long summer's day—a bewildering phantasmagoria of strange sights, a din of unearthly music, that almost caused the reason to waver, and make one believe that one was indeed in the magic realm represented by the actors, a dreadful world, affording but dismal prospects; being even as these Buddhists regard this present existence of ours, and of which, if it were thus, one would indeed be well quit. For the principal motive of this mystery play appeared to be the lesson that the helpless, naked soul of man has its being in the midst of a vast and obscure space full of malignant demons—the earth, the air, the water crowded with them—perpetually seeking to destroy him, harassing him with tortures and terrors; and that against this infinite oppression of the powers of evil he can of himself do nothing, but that occasionally the exorcisms or prayers of some good lama or incarnation may come to his assistance and shield him, and even then only after a fierce and doubtful contest between the saint and the devils. And only for a time, too, can this relief from persecution endure, for all the exorcisms of all the saints are of little avail to keep back the advancing hordes. The shrieking demons must soon close in upon the soul again. (1891)

E.F. KNIGHT[38]

## 4. The four noble truths

What is the good of this universe? This is a question to which
Buddha gave no indecisive answer. To his disciples he said, 'What
think ye, disciples, whether is more, the water which is in the four
great oceans, or the tears which have flown from you and have been
shed by you while ye strayed and wandered on this long pilgrimage?' Yet according to Buddha all these tears had been shed in vain.
Not one tear need be shed if mankind had but knowledge of the
Four Noble Truths. It was not ignorance of God and of the Soul that
sent man through the weary pilgrimage of life and endless rebirths.
It is ignorance that life is suffering arising out of desire, and that this
suffering ceases on cessation of desire. This is the central and
fundamental doctrine of Buddhism, contained in the ever repeated
teachings of the Four Noble Truths:

1. That life from birth to death is crowded in with suffering.
Suffering is 'the hankering after corporeal form, after sensations,
perceptions, conformations, and after consciousness.'
2. That desire or thirst for power, for pleasure, for being,
leads from birth to rebirth with their sufferings.
3. That all sorrows cease when this desire or thirst is extinguished.
4. That there is a path which, if followed, leads to a cessation
of suffering. This is an eightfold path of right belief or faith, right
aspiration, right speech, right action, right living, right effort,
right thought, and right meditation.

The Buddha essays in these Four Noble Truths no metaphysical
speculations over the why or the wherefore of the universe. A
fivefold craving after form, sensation, perceptions, conformations,
and consciousness is all that Buddha's simple teachings set before
his disciples. The Four Noble Truths held in themselves a code of
ethics whereby all people, irrespective of caste or religious belief,
could become free in this world from the pains and sorrows of life. It
was ignorance of the cause of suffering and ignorance of the path to
the cessation of suffering that the Buddha spent forty-five years of
his lifetime in efforts to eradicate. To obtain freedom from desire
and actions which attached themselves to desires, the Buddha
preached no doctrine of extreme asceticism so common in India
from the earliest times. A monastic middle-life was ordained for

those who sought freedom from ignorance, but who might find the allurements of the world too strong for a life of contemplation. By a life of intense concentration of thought and self-culture each man could find for himself the truth of the Buddha's contention that when ignorance ceased actions would lose their potency by non-attachment to outside objects and pleasures. For those Buddhists who remained in the world, as lay members of the order, there was given a moral code by the observance of which they rose above the trammels of caste, above priestly superstitions. Further, the lower classes of the people, in accepting Buddhism, gained the proud position of belonging to a saintly, dignified, and widely revered order. The natural disposition of the lay members to store up merit by charity and good deeds was met to the full in the ample opportunities they had of giving of their alms for the support of the wandering Buddhist monks. Buddhism set before the people ideals of charity, chastity, and self-repression—ideals ever revered in the best of Indian belief and in the best of Indian literature. The question of the existence or non-existence of a Soul found no place in the primitive teachings of Buddhism. The question of the existence of a God was ignored, as were all questions of social rank or caste. None of these questions in any way affected the teachings of the Buddha.

To the simple teachings of the Buddha after ages added learned discussions on every conceivable cosmological, psychological, and even ontological problems that perplexed the thought of their times. The piety, or vanity, of these ages ascribed all their wordy disquisitions to the Buddha, and laid them as tributes of reverence at his feet. The Buddha had ever consistently refused to be drawn by his disciples into any definite statements or metaphysical discussions regarding the nature of the Atman, or Soul, or even respecting the question of the existence or non-existence of a future life after death. It is even suggested that he was not responsible for the first annunciation of the principle underlying the grouping of the Four Noble Truths, for 'these Four Noble Truths are nothing more than the four cardinal principles of Indian medical science applied to the spiritual healing of mankind.' (1915)

R.W. FRAZER[39]

# C. JAINISM

## 1. The ancient Jain temples, Ajmer

'I ask'd of *Time* for whom *those* temples rose,
That prostrate by his hand in silence lie;
His lips disdain'd the myst'ry to disclose,
And borne on swifter wing, he hurried by.
The broken columns *whose*? I ask'd of *Fame*:
(Her kindling breath gives life to works sublime;)
With downcast looks of mingled grief and shame,
She heaved the uncertain sigh, and follow'd *Time*.
Wrapt in amazement o'er the mouldering pile,
I saw *Oblivion* pass with giant stride;
And while his visage wore *Pride's* scornful smile,
Haply *thou know'st*, then tell me, *whose* I cried,
*Whose* these vast domes that ev'n in ruin shine?
I *reck not whose*, he said: they *now are mine*.' (1829)

JAMES TOD[40]

## 2. The sacred mountain

Paras-nath is a mountain of peculiar sanctity, to which circumstance
is to be attributed the flourishing state of Maddaobund. The name is
that of the twenty-third incarnation of Jinna (Sanscrit 'Conqueror'),
who was born at Benares, lived one hundred years, and was buried
on this mountain, which is the eastern metropolis of Jain worship, as
Mount Aboo is the western (where are their libraries and most
splendid temples). The origin of the Jain sect is obscure, though its
rise appears to correspond with the wreck of Boodhism throughout
India in the eleventh century. The Jains form in some sort a
transition-sect between Boodhists and Hindoos, differing from the
former in acknowledging castes, and from both in their worship of
Paras-nath's foot, instead of that of Munja-gosha of the Boodhs, or
Vishnoo's of the Hindoos. As a sect of Boodhists their religion is
considered pure, and free from the obscenities so conspicuous in
Hindoo worship; whilst, in fact, perhaps the reverse is the case; but
the symbols are fewer, and indeed almost confined to the feet of
Paras-nath, and the priests jealously conceal their esoteric doctrines. (1854)

JOSEPH DALTON HOOKER[41]

## 3. Sect of Jainas

The *Jainas* or *A'rhatas,* followers of Jina or Arhat (terms of like import), are also denominated *Vivasanas, Muktavasanas, Muktambaras* or *Digambaras,* with reference to the nakedness of the rigid order of ascetics in this sect, who go 'bare of clothing,' 'disrobed', or 'clad by the regions of space.' The less strict order of *Swetambaras* 'clad in white,' is of more modern date and of inferior note. Among nick-names by which they are known, that of *Lunchita-kesa* occurs. It alludes to the practice of abruptly eradicating hair of the head or body by way of mortification. Parswanatha is described as tearing five handfuls of hair from his head on becoming a devotee.

According to the *Digambara Jainas,* the universe consists of two classes, 'animate' and 'inanimate' (*jiva* and *ajiva*), without a creator or ruling providence (*iswara*). They assign for the cause (*Karana*) of the world, atoms, which they do not, as the *Vaiseshikas,* distinguish into so many sorts as there are elements, but consider these, viz. earth, water, fire, and air, the four elements by them admitted, as modified compounds of homogeneous atoms. (1873)

H.T. COLEBROOKE[42]

# D. ISLAM

## 1. The Moors of Surat

The *Moors* with a very rigid and avowed Abstinence, observe every Year one Month, a Fast, which they term the *Ramezan*; during which time they are so severely abstemious, that they stretch not their Hands to either Bread or Water, 'till the Sun be set, and the Stars appear'; no, not the Youths of 12 or 13 Years of Age. Which makes the Penance so much the more rigorous and troublesome, in that a draught of Water in those warm parching Climates is so very necessary, and so refreshing to such as are ready to faint with Thirst. This Fast is not kept always at the same Season of the Year, but begins its date Annually more early by Eleven Days. When I was at *Suratt,* this mortifying Custom was about the Month of *September,* at which time the *Moors* would begin to refresh themselves about the close of the Evening, and Eat then freely; and by an Early

Collation in the Morning, before the dawning of the Light, prepare
themselves for the drought and heat of the following Day. The
Almighty, they told us, requir'd from *Mahomet,* that his followers
should be oblig'd to this Austerity, the whole Circuit of the Year;
but that the Holy Prophet, in compassion to the Faithful, obtain'd
from God the confinement of it only to a Month, which would
therefore highly aggravate their Crime, if they neglected the Dedi-
cation of so small a portion of the Year to this Religious Abstinence,
tho' the observance of it had been injoyn'd after a more rigorous
manner than it is. And to add to the Sanctity of this Celebrated and
solemn Fast, their *Mullahs,* acted with a sacred Zeal, and lively
concern for the Souls of the People, will at this time spend whole
Nights in the *Musseets,* in chanting aloud alternately their Divine
Hymns,' till the approach of day breaks up their Devotions: And so
they compleat their Fast, according to the strictest Rules of the most
rigid *Asceticks,* by mixing Prayers and Watchings with their Abstinence; in which, as well as in their Publick Prayers and Religious
Worship, they tie themselves up to a very nice and devout strictness,
and behave themselves with all those decencies of Respect, with
that astonishing Reverence in the *Musseets,* as not to defile them
with either their Eyes or Lips; not daring so much as to turn their
Heads to gaze about, or utter the least word to one another. Which
profound Respect casts an obloquy and deserv'd Reproach upon
some Professors of a much purer Religion, and more Holy Faith,
whose careless Deportment and familiar Address discountenance
all the Religious decorum of Prayers, and might tempt those Heathens to conclude, that our Devotions were rather some light Diversion, than the effects of serious and sacred Thoughts. (1689)

J. OVINGTON[43]

## 2. The faith of Islam

Vague ideas concerning the faith of Muhammadans exist in the
minds of those who have not studied the religions of the East. Living
side by side with the Hindus, the Muslim sometimes gets the credit
of being an idolater. Those who know that he follows the teaching of
a book of scripture called the Quran, and reveres a Prophet named
Muhammad, are nevertheless sometimes ignorant of the fact that
the Muhammadan, the Jew, and the Christian all believe in the
broad historical outline of the Old Testament; and acknowledge the

Patriarchs and Moses, the legend of Adam and Eve, their life in the Garden of Eden, and their fall.

The interpretation of the Old Testament by the teachers of the three creeds varies considerably. The Christian accuses the exponent of Muhammad's doctrines of overlaying the simple tale of the Patriarchs with tradition for which there is no historical foundation. The Muhammadans, on the other hand, complain that the Christians have perverted the truth and shorn sacred history of all its details. However much they may differ in this respect, the general acceptance of the outlines by all three should create a sympathy between them which could not exist between the heathen and any one of the believers in the Old Testament Scriptures.

Muhammad was born to a degenerate faith into which gross error had crept. His spirit revolted against the error and he rose as a reformer, calling for a drastic reformation. His preachings drew a large following, and he was made a leader; his sayings and writings were collected in a book. The book received the name of the Quran. It was believed that Muhammad wrote it at the dictation of the angel Gabriel, who brought the message direct from God. Rules were laid down for the conduct of the individual as well as for the community. They related to prayer, fasting, ablutions, cleanliness, diet, and other matters connected with daily life. Moses gave the same kind of rules to the Israelites. In these days some of them would be called the practice of eugenics rather than religious observances.

The Quran is highly venerated; and the followers of the Prophet learn it by heart. Some of the religious exercises consist of a repetition of its words. Sentences must be said over and over again, the greatest care being taken to pronounce every syllable correctly. As to the interpretation of the Quran, the Muhammadan is not asked to think for himself. He is to follow example and precept blindly, as others have followed before him.

One of the earliest disciples of the Prophet was observed to ride his camel several times round a rock. He was asked why he did so. He replied that he did not know; he had seen the Prophet do it and was following his example. His conduct met with approval and commendation. He was exhibiting in his action a faith worthy of imitation; it was placed on record, that it might be a lesson to those who should come after.

There are five acts that are called the five pillars of islam. They should be performed by all good Muhammadans. They are the confession of faith; the periods of prayer; the fast of Ramazan; the giving of prescribed alms; the pilgrimage to Mecca. In addition to these there is circumcision, purification, obedience to parents, etc.

What a Muhammadan may not do is to eat forbidden food or act in any way contrary to the directions of the Quran and the Traditions. When he is in doubt, he is to abstain from the contemplated deed.

The part of the Muhammadan's life that impresses the stranger most is his obedience to the call of prayer. If he is within hearing of the cry of the Muezzin, he goes to the mosque, puts off his shoes, and prostrates himself within the building. If, however, he happens to be working, travelling, or amusing himself where no mosque is at hand, he stops as the sun nears the horizon, spreads his carpets and says his prayers, indifferent to what the world may think or say.

Three or five periods are observed for prayer. The three are sunrise, sunset, and night. The odd numbers are curious. The Muslim believes that the Deity loves odd numbers. 'God is odd; He loves the odd,' said a Tradition. The Muhammadan is careful to use odd numbers on every occasion; in the repetition of his prayers, in the date that he chooses for starting on a journey or for beginning a work, and in every other matter wherein a number enters, he shows his preference for the odd figure. (1914)

F.E. PENNY[44]

# E CHRISTIANITY AND CHRISTIAN MISSIONARIES

## 1. Akbar and Christianity

Not to go into too many details, the Fathers frequently and freely admonished the King; but their conscientious readiness in doing this never lessened, still less put an end to, the kindly friendship of the King towards them. Nay more, when the King perceived that it was the sincerity of their hearts that led them to feel themselves free to correct him, he took it in such good part that he always seemed not only to favour them, but to heap honours upon them in his desire to show his affection towards them. For when they saluted him, which they did with uncovered heads, he answered with a nod and a bright smile. He did not allow them to keep their heads uncovered when they were in his presence. When a council was being held, or when he summoned them to his private audience-chamber for familiar conversation, he used to make them sit beside him. He shook hands with them cordially and familiarly. He frequently left the public audience-chamber to converse with them in private. Several times he paced up and down with his arm round Rudolf's shoulders. Once, when he was in camp, he desired another of the priests, in the middle of a crowd of his nobles, to help him fasten on his sword, which service the Father performed, amidst the envy and wonder of all the courtiers. He wished the priests to be sharers of his inmost thoughts, both in good and ill fortune—no common mark of love and kindness. He ordered his door-keepers to grant them entrance, whenever they wished, even into the inner courtyard of the palace, where only the most distinguished nobles had the right of entrance. He sent them food from his own table—a mark of distinction which he is said never to have conferred upon anyone before. He visited one of the Fathers when he was ill, and greeted him in Portuguese as a sign of respect. There would have been no end to his gifts, had the Fathers not frequently told him that all they needed was food and clothing, and these of the most simple description. This reply pleased him so much that he repeated it publicly: and each month sent them as much money, under the guise of alms, as he thought would be sufficient for their daily expenses. (1581)

FATHER ANTONIO MONSERRATE[45]

## 2. The Christians of India

The Christians of India, vulgarly named the Christians of Saint Thomas, because by his preaching they are supposed to have beene converted to Christian Religion (and his bodie as is thought, remayneth among them, buried in the Citie of Maliapar on the Coast of Choromandel) inhabit in the neerer part of India: namely, in that great Promontory, whose base lying betweene the Outlets of the Rivers Indus and Ganges, stretcheth out the sides farre toward the South (well nigh 1000 miles) till meeting in the point of Comori, they make, together with the base line forementioned (betwixt Cambaya and Bengala) the figure almost of an Equilaterall Triangle. In the more Southerly part of this great Promontory, I say neerer to Cape Comori, about the Cities of Coulan and Cranganor on the West side, and about Maliapar and Negapatan, on the East

side, doe these Christians of Saint Thomas dwell, being esteemed
afore the Portugals frequented those parts, about 15000 or 16000
Families, or after anothers account 70000 persons: but on the West
Coast, the farre greater number of them is found, and especially
their habitation is thickest, about Angamale, 15 miles from the Citie
Cochin Northward, where their Archbishop keepeth residence.

Now as touching their government: Their Archbishop till twentie
yeeres since or little more, acknowledged obedience to the Patriarch of Mozal, by the name of the Patriarch of Babylon, as by
those Christians of India he is stil tearmed: and certainly that the
Patriarch of Mozal, challengeth their obedience, as being of his
jurisdiction, appeareth by the profession of Abil-Isu, a Patriarch of
Mozal, of Pope Pius the Fourth his Investing (Anno 1562) as is to
bee seene in Sanders Booke de visibili Monarchia. But then, the
Archbishop of these Indians, revolting from his former Patriarch,
submitted himselfe by the Portugals perswasion, to the Bishop of
Rome, retayning notwithstanding, the ancient Religion of his Countrey, which was also permitted by the Pope. In so much, that in a
Synod held in Goa, for that purpose, hee would not suffer any
alteration to bee made of their ancient Ties or Religion, as one that
lived in those parts at that time hath recorded. But that Bishop
being dead, his successour in another Synod, held by the Archbishop at Goa, at Diamper, not farre from Maliapur, Anno 1599
made profession, together with his Suffragans, and Priests, both of
the Roman obedience and Religion, renouncing in such direct sort,
the Patriarch of Mozal, and Nestorianisme, that they delivered up
all their Bookes, to the censure of the Archbishop of Goa, and
suffered their Lyturgie, in the points that rellished of Nestorianisme
to bee altered, even in such sort as now it is to be seene in the last
Edition of Bibliotheca veterun Patrum. (1625)

SAMUEL PURCHAS *(comp.)*[46]

## 3. Only one church

It will hardly be believed that in this splendid city [Calcutta], the
head of a mighty Christian empire, there is only one church of the
establishment of the mother country, and that by no means conspicuous, either for size or ornament. It is also remarkable, that all
British India does not afford one Episcopal See, while that advantage has been granted to the province of Canada; yet it is certain

that from the remoteness of the country, and the peculiar temptations to which the freedom of manners exposes the clergy, immediate Episcopal superintendence can no where be more requisite. From the want of this it is painful to observe, that the characters of too many of that order, are by no means creditable to the doctrines they profess, which, together with the unedifying contests that prevail among them even in the pulpit, tend to lower the religion, and its followers, in the eyes of the natives of every description. If there be any plan for conciliating the minds of the natives to Christianity, it is so manifestly essential it should appear to them in a respectable form at the seat of Government, that I presume all parties will allow, that the first step should be to place it there upon a proper footing. (1802-6)

GEORGE VISCOUNT VALENTIA[47]

## 4. Malabar Christians

We learn from the Portugueze writers, that these Christians possessed upwards of one hundred villages, situated mostly in the mountainous part of the southern division of Malabar. Their habitations were distinguished from those of the Hindoos by being mostly solid buildings, and collected in villages; not scattered and dispersed as those of the brahmins and Nairs. They obeyed their Archbishop, both in ecclesiastical and civil matters, paying a very moderate tribute to the different rajahs in whose territory they lived, who very little interfered in their concerns. When any complaints in civil affairs were preferred to the Archbishop, he used to appoint arbitrators or judges, whose sentence was final; they never condemned any person to death, and most crimes were expiated with pecuniary fines. They paid no tithes to their clergy, but at weddings they offered the tenth of the marriage gifts to their churches. On these occasions they were very profuse and ostentatious, and celebrated their nuptials with great pomp; it was then principally that they made a shew of the privileges granted to them by one of the PERUMALS; as of the bride and bridegroom riding upon elephants, of having the hair ornamented with flowers of gold, of musical instruments, also of flags of different colours carried before them. They all wore swords and targets, and some of them had firelocks; they were great marksmen, and from their eighth year frequented the firing schools: husbandry and trade were their principal occupations, and, next to the brahmins, the St Thome Christians furnished the greatest quantity of pepper to the Portugueze. (1812)

JAMES FORBES[48]

## 5. A native church

The church [in Sirdhana] is not an ungraceful building, though its architecture is mixed. It is built entirely for display, however, and will hold a very small congregation in proportion to its external dimensions. Its decorations within are very paltry, and about the altar there is a great deal of tinsel frippery and tasteless ornament, better fitted for a theatre. One slab of white marble there is, which is deservedly admired for the beauty of its mosaic work, being inlaid with precious stones, in the style of the Tajh Mahal at Agra. (1831–6)

THOMAS BACON[49]

## 6. Missionary work of Dr Wolff

Wolff proceeded from thence [Connanore] to Combaconum, where he was most hospitably entertained by the Portuguese commander; for this place belongs to the territory of Goa. The priest of the place, Father Antonius Cajetanus, an enlightened gentleman, received him with the greatest kindness. Wolff presented him with a Portuguese Bible, and it must be said, to the honour of that priest and his whole congregation, that they informed Wolff, with delight, that the Inquisition was abolished.

He then left Combaconum, and arrived, on the 31st of October, 1833, at Goa. Wolff cannot conceal his feeling of joy, when he saw on the highroad there the cross of Christ planted; and heard the bells of the churches ringing in every village; and beheld Christian churches erected instead of the idols of Hindostan. He could not help exclaiming, 'Behold! the triumph of the cross over idolatry,'—recollecting, at the same time, that these churches were established through the flaming words of the Gospel, preached by the great Francis Xavier (as he was informed by the priests of and around Goa), and not by a sword of steel! nor by an *auto-da-fe*! in which the body is given to the flames of fire, and the soul to the eternal flames of hell.

Wolff then took a boat, and went on the river to Pangim, which is the place of residence of the Viceroy of Goa. The Secretary of Government, Nunez by name, and of Jewish descent, gave to Wolff a letter to the Provincial of the Augustinian Monastery in New Goa.Whilst he was writing this letter, some officers of the Portuguese army entered the room, and asked the Secretary, 'When will that extraordinary man, Wolff, come, the Protestant Xavier?' Nunez replied, 'Here he stands before you, alive!' They all took off their caps (for the Portuguese officers wear caps), and expressed their joy at seeing him 'whom they had admired for years.'

Wolff then went with the letter to the Augustinian Monastery, when the Provincial, who was of the Jewish family of Picciotto, with the rest of the monks, received him with the greatest kindness, and assigned to him a most beautiful room. The first observation made to him by the Father Provincial was, 'I hope, Senhor Wolff, that you will give a more favourable account of us than Claudius Buchanan has done (though he spoke with justice), for the Inquisition is now abolished.' Then he proceeded, 'Oh! I can see before me that great man, Buchanan, intruding himself into the very tribunal-room of the Inquisition, just at the very moment when Joseph a Dolorosis, was pronouncing a death-sentence on a poor old woman. There Buchanan stood, with arms folded over his breast, undaunted, and said, "I am sent here by Government to watch your proceedings, and I have to report all I see. This woman is your victim!"'

Now, it is very remarkable that Mr. Simeon, though an intimate friend of Buchanan, believed that he had over-coloured his account. Yet, at Goa, Wolff, heard an account condemnatory of the Inquisition, given by the monks themselves, in even stronger terms than Buchanan has given in his *Researches*.

The Provincial then made this just remark, that 'It was right that the Church should watch over the integrity of her faith, being, at the same time, helped by her members; but, allowing all this, judicial proceedings ought to be public; the accusers ought to be known; and none ought to be put to death on account of his religion. Thanks be to God,' continued the Provincial, 'the Inquisition was abolished in 1810; and the man, with a heart hard as stone, has left Goa, and we are free.'(1833)

JOSEPH WOLFF[50]

## 7. Bad character of native converts

If it should so happen that any natives are converted, they are so to answer their own purposes, and become worse than they were before. Can there be a greater set of rascals, drunkards, thieves and reprobates than the generality of native Christians? And they profess to be Christians, too! They are looked upon by their fellow countrymen as the most degraded of all castes. The worst characters in our regiments are Christians! And it is no uncommon thing to have some such remark as the following made. 'He is a great blackguard, he is a *parriah Christian!'* A servant presents himself for employment, and is asked what caste he is? The reply is 'I master's caste, I Christian, sar.' He is not taken, because all Christians, with but few exceptions, are looked upon as great vagabonds. (1850)

ALBERT HERVEY[51]

## 8. Among the missionaries

Now that I have lived several years in India, visited such widely different parts of it, and mixed with all castes and creeds, I have quite revised some of the preconceived notions I brought with me. One of these relates to the missionaries, and I must tell you how much impressed I have been by finding how universally respected the missionaries in general are by all classes of the Indian people.

This is quite the reverse of what people in England who have not lived in India believe to be the case. In England, one very frequently hears it said: 'I never subscribe to missions. Missionaries cause trouble wherever they go.'

Not long after I arrived in India I heard an English official speak against missionaries, and was surprised to hear a Brahmin gentleman take up their defence, saying: 'They do more good than any one else. They work very hard, and not for their own profit. They never enrich themselves. They often die young, and always die poor.'

Then turning to me he added: 'You may be surprised to hear it, but though few educated Hindus become Christians, they have a great respect for missionaries.'

I replied: 'I am glad to hear it, and I see that Christian philanthropy is appreciated. In India it cannot be said: "First the missionary, then the gunboat." It is rather: "First the missionary, then the schools and hospitals." '

Many English people will say speaking of the Indian people: 'Our religion is good for us, and their religon for them.'

I heard an English lady who had expressed this opinion say soon afterwards in reference to servants: 'Oh! any one of them would murder us for eight annas (sixpence).'

'And yet,' I rejoined, 'you say that a religion which would not restrain them from doing that is good enough for them, and they do not need to be taught better!'

I was reminded of Voltaire, who would not allow his atheist companions to talk against religion while at a dinner-table. 'Wait till the servants have gone out of the room,' he said. 'It is only their religion that keeps them from murdering us in our beds to-night, and making off with the money and valuables.'

One has only to talk with Indian people, or with missionaries or others who know them well, to find out that Hinduism is (certainly among the uneducated) chiefly a matter of ceremonies, and no check on conduct.

If you hear people saying that Hindus should be let alone and do not need to be taught, or to have their moral standard raised, pray tell them the following true story. It was told me by the wife of the Judge who tried the case.

A childless wife, fearing that, if she bore him no children, her husband would take a second wife (which the Hindu religion allows), went to a holy man or priest, an ascetic, to ask his advice as to what she could do to make the gods propitious.

The holy man told her to kill a little girl under ten years of age, take out her liver, fry it and eat it, and it would have the desired effect; she would have a son.

The woman obeyed these instructions.

The murdered child's corpse she hid under a stack of corn-stalks near the hut; the odour of the decomposing body attracted attention, the crime was discovered, and the woman brought to justice. The Judge sentenced her to be hanged. He was blamed for condemning her to the supreme penalty. It was said the woman was so grossly ignorant that she did not understand how foul a crime she had committed. The Judge refused to commute the sentence, for he said: 'The superstition which led to the crime is widespread. Not long ago another woman was sentenced to penal servitude for a similar crime, and I was told the woman I have lately condemned showed no fear when arrested, saying: "At worst the Judge Sahib will only send me across the *kala pane*"—i.e. send her across the sea to the penal settlement in the Andaman Islands. Only when it becomes known that death is the penalty will such crimes cease.'

Her decision was appealed against, but the High Court upheld it, seeing the force of his argument. The sentence of death was carried out.

The 'holy man' who advised the crime was perhaps the worst offender. But to catch him was an impossibility. He would be hundreds of miles away, or adopt fifty different disguises. All classes of natives would shelter him; they would be afraid of offending him, lest they might draw his curse upon them.

Was he not a holy man?

I have seen natives of India of respectable standing throw themselves at the feet of such a one, and ask his blessing, though he was very drunk at the time, and known to be a debauchee.

'In what did his holiness consist?' you may ask.

Perhaps he did not live in a house, and abstained from some kinds of food, or could recite long portions of the Vedas.

He certainly did no work, nor did he clothe himself decently.

The holy men among the missionaries are a very different type. Their self-denial is shown in teaching the ignorant, tending the leper, feeding the famine-stricken, or working in many other ways for the good of others, working strenuously on what is only just a living wage, and some of them at their own cost. Many of them are men whose abilities would have won them wealth and distinction in any profession they had chosen to enter, such as Dr. Pennell, the C.M.S. missionary at Bannu, on the northern frontier, who was said to be worth a regiment of soldiers to the Government as a peacemaker, on account of his influence with the turbulent frontier tribes to whom he devoted his life.

Then there are the two Mission doctors in Cashmere, the Neves, and the C.M.S. doctor at Quetta, who are widely known and revered; and Dr. Wanless, of the American Presbyterian Mission at Miraj, who is a power in the land, and whose fame as a surgeon has spread throughout India. He possesses the finest and best equipped operating-room in the Presidency, the gift of a gentleman of Philadelphia, who says it is the best investment he ever made. Had Dr. Wanless done nothing else, it would have been an achievement to be proud of, to have performed (as he has during his stay at

Miraj) two thousand successful operations for cataract, and given sight to two thousand people.

It must, however, be said that though medical missionaries are greatly respected, and hundreds' of thousands of natives of India take advantage of their skill, very few of the natives are led to accept Christianity. They may learn to respect it, but for the most part they say: 'Our religion for us, yours for you.' Many high-class Hindus like their wives to be visited by missionary ladies, and say: 'They will learn nothing but what is good from you.' But should one of the Hindu ladies become a Christian, an uproar would ensue.

Hindus want the fruit without the root—Christian virtue without Christ.

Yet when one thinks of the penalties incurred by a high-caste native of India who forsakes the religion of his race, there is perhaps no reason to wonder that so few accept Christianity. The English Government has been so anxious to be fair to all denominations, to show no preference to Christians, that it has perhaps allowed the scale to dip a little on the other side. One who becomes a Christian is first an outcast from the Hindu community. and, second, cannot inherit his share of the family property. This last seems an injustice. It needs very strong religious convictions to enable a man or woman to cast themselves off from family ties, which are very binding among Hindus, and to give up his means of living. It will be long before he feels one with the English Christian Community; there can only be superficial intercourse between them. Amongst the natives of India, rich and poor, *if of the same caste*, are to a certain degree, equal. When Hindus of any class become Christians they think they have become of the same *caste* as the English, and consider themselves on an equality with the English. This is really the root of the complaints against native Christian servants, and the source of the advertisements frequently seen, ending 'No Christians need apply.'

Christian servants are often too familiar in their manner. They think: 'We have been baptized. Now we are the same caste as the Sahibs.'

The greater number of Indian natives who form the native Christian community are of the lowest classes, Out-castes (people of no caste), and have had everything to gain and nothing to lose by becoming Christians.

In spite of the defects of Christian servants, and failure of some native Christians to act up to the standard of Christian conduct, the efforts of Christian missionaries are beginning to meet with recognition from Government. (1913)

G.C. DYSON[52]

# 4. The People

## A. ROYALTY

### 1. Kanishka, king of Gandhara

In the four-hundredth year after the *Nirvana* of Tathagata, Kanishka, king of Gandhara, having succeeded to the kingdom, his kingly renown reached far, and he brought the most remote within his jurisdiction. During his intervals of duty he frequently consulted the sacred books of Buddha; daily he invited a priest to enter his palace and preach the law, but he found the different views of the schools so contradictory that he was filled with doubt, and he had no way to get rid of his uncertainty. At this time the honoured Parsva said, 'Since Tathagata left the world many years and months have elapsed. The different schools hold to the treatises of their several masters. Each keeps to his own views, and so the whole body is torn by divisions.'

The king having heard this, was deeply affected and gave way to sad regrets. After a while he spoke to Parsva and said, 'Though of no account personally, yet, thanks to the remnant of merit which has followed me through successive births since the time of the Holy One till now, I have come to my present state. I will dare to forget my own low degree, and hand down in succession the teaching of the law unimpaired. I will therefore arrange the teaching of the three *pitakas* of Buddha according to the various schools.' The honourable Parsva replied, 'The previous merit of the great king has resulted in his present distinguished position. That he may continue to love the law of Buddha is what I desire above all things.' (A.D. 629)

HIUEN TSIANG[53]

### 2. The mightiest King

The king [of Bisnagar, South India] is the mightiest King in India, and hath twelve thousand Women, foure thousand of which attend him on foot withersoever he goeth, and are busied in the service of his Kitchin; foure thousand others ride on Horses, or are carried in Litters; two thousand are to burne with him, which is holden a great honor. (1444)

NICOLO DI CONTI[54]

## 3. The king of great dignity

This king of the Ioghe [Jogi] is a man of great dignity, and has about thirty thousand people, and is a pagan, he and all his subjects; and by the pagan kings he and his people are considered to be saints, on account of their lives, which you shall hear. It is the custom of this king to go on a pilgrimage once in every three or four years, like a pilgrim, that is, at the expense of others, with three or four thousand of his people, and with his wife and children. And he takes four or five coursers, and civet-cats, apes, parrots, leopards, and falcons; and in this way he goes through the whole of India. His dress is a goat skin, that is, one before and one behind, with the hair outwards. His colour is dark tawny, for the people here[1] begin to be more dark than white. They all wear a great quanity of jewels, and pearls, and other precious stones, in their ears, and they go dressed all 'apostolica (i.e. in a loin cloth, langoti), and some wear shirts. The king and some of the more noble have the face and arms and the whole body powdered over with ground sandalwood and other most excellent scents. (1502–8)

LUDOVICO DI VARTHEMA[55]

## 4. Characteristics of Akbar

This Prince [Akbar] is of a stature and a type of countenance well-fitted to his royal dignity, so that one could easily recognize, even at the first glance, that he is the King. He has broad shoulders, somewhat bandy legs well-suited for horsemanship, and a light-brown complexion. He carries his head bent towards the right shoulder. His forehead is broad and open, his eyes so bright and flashing that they seem like a sea shimmering in the sunlight. His eyelashes are very long, as also are those of the Sauromates, Sinae, Niphones and most other north-Asiatic races. His eyebrows are

---

[1] A city, described near Cambay in Deccan.

'The King's Elephant in the Great Sowari at Baroda', drawn by Emile Bayard

not strongly marked. His nose is straight and small, though not insignificant. His nostrils are widely opened, as though in derision. Between the left nostril and the upper lip there is a mole. He shaves his beard, but wears a moustache like that of a Turkish youth who has not yet attained to manhood (for on reaching manhood they begin to affect a beard). Contrary to the custom of his race he does not cut his hair; nor does he wear a hat, but a turban, into which he gathers up his hair. He does this, they say, as a concession to Indian usages, and to please his Indian subjects. He limps in his left leg, though indeed he has never received any injury there. His body is exceedingly well-built and is neither too thin ncr too stout. He is sturdy, hearty and robust. When he laughs, his face becomes almost distorted. His expression is tranquil, serene and open, full also of dignity, and when he is angry, of awful majesty. When the priests first saw him he was thirty-eight years of age. It is hard to exaggerate how accessible he makes himself to all who wish audience of him. For he creates an opportunity almost every day for any of the common people or of the nobles to see him and converse with him; and he endeavours to show himself pleasant-spoken and affable rather than severe toward all who come to speak with him. It is very remarkable how great an effect this courtesy and affability has in attaching to him the minds of his subjects. For in spite of his very heterodox attitude towards the religion of Muhammad, and in spite also of the fact that Musalmans regard such an attitude as an unforgivable offence, Zelaldinus [Akbar] has not yet been assassinated. He has an acute insight, and shows much wise foresight both in avoiding dangers and in seizing favourable opportunities for carrying out his designs. . . . (1582)

FATHER ANTONIO MONSERRATE[55a]

## 5. *Character of Tippoo Sahib*

Taking the whole of the circumstances into one glance, it may be judged what the Captain's feelings must have been on finding himself once more a prisoner. Hyder Ali, who was, when compared with the worst despots of the European world, a monster, must yet be considered, when put in comparison with his succssor Tippoo, as mild and merciful. Hyder, from policy and hypocrisy, shewed some lenity to the prisoners who fell into his hands. Instances are known where British captives have broke through the crowd that surrounded him into his presence for protection—when he has hypocritically feigned anger, threatened the persons who had treated them ill, reprobated severity, and sent them off satisfied for the present. Tippoo, on the contrary, was so perfectly savage, that cruelty seemed to be, not only the internal habit of his soul, but the guide of all his actions, the moving principle of his policy, the rule of his public conduct, and the source of his private gratifications. (1796)

DONALD CAMPBELL[56]

## 6. Wives of a Rajah[1]

It is the custom of this great country, that the wives of the Rajah always sit on the left side of the throne. They have neither diamonds, nor cats-eyes, nor rubies, nor agates: yet they are beautiful, and their dress is bewitching. Some looked tall and others short, but I did not see them stand; they appeared happy, and glistened like fish fresh caught.

> Such! proud Bengala's King and court,
> Where chiefs and champions brave resort,
> With ladies happy, gay, and free,
> as fishes in Bengala's sea!
>
> One beauty shone amid the throng,
> I mark'd her nose so fair and long,
> So fitted to her pretty pole,
> Like a nice toad-fish in its hole.
>
> One beauty small, amid the row,
> Did like the fair *Sanangin* show;
> None softer smil'd amid them all;
> Small was her mouth, her stature small,
> Her visage blended red and pale,
> Her pregnant waist a swelling sail.
>
> Another's face look'd broad and bland,
> Like pamflet floundering on the sand
> Whene'er she turned her piercing stare,
> She seemed alert to spring in air.
>
> Two more I mark'd in black array,
> Like the *salisdick* dark were they;
> Their skins, their faces fair and red,
> And white the flesh beneath lay hid.

[1] Written on a visit to the Government House in Calcutta.

These pretty fish, so blithe and brave,
To see them frisking on the wave!
Were I an angler in the sea,
These fishes were the fish for me!!

(1811)                                          IBRAHIM[57]
                              (A merchant from the Malay countries)

## 7. *The Rajah Govind Buckish's reception and house*

Last night about seven o'clock we proceeded to the residence of the
rajah, which is nearly opposite the great mosque. We were received
by him at the door, and conducted into a very handsome veranda,
well lighted with chandeliers; in front of it a large piece of water, and
fountains, on the other side of which, reflected in the water, was a
very splendid illumination, with many globes and differently shaped
figures formed of lamps, continually revolving, which had a very
beautiful effect. The floor of the veranda was covered with white
cloth, and Captain Sydenham took off his shoes before he went
upon it; but I declined following his example, being in boots, and
having appeared in them at the court of Delhi before the king. This
point was settled by Lord Lake stating, after the battle of Delhi,
when he was to appear before Shah Allum, that boots were a part of
his dress as a soldier, and that he could not appear without them. It
is curious how directly opposite our ideas on this subject are to those
of the natives in India. A Mahometan servant will hide himself,
should he be without his turban when you come upon him unpre-
pared, and he dare not enter your room without leaving his shoes at
the door. What a revolution must take place in England before the
footman may with propriety come into a room with his hat on, and
without his shoes! The rajah brought his son, a fine boy, to see the
show, telling us that his other child was ill with the small pox. After
seeing some very bad mimics, we were informed that our dinner was
ready, and proceeded to another court, where in a veranda, very elegantly lighted, we found a table furnished with captain Sydenham's
plates, knives, forks, spoons, glasses, etc. these not being known in
the east, where they always eat, and even help you, with the right
hand. An excellent Persian dinner was served up, consisting of some
very good dishes; and the bread, with poppy seeds in the crust, was
very delightful. Our repast had, however, one advantage over those
of Persia; our beverage being madeira, hermitage, and claret; at

which after sitting an hour, we sent to inform the rajah we were
about to return to the veranda. Some bad fireworks were exhibited
being inferior to the generality, as the natives are very successful in
these matters, but the short notice I had given did not permit the
powder to dry. After we had seen these, a celebrated singer was
introduced, who sung tolerably well, not only Persian, but Hindoo
songs, accompanied by tom-toms, and two instruments not unlike
guitars. This man, with the set of mimics, and two sets of nautch
women, are always in the rajah's pay, and are part of his household
and state. He receives 300 rupees a month, equal to £37, and the
mimics and nautch women from 300 to 400 a set. I am told that a
singer, a woman at Hyderabad, is in such repute, that she will not
sing under 500 rupees a night. She must be the Catalani of the east.
These mimics are the worst kind of buffoons, and accompany their
acting by silly remarks, and execrable attempts at wit. I recollect
seeing a set when I was in Hindoostan in 1815, who, in ridicule of
our cutchery or court of justice, went through a trial, in which the
judges were supposed to be Europeans. The offender, when about
to enter on his defence, is interrupted by a servant who announces
that dinner is ready, and the judges start up, pronounce the prisoner
guilty, condemn him to be hanged, and run off to table. It is almost
needless to remark how little this buffoonery is justified by the
actual practice of our courts in India, and the classical English
reader will at once apply to this specimen a line of one of our great
poets. Yet the performance, however it may be regarded as a piece
of impertinence, is a proof among many others of the mildness and
toleration of the British government; since even the public actors
feel that they can take such liberties with impunity. After several
songs, our singer stated that he had been in Calcutta, and knew an
English song; and to my surprise, began to the same tune as that in
which he had been chanting his Persian,

> I care for nobody,
> Nobody cares for me.

This was all he knew, and was well enough; but in repeating it
several times it became

> I care for no-
> -body no ca-
> -re for me, I
> -care for nobo-
> dy no ca

to my infinite amusement. The rajah, I thought, fancied I was treating his singer with great disrespect on my laughing at him, and, to raise him and his *metier* in my opinion, began a long story about a singer who was performing before Nadir Shah after his capture of Delhi. At a nautch given to the conqueror by his prisoner Mahmumed Shah, the former was to pleased with him, that he promised to give him any thing he asked. The patriotic and disinterested singer immediately answered, 'the occupation of the city by your army has raised the price of flour to an exorbitant height; make it cheaper.'

After we had seen both sets of nautch women and more fireworks, we took leave, and the rajah presented me with presents similar to those I had given him the day before, with the exception of two small bottles of attar of roses, and immense wreaths of roses thrown round our necks. (1817)

LT. COL. FITZCLARENCE[58]

## 8. High mass and grand fete at Christmas

The Begum [Sumroo] usually gives a grand *fete,* which lasts three days, during Christmas, and to which nearly all the society of Merat, Delhi, and the surrounding stations is invited. I have by me one of her circulars: 'Her Highness the Begum Sumroo requests the honour of——'s company at Sirdhana, on Christmas Eve, at the celebration of High Mass, and during the two following days, to a nautch and a display of fire-works.' Here the burden of the exhibition is distributed pretty equally between our good friend the Bishop, the *Nauchnies,* and the fire-works. Of these spectacles, most who have witnessed them agree that the religious pageantry has the lead, in point of display and finery.

Tents are prepared in the palace-garden for the accommodation of visitors, and every luxury which a profuse outlay can secure is provided for the company; the tables are sumptuously spread, the viands and the wines are alike excellent. Upon these grand occasions, the Begum usually honours the guests by presiding at the table; but she does not herself partake of any food in their presence. Not only are the numerous visitors entertained in this magnificent style, but the whole host of their followers and train are also feasted and feted, in a manner equally sumptuous in proportion to their conditions. When we recollect who the Begum originally was, the diabolical character of her husband, his perpetration of the mas-

sacre at Patna, and the many acts of crime and tyranny which she has
herself committed, it is strange thus to find an enlightened British
community, the victors of the soil, doing homage and seeking favour
at her foot-stool, or even condescending to partake of her hospitality. (1831–6)

THOMAS BACON[59]

## 9. *A meeting with Maharaja Runjeet Singh*

G. went to meet Runjeet at seven this morning, and F. joined them
on her elephant as they went through our street. I did not set off in
the carriage till past eight, and when I got to the ground I was still
too early, for Runjeet, instead of being satisfied with a general view
of the line, insisted on riding down the whole of it, about three miles,
and inspecting every man.

F., Major W., C., and I waited at the flagstaff till their return,
which was a beautiful sight (I mean their return was beautiful, not
our waiting).

Old Runjeet looks much more personable on horse-back than in
durbar, and he is so animated on all military matters that he rides
about with the greatest activity. G. and he, and their interpreter,
finally settled themselves at the flagstaff, and there G. sent for F.
and me to come on our elephants to them.

In front there was the army marching by. First, the 16th Hussars,
then a body of native cavalry, then the Queen's Buffs, then a train of
Artillery drawn by camels, then Colonel Skinner's wild native
horsemen with their steel caps and yellow dresses—the band of each
regiment wheeling off as they passed, and drawing up to play
opposite to Runjeet.

Behind us there was a large amphitheatre of elephants belonging
to our own camp, or to the Sikhs, and thousands of Runjeet's followers all dressed in yellow or red satin, with quantities of their led
horses *trapped* in gold and silver tissues, and all of them sparkling
with jewels. I really never saw so dazzling a sight. Three or four
Sikhs would look like Astley's broke loose, but this immense body
of them saves their splendour from being melodramatic. The old
man himself wears a sort of red stuff dress with a little edging of the
commonest grey squirrel's fur, and a common red muslin turban.
His horse, too, had less gold about it than any other. He was quite
delighted with the review, and at the end of it his servants put down

before him eleven bags, each containing 1,000 rupees, to be distributed among the troops. When everything was done, all the chief people went to one tent, which we had pitched on the ground, where there was a *dejeuner a la fourchette* and the right things. (1838)

EMILY EDEN[60]

## 10. Akbar, the greatest Mogul

At Agra, Akbar, the greatest of all the Mogul sovereigns, descendant of Baber and Timur, and of tribal connection with Genghis Khan, becomes a very real personage. He lived in that age of great sovereigns when Henry IV, Philip II, and Queen Elizabeth ruled in Europe. He has been called the Marcus Aurelius and the Frederick the Great of India, and he was the greatest builder the country had then known.Forts, palaces, tombs and whole cities sprang up by his command, and at his court literature, art, and all religions were honoured. Brahmans. Mohammedans, Sikhs, Jains, and Catholic priests expounded and argued with him in a first parliament of religions, and, regarding them all impartially, he devised a universal theory, a compromise creed which his vizier and not a few courtiers adopted. He himself worshipped the sun every morning, as representative of the divinity which animates and rules the world. He was a strenuous sort of ruler too, walking twenty and thirty miles a day, to the dismay of his courtiers; and once he rode from Ajmir to Agra in two days, covering the two hundred and twenty miles by innumerable relays of fast horses. Akbar wrote his memoirs, in worthy emulation of Baber, whose autobiography in illuminated Persian text is treasured in the Agra College library.

In the usual reverse order of all Indian sight-seeing, we first saw Akbar's tomb, and then his City of Victory. The tomb is at Secundra, a suburb of Agra. A great red sandstone gateway admits one to the flagged court, and the impressive pillared pavilion, rising story upon story, after the oldest Buddhist constructions, covers the remains of the greatest of the Moguls. A pierced marble screen walls the upper terrace, where the white sarcophagus, covered with carving, lies open to the sun and sky, the intended white dome never having been completed by Akbar's successors. The real tomb is reached by a sloping passageway, and the monarch lies in a grave scooped in the earth like the graves of his desert-chief ancestors. (1903)

ELIZA RUHAMAH SCIDMORE[61]

# B. THE COMMON MAN

## 1. The Indians

Their favourite mode of exercising the body is by friction, applied in various ways, but especially by passing smooth ebony rollers over the skin. Their tombs are plain, and the mounds raised over the dead lowly. In contrast to the general simplicity of their style, they love finery and ornament. Their robes are worked in gold, and ornamented with precious stones, and they wear also flowered garments made of the finest muslin. Attendants walking behind hold up umbrellas over them: for they have a high regard for beauty, and avail themselves of every device to improve their looks. Truth and virtue they hold alike in esteem. Hence they accord no special privileges to the old unless they possess superior wisdom. (302–298 B.C.)

MEGASTHENESE[62]

## 2. Brahmins of Calicut

It is a proper, and at the same time a pleasant thing to know who these Brahmins are. You must know that they are the chief persons of the faith, as priests are among us. And when the king takes a wife he selects the most worthy and the most honoured of these Brahmins and makes him sleep the first night with his wife, in order that he may deflower her. Do not imagine that the Brahmin goes willingly to perform this operation. The king is even obliged to pay him four hundred or five hundred ducats. The king only and no other person in Calicut adopts this practice. We will now describe what classes [or castes] of pagans there are in Calicut.

The first class of pagans in Calicut are called Brahmins. The second are Naeri [Nairs], who are the same as the gentlefolks amongst us; and these are obliged to bear sword and shield or bows or lances. When they go through the street, if they did not carry arms they would no longer be gentlemen. The third class of pagans are called Tiva [Tiyan], who are artisans. The fourth class are called Mechua [Mukkuvan], and these are fishermen. The fifth class are called Poliar [Pulayan], who collect pepper, wine, and nuts. The sixth class are called Hirava [Vettuvan], and these plant and gather in rice. These two last classes of people, that is to say, the

Poliar and Hirava, may not approach either the Naeri or the Brahmins within fifty paces, unless they have been called by them, and they always go by private ways through the marshes. And when they pass through the said places, they always go crying out with a loud voice, and this they do in order that they may not meet the Naeri or the Brahmins; for should they not be crying out, and any of the Naeri should be going that way and see their fruits, or meet any of the said class, the above mentioned Naeri may kill them without incurring any punishment; and for this reason they always cry out. (1502-8)

LUDOVICO DI VARTHEMA[63]

## 3. The Hindoos

When I visited the Hindoo villages in the Concan, and enjoyed the pleasant interview with Ragojee Angria and Govindsett, mentioned on my journey through that district, I was charmed with the simple manners of the brahmins, the liberal sentiments of the prince and his philanthropic vizier, the venerable Mahomedan at Ram-Rajah, and many other amiable characters, replete with novelty and interest. I wrote from first impressions, in the same manner as I afterwards pourtrayed the natives of Malabar, and the inhabitants of Surat and the northern cities, where I occasionally resided; especially while sojourning in the Mahratta camp, and travelling to Ahmedabad, through the delightful province of Guzerat. In my letters on those occasions, I related events as they occurred, without much reflection, or comparison with other countries. Every incident had the charm of novelty; and, like some other travellers, I might have viewed passing events superficially, and formed hasty conclusions.

In subsequent situations, particularly when collector of Dhuboy, and acting as judge in that district, I had much greater opportunities of scrutinizing the Hindoo character. In this investigation my opinion materially changed, and a further intercourse with the religious brahmins at Dhuboy and Chandode, did not raise them in my estimation. Nor did the moral conduct of the Yogees, Senassees, and other devotees frequenting the jattaras of the Nerbudda, prejudice me in their favour. But when I developed the character of the secular brahmins and Hindoos of various description, employed in the revenue department from the consequential zemindar to the village patell, how was I astonished! Their cruelty, avarice, craftiness, and duplicity, occasioned a thousand grievances, which I could neither counteract nor redress; and displayed such shocking traits, rooted and strengthened by religious opinions, prejudice of caste, and habits of oppression, as baffled all my endeavours to relieve the poor ryots, suffering under their tyranny. (1813)

JAMES FORBES[64]

## 4. The Aryan population

It is a bad thing for a race to be able to get other people to do its work during three thousand years. The higher classes of Hindu society, by their inbred dislike and contempt for manual industry, disabled themselves from becoming a wealthy or powerful people, and are at this moment being ousted from many posts of emolument by the despised mixed multitude who have for ages done the work of the country, but who now for the first time are secured by an impartial government in the fruits of their labour. Even in education, the immemorial monopoly of the Brahmans, the competition of the non-Aryan element is beginning to be felt. In the Beerbhoom public school, which stands first of three hundred educational institutions in the south-west division of Lower Bengal, a man belonging to what used to be considered a very degraded caste is now head-master; and throughout the whole country, thousands of Brahman boys are instructed by teachers whose family names (Dass) proclaim them the descendants of the enslaved aboriginal tribes (Dasyu). Accustomed to look upon toil as a mark of slavery, the Hindus have never worked more than was necessary to supply their wants. Capital, therefore, the surplus of production above consumption, has never existed; and in the absence of capital, any high advance in material civilization is impossible. Another element of such an advance, co-operation, has been equally unknown. Division of labour, in its literal sense of giving to every man a separate employment, has indeed been carried to its utmost length; but the division of labour, in its economical signification as a method of co-operation, has been rendered impossible by the contempt which divides man from man. On this subject, false appearances, and inaccurate names for these appearances, have led many writers into error. Division of labour, as a term of Political Economy, means a division of processes in order to attain an ultimate combination of results. Division of labour, as predicable of Indian art or manufacture, means a division of results (each man being able to do only one thing) effected by a combination of processes (each man performing the whole of the processes requisite to produce the single result). The Indo-Aryans have paid a heavy penalty for debasing the humbler children of the soil, by that stagnation and incapability of national advancement which has formed the most conspicuous difference between them and other families of the same noble stock. They refused to share their light with the people who dwelt in darkness, and for ages any further illumination has been denied to themselves.

But this has not been their whole punishment. In the pride of intellect, they condemned a people strong-armed, but of meagre intelligence, to perpetual slavery while living, and refused them admittance to their own bright world when dead. Hence the reticence of the Bengali people, each caste keeping its sympathies for its own members, dreading the classes above it as conquerors or tyrants, and disdaining to admit the classes below it into its confidence. In their turn, the Aryan population of India has been subdued by successive waves of conquerors, inferior to them in their boasted intellect, but able to wield the sword with a more powerful right hand than is given to a people who shift the labour of life on servile shoulders. Afghan, Tartar, and Mogul, found the Indo-Aryans effeminated by long sloth, divided amongst themselves, and devoid of any spirit of nationality. Thus for seven centuries has providence humbled the disdainful spirit of Hinduism beneath the heel of barbarian invaders, grinding together all classes of people as upon the nether millstone, and slowly bringing on the time foretold in the Sanskrit Book of the Future (the Bhavishya Purana), when the Indian people shall be of one caste, and form one nation. That this time is now not far off, no one who is acquainted with the Bengalis of the present day will doubt. They have about them the capabilities of a noble people. What they want is social amalgamation, to be effected, not as the Sanskrit prophet predicts, by the universal corruption of the Indian races, but as the Christian devoutly hopes, by their universal regeneration. (1868)

W. W. HUNTER[65]

## 5. *An enlightened Hindu landholder*

My destination was Bhowal, where lived an enlightened Hindu land-

holder, called Kali Narain Rai, who was anxious to be on good terms
with the official and all other Europeans of respectability. A large
portion of his estate was situated in the forest jungle; but he resided
on some clear land at the south-eastern edge of it, where he had his
old ancestral residence, family temple, etc., etc.

He had also, with true Oriental hospitality, added to his house a
building in the European style, for the use of Europeans; and in this
my wife and child, whom I had taken with me, and myself were
located. He did not appear at first, as he said he would pay his
respects to us after we had bathed and breakfasted. The walls of his
drawing-room were covered with some ten engravings of English
pictures, and I was amused to observe that they were all duplicates.
There were two of 'The Monarch of the Glen,' two of 'Bolton
Abbey in the Olden Time,' two of 'The Meeting of Blucher and
Wellington after Waterloo,' etc., etc. I suppose he must have procured them through some native agent in Calcutta.

In due time he came in, and, after some conversation, took my
wife to see his wives, into whose presence I, of course, was not
permitted to go. She told me there were three of them, of very
different ages, and all exceedingly pretty. He had had children by
each, and explained to her which belonged to which. All this she
thought rather curious.

As I have observed before, we English in India are accused of
keeping aloof from native society; but the blame does not rest with
us. It is attributable to caste prejudices, and the seclusion of women.
Here was this man, most anxious to be civil and hospitable; but his
religion forbad him to let me see his wives or daughters, and himself
to eat or drink with me. Probably, also, he underwent a purification
after each interview, for he was a high Brahmin. However, as I
stayed some days here, and had about two interviews with him daily,
we gradually became very confidential. (1878)

AN EX-CIVILIAN[66]


## 6. The titles of honour

Sri 108 Matparamahansaparivrajakacharyaswamibhaskarananda-
saraswati.

You do not put 'Esq.' after it, for that is not necessary. The word
which opens the volley is itself a title of honour—'Sri.' The '108'

stands for the rest of his names, I believe. Vishnu has 108 names which he does not use in business, and no doubt it is a custom of gods and a privilege sacred to their order to keep 108 extra ones in stock. Just the restricted name set down above is a handsome property, without the 108. By my count it has fifty-eight letters in it. This removes the long German words from competition; they are permanently out of the race. (1896)

MARK TWAIN[67]

## 7. The Indian people

In this connection it may be observed that there is nothing more misleading than to accept as authoritative the statements about India and its peoples, which are made by those who base their claim to be heard on a long residence in Calcutta, or any other Presidency town. It has to be borne in mind that India, with all the differences that exist between different parts of the country, has this common feature throughout, that it is an agricultural country, consisting mainly of villages, smaller or greater, scattered over its hills and plains. In the Presidency towns one sees, no doubt, many Indians gathered together; but they have separated themselves, either recently or at a more remote period of their family history, from the great occupations and interests of the people of India. They have come together, some of them, for the acquisition of Western learning which the great mass of their countrymen do not value and are inclined to think as little suited to an Indian as the peacock's feathers to the jackdaw of the fable.

Some of them have come for the study and practice of law, of which the great mass of their fellow-countrymen are ignorant and suspicious; some of them for the sake of commerce, in which the great mass of their countrymen have no intelligent interest or direct concern. Their habits of life in the town are altogether different from the habits of the country; and there is no tie that binds the professional and commercial classes of the capital cities to the people of the country generally. The former do not understand the latter; and the latter, while they may, where necessity compels them, utilize, the services of the former, are by no means as a rule in frank and intelligent sympathy with them.

It is a common saying among people in Bengal that there is no one more ignorant of the people of the interior and of their affairs than the man whose training and career are confined to Calcutta; and I daresay the statement is true. The man who lives a town life in Great Britain generally keeps up some connection with the country. He pays periodical visits and tries to live the country life and get into touch with the country people and their concerns; he spends there many of his weekends and sometimes weeks at a time; and when there he throws himself deliberately into the life of the country, and lives as if himself of its people. On the other hand, the man whose life work is done in the Indian Presidency town, ordinarily goes to the country far too little; and, even when he does go there, he lives apart from the people in the aloofness which his sense of educational superiority and want of community of interest lead him to adopt. He has not, and does not care to have, much sympathy with or knowledge of the country and the country people.

When this great barrier between the people of the town and the people of the country is taken into consideration, as well as the great differences of races and religion that exist throughout India, one begins to realise something of the difficulty of dealing with Indian questions. The sources of information to the man who does not travel about and live among the people of the country, who, as a rule, are silent and invisible to those who do not make an effort to hear and see them, are the newspapers and orators of the great cities. These men talk as freely and as fully in regard to matters of which they are entirely ignorant as in regard to matters with which they may claim some acquaintance. (1911)

ANDREW H.L. FRASER[68]

## C. ANGLO-INDIANS AND CHRISTIANS

### 1. A panic among the coolies

Three short marches brought us to Taien, the proposed field of our action. We had ridden on before our servants and the *koolies* who were carrying our baggage; and Sackville, who had recovered his spirits, was playing all sorts of pranks for my amusement. Among other accomplishments, upon which he prided himself, was the art of imitating various birds and beasts; and while waiting for the arrival of our tents and camp-equipage, he proposed to waylay and frighten our followers. Secreting ourselves, therefore, in a patch of underwood, overlooking the track up which we had ridden, we lay in ambush, perfectly silent, until the first man made his appearance, under a load that would have better fitted the back of an elephant. Sackville uttered a terrible roar—'*Urra! Urra!–Wa! Wa!*' screamed the man, as he dropt his burden and ran off, as fast as terror could drive him, to the village for protection. Two minutes afterwards, a second appeared. '*Wa! Wa!*' said he, solioquising aloud, 'Ram Chundur has grown weary of his *bojh*, or some prowling tiger has taken a fancy to his ugly person. Well, so much the better; he won't want me.' A thundering bellow from Sackville made him too drop his load, and thus he stood for a moment petrified with fright, trembling from head to foot, with his eye fixed upon the thicket where we lay; then, taking a bound over the edge of the road, away he went scrambling and tumbling down the *khud*, at the imminent risk of his neck. (1833)

THOMAS BACON[69]

## 2. Anglo-Indian comforts

During that period of the year which is, by a pleasant fiction, called the 'cold season' in Calcutta—extending from December to February—the temperature is bearable. The European can then walk out in the mornings and evenings with comfort, walk out and enjoy the exercise, or ride briskly and not feel himself gradually sinking into a state of liquefaction. He must not, even then, however, tempt the sun's rays during the heat of the day; if he do, medical men 'will not be answerable for the consequences.' It is the 'cold season,' to be sure, but it is the Calcutta cold season, and, in such a climate, we must expect to exist only, not to enjoy.

The musquitos, too, during this cold season, swarm by thousands into the houses; they are driven in by the *cold,* any old yellow-faced, liver-diseased Anglo-Indian will gravely tell you; nay, not only gravely tell you so, but positively appear aggrieved if you do not appear at least to believe it. Those only who know what the delights of being a favourite with the musquitos are, can fancy the incessant state of activity in which the devoted object of their attentions is kept during a long evening.

The large fan which, for three-fourths of the year, swings heavily backwards and forwards in the room, suspended from the ceiling, is now at rest, and the little plagues have it all their own way. They persist in settling on your hands, or tapping your forehead, with a perseverance which, if you be an entomologist, will considerably enlighten you as to the nature of insects generally. You find that a flourish of your handkerchief is one of the best means of preventing their settling—they cannot endure a breeze, and they dislike being caught in the folds of even a cambric or silk trap—so you flourish your handkerchief, innocently, often.

If you have the misfortune to wear shoes, they will soon discover the fact, and settle accordingly upon the instep and by the side of the foot—they prefer the fleshy portion. By skilfully manoeuvring your feet, however, you easily detach them or prevent their settling effectually, that is, by gliding one foot over the other softly and leisurely, as if you meant nothing particular. Acute smarts you must expect, for, to be a favourite with the musquitos, is an honour involving much that is disagreeable, like many other honours—acute smarts, followed by intense itching; but you see old Anglo-Indians making light of musquitos, and you do not like to be considered a grumbler, so you say nothing about your own sufferings, feeling none the less, however.

One cannot be always flourishing his handkerchief about, gracefully or ungracefully; one cannot be always sliding the right foot over the left, and the left over the right, quickly or slowly. There is a limit beyond which the most determined musquito-hater cannot carry these resources, but there is no limit to the ravages of the little blood-sucker. When you take your stockings off at night, you will be able to trace the outline of the shoe upon your foot, by the bites, the little red spots forming the centres of small circles of inflammation; the neat way in which these bites will be found crossing your instep and running round by the side of the foot to the heel, will enable you to decide at once as to whether your shoe is properly and evenly cut.

Nor is it during the 'cold season' only that the musquitos thus abound in the houses. During the months of August and September, that is, after the rains, they are to be encountered in swarms. You have then, however, the resource of the large fan swinging over your head, and by sitting beneath it, the upper portion of your figure is safe from their attacks, as long as a sufficient current of air is kept up to drive them off, which will be as long as the fan-puller is awake. As to your nether limbs, if you wear shoes after the first few days of Calcutta life, you must then be one whom experience will *not* teach, and if you do not have a pad at the knee, beneath your tightly-drawn nether garments, to prevent the little monsters from assailing you there, it is your own fault.

'Our Bedroom', drawn by Captain G. F. Atkinson

Nor will you heedlessly sit on an open-worked cane-bottomed chair any longer than is necessary to convince you that you have made a mistake. However large the company, and however stiff, be not afraid to convey your person at once to a softer horse-hair or leather-covered seat. True, every one is well aware why you have moved—never mind that,—that old Anglo-Indians may smile a little internally or externally, but all those who have not become yellow with 'liver' (as the disease of that organ is curtly called in Calcutta), will sympathize with you—ladies as well as gentlemen—for musquitos know no distinction of sex, and would as soon commit their depredations on the shapely ankle of the belle of the season, as on the nose of the moustachoed and bewhiskered officer who solicits her hand for a dance. (1855)

WILLIAM KNIGHTON[70]

## 3. The Kitmutgars

When from the palkee I descend,
    Too weary to rejoice
At sight of my Mofussil friend,
    I cry with feeble voice,
Ere yet within the genial tub
    I plunge my clammy brow;
'Qui hye, Mahommed, brandy shrub,
    Belattee pawnee lao!'

As from Cutcherry home I spin,
    Worn with the ceaseless rout
Of mookhtars quarrelling within
    And chokeydars without,
My servant catches from afar
    The mandate, 'Juldee jao'.
'Hullo, there! Brandy, kitmutgar!
    Belatee pawnee lao!'

And when, a poor forsaken brute,
    On fevered couch I toss;
No man of medical repute
    Within a hundred coss;
One sovereign remedy I know,
    Whose virtues all allow;

'Qui hye, Mahommed, Brandy do!
Belattee pawnee lao!' (1863)

H. BROUGHTON[71]

## 4. Christians of St. Thomas

The gathering in of the 'Christians of St. Thomas' would indeed be a grand harvest. May God be pleased to give it to His Church!

In all my dealings with the native Christians of Southern India, nothing struck me so much as their delight in a seemly ritual. With that of Rome constantly before them, with the Eastern ritual of processions and grand displays, they are already acquainted; and they long for a ritual in their religious worship, which shall show forth to them 'the beauty of holiness.'

This will be the *key-note,* I am persuaded, of the conversion of thousands to the Catholic Faith; and it is, and has been, the key-note which has won for Rome her innumerable converts of the present day.

Yes! great and glorious would be such a harvest, already ripe for the gathering.

> Work to be done; a Master to be served;
> Fields white for reaping; judgment hard at hand;
> O Lord! what thoughts are these!

The Malabar Church possesses . . ., the three-fold ministry—bishop, priest, and deacon. They have always used for sacred purposes the Syrian tongue, a dialect of which was the language of Judea when our blessed Lord was upon earth. Bishops in regular succession under a Metropolitan have ruled their Church, which at one time amounted to 16.000.

A liturgy and other common prayers in Syriac mark their adherence to primitive antiquity.

Their infants have been baptized from time immemorial; and whilst observing a considerable degree of ceremonial they abhor the use of images in worship. (1870's)

A RETIRED CHAPLAIN[72]

# D. THE PARSIS

## 1. The Parsis at Surat

In Surat there is a class of men called Parsis, worshippers of fire, who in former days were inhabitants of Persia. But when first the Mahomedan religion got into Persia, the king tried to force them to become Mahomedans. For this reason they sent an embassy to the Hindu prince of Surat, asking him to grant them permission to emigrate into that country with their families, where they would become his permanent subjects. The Hindu prince received the embassy and allowed them to come, on condition that they should neither slaughter cows nor eat cows' flesh. He promised them the same rights as his other subjects. They came to Surat, where unto this day there are number of them, as also in different villages, and in the Portuguese territory adjacent to Damao [Daman].

Their religious belief is such that, if through misadventure anyone's house takes fire, on no account will he allow the fire to be interfered with or extinguished, it being, according to them, the greatest good luck and cause of rejoicing that he could have, he believing that his gods have conferred on him as especial gift and favour, in return for the adorations he has paid to them. And it ever, through negligence, the fire goes out in any of their houses, a fire that all of them maintain with especial care, there is great lamentation, much more than they would make if their nearest relation had died. After such a mishap the owner has recourse to his priest, begging his pardon for the crime he has committed in allowing the extinguishment of his household fire. The usual penance imposed is that the culprit must invite a number of families of the highest position among them. When these have all collected, well-washed and well-clad, they go off to the priest's house, and he, in their presence, makes a speech to the house-holder, and at the end of it delivers fire from his own house. This they carry, with a grand array of trumpets and drums, and arriving at the sinner's house, he is obliged to give them all a feast. These people have made a vow never to go upon the sea, in order not to defile it, since the sea unfailingly induces vomiting; and in gratitude for the benefits it has done to them they hold it in this great respect. (1652)

NICCOLAO MANUCCI[73]

## 2. The Parsis at Surat

Besides the *Moors* and the *Bannians,* and these *Faquirs,* which belong to both Professions, the *Persies* are a Sect very considerable in *India,* of whom the Tradition is, that coming from *Persia* in a Tempest, at the time that *Mahomet* and his Followers gave Laws to the *Persians,* (which they were unwilling to submit to) they were driven to that distress, that they almost despair'd of Life, 'till hearing a Cock Crow, and espying Fire at Land, they recover'd their hopes of safety, and gain'd a speedy Arrival. The Cock therefore is as much esteemed by them as the Cow is by the *Bannians,* of the lives of both which, they are the zealous Patrons and Protectors. For the Worshipping of Fire seems to be the Ancientest instance of Idolatry in the World, inasmuch (as some think) that *Cain,* after he was banished from the presence of the Lord, turned a downright Idolater, and then introduced the Worship of the Sun, as the best resemblance he could find of the Glory of the Lord, which was wont to appear in a flaming Light. And in after-times, they Worshipped Fire in the Eastern Counties as the best Emblem of the Sun, when it was absent. Nor was the Vestal Fire ever more Sacred, than all other Fires are with the *Persies,* the extinction of which, if it is voluntary, is a Crime as hainous, as if the vital Heat of the Cock or some other beloved Animal were destroy'd; so that if their Houses were on Fire, they would sooner be persuaded to pour on Oyl to increase, than Water to asswage the Flame. If a Candle is once lighted, they would judge the Breath of him more than Pestilential, that durst attempt to blow it out. And a *Persy* Servant, who is commanded to bring a hot Steel, and warm with it a Bowl of Punch, will plead his Excuse, and that he dare not hasten the coolness of the Steel by a violent abatement of the Heat. The active Flame must be allow'd to live, whilst there's any Fuel for it to feed on; if the Fire is once kindled, all care is taken that it comes to a natural Expiration, and no violence allow'd to bring it to a period sooner. Another account we have for their respect of Fire, is, that their great Law - giver, *Zertoost,* was taken into Heaven, and brought from thence Fire with him (*Prometheus* like) which he commanded his Followers afterwards to Worship.

They have other Fables concerning *Abraham,* that he was once in the Devil's Power, who expos'd him to the Flames, but the kind Fire would not fasten on him; from which they infer the great unreasonablenes of destroying that Element, which was so averse, (notwithstanding all its Fury) from hurting *Abraham* their Friend; the Reason of this may be, because that *Abraham* came from the Land of Ur, which signifies Fire, which might give the occasion for the Fable of his Escaping the Fire.

They own and Adore one Supreme Being, to whom, as he is the Original of all things, they dedicate the first Day of every Month, in a solemn observance of his Worship. And enjoin, besides these, some others for the Celebration of Publick Prayers.

At their solemn Festivals, whither an hundred or two sometimes resort, in the Suburbs of the City, each Man according to his Fancy and Ability, brings with him his Victuals, which is equally distributed, and eat in common by all that are present. For they shew a firm Affection to all of their own Sentiments in Religion, assist the Poor, and are very ready to provide for the Sustenance and Comfort of such as want it. Their universal Kindness, either in imploying such as are Needy and able to work, or bestowing a seasonable bounteous Charity to such as are Infirm and Miserable; leave no Man destitute of Relief, nor suffer a Beggar in all their Tribe; and herein so far comply with that excellent Rule of *Pythagoras, to enjoy a kind of Community among Friends.*

These *Persies* are by another Name term'd *Gaures,* or Worshippers of Fire, because of their Veneration for that Element; and were Transported into *India,* when *Calyf Omar* reduc'd the Kingdom of *Persia,* under the Power of the *Mahometans;* and they profess the Ancient Religion of the *Persians.* But their Religion spread it self more Westerly, it seems than *Persia;* . . . But I believe what remains of this Cast, are most of them in the Kingdom of the *Great Mogul.* But we read of some in *Persia* of great Antiquity. For near *Yesd* in the Province of *Ayrack,* (or *Hierack Agemi*) which yields the richest and Fairest Tapestries of all *Persia,* and of the World; and on the Mountain *Albors,* there are yet some Worshippers of Fire, who are said to have used it above 3000 Years.

They are not quite so Abstemious in their Diet as the *Bannians,* but Superstitiously refuse to drink after any Stranger, out of the same Cup. *Hindoes* will eat of one kind of Flesh, some of another, but all refrain from Bief, out of respect to Kine.

In their Callings they are very Industrious and diligent, and careful to train up their Children to Arts and Labour. They are the principal Men at the Loom in all the Country, and most of the Silks and Stuffs at *Suratt,* are made by their Hands. The High-Priest of the *Persies* is called *Destoor,* their Ordinary Priests *Daroos,* or *Harboods.*

I shall not mention their Marriages, which much resemble the manner of the *Bannians,* but proceed only to a Description of their

way of Burying, which is this. The noblest Sepulture which they
fancy they can bestow upon their deceased Friends, is exposing
them to be devour'd by the Fowls of the Air, and bestowing their
Carcasses on the Birds of Prey. After the Body is for some time
dead, the *Halalchors* (which are a sort of sordid *Indians*) take and
carry it out upon a Bier into the open Fields, near the place where it
is expose'd to the Fowls of Heaven. When 'tis there decently deposited upon the Ground, a particular Friend beats the Fields and
neighbouring Villages, upon the hunt for a Dog, 'till he can find one
out; and having had the good luck to meet him, he cherishes and
intices him with a Cake of Bread, which he carries in his Hand for
that purpose, 'till he draws him as near the Corps as he is able; for
the nearer the Dog is brought to the dead Body, the nearer are its
approaches to Felicity. And if the hungry Cur can by bits of Cake be
brought so nigh the Deceased, as to come up to him, and take a
piece out of his Mouth, 'tis then an unquestionable Sign, that the
Condition he died in was very happy; but if the timorous Dog
startles at the sight, or loaths the Object, or being lately well fed, has
no Stomach to that ordinary Morsel, which he must snatch out of the
dead Man's Jaws, the Case then with him is desperate, and his state
deplorable. The poor Man whom I saw, was by these Prognosticks,
very miserable; for the sturdy Cur would by no means be inticed to
any distance near him. When the Dog has finisht his part of the
Ceremony, two *Daroos,* at a Furlong's distance from the Bier,
stand up with joined Hands, and loudly repeat for near half an hour,
a tedious Form of Prayer by Heart; but with such a quick dispatch,
that they scarce drew Breath all the while, as if they had been under
some invincible necessity of running over the Words in such a time.
All the while they were thus gabling, a piece of White Paper fasten'd
to each Ear, o'erthwart the Face, hung down two or three Inches
below the Chin; and as soon as they had ended their Petitions, the
*Halalchors* took up the Corps, and conveyed it to the Repository,
which was near; all the Company ranking themselves by two and
two, and following it with joined Hands. The place of Sepulture is in
the open Fields, within a Wall built in form of a Circle, about twelve
Foot high, and about an hundred in the Circumference; in the
middle of which was a Door of Stone about six foot from the ground,
which was open'd to admit the Corps. The Ground within the Walls
is rais'd above four Foot, and made shelving towards the Centre,
that the Filth and Moisture which are drain'd continually from the

Carcasses. may by an easie passage descend into a Sink made in the
middle to receive them. The Corps therefore was left here, and all
the Company departing thence, betook themselves to a Rivolet that
run near the place for Ablution, to cleanse themselves from what
defilements, on this Melancholy occasion, they might have contracted; and retir'd afterwards to their proper Habitations in the
City, from whence this place is distant about a Mile. But within the
space of a Day or two after, some of the nearest Relatives return
against hither, to observe which of the Eyes of their deceased Friend
was first pickt out by the hungry Vultures; and if they find that the
right Eye was first seis'd on, this abodes undoubted Happiness; if
the left, they then are sorrowful, for that's a direful sign of his
Misery.

The *Persies* are very nice in the preservation of their Hair, and
careful to preserve whatever is cut of their Heads or Beards, that
nothing of it be lost or carelessly thrown about, but once a Year be
decently laid in their Burying place. A description of which, tho' it
be drest with nothing but Horrour, yet may here properly be in-
serted. (1689)

J. OVINGTON[74]

### 3. *A particular custom of Bombay at the death of a person*

As the *Gentoos* burn their dead, one would think that the *Persees,*
who are so fond of worshipping their deity under the representation
of fire, should be desirous of having their dead bodies committed to
that element, wherein they suppose their creator principally to
reside. But contrary to this, and to the custom of all other nations in
the world, they neither burn nor bury their dead, but cast them out
in the open air, to be exposed to the several elements, where they
are soon devoured by eagles, vultures, and other birds of prey. The
principle they go upon is, that a living man being compounded of all
the elements, it is but reasonable, after he is dead, that every
particular element should receive its own again. On the top of
*Malabar-hill,* in this island of *Bombay,* are two round buildings, on
purpose for receiving the dead bodies of the *Persees,* which are
placed and remain there till the bones are clean picked by the birds.
A guard constantly stands within a small distance of the place, who
is very much displeased if you offer to approach the buildings; and
for this reason, lest by your going too near, you disturb the vultures
in their preying upon the dead bodies. One afternoon however, I

resolved to satisfy my curiosity so far as to peep into one of these edifices. I perceived several dead bodies; but there was little flesh left upon the bones; and that little was so parched up by the excessive heat of the sun, that it did not emit those stinking *effluvia* which there was reason to expect. It was owing probably to the same cause, that the bones were rendered quite black.—Upon the whole, this is a most odious and abominable custom, and the reason they give for following it, is truly ridiculous. (1754)

EDWARD IVES[75]

## 4. *Character of the Parsees*

From the length of time which Bombay has been under the control of Europeans, the Persees, since their arrival there, have adopted little of the Asiatic manners. They indeed wear the dress, which they informed me had been adopted on their arrival, but they eat and drink like the English. Ardiseer Dady, one of their richest members, gave me a most magnificent entertainment. The table for the Europeans was chiefly covered with English cookery, but they sent me from their own several dishes, which were very highly seasoned, and good. The wines were excellent; but when I adjourned to their table, I was not a little astonished to find liqueurs placed opposite each Persee, which they drank in glasses as freely as wine, and which, though they sat late, seemed to have no effect on them. Their houses are furnished with a profusion of English looking-glasses, prints, and paintings. They always light them up remarkably well; but on this occasion the whole gardens were illuminated with torches and lamps, which had a most brilliant effect. The band playing in the verandah, and the crowd of differently dressed people had the semblance of an English masquerade. We had a very good set of nautch-girls, which much pleased Sir James Mackintosh, who had not before seen this Asiatic amusement. Coffee and tea, pawn and attar, lavender water, and other perfumes, completed the melange of this Anglo-Asiatic entertainment, from which we departed about midnight.

To the credit of the Persee humanity, they provide for all their poor; and to the credit of their private morals, there is not a single prostitute, or mistress to a gentleman, of their cast, in the settlement. They are generous and splendid in the higher orders; and in the lower, active and intelligent, far surpassing as servants the

Mussulmauns or Hindoos. They mostly speak English with propriety. In their persons they are a handsome race, fairer than the natives, though not possessing the clear skin of the Europeans. In their manners they are uniformly conciliatory and mild. I confess that I infinitely prefer them to any race of people in the East subject to the British control. They have numerous temples to Fire, but their priests seem to have no authority in temporal concerns, nor much spiritual control. Their religion is tolerant, and, as far as it throws no impediment in the way of the public service, must be considered politically as a good one. (1809)

GEORGE, VISCOUNT VALLENTIA[76]

## 5. Parsees in British India

The Parsees in British India enjoy every privilege, civil and religious. They are governed by their own *panchait*, or village council. The word *panchait* literally means a council of five, but that of the Guebres in Bombay consists of thirteen of the principal merchants of the sect; these were chosen originally by the people, confirmed by the government, and have continued hereditary. This little council decides all questions of property, subject, however, to an appeal to the recorder's court; but an appeal seldom happens, as the *panchait* is jealous of its authority, and is consequently cautious in its decisions. It superintends all marriages and adoptions, and inquires into the state of every individual of the community; its members would think themselves disgraced if any Parsee were to receive assistance from a person of a different faith; accordingly, as soon as the children of a poor man are old enough to marry, which, in conformity to the Hindoo custom, is at five or six years of age, the chief merchants subscribe a sufficient sum to portion the child; in cases of sickness, they support the individual or the family, and maintain all the widows and fatherless.

The *panchait* consists both of dustoors and laymen; all religious ceremonies and festivals come under its cognizance, together with the care of the temples, the adjusting the almanack, and the subsistence and life of the dogs. I could not learn with certainty the origin of the extreme veneration of the Parsees for this animal; every morning the rich merchants employ koolis to go round the streets with baskets of provision for the wild dogs; and, when a Parsee is dying, he must have a dog in his chamber to fix his closing eyes upon.

Some believe that the dog guards the soul, at the moment of its separation from the body, from the evil spirits; others say that the veneration for the dogs is peculiar to the Indian Guebres, and that it arose from their having been saved from shipwreck in their emigration to India, by the barking of the dogs announcing their approach to the land in a dark night.

The Parsees use some solemnities when they name their children, which is done at five or six months old; when the muslin shirt is put on the first time, a sacred fire is lighted, prayers are repeated, and the name is given. Since their intercourse with Europeans, they persist in calling this ceremony christening, because it is performed when the first or proper name is given; the second name is a patronymic; thus, *Norozejee Jumsheedjee,* is Norozejee the son of Jumsheedjee.

The Parsees are the richest individuals on this side of India, and most of the great merchants are partners in British commercial houses. They have generally two or three fine houses, besides those they let to the English; they keep a number of carriages and horses, which they lend willingly not only to Europeans, but to their own poor relations, whom they always support. They often give dinners to the English gentlemen, and drink a great deal of wine, particularly Madeira. The Guebre women enjoy more freedom than other oriental females, but they have not yet thought of cultivating their minds. Perhaps this is owing in great measure to the early marriages which, in compliance with the Hindoo customs, they contract. By becoming the property of their husbands in their infancy, they never think of acquiring a further share of their affection, and, with the hope of pleasing, one great incitement to mental improvement is cut off. (1811)

MARIA GRAHAM[77]

# E. WOMEN

## 1. Duties of women and wives

> In childhood must a father guard his daughter;
> In youth the husband shields his wife; in age
> A mother is protected by her sons—
> Ne'er should a woman lean upon herself

A faithful wife who wishes to attain
The heaven of her lord, must serve him here
As if he were a god, and ne'er do aught
To pain him, whatsoever be his state,
And even though devoid of every virtue.

She who in mind, speech, body, honours him,
Alive or dead, is called a virtuous wife.

Be it her duty to preserve with care
Her husband's substance; let her too be trusted
With its expenditure, with management
Of household property and furniture,
Of cooking and purveying daily food.

Let her be ever cheerful, skilled in all
Domestic work, and not too free in spending.

Drink, bad companions, absence from her lord,
Rambling about, unseasonable sleep,
Dwelling in others' houses, let her shun—
These are six things which tarnish woman's fame.

Whatever be the character and mind
Of him to whom a woman weds herself,
Such qualities her nature must imbibe,
E'en as a river blending with the sea.

Women, united by the marriage tie
To men they love, in hope of virtuous offspring,
Worthy of honour, eminently blessed,
Irriadiate the houses of their lords,
Like shining lights or goddesses of fortune.

Then only is a man a perfect man
When he is three—himself, his wife, his son—
For thus have learned men the law declared,
'A husband is one person with his wife.'

Fidelity till death, this is the sum
Of mutual duties for a married pair.

And if the wife survives, let her remain
Constant and true, nor sully her fair fame,
E'en by the utterance of another's name.

(?600 BC-AD 300?)                    MANU

*Translated by Monier Williams*[78]

## 2. *The Hindoo widow*

Having hired a small covered boat, rowed by four men and steered by a fifth, I left Calcutta on a visit to my friend Mr. Fletcher at Santipore, sixty miles higher up the Ganges. In the evening, the tide running up, the boatmen pushed off into the middle of the stream and began rowing. As long as light continued I observed the many objects of my interest which this part of the river presented—boats in great numbers and of various size and form, engaged in the internal commerce of the country, and others heavily laden with supplies for the markets of the great British metropolis.

Soon after dark I crept under the low flat roof of my little boat and went asleep on a mattress my servants had spread for me.

I got up soon after daybreak and went upon the forepart of the boat, between the roof and the rowers, to enjoy the coolness of the morning air. When I had been here about half an hour I observed on the shore to our left several persons coming from the interior to the river, and others standing together near it, a sight so usual at this time of the day that it did not strike me as at all singular. As, however, we came nearer, some singularity was observable, for the people did not enter the river to bathe. I therefore noticed them more attentively, when the discovery of a *pile* which I could perceive amongst the crowd at once suggested a painful solution of what was passing, and the opinion of my boatmen removed all doubt. It was certainly a suttee, or burning of a Hindoo widow, that was about to take place. Though feeling a great repugnance for painful sights, I determined to avail myself of an opportunity which so seldom offers itself to a native of Europe of *seeing* one of the most remarkable customs of the East. I accordingly directed the boat to be steered towards the people, and soon landed amongst them, close to the body of the deceased Hindoo, which had apparently just been placed at the edge of the water, with which some Bramins, or persons of the family, were then washing it. The deceased appeared to have been about thirty-five years of age, and to have been rather a tall man. I did not learn what his illness had been, but he was reduced almost to a skeleton. He was lying on his back on a small bedstead, with his knees up, and was quite uncovered, excepting a cloth about his middle. I looked about for his widow, but could see no one distinguishable by anything particular from the rest of the females. Walking a few yards up the shore I saw the pile. It was

'A Suttee', from a drawing in Nolan's *History of the British Empire in India*

about 4½ feet high, something less in width, and about 5½ feet in length. The bottom part was composed of dried faggots, upon which was a thick layer of dried palm-leaves, rushes, and stalks of sugar-canes. While I was standing here the circle of people who surrounded the pile, looking at the preparations, opened towards the river, and the dead body was brought through on the bedstead, and after having been put down for a minute near the pile, was lifted up and placed upon it, the head towards the south, the face turned towards the Ganges.

During these proceedings I was standing about ten feet from the north-west angle of the pile, in the inner line of the circle formed by the people. Looking now to my right I perceived the unfortunate woman. She was sitting between two young children, a little within the circle and immediately opposite the middle of the western side of the pile. A white cloth fell from the top of her head over each cheek, but her face was partly visible where I stood.

As she sat, her elbows rested upon her knees, her hands supporting her head. Her eyes, half closed, were fixed upon the ground, but without taking notice of anything. Several women whom I supposed to be her relations and friends, were sitting or standing behind her, but there was no communication of any kind between them and the widow, nor between the latter and her children; not a tear was shed nor a word spoken.

After a few minutes the woman rose, and some Bramins, stepping forward, put into her hand a cloth containing something, and then ranged themselves partly behind her, partly by her side, some of the women doing the same. In this movement I lost sight of the children, and supposed that they had been secretly withdrawn by some one of the family or of the attendants. Followed by the Bramins and women, she now began to walk gently within the circle to the left, distributing as she went the contents of her cloth. She would necessarily pass close to me, and this circumstance seemed to favour the little chance there was of saving her life. I determined to attract her attention as she passed me and to be guided by the results as to any further interference. When, therefore, she came to where I was standing, I stepped forward and held my hand towards her as expressive of a desire to share the farewell offering she was giving away. The unexpected appearance of an European, whom she now saw for the first time in all probability in her life, undoubtedly surprised her, although her feelings seemed too deadened by the circumstances of her situation to be susceptible of much impression. She had not raised her eyes from the ground to look at the persons she passed, but my advancing, together with my dress, caused her to look at me while she put a small quantity of burnt rice into my hand. She appeared to be about twenty years of age and had the regular delicate features so usual among the native women of India. Having received her rice as graciously as I could, I allowed her to pass on. I considered, however, what had occurred as so favourable that I resolved to speak to her when she came to me again, for I understood that she was to walk round three times.

Having proceeded slowly round the pile she came to the part where she had been seated with her children, and a few steps more brought her near to me a second time. I again advanced as she approached, and having again received a few grains of rice, which she seemed quite prepared to give me, I expressed my grief at her intention, and entreated her to relinquish it for the sake of her children, for whom as well as for herself I promised provision and protection. Although she said nothing, I thought her look seemed to express thankfulness for the proposition she had heard. I had not time to say more, the pressure of the Bramins, watchful lest their victim should escape, obliging her to move on.

Having once more completed her round and come to where I stood, she herself turned to put some rice into my hand. I eagerly seized the last opportunity I should have of renewing my exhortation, promising her a pension for life and provision for her children. Though her head remained inclined towards the ground, she looked at me while I spoke, and her countenance impressed me with the assurance that if she had been free from the fatal influence which surrounded her it would not have been difficult to turn her from her resolution. Pressed on as before, she turned her eyes from me and moved forwards.

The last scene of this shocking tragedy was now approaching. The procession did not quite complete the third round, for having reached the head of the pile the widow advanced to the side of it next the river, when two men, laying hold of her, raised her in their arms and laid her upon it, with her face towards the face of her dead husband. It was, however, found that the bent knees of the latter prevented her being placed sufficiently near the corpse to be tied to it. As soon as the bystanders perceived this difficulty there was a considerable rumour amongst them. Some called out that the woman had better be placed behind the man, others observing that she was now in her proper place. After some discussion the former arrangement was decided on, and the miserable woman was again lifted up and carried round to the opposite side, where she was placed close to the back of the deceased, her face towards him. A rope which had been put under the dead body being passed also under and then over her's, the two—the living and the dead—were tied firmly together. Dry combustible materials, similar to those on which the bodies rested, were now heaped over them, and I entirely lost sight of the woman.

When the pile had been thus raised about eighteen inches more, two long bamboos were fastened to pegs in the ground on one side, and being passed over it were depressed till their ends reached the other pegs, to which also they were secured. The pressure upon the pile by these means was very considerable, and would effectually prevent the woman from rising. Indeed, it seemed to me doubtful whether the quantity of stuff piled upon her and closely pressed down would not smother her, and happily rescue her from a more painful death. There was, however, scarcely time allowed for this, for as soon as the bamboos were fastened down, fire was brought from a small burning heap that was ready for the purpose, and applied, amidst the shouts of the people, first to the head of the pile, then at the bottom, and afterwards to different parts of it. The ignition was immediate, and to increase its action and direct the flames through the middle, ghee, a sort of liquid butter, was poured upon the top. There was no shouting after the first exclamation on lighting, but the noise was still considerable, seeming, however, to be accidentally occasioned by the talking and observations of the people rather than studiously produced to conceal the shrieks of the woman. Indeed, the way in which she was covered up and pressed down would render her cries very feeble; nor, if they did reach the ears of the bystanders, would they be likely to excite either horror or pity, for I saw not a single countenance that testified either of these feelings. The flames were so excited as the ghee flowed down upon them that they quickly pierced through the crackling faggots, and must, as far as I could judge, have reached the poor woman in less than two minutes after the pile was lighted; and though their rapidly-increasing progress would soon put an end to her sufferings, these for some seconds must have been dreadful. At length they made their way through the top of the pile, and the whole was one

general blaze. There could be little doubt that ine agonies of the
wretched widow were now over; but this desirable fact was rendered unquestionable by a circumstance which occurred shortly
after. It was an explosion in the pile, like the discharge of a pistol.
Had this happened sooner I should have concluded that gunpowder
had been put amongst the materials to accelerate their combustion.
The noise was followed by clamorous expressions of satisfaction
amongst the spectators. Upon my asking a Hindoo near me what all
this meant, he said that the skull of one of the dead had burst, and
that the people had shouted because this occurence was a favourable omen. In a few moments more there was a similar explosion,
followed by a similar burst of satisfaction round the whole circle.

The pile was soon after reduced to a burning heap of fragments
and ashes about two feet high, and not knowing what new horrors its
further reduction might disclose, I made my way through the people
behind me and went on board my boat, not certainly to partake of
the breakfast my servants were about to prepare for me, nor to
dismiss from my thoughts the spectacle I had seen. (1792)

THOMAS TWINING[79]

## 3. Indian women

The ghauts – flights of steps to the river – of which every town on
the Ganges boasts of three or four, always present an animated
scene to the acquatic passenger. At all hours of the day, but more
particularly in the morning, they are thronged with busy crowds of
Hindoos, who are certainly the most cleanly people in the world.
The Brahmin may be seen standing up to his knees in the holy
stream, with depressed head, and hands in the attitude of prayer; or
carefully washing the symbolical thread, the badge of his sacred
caste. Women with their graceful garments, and still more graceful
persons, and with their well-poised water-vessels on their heads,
glide up and down the steps in execution of their duty, the drudgery
of the menage. It does one's heart good to see these elegant creatures cheerfully performing their domestic offices, and rendering
even labour graceful. You may talk of your Frenchwoman's
walk – it may be pretty – indeed, it is so; but is it natural? She goes
pitter-patting along as though she feared at each step to burst her
shoe. My Indian daughter of nature has no shoe to burst; but she
plants a very pretty bare foot with precision, yet lightness; and floats

past, unencumbered with the weighty vase, which her slender neck seems almost too fragile to support.

A little apart from the town and the public haunts of man, females, singly or in pairs, may be seen stealing down to the river, like Musidora, to bathe their 'fervent limbs in the refreshing flood'; like her, unconscious of any treacherous Damon, after a hasty glance up the bank and along the shore, they disengage themselves in an instant from their simple garment, and plunge into the stream.

This dress of the women consists of but one piece of cloth, the sarree; it is fastened round the waist, and thrown over the head and across the bosom. Simple though it be, this attire is infinitely more graceful, and even more decent, than the evening costume of the belles of more sophisticated regions.

I have often been amused by, and marvelled at, the total absence of all visible sympathy or gallantry between the Hindoo men and women in public. In Europe, on occasions like these conventions on the Ghaut, there would doubtless be free scope given to badinage, ribaldry, and practical jokes; but the orderly Hindoo plods through his prayers and ablutions perfectly indistrait by the vicinity of his fair neighbour, whom he suffers to raise the ponderous water-vessel to her head, without dreaming of offering assistance. (1829)

CAPT. GODFREY CHARLES MUNDY[80]

## 4. Women in India

Woman, as a mother, while the husband lives, is seldom allowed in India to bear any rule in the family: children are without natural affection; so that the place assigned to females in Hindoo society is, to appearance, abject in the extreme. The institutes of Menu, whose inspiration is as unquestioned as his legislative supremacy is universal among them, do indeed direct that the female who is to be chosen for the wife should not be reproachable for reddish hair, or too much or too little of the proper shade, for a deformed limb or inflamed eyes, for being immoderately talkative, or for being troubled with habitual sickness; while her name must be neither that of a constellation, a tree, nor a river, of a barbarous nation, nor of a mountain, of a winged creature, a snake, nor a stone, nor of any image which occasions terror. Besides an agreeable name, she must possess a form which has no defect; she must walk gracefully – like a young elephant; her teeth must be moderate in number and in size and her body of exquisite softness. But there are no rules for the virtues of the heart, the degree of knowledge, the habits of the mind, or the graces of benevolence; and little wonder! Could they gather grapes of thorns, or figs of thistles? In childhood's years a female must be dependant on her father; in youth, on her husband; and, should she survive his decease, her dependance must be on her sons. The nature of this dependance may be imagined, when it is added, that at no period of life, in no condition of society, should a woman do any thing according to her own mere pleasure. Their fathers, their husbands, their sons, are verily called their protectors; but it is such protection! day and night must women be held by their protectors in a state of absolute dependence. A woman, it is affirmed, is never fit for independence, or to be trusted with liberty; for she may be compared to a heifer on the plain, which still longeth for fresh grass. They exhaust the catalogue of vice to affix its epithets to woman's name:—infidelity, violence, deceit, envy, extreme avariciousness, an entire want of good qualities, with impurity, they affirm, are the innate faults of womankind. And their deity has allotted to women a love of their bed, of their seat, and of ornaments, impure appetites, wrath, flexibility, desire of mischief, and bad conduct. Though her husband be devoid of all good qualities, yet, such is the estimate they form of her moral discrimination and sensibilities, that they bind the wife to revere him as a god, and to submit to his corporeal chastisements, whenever he chooses to inflict them, by a cane or a rope, on the back parts. The observation was justly deduced from the facts of woman's history in India, when the historian said, a state of dependence more strict, contemptuous, and humiliating, than that which is ordained for the weaker sex among the Hindoos, cannot easily be conceived: and to consummate the stigma, to fill up the cup of bitter waters assigned to woman, as if she deserved to be excluded from immortality as well as from justice, from hope as well as from enjoyment, it is ruled that a female has no business with the texts of the Veda–that having no knowledge of expiatory texts, and no evidence of law, sinful woman must be foul as falsehood itself, and incompetent to bear witness. To them the fountain of wisdom is sealed, the streams of knowledge are dried up; the springs of individual consolation, as promised in their religion, are guarded and barred against women in the hour of desolate sorrow and parching anguish; and cast out, as she is, upon the wilderness of bereavement and affliction, with her impoverished resources, her water may well be spent in the bottle; and, left as she is. will it be matter of wonder that, in the moment of despair, she should embrace the burning pile and its scorching flames, instead of lengthened solitude and degradation, of dark and humiliating suffering and sorrow? (1839)

J.W. MASSIE[81]

## 5. *Water carrying by women*

Benares is seen to great advantage from Ramnuggur, on the opposite bank of the Ganges. Its appearance is strikingly grand and picturesque; the ground is covered with buildings even to the water's edge, and some of the ghats, which are constructed of large blocks of red chunarstone, have a flight of thirty or forty steps leading down to the river. Here a most animated scene generally presents itself. Men and women, boys and girls, may be seen bathing early in the morning, and evening and, during the cold season, also in the middle of the day; for the cold does not deter even the gentler sex from adventuring into the river. Hither, too, resort the girls and young women of Benares, to fetch water from the sacred stream. Their figures are elegant and their stature erect. They all carry two or three water-pots on their heads, each successive pot being smaller than the one beneath it. Having dipped them into the stream, and filled them with water, they replace them upon their heads, and return homewards. This habit of carrying their gharahs, or jars, filled with water, from their early youth, may account, in a great measure, for their graceful carriage. They balance their pitchers so equally as not even to require any assistance from the hand. The sight of these women, with their water-pots, powerfully recalls to mind passages in Holy Writ; and many of them refer to periods of so ancient a date, that we cannot avoid coming to the conclusion that the Hindoos are a people of great antiquity. (1845–6)

W.W.W. HUMBLEY[82]

## F. FARMERS

## 1. *Rajpoot landlords*

The lands of Poknapoor are all divided into two equal shares, one

held by *Dewan* and the other by *Ramnath,* who were both among
the people with whom I conversed. Teekaram, who has a share in
Dewan's half, mentioned that about thirteen years ago the Amil,
Khwaja Mahmood, wanted to increase the rate of the Government
demand on the village from the four hundred, which they had long
paid, to four hundred and fifty; that they refused to pay, and Hindoo
Sing, the Rajpoot tallookdar of Rehreea, one koss east of Poknapoor, offered to take the lease at four hundred and fifty, and got
it. They refused to pay, and he, at the head of his gang of armed
followers, attacked, plundered, and burnt down the village, and
killed his, Teekaram's brother Girdharee, with his two sons, and
inflicted three severe cuts of a sabre on the right arm of his wife,
who is now a widow among them. Hindoo Sing's object was to make
this village a permanent addition to his estate; but, to his surprise,
the Durbar took serious notice of the outrage and he fled into the
Shajehanpoor district, where he was seized by the magistrate, Mr.
Buller, and made over to the Oude authorities for trial. He purchased his escape from them in the usual way; but soon after offered to
surrender to the collector, Aboo Torab Khan, on condition of
pardon for all past offences.

The collector begged the Brahmins to consent to pardon him for
the murders, on condition of getting from Hindoo Sing some fifty
beeghas of land, out of his share in Rehreea. They said they would
not consent to take five times the quantity of the land among such a
turbulent set; but should be glad to get a smaller quantity, rent-free,
in their own village, for the widow of Girdharee. The collector gave
them twenty-five beeghas, or ten acres, in Poknapoor; and this land
Teekaram still holds, and out of the produce supports the poor
widow. A razenamah, or pardon, was given by the family, and
Hindoo Sing has ever since lived in peace upon his estate. The lease
of the village was restored to the Brahmin family, at the reduced
rate of two hundred and fifty, but soon after raised to four hundred,
and again reduced to two hundred and fifty, after the devastation of
Bahadur Sing and Bhoder Sing.

These industrious and unoffending Brahmins say that since these
Rajpoot landholders came among them, many generations ago,
there has never been any peace in the district, except during the
time that Hakeem Mehndee held the contract, when the whole plain
that now lies waste became a beautiful *chummun* (parterre); that
since his removal, as before his appointment, all has been confu-

'Mountaineers of the Himalayas Halting to Smoke' drawn by T. M. Baynes

sion; that the Rajpoot landholders are always quarrelling either among themselves or with the local Government authorities; and, whatever be the nature or the cause of quarrel, they always plunder and murder, indiscriminately, the unoffending communities of the villages around, in order to reduce these authorities to their terms; that when these Rajpoot landholders leave them in peace, the contractors seize the opportunity to increase the Government demand, and bring among them the King's troops, who plunder them just as much as the rebel landholders, though they do not often murder them in the same reckless manner. They told me that the hundreds of their relatives who had gone off during the disorders and taken lands, or found employment in our bordering districts, would be glad to return to their own lands, groves, and trees, in Oude, if they saw the slightest chance of protection, and the country would soon become again the beautiful parterre which Hakeem Mehndee left it thirty years ago, instead of the wilderness in which they were now so wretched; that they ventured to cultivate small patches here and there, not far from each other, but were obliged to raise small platforms, upon high poles, in every field, and sit upon them all night, calling out to each other, in a loud voice, to keep up their spirits, and frighten off the deer which swarmed upon the grass plain, and would destroy the whole of the crops in one night, if left unprotected; that they were obliged to collect large piles of wood around each platform, and keep them burning all night, to prevent the tigers from carrying off the men who sat upon them; that their lives were wretched amidst this continual dread of man and beast, but the soil and climate were good, and the trees and groves planted by their forefathers were still standing and dear to them.
(1849-50)

WILLIAM HENRY SLEEMAN[83]

## 2. Indigo planters and the ryots

Being surrounded by Indigo Planters in this Zillah, the ryots of each village are forced to take advances; if a ryot refuses, lattials [hired ruffians] are sent, numberless as locusts, and his cattle are impounded and carried to the factory, or the factory's ploughs are sent, and the ryot's recently sown rice is ploughed up, and indigo sown by force; from fear of this, the ryots rather yield to the evil, and take the advances, though with reluctance. When advances are made, the ryots receive two rupees per beegah, but from the time of leaving the factory, to cutting the crop and carrying it to the vats, there is nothing but giving salamis and bribes, and thus all the money goes away. For to the Dewan eight annas have to be given for salami; to the Ameen and Dagiddar eight annas each; to the ticcah Dagiddar four annas; and at the manufacturing time some eight annas must be given to the various servants. Besides this, if a bullock strays into the indigo, the ryot has with folded hands to pay a fine according to their wishes. If the ryot does not submit to all this, he cannot cultivate any land for the support of his family, nor can he remain in his native place, but must flee from village to village.

Even when there is a full crop on the land, for which the advance was made, the amlahs, at the time of the accounts being made up, manage to pay only a fourth part of what is due; consequently the advance not being balanced, the ryot has to sow again each successive year for the debt carried against him, and he has to sell other crops or produce, in order to pay the rent for this very indigo ground, otherwise he will be beaten to death; besides all the labour of the ryots for indigo is lost-labour. It is owing to this oppression and fruitless labour, that the ryots are so very poor. We know to a certainty, that for the fertility of ground, and the industry of the peasantry in Bengal, the latter could rise to opulence, if no one deprived them of the fruit of their labour; and they could with ease pay the government taxes.

Besides this, the planters have also thousands of beegahs of *Nij abad,* (i.e. their own cultivation) within the borders of each factory. For cultivating this, they send lattials to each village, and bring the ryots with their ploughs and bullocks there without paying them; in like manner they force them to house the indigo without due remuneration. If a poor man refuses, either because he has to attend to his own work, or because he has nothing to eat, unless he gets his day's hire, he is shamefully abused and beaten and forced to go. Coming home at night, nothing remains for him and his starving family but lamentation, because without his daily wages they cannot live. (1859)

F. SCHURR[84]

## 3. *Agricultural community and debt*

One of the greatest evils connected with agricultural life in India is the indebtedness of the people, and the difficulty that they have in obtaining command of capital for carrying on agricultural work and effecting improvements. The indebtedness of the people has long attracted the attention of the Government and of those who are in any way interested in their welfare. It is not easy to understand why there should be so large a proportion of the agricultural community involved in debt; for there are so many careful and prudent persons among the agricultural classes that many who know them would be inclined to say that habits of prudence and thrift characterise the people generally. That the Hindu is not necessarily improvident and unthrifty is manifested by the many cases that one sees of lives conducted on sound business principles; and yet it cannot be denied that indebtedness is, to an extraordinary degree, characteristic of the agricultural classes.

There is one reason for this which is manifest on the face of it to any one who has practical experience of the life of the people, namely, that it is practically impossible for any man or any family that has once fallen into debt to recover. Therefore, generation by generation there is a tendency for indebtedness to increase. It is not the policy of the money—lender to sell up the debtor except under special circumstances. He will sell him up if he desires for himself, or for any one in whom he is interested, the property which the debtor owns; or he will sell him up when the debtor has become so involved as to be unable to pay what he regards as adequate interest for the money he has lent; but he will not ordinarily sell him up so long as he can extract from him a good profit in the shape of interest. Then, again, there is something in the climate in India that is against any great or special effort. The routine of life is as much as most men desire: special effort is irksome. Thus it is that, from generation to generation, the debt descends, sometimes without increasing in volume to any very appreciable extent, but without diminishing. There is one thing the creditor does not like in a debtor who has property such as to form anything like reasonable security: that is repayment of the loan, and the conditions of the debt are generally such as make the repayment of the principal very difficult. (1911)

ANDREW H.L. FRASER[55]

# G. TRIBALS

## 1. *Lepchas*

An attentive examination of the Lepcha in one respect entirely
contradicts our preconceived notions of a mountaineer, as he is
timid, peaceful, and no brawler; qualities which are all the more
remarkable from contrasting so strongly with those of his neighbours to the east and west: of whom the Ghorkas are brave and
warlike to a proverb, and the Bhotanese quarrelsome, cowardly,
and cruel. A group of Lepchas is exceedingly picturesque. They are
of short stature—four feet eight inches to five feet—rather broad in
the chest, and with muscular arms, but small hands and slender
wrists. The face is broad, flat, and of eminently Tartar character,
flat-nosed and oblique-eyed, with no beard, and little moustache;
the complexion is sallow, or often a clear olive; the hair is collected
into an immense tail, plaited flat or round. The lower limbs are
powerfully developed, befitting genuine mountaineers: the feet are
small. Though never really handsome, and very womanish in the
cast of countenance, they have invariably a mild, frank, and even
engaging expression, which I have in vain sought to analyse, and
which is perhaps due more to the absence of anything unpleasing,
than to the presence of direct grace or beauty. In like manner, the
girls are often very engaging to look upon, though without one good
feature: they are all smiles and good-nature; and the children are
frank, lively, laughing urchins. The old women are thorough hags.
Indolence, when left to themselves, is their besetting sin; they detest
any fixed employment, and their foulness of person and garments
renders them disagreeable inmates: in this rainy climate they are
supportable out of doors. Though fond of bathing when they come
to a stream in hot weather, and expert, even admirable swimmers,
these people never take to the water for the purpose of ablution. In
disposition they are amiable and obliging, frank, humorous, and
polite, without the servility of the Hindoos; and their address is free
and unrestrained. Their intercourse with one another and with
Europeans is scrupulously honest; a present is divided equally
amongst many, without a syllable of discontent or grudging look or
word: each, on receiving his share, coming up and giving the donor a
brusque bow and thanks. They have learnt to overcharge already,
and use extortion in dealing, as is the custom with the people of the

plains; but it is clumsily done, and never accompanied with the
grasping air and insufferable whine of the latter. They are constantly armed with a long, heavy, straight knife, but never draw it on
one another: family and political feuds are alike unheard of
amongst them.

The Lepcha is in morals far superior to his Tibet and Bhotan
neighbours, polyandry being unknown, and polygamy rare. This is
no doubt greatly due to the conventual system not being carried to
such an excess as in Bhotan, where the ties of relationship even are
disregarded.

Like the New Zealander, Tasmanian, Fuegian, and natives of
other climates, which, though cold, are moist and equable, the
Lepcha's dress is very scanty, and when we are wearing woollen
under-garments and hose, he is content with one cotton vesture,
which is loosely thrown round the body, leaving one or both arms
free; it reaches to the knee, and is gathered round the waist: its
fabric is close, the ground colour white, ornamented with longitudi-
nal blue stripes, two or three fingers broad, prettily worked with red
and white. When new and clean, this garb is remarkably handsome
and gay, but not showy. In cold weather an upper garment with
loose sleeves is added. A long knife, with a common wooden
handle, hangs by the side, stuck in a sheath; he has often also a
quiver of poisoned arrows and a bamboo bow across his back. On
his right wrist is a curious wooden guard for the bowstring; and a
little pouch, containing aconite poison and a few common implements, is suspended to his girdle. A hat he seldom wears, and when
he does, it is often extravagantly broad and flat-brimmed, with a
small hemispherical crown. It is made of leaves of *Scitamineæ*
between two thin plates of bamboo-work, clumsy and heavy; this is
generally used in the rainy weather, while in the dry a conical one is
worn, also of platted slips of bamboo, with broad flakes of talc
between the layers, and a peacock's feather at the side. The umbrella consists of a large hood, much like the ancient boat called a
coracle, which being placed over the head reaches to the thighs
behind. It is made of platted bamboo, enclosing broad leaves of
*Phrynium*. A group of Lepchas with these on, running along in the
pelting rain, are very droll figures; they look like snails with their
shells on their backs. All the Lepchas are fond of ornaments,
wearing silver hoops in their ears, necklaces made of cornelian,
amber, and turquoise, brought from Tibet, and pearls and corals

from the south, with curious silver and golden charm-boxes or amulets attached to their necks or arms. These are of Tibetan workmanship, and often of great value: they contain little idols, charms and written prayers, or the bones, hair, or nail-parings of a Lama: some are of great beauty, and highly ornamented. In these decorations, and in their hair, they take some pride, the ladies frequently dressing the latter for the gentlemen: thus one may often see, the last thing at night, a damsel of discreet port, demurely go behind a young man, unplait his pig-tail, teaze the hair, thin it of some of its lively inmates, braid it up for him, and retire. The women always wear two braided pig-tails, and it is by this they are most readily distinguished from their effeminate-looking partners, who wear only one. When in full dress, the woman's costume is extremely ornamental and picturesque; besides the shirt and petticoat she wears a small sleeveless woollen cloak, of gay pattern, usually covered with crosses, and fastened in front by a girdle of silver chains. Her neck is loaded with silver chains, amber necklaces etc. and her head adorned with a coronet of scarlet cloth, studded with seed-pearls, jewels, glass beads, etc. The common dress is a long robe of indi, a cloth of coarse silk, spun from the cocoon of a large caterpillar that is found wild at the foot of the hills, and is also cultivated; it feeds on many different leaves, Sal (*Shorea*), castor-oil, etc. (1848)

JOSEPH DALTON HOOKER[86]

## 2. The Gonds

We have a few architectural remains and inscriptions that tell of Aryan chiefs holding power in parts of the Narbada valley and the central plateaux, between the 5th and the 14th centuries. But who and what they were, and what was really their position, there is nothing to show. Remains of religious edifices surrounded by fortifications point to the probability of their having been the heads of isolated bands of the warlike caste, protecting settlements of missionary priests, and perhaps, by superior courage and arms, holding in nominal subjection the aboriginal tribes around them. Traditions exist of a pastoral race, to whom is attributed every ancient building that cannot be otherwise accounted for. It is highly probable that the cow was unknown to the aborigines before it was brought by their Aryan invaders. Tradition would probably fix on so striking a feature as the possession of herds by those early colonists; and thus it does not seem necessary to suppose the existence of any peculiar pastoral people, distinct from other Aryan settlers in these central regions.

But what these early immigrants may really have been is unimportant. For, when first the light of true history breaks upon the country, at the period of its contact with the invading Mahomedan in the 14th century, all of them had ceased to have any separate existence. Most probably they had been absorbed in the great mass of the aboriginal tribes who surrounded them: and we find the country then called by the name of Gondwana, from the tribe of Gonds who chiefly inhabited it. The petty tribal chieftainships, into which, there is reason to believe, it had formerly been divided, had then been united into three considerable principalities, under the sway of chiefs whom all the evidence we have proves to have been of mixed aboriginal and Hindu (Rajput) descent. Architectural remains, and the recorded condition of the country at the time mentioned, show that these little kingdoms had acquired a considerable degree of stability and development; and it has often been wondered how a tribe of such rude savages as the Gonds could have reached a stage of civilization at that early period so greatly above anything they have since shown themselves to be capable of. The explanation seems to lie in the circumstance mentioned. The real establishers of these courts, and introducers of the arts, were not Gonds but Hindus.

It is the custom in all families which trace their lineage to the fountain-head of Hindu aristocracy among the Rajput clans of Rajasthan to retain, like the Celtic chieftains of our own country, family bards, whose duty it is to record in a genealogical volume, and recite on great occasions, the descent and family history of their patrons. The bardic office is hereditary, and where the lineage of the family is really ancient the bard is generally also a descendant of the bards of the original clan. Often he is the chief bard of the clan itself, and resides with its hereditary head at the family seat in Rajasthan, visiting at intervals the cadet branches of the house to record their domestic events. In Gondwana numerous chiefs now exist who claim either a pure descent from Rajput houses, or more frequently admit their remote origin to have sprung from a union between some Rajput adventurer of noble blood and one of the daughters of the aborigines. Few of them are admitted to be pure Rajputs by the blue-blooded chiefs of Rajasthan; but all have their bards and genealogies. These, like such documents in all countries often go back to fabulous times, and are overlaid with modern fiction; but the legendary portion of the bardic chronicle can generally be separated with little difficulty from a solid residue of probable fact.

The general conclusion to be drawn from the evidence of these writings, supported as they are by tradition and later history, is that during the 14th and 15th centuries, and it may be even earlier, a great immigration of the Rajput clans took place into the country of the aborigines. The Mahomedan invaders of Upper India were then pressing hard on the country between the Ganges and the Narbada rivers occupied by the Rajputs; and it was doubtless the recoil from them that forced these colonies of Rajputs southwards into the wilds of Central India. Here it would seem that they generally formed matrimonial alliances with the indigenous tribes. The superior qualities of the Aryan race would soon assert themselves among such inert races as these aborigines; and there is little doubt that before the arrival of the Mahomedans, not only the heads of what have been termed the Gond kingdoms, but also many of the subordinate chiefs, were far more Hindu than aboriginal in blood. The unfailing evidence of physical appearance supports these indications of tradition. Most of the chiefs possess the tall well-proportioned figure and light complexion of the Hindu, but allied with more or less of the thickness of lip and animal type of countenance of the pure aborigine. The mass of the tribes on the other hand are marked by the black skin, short squat figure, and features of the negretto race of humanity. Between them are found certain sections of the tribes, who would seem to have been also imbued with something of the foreign blood, though in a less degree than the chiefs. Like the latter they affect much Hindu manners and customs; and it is probable that they too are the results of some connection in long past times between immigrant Aryans and the indigenous tribes. (1872)

JAMES FORSYTH[87]

## 3. *The Sontals*

The Rajmahal Mountains, which are sometimes supposed to form part of the range of the Vindhyas, compose a completely isolated group of that chain, and belong to an absolutely distinct geological formation. They extend in a northerly direction on the western frontier of Bengal from Birbhoum to the Ganges. They are inhabited by the Sontals—a primitive race which seems to belong to the same family as the Gounds—and by the Malers, a tribe of a still more primitive type. The Sontals are industrious, and, unlike the other aboriginal races, occupy themselves with agriculture; and they inhabit villages which are generally composed of about a hundred huts, very elegantly built of plaited bamboo, with rounded roofs and verandahs. Of a proud and intrepid nature, they seem very jealous of their independence, which they have defended many times even against the English themselves. Their costume is of the simplest description—a turban, and a piece of linen round the loins, for the men; and a piece of stuff rolled round the legs and the bust, for the women, who adorn themselves besides with innumerable necklaces of glass and of shells (cowries) and heavy brass bracelets.

The religion of the Sontals is a coarse naturalism. Wooden beams, squared and painted with red ochre, supporting a sort of rough lingam, are their idols; they offer up sacrifices of buffaloes, and more frequently still of goats. The priest, or sacrificer, strikes off the head of the animal with a single blow of a long knife, and then sprinkles the idol and the people present with the blood of the victim. At the entrance to the villages, and near their idols, they raise light platforms of bamboo, on which they place trophies of the animals of the forest. They are bold hunters, and in recent years have destroyed the numerous herds of elephants which infested the mountain and ruined their harvests.

The Sontals are divided into tribes, under the rule of elected chiefs, who are aided by a council of elders in the administration of public business. Their number at the present time is calculated at eighty-five thousand.

The Malers, who inhabit the higher parts of the Rajmahals, are very inferior in physical and moral qualities to the Sontals, who, having been themselves expelled from the plain by the Thibetian and Aryan races, have driven them into the most inaccessible parts of the mountain. (1875)

LOUIS ROUSSELET[88]

## 4. Wild men of the woods

There are some curious specimens of humanity to be found dwelling among the forests about the Chipla, called 'Razees,' compared with whom the villagers are quite civilised. As they are few in number, and hardly ever visit the villages, I much regretted not having had an opportunity of becoming personally acquainted with them. The villagers described these 'junglee admi' (wild men of the woods), as they termed them to me, as being almost on a par with the beasts of the wilds they inhabit, subsisting chiefly on what they can secure with their bows and arrows, and by snaring. I at first suspected their existence to be a myth, until I afterwards learnt on good authority that it was a fact. My old friend Colonel Fisher, senior Assistant Commissioner of Kumaon, gave me the following short account of these interesting barbarians. 'They were the original indigenous inhabitants of the country about there, but the persecutions to which they were subjected by the Kumaon Rajas, and especially by their neighbours the Goorkhas, were so cruel, that they abandoned their hamlets and retired into the wildest and least inhabited parts of the country, and lived on wild roots, fruits, and fish, and game, and lost all recollection even of their language. They had a language of their own, but it is quite extinct now; in fact, I was told by the Rajwar of Askote, they themselves have entirely disappeared from Kumaon, though there may be a few yet on the banks of the Sarda in our territory, or the thick jungles on the Nepal side of the river. The last time I saw a man and woman of the tribe was at Askote in 1866 and they were caught for my special benefit. We gave them a few rupees, but they seemed to value them as much as apes! They would eat anything given to them; and both the man and the woman wore long hair down the back, and used leaves stitched together for clothing.' From this, the condition of these remnants of an almost lost race appears to have been still much the same as, we may suppose, was that of Adam and Eve after the fall. (1889)

DONALD MACINTYRE[89]

## 5. *The Kukis, Tongkhuls and Kupoes*

Our short stay in Silchar came to an end very soon, and we were on our way to Manipur in real earnest by the end of the third day. The first two marches out to the Jhiri were uneventful, and we then found ourselves on the banks of the river, with a vast expanse of forest jungle before us to be traversed the following day. Unluckily, it rained all that night, and when the morning arrived it was still damp and drizzling. We changed our coolies here, and got Nagas (hillmen) to carry the baggage. They were fine-looking men, belonging to the various hill tribes about Manipur. They were Kukis, Tongkhuls, and Kupoes, and they seemed to my uninitiated eyes very alarming people indeed. They wore very few clothes, and their necks were adorned with many necklaces made of gaudily-coloured glass beads. Their ears were split to a hideous extent, and in the loops thus formed they stuffed all kinds of things—rolls of paper (of which they are particularly fond), and rings of bamboo, which stretched them out and made them look enormous.

Their hair was cut in different ways. The Tongkhuls' heads were shaved with the exception of a ridge along the top, which extended to the nape of the neck, and gave them the appearance of cockatoos.

The Kukis' hair was long, and gathered up into a loose and very untidy knot at the back of their heads, and the Kupoes had theirs cut so that it stuck out all round their heads and made them look as though they had fur hats on. *They* made no fuss over the Memsahib's trunks, and I was much amused at the way they all rushed for the bath, which had a flat cover to it, and was easy to carry and cool against their backs. (1891)

ETHEL ST. CLAIR GRIMWOOD[90]

# H. COOLIES AND SERVANTS

## 1. *Indian Servants*

The *Indians* in general are very temperate in eating and drinking; they seldom use strong liquors, unless prescribed by way of physic. Their food is chiefly boiled rice, with now and then a little fish, and mutton or fowl dressed in a *Currey,* as they call it, which is very warm to the palate. This, I have reason to think, they also feast on with great moderation. The *Gentoo* castes never eat beef; they pay adoration to the image of the cow, and have a proverb among them, 'that they would as soon taste of the flesh of their parents, as of that animal.' One strong evidence of the temperance of these people is their hands, which, if touched by chance, you will be sure to find very cold, even in the middle of the hottest day; while the hands of the *Europeans* are burning with an excessive heat, partly the effect perhaps of our intemperate way of living. Let me add too, that the

*Indians* are a very quiet, inoffensive people; and at some distance from the sea-shore, we were told, that we should also find them honest and sincere. On the coast, they will make use of a thousand tricks, and stratagems, to over-reach a stranger. But for this we may thank ourselves, who first sullied their purity, and debauched their manners. They probably had never known the crime of cheating, had they not first learned it from the tricking *European*. Among the lower *castes* the poor women do all the drudgery; they get all the fodder for the gentlemen's horses in the fort, and are obliged to bring it some miles. They likewise grind all the rice used in their own houses; fetch wood and cow-dung to burn; and as the water near the fort is brackish, they are daily necessitated to go a mile or two to a good well, and to bring a large pitcher of this element upon their heads for the use of the gentlemen of the factory. I have more than once seen a line of 40 or 50 of them in a morning, engaged in this laborious employment. Their dress is much the same as that worn by the women at *Fort St. David*; and that of the higher *castes,* at both places, differ nothing from the lower, except that the wrapper which goes round the loins of the former is made of finer stuff, and that they commonly cover their breasts with a silk handkerchief. It is very seldom that any of the women, unless those of the lowest rank, can be seen, being forbidden by their *caste* to stand anywhere to be gazed upon by strangers. In our morning walks, indeed, we sometimes saw them standing without their houses for the benefit of the fresh air, but upon the first sight of us, they never failed to run in, and shut and bolt their doors. We could not but remark too, that whenever we had occasion to go into a shop, our guide always gave us a hint to stand a little while at the door, while he stepped in; and he made no scruple to confess, that his motive for doing it, was to clear the house of the women before we entered.

Much has been said in regard to servants in this country: some speak highly in their favour, while others equally depreciate them. The service of any one of them is exceedingly cheap, but the number which you are obliged to keep, makes it dear in the end. Perhaps it may seem surprising, though true, that an *European* gentleman or merchant in a considerable way of business, cannot hire less than a dozen or fifteen; for as they are almost all of different *castes,* the higher are not permitted to do the least thing which is the business of an inferior caste. They all wear turbans; the principal servants commonly dress neat and clean, in a robe of fine cotton cloth, or muslin, particularly the *Gentoos,* whose religion enjoins much bodily purification; and therefore the first thing they do in a morning is to go down to the river's side and wash, and afterwards to say their prayers on the banks. If you ask them what they pray for, they will be sure to say, *'For master'*—and *'that God Will shew favour for master, that master may shew favour for them.'* They are an artful cunning people, and very ready at returning an answer. We met with a thousand instances of this sort, during our stay in the *East Indies.* (1755)

EDWARD IVES[91]

## 2. Coolies

I set out early this morning in company with Sir Robert and Lady Colquhoun for Chilkea. Mr. Traill had lent me a couple of tents for this journey, which, with a good deal of my heavier baggage, had been sent on the day before. A still greater number of coolies were necessary than in my ascent from Bamoury [near Almorah U.P.], partly on account of some presents of honey, etc., which I had received, and which required to be carried, like the rest, on men's heads, partly because, from the wild and uninhabited character of some part of the country which we were to traverse, I was obliged to give up two mules for the transport of the provisions and necessaries of the coolies themselves. We had a good deal of plague and trouble in dividing the loads to be carried by each man, and were harassed by pitiful complaints, from almost all, of their inability to go through such an expedition, and by their entreaties to be left behind. It seems singular that, among so poor a people, with whom a job of work might at first seem no trifling object, this reluctance should exist, since the rate at which, according to the regulations of Government, their labour is repaid on these occasions, being arranged at two annas for each march, with a similar sum for their return home, exceeds the average rate of agricultural labour through India, and is much above any thing which they were likely to have earned at home. Yet so it is, that they are always pressed to this service; that they almost always endeavour to excuse themselves; that they are apt to desert the first opportunity, even to the forfeiture of their legal hire; and which tells well for their honesty at least, that, when any suspicion exists that they feel peculiar reluctance, no way is found so efficacious to keep them, as to pay them their money in advance. I can understand their aversion to this employment during the rainy season, when it is really at the risk of life that people descend into the Terrai, or the lower valleys of this province. But at present, though they may encounter hardship and fatigue, there is, literally, no danger; and I can only account for their reluctance, by supposing that as yet there exists in Kemaoon no sufficient occupation for coolies to induce any number of men to addict themselves to this pursuit alone, and that other peasants feel unwilling to separate from their families, and desert their usual routine of industry, for an uncertain and fatiguing, though profitable employment. (1824)

REGINALD HEBER[92]

## 3. The Motiyas and the servants

Beyond the Bazars [of Calcutta] I have named, I know of none other worth your notice, but in quitting them will take the opportunity of informing you by what means purchases, therein made, reach their destination; for by that politico-religious system of thing which characterizes the fabric, not alone of Hindoo life, but, by amalgamation, of Moosulman also, and securing to all classes, without fear of innovation, the employment to which, either by caste or education, they were intended, none but *Motiyas*, or porters, will carry any parcel which may be too bulky for the hands; the servants, generally, not even taking so much into consideration, but, if left to themselves will, as a perfect matter of course, hire a porter for the merest trifle which may have been purchased, and return home, themselves, empty-handed.

The Basket-ware of the country, accordingly, is of that kind adapted only for being borne upon the head; and upon the head, I should state, is the only manner in which a Motiya, whether by force of custom, or of 'caste,' would ever dream of carrying his load, although it were even demonstrated to him that another method would be easier.

The Motiyas, however, are not people of any particular class, caste, or creed, but a collection of poor men from all parts of Bengal, who, whether professionally porters, having no other calling, or peasants in time of dearth, or other distress oft attending an agricultural life, take this means of seeking a livelihood in Calcutta. The latter people, possibly, having, after some months, scraped a dozen

or fifteen Roopees together, return to their families—pay their
rents—prepare their little plots of ground against the next season,
and which perhaps in like way they again leave to the care of their
wives or children, whilst they, once more, try their fortunes in the
city.

Motiyas (or coolies) are employed not alone for conveying loads
but for any little domestic labour which may not interfere with their
religious prejudices; and as their services are to be procured at a very
trifling remuneration (about 4 Roopees per month), they form a
very useful body of people. Upon occasion of moving house, it is, in
general, but necessary for a servant to step outside the gate, for a
few moments, to gather a body of them sufficiently numerous to
carry away the whole premises.

In addition to coolies—to whose honesty and fears we cannot
always trust, and who, from the number required upon such occasions, become both inconvenient and expensive—we have carts,
which for roughness, simplicity, awkwardness and noisiness, I
would match against any carts in the world. They are formed of
bamboos fastened together with something of that freedom of style
which characterizes a bundle of faggots, and they are drawn by a
pair of bullocks,—their galled necks (in front of the hump where the
wooden yoke rests) and *twisted,* and even *mutilated* tails, which are
used both as instruments of guiding and goading, often exhibiting
alike a lamentable proof of the vile inhumanity of their owners, and
the inefficiency of our Police, to which, however, I live in the desire
and hope of yet seeing attached, a 'SOCIETY FOR THE PREVENTION
OF CRUELTY TO ANIMALS.' I can fearlessly assert—despite the enjoined humanity of 'the Faithful'—the belief in the doctrine of the
metempsychosis existing amongst many of the Hindoos, and the
tender mercies and extravagant example of the sensitive Jaina
devotees who cover their mouths with cloths, lest an insect be
swallowed, and sweep the earth before them lest they destroy
another under feet—that hardly a country in the world stands more
in need of one.

Let us proceed with the domestics.

The smart, but, not uncommonly, somewhat dissipated looking
individual who here presents himself to your notice in the KHID-
MUTGAR—the aspirant to the honors and emoluments of a khansa-
manship, and to whom I have already referred.

In houses where servants are numerous this man's sole duty

consists in bringing meals on table and attending there. He does not even wash the crockery, that duty devolving upon an under servant, whom I shall hereafter describe. Amongst the opulent there may be seen a khidmutgar to each member of the family; amongst the extravagant even two, but a couple, or perhaps three, form the usual domestic complement, and in families where means are circumscribed, there will probably be but one. In the service of a bachelor of moderate income, he is a general attendant upon his master's person, wardrobe and apartment.

At both public and private dinner parties the khidmutgars accompany their masters to the festal board, where, standing behind each chair, dressed in liveries of Eastern fashion, or more commonly in pure white linen with white turbans, which amongst the higher classes are sometimes decorated with a narrow gold or silver band, surmounted by the crest of the family, they present a very extraordinary and imposing array.

At one period these men, on the score of religious prejudice, as Moosulmans, refused to bring pork upon table, and the matter was long conceded, until so many having being detected not only touching but *eating* it, the objection was *overruled,* and the pork *carried.*

The wages of a khidmutgar vary from six to ten roopees per month.—The higher pay can only be expected in a service where fashionable habits, fashionable hours, and late dinner or supper parties, may draw more largely upon the time, attention, and wardrobe of the men.

We next have the BAWURCHEE or cook, who may be either a Moosulman, a Portuguese, a Mug, or a Hindoo of a particularly low caste, termed *cowra.*

With the disadvantages of apparatus I have already pointed out to you, this man, if at all skilful, really performs wonders; more particularly when it is remembered that. unless a Mug or a Portuguese, he never tastes when he cooks, and can only form on opinion of the success of his labours by the scolding or the commendation he may receive from his employers.

The wages of a cook vary not so much according to the rank of the master, as to his means and his love of good living, for which some men are willing to pay not a little handsomely. From six to twelve roopees may be stated as the common amount of their pay, but I have heard of their receiving twenty-five.

Here we have the MUSHALCHEE.—literally 'Torch-bearer,' such

being this man's real office whilst travelling with his master; but
when in camp, being a Moosulman, he becomes an understrapper to
the cook and khidmutgars: tends the spit. and cleans the knives,
forks, plate and crockery.—In Calcutta, therefore, the dispenser of
light, and scarer of tigers, dwindles into a scullion!

It is not in every house, however, that a Mushalchee is now to be
found. It is surprising to note the economizing changes which, by
reference to old customs, will be found to have taken place, within
the last few years, in Europeans' establishments. I may have occasion to notice this again hereafter, and need only add, with reference to the Mushalchee, that in numerous private families, cooks
and khidmutgars have been found not to have so much to do as to
require an assistant on a salary of four roopees per month.

Fifth on the roll of this domestic corps I may name the HOUSE
BEARER, who is a Hindoo. He will, therefore, neither touch your
food nor do any work connected with it or the table during dinner
time; one class of bearers (the *Ooriah*) having gone so far as during
that period, to refuse to pull the Punkah, by reason of its suspension
over the unhallowed viands!

The bearers are of three kinds; the *Rouwanee,* the *Ooriah,* and
*Bengalee;* and the principal man amongst any set of them serving in
a house—one who is a supposed master of the craft—is termed the
Sirdar, signifying head or chief. A house-bearer alone, however, or
with one or two mates or assistants, is, in the present day, more
usual than a whole set,—unless. as I have already explained, attached to a private *palkee.* Of the three kinds of these men that I
have named, the *Rouwanee* are more commonly met with in house
service than either the *Ooriah* or *Bengalee,* but all three are fitting
for the office. The *Ooriah,* characteristically speaking, are the most
sober, and the *Rouwanee* the least sober, but the most trustworthy
and active.

The duty of the house-bearer entirely depends upon the rank,
means, and habits of his master. In the service of the opulent, where
he is sure of having a mate or several under-bearers, he becomes a
very important personage. In no case does he ever touch the palkee,
but in this he ranks as confidential body-servant,—attends his master when dressing—possesses a degree of control over the other
servants—has charge, probably, of the silver and the stores (in
preference to the khansaman) and the entire responsibility of the
whole of his master's property,—acting, in short, to both married

and single men, as *valet de chambre*. To these duties are added—although performed not by himself but his assistant—those of cleaning the furniture, the rooms, and the shoes,—trimming the lamps, attending to the bachelors' beds and bedrooms, going errands and bringing the hot water to the tea-table—a self-imposed office, I believe, and the only exception, a trifling one, to what I have stated in reference to Hindoo non-attendance at the meal table. The wages of sirdars or house bearers range from six to ten roopees per mensem; of their mates from five to seven, and of ordinary bearers from four, for *Rouwanee,* to five, for *Ooriah,* as I have already stated.

Of more imposing front, more fearless mien, and gay attire, in which turban and sash divide the glowing beauties of scarlet, pink, purple and yellow here stands 'our castle's warder,'—the DURWAN (properly *Durban*) or door-keeper. He is generally a Hindoo of the north-west provinces. In Calcutta he is commonly designated—'an up-country man;' which indefinite term seems to imply something to which a degree of respect is attached, unassociated with what may be termed the lowlanders, that is of the same class. The people of the upper provinces have decidedly succeeded in gaining for themselves an estimation not evinced towards their brethren in Bengal. I am anxious, however, that my observation should be understood as limiting the comparison to the middle and lower rank on either side. If extended to the higher and well educated, I should assuredly reverse the order of precedence in favour of the native of Bengal. With reference, then, to the northerns, certain it is that these people regarded as possessing personal courage, pride, and honesty, are generally found in situations of supposed danger and trust, where, of course, such qualities are the most needed. With climate more bracing, and habits of physical culture somewhat akin to the gymnastic recreations of the ancients, they possess a degree of personal strength and vigour almost unknown to the Bengalees, and favourable, as I presume, to a corresponding mental energy and independence. By mental energy I do not mean more than the predominance of what Phrenologists ascribe to the faculties of *combativeness,* and *firmness,*—the first conferred '*to meet and subdue physical and moral obstacles,*'—the second giving '*determination to our purposes,*' which, united to a generous and educated mind, lends nobility, but to graceless ignorance a ruffianly brutality.

The superiority of appearance which these men generally present is very striking. Independently of hosts of remarkably fine looking fellows who may be seen amongst our Rajpoot, Puthan and other Sipahees, both Hindoo and Moosulman, from Lucknow and elsewhere, in Fort-William and at Barrackpore, I have observed many of the men retained as *Burkendazes* and *Durwans* whose persons, not hidden and disguised by stiff uniform, but gracefully girded in the twisted folds of a single garment, might form no mean academy figures as models for Roman and Grecian Athletae.

A little building—I might say den—with one door and no window, unless a hole of a few inches in diameter to allow the escape of the smoke from his cooking fire, may be called such, situated at the side of the gate or possibly under the arch of it, according to the form of the premises, marks the residence of the Durwan,—for whose comforts, I will just add, our builders might take shame for not shewing a little more consideration. There, seated at the entrance, his sword and shield—the necessary companions of his travels, but now useless encumbrances—pendent from the wall, a pair of heavy *Mooghdurs* or dumb-bells, the instruments possibly of his morning and only exercise, being visible in some corner, he remains the whole day, the lazy guardian of the place, giving notice of the arrival of visitors by ringing a hand bell, or striking a gong, and allowing nothing to pass from out the door without an order therefor.

In houses, however, where the custom is enforced, or many valuables are kept, his duty extends further, and consists in searching the persons of the servants ere leaving: sad comment! humiliating process! and one the necessity for, or, at least, the utility of which, in private houses, with a proper system of reference for character and responsibility in office, I very much question. The *evil* must be as apparent as that of corporal punishment in the army and navy. Rob a man of his self-respect and the very foundation of his principles is sapped and endangered.

Some time back it was proposed to establish in Calcutta '*An Office for Servants,*' from whence they might be obtained with some reference or security as to character, but it failed of any thing like general support, and has, I believe, as too many other of our Calcutta schemes have done, fallen to the ground.

One other matter in connection with this man's duty I cannot help noticing and regretting. I allude to the custom, common in fashionable life (not with all, be it understood) of being '*Not at home*' during certain hours of the day.

I am far from assuming that people should not have their hours of quiet and retirement, but I cannot conceive that to put an untruth into the mouth of the door-keeper is either a right or a necessary method of securing them. It is unnecessary, because the shutting of the gate is a usage not only well understood amongst fashionable people, but with very many the only means adopted and because with none or few would the firm but respectful assurance of 'engaged' or 'not at leisure' be otherwise than as effectual as an untruth. An up-country Durwan might be disciplined in this matter to turn away his very master from the door!

Under the present system the Durwan probably receives a vague order of exception to some particular person—but it is more than probable that he blunders, or some one member of the family has made an actual engagement against an hour at which another orders the gate to be shut. Thus after the door-keeper's positive assurance of *'koee hy nuhee ghur mey—sub koee bahir geir,'*—(no one is at home—all are gone out), it sometimes happens that through want of method and forethought the order has to be recalled, and the man is under the necessity of confessing to an untruth as the visitor is quitting the door,—or in the event of no such timely discovery, an apologetic note is received the next day 'extremely regretting the *foolish blunder* of the servants, etc.'—We preach to the natives of integrity and truth, and make our servants the medium of the violation of our own precepts; for as there is not as yet any fixed enactment 'for the better and more securely' understanding the *degrees* of falsity, we cannot expect that every one, more particularly the uneducated, will comprehend such nicities of variation as those of *colour*—a prismatic distinction which Mrs. Opie laboured so industriously to overthrow. Were a small board, conventionally superscribed with the proper intimation in English, either hung on the gate, or placed in the hand of the Durwan it would at least prevent all mistakes on the part of new arrivals, and of all others upon whom the verbal politeness of truth might, like the pearls of scripture, be cast away.

Next in order of the regular household may be introduced one whose name might place him at the head of a *royal* household,—the humble knight of the broom, being dignified with the title of 'Prince,'—such being the signification of the term MEHTUR.

This man is of the lowest grade, or caste, of Hindoos, and who yet are divided and sub-divided into classes or shades of rank and purity, resembling the list of precedence in the British peerage, from the blood royal duke to the youngest sons of esquires. As I need not, however, entertain you with a running commentary on the gradation, it will suffice if I state that amongst the Mehturs there are those who will eat of the food which goeth from the master's table, whilst others would hold themselves defiled by so doing; and certain menial offices in no way objectionable to the one would be pollution to the other. The generality of house Mehturs, for instance, would not touch a dead animal, such duty, save where the Mehtur is of a particular class, being left to the *Domes*, a set of people employed in Calcutta by the Police to sink dead bodies discovered floating in the river, to remove all carcasses, and kill all stray dogs found in the streets; whilst, on the other hand, these men would not touch food belonging to, or handled by, the Mehtur!

Of the immutability of station or profession amongst the Hindoos, and of the consequent, and frequently to be seen, contrast of manners, mental capacities and physical appearance, with their actual and unalterable.position, the Mehtur affords a fair illustration. If, which is often, if not always the case, he be a native of the upper provinces, though holding the lowest office in the house, he will very probably, in his manners and languages, be the greatest gentleman in the whole circle of domestics! and, in equal likelihood, serve in his appearance, with broom in hand, to recall to mind the image of Hercules with the distaff!

Here is a domestic in whom I doubt not your interest is already awakened. Her duty speaks for itself.—An AYAH—*Nurse,* or *Lady's Maid*—for she is indifferently either one or the other—will, I may venture to assert, be found in every European family throughout India. From these I may except the poor British soldiers' wives, who, trained in their native land to labour and endurance, may be seen with umbrella over head, and infant in arms, trudging their way on foot to the bazaars, or home to their quarters in the Fort.

The labour of nursing and attending to a child the whole day in a hot climate, requires, you will believe, to be fully known to be fully appreciated; and the necessity which thus exists for the services of a native nurse increases the trouble of every parent, solicitous for the right culture of a child's mind, in the anxiety to eradicate, or check the growth of unamiable habits and traits of character which are too often and imperceptibly contracted during its association with the servant.

Of the Ayahs it may be sufficient to observe, that, no better educated than their countrymen, you cannot expect from them other than mere labour divested of mind and judgment. Guided alone by the capriciousness of their own impulses, and by hereditary customs, I have seldom seen them command the respect of their *own* children, and never those of their mistresses.

We reap not, however, where we have not sowed, nor whilst the 'great gulf,' of which I have already spoken, exists between Europeans and their dependents, are these evils likely to be remedied. Children seldom see any thing in the manners of their parents towards the servants to impress their minds with any strong feelings of respect for them; the natives are, with very rare exceptions, the *only servants* whom they see in the country, while the strong distinguishing mark of complexion, in children's minds, of course, makes the line of demarcation more unhappily definite. The servants themselves seldom or never interfere with or thwart the children because parents have never been induced to place either confidence or authority in them, and this for several good reasons;—ignorance, superstition, and immorality, added to the substitution of mere impulse for reason, are regarded as the unhappy concomitants of their characters: they have not, therefore, been allowed any exercise of judgment or authority lest they take advantage of the privilege and act injudiciously through ignorance or caprice. But this is not all. Independently of any such judicious motives, and I fear often apart altogether from them, aristocratic feelings of pride in many instances lead Europeans, East Indians, and particularly native parents (of families of respectability and distinction) to desire that menials should in no way correct or thwart their superiors. In illustrations of this, our good sister M—— here, to whose observations and judicious hints I am indebted for the remarks I have—with greater confidence therefore—ventured, says that she has known parents highly offended with their servants for authoritatively desiring their children to be washed and dressed, or for speaking to them in any other manner than that in which the servants would address their master or mistress!—and that she has also known parents who would not allow their children to do the most trifling act of service for a servant,—such, for instance, as informing one man that he was required by another. These restrictions, though there may be cases in which they are necessary, yet, when enforced commonly, and without discrimination, towards

servants of opposite or various characters, as they often are, naturally lead to that diffidence and reluctance to act, and that irresolute-
ness, even when duty seems imperatively to demand an effort on the
part of the servant, of which I now complain.—Thus is completed
that 'atmosphere of circumstances' in which servants are degraded
and children are educated to domineer. (1849)

AN ARTIST IN INDIA[93]

## 4. Coolie who propels a vehicle

One of the first things to be obtained at Simla is a small vehicle
called a rickshaw, said to be of Japanese origin. It resembles a bath
chair with a hood and is propelled by coolies, two in front and two
behind. All ladies with the slightest pretension to *bon ton* have their
coolies dressed in neat knickerbockers, tunic and cap or turban, and
there is much emulation as to who shall have the best dressed 'stud.'
Just before my arrival there had been a show of jampanni costumes
and prizes had been awarded; indeed our hotel boasted of shelter-
ing the lady whose taste had thus been signally approved, and many
of the inmates felt a kind of honour reflected on themselves by their
connection with the house.

Jampannis do not of course wear this elegant costume all day,
only when they perambulate mem-saheb. They are engaged by the
month and are expected to take madam out at all times and seasons.
(*c.* 1891)

CHRISTINA S. BREMNER[94]

# I. FAKIRS AND SADHUS

## 1. The Fakirs near Surat

Two Miles distant from *Suratt* is a very delightful place, nam'd
*Pulparrock*, adorn's with pleasant Walks and Groves of Trees, near
the gentle Streams of the River *Tappy*. The Ground is all very even,
except only near the Banks of the River, where the rising Hills
enlarge the prospect upon the Water. And the Hot Air is temper'd
by the shady Walks under the spreading Branches, and the nearness
of the Current of the Water gliding by. For these Religious *Santones*
here, as well as in *Europe,* are industrious in culling out the most

delightful Habitations in the Country, and taking up their Abode where ever either Art or Nature Invite their Residence by a commodious pleasant Dwelling. For there is not any place near *Suratt,* that yields either the Beauty, or the Delight that *Pulparrock* affords.

The Original of these Holy Mendicants is ascrib'd, according to their Account, to a certain Prince named *Revan,* who quarrell'd with *Ram,* a Knowing and Victorious Prince; and being Conquer'd and depriv'd of all by a certain Ape named *Herman,* or *Hanneman,* which was his Assistant on Earth, spent the remainder of his Days in Pilgrimage, and rambling, without any Maintenance either to himself or his Followers, but what was given them in Charity: It was for the good Services done to Ram in his Life time by the Apes, that they are in so great Esteem both with the *Moors* and *Gentiles* in the *Indies*; and this arch unlucky Creature is in that Repute among them all, that they seriously declare, *were the Blood of one of them spilt upon the Ground, the Earth would suddenly become unfruitful, and the Judgment upon it would be at least a Years Famin.* And therefore when a large Ape had broke loose from the *English* Factory at *Suratt,* and skipping to and fro' had snatch'd away several things of value, and in his Anger had bit a Child or two so sorely, that they afterwards died of the Wounds (as it was reported), yet was it an inexcusable Crime at the same time for any violent Hand to touch him.

These Philosophical Saints have since the first forming of their Order, assum'd a liberty of taking that by violence, which they find is denied their civil Requests, and sometimes force a Charity from the People, when Intreaties cannot prevail, especially in the Country Villages. For their numbers render them imperious, and upon pretension of extraordinary Sanctity, they commit a thousand Villanies unbecoming their Profession. They imitate the *Romish* Orders in Vows of Piety and Celibacy, and in their Pretensions to a strange Intimacy, and prevailing Interest with Heaven. Thus they endeavour to raise their Veneration and Respect; thus they acquire constant Homage and Address, daily Applications, and large Presents from the People. And some, by a seeming neglect of themselves, indulge their Bodies, and pamper their Ambition the more.

They are called *Faquirs* by the Natives, but *Ashmen* commonly by us, because of the abundance of Ashes with which they powder their Heads, and mix with their Hair, which falls down sometimes to the middle of their Backs. They use no Pillabers to repose their Heads

'The Sunyasees' drawn by William Taylor

on, but lay them unconcernedly upon the Ground, where they gather a constant supply of Dust and Filth, which makes them (in their Opinion) of a very becoming appearance, because it is squalid, but gives the Ascetick or votary in our Eyes a very disagreeable and sordid Aspect.

Of this Persuasion and kind of life, are several sorts both among the *Gentiles* and the *Moors*; some of whom shew their Devotion by a shameless appearance, and walking naked, without the least Rag of Cloth to cover them. And even at Mid-day, and in the heart of the City, and places of chief Concourse, will they walk the Streets, as shameless and unconcern'd, as if they were Cloathed all over. The constant sight of them in the City, which offers itself at every turn, abates that bashfulness in the Spectators, which such an immodesty might be apt to create, and diverts neither Sex from their Society, from a familiar Conversation and Intimacy with them; and Custom has wore off all that Coyness even in the Women, which would be startled at such an immodest Spectacle at first.

Others make solemn Vows of continuance in such and such kind of Postures all the days of their life, and will never move from them to alter them, tho' the Pains are never so violent, which seem to be attended with so much Torture, as would even force them to forbear. For these are Penitentiaries in earnest, without any Mask or possible appearance of Deceit, and voluntarily mortifie their Limbs, and distort their Joints to a perfect Dislocation. For by the Delusions of Satan, these infatuated Votaries are possessed with a wretched Opinion of making themselves unspeakably happy hereafter, by these insufferable Torments here: and the Enemy of Mankind, impatient of Delays in exercising his infernal Cruelty, persuades them to undergo these Torments which will end in making them Meritorious Saints, and that by these horrid Punishments they may secure a future larger Bliss. (1689)

J. OVINGTON[95]

## 2. *Hindu mendicants*

The two Bhaderpoor rivers were the general rendezvous of travellers, in their way to the eastern hills, or coming from the interior to the sacred shrines of Guzerat, and on the latter account very much frequented by Hindoo devotees, and pilgrims of every caste. There I beheld, assembled in the same pandaul, or reposing under the friendly banian-tree, the Gosannee in a state of nudity, and the Yogee with a lark or paroquet, his sole companion for a thousand miles; the Guroo, of the first rank in the brahminical hierarchy, travelling with oriental pageantry to visit the temples and superintend the seminaries, meeting the brahmacharee, with a covered mouth and nostrils, that he may not inhale an animalcule; and a soft broom in his hand to sweep the ground, that he may not tread on an insect. There also were religious enthusiasts reduced to a skeleton by abstinence, or almost bursting under a vow of swallowing so many maunds of consecrated ghee. One resting from turning over his body in a rolling posture, another imploring food from others, by having rendered himself incapable of lowering or moving his arms in consequence of superstitious devotion. But it would be endless as well as needless to enlarge further on these enthusiasts, so often mentioned in these memoirs; except that in the eastern parts of my districts, attracted no doubt by the sacred fanes at Dhuboy and Chandode, they were more abundant than I ever saw them elsewhere, and seemed to have acquired an unusual degree of consequence. The annexed engraving exhibits two of these singular characters, drawn from life, meeting near the ford of a river; the one accompanied by his faithful lark, nearly in the state of the ancient Gymnosophists; the mouth of the other covered with a cloth to prevent the death of an insect. The next engraving represents a further variety of these deluded fanatics, also taken from nature.

Far be it from me to cast a general reflection on these mendicants, but respecting the majority, those who have had the best opportunities of knowing them, will, I am confident, coincide in Dr. Fryer's remark, made a hundred and fifty years ago, that 'most of them are vagabonds, and the pest of the nation they live in: some of them dwell in gardens and retired places in the fields, in the same manner as the seers of old, and the children of the prophets did. Their habit is the main thing that signalizes them more than their virtue; they profess poverty, but make all things their own wherever they come. All the heat of the day they idle it under some shady tree, at night they come in tropps, armed with a great pole, a mirchal [a fan made of peacock's feathers] or peacock's tail, and a wallet, more like plunderers than beggars: they go into the market, or to the shopkeepers, and force an alms, none of them returning without his share. Some of them pass the bounds of a modest request, and bawl out in the open streets for an hundred rupees, and nothing less will satisfy them. They are clothed with a ragged mantle, which serves them also for a mattress; for which purpose some have lions', tigers', or leopards' skins to lay under them; the civilest of them wear flesh-coloured vests, somewhat like our brickmakers' frocks, and almost of that colour. The merchants, as their adventures return, are bountiful towards them; by which means some of them thrive upon it. These field-conventiclers, at the hours of devotion, beat a drum, from them called the fakeer's drum. There are enough of these strollers in Surat to make an army, insomuch that they are almost become formidable to the citizens; nor is the governor powerful enough to correct their insolence; for lately setting on a nobleman of the Moors, when his kindred came to demand justice, they unanimously arose in defence of the aggressor, and rescued himfrom his deserved punishment'. (1781)

JAMES FORBES[96]

## 3. The Aghoris

I was much more annoyed, however, at not being able to reach the shrine of Kalka, which tradition and universal report had clothed with something mysterious; and as I had signified to Lalla Joshea, the Guicowar's agent, my determination at all hazards to penetrate to this dread spot, in spite of his warnings, he and the rest very gravely imputed my sudden lameness to this profane resolution. To this awful *penetralium* the pilgrim never ventures, and the legend relates, that whoever has been so fool-hardy, has paid dearly for his temerity. A stranger was said always to join the sacrilegious visitor *en route,* who, on throwing aside her *incog.,* proved to be the dread Mother herself. Her rites are performed by the hideous Aghori, whose patroness she is, as *Aghoriswara Mata;* and it was a strong desire to unkennel some of these cannibals which tempted me to prolong my rugged pilgrimage to the Kalka Sikra, which in other respects has nothing attractive. At one time, they existed in these regions in some numbers; but, like brutes of the most noxious kind, they were only found in the wildest retreats, in the mountain-cave, or the dark recesses of the forest. Having elsewhere touched on the subject, I shall here only seek to establish the facts by some additional anecdotes.

The Ogur Sikra was called after one of these Murdi-khor, or man-eaters, who there established himself. Gazi was the name of one of these brutes, who used occasionally to quit his mountain-lair for the plain, to indulge his appetites. The last time he was seen, a live goat and an earthern vessel full of *shraub* were placed before him. He tore up the animal with teeth and nails, gorged, drank, slept amidst the offals, awoke, again gorged and drank, and then returned into the forest. In 1819, I appealed to my friend Mr. Williams (now with me) regarding these monsters. The following was his answer: 'When I was in Cattiawar, there were three or four men who literally lived like wild beasts, realizing the story of Nebuchadnezzar, except that they also ate raw and human flesh. One of these devils came, I think in 1808, to Baroda, and actually ate the arm of a dead child. Another came into the camp of the Sirsohoh of Cattiawar, in 1811, but he was not suffered to remain, although they covered him with shawls, etc. At one of the Jatras at Girnar, one of these Aghoris came to the rock amongst the pilgrims, who made *pooja*, or worship, to him, and clad him with shawls, turbans, rings, etc. He sat for some time, and at length, with an idiotic laugh, sprung up, and darted into the forest.' I was told that, not many months ago, one of the wretches issued from his retreat, and finding a Brahmin's boy who had strayed a little way from the temple, brought him down with a stone, but having only broken his leg, his cries summoned some one to his rescue. The Aghori fought for his prey, was mauled, and left for dead. Since this, they have kept still closer, and this last offender is said to have quitted the forest of Girnar altogether. (1808–11)

JAMES TOD[97]

## 4. *Fakirs of Juggernauth*

Passing through the town (Pooree), I observed several fine tanks, in which crowds of men, women, and children were bathing—yet one of the bearers assured me that he had often seen large alligators raise their heads above the surface when the weather was sultry. Like other holy places, Juggernauth is infested by those sanctified vagabonds, Fakirs, with the numerous branches of Gossains, Byraghees, Suniassees, etc, into which their important profession ramifies. At every turn, along every dead wall, under each banyan or peepul tree, the naked, squalid and painted bodies, matted and sunburnt hair, and distorted limbs of this race of Gymnosophists disgust the eye of the traveller; whilst his ear is deafened by their vociferated and often insolent demands for charity. My heart and purse were always alike closed against these chartered mendicants, who reap harvest sufficient from the superstition of their fellow-countrymen. (1832)

GODFREY CHARLES MUNDY[98]

## 5. A self torturing fakir

The word 'Fakir' (pronounced Fa-keer, with the *a* broad) is an Arabic term signifying 'poor', or a 'poor man', because they profess to have taken the vow of poverty, and, in theory, hold themselves above the necessity of home, property, or money, realizing their living as a religious right from the people wherever they come.

Some wander from place to place, some go on pilgrimages, and others locate themselves under a great banyan tree, or in the depths of a forest in some ruinous shrine or tomb, or on the bank of a river, and there receive the homage and offerings of their votaries.

I have often stood and looked at them in the wild jungle, miles away from a human habitation, filthy, naked, daubed with ashes and paint, and thought how like they seemed to those wretched creatures whom a merciful Saviour released from the power of evil spirits, and so compassionately restored to decency, to friends, and to their right minds.

Some few of these Fakirs are undoubtedly sincere in their profession of giving up the world, and its social and domestic relations, to embrace lives of solitude, mortification, or self-torture, or to devote themselves to a course of religious contemplation and asceticism; others of them do it from a motive of vain-glory, to be honored and worshiped by their deluded followers; while both of these classes expect, in addition, to accumulate thereby a stock of merit that will avail them in the next transmigration, and hasten their absorption into Brahm. But no one who has seen and known them can doubt that the great majority of the Fakirs are impostors and hypocrites.

A glance at the picture will enable the reader more fully to understand the descriptions which follow. These wear some clothing, but not much. The hair of the head is permitted to grow—in some cases not cut, and evidently not combed—from the time when they enter upon this profession. It grows at length longer than the body, when it is wound around the head in a rope-like coil, and is fastened with a wooden pin. The figure on the left hand of the picture in front is one of these. Having some doubts whether there was not some 'make-believe' in the huge roll, I questioned a Fakir one day about it. Seizing the big pin, he pulled it out, and down fell the long line of hair trailing after him. It was, sure enough, all his own hair.

But even these are not the worst of the class. Quite a number of them give up wandering and locate, and engage in the most amazing manifestations of endurance and self-torture. A few must be mentioned. One will lash a pole to his body and fasten the arm to it, pointing upward, and endure the pain till that limb becomes rigid and cannot be taken down again. The pole is then removed. I saw one of them with *both* arms thus fixed, his hands some eighteen inches higher than his head, and utterly immovable. Some of them have been known to close the hand, and hold it so until the nails penetrated the flesh, and came out on the other side. Tavernier and others give engravings of some who have stood on one leg for years, and others who never lie down, supported only by a stick or rope under their armpits, their legs meanwhile growing into hideous deformity, and breaking out in ulcers. Sticking a spear through the protruded tongue, or through the arm, is practiced, and so is hook-swinging—running sharp hooks through the small of the back deep enough to bear the man's weight—when he is raised twenty or thirty feet into the air and swung around. Some will lie for years on beds of iron spikes ... reading their Shaster and counting their beads, while their ranks furnish many of the voluntary victims who have immolated themselves beneath the wheels of Juggernaut. But there are tens of thousands of them who take to the profession simply because it gives them a living off the public, and who are mere wandering vagabonds.

Many of them are animated by another class of motives. These hunger for *fame*—they have become Fakirs for the honor of the thing—are willing to suffer that they may be respected and adored by those who witness in wonder the amazing self-tortures which they will endure. An instance which may be worth relating will illustrate this aspect of the subject. It was turned into verse by a humorous Englishman when the case occurred, and we present it here. One of these self-glorifying Fakirs, after graduating to saintship by long years of austerities and extensive pilgrimages, took it into his head that he could still further exalt his fame by riding about in a sort of Sedan chair with the seat stuck full of nails. Four men

'A Self-torturing Fakir', from Butler's *The Land of the Veda*

carried him from town to town, shaking him as little as possible. Great was the admiration of his endurance which awaited him everywhere. At length (no doubt when his condition had become such that he was for the time disposed to listen to some friendly advice) a rich native gentleman, somewhat sceptical as to the value and need of this discipline, met him and tried very earnestly to persuade him to quit his uncomfortable seat, and have mercy upon himself. But here let Mr. Cambridge give the reasoning of the kind-hearted native, and point the moral of the story. He says to the Fakir:

'Can such wretches as you give to madness a vogue?
Though the priesthood of *Fo* on the vulgar impose
By squinting whole years at the end of their nose—
Though with cruel devices of mortification
They adore a vain idol of modern creation—
Does the God of the heavens such a service direct?
Can his Mercy approve a self-punishing sect?
Will his Wisdom be worshiped with chains and with nails,
Or e'er look for his rites in your noses and tails?
Come along to my house, and these penances leave,
Give your belly a feast, and your breech a reprieve'.

This reasoning unhinged each fanatical notion,
And staggered our saint in his chair of promotion.
At length, with reluctance, he rose from his seat,
And, resigning his nails and his fame for retreat,
Two weeks his new life he admired and enjoyed;
The third he with plenty and quiet was cloyed;
To live *undistinguished* to him was the pain,
An existence unnoticed he could not sustain.
In retirement he sighed for the fame-giving chair,
For the crowd to admire him, to reverence and stare:
No endearments of pleasure and ease could prevail,
He the saintship resumed, and new-larded his tail. (1873)

WILLIAM BUTLER[99]

## 6. *The saint and his crocodiles*

The sight of the neighbourhood of Kurrachee, is the crocodile saint and his crocodiles. The track to Peer Mugger runs along an open billowless plain, all along which the campanile is visible, till you strike a low spur of hills running down into the sea. This little range is pierced by a pass invisible until you reach it, and at a short distance on the other side, is situated a small pond surrounded by a low mud wall, and situated in the middle of palm trees. A wild tulip tree hangs over the puddle, which is not a dozen yards long or half-a-dozen broad; and close by on a hillock overlooking it is the little tomb place, wherein the saint lives and prays and collects rupees from his visitors. I was looking at the pond and asking where the crocodiles were, when I saw what looked like a log of wood moving on the sand just beneath my eyes and not two yards away. This was one of the reptiles, and by and by a Mussulman, called the 'padre', came down and summoned his pets, whereon they all ran into the water, the level of which they raised several inches by their united bulk. One only was refractory, and the 'padre' beat him over the head with a stick. I remember a dignitary of the Church of India, now deceased, telling me that he had such influence with the people of the country that when he laid his hands on their backs they burst into tears. This 'padre', with more practical persuasion, laid his stick on the back of his recalcitrant pet, who did not burst into tears in spite of the proverbially lachrymose disposition of the crocodile, but opened his jaws and hissed loudly and looked as if he would bite the 'padre' but abstained from the actual commission of such sin. Inside the thick and dirty water, the heads of these beasts appeared sticking out like shapeless little rocks. Though their mouths were shut the teeth in their lower jaws protruded, growing seemingly in random fashion without any regard to order or uprightness, just like almonds in a piece of nougat. One of the attendants, when questioned, said that these reptiles, of which there were 80 more or less by his account, were created by the saint by a mere act of volition, a power which fortunately is not possessed by many. What particular connection they had with the holy tomb, or with religion in general he could not say, and I cannot help thinking that, they are a mere speculation, their proximity to the tomb an accident, their sanctity fortuitous, their *raison d'etre* an excuse for a collection, the only religious association to which they can rightly lay claim. (1889)

JOHN DAVID REES[100]

## J. JUGGLERS AND SNAKE CHARMERS

### 1. The snake–charmer

Near my friend T——'s house, in the fort of Asirgarh, to which we returned for a few days, were several small out-houses in which his

'The Fakirs of India' from Butler's *The Land of the Veda*

dogs and poultry were kept. He had some very handsome and valuable English dogs; one of these was found dead one morning and brought out for inspection, and as he had been in good health and spirits the evening previous, his sudden death, as well as that of some game fowls in the room adjoining, was unaccountable. We closely examined their dormitories, but could discover nothing suspicious, but some rat-holes in the chunam of the floor; one of the fowls, however, on being denuded of his feathers, exhibited such unmistakable marks of having succumbed to snake bite, that a snake charmer from the city of Burhanpur was sent for, and soon made his appearance.

The man had with him the usual equipment of a basket and flageolet made, apparently, from a long thin gourd; for clothes he had the common waist-cloth round his loins, and a scanty rag across his shoulders. My friend commenced by having him searched, and when assured he had nothing about him but what nature gave, he was told what had occurred, and taken to the rooms that had proved so fatal. Before commencing work, however, the charmer stipulated that any snake or cobra that he might capture should not be killed. As all of us were aware that the snake represents an incarnation of the Hindu deity, this was agreed to, and accordingly, before us all and under close surveillance, the man entered one of the rooms with nothing but his pipe and a waist-cloth. He examined the rat-holes, and selecting one he commenced piping a reedy monotonous treble for some five or six minutes, when a cobra's head slowly emerged from the hole. With a forked stick he at once pinned the snake to the ground, and seizing it with the other hand behind the head, drew him gently out of the hole.

This we saw him do as distinctly as sharp eyes within six feet of the operation could assure us. He then went to two other of the small rooms, repeating his first performance. On one he was unsuccessful, or it had no occupant; from the other he drew another but a smaller cobra, which he slipped, as before into his basket outside. We all now proceeded to the front of the house, and two chickens being brought, the man commenced again playing before the closed basket containing the snakes, and then, slowly lifting off the lid partially, he presented one of the birds at the opening, which was immediately struck by one of the snakes, and released immediately. In three minutes the fowl, after running about freely, began to stagger, then run round, and fell and died within five minutes, for it was timed, watch in hand. If anything that one actually sees is convincing of a fact, this surely ought to have assured us that the man had actually enticed unsophisticated snakes from their retreat; and none of those who witnessed the feat entertained, I believe, a doubt on the subject. The doctor, moreover, 'to make assurance doubly sure,' had one of the snake's jaws opened, and we saw distinctly the two fangs, one on each side of the upper jaw. (c. 1825–50)

T.G. FRASER[101]

## 2. Indian jugglers

As for some of the feats of Indian jugglers, they are totally destitute of any element of conjuring. Take, for example, that which is possibly best known to fame—the sword-swallowing performance. No sleight of hand or artful machinery is exhibited in this; there is literally no deception: the juggler throws his head back so as to obtain a reasonably straight course of some eighteen inches from his thorax downwards, and then, employing so much of his internal economy as a scabbard, inserts therein the instrument that is accepted as a sword—that is to say, an instrument closely resembling the pointless and edgeless cutlass of the British sailor or bandit of melodrama. The performance is, in short, an uncomfortable one for all concerned, but not otherwise remarkable.

Lucknow used to boast of its special swallowers—unpleasant people who could gulp a billiard-ball or half-a-dozen birds of the avidwat order and reproduce them on demand. Once I witnessed this performance and was more than satisfied. I saw the birds pass through the hideous and gaping entrance to the juggler's maw, and anon come forth fluttering from that human cavern and spread their wings in flight. I saw a turkey's egg travel the same darksome route and return to the light of day; and the only emotion, besides disgust, that I experienced was envy of that juggler's capacity for taking pills.

The Indian juggler, when an expert in his profession, deftly acquits himself in sundry efforts of sleight of hand and performs some few tricks that are so decidedly overt as that mango-tree swindle (one of the famous tricks of Indian jugglers, in which they plant a mango-stone . . . . flowers and fruit), but at the best he is a

'Jugglers', from Rousselet's *India and its Native Princes*

feeble entertainer. (1870–6).

EDWARD BRADDON[102]

## 3. Snake-charmers

The tricks played upon the monkeys were by no means commendable. One day some snake-charmers came, with their little flat-muffin-shaped basket full of detestable reptiles. One of these baskets, containing a lively cobra, was carefully tied round the largest monkey's neck, and then Jackoo was let go, and, of course, proceeded to do his best to get rid of the encumbrance. In effecting this, tugging at the basket with hands and feet, the lid flew off, and the cobra, tumbling out, arose in angry majesty with expanded hood, and with fierce threatenings, close to poor Jackoo! There is nothing of which a monkey has so great a horror as of a snake. Jackoo fainted! It may seem incredible; but such was the fact. The shock was too much for his nerves, and he collapsed. The assembled griffs revived him by pouring gin down his throat.

The snake-charmers brought with them large earthen pots full of black scorpions, which they handled in the most unconcerned manner; putting their hands in, and pulling out one scorpion after another for our inspection. The black scorpions grow to a great size: they are sometimes met with from nine to ten inches in length, but are not by any means so dangerous as the small semi-transparent, yellow or white scorpion. Once, in the jungle, I saw a shikarry stung by a black scorpion. He was walking in front of me down a rocky hill; suddenly, while picking his way among the loose stones, he stopped, and, making a terrible grimace, forked up his foot, and began to rub it with earth. He then pointed to a large black scorpion, which, tail over back, was crawling out of the path, and which he viciously smashed up with his billhook. After a minute of hard rubbing and wry faces, he again addressed himself to the road, and appeared to suffer no further inconvenience. (1885)

E. F. BURTON[103]

## 4. Man-killings by snakes

In India, the annual man-killings by snakes are as uniform, as regular, and as forecastable as are the tiger average and the suicide average. Any one who bets that in India, in any three consecutive years, the snakes will kill 49,500 persons, will win his bet; and any one who bets that in India in any three consecutive years the snakes will kill 53,500 persons, will lose his bet. In India the snakes kill 17,000 people a year; they hardly ever fall short of it; they as seldom exceed it. An insurance actuary could take the Indian census tables and the government's snake tables and tell you within sixpence how much it would be worth to insure a man against death by snake-bite there. If I had a dollar for every person killed per year in India, I would rather have it than any other property, as it is the only property in the world not subject to shrinkage. (1896)

MARK TWAIN[104]

## K. PARMAHANSAS, BUNJARAS AND THE PINDAREES

### 1.  Parmahansas—a caste that eats human flesh

I will go a step farther, and say that not only do *Hindus,* even *Brahmans,* eat flesh, but that, at least, one sect eat *human* flesh. I know only of one sect, and that, I believe, few in numbers, that doth this; but there may, for aught I can say, be others, and more numerous. They do not, I conclude (in our territory, assuredly not), kill human subjects to eat; but they eat such as they find in or about the *Ganges,* and perhaps other rivers. The name of the sect that I allude to is, I think, *Parmahansa,* as I have commonly heard it named; and I have received authentic information of individuals of this sect being not very unusually seen about *Benares,* floating down the river on, and feeding on, a corpse. Nor is this a low despicable tribe, but, on the contrary, esteemed—by themselves, at any rate, a very high one. Whether the exaltation be legitimate, or assumed by individuals in consequence of penance, or holy and sanctified acts, I am not prepared to state, but I believe the latter; as I have known other instances where individuals of different sects, by persevering in extraordinary piety, or penance, have been deemed in a state incapable of sin.—The holiness of the actor sanctified the act, be it what it may; or, as we say, to the pure all things are pure: but I never heard of these voluptuous saints carrying their devotion or impudence to the disgusting extravagance under our consideration. They are still much respected; more, however, under all their shapes, by women than men.

I will finish my notice of the *Parmahansa* by observing, that my information stated, that the human brain is judged by these epicurean cannibals as the most delicious morsel of their unsocial banquet. (1810)

EDWARD MOOR[105]

## 2. *The Bunjaras*

The appellation by which this race [Bunjaras] is known, is probably a compound Hindoo word expressive of their habit of *burning the woods,* or from their *living in the woods.* They are divided into four classes, which have branched into numerous families, and whose language, habits, and manners differ from those of the Deccan nations so materially, as at once to stamp them as foreigners. They however appear to have adopted the dress of the Murhuttas, the most northern of the Deccan people; and it is fair to infer from this fact, which comes in confirmation of their own oral traditions, that they first settled in that country, but the precise period of their arrival remains in obscurity, although it is probable they accompanied the first Mahomedan armies which so frequently invaded the Deccan from Hindoostan in the fourteenth century. To the dress of the Murhuttas the Bunjara women have added massive rings of ivory, either plain or dyed, round their arms, which they have substituted for lighter metallic bracelets; and the men wear at the end of the strings with which they fasten their short drawers round the waist, a profusion of heavy and gaudy-coloured tassels, and are easily distinguishable by these peculiarities of dress . . .

I shall give some account of their manners and habits. In the first place, the Bunjara, born in the open field and bred up in a camp, braves the heat of a vertical sun, and the bleak blast and deluge of the rainy season, from the time of his birth. In this life he acquires a robust constitution, a fierceness of manner and disposition, and a freedom of thought and action, which combine to render him athletic, hardy, and brave. The women are much of the same character, and are remarkable for their extreme want of beauty. The care of the former is to tend his cattle; of the latter, to perform the menial and culinary offices, and to rear the children. The dress of both, as I have before remarked, appears to resemble that of the Murhuttas; and the arms of the men consist principally of a sword, frequently double-edged, and a shield or else a spear, and sometimes a matchlock. They are constantly attended by dogs of a peculiar breed, resembling our English rough shepherd's dog, but considerably larger and handsomer; their colour, which is generally sandy or grey, and the length of their harsh wiry hair, evidently point them out of a wild breed, or, more properly speaking, indicate their habits of dwelling in the air. With these animals, which are famous for their docility and attachment, as well as their intrepidity in attack and courage in long chases, they hunt hares and wild boars, whose flesh they prize highly; and in the rainy season are often successful in taking deer, which they also eat.

In marching with convoys of grain or merchandise, they are particularly careful to count each bag both at loading and unloading; and in cases of expected attack, they pile them up breast-high with their cattle inside, and have been known to fight with unparalleled desperation and courage. In attending armies, they generally leave their women and children in some station of their own country. The grant that they pretend to have received from Ourungzeeb, for 'the thatch of houses; the seizure of well-drawn water; and plunder in the enemy's country,' has furnished them with pretexts for their general predatory habits. Wherever they go in times of peace, they are most cruel robbers in the highways; for they seldom spare the life if any resistance is made, or there is the slightest chance of discovery; while in times of war, it has been frequently found necessary to defend the villages of our own and the enemy's country on the flanks, by protecting them with safeguards; but no inducement will lead individuals to tell to what tauda* they belong; nor will the naigst of the taudas they belong to, either acknowledge them or revenge their cause. Theft by them, as among the Spartans, is not considered as a crime, but detection brings with it its own punishment. A remarkable instance both of their depravity and of their principles of honour in this respect, took place in the Murhutta campaign in 1803. One evening, an order reached Colonel Stevenson from General Wellesley, to send to him, during that night, five hundred bullock-loads of grain for his cavalry, in order that the convoy might make good its way in the dark without being intercepted by the enemy, which it probably would have been in the day. The commissary's native agent was immediately sent to dispatch the forage; and attended by a few troopers was proceeding towards the Bunjara camp, when his ear was assailed by the cries of some one in distress, he immediately went towards the spot and saw two Bunjaras with their swords drawn, and in the act of putting to death one of the camp settlers: they were immediately pursued, overtaken, and on the following day executed in front of all the Bunjara naigs, who maintained that they knew them not, and the culprits refused to give any account of themselves.

A similar circumstance happened a very short time ago with respect to Major Mackintosh, the commissary-general of the Nizam's subsidary force, on his way from Madras to Jalua, near the town of Nulgonda, with five Bunjaras; who after having robbed him of every thing in his palankeen, and breaking it to pieces, left him without taking his life, probably owing to the intrepidity of that officer, who, having the advantage of speaking the language, argued with them on the folly of putting him to death; which they at first attempted by running their pikes through his palankeen while he was in it, and which he told them would do them no good, but certainly lead to their discovery. They were afterwards taken and brought to Hydrabad while I was there in October last, but they refused to give any account of themselves.

Such is the outline of the Bunjara history. If we consider their domestic and wandering habits merely, we cannot but view them as the most barbarous description of inhabitants in a country otherwise in a state of civilization; while if we look upon them as members of the commonwealth in a public point of view, we shall be inclined to admit their general utility to the state, either by promoting commerce or maintaining armies in the field in every contiguous territory. (1813)

JOHN BRIGGS[105a]

*The clan or a group.
†Leaders or chiefs.

## 3. The Brinjarrees

At Rahtgurh we found a bungalow, and made a halt. Rahtgurh is situated on the steep banks of the beautiful river Bhina, which is crossed at this point by a superb viaduct; and it commands a fine panorama. At the distance of about half a mile towards the east stands the ancient citadel of Rahtgurh (Castle of Night), with its battlemented ramparts, its gates, and its ruins of palaces and temples; at its foot lies the little town, surrounded with trees and cultivation. The plain is inclosed by grand mountains, whence sprang high columns of smoke, causing them to resemble so many volcanoes; they were the burning jungles, surrounding us during the night with a circle of flames. During the day we witnessed the passage of a caravan of Brinjarrees. Few sights are more picturesque than these caravans on the march, with their thousands of oxen, and their escorts of men of warlike aspect and strangely attired women. The whole family is there; the infant being slung to the back of its mother, and the young children perched on the milking cows, which carry besides all the household utensils. To the old man, who is a member of the council is reserved the honour of mounting a starveling pony. They are said to practise the abduction of male children and female infanticide. Their utility as carriers is incontestable, and has earned for them the protection of the English Government, which constantly employs their services. They are fated, however, to see their occupation monopolised by the railroads at no very distant period, when they will be compelled to abandon their wandering life. They are reckoned as numbering at the present time some hundreds of thousands; but, to say the truth, these figures have never yet been confirmed by any regular census.

On attentively considering the type of these Brinjarrees, their manners and some of their customs, such as the necromancy practised by the women, their primitive marriage ceremonies, and the practice charged against them of stealing children, many travellers have persisted in recognising them as the parent branch of that wandering race which, under the names of Bohemians and Zingaris, have spread themselves all over Europe. Whatever may be the probabilities in favour of such an hypothesis, this interesting question can only be solved by a minute observation of the customs of the Bohemians of Europe, and especially by the study of their idioms and their legends; all of which are researches still remaining for the most part to be undertaken. (1875)

LOUIS ROUSSELET[106]

## 4. Of the Pindarries

The Pindarries have been compared to the first Mahrattas; but, though alike in character and habits, there were essential points of difference. The adherents of Sevajee and his successors were united and animated by the ties of brotherhood, as well as by the prejudices

'Brinjarees on the March', drawn by C. Laplante

of religion. They were of one tribe, and almost of one province. They were not impelled by the mere love of plunder, and the ambition of a martial chief; they had the more legitimate, and, therefore, the more permanent motives, of attachment to their native soil and to the religion of their fathers, with the consequent resentment against the intolerant and oppressive rulers by whom they were assailed. These causes, though they might have checked the increase of their numbers, gave them an union of interest and action, which was unknown to the Pindarries. It was, however, one of the greatest evils attending the growing numbers of the latter, that, though divided, and only susceptible of union through the existence of some common principle of action, they became, from the very looseness of their composition, a nucleus to attract what was floating and unattached in the community; and thus presented, at all moments, a mass of materials which an able and popular leader might use, either for the destruction of others, or for his own aggrandisement.

The Pindarries, when they came to a rich country, had neither the means nor inclination, like the Tartars, to whom also they have been compared, to settle and repose. Like swarms of locusts, acting from instinct, they destroyed and left waste whatever province they visited. Their chiefs had, from grants or by usurpation, obtained small territorial possessions; but the revenues of their land were never equal to the maintenance of one-tenth part of their numbers, and they could, therefore, only be supported by plunder: their force, within the last twenty years that they were settled in Central India, has been computed at from twenty to thirty thousand horse of all descriptions. But it was evidently impossible to form a correct estimate of a body whose numbers were so continually varying, who were diminished by misfortune and swelled by success, who coalesced, from similarity of habits and condition, with every chief who was tempted, by the weakness or the oppression of the power he served, to throw off his allegiance, and to become a freebooter. It is also to be observed, that the Pindarries were fed and nourished by the very miseries they created; for, as their predatory invasion extended, property became insecure, and those who were ruined by their depredations were afterwards compelled to have recourse to a life of violence, as the only means of subsistence left them. They joined the stream which they could not withstand, and endeavoured to redeem their own losses by the plunder of others. Such facts as these rendered fallacious all calculation regarding the numerical strength of the Pindarries, who were, indeed, so amalgamated with the whole of the loose part of the military population of India, that it had become a system, not a particular force, that was to be subdued.

Lines of defence against the ravages of the Pindarries, and partial expeditions against their leaders, were equally ineffectual to remedy this evil; for, while efforts were made to crush one head of the hydra, others arose; and the resources of those governments which tried to suppress them, were vainly wasted against an enemy who had every thing to hope from success, and whose condition defeat did not render more desperate. To understand this fact, it is necessary to advert to the mode of warfare pursued by these freebooters. When they set out on an expedition, they placed themselves under the guidance of one or more chosen leaders, called Lubbiriahs, who were selected on account of their knowledge of the country that it was meant to plunder. The Pindarries were neither encumbered by tents nor baggage; each horseman carried a few cakes of bread for his own subsistence, and some feeds of grain for his horse. The party, which usually consisted of two or three thousand good horse, with a proportion of mounted followers, advanced at the rapid rate of forty or fifty miles a-day, neither turning to the right nor left till they arrived at their place of destination. They then divided, and made a sweep of all the cattle and property they could find: committing at the same time the most horrid atrocities, and destroying what they could not carry away. They trusted to the secrecy and suddenness of the irruption for avoiding those who guarded the frontiers of the countries they invaded; and before a force could be brought against them, they were on their return. Their chief strength lay in their being intangible. If pursued, they made marches of extraordinary length (sometimes upwards of sixty miles), by roads almost impracticable for regular troops. If overtaken, they dispersed, and reassembled at an appointed rendezvous; if followed to the country from which they issued, they broke into small parties. Their wealth, their booty, and their families, were scattered over a wide region, in which they found protection amid the mountains, and in the fastnesses belonging to themselves and to those with whom they were either openly or secretly connected; but no where did they present any point of attack; and the defeat of a party, the destruction of one of their contonments, or the temporary occupation of some of their strong-

holds, produced no effect, beyond the ruin of an individual freebooter, whose place was instantly supplied by another, generally of
more desperate fortune, and therefore more eager for enterprise.

The Pindarries, who had arisen, like masses of putrefaction in
animal matter, out of the corruption of weak and expiring states,
had, fortunately, none of those bonds of union which unite men in
adversity. They had neither the tie of religious, nor of national
feeling. They were men of all lands and all religions. They had been
brought together less by despair than by deeming the life of a
plunderer, in the actual state of India, as one of small hazard, but of
great indulgence. A body so constituted, and of such a character,
could only be formidable when considered as part of a distempered
community, with every branch of which they were more or less
connected. In this view they had importance, whether we refer to
the dangerous contagion of their example, or the probability that
they would early triumph over what little remained of government
in Central India, and swell their bands with all its military
population . . .

The Pindarries were principally dangerous from their existing
among governments, none of which was powerful enough to subdue
them, and their being themselves constitutionally incapable of settling into a community, possessing any interest in the general tranquillity; but this condition, while it made them formidable to weak
and distracted states, rendered them incapable of resisting the
resolute attack of a strong and vigorous government. Superficial
observers thought it would be difficult, if not impossible, to destroy
these freebooters. But it was evident that they could not exist
without a home or without support. To drive them from the territories they possessed, to identify with them all who gave them aid
or protection, was the only mode by which the great and increasing
evil could be remedied. No measures were ever more wisely plan-
ned, more vigorously pursued, or more successfully accomplished,
than those adopted for their suppression. There remains not a spot
in India that a Pindarry can call his home. They have been hunted
like wild beasts; numbers have been killed; all have been ruined.
Those who adopted their cause have fallen. They were early in the
contest shunned like a contagion, and even the villagers whom they
so recently oppressed, were among the foremost to attack them.
Their principal leaders have either died, submitted, or been made
captives; while their followers, with the exception of a few, whom

the liberality and consideration of the British government have
aided to become industrous, are lost in that population, from whose
dregs they originally issued. A minute investigation only can discover these once formidable disturbers, concealed as they now are
among the lowest classes, where they are making some amends for
past atrocities, by the benefit which is derived from their labour in
restoring trade and cultivation. These freebooters had none of the
prejudices of caste, for they belonged to all tribes. They never had
either the pride of soldiers, of family, or of country, so that they
were bound by none of those ties which, among many of the communities in India, assume an almost indestructible character. Other
plunderers may arise from distempered times; but, as a body, the
Pindarries are so effectually destroyed, that their name is already
almost forgotten, though not five years are passed since it spread
terror and dismay over all India. (1823)

JOHN MALCOLM[107]

# 5.  Social Life

## A. DANCES

### 1. *Invitation to a nautch*

I received a printed card on the occasion [Durga Puja], which I transcribe: 'Maha Rajah, Rajkissen Bahaudur, presents his respectful compliments to *Mrs Gram,* and requests the honour of *his* company to a nautch (being Doorga Poojah), on the 5th, 6th, and 7th of October, at nine o'clock in the evening.' Having never seen a nautch, I did not decline the Maha Rajah's invitation; but on the evening of the fifth I went, with a small party, to the assembly, and received more amusement than I expected. The Maha Rajah has a fine house at the end of Chitpore bazar. The room into which we were ushered was a large square court, covered in for the occasion with red cloth, to which a profusion of white artificial flowers was fastened. Three sides of the court are occupied by the dwelling-house, the walls of which are adorned by a double row of pillars in couplets, and between each couplet is a window. The fourth side is occupied by the family temple, of a very pretty architecture; the arches which support it are not unlike those used in England in Henry VII's time, with cinquefoil heads. A flight of steps leads to the viranda of the temple, where Vishnu sat in state, with a blaze of light before him, in magnificent chandeliers. When we entered there were some hundreds of people assembled, and there seemed to be room for as many more. The dancing was begun, but as soon as our host perceived us he led us to the most commodious seats, stationed boys behind us with round fans of red silk, with gold fringe, and then presented us with bouquets of the mogue and the rose, tied up in a green leaf, ornamented with silver fringe. A small gold vase being brought, the Maha Rajah, with a golden spoon, perfumed us with ottur, and sprinkled us with rose-water, after which we were allowed to sit still and look on. The first dancers were men, whom by their dresses I took for women, though I was rather surprised at the assurance of their gestures, which had nothing else remarkable in them. These gave way to some Cashmerian singers, whose voices were very pleasing. They were accompanied by an old man, whose long white beard and hair, and fair skin, spoke a more northern country than Bengal. His instrument was a peculiarly sweet-toned guitar, which he touched with skill and taste, to some of the odes of Hafiz and some Hindostanee songs. I was sorry when they finished, to make way for a kind of pantomime, in which men personated elephants, bears, and monkeys. After this some women danced; but though they were pretty, and their motions rather graceful, I was disappointed, after hearing so much of the nautch-girls of India. One of them, while dancing in a circle, twisted a piece of striped muslin into flowers, keeping each stripe for a different coloured flower. The last amusement we staid to partake of, was the exhibition of a ventriloquist (the best I ever heard), although the Maha Rajah pressed us to remain, saying that he had different sets of dancers, enough to exhibit during the whole night. I was pleased with the attention the Rajah paid to his guests, whether Hindoos, Christians, or Mussulmans; there was not one to whom he did not speak kindly, or pay some compliment on their entrance; and he walked round the assembly repeatedly, to see that all were properly accommodated.

I was sorry I could not go to his nautch the next night, where I hear there was a masquerade, when several Portuguese and Pariahs appeared as Europeans, and imitated our dances, music, and manners. I grieve that the distance kept up between the Europeans and the natives, both here and at Madras, is such, that I have not been able to get acquainted with any native families as I did at Bombay. (1811)

                                                    MARIA GRAHAM[108]

## 2. Nautches

The nautch of my experience may be briefly described thus: Scene—the courtyard of the host's house, covered in temporarily by an awning of some sort which has no pretensions to be watertight. In the place of honour the host smoking a hookah, and all round the yard a dusky crowd of hookah-smokers, squatted upon the ground for the most part, but as to a few honoured with chairs. Behind the host and guests a score or so of retainers, whose mission it is to purvey *pan supari* when the entertainment shall be concluded, or to

sprinkle diluted attar upon the more important of the people present, or to bring *gools* or *chillums* for the hookah, etc. In the centre
of the courtyard, which is carpeted or matted for the occasion, the
nautch girls, with their attendant orchestra, find their stage. In front
sit the girls when the exigencies of the dance do not claim their
services; behind them the three or four makers of noises, who by a
pleasant irony are described as musicians, and where the instruments (old-time as the pipes of Pan and Appollo's dried-up turtle)
consist of a stringed affair that rudely burlesques a Lowther Arcade
fiddle, a reed arrangement potent of discord, and the tom-tom that a
poet has dignified under the style and title of the Indian drum. The
girls—the Bayaderes of romance—are unprepossessing females who
would be menials in some household if they were respectable: some
of them fat and middle-aged; none of them remarkable for beauty.
The musicians—save the mark—are scoundrels to a man, and
would be convicted by a jury of physiognomists of any crime
charged against them.

The smoke of a hundred hookahs rises and hangs as a pall over
the throng. The musicians make hideous sounds, which have a sort
of rhythm about them because of the time-beating of the constant
tom-tom. A nautch-girl rises and proceeds to jingle music from her
anklets by a monotonous shuffle round the stage, while she sways
hither and thither and waves her arms, until she is relieved by
another girl, who shuffles and sways and waves in the approved
manner, and so *da capo*. Or, by way of change, a siren rises and
emits vocal sounds of such power that when she brings out a high
note (and she is as full of high notes as a confidential bank clerk) one
sees the muscles of her throat throb again. And so the intellectual
sport proceeds for hours until the regulation quantities of discord,
smoke, and smell have been enjoyed. That is the Indian nautch.
(1870–6)

EDWARD BRADDON[109]

## 3. The cathacks and the egg-dance

The male dancers, who are called cathacks, were fine tall young
men, from eighteen to twenty years of age; and, attired in a very rich
costume, they executed the very same dances as the nautchnis, with
great agility and much grace. Still it was rather a ridiculous spectacle
to see those great, powerful young fellows balancing themselves to

the sound of little bells, and executing poses plastiques with their scarves. But is it, after all, more ridiculous than the pirouettes of our opera-dancers?

Another dance, infinitely more graceful and interesting, was the egg-dance. This is not, as one might expect from the name, a dance executed upon these fragile articles.

The dancing-girl, dressed in the ordinary female costume of the women of the people, a bodice and very short sarri, carries on her head a wicker wheel of tolerably large diameter, placed in a perfectly horizontal manner on the top of the crown; and round this wheel threads are attached at equal distances, provided at their extremities with a slip knot, which is kept open by means of a glass bead. The dancing-girl advances towards the spectators, holding a basket filled with eggs, which she hands to us so that we may verify that they are real eggs and not imitation.

The music strikes up a monotonous and jerking measure, and the dancer begins turning herself round with great rapidity. Then, seizing an egg, she inserts it in one of the slip-knots, and with a sharp movement jerks it so as to tighten the knot. By means of the centrifugal force produced by the rapidity of the dancer's circular movement, the thread holding the egg is stretched out so that the egg is placed in a straight line with the prolongation of the corresponding spoke of the wheel. One after the other the eggs are thrown into the slip-knots, and they soon form a horizontal aureola round the head of the dancing-girl. At this point the dance becomes more and more rapid, and the features of the dancer can with difficulty be distinguished. It is a critical moment: the least false step, the slightest stoppage, and the eggs would be smashed one against another.

But, now, how is the dance to be interrupted? how is it to be stopped? There is only one way, and that is by withdrawing eggs in the same manner in which they have been fixed there; and, in spite of all appearances to the contrary, this last operation is the more delicate of the two. The dancer must with one single clear and precise movement seize the egg and draw it towards her; it is evident that, if the hand were carelessly to place itself within the circle, it would suffice for it to touch one of the threads only for the general harmony to be suddenly broken. At last all the eggs are successfully withdrawn; the dancer stops abruptly; and, without seeming in the least degree dizzy from the constant whirling, she advances with a firm step towards us, and presents us with the eggs contained in the

'The Egg-dance', drawn by Emile Bayard

basket, which are broken on the spot into a plate, by way of proving the complete absence of all trickery. (1875)

LOUIS ROUSSELET[110]

## 4. *Nautch dances*

The ladies of my old friend's family were ranged round the large central room in dresses of light gauzy muslins or silks delicately embroidered, and dyed with all the loveliest tints imaginable, rose colour predominating. The effect was like a garden of beautiful flowers. The gentlemen wore black coats and hats of the well-known Parsee fashion, with trousers of crimson or white. In the centre of the apartment sate the two nautch girls, Wazil-Bukhsh, a Mohammedan, and Krishna, a Hindu, both amazingly arrayed in skirts of scarlet and gold, with saris of bright hues, plentifully spangled, tight gilded trousers, and anklets of silver and gold bells, which make a soft tinkling at every movement of the small brown feet. Behind them stand their three musicians, one playing the saringi, a sort of violin, the other the tamboora, a deep-sounding kind of violoncello, and the third provided with a bass and treble drum tied round his waist on an ornamented scarf. The girls rose to their feet, salaamed, and one of them began a slow *pas,* advancing and retreating with rhythmical waving of hands and measured beat of foot, which the other dancer then repeated. Next followed a song, or series of songs, delivered in high head notes, and principally of an amatory character. 'My beloved is absent, and by day there is no sun in the sky, no moon for me at night! But he is coming, ek hath Khali—"with one hand empty"—yet in that he carries me back my heart.' Then Krishna sang the 'Taza ba Taza,' the musicians advancing and retreating with her tinkling paces, leaning over the absorbed performer, and seeming in the intensity of their accompaniment to nurse the singing and draw it forth note by note. After this the Muslim girl and her Hindu sister executed together a famous dance called the 'Kurrar,' which consists of a series of character pictures. They placed conquettish little caps of spangled velvet on their black hair, and acted first of all the Indian *jeune amoureux,* adjusting his turban, stroking his moustache, and pencilling his eyebrows. Then it was Govinda, one corner of the sari twisted up to represent the *bansula,* on which the light-hearted god piped to the shepherdesses, and Radha listening and singing. Next—to the same never-ending rise and fall of the amorous music—Wazil Bukhsh became a love-sick maiden in the jungle, picking blossoms to fasten in her hair, and Krishna followed, enacting a serpent-charmer. Blowing on the beaded gourd that snake music which brings the hooded cobra forth from his deepest hole, she swayed her lithe body over the imaginary reptile, chanting the notes of the dreamy, bewildering, beguiling song; bent herself over the half entranced snake, coaxing him out with long, low, weird passages of wild melody, until the charm was supposed to have triumphed, the serpent was bewitched and captured; whereupon Krishna rose to her feet and, drawing the glittering fringe of her sari over her forehead, expanding it with both hands, so as to resemble a cobra's hood, she finished with the snake-dance, amid cries of 'Shabash' (well done)! which were acknowledged with deep salaams. (1886)

EDWIN ARNOLD[111]

## B. FESTIVALS

### 1. Festival of Nauroz

On the present occasion this nine days' festival [Nauroz] was celebrated by Zelaldinus [Akbar] with such lavish expenditure of money, with such magnificence of clothing, ornament and all manner of appurtenances, and with such gorgeous games, that the like, as we were told, had not been seen for thirty years. For the walls and colonnades of the palace courtyard were decorated with hangings of cloth of gold and silk. Games were held and pageants conducted each day. The King himself was enthroned on a high golden throne approached by steps. He wore his crown and insignia of royalty. He distributed gifts to many generals who had accompanied him on the campaign; and he gave instructions that all classes of the citizens should be bidden to show their joy either by leaping, singing or dancing. He welcomed all who came to see the festival with largess, free supply of wine, and free banquets. Hence whole communities of Jogues arrived, with their chiefs. These men were evidently devoted to religion in appearance rather than in fact; for they profanely and frivolously laid aside all pretence of piety, danced impudently and shamelessly, and fulsomely flattered the King in the songs they sang. (1582)

FATHER ANTONIO MONSERRATE[111]

## 2. Season of festivals

This is the season of festivals; I hear the tomtoms, drums, pipes, and trumpets in every corner of the town, and I see processions in honour of Kali going to a place two miles off, called Kali Ghaut, where there has long been a celebrated temple to this goddess, which is now pulled down, and another more magnificent is to be erected in its place. In all the bazars, at every shop door, wooden figures and human heads, with the neck painted blood-colour, are suspended, referring, I imagine, to the human sacrifices formerly offered to this deity, who was, I believe, the tutelary goddess of Calcutta. Three weeks ago, the festival of Kali, under the name and attributes of Doorga, was celebrated. On this occasion her images, and those of some other divinities, were carried in procession with great pomp, and bathed in the Hoogly, which, being a branch of the Ganges, is sacred. The figures were placed under canopies, which were gilt and decked with the most gaudy colours, and carried upon men's heads. Several of these moving temples went together, preceded by musical instruments, banners, and bare-headed Bramins, repeating *muntras* (forms of prayer). The gods were followed by cars, drawn by oxen or horses, gaily caparisoned, bearing the sacrificial utensils, accompanied by other Bramins, and the procession was closed by an innumerable multitude of people of all castes. This feast lasted several days. (1811)

MARIA GRAHAM[112]

## 3. A festive crowd

One of the Hindoo festivals in honour of the goddess Kali commenced this evening. Near the river a crowd was assembled round a stage of bamboos, 15 feet high, composed of two upright, and three horizontal poles, which last were placed at about five feet asunder. On this kind of ladder several men mounted, with large bags, out of which they threw down various articles to the standers, who caught them with great eagerness; but I was too far off to ascertain what they were. They then one by one raised their joined hands over their heads, and threw themselves down with a force, which must have proved fatal had not their fall been broken by some means or other. The crowd was too dense to allow of my discovering how this was effected; but it is certain they were unhurt, as they immediately reascended, and performed the same ceremonies many times.

On the 10th [April] we were awakened before day-break, by the discordant sounds of native musical instruments, and immediately mounted our horses, and rode to the Meidan. As the morning advanced we could see an immense crowd coming down the Chowringhee road, which was augmented by persons joining it from all the streets and lanes of the city. We entered the crowd, taking the precaution of making the saees walk close by my horse's head, who was frightened at the music, dancing, and glare of torches, accompanied at intervals by the deep sound of the gong.

> The double double peal of the drum was there,
> And the startling sound of the trumpet's blare,
> And the gong, that seemed with its thunders dread
> To stun the living, and waken the dead. (1824)

(MRS) REGINALD HEBER[113]

## 4. Annual fairs

Before setting out on our journey towards the Himmalah we formed once more an agreeable party to visit the marble rocks of the Nerbudda at Beraghat. It was the end of Kartick (October) when the Hindoos hold fairs on all their sacred streams, at places consecrated by poetry or tradition as the scene of some divine work or manifestation. These fairs are at once festive and holy—every person who comes enjoying himself as much as he can, and at the same time seeking purification from all past transgressions by bathing and praying in the holy stream, and making laudable resolutions to be better for the future. The ceremonies last five days, and take place at the same time upon all the sacred rivers throughout India; and the greater part of the whole Hindoo population, from the summits of the Himmalah mountains to Cape Comorin, will I believe, during these five days, be found congregated at these fairs. In sailing down the Ganges one may pass, in the course of a day, half a dozen such fairs, each with a multitude equal to the population of a large city, and rendered beautifully picturesque by the magnificence and variety of the tent equipages of the great and wealthy. The preserver of the universe (Bhugwan) Vishnoo is supposed, on the 26th of Assar (June), to descend to the world below (Putal), to defend Raja Bull from the attacks of Indur, to stay with him four months, and to come up again on the 26th Kartick (October). During his absence almost all kinds of worship and festivities are suspended; and they recommence at these fairs, where people assemble to hail his resurrection. (*c.* 1830's)

WILLIAM HENRY SLEEMAN [114]

## 5. *Mohurrum*

I have just learned the origin of the Mohurrum. It is a festival, or rather commemoration of the death of Hussein and Houssein, the sons of Ali, Mohammed's nephew. These two were pursued towards the desert by their enemies; they took shelter in a well, and a spider immediately wove a web across the top. Their enemies came up, and, seeing the web, thought that Houssein and Hussein could not be in the well. However, one of them looking down observed a number of lizards all hastening up the sides, so then they thought there must be some one at the bottom who frightened the lizards, and, searching, they got up the two brothers and killed them. It is to commemorate this fact that they have instituted the festival of the Mohurrum, and in consequence the Mohammedans all reverence the spider, while they kill the lizard. (1843)

T. ACLAND [115]

## 6. *Holi*

At the festival of the Hooli, which is particularly dedicated to Krishnu, images of the deity are carried about on elephants, horses, in palkees, etc. The songs are exclusively in honour of Krishnu, and hailing the return of the season, personified under the name of Vasanta, generally pronounced Bessant. Kama, the god of love, is the son of Krishnu.

The Hooli was celebrated by the natives with due glee; they threw abeer (red powder) into each other's faces, and then squirted orange-coloured water over it; people were also sent on April-fool errands. Colonel Gardner avoided appearing amongst the people during this festival, and I imitated his example. The orange-coloured water is tinged with the flowers of the dhak tree; the abeer is flour made from the singharra (water-nut), and dyed with red sanders; the roots of the singharra are loosened by means of ropes fastened between two boats, with several men in each; and iron prongs are used in collecting them. (1850)

FANNY PARKES [116]

## 7. Dewali

This Feast of Lamps, known in India as the 'Dewali', is by no means peculiar to that country. It has been known, from remote ages, alike in Europe, Asia, and in Africa. 'When we reflect', writes Colonel Tod, in his 'Annals of Rajasthan', 'that the Egyptians, who furnished the Grecian Pantheon, held these solemn festivals, also called the Feast of Lamps, in honour of Minerva at Lais, we may deduce the origin of this grand Oriental festival from that mother country in Central Asia, whence the Dewali radiated to remote China, the Nile, the Ganges, and the shores of the Tigris; for the Shebrat of Islam is but the Feast of Lamps of the Rajpoots.' Mr. Ward, in his 'View of the Hindoos', gives but a meagre account of this festival, and admits that he cannot trace its origin. 'In the month Kartiku', he says, 'the Hindoos suspend lamps in the air on bamboos, in honour of the gods and in obedience to the Shasters. I cannot learn any other origin of the custom than this—that as the offering of lamps to particular gods is considered as an act of merit, so this offering to all the gods, during the auspicious month of Kartiku, is supposed to procure many benefits to the giver.' The Chinese, however, have a theory of their own with respect to this custom, which is sufficiently definite if nothing else. The people ascribe the custom to 'an accident that happened in the family of a famous Mandarin, whose daughter walking one evening on the shore of a lake fell in and was drowned. The afflicted father with his family ran hither and thither, and the better to find her, he caused a great number of lanterns to be lighted. All the inhabitants of the place thronged after him with torches. The year ensuing they made fires upon the shores on the same day. They continued the ceremony every year—everyone lighted his lantern; and by degrees it grew into a custom.' This is taken from a work published many years ago, on the 'Present State of China,' and quoted in the notes to Moore's 'Lalla Rookh.' The poet, who adopts this view of the case, is obviously at issue with the historian. Instead of China having borrowed the custom from Central Asia, Central Asia, according to Moore, borrowed it from China. When Lalla Rookh is journeying in state to Bokhara, we are told that on her arrival, one night, at the place of encampment, she was 'surprised and delighted to find the groves all around illuminated, some artists of Yamtcheou having been sent on previously for the purpose. On each side of the green

'The Moharum: The Taboots on the Shore of the Back Bay at Bombay', drawn by Emile Bayard

alley which led to the pavilion, artificial sceneries of bamboo-work
were erected, representing arches, minarets, and towers, from
which hung thousands of silken lanterns, painted by the most delicate pencils of Canton. Nothing could be more beautiful than the
leaves of the mango-trees and acacias, shining in the light of the
bamboo scenery, which shed a lustre round as soft as that of the
nights of Peristan . . .' On the whole, the poet of 'Lalla Rookh' is
wonderfully correct in his Oriental imagery; but it may be doubted
whether any master of the ceremonies in Central Asia would have
sent to China for coloured lamps.

Colonel Tod states that in Rajpootana, the Feast of Lamps is in
honour of Lachsmi, the wife of Vishnu. 'As Lachsmi,' he says, 'was
produced at the "churning of the ocean," and hence called "one of
the fourteen gems," she is confounded with Rembha, chief of the
Apsaras, the Venus of the Hindoos. Though both were created from
the froth *(sara)* of the waters *(ap)*, they are distinct as the representation of riches and beauty can be.' And the writer adds with
reference to the festival, 'On this day, it is incumbent on every
votary of Lachsmi to try the chance of the dice; and from their
success in the Dewali, the prince, the chief, the merchant, and the
artisan, foretell the state of their coffers for the ensuing year.'
(1867)

JOHN WILLIAM KAYE[117]

## 8. *Observance of ritual*

To pray and serve yet not be pure,—
    In dirty pot to place good food,—
To worship God while sins endure,—
    Can never turn to good.

Our sins grow ever from our deeds,
    Nor owe their birth or death to place.
'Tis better, then, to see our needs
    Than look to works for grace.

Why dost thou long for holy springs,
    Or seek at Kasi saintlihood?
Can sinful man obtain the things
    That Kasi gives the good?

Though hypocrites should meditate,
  And perfect keep the outward law,
They ne'er attain the holy state;
  But sink in hell's dark maw.

The sanctity that God counts right
  Is not in sky or deserts rude;
'Tis not where holy streams unite:—
  Be pure—thou viewest God. (1872)

                                    CHARLES E. GOVER[118]

## 9. Feasts of fear and love

Here are drawn up two or three hundred Sapwallahs, or serpent-charmers, each having in front of him a basket containing several cobra capellas. The pious Hindoos bring them bowls of buffalo's milk, of which these reptiles are very fond, and which the charmer gives them to drink. Each bowl is quickly surrounded by a circle of cobras, which, with their heads immersed in the liquid, remain perfectly motionless. From time to time the Sapwallah takes one away to make room for another; and it is curious to witness the fury of the deposed animal, which draws itself up, and swells out its hood. The circle of charmers is surrounded by a crowd of spectators, who contemplate the scene. The reptiles swarming about the bowls, and the men half naked, or covered with coloured tinsel, who handle them without the slightest fear, form a very original spectacle. These singular proceedings continue all day, during which a large number of cobras are abundantly regaled with milk. At night the houses are illuminated; processions accompanied by torches pass through the streets; and on every side there resounds a fearful din of cymbals, toms-toms, and hautboys.

This fete is generally held in July or August, the season when the cobras are most dangerous; and their instinctive dread has induced the people to choose this time to appease the wrath of these terrible demi-gods.

The feast of Naryal Puranama, or of the Full Moon of the Cocoa-nuts, is one of the most important of those celebrated at Bombay. It is usually held towards the latter end of September, and is supposed to mark the termination of the rainy season. Although purely a Hindoo festival, all the races of the island unite together in

'Snake Men', drawn by Charles Gold

its celebration. An immense concourse assembles on the shore of the Back Bay. The top of the bank is covered with tressels and carracks, and for two days this place, usually a perfect desert, presents a most picturesque and animated spectacle. Every one approaches the sea, or even enters it up to mid-leg, and casts some cocoa-nuts as far as possible into the water. To this offering he adds a short prayer, in which he invokes the sea, and prays it to keep all danger far away from those who are going to undertake long voyages. Before he comes out, he further throws into the sea a crown of flowers, by way of thanking it for having accepted his tribute.

Thousands of cocoa-nuts are thus thrown into the bay during those two days, for a considerable section of the population of Bombay get their living by the sea, and have an interest in its being favourable to them. Fishermen, sailors, ship-owners, women and children, all come to pray to it, and implore its clemency. This custom, in all its primitive simplicity, is very touching, and shows that the Hindoo, in his religion, forgets neither that which he loves, and which is a source of benefit to him, nor that which he fears, and whose resentment must be appeased. (1875)

LOUIS ROUSSELET[119]

# C. MARRIAGE

## 1. Child marriages

We found Marriages great store both in Towne and Villages in many places where wee passed, of Boyes of eight or ten yeares, and Girles of five or sixe yeares old. They both doe ride upon one Horse very trimly decked, and are carried through the Towne with great piping and playing, and so returne home and eat of a Banquet made of Rice and Fruits, and there they dance the most part of the night, and so make an end of the marriage. They lie not together untill they bee ten yeares old. They say they marrie their Children so young, because it is an order, that when the man dyeth, the woman must be burned with him: so that if the Father die, yet they may have a Father-in-law to help to bring up the Children which be married: and also that they will not leave their Sonnes without Wives, nor their Daughters without Husbands. (1583–91)

RALPH FITCH[120]

## 2. Marrying within tribe and trade

They [Indians] call a man Adam, from our first father Adam, whose wife tempted with the forbidden fruit, tooke it as they say and eate it downe, but as her husband swallowed it, the Hand of God stopped it in his throat, whence man hath a Bunch there, which women have not, called by them Adams Apple. As anciently among the Jewes, their Priesthood is hereditarie; for every Bramins sonne is a Priest, and marries a Bramins daughter; and so among all the Gentiles, the men take the daughters of those to bee their wives which are of their Fathers Tribe, Sect, and Occupation. For instance, a Merchants sonne marries a Merchants daughter. And every mans sonne that lives by his labour, marries the daughter of him that is of his owne profession, by which means they never advance themselves. These Gentiles take but one wife, of which they are not so fearefull as the Mahometans of their multitude, for they suffer them, to goe abroad. They are married yong, at six or seven yeeres old (their Parents making the Contracts) and about twelve come together. Their Nuptials, as those of the Mahometans, are performed with much pompe and jollitie. (1616)

EDWARD TERRY[121]

## 3. Second marriages not for women

Second marriages, which are indulg'd to the Men, are solemnly prohibited the Women, because this engages their Fidelity so much the more to the first Lovers, in that they are debarr'd all Hopes and Prospect of all others. But with this Additional Severity upon the young Maids, whose Husbands die before they cohabit, that they are obliged to a disconsolate Virginity all the Days of their Lives; and must never contract with another Man, tho' they are unfortunately Widows at Six or Seven Years of Age.

Polygamy likewise, besides second Marriages, is allowed the wanton Husbands, who notwithstanding are not often so very Amorous as to prosecute that Liberty, or rather Thraldom, to more Wives than one at once. The nature of the Climate inclines them much to this Amorous Passion, which stings them with impatient Desires, and makes them restless by Delays; and yet tho' Marriage upon this account is so very necessary and agreeable, they do not think that the variety of Women will compensate for the double Burthen and Inconvenience of them in a Family; nor do they imagin that it's worth their while to satisfie the fervour of their wandring

Desires, that is attended with such a train of mischievous Consequences. A merry *Bannian* was wont often to complain of this Folly, of engaging with two Wives at once, and venturing too hastily upon a double Marriage, because the fondness of the two Wives provoked them to continual Feuds and Jealousies. For he could never enjoy the one without disturbance to the other, whose Passions were presently alarm'd upon any token of Kindness extraordinary. When he was wheedled into a liking of the one, the other would pout and ask him if he meant to forsake her? And if he was going that way, would hold him by the Coat, and pull him back to her. This urg'd to him, that she was the Wife of his Youth, that they had contracted a long and intimate acquaintance, and his first solemn Engagements were made to her: The other replies to him, that she now ought to partake more liberally of his Favours, and his Thoughts should incline more kindly towards her, since the other possess'd him so long before. Thus the distracted Husband was twitted on both sides, and at a stand many times which way to turn for his own tranquility and their satisfaction, and often in his *Indian* English confest, *English fashion, sab, best fashion have, one Wife best for one Husband.* (1689)

J. OVINGTON[122]

## 4. *Hindu marriage ceremony*

Another instance, though of a less serious nature, occurred in the person of a palankeen bearer in our service, who asked leave to go to his village and be married. This was the only time of the year they do marry. His master told him that he could not spare him immediately, but that, before the marrying season was over, he should go. '*A, eha Saheb,*' 'Very well, Sir,' replied the bearer, 'next year will do as well.' Hence it may be concluded that parties in this country do not *always* marry from attachment; in fact, girls are betrothed by their parents before they attain their seventh birthday, without regard to difference of age in the man—being of the same *caste* is quite sufficient. When all arrangements are made, the bride elect, decked out in all her finery, is introduced to her intended husband, and then retires to feast with the females of both families; while the males regale separately for two or three days, or as long as the parents of the girl can afford it. They then return to their several occupations; and she is allotted an apartment in her father's house, out of which she must not stir again unveiled. About three years after this ceremony, she is supposed capable of managing a family, and the husband returns to claim her. The head man of the village is then applied to, who draws up the marriage contract, which he signs himself, and several other witnesses. They send cardamum seeds, as notices of invitation, (or cloves, if they are rich,) to all the persons they wish to see, notifying by a special messenger the day the marriage is to take place. These tokens are sent three days previous to the grand entertainment; but a smaller one is provided on the two former days, when none but very intimate friends are expected. On the second day, the women (all except the bride, and any sister or relative that she may have under seven years of age) go in procession to the house of the bridegroom, and tinge his head and the palms of his hands with *mindy* [henna], a sweetsmelling shrub, which, when bruised and mixed with water, produces a beautiful red colour. After this operation he adorns his person by putting on a yellow turban and waistband, with a pair of yellow cloth shoes, and mounting a horse or poney as gaily caparisoned as himself, returns with some of his own friends at the head of the procession, when, as I before mentioned, the parties regale themselves—the men on the outside of the house, under an awning erected for the occasion, the women within. Every member of the family to which she belongs, feels it incumbent upon them on this occasion to present some pledge of friendship. I have seen the daughter of a rich merchant, or of a banker, go off with two or three loaded waggons in her suite. The bridal party spend most part of their time in feasting, smoking, and parading the streets, accompanied by all sports of noisy instruments, to the great annoyance of the more peaceable inhabitants, particularly at night. The bride is conveyed from her father's house in a kind of covered cart, with curtains drawn closely round, (in which she contrives sometimes to make a small fracture just to peep through,) to that of her husband, attended by himself and his friends, some on horseback, some on foot, (but every one sports a little bit of yellow upon his person,) firing matchlocks, flourishing swords, and scampering round the bride's carriage with every demonstration of joy. Many other vehicles filled with company follow in her train, and the ceremony concludes with a wedding supper. The practice of using *mindy* is not confined to marriage ceremonies: no woman in Hindostan considers herself dressed without it. They rub it inside their hands and fingers, as well as at the roots of their nails, both of fingers and toes; while to heighten the brilliancy of

'Hindu Marriage Ceremony', drawn by Solvyns

their eyes, they describe a black line close to the edge of the lid with
a powder mixed in water, called *Soolmah:* this they perform by
dipping a small wooden bodkin into the mixture, and drawing it
gently along the eye-lash when the eye is closed.

This must have been an ancient custom in the East, for it is spoken
of in the second book of Kings, 'She put her eyes in painting.' They
also consider long hair as one of their principal ornaments, cutting it
only when the moon is in the increase; and it cannot be denied that
these women have the finest hair of any in the world; perhaps the
quantity of oil which they daily apply to the roots, may be an
additional reason for its being so extremely soft and luxuriant.

The Hindoos are uniformly tenacious in whatever respects ancient custom, but particularly so in regard to the difference of *caste*.
A young Hindoo girl, of superior beauty, had by chance been seen
and admired by a youth of the same religion, but of inferior *caste*.
Knowing the latter to be an insurmountable barrier to the parents'
consent, he at length prevailed on her to elope with and marry him
in his own village. Her family soon discovered their retreat, and
contrived by a stratagem to get her again in their power. Accordingly, her mother was despatched to negotiate the pretended reconciliation, and prevail on her to return, in order that the marriage
might be properly celebrated at her father's house. The poor girl,
delighted at the prospect of so fortunate an issue, readily accompanied her mother, and was received by her father and brother with
open arms. When three days had elapsed, and no marriage feast
been proclaimed, she began to suspect the treachery, and determined on seizing the first opportunity of returning to the husband
she had chosen. A favourable one seemed to present itself; but she
had not been gone long, before she was overtaken by her brother,
who affected to sympathise with, and offered to see her safe home.
The road lay through an unfrequented path, which taking advantage of, he drew his sword, and severed her head from the body. She
was found the next morning weltering in her blood. The father and
brother were immediately apprehended, and, wonderful to relate,
not only confessed the crime, but exulted in the accomplishment of
it: nor was it in the power of the Judge to punish them; for,
unhappily, the Mahometan law, by which natives of every description are tried, is so arbitrary as to invest parents with unlimited
authority over their children, even to the depriving them of life; and
it being proved in evidence that the son only obeyed his father's

orders, they were both acquitted. (1804-14)

A. DEARE[123]

## 5. *Marriages in India*

Certain it is that no Hindoo will have a marriage in his family during the four months of the rainy season; for among eighty millions of souls, not one doubts that the Great Preserver of the universe is, during these four months, down on a visit to Rajah Bull, and, consequently, unable to bless the contract with his presence. Marriage is a sacred duty among Hindoos, a duty which every parent must perform for his children, otherwise they owe him no reverence. A family, with a daughter unmarried after the age of puberty, is considered to labour under the displeasure of the gods; and no member of the other sex considers himself *respectable*, after the age of puberty, till he is married. It is the duty of his parent or elder brothers to have him suitably married; and if they do not do so, he reproaches them with his *degraded condition*. The same feeling, in a less degree, pervades all the Mahomedan community; and nothing appears so strange to them as the apparent indifference of old bachelors among us to their *sad condition*! Marriage, with all its ceremonies, its rights and its duties, fills their imagination from infancy to age; and I do not believe there is a country upon earth in which a larger portion of the wealth of the community is spent in the ceremonies, or where the rights are better secured, or the duties better enforced, notwithstanding all the disadvantages of the laws of polygamy. Not one man in ten can afford to maintain more than one wife, and not one in ten of those who can afford it will venture '*upon a sea of troubles,*' in taking a second, if he has a child by the first. One of the evils which press most upon Indian society, is the necessity which long usage has established of squandering large sums in marriage ceremonies. (*c.* 1830's)

WILLIAM HENRY SLEEMAN[124]

## 6. *A marriage*

1835, *March 18th*—Before entering on a description of the marriage ceremonies, it may be as well to explain the singular manner in which Colonel Gardner's family has intermarried with that of the Emperor of Delhi, which the annexed pedigree will exemplify.

William Gardner, Esq., of Coleraine, left a son.

William Gardner, Esq., Lieut.-Colonel in the 11th regiment of Dragoons. He married Elizabeth, daughter of Valentine Farrington, Esq., and had issue Valentine, born 1739, Allan, and other children. Allan was created a baronet, and afterwards elevated to the peerage in Ireland in 1800; and created a peer of the United Kingdom, 1806.

Valentine, the eldest son, a Major in the army, married, first, Alaida, daughter of Robert Livingstone, Esq., by whom he had a son, William Linnaeus, Captain in the army; and, secondly, Frances, daughter of Samuel Holworthy, Esq., by whom he had another son Valentine.

Colonel William Linnaeous Gardner married Nawab Matmunzelool-Nissa Begam Delme, and by her had two sons, Allan and James, and a daughter; the last mentioned died young.

Allan, the eldest son, married Beebee Sahiba Hinga, and left one son, Mungo, who died young, and two daughters, Hirmoozee and Susan. Hirmoozee married her relative, Steward William Gardner, Esq., son of Rear-Admiral Francis Gardner, the brother of Allan Hyde Lord Gardner. Susan, the second daughter, or Shubbeah Begam as she is called, is the one whose marriage is on the *tapis*.

James Gardner, the second son of Colonel William Linnaeus Gardner, married, first, Beebee Sahiba Banoo, by whom he had one son, Hinga, and two daughters, Alaida, the Morning Star, and the Evening Star. He married, secondly, Mulka Humanee Begam, and by her had four children, two sons and two daughters: Suliman and William Linnaeus; Nashaba Begam, and another girl.

Mirza Suliman Sheko, son of Shah Allum, the late Emperor of Delhi, and brother of Akbar Shah, the present Emperor, has a numerous family. Two of the daughters were celebrated for their beauty: one of them, Mulka Humanee Begam, married her cousin, Mirza Selim, the son of Akbar Shah, from whom she was divorced: she married, secondly, Mr. James Gardner. Sultana Boa, the other daughter, married Nusseer-ood-Deen Hvdur, the King of Oude. Mirza Unjun Sheko, son of Mirza Suliman Sheko, and half-brother of Mulka Begam, is engaged to Susan Gardner, as before mentioned.

Colonel Gardner was exceedingly unwilling to allow the marriage of his grand-daughter with the young prince, but the old Begam, his wife, had set her heart upon it. He would rather have seen her married to a European gentleman; but the Begam, who is an adopted daughter of the Emperor of Delhi, is delighted with the match,—in *her* eyes a fine alliance.

I must describe the bride, Susan Gardner, or, as she is called in the zenana, Shubbeah Begam, every lady having her name and title also. She had been cried up by the people at Agra as a great beauty, and Colonel Gardner had received several proposals for her, both from European and native gentlemen. She was also described as very accomplished for an inhabitant of four walls, being able to read, and write, and keep accounts with gram. She is about twenty years of age, very old for a bride in this country, where girls marry at eleven or twelve, and the proverb describes them as 'shrivelled at twenty'.

My surprise was great when I saw her in the zenana. Her complexion is pale and sallow, her face flat, her figure extremely thin, and far from pretty. Her flatterers called her 'so fair!' but she has not the fairness of a European, or the fine clear brown of some Asiatic ladies: her manners were also admired, but I did not like them, nor did she move stately as an elephant, an epithet applied to a woman having a graceful gait.

Unjun Sheko, the bridegroom, who is about twenty years of age, is a remarkable handsome man; his black curling hair hangs in long locks on each side his face; his eyes very large, long, and bright; his features fine; his complexion a clear brown; his figure the middle size; and like all natives, he wore a beard, moustache, and whiskers. His three brothers, who came to the wedding with him, are ugly, low caste looking men. Unjun's manners are good, theirs are cubbish. For four or five years he has been trying to bring about this marriage; but Colonel Gardner opposed it on account of his extravagance. His father, Suliman Sheko, has refused to give one rupee to the young couple, so that the whole expense of the wedding falls upon Colonel Gardner: he pays for both sides. The young prince has only an allowance of 100 rupees a month! Natives, especially native women, are curious beings; the whole pride of their lives consists in having had a grand wedding: they talk of it, and boast of it to the hour of their death. Colonel Gardner said, 'If I were to give Shubbeah the money that will be fooled away in display at this marriage, I should make her miserable; she would think herself disgraced; and although by custom she is not allowed to stir from her room, or to see the sight, still it will charm her to hear the road was lighted up for so many miles, the fireworks were so fine and the procession so grand! She would have this to talk of in preference to the money, even if she were forced to deprive herself of half her food all her life; she is a pakka Hindostanee!' They were horrified at my description of an English marriage. A carriage and four, attended by five or six other carriages, made a good wedding; when the ceremony had been performed by the padre, the bride and bridegroom drove away: no procession, no fireworks; the money put in the banker's hands, the parents gave a dinner and ball, and all was finished.

The Begam was in a perfect agony from morning till night, lest any one thing should be forgotten,—lest any, even the smallest gift might be omitted; if it were, the people would say, 'What a shabby wedding!' and, in spite of all the expense, she would lose her good name.

It would be utterly impossible for me to recount the innumerable ceremonies performed at the wedding of a Muhammadan; the following are a few of the most remarkable.

*March 12th*—The ceremonies began: In the first place, the bridegroom's party, consisting of Mr. James Gardner, Mulka Begam, Mrs. B——, and Mr. V.——, went into tents four miles distant; while the bride's party, consisting of Colonel Gardner, his Begam, the bride, and myself, remained at Khasgunge. We had also, in the outer house, Mr. Valentine Gardner, a party of English gentlemen, and the old Nawab of Cambay. It appeared curious to me to sit down to dinner with these gentlemen, who were all attired in native dresses, and do the honours, at times when my dear Colonel Gardner was too unwell to quit the zenana, and join the dinner party in the outer house. The turban is not a necessary appendage to Asiatic attire; in all friendly or familiar intercourse the skull cap is worn,—the turban in company; it is disgraceful to uncover the head.

But to return to my story. About 3 p.m., Mulka Begam came in procession to bring the bride's dress, which is a present from the bridegroom. The procession consisted of elephants, raths (four-wheeled native carriages drawn by bullocks), palanquins, led horses etc.; and one hundred trays, carried on men's heads, containing the dress for the bride, sweetmeats, and basun (flour of gram), wherewith to wash the lady. Mulka Begam came in a covered palanquin, screened from the gaze of men.

I, as in duty bound, had made my salam to Shubbeah Begam, and was in attendance in the zenana, to receive the bridegroom's party.

Women of the lower class, on entering the female assembly, must not say 'salam'; if the hostess be a lady of rank, they perform kudumbosee (the ceremony of kissing the feet) to her, and merely make salam to the rest. When going away they request permission, in the same way as the men in the male assembly, and take their departure.

Kudumbosee, or the ceremony of kissing the feet, is, rather, to touch the feet of the hostess with the right hand, and then kiss the latter, or, more generally, make salam with it; while her ladyship, scarce allowing it to be done, out of politeness and condescension, withdraws her foot; and, taking hold of her hands, says, 'Nay, don't do that!' or 'Enough!' 'Long may you live!' 'Come, be seated!' Or, if she be married, 'May God render your *sohag* durable!' *i.e.* May God preserve your husband: if he be dead, 'May God cause your end to be happy!'

The men of the better ranks of society, however, when coming in or going away, say, 'Salam, bundugee tuslemat!' *i.e.* 'My blessing, service, or salutation to you!' according to the rank of the lady of the house.

The salam made by females is not like that of the males—touching the forehead with the right hand—but it consists in touching the *puttee*, or hair above the right temple.

Speaking of men entering a zenana, the place is considered so sacred, that, in a native family, only the nearest male relatives, the father and grandfather, can unrestrainedly obtain admission; the uncles and brothers only on especial occasions. The bride was once allowed to be seen by the brothers of Mirza Selim, her betrothed husband; but he requested that no other persons but Colonel and Mr. James Gardner might behold her, and said, after marriage, he should not allow her to be seen even by his own brothers.

The trays containing the presents, brought in procession from the Prince, were received by the female slaves, conveyed by them into the zenana, and placed before Colonel Gardner's Begam and the Princess Mulka. It is a custom never to send back an empty tray; if money be not sent, part of the contents of the tray is left, fruit, flowers, etc. The presents were displayed on the ground before the bride, who was sitting on a charpai, wrapped in an Indian shawl, hiding her face, and sobbing violently; I thought she was really in distress, but found this violent sorrow was only a part of the ceremony. Mulka Begam took a silver bowl, and putting into it sandalwood powder and turmeric and oil, mixed it up, whilst both she and Colonel Gardner's Begam repeated with great care the names and titles on both sides; it being unlucky if any name be forgotten, as any evil that may chance to befall the bride hereafter would be occasioned by forgetfulness, or mistaking the name over this oily mixture. The bride was then rubbed from head to foot with it; how yellow it made her, the turmeric! The natives say it makes the skin *so beautiful, so yellow,* and so soft: it certainly renders the skin deliciously soft, but the yellow tinge I cannot admire. After this operation was performed, all the mixture was scraped up, put into the bowl, and mixed with more oil, to be sent to the Prince, that his body might be rubbed with it—this is considered a compliment!

The bridal dress was then put on Shubbeah; it was of yellow gauze, trimmed with silver; the pajamas of red satin and silver. The faces of the attendants were smeared by way of frolic with the oily mixture, and the bridegroom's party returned to their tents. I must not forget to mention that from the moment the bride is rubbed with this turmeric, she is a prisoner for ten days; not allowed to move from her charpai, on which she sits up or sleeps. Twice a day she is rubbed with almond soap, mixed with turmeric, etc. All this time she is never allowed to bathe; she is fed on sweet-meats, and not allowed to touch acids, or vinegar, etc.: even pan is almost denied; but I fancy, without it an Asiatic lady would fret herself to death. And in this horrible state, a girl is kept during all the gaiety of the wedding; never allowed to move; to make her skin soft and yellow, and to render her sweet-tempered, I suppose, by feeding her with lumps of sugar!

As soon as the bridegroom's party were gone, Colonel Gardner requested me to go in procession, with his pretty grand-daughter, Alaida (the Morning Star), to the Prince's tents, to escort the dress of the bridegroom, sent as a present by the bride. We went accordingly in full procession, as described before, taking back the oily mixture. Mulka Begam received us at the Prince's tent; he was placed on a silver footstool; Mulka took off his upper dress, and rubbed his face and arms with the mixture; she then arrayed him in a dress of yellow and orange muslin, a red turban, and red silk pajamas, in which attire he looked very handsome.

Before him sat three women, the Domnee, playing and singing bridal songs; I saw the Prince turn very red; he looked at the women, and said something in a low tone to Mulka Begam, who

answered,—'The mem sahiba knows they are singing galee (abuse);
but she does not understand Hindostanee sufficiently to comprehend their songs.' The language of the songs is complete *slang*.
Yellow powder, mixed with water, was then thrown in frolic at all
the people; I made my salam, quitted the tent, and finding a gentleman in waiting ready to drive me back, returned to Colonel
Gardner's, leaving the rest of the party to play and sing all night.
Thus ended the first day of the ceremonies. (1835)

FANNY PARKES[125]

## ·D. PROCESSIONS

### 1. A nuptial procession

We were amused by the sight of a splendid nuptial procession, on
account of the betrothal of the son of a neighbouring Raja to the
daughter of a Thakoor. The little boy passed on an elephant, with a
long array of kettle-drums, trumpets, and standards before him as
well as a very handsome palanquin, in which two brothers, still
younger than himself, were conveyed. In his passage through the
streets of the town, fire-works were let off at intervals, and all the
roofs of the houses, as well as the ramparts of the fort, were covered
with spectators. The towns-people were very civil in securing us a
good place, and seemed pleased with the interest which I felt in the
show, and with my wishing the little bridegroom 'good luck.' They
told me that he was to be taken for that evening to the house of his
new father-in-law, where the ceremony of affiancing took place, but
that he and the little girl were to remain for some years with their
respective parents, when the second and real marriage would be
celebrated. (1825)

REGINALD HEBER[126]

### 2. The tanda

The *tanda* or caravan, consisting of four thousand bullocks, has
been kept up amidst all the evils which have beset this land, through
Mogul and Mahratta tyranny. The utility of these caravans, as
general carriers to conflicting armies, and as regular tax-paying
subjects, has proved their safe-guard, and they were too strong to be
pillaged by any petty marauder, as any one who has seen a Bunjarri
encampment will be convinced. They encamp in a square; their
grain-bags piled over each other breast-high, with interstices left

for their matchlocks, make no contemptible fortification. Even the
ruthless Toork, Jemshid Khan, set up a protecting tablet in favour of
the Charuns of Murlah, recording their exemption from *dind*
contributions, and that there should be no increase in duties, with
threats to all who should injure the community. As usual, the sun
and moon are appealed to as witnesses of good faith, and sculptured
on the stone. Even the forester Bhil and mountain Mair have set up
their signs of immunity and protection to the chosen of Hinglaz; and
the figure of a cow and its *kairie* (calf), carved in rude relief, speak
the agreement that they should not be slain or stolen within the
limits of Murlah. (1832)

JAMES TOD[127]

## 3. The grand display

The bride is denominated dulhan on the day of Sachak, and the
bridegroom dulha. The poor dulhan is kept in strict parda on her
charpai; the dulha ought by law to be equally confined, but he
generally contrives to amuse himself during the time. After the
bride and bridegroom had been rubbed a certain number of days
with the oily mixture, the time appointed for the second day's
ceremonies arrived; which is called the Sachak. Mulka Begam and
the prince arrived in procession. The bridegroom's party were
dressed out in all their bravery. The party of the bride wore their old
clothes, and looked as deplorable as possible. This was according to
custom, and therefore strictly observed. On this day it is the fashion
for the bride's mother to appear in an undress, and even that soiled!
The procession consisted of elephants in all their crimson and gold
trappings, led horses, English and Arab nalkis, a sort of litter used
by people of rank, palanquins, and raths (native bullock carriages),
etc. A number of men dressed up as horses were prancing about,
kicking and playing antics, and two hundred gharas (eastern vessels) filled with sweetmeats, which looked very gay from being
covered with silver-leaf, were carried on the heads of two hundred
men.

The platforms for the nach women were the most curious part of
the procession, they are called takhti-rawan, a sort of travelling
throne, formed of bamboo, square in form, over which was spread
an awning ornamented with crimson, and gold, and silver, and
supported by four bamboos, one at each angle of the platform. On
each travelling throne sat a native musician, playing on a kettle-

drum, and before him danced two nach women; the girls twirled and
nached with all their might and skill. The platforms were *carried on
the heads* of a number of men in the procession, and had a curious
and singular effect; the situation was a very unsteady one for the
dancing girls, one of whom became giddy and tumbled down upon
the heads of the crowd of people below. In this fashion ten stands,
containing twenty nach girls and ten musicians, were carried on
men's heads to the sound of kettle-drums. When Mulka had
brought in the procession, and the company were seated, atr of
sandal-wood was put on each person's face, and a necklace of silver
tissue around their necks. The same three vile old women began
their songs of abuse; abusing the prince, the Begams, and myself;
but as it was the custom, no one could be angry. I could only guess
the sort of abuse; I could not understand it, never having heard it
before. The prince's yellow dress, now quite dirty, was on him still;
according to custom, *over* it was put on a dress of cloth of gold and
crimson. In front of his turban the jewelled jika was placed, and on
his arms valuable bazubunds—armlets of precious stones. All this
time the poor little bride was kept in her oily attire on her charpai,
and not allowed to stir. She only heard the noise and uproar of the
procession. Mulka's dress was very elegant. (1835)

FANNY PARKES[128]

## 4. *Religious processions*

Many of my countrymen, full of virtuous indignation at the outrages
which often occur during the processions of the Mohorum, particularly when these happen to take place at the same time with some
religious procession of the Hindoos, are very anxious that our
government should interpose its authority to put down both. But
these processions and occasional outrages are really sources of great
strength to us; they show at once the necessity for the interposition
of an impartial tribunal, and a disposition on the part of the rulers to
interpose impartially. The Mahomedan festivals are regulated by
the lunar, and those of the Hindoos by the solar year; and they cross
each other every thirty or forty years, and furnish fair occasions for
the local authorities to interpose effectually. People who receive or
imagine insults or injuries, commonly postpone their revenge till
these religious festivals come round, when they hope to be able to
settle their accounts with impunity among the excited crowd. The

mournful procession of the Mohurum, when the Mahomedans are
inflamed to madness by the recollection of the really affecting
incidents of the massacre of the grandchildren of their prophet, and
by the images of their tombs, and their sombre music, crosses that of
the Hoolee, in which the Hindoos are excited to tumultuous and
licentious joy by their bacchanalian songs and dances every thirty-
six years; and they reign together for some four or five days, during
which the scene, in every large town, is really terrific. The processions are liable to meet in the street, and the lees of the wine of the
Hindoos, or the red powder which is substituted for them, is liable to
fall upon the tombs of the others. Hindoos pass on, forgetting in
their saturnalian joy, all distinctions of age, sex, or religion, their
clothes and persons besmeared with the red powder, which is mois-
tened and thrown from all kinds of machines over friend and foe;
while meeting these come the Mahomedans, clothed in their green
mourning, with gloomy downcast looks, beating their breasts, ready
to kill themselves, and too anxious for an excuse to kill anybody
else. Let but one drop cf the lees of joy fall upon the image of the
tomb as it passes, and a hundred swords fly from their scabbards;
many an innocent person falls; and woe be to the town in which the
magistrate is not at hand with his police and military force. Proudly
conscious of their power, the magistrates refuse to prohibit one class
from laughing because the other happens to be weeping; and the
Hindoos, on such occasions, laugh the more heartily to let the world
see that they are free to do so. (1844)

WILLIAM HENRY SLEEMAN[129]

## E. BAZAARS

### 1. Bazaars in Delhi

Here [in Delhi] the costly merchandise is generally kept in
warehouses, and the shops are seldom decked with rich or showy
articles. For one that makes a display of beautiful and fine cloths,
silk, and other stuffs striped with gold and sliver, turbans embroidered with gold, and brocades, there are at least five-and-twenty
where nothing is seen but pots of oil or butter, piles of baskets filled
with rice, barley, chick-peas, wheat, and an endless variety of other
grain and pulse, the ordinary aliment not only of the *Gentiles,* who
never eat meat, but of the lower class of *Mahometans,* and a considerable portion of the military.

There is, indeed, a fruit-market that makes some show. It contains many shops which during the summer are well supplied with dry fruit from *Persia, Balk, Bokara,* and *Samarkande*; such as almonds, pistachios, and walnuts, raisins, prunes, and apricots; and in winter with excellent fresh grapes, black and white, brought from the same countries, wrapped in cotton; pears and apples of three or four sorts, and those admirable melons which last the whole summer. These fruits are, however, very dear; a single melon selling for a crown and a half. (1656–68)

FRANCOIS BERNIER[130]

## 2. Bazaar, or market scene

The figure in the foreground, resting upon a staff, and holding in his left hand a kind of gourd scooped into the form of a lota (which is a brass utensil common throughout Hindostan), represents an Indian beggar. He lives upon the contributions of his fellow-man. Here and there a little flour is put into his pot, always kept held out to receive whatever the charitably disposed may give him. In this way the beggar soon picks up enough for a meal, which is a very simple one. He wants but water, and adding it to the flour, makes for himself a few cakes called chapatties. These are heated; and then, with a drought of water to assist the repast, the Faqueer settles down to enjoy himself. What the beggar is in England, the Faqueer is in India; with this difference, that whereas the former is considered next akin to a vagrant, and (though often deserving of the alms which he solicits) is held in the very lowest esteem, the latter, taking religious devotion as the apparent basis of his conduct, is not only tolerated as a privileged member of society (imposter would be a better word) but is, on account of his prescribed austerities, even regarded with honour and respect. These Faqueers are, in many instances, sad rogues, and very immoral. Religion with such is merely a cloak for every species of wickedness. Some coat themselves over with all kinds of filth, and in consequence become objects of disgust. Some there are who, completely wrapped up in the benighting folds of idolatry, with fervency and zeal undertake and perform penances which excite our wonder, hoping thereby to ensure for themselves endless happiness in heaven. It is a fearful sight, indeed, when we see the human mind, formed to look up to God with simple veneration, gratitude, and love, as the author of its

'A Bazaar or Market Scene', drawn by Charles Richard Francis

existence, prostrating its powers to a level with those of the beasts, over whom it was, by the Fiat of that God, constituted lord. The author once saw in central India a Hindoo devotee standing upon one leg, with the other doubled, and fastened to his body. With the right hand he held a rope, which was attached to a branch of the tree under which he was standing; the other hand was free. In this position the wretched creature had been fixed for seven years! He had inflicted the penance upon himself as a sacrifice which, he hoped, was pleasing to his Gods. The muscles had, of course, become perfectly rigid, and considerably reduced in size. The necessaries of life were supplied by neighbouring villagers, who admired the Faqueer's devotion. Indeed, so far as assistance was needed, he always had it. Contrasting the withering effects of the religion of the Hindoo with those produced by the practice of a pure and elevated Christianity, how fervently ought we all to long for the time, when India shall appreciate the full blessings of the Gospel of Christ, and become emancipated from the trammels of Paganism by which she is now so closely fettered!

To the right of the beggar is seen a female carrying a child upon her hip. This is a very common custom: often do the native women, when they leave their houses to draw water, take with them in this way a child that is either too young to be left, or who is especially dear.

The market scene here represented was sketched at Poshkur. The structure of the buildings is different to that which is usually met with throughout the plains of India. Here, however, as elsewhere, native character remains the same; and the author has endeavoured to depict a somewhat amusing scene which occurred during his stay in the town. A grain-seller was seated in the market place, quietly talking with a traveller from Delhi; suddenly there stopped in front of them an elderly female, a vendor of earthern pots, who began to pour forth a torrent of language evidently of a very angry nature. It appeared that she was explaining to the traveller (whom she had never before seen), the nature of some fancied wrongs. She probably thought that he, having seen a little of men and manners in his travels, would be likely to give an impartial opinion upon the merits of the case. Her story, however, had the effect of eliciting smiles from all around, rather than sympathy. The word Bazaar naturally raises in the mind of an Englishman the idea of a place similar to the Pantheon, or the Bazaar in Soho Square. We merely require to take

it in a general sense, to understand its meaning at once. The word
Bazaar is Persian, and implies market. In India it is a market of
provisions; in England one of fancy goods. (1848)

CHARLES RICHARD FRANCIS[131]

## 3. The Chandney Chowk

Leaving the Fort, you find yourself in a broad, cleanly-looking road,
along which we will pass, and diverge into the town itself. Traversing some narrow streets, crowded with busy people, and lined by the
funniest of shops, gaily painted, and at this early hour of the morning well filled with customers, we emerge presently into *the*
thoroughfare of Delhi—the Chandney Chowk. Here the shops
present a very improved appearance over the generality of native
bazaars, and there is a manifest air of well-to-doism prevailing.
Extending nearly its entire length is an avenue of fine shady trees,
and on either side are several buildings, very pretentious in point of
decorative art: the cornices and walls being raised in rich arabesque
stuccoed relief, and ornamented with floral designs in pigment. But
the decoration is necessarily of very temporary duration, and needs
frequent renewal. The majority of the houses and shops, however,
are unornamented, and of a most heterogenous character, as much
so in their outer appearance as in the nature of their contents, which
embrace every known oriental art-manufacture; their neatly-
clothed turbaned owners outside, beseeching (in Parsee-English)
an inspection of their wares, and playing no unimportant part in
the general picturesqueness and effect of the scene.

Most of the houses have shallow projecting balconies of a highly
insecure appearance, in which, in the cool of the evening, the native
'merchant,' or shop-keeper, and his family may be seen enjoying
their *otium* over a *hubble-bubble,* and clad in the most invitingly
cool deshabille of white flowing muslin. (1866)

F.F. WYMAN[132]

## 4. Shops in Calcutta

In the first number of this work, a graphic representation was given
of a bazaar, or street of shops, in the outskirts of Calcutta. The
present illustration deals in detail with a component of one of the
great bazaars—a single Indian shop, at which the necessaries of life,

'A Native Shop in a Calcutta Bazaar', drawn by William Simpson

as rice, peas, and other kind of grain, are sold. These great marts,
with the exception of the China Bazar (or rather Bazaars, for there
are the 'Old China Bazaar' and the 'New China Bazaar'), are little
visited by Europeans. In these, however, is to be found every article
of household equipment—beds, tables, chairs, couches, glass, crockery, knives and forks, tablelinen—to say nothing of endless supplies of beer and wine and 'oilman's stores.' In some of the shops the
produce of the Celestial Empire is sold by Chinamen; but the
majority are presided over by Bengalees, and 'Europe goods' are
the principal articles of merchandise. To the 'griffin,' or newly-
arrived Englishmen, a visit to the China Bazaar is the source of
considerable amusement. The shopkeepers speak the English language, and can write it, too, with sufficient correctness for all
purposes of trade. Their almost invariable system is to ask, in the
first instance, more than they expect to receive, or are contented to
get, for their goods. Fortified by a knowledge of this little fact, the
purchaser resorts at once to the process of 'cheapening' every article
that is offered, bidding, perhaps, as much under, as the 'asking
price' is over, the real value of the goods. The result is generally a
compromise, by which the goods are obtained at about one half the
price that was first demanded from the customer. This kind of direct
personal intercourse between native sellers and European buyers is
limited to such goods as I have indicated above—the ordinary
articles of food in daily consumption, as meat, fish, vegetables, etc.
being purchased in the bazaars by our native servants. Europeans
are generally charged for such purchases more than their market
value; but when an Englishman has endeavoured to market for
himself he has almost always found the experiment a failure. (1867)

                                    JOHN WILLIAM KAYE[133]

## F.  BURNING GHATS AND BURIAL GROUNDS

### 1.  *Funeral customs*

When a person dies, those who attend the funeral raise lamentable
cries and weep together. They rend their garments and loosen their
hair; they strike their heads and beat their breasts. There are no
regulations as to dress for mourning, nor any fixed time for observing it.
    There are three methods of paying the last tribute to the dead: (1)

by cremation—wood being made into a pyre, the body is burnt; (2) by water—the body is thrown into deep flowing water and abandoned: (3) by desertion—the body is cast into some forest-wild, to be devoured by beasts.

When the king dies, his successor is first appointed, that he may preside at the funeral rites and fix the different points of precedence. Whilst living they give [their rulers] titles according to their character [virtue]; when dead there are no posthumous titles.

In a house where there has been a death there is no eating allowed; but after the funeral they resume their usual [habits]. There are no anniversaries [of the death] observed. Those who have attended a death they consider unclean; they all bathe outside the town and then enter their houses.

The old and infirm who come near to death, and those entangled in a severe sickness, who fear to linger to the end of their days, and through disgust wish to escape the troubles of life, or those who desire release from the trifling affairs of the world and its concerns [the concerns of life], these, after receiving a farewell meal at the hands of their relatives or friends, they place, amid the sounds of music, on a boat which they propel into the midst of the Ganges, where such persons drown themselves. They think thus to secure a birth among the Devas. Rarely one of these may be seen not yet dead on the borders [of the river]. (625–45)

HIUEN TSIANG[134]

## 2. Mohammedan tombs

Now concerning their burials: every Mahometan of Qualitie in his life time, provides a faire Sepulcher for himselfe and kindred, encompassing with a firme wall a good circuit of ground, neere some Tanke (about which they delight for to burie their dead) or else in a place nigh Springs of Water, that may make pleasant Fountaynes, neere which hee erects a Tombe round or square, vaulted upon Pillars, or else made close, to be entred with Doores, under which are the bodies of the dead interred. The rest of the ground they plant with Trees and Flowers, as if they would make Elysian fields, such as the Poets dreamed of, wherein their soules might take their repose. They burie not within their Churches. There are many goodly Monuments of this kinde richly adorned, built to the memorie of

such as they have esteemed Saints, of which they have a large
Kalender. In these are Lamps continually burning, whither men
transported with blinde devotion daily resort, there to contemplate
the happines these Pieres (for so they call them) enjoy. But among
many faire Piles there dedicated to this use, the most excellent is at
Secandra, a Village three miles from Agra. It was beganne by
Achabar-sha, this Kings Father, who there lyes buried, and finished
by this present King, who meanes to lye beside him. (1616)

EDWARD TERRY[135]

## 3. Funeral ceremonies

All Hindus burn their dead, except the infamous sect of the Lingam.
These bury the bodies, not in their temples—for that, in this country, would be the most abominable sacrilege that could be
committed—but in a field distant from their dwellings. As to all
other castes, they also burn them in a field distant from the town or
village, which each locality has set apart expressly for this purpose.

The mode of burning the body is as follows: First of all, no
Brahman, however rich he may be, is allowed to die within his
house, for in their belief all within it would be thereby defiled. This
is the reason that before he expires they carry him into a courtyard,
and there place him under a sort of gallery, which every house has
for the purpose. Should it happen that the Brahman dies a sudden
death within the house, they carry the body at once, with all imaginable haste, and place it under the gallery alluded to. Then, breaking
all the earthen vessels in the house, all the inmates quit it, and do not
re-enter it until it has been well rubbed over with cowdung, and
until, as one may say, the interdict has been removed by a number of
ceremonies, used by them for this purpose.

When a Brahman dies, all his female relations and female friends
stand in a circle, and with their stomachs bared beat themselves
severely with their two hands, weeping for the dead; and, moving
round, they sing a song learnt for the purpose. It is extremely well
suited to the conditions of the time and place in which they find
themselves. After they have been round three times in this fashion,
they bathe the body, dress it in new clothes, put some ground
*sandal*-wood on the forehead, and then deposit it in a sort of coffin
which is quite open. It may be interjected here that this coffin is
made just as our hand-barrows for manure, constructed like them

from pieces of wood tied together with straw. Then four Brahmans carry the body to the burning-ground. They are preceded by a sort of shrine, highly ornamented and covered with flowers. Having arrived at the cemetery, they perform for him all the usual ceremonial, and burn him with all the solemnities that I have remarked upon in regard to their marriages.

After the body has been burnt, the Brahmans bathe their bodies, and wash the pieces of cloth which they used for clothing themselves. All dripping as they are, they put these on again and return home. Thence they proceed to the house of the deceased, where a feast is given. On that day it is served under some palm-trees, which they say represent the deceased. There for the space of ten days all the friends and relations weep for the deceased; each of the nearest relations gives a sort of petticoat they call a *panes (punjam)* to the deceased's widow, and his brothers subscribe and give her a half-moon of silver.

On the tenth day, after loud lamentation, the deceased's widow flings her arms round the neck of another widow, weeping and displaying all imaginable signs of grief. Meanwhile, all the other widows present cut off the piece of gold attached to her neck, which they call a *tali*. It should be noted that no married women may take part in this act, which constitutes the woman a widow.

Every year upon the anniversary of her husband's death a young widow performs a holocaust, feeds four or five Brahmans, and if she is rich she also gives them clothes. She does the same every month at the new moon, but with less expense and formality. Whatever is essential in funerals of the Brahman caste is also common to the other castes. This is the reason that I shall not say anything special about them, and I pass on to the opinions held about Europeans, known to them under the name of Farangis. (1653–1708)

NICCOLAO MANUCCI[136]

## 4. *The Dutch burial-ground*

But, we are amid Tombs—in the Dutch burial-ground: fewer in number but greater in variety are the monuments, shrouded by the wild custard-apple trees that luxuriate here in wantonness, or embraced by some wild parasite, which the scorching heat of October has not been able to destroy. The cemetery occupies rather an elevated site; and, as the area is entered, to the left may be noticed

'The Burning Ghat at Calcutta', *Illustrated London News*, 25 Oct. 1879

a small hut tenanted by a gardener and his family, who maintain a thriving livelihood by the proceeds of the fruit grown here, and the *mendhi (Lawsonia inermis)* dried within the shade of the larger sarcophagi. Grand, noble, for the expanse of ground it covers, its height, its peculiar style of sculpture—is the mausoleum erected over the last resting-place of M. VAN REEDE, whom Oriental History pays the tribute of eulogy in denominating the *Moecenas of Malabar*. At a period when European residents in India wholly directed their attention to mercantile adventure, or attempted political aggrandizement, *he* could spare the leisure to devote to scientific research; and his labors have provided Holland with many valuable manuscripts and other equally important curiosities, while some of his statements still challenge enquiry. His *Hortus Indus Malabaricus,* a work in twelve volumes folio, is an evidence of his literary exertions. It was Baron Reede's translation of the Copper inscriptions in the Jewish Synagogue at Cochin which elicited that severe scrutiny on the part of Dr. CLAUDIUS BUCHANAN (who accompanied the Marquis of Wellesley to India) into their originality. Several other circumstances in relation to the government and private department of this extraordinary man are before the public, but they fall within the compass of a graver work than the present.

A figure approaching that of the decagon with pillars running along the open varanda, compass a walled apartment pierced with carved wooden windows: in the centre of this chamber a single tomb-stone marks a vault with more occupants than the Dutch official. Three of the niches around the room are indulged with wooden tablets: one, hanging above the head of the tomb, recounts the subjoined particulars of M. Van Reede; another facing it is scarcely legible; while one portion of the third—which is placed midway—dangles by a nail upon the wall, and its remnant is to be seen without among a lot of rubbish and dried mendhi. A spiral stone stairway leading directly from, and to the left of the tomb, conducts to the strong exposed terrace, with plain columns supporting a cupola of no particular school of design—though the Islamite style has doubtless been studied throughout—but combining a taste for the fanciful and an anxiety for the superb. STAVORINUS writing in 1775, remarks —'The burying-place of the Dutch merits the attention of the traveller, as there is scarcely any grave that has not a tomb with lofty spires upon it; the meanest have a grave-stone with a sculptured epitaph. That of M. Van Reede,

Commissionary General of the East India Company over the Western Factories, excels all the others in largeness of dimension, elegance of architecture, magnificence of ornament, and richness of material, and is kept in repair at the expence of the Company; for which purpose not long ago, about six thousand rupees, or nine thousand guilders, were charged in account to the Company.' The English translator of his work adds a note worth the transcribing—'When *Thevenot* was at Surat, this monument was then building: *Ovington* mentions it and calls it a noble pile.'

*The Inscription*
HIER RUST
HEI LICHAAM VAN
ZYN HOOG EDELHEYT
D.H.—*Hendrik Adriaan*
*Baron Van Reede*
TOT *Drakesteyn* HEERE VAN
*Meydiegt*
ONDER DE ORDRE VAN DE RIDDER
SCHAB EN UYT DE SELVE ORDRE
GECOMMITTEERD IN DE ORDINARIS
GEDEPUTEER DE VAN D'ED ..MOGEND
HEEREN STAATEN S LANDS VAN
*Utregt*
COMMISSARIS VAN DE GENERALE
NEDERLANDER GEOCTROYEER DE
OOST INDISCHE COMPAGNIE OVER
*India*
REPRESENTERENDE IN DIER QUALITE
De VERGADERINCE DER ED ..H ...
XVII ..
OVEBLEDER DEN 15 ..DECEMBER.
AO 1691
OP't SCHIP DREGTERLANT ZYLENDE
VAN *Cochim* NAAR *Souratta*
OP DE HOOGLE VAN DE ENGELSE
STERKTE *Bombai;*
OUD ON GEVAER
*56 Jaaren.*

The armorial bearings painted on a black field upon two pieces of wood, cut in lozenge form, may be discovered amid a heap of broken timber without the mausoleum—the painting is sadly defaced. The only portion which could be deciphered of the slab facing M. Van Reede's epitaph runs to the following purport.

BASTIANA THEODORA D'LE BOUCQ
*Grenulinni van den E.: E: Agtl: Heer*
JAN SCHREUDER
*Directeur en Opper Geluder*
7 MAY 1743.

A Ship's Steward—who is reputed to have been the father of a Prince of Orange, and a vicious wine-bibber—is said to have had a tomb here, crowned by a clay punch-bowl, in which his favourite drink was mixed once a week by his friends to regale upon; each point of the tomb was also furnished with the resemblance of a sugar-loaf. The tomb upon Stavorinus's visit was in decay. Carelessness and time have worked both sufficiently and efficiently in this desolation. It was mentioned to me, that the Dutch Government at one time allowed a trifling annuity to the Roman Catholic clergyman here to look after the cemetery: distance (coupled perhaps with other and less disagreeable circumstances) appears to have blunted those sensitive impressions which early associations had fostered, and this gratuity has been permitted to lapse, followed by neglect on the part of the priest to the trust with which he had once been charged. (1847)

HENRY GEORGE BRIGGS[137]

# 6. Poverty

## A. GENERAL

### 1. Misery of the poor

Where such acts of injustice and oppression are committed with
impunity, it is not wonderful that there should be much misery
among the poorer orders of the community. When grain is dear,
hundreds of poor families are driven to the most distressing shifts
to obtain a bare subsistence. At such times I have seen women
and children employed in picking out the undigested grains of corn
from the dung of the different animals about the camp. Even now,
when grain is by no means at a high price (wheat being sold in the
market for thirteen *seers* for the rupee), it is scarcely possible to
move out of the limits of our own camp, without witnessing the most
shocking proofs of poverty and wretchedness. I was returning from
a ride the other morning, when two miserable looking women
followed me for charity: each had a little infant in her arms; and one
of them repeatedly offered to sell hers for the trifling sum of two
rupees. Many of our Sipahees and servants have children whom
they have either purchased in this manner, or picked up begging,
among our tents. In adopting these little wretches, however, they
have so often been taken in, that they are now more cautious in
indulging their charitable propensities. The poor people of the army
finding that a child, who told a piteous tale and appeared to be
starving, was sure to find a protector in our camp, used, in hard
times, to send their children out to beg; and when better able to
support them themselves, would pretend to discover their lost
infants, and reclaim them. (1809)

THOMAS DUER BROUGHTON[138]

### 2. The sepoy: his extreme poverty

Turn we now to a sepoy on the line of march. We will suppose him in
the ranks. We have seen his means of subsistence; we know how he

feeds, how he is clothed, and how he can undergo his duties in garrison. Now let the reader patiently follow me a little longer, and I will show him the miseries, the privations, and the fatigues to which he is exposed while marching. Before starting, a sepoy generally receives an advance of pay; perhaps he has it in full, or only half, according to the pleasure of the commanding officer, or the distance he has to go. With this advance of pay he has to clear himself from the station (for probably he has incurred debts), besides paying an advance equal to one half, or altogether, as the case may be, for the means of conveying his goods and chattels, as well as his numerous family, some of whom, particularly the young and aged, are unable to walk.

Exclusively of all this, he has to provide the means of sustenance for himself and dependants, and that with a total of perhaps two rupees in his pocket, for a journey of about two or three or four hundred miles! How can he do this? Impossible! He must starve and so must his family; at all events, they must from sheer necessity feed themselves upon the most economical plans that they can possibly devise.

Curry and rice are luxuries they dare not think of. Plain boiled rice is not so expensive, and of that they sometimes do manage to have a treat, about two mouthsful each. Bread or biscuits, or *chuppatees* (cakes made of rice flour), are quite out of the question. Butter-milk with a green chili after it, and now and then a bit of salt fish by way of a relish, is generally their sole food; and parched peas, or raw *chenna* (or grain), forms a kind of variety which they chew, resembling the cud of bitter poverty in every sense of the word.

Upon this sort of diet have they to support nature, and be fit for the duties to which they are called in the camp and on the route. The sepoy has to take his tour of guard once every three days (sometimes oftener), exposed at nights to the damp chilly dew, and perhaps be drenched with rain, being obliged to remain so for hours together during the whole night, and march the next morning without change of clothes, and without any food or other description of creature comfort, save a pot full of that abominable trash, butter-milk.

On arriving at the next stage, he has no comfortable breakfast, no hot coffee, no dram, nothing except some cold rice and water of the preceding day to satisfy his hunger. All this time he has to carry his pack, firelock, and accoutrements; his chaco, his pouch full of ball cartridges; the body emaciated and rendered feeble from want of proper sustenance; how is it possible for the wretched man to go through all this without breaking down? (1833–42)

ALBERT HERVEY[139]

## 3. On the growing poverty of India

It is admitted on every hand that India has increased in wealth in the large towns, that is, in about one-tenth of her total population, though even there it may be doubted whether any but the capitalistic classes, bankers, moneylenders, contractors, large merchants, have, in this respect, profited appreciably by British rule. But what of the remaining nine-tenths—the vast agricultural and rural population, classes that never have thriven under British rule at home, whether we examine them in England, Scotland, or Ireland? The problem is not an easy one, for the conditions of life vary so greatly in Britain and India that the standards of comfort do not seem reducible to a common denominator.

We learn that the English standard of comfort among the labouring classes has increased since the time of Henry VII, because shoes and stockings are now a necessary, not a luxury, that mattresses and feather beds and pillows are now quite common where formerly a truss of hay did duty. But in India we have hardly any data to judge by, 'mean folk' were even less observed in the East than in the West, not to mention that the standard of comfort does not run to piling clothes on one's person in the East, still less to feather beds.

It must be a perception of the difficulty of finding facts on the subject and of marshalling them so as to elicit any meaning or definite conclusion, that makes optimists favourable to English rule and its immense benefits, have recourse not to an attempt to compare standards that are hardly comparable, but to a totally different class of facts, facts which cannot be controverted except as to the bearing they have on the subject under consideration.

India's prosperity under our rule is commonly as much assumed as are Euclid's twelve axioms. Should any bold Griffin at any Anglo-Indian dinner-table decline to admit the assumption, of course merely in jest, any one of the following is supposed to prove the conclusion completely; the whole taken together form an imposing array of premises leading irresistibly to the conclusion for which the bold one demanded proofs. There has been a rise in rents under our rule; population has increased; so have exports and imports; produce has risen in price; railways, bridges, irrigation canals and other public works have increased at an unprecedented rate; the government takes only a small share of the gross produce of the cultivators, probably one-sixth or even a seventh. Only the last of these can be disproved; but even if all the other statements could be fully established, there is not one of them that fully proves the conclusion desired . . .

During the last thirty years much anxiety has been caused to the Indian government by frequently recurring famines, causing enormous loss of life, famines unequalled in severity during England's connection with India. From 1802 to 1854 there were thirteen famines with a probable loss of 5,000,000 lives. It will be remembered that the Mutiny forms a unique epoch in India's history, it marks the end of government by the famous East India Company, the assumption of all its powers by the Crown, the commencement of rapid steam navigation. which now brings Bombay within sixteen days of London. an immense impetus to trade between Indian and foreign lands, the development of the centralisation mania, and of railway communication. It is Modern as distinguished from Ancient India. What may be the exact bearing of some of these particulars upon the question of the increasing poverty of the Empire it is not easy to shew. But it is indisputable that between 1860 and 1879 sixteen famines occurred, and 12,000,000 lives were lost. The figures are the official admission. Probably the loss was 18,000,000 or 20,000,000. It may be that the terrible scourge has now done its worst, and will not reappear for long years to come, or it may be that India is growing poorer and weaker, and succumbs more readily and unresistingly when gaunt famine stalks the land. Even the government admits 'that a good harvest yields just sufficient food for the people, and thousands of lives depend each autumn on a few inches, more or less, of rainfall. The government may, by great efforts, feed the starving in time of actual famine; but *it cannot stop the yearly work of disease and death among a steadily underfed people'* (Imperial Gazetteer of India, iv. 168). A wonderful admission, and calculated to induce men to hope great things of the government that can make it.

Between smiling plenty and the havoc wrought by the famine spectre is an entire scale of life; it is certain that India lies at the meagre end of it. The greatest authority on matters Indian, the

Director-General of Indian statistics, and author of the Gazetteer of India, Sir W.W. Hunter, after admitting the poverty of four-fifths of India, declared that the remaining fifth, or forty millions of the people are half starved, obtaining only one full meal a day where two are necessary and sometimes not even that. Entire unanimity exists as to this state of semi-starvation, and many commissioners and collectors are of opinion that physique is visibly deteriorating, an opinion shared in some districts by the recruiting officers of the army . . .

Another proof of India's increasing poverty lies in the fact that whereas food has risen in value, wages have remained stationary, except perhaps among certain classes of labour in the great cities. The foreign buyer goes to the Indian villages, buying up immense quantities of wheat and other cereals, and by entering into competition with native consumers, forces up the price. To pay his taxes and rent the producer must grow the crops which the buyer will buy most readily, and thus it is observed that where formerly millet, bajra, rice were grown, now cotton, opium, indigo, jute have taken their place. Thus articles are grown for export to England instead of the food of the people; railways are made to carry off this 'surplus' produce, steamers await its arrival at the ports, coolies, in most slender attire, store it in the ship's holds for four annas a day, and India's trade grows enormously, an overwhelming proof of her prosperity under British rule. This very day (May 30th, 1891), turning to the commercial column of a provincial paper, I observe that:—'The shipments of Indian wheat from Bombay for the first four months of the present year have been unprecedentedly large, and the total for the year bids fair to beat the record.' The *Times of India* remarks:—'Never since 1874 (a terrible year of famine), when the wheat trade practically began, have the receipts of wheat in Bombay been so large, or nearly so large, as in the first four months of the current year—that is, from 1st January to 30th April, 1891. They have reached during that period the enormous total of 198,097 tons as compared with 97,420 in the corresponding four months of the previous year; 178,686 in the same period of 1886, in which year the shipments were larger than had ever before been known.' A truly delightful picture, always supposing it is *surplus* food India is sending us, for it must not be forgotten that one-fifth of her population is starving. And what does England send India in return for food and raw material for manufacturers? Turning to the

Statistical Abstract for 1888–89, we find that India imports (always at a loss: for every £100 exported, £70 imported) apparel, coal, manufactured cotton, machinery, metals, provisions for the Saheb log, railway plant, silk, etc. Railway plant and cotton cloth for India's starving millions when they care little about the first and cannot afford the second!

No fairly thoughtful person can here help asking why India sends to England the very food she needs for her own people, receiving in return things she could dispense with quite well. The answer lies to hand. India is very heavily taxed by England, taxation is twice as heavy per head as at home, and India must grow those crops which will pay that taxation, the summing up of home charges, guaranteed railways, interest on British capital, profits of Indian trade in British hands, and so forth. India sends out her crops because she cannot afford to eat them. 'Increasing exports,' said a Bengal civil servant in giving evidence with regard to the Orissa famine of 1863, 'are by no means a conclusive test of the prosperity of India, often the reverse, because they are very largely compulsory. The province of Orissa was depleted of produce which was exported to pay the government taxes.' Another government official says:—'The export trade is as brisk as ever. This is a great cause of the present scarcity. The grain grower is always in debt to the grain merchant, and is bound to deliver so much rice after each harvest. He may be starving, but that is no affair of the grain merchant.' A third somewhat timidly observes that the 'railway may be carrying off more than it is safe for the agricultural class to part with.' Says Sir W.W. Hunter:—'If all the poorer classes in India ate two full meals every day, the surplus for export would be much less than at present.' (1891)

CHRISTINA S. BREMNER[140]


# B. POPULATION

## 1. Population of India

Speaking of the natives reminds me of the subject of the population of India, which is very much exaggerated. It cannot be compared, in proportion to the extent of the country, to that of England. There are said to be 40,000 natives in Midnapore, though I much doubt

the fact; and then on every side, farther than the eye can reach,
extends a vast expanse of thick jungle (that is, bushes growing so
close together as to be altogether impassable, and full of tigers,
deer, leopards, buffaloes, elephants, etc); and as the same is the
case throughout the whole of India, I should think that nine-tenths
of the country consists of thick, close jungle, or enormous swamps.
Here and there, amidst all this, is found a small native village,
composed of a few huts; but the population in such places is probably not above one in thirty square miles on the average; this is, of
course, a mere rough guess. (1842)

T. ACLAND[141]

## 2. *Increase of population*

Increase in population is an equally unreliable argument, especially
in a country that is miserably poor. In Ireland, up to the potato
famine of 1847, population increased to a large extent under a
government that no candid person will pretend achieved the happiness or prosperity of the people. Famine commissioners in India
pointed to over-population as a powerful factor in the awful misery
of Behar, Orissa, and Bengal. But indeed any arguments based on
population could not be of great value. No complete census of
British India was made till 1872; by improved methods more people
might be counted on a second and third occasion than on a first.
Some excellent authorities are of opinion that the Indian population
is a very stationary one, more so than might reasonably be expected
after many years of settled government. (1891)

CHRISTINA S. BREMNER[142]

# C. SLAVERY

## 1. *Slavery and purchase of children*

The poorer Malabars live on rice, salt-fish, and jagree; which is a
coarse sugar produced from the cocoa-nut tree, wholesome and
nourishing; those who cannot afford rice, content themselves with
natchnee, a grain of inferior quality. The despotism of the government frequently occasions an artificial famine, and the inhabitants
fly the country: a real famine is sometimes attended with dreadful
consequences. Rice is sown at the commencement of the rains;

which do not always fall as expected, and in some instances they have been entirely withheld for a whole season. Should the ground be only partially inundated, the ear droops, and yields but half a crop. On such occasions the poor wretches are driven by hunger to Anjengo, and other sea-ports, where you see a youth selling himself for sustenance, a mother offering her infant son for a bag of rice, and a desponding father parting with his wife and children for forty or fifty rupees.

Malabar children are generally a cheap commodity at Anjengo; at the end of the rainy season, when there was no particular scarcity in the interior country, I purchased a boy and girl about eight or nine years of age, as a present to a lady at Bombay, for less money than a couple of pigs in England: I bought the young couple, laid in two months provision of rice and salt-fish for their voyage, and gave each of them four changes of cotton garments, all for the sum of twenty rupees, or fifty shillings. English humanity must not pass a censure on this transaction: it was a happy purchase for the children; they were relieved from hunger and nakedness, and sent to an amiable mistress, who brought them up tenderly, and, on leaving India, provided for their future comfort; whereas, had I refused to buy them, they would assuredly have been sold to another, and probably have experienced a miserable bondage with some native Portugueze Christian, whom we do not reckon among the most merciful task-masters.

A circumstance of this kind happened to myself: sitting one morning in my veranda, a young fish-woman brought a basket of mullets for sale; while the servant was disposing of them, she asked me to purchase a fine boy, two years of age, then in her arms: on my upbraiding her want of maternal affection, she replied with a smile, that she expected another in a few weeks, and as she could not manage two, she made me the first offer of her boy, whom she would part with for a rupee. She came a few days afterwards, with a basket of fish, but had just sold her child to Signor Manoel Rodriguez, the Portugueze linguist; who, though a man of property and a Christian had thought it necessary to lower the price to half a rupee. Thus did this young woman, without remorse, dispose of an only child for fifteen pence! (1812)

JAMES FORBES[143]

## 2. Slave girls for sale

Upon our return to our tents, we found there a man waiting our arrival with a very different sort of merchandise to any we had hitherto seen. He had with him two young girls, whom he had brought down from the Punjab, and these he was anxious to dispose of as slaves; offering the eldest, who was the least comely of the two, and about sixteen years of age, for one hundred and fifty rupees; and the other, who had really some pretensions to beauty, and was younger by about four years, for two hundred. The poor little things, putting their hands before them, in an attitude of supplication, begged earnestly that we would purchase them, declaring that otherwise they should starve, and vowing to be faithful and obedient to us. Finding that we were not inclined to become purchasers, the man took them away, and the same proffer was made at every tent: they were ultimately purchased by a native gentleman, residing in the neighbourhood of Delhi, for about half the sums above-mentioned. This traffic in slaves is considered to have been long since abolished, but it is still surreptitiously practised throughout the upper provinces, and at any of these fairs, girls may be purchased: they are generally from Georgia, Cashmere, Kabul, the Punjab, or Moultan. (1837)

THOMAS BACON[144]

## 3. A nice little purchase

I have made such a nice little purchase to-day—two little girls of seven years old. rather ugly, and one of them dumb. I gave three pounds for the pair—dirty cheap! as I think you will own. They are two little orphans. The natives constantly adopt orphans—either distant relations, or children that they buy—and generally they make no difference between them and their own children; but these little wretches were very unlucky. They belonged to a very bad man, who was serving as a substitute for a sick servant whom we sent back to Calcutta. This man turned out ill and got drunk, upon which all the other Mussulmauns refused to associate with him, and he lost caste altogether. Giles was very anxious to get rid of him, as a drunken Mussulmaun is something so shocking we are all quite *affected* by it. On Monday he gave us an opportunity to leave him at Kurnaul. I had tried to get hold of these children at Simla, hearing they were very ill-used, and that this man was just going to take them down to Delhi to sell them into the palace, where thousands of children are *swallowed up*. Luckily, his creditors would not let him go, and I told A. to watch that he did not carry off the little girls; so to-day he sent word I might have them if I would pay his debts, and the baboo has just walked in triumphantly with them. They have not a stitch of clothes on; and one of them is rather an object, the man has beat them so dreadfully, and she seems stupified. I hope to deposit them finally at Mrs. Wilson's orphanage near Calcutta. (1839)

EMILY EDEN[145]

# 7. Law and Order

## A. THUGS AND ROBBERS

### 1. *The Phansigars*

A gang of Phansigars consists of from ten to fifty, or even a greater number of persons, a large majority of whom are Mussulmans; but Hindus, and particularly those of the Rajput tribe, are often associated with them. Bramins, too, though rarely, are found in the gangs. Emerging from their haunts, they sometimes perform long journeys, being absent from home many months, and prowl along the eastern and western coasts to Hyderabad and Cape Comorin. In general, however, they do not roam to such a distance, but make one or two excursions every year. Their victims are almost exclusively travellers whom they fall in with on the road. Each gang has its sirdar or leader, who directs its movements. Of a numerous gang, some usually remain at home, while the rest are engaged in the work of pillage and murder. Those that are abroad are often divided into separate parties of ten or fifteen persons, who either follow each other at some distance, or, the parties taking different routes, they rendezvous at an appointed place in advance, measures being at the same time taken to secure a speedy junction of the gang, should this be requisite for the purpose of attacking several travellers at once. Different gangs sometimes act in concert, occasionally apprising one another of the approach of travellers whose destruction promises a rich booty.

Phansigars have the appearance of ordinary inoffensive travellers, and seldom assume any particular disguise. They indeed not unfrequently pretend to be traders, and there is reason to believe that they sometimes come from the Dukhun clothed in the garb of Bairagis. Formerly, when Phansigary was practised to a greater extent, and in a more daring manner than at present, the leader, especially if enriched by former spoliations, often travelled on horseback, with a tent, and passed for a person of consequence or a wealthy merchant, otherwise he appeared at first in a more humble

'My Second Victim', from Taylor's *Confessions of a Thug*

character, and assumed in the course of his rapacious progress one
of more importance, as he became possessed of horses and bullocks,
which while they afforded him carriage for the plundered property
subserved the purpose of giving countenance and support to his
feigned character.

Phansigars are accustomed to wait at Choultries on the high
roads, or near to towns where travellers are wont to rest. They
arrive at such places and enter towns and villages in straggling
parties of three or four persons, appearing to meet by accident and
to have had no previous acquaintance. On such occasions, some of
the gang are employed as emissaries to collect information, and
especially to learn if any persons with property in their possession
are about to undertake a journey. They are often accompanied by
children of ten years of age and upwards, who, while they perform
menial offices, are initiated into the horrid practices of the Phansigars, and contribute to prevent suspicion of their real character.
Skilled in the arts of deception, they enter into conversation and
insinuate themselves, by obsequious attentions, into the confidence
of travellers of all descriptions, to learn from them whence they
come, whither and for what purpose they are journeying, and of
what property they are possessed:— thus—
   —under fair pretence of friendly ends,
   and well placed words of glozing courtesy,
   Baited with reasons not unplausible,
   Wind them into the easy-hearted man;
   And hug them into snares. (1816)

                              RICHARD C. SHERWOOD[146]

## 2. *The plight of the bazaars*

   ... Form a huge torrent rolling into one:
   Stumbling I cross this bridge, impelled by fright
   Lest I perchance should be kept out all night—
   For soon as night has settled o'er the plains
   Each merchant shuts his door with double chains

   And homeward wends to count his store of gold,
   And see what hopes his Ledger can unfold.
   While not a soul about Tank Square we meet
   Gangs of *Dacoits* infest each distant street,
   The wildest *jungul* being safer far

Than Potuldunga or than Sham Bazar
Alas for him whom business may detain
Near Chunam Gully or Nulpokur Lane!
Out start four Chinamen each with a knife
And threatening cry 'Your money or your Life'! (1831)

A.H.E. BOILEAU[147]

## 3. *Kassee: the consecrated pick-axe*

At first Thugs were allowed by *Davy*, according to their creed, to leave on the ground the bodies of the persons murdered, but were prohibited from looking back to see how she disposed of them. A slave on one occasion looked back, and saw her occupied in throwing them into the air, without any clothes on her body. She was naturally very angry and bid them in future to bury the bodies themselves; but to use in making the graves pick-axes duly consecrated. On ascertaining from the priest or elder of the gang a lucky day for the purpose, the leader of the gang goes to the blacksmiths, and having closed the door that no other person may enter, gets him to make the axe in his presence, without touching any other work till it is completed.

On a day fixed, either Friday, Monday, Tuesday, or Wednesday, they give it the *dhoop* or incense offering. The place chosen must be either inside a house or tent, so that the shadow of no living thing may fall on and contaminate the axe. The Thug most skilled in the ceremonies, sits down with his face to the west, and receives the pick-axe on a brass dish. A pit is dug in the ground, and the pick-axe is washed with water which falls into this pit. It is afterwards washed with a mixture of sugar and water. Then with *dehee* or sour milk, and lastly with ardent spirits; all falling successively from the pick-axe into the pit. It is then marked from the head to the point with seven spots of red lead, and placed on the brass dish, containing an entire cocoanut, some cloves, pawn leaves, gogul gum *(amyris agollacha)*, inderjon, some seed of the sesamum, white sandal wood, and sugar. In a small brass cup close by, is some ghee. They now kindle a fire from some dried cow dung, and some wood of the mango or byr tree, and throw in upon it the above named articles, except the cocoanut; and when the flame rises, they pass the pick-axe seven times through it, the officiating priest holding it in both hands. He now strips the cocoanut of its outer coat, and placing it on the

'Thugs in the Prison of Aurangabad', drawn by A. Gusmand

ground, holds the pick-axe by the point in his right hand, and says 'Shall I strike?' All around reply yes. He then says 'all hail mighty *Davy*, great mother of all!' and striking the cocoanut with the but end of the pick-axe, breaks it in pieces, on which all exclaim 'All hail *Davy* and prosper the Thugs!' They throw all the shell and some of the kernel into the fire, tie up the pick-axe in a clean piece of white cloth, and placing it on the ground to the west, all face in that direction and worship it. This done they all partake of the kernel of the cocoanut, and collect all the fragments and put them into the pit, that they may never after be contaminated by the touch of any one's foot. If after this ceremony the *Thibaoo,* or auspice on the right is seen or heard, the sacrifice has been approved. If the *Pilhaoo,* on the left, it is not; and if the cocoanut is not severed at one blow, the deity is considered to have disapproved, and another day is appointed for the ceremony to be performed over again. Henceforward the pick-axe is called the *Kassee,* or *Mahee,* instead of *Kodalee.* The Jemadar keeps it with great care, and before every expedition the ceremony must be repeated.

It is given to the shrewdest, cleanest and most sober and careful man of the party, who carries it in his waist-belt. While in camp he buries it in a secure place, with its point in the direction they intend to go; and they believe that if another direction is better its point will be found changed. They say that formerly they used to throw it into a well, and that it would come up of itself when summoned with due ceremonies; but since they began to do what was forbidden, and neglected what was enjoined, it has lost that virtue. They say that it has it still among some classes of Thugs in the Duckun who have adhered more rigidly to their rites and usages. No foot must touch the earth under which it lies buried; nor may the pick-axe be touched by any man in an unclean state, or by any unclean animal or thing. The burnt offering is repeated on certain holydays, and whenever they have been long without a victim. After every grave made with it, it must be bathed with certain ceremonies.

The oath by the *Kassee* is, in their esteem, far more sacred than that by the Ganges water or the Koran, and I have known men who have been in prison twenty years, entertain the firmest conviction that perjury on the *Kassee,* when the oath has been administered with due ceremony, must inevitably cause the death of the person within six days, or involve him in some great calamity. I have talked with hundreds who have told all their secrets, and I never yet met a

Thug that did not, up to the last moment of his existence, believe the same. They never under any circumstance lose their confidence in the *Kassee*; and if it fail them, they attribute it to accidental neglect of the prescribed ceremonies. In prison, when administering an oath to each other in cases of dispute among themselves, I have known them frame the image of the *Kassee* out of a piece of cloth, and consecrate it for the purpose. The deponent puts his hand on it while he deposes, or holds it in both hands, and after having sworn he drinks water in which the *Kassee* has been washed, or he goes before the image of *Davy* with the *Kassee* in his hands and swears.

If the *Kassee* at any time falls from the hands of the man who carries it, it is a dreadful omen, and portends that he will either be that year killed, or that the gang will suffer some grievous misfortune. The gang must deprive him of his office, return home, or change the road, and consecrate the *Kassee* anew; and no other party will ever encamp or associate with one whose *Kassee* has so fallen, lest they should be involved in the calamity. Many are the curious stories they relate to illustrate all this. (1836)

WILLIAM HENRY SLEEMAN[148]

## 4. Robbers and thieves

As in Tehree, so here, the pickpockets constitute the entire population of several villages, and carry their depredations northward to the banks of the Indus, and southward to Bombay and Madras. But colonies of thieves and robbers like these, abound no less in our own territories than in those of native states; there are more than a thousand families of them in the districts of Mozuffeernugur, Saharunpore, and Meerut, in the upper Dooab, all well enough known to the local authorities, who can do nothing with them. They extend their depredations into remote districts, and the booty they bring home with them they share liberally with the native police and landlords under whose protection they live. Many landholders and police officers make large fortunes from the share they get of this booty. Magistrates in our districts do not molest them, because they would despair of ever finding the proprietors of the property that might be found upon them; and if they could trace them, they would never be able to persuade them to come and 'enter upon a worse than sea of troubles,' in prosecuting them. These thieves and robbers of the professional classes, who have the sagacity to avoid plundering near home, are always just as secure in our best regulated districts, as they are in the worst native states, from the only three things which such depredators care about—the penal laws, the odium of the society in which they move, and the vengeance of the god they worship; and they are always well received in the society around them, as long as they can avoid having their neighbours annoyed by summonses to give evidence for or against them in our courts. They feel quite sure of the good will of the god they worship, provided they give a fair share of their booty to his priests; and no less secure of impunity from penal laws, except on the very rare occasions when they happen to be taken in the fact, in a country where such laws happen to be in force! (1844)

WILLIAM HENRY SLEEMAN[149]

## 5.  The Murder-lists

The Oude bands seldom went out of their own country, but they did a thriving business within its borders. So did outside bands who came in and helped. Some of the Thug leaders of Oude were noted for their successful careers. Each of four of them confessed to above 300 murders; another to nearly 400; our friend Ramzam to 604—he is the one who got leave of absence to attend a wedding and went thugging instead; and he is also the one who betrayed Buhram to the British.

But the biggest records of all were the murder-lists of Futty Khan and Buhram. Futty Khan's number is smaller than Ramzam's, but he is placed at the head because his *average* is the best in Oude-Thug history per year of service. His slaughter was five hundred and eight men in twenty years, and he was still a young man when the British stopped his industry. Buhram's list was nine hundred and thirty-one murders, but it took him forty years. His average was one man and nearly all of another man per month for forty years, but Futty Khan's average was *two* men and a little of another man per month during his twenty years of usefulness.

There is one very striking thing which I wish to call attention to. You have surmised from the listed callings followed by the victims of the Thugs that nobody could travel the Indian roads unprotected and live to get through; that the Thugs respected no quality, no vocation, no religion, nobody; that they killed every unarmed man that came in their way. That is wholly true—with one reservation. In all the long file of Thug confessions *an English traveller is mentioned but once*—and this is what the Thug says of the circumstance:

He was on his way from Mhow to Bombay. *We studiously avoided him.* He proceeded next morning with a number of travellers *who had sought his protection*, and they took the road to Baroda.

We do not know who he was; he flits across the page of this rusty old book and disappears in the obscurity beyond; but he is an impressive figure, moving through that valley of death serene and unafraid, clothed in the might of the English name.

We have now followed the big official book through, and we understand what Thuggee was, what a bloody terror it was, what a desolating scourge it was. In 1830 the English found this cancerous organization embedded in the vitals of the empire, doing its devastating work in secrecy, and assisted, protected, sheltered, and hidden by innumerable confederates—big and little native chiefs, customs officers, village officials, and native police, all ready to lie for it, and the mass of the people through fear, persistently pretending to know nothing about its doings; and this condition of things had existed for generations, and was formidable with the sanctions of age and old custom. If ever there was an unpromising task, if ever there was a hopeless task in the world, surely it was offered here—the task of conquering Thuggee. But that little handful of English Officials in India set their sturdy and confident grip upon it, and ripped it out, root and branch! How modest do Captain Vallancey's words sound now, when we read them again, knowing what we know:

The day that sees this far-spread evil completely eradicated from India, and known only in name, will greatly tend to immortalize British rule in the East. (1896)

MARK TWAIN[150]

## 6. Thuggee

It has been remarked that an interesting book might be written on the crimes in India which have been 'repressed,' only to appear again in some novel form. This is the case with Thuggee, which, when put down by General Sleeman and the officers who worked with him, has appeared again in the form perhaps quite as dangerous of Road Poisoning. Both these forms of crime, however, seem to have gone on side by side from a very early period.

The early Hindus were familiar with the use of the Naga-pasa, or 'dragon noose.' We find in the Epics that the demons who fight with the gods are thus armed. Strangling of travellers prevailed from a very early time. In the Ellora cave-temple, which was constructed about 760 A.D., we have a Thug represented strangling a Brahman who is worshipping the emblem of Siva, whereupon the god comes to his rescue and kicks down the Thug. Firoz Shah, near the end of the fourteenth century, captured some thousand Thugs near Delhi, and in his usual merciful way contented himself with deporting them to Bengal.

Early in the last century, to quote Sleeman, 'the annually returning tide of murder swept unsparingly over the whole face of India, from the Sutlej to the sea. One narrow district alone was free, the Concan beyond the Ghauts, whither they never penetrated.'

One gang lived close to his court-house, and he often encamped in the grove near Narsinghpur, one of the greatest places of slaughter in India.

The river Thugs committed fearful slaughter among the boating population.

'Two hundred and fifty boats full of river Thugs,' writes Sir J. Hooker, 'in crews of fifteen, infested the Ganges between Benares and Calcutta during five months of the year, on pretence of conveying pilgrims. Travellers along the bank were tracked, and offered a passage, which, if refused in the first boat, was probably accepted in some other. At a given signal the crew rushed in, doubled up the decoyed victim, broke his back, and threw him into the river, where floating corpses are too numerous to elicit even an exclamation.'

All along the main routes Sepoys returning home on leave, merchants conveying treasure, dancing-girls on their way to marriage-feasts were ruthlessly murdered. Sleeman's Thuggee map of Oudh shows 274 murder stations; one man confessed that he had been engaged in 931 cases.

These gangs of assassins regularly took the field after the Dasehra Festival at the close of the rainy season. They acted, as they believed, under the sanction and with the aid of the goddess Kali, who has her most noted shrine at Bindachal, near Mirzapur, where the Vindhyan hills overshadow the Ganges valley. Here the *Roomal,* or handkerchief used in strangling, and the mattock with which the grave of the victim was dug, were solemnly blessed by the temple priests, who received a liberal share of the plunder. The Musalman

Thugs in the same way owed allegiance to the Saint Nizam-ud-din Auliya, whose beautiful tomb is one of the chief architectural gems of old Delhi. One class of these Thugs, known as the Tasmabaz, or those who played the game of 'Stick and garter' familiar at country fairs, where the player has to push a stick into the exact central fold of a twisted strap, are said to have owed their skill to the teaching of an English soldier named Creagh.

At length, when the matter was taken up by our Government, informers were induced to reveal the organisation of the gangs. They were hunted down by the police like wild beasts. Many were executed, and the less guilty were interned for life. By these operations this form of crime disappeared for a time. How far these miscreants were connected with the road-poisoners of our day has been much debated. James Forbes, a good authority in such matters, was of opinion that the more experienced Thugs used the cord, the less intelligent poison; and Dr. Chevers believed that when the raid began, the Thugs abandoned strangling and had recourse to drugs. But while these two classes of crime are in some respects similar, there is a clear difference in the methods. The road-poisoners formed small isolated gangs, and never possessed the elaborate organisation characteristic of the Thugs. It is only Thevenot who describes the Thugs of his day taking women with them to entice travellers. This Sleeman denies to have been the habit of the Thugs, and it is probable that Thevenot's Thugs were really poisoners. Thugs, again, were specially directed to spare women, while the chief victims of the poisoners were dancing-girls. Lastly, there is no word for poison in the Thug argot. A connection between these two classes of crime has been traced in the custom of sacrificing to a god or making offerings to a saint before undertaking an enterprise. But this is a habit with other classes of criminals, and has no resemblance to the organised religious meetings of the Thugs.

The methods of the modern poisoner much resemble those of the Thug. Sometimes he is accompanied by a family, real or pretended; sometimes he masquerades as a wandering Fakir, or to facilitate his operations as a Brahman cook, from whose hands any traveller may eat. Sometimes he pretends to be a pilgrim tout, or a marriage agent in search for a bride, or he hangs on to a band of dancing-girls, or a party of Kabul merchants bringing Turkestan horses for sale. His chief hunting-ground is the *Serai*, or native inn, where he offers to assist travellers in procuring or cooking food, and is thus enabled to drug their cakes or rice. He almost always uses Dhatura or *Stramonium,* occasionally *Nux vomica.* General Sleeman believed that the road-poisoners always intended to take life; but Colonel Hervey denies this, and asserts that their real object was to promote insensibility sufficient to cover their escape. This is probably the intention of the criminals of our time: but often through a mistake in the amount of the dose, fatal results follow the administration of the drug. The extent of their operations may be judged by the case of Shara-ud-din, the most noted poisoner in recent times. He had been a policeman, and learnt the trade in jail. He confessed to sixty-nine cases of poisoning, and said that he had committed hundreds, the details of which he could not remember.

The extension of railway travelling has, by providing facilities for escape, greatly assisted this class of crime. It is checked only by the constant efforts of a well-organised detective service, and when repressed in one direction soon reappears elsewhere. If the vigilance of our police were relaxed, it would soon become as serious an evil as the old associations of the Thugs. (1906)

WILLIAM CROOKE[151]

## B. CONVICTS AND THEIR EXECUTION

### 1. *Aurangzeb's measures against wine*

Among the other disorders, Aurangzeb observed that in Hindustan, chiefly in Dihli, there was great licence among Mahomedans and Hindus in the consumption of wine, although most repugnant to this king, who declared himself a strict follower of the Quran. This licence began in the time of Jahangir. Akbar was the first to give leave to the Christians to prepare and drink wine; but in his time the Mahomedans did not drink. The evil example of Jahangir established this custom among the Mahomedans. In the days of Shahjahan they drank with full liberty, just as if drinking water, encouraged by Dara's example. Nor did Shahjahan, although not a drinker himself, care to remedy this disorder, but left everyone to live as he pleased, contenting himself with passing his days among women, as I have already said.

It was so common to drink spirits when Aurangzeb ascended the throne, that one day he said in a passion that in all Hindustan no more than two men could be found who did not drink, namely,

himself and 'Abd-ul-wahhab, the chief *qazi* appointed by him . . .
But with respect to 'Abd-ul-wahhab he was in error, for I myself
sent him every day a bottle of spirits *(vino)*, which he drank in
secret, so that the king could not find it out. Aurangzeb wished to
repress this disorder, and therefore ordered that all Christians,
excepting physicians and surgeons, should leave the city and remove to near the park of artillery, which was beyond the suburbs at
one league's distance from the city. There they had leave to prepare
and drink spirits on condition they did not sell them.

After the issue of this order he directed the *kotwal* (chief of
police) to search out Mahomedans and Hindus who sold spirits,
every one of whom was to lose one hand and one foot. Without fail
the *kotwal* went out to search for the vendors, although himself one
of the consumers. One day I saw him carry out such a sentence on six
Mahomedans and six Hindus; after the punishment he ordered
them to be trailed to a dung-heap, leaving them there to die dis-
creetly. This penal order was in force for a time, so that no vendors
were to be found; for whenever the *kotwal* suspected that spirits
were made in any house, he sent his soldiers to plunder everything
in it. The regulations were strict at first, but little by little they were
relaxed; and during the period of strictness the nobles, who found it
hard to live without spirits, distilled in their houses, there being few
who do not drink secretly.

I have said that the Christians had leave to prepare spirits for their
own consumption, but were prohibited selling them. On this account sentinels were kept over them to watch that they did not sell.
In spite of this, the gain being great, they did not refrain, by
resorting to a thousand expedients, from selling them on the sly,
although when the offence was discovered the *kotwal* used to send
and plunder the house, the still being hung round the offender's
neck, and then he was taken through the streets chained, and
buffeted on his way to the *Kotwal's* house. On arrival there half
dead he was locked up in prison, and only released after many
months with a fine and a beating. (1653–1708)

NICCOLAO MANUCCI[151a]

## 2. *Native tribunals*

I believe that as little falsehood is spoken by the people of India, in
their village communities, as in any part of the world with an equal

area and population. It is in our courts of justice where falsehoods prevail most, and the longer they have been anywhere established, the greater the degree of falsehood that prevails in them. Those entrusted with the administration of a newly-acquired territory, are surprised to find the disposition among both principals and witnesses in cases to tell the plain and simple truth. As magistrates, they find it very often difficult to make thieves and robbers tell lies, according to the English fashion, to avoid running a risk of criminating themselves. In England, this habit of making criminals tell lies, arose from the severity of the penal code, which made the punishment so monstrously disproportionate to the crime, that the accused, however clear and notorious his crime, became an object of general sympathy. In India, punishments have nowhere been, under our rule, disproportionate to the crimes; on the contrary, they have been generally more mild than the people would wish them to be, or think they ought to be, in order to deter from similar crimes; and in newly-acquired territories they have generally been more mild than in our old possessions. The accused are, therefore, nowhere considered as objects of public sympathy; and in newly-acquired territories they are willing to tell the truth, and are allowed to do so, in order to save the people whom they have injured, and their neighbours generally, the great loss and annoyance unavoidably attending upon a summons to our courts. In the native courts, to which ours succeed, the truth was seen through immediately; the judges who presided could commonly distinguish truth from falsehood in the evidence before them, almost as well as the sylvan gods who sat in the peepul or cotton trees; though they were seldom supposed by the people to be quite so just in their decisions. When we take possession of such countries, they, for a time at least, give us credit for the same *sagacity,* with a little more *integrity.* The prisoner knows that his neighbours expect him to tell the truth to save them trouble, and will detest him if he does not; he supposes that we shall have the sense to find out the truth whether he tells it or not, and the humanity to visit his crime with the measure of punishment it merits, and no more.

The magistrate asks the prisoner what made him steal; and the prisoner enters at once into an explanation of the circumstances which reduced him to the necessity of doing so, and offers to bring witnesses to prove them; but never dreams of offering to bring witnesses to prove that *he did not steal,* if he really had done so—because the general feeling would be in favour of his doing the one, and against his doing the other. (*c.* 1830's)

WILLIAM HENRY SLEEMAN[152]

## 3. *Prison system of India*

*Prison Labour.*—The question of the employment of prisoners has been much and constantly discussed and considered in India. Prior to 1838, the chief occupation of criminals was extra-mural, either in making Imperial roads, or in station improvements. In the former they were employed in considerable numbers, were encamped or hutted, and were in charge of engineer officers. In the latter they were under the immediate charge of the district magistrates. During the enquiries which were ordered by the Government of India, it was elicited that this mode of employing prisoners was extremely unhealthy, that it was liable to great abuse, and was, in fact, much abused; that it was characterised by an entire absence of penal discipline; and that, while it was of questionable advantage to the state, it was abundantly detrimental to the criminals.

The intra-mural employment of prisoners was chiefly in prison occupations, and so much under the control of prison subordinates as to be generally abused, the rich, and those of high caste, purchasing or obtaining immunity; the poor, low caste, and friendless, being subject to tyranny and oppression. To remedy this, the Prison Discipline Committee of 1838 recommended the cessation of out-door work, and the general introduction of in-door labour in dull, wearisome, monotonous tasks, the evident intention of which was to inflict as much personal pain as could be safely inflicted without injury to health. Tread-wheels and cranks were accordingly introduced tentatively in Calcutta and at Deegah, but they failed, and were speedily abandoned.

At that time the doctrine of making prisons a terror to evildoers by measures of coercion and severity, was in full force. The higher aim of reformation was neither entertained nor practised.

In 1843, the introduction of remunerative industry was enjoined by the Government of India, then administered by the late Earl of Ellenborough. The labour was to be regulated by taskwork, each task being at least equal in amount to that performed by a fairly skilled artisan of the same class. It was to be sufficiently severe to keep the prisoners actively employed during the day, with the intervals necessary for food and rest. It was not to be repugnant to the castes and religious customs of the prisoners.

Rules were subsequently framed, and are now in force, to classify the labour, to apportion it as much as possible to the sentence and crime of the prisoner, and to make it an instrument of reformation. This latter is accomplished by teaching each prisoner some form of handicraft that will enable him to earn an honest livelihood on release, and, by inculcating habits of industry, to counteract the idleness which is the proximate cause of much of the vice that leads to crime.

Remunerative prison industry as an instrument of reformation, is the basis of the system of prison labour now in force throughout India. It is not carried out with the precision and perfection of which it is susceptible, from the absence of properly constructed prisons, from the miserable economy which has reduced the establishment of gaols throughout India to a pitch bordering on positive ineffi- ciency, from the large number of short sentences awarded by the criminal courts, in which it is impossible to teach any trade or handicraft, and from a majority of the prisoners throughout India belonging to the agricultural classes, who neither can nor will follow any other pursuit on release.

As the whole of the prisons in India are under State control, most of these defects could be readily remedied.

In so extended and poor a country as India financial considera- tions are undoubtedly of primary importance, and cannot be rightly or safely disregarded in dealing with all such questions.

But it can be shown and has been proved in practice, that by a wise regulation of prison labour all the ends intended by the addi- tion of this condition to criminal sentences can be fully accomp- lished, and the prisons be made at the same time entirely self- supporting. One presidency in India has for several years repaid about 40 per cent of the whole cost of its prisons, and some gaols in the same presidency have been and are entirely self-supporting. An extension of the system which I long and earnestly pressed upon the attention of the Government, would have recouped to the State the whole of the outlay on the prisons, would have converted unprofitable consumers into profitable producers, would have of- fered to the largest and most important section of the criminal community the means of securing an honest livelihood on release, would have provided the means of gradually rebuilding the whole of the prisons in the manner required by our present knowledge of the subject, without causing the financial pressure that is a source of public discontent and consequent danger in India, and would have removed the reproach from the prison system of that country which must ever attach to it under the system of association. This is, in all countries and at all times, an undeniable source of demoralisation. India is no exception to the rule.

The chief objections to remunerative prison labour are, that it does not provide the hard work intended by the criminal law, that it enters into injurious competition with free labour of the same kind, and that it makes the prison a stepping-stone to fortune, and thus places the prisoner in a better position than the honest labourer of the same class.

The obvious answers to these objections are, that the severity of labour consists rather in its continuance, and the constant care and attention exacted by all forms of work in which more or less of skill is required, than in the mere exercise of unreasoning muscular force. The limits of the latter are soon reached, and demand prolonged intervals of rest which are injurious to discipline. They excite feelings of anger and resentment destructive of the moral sentiments which are the sole agents of reformation. They are in reality torture in disguise, and not warranted either by the Christianity we profess, or the civilisation to which we lay claim.

That remunerative prison industry enters into competition with free labour is undoubted, and I conceive that it has a perfect right to do so. The interests of the community at large are superior to those of sections or individual members of that community. Prisons must be maintained at the public cost; this cost falls upon the honest and well-conducted members of society; and if the prisoners can be made to diminish the burden by the exercise of compulsory industry, it is not only a most legitimate retribution to exact, but the State is bound to resort to it as a measure of general policy. To teach the prisoner a handicraft, and thus enable him to gain an honest livelihood on release, will merely restore him to the place that he would have occupied, had he not taken to evil courses. It creates nothing new. It adds to the stock of public virtue, and diminishes to a like extent that of corroding vice. For that reason, if there were none others founded on more general economic considerations which it is foreign to the immediate purpose of this paper to refer to, the use of remunerative prison industry as an important measure of reformation, is not only justified but enjoined.

That a gaol can, in any well-regulated system of prison discipline, ever become a productive school of industry in which a poor and honest labourer should desire to graduate, can only result from grave mismanagement, such as I believe nowhere to exist. The necessary and accessory inconveniences of imprisonment, viz., the entire loss for the time of personal liberty, the consequences immediately resulting from this loss, disruption of family and social ties, destruction of business, a compulsory state of existence in all matters, the necessity of conforming to strict regulations which are and must from their nature be distasteful, a compulsory dietary, uncomfortable means of repose, total exclusion of society, and enforced labour in uncongenial pursuits, are all immediate, tangible, well-understood evils. That there is a desire to encounter them with the remote prospect of learning a trade or handicraft in any section of the honest community at home or abroad, I do not believe.

Within the last two years the out-door employment of convicts has been revived in India, and large gangs of them are now engaged on canal works. If the intention of convict labour were merely to furnish hard work and to recoup the cost of maintenance, and if the essential conditions of prison discipline are to be entirely ignored, this system is sound and logical. But if, as I firmly believe ought to be its intention, the labour is to be a means of an end, viz., the reformation of an offender by the inculcation of habits of order and industry, and by the possession of the skill and knowledge necessary to earn an honest livelihood on release, then I hold the system to be unsound, and to be a retrograde measure.

*Prison Dietaries.*—The dietaries for prisoners in India vary somewhat in detail in every province and presidency. They are, as a rule, based upon the food in use among the lowest classes of the different people, and are so regulated as to maintain health and strength without the introduction of a single article that is considered to be a luxury. Prisoners are weighed on admission and discharge, and provision is made in the gaol rules of some parts of India to weigh them whenever there is reason to believe that the dietary is, from any cause, productive of disease, a loss of weight being a rough test of deficient quantity or improper quality of food. In such circumstances the surgeon of the prison has power to change the dietary in the way that may be needed for the health and strength of the prisoners—a special report of every instance in which this is done being made to the head of the prison department. to ensure that such power is not abused.

A penal dietary has, after careful experimental inquiry, been recently introduced for short-term prisoners, and for serious breaches of gaol discipline, which used, heretofore, to be punished by flogging. This also is carefully guarded to prevent its being a source of injury to health, and thus in excess of the punishment awarded by the law.

Tobacco, opium, and all narcotics and stimulants to which natives of India have been accustomed from the earliest age, are strictly prohibited in Indian prisons. That the sudden withdrawal of any accustomed luxury may not be attended with injury to health, all prisoners who have indulged to excess in such luxuries or vices, are placed under observation, and the medical officer of the prison has full power either to continue the indulgence in gradually diminishing quantities, or to subject the sufferers to such dietetic and other treatment as he may consider to be necessary, to enable them to bear the entire privation with impunity.

There is no restriction in hospital dietaries as to all reasonable changes in quantities of food that medical officers consider necessary for the cure of disease, or restoration to health and strength.

The subject of prison dietaries in India has frequently been investigated with great care in consequence of their important relations to health. The practical rule of guidance has been to give all that is really required for health and strength, and, this end being kept steadily in view, to withhold everything that would place the prisoner in a better position than the poor and honest in his own walk of life.

The action of the Government of India in this important matter has always been guided by a wise and laudable humanity.

*Prison Punishments.*—The punishments for breaches of gaol discipline in force in India, are: the imposition of fetters, separate confinement, flogging, penal labour, and a penal dietary.

In some parts of the country, from the extreme insecurity of the prisons, all heinous offenders, and some persons under trial, are ironed to prevent escape—a harsh proceeding caused by the absence of properly-constructed prisons. This proceeding has recently been legalised—a reproach to the legislation of the country.

When the prisons are tolerably secure, fettering is employed for the punishment of breaches of gaol discipline.

Separate confinement is resorted to where the means exist; but the provision of cells is so inadequate, even for this purpose, that recourse is had to flogging to an extent that is lamentable.

There is no doubt that this is a brutal and degrading form of punishment. and one that should be strictly reserved for the very few cases in which all more humane and proper means of enforcing discipline fail, after full and fair trial.

Penal labour exists and is enforced in some of the Indian prisons, but not to any great extent. It consists of such tasks as are mere exercises of muscular power, which can only be continued with safety for short periods. It contains no reformatory element, and stands little above flogging in its penal value. It cannot be pushed to any great extent in India without undermining health and strength—hence is regarded with mistrust and dislike by all humane and skilled prison officials. Speculative prison disciplinarians are much enamoured of this mode of employing prisoners generally. They cannot exhibit graver ignorance of the ends and objects of imprisonment. . . .

A penal dietary has recently been introduced generally. This was impracticable so long as the prisons were in the personal charge of judicial officers who had not time to attend to them. In these circumstances it became an instrument of illicit gain to corrupt prison subordinates, and a source of lamentable sickness and mortality from insufficient quantity and improper quality of food. It was only re-introduced after careful experiment, and for its proper working demands constant and close supervision, lest it should be again abused.

All returns of punishment in gaols are furnished in Bengal, monthly, to the head of the prison department, and are carefully scrutinised by that officer to see that the rules are enforced with discretion and humanity. Abuses are immediately corrected, and care is taken that the ends of justice are not defeated, so far as can be accomplished by vigilance in general supervision. (1872)

FREDERIC J. MOUAT[153]

## 4. Criminal executed by an elephant

This punishment is one of the most frightful that can possibly be imagined. The culprit, bound hand and foot, is fastened by a long cord, passed round his waist, to the elephant's hind leg. The latter is urged into a rapid trot through the streets of the city, and every step gives the cord a violent jerk, which makes the body of the condemned wretch bound on the pavement. The only hope that remains for the unhappy man is to be killed by one of these shocks; if not, after traversing the city, he is released, and, by a refinement of cruelty, a glass of water is given him. Then his head is placed upon a stone, and the elephant executioner crushes it beneath his enormous foot.

Very strict etiquette prevails at this Court,* and the most scrupulous politeness is observed; only a few curious usages differ from those to which we are accustomed. Thus, it is expressly forbidden for any one whomsoever to sneeze in the royal presence: he who transgressed this rule would be rigorously punished, for his conduct would oblige certain improprieties, which are carefully banished from society amongst us, are here considered perfectly innocent. If the king commits one of them, the courtiers do not fail to felicitate him, after our old fashion of exclaiming 'God bless you!' on such occasions. It is also a mark of good breeding, whenever the king yawns, to snap the fingers, in order to keep off every insect that might seize the opportunity of entering his august mouth. (1875)

LOUIS ROUSSELET[154]

## 5. The reformatory

I have done into English one of the simple Tamil lyrics of the Reformatory. My translation is free, but it reproduces the sense, and I daresay the quality, of the original.

> Before the sun has lit the skies
> With rosy light, we early rise,
> And first we supplicate the Lord
> That he may health and help afford.
> When thus prepared with thankful heart
> To run our course, the day we start,
> Each to his labour to address
> Himself, nor lie in idleness.
> Some, happy they, 'neath plantain shade
> Delve in the yielding earth with spade,
> While many more unceasingly
> The weaver's shuttle deftly ply.

* At Baroda

'Criminal Executed by an Elephant at Baroda', drawn by Emile Bayard

Others the molten iron know
To fashion with unerring blow,
And nimble pairs of hands are made
To learn the useful tailor's trade.

We all are busy, all confess
That sin begins with idleness,
That those who work with all their might,
At least in that, are doing right.

Thus when our sojourn here is o'er,
And we, reformed, are free once more,
In after life we always mean
To be good boys, and bless the Queen. (1886–90)

J.D. REES[155]

# C. ADMINISTRATION OF JUSTICE

## 1. Akbar's justice

The King's [Akbar's] severity towards errors and misdemeanours committed by officials in the course of government business is remarkable, for he is most stern with offenders against the public faith. Hence all are afraid of his severity, and strive with all their might to do as he directs and desires. For the King has the most precise regard for right and justice in the affairs of government. In accordance with Musalman practice cases are decided by a double process before two judges. However by the King's direction all capital cases, and all really important civil cases also, are conducted before himself. He is easily excited to anger, but soon cools down again. By nature moreover he is kindly and benevolent, and is sincerely anxious that guilt should be punished, without malice indeed, but at the same time without undue leniency. Hence in the cases in which he himself acts as judge the guilty are, by his own directions, not punished until he has given orders for the third time that this shall be done. During the campaign against the king of Chabulum, twelve deserters to the enemy were captured in an ambush near the Bydaspes and brought before the King. He pronounced judgment upon them; some were to be kept in custody in order that their case might be more thoroughly investigated, whilst some were convicted of treachery and desertion and handed over

for execution. One of these latter, as he was being hustled off by the
executioners, begged for a chance to say something. 'O King,' he
said, 'order me not to the gibbet, for nature has bestowed upon me
marvellous powers in a certain direction.' 'Well,' said the King, 'in
what direction do you thus excel, O miserable wretch?' 'I can sing
beautifully.' 'Then sing.' The wretched fellow then began to sing, in
a voice so discordant and absurd that everyone began to laugh and
murmur, and the King himself could scarcely control his smiles.
When the guilty man perceived this, he put in, 'Pardon me this poor
performance, O King. For these guards of yours dragged me along
so roughly and cruelly, on a hot and dusty road, and pummelled me
so brutally with their fists, that my throat is full of dust, and my voice
so husky that I cannot do myself justice in singing.' The King
rewarded this witty saying with such signal grace that for the sake of
this one man he pardoned both the fellow himself and his companions. (1582)

FATHER ANTONIO MONSERRATE[155a]

## 2.   *Jahangir's court of justice*

The Emperour stiles himselfe, the King of Justice, the light of the
Law of Mahomet, the Conquerour of the World. Himselfe moder-
ates in all matters of consequence which happen neere his Court, for
the most part judging, secundum allegata and probata. Tryals are
quicke and so are Executions, hangings, beheading, impaling, killing with Dogges, by Elephants, Serpents, and other like according to the nature of the Fact. The execution is commonly done in the
Market place. The Governours in Cities and Provinces proceed in
like forme of Justice. I could never heare of Law written amongst
them: the King and his Substitutes will is Law. His Vice-gerents
continue not long in a place, but to prevent popularitie receive
usually a remoove yearely. They receive his Letters with great
respect: They looke for Presents from all which have occasion to use
them; and if they be not often visited will aske for them; yea, send
them backe for better exchange. The Cadee will imprison Debtors
and Sureties, bound with hand and Seale: and men of power for
payment will sell their persons, wives, and children, which the
custome of the Land will warrant.

The King shewes himselfe thrice a day; first at Sunrising at a
Bay-window toward the East, many being there assembled to give

him the Salam, and crying, Padsha Salament, that is, Live, O King:
At noone he sees his Elephants fight or other pastimes. A little
before Sunset, he shewes himselfe at a window to the West, and the
Sunne being set, returneth in with Drums and wind Instruments, the
peoples acclamations adding to the consort. At any of these three
times, any Sutor holding up his Petition to be seene, shall be heard.
Betwixt seven and nine he sits privately attended with his Nobles. (1616)

EDWARD TERRY[156]

## 3. Administration of justice in British India

Of the actual system for the administration of justice to the native
subjects of British India, I wish to speak with respect; because it
originated and has been continued in the purest intentions. On the
political question I presume to risk but one short observation. It is
impossible to separate the political tendency of laws from the genius
of the government from which they emanate. The spirit of the
English constitution assigns to the mass of the people an extensive
control over the exercise of public authority; and deems the executive government to be the representative of the public will. This
spirit pervades the whole body of its laws; these laws necessarily
reflect back, and reproduce the principles from which they spring:
and it is matter for grave reflection, that if this species of reaction
should ever be produced in India, from that moment it is lost to this
country for ever. The efficient protection of our native subjects in
all the rights which they themselves consider to be essential to their
happiness, is certainly the most sacred and imperious of all our
duties; and it is on this express ground that our present regulations
considered as a system of jurisprudence for the south of India,
appear to me to require a radical reform.

The English civil code professes to govern the Hindoos by their
own laws: the distinction of castes, which is absolutely the key-stone
of Hindoo law, has unfortunately either not been recognized at all in
our laws and regulations, or indirectly treated with contempt; thus
insulting the higher, without gratifying the lower classes; and, added
to the novelty of our forms, exciting in both the apprehension of
further change. It would be absurd and unjust to impute to the
authors of this system the intention of proselytism; and it can only
be lamented that it has contributed, among other causes, to produce

the belief of such an intention. But if, as some publications give reason to believe, such views have really been entertained by other persons, it will be incumbent on sober thinkers seriously to consider that, exclusively of the excess of visionary folly, it is a most unmanly, ungenerous, and unchristian deception, to veil this object under the pretext of respecting the civil and religious customs and prejudices of the people; for all their prejudices, all their opinions, and all their customs, from the most trifling to the most important, are absolutely incorporated with their religion, and ought all to be held sacred.

The founder of a philosophical Utopia would certainly reject with abhorrence a system which tends to enslave the human mind, and to entail hereditary degradation on a large portion of his citizens. But we are not here discussing a speculative theory; the objects in our contemplation are not metaphysical entities to be moulded into ideal forms; but human beings, already fixed in stubborn and immoveable prejudices, to which any system founded in wisdom and humanity must necessarily conform. It is not the question, it never can be a question, whether the English or the Hindoo code of religion and jurisprudence be entitled to the preference; but whether the Hindoo law and religion, for they are one and the same, are, or are not, to be maintained, or whether we are at liberty to invade both. If we profess to govern the Hindoos by their own laws, let us not falsify that profession by tearing them up by the roots, on the pretence of pruning and amending them. They are no longer Hindoo if they are subject to innovation. Before quitting this branch of the subject, it may be useful (for the sake of illustration) to examine the reasonableness of interfering with the most exceptionable of all their institutions. It has been thought an abomination not to be tolerated, that a widow should immolate herself on the funeral pile of her deceased husband. But what judgment should we pronounce on the Hindoo, who (if any of our institutions admitted the parallel) should *forcibly* pretend to stand between a Christian and the hope of eternal salvation? And shall we not hold him to be a driveller in politics and morals, a fanatic in religion, and a pretender to humanity, who would *forcibly* wrest this hope from the Hindoo widow? To return to the question of caste. To equalize them is impossible: to attempt it, offensive beyond all endurance to those whom we would exalt, as well as to those whom we would debase; and if we possessed the power, to exercise it would be a gross and intolerable oppression. That our regulations, where they do extend,

'Our Judge', drawn by Captain G. F. Atkinson

and where they have not yet reached, are considered with terror as
the instruments of a foreign rule, and that the Hindoos neither do
nor can feel that they are governed by their own laws, seems to have
been distinctly foreseen by that able and learned officer, major
Leith, judge advocate general, who aided in the first compilation of
the judicial regulations of Fort St. George. In a preliminary report
he deprecates the idea of sudden innovation, and observes, 'that the
system ought rather to grow out of the first germ, than start at once,
full grown, like Minerva from the head of Jupiter, shaking a lance
and aegis at the astonished native. They will arise gradually, as the
best laws ever have done, out of the manners and habits of the
people, meliorating, and reflecting back, the principles they have
derived from them.'

'If Anglo-Indian legislators would throw off a little of that, which
they somewhat too largely ascribe to the natives of India, namely,
the prejudice of education, they would find the rules of the proceeding prescribed by the Hindoo code (with all its numerous imperfec-
tions on its head), combined with the local customs, or common law
of India, not ill adapted to the state of society to which it is intended
to apply; and in the *panchaiet,* or Indian jury, which is (or rather
was) universally established in the south as the common law of the
land, an admirable instrument of practical decision.'

To the last paragraph its intelligent author adds this note: 'The
*panchaiet,* or Indian jury, is an institution so entirely neglected, or
misunderstood, that I believe its existence is now, for the first time,
presented to the notice of the English reader.' I am happy to find
this excellent judge passing so favourable an opinion on the only
mode of administering justice I adopted during my residence at
Dhuboy; as will appear in the chapter set apart for that subject,
under the name of *panchaut,* or the *'decision of five.'* I was delighted
with so simple and effectual a mode of satisfying all parties, and in
confirmation of the colonel's remark, I must observe, that it was an
institution perfectly new to me, and appeared to be so to all my
European visitors. (1813)

JAMES FORBES[157]

## 4. *Settlement of quarrels and litigations*

Intestine discord, or serious disputes ending in murder, or the usual
effects of revenge, are very rare. Quarrels and litigation are usually

settled by the arbitration of men appointed by the parties, or whose character gives them a sort of claim to such a distinction, and are generally the elders and chief men of villages. When such arbitration fails of effect, or is regretted by either party, the case is referred to the prince or governor of the province or district (who have various designations in their respective countries), before whom the trial by ordeal is performed, for which several means are used. A small copper coin is thrown into a pan of boiling oil, out of which he who professes to clear his innocence or right must take it with his naked hand; or he must, unhurt, hold a red hot ball of iron in the palm of his hand; or, each party taking a goat, gives poison to the animals, and that which survives denotes the owner's innocence, or gains his cause. The wuzzeers, or ministers of the chief, settle all minor causes, and from them there is always an appeal to the superior. (1815)

JAMES BAILLIE FRASER[158]

## 5. Want of a code of laws for British India

I may conclude these reflections with one more, obviously exemplifying the real nature of our government of the sword. Although far advanced into the second century of our sway, no Justinian has yet appeared to condense into a simple form those vast, accumulating, and crude materials called 'Regulations.' Is it that the period of one, or at most two lustres, accorded to our ephemeral governors, is too limited for its accomplishment; or does the pusillanimous maxim, 'a little knowledge is a dangerous thing,' operate to prevent it? Let us hope that this anomaly in our administration may be removed, and that vanity, if no better feeling, may stimulate some future vicegerent to immortalize himself by the formation of a legal code, which may be at once adapted to the comprehension and guidance of the people, and a fitting record of our supremacy when the Atlantic shall roll between us and the governed.

The difficulty of framing a code of laws which may be applicable to the condition of the complicated masses under our rule, may be urged in palliation of its total omission; but this plea cannot be deemed valid in the absence of all experiment with the extensive provinces adjacent to the seat of Government, as laws framed for these could always be modified to meet a further extension of territory. As regards our tributary or subsidiary connections, the

political treaties must necessarily form the basis of our relations and
conduct with them; but even these might be reduced to something
like uniformity, and instead of the eccentric movements now given
by individual will, be made to harmonize with one general design.
(1839)

JAMES TOD[159]

## 6.  *One sells his rice at any price*

> A paddy-buyer, purse in hand,
> Comes to a store, and to a stand.
> 'I want to buy some rice,' says he,
> 'A sample of it let me see.'
> The paddy-seller is not slow
> A little measure-ful to show.
> The buyer asks, 'Have you no more?'
> The seller says, 'This is the story:'
> Pagodas one or ten will buy
> No other rice than now you spy.'
> The neighbour pays pagodas ten,
> And says he'll soon be here again.
> And back he comes, with bullock strong,
> To fetch his purchase before long,
> And, like a man of means and mirth,
> Demands his ten pagodas' worth.
> The dealer brings the measure small,
> And says, 'Pour out, and take it all.'
> 'This all for ten pagodas!' cries
> The purchaser. The cheat replies,
> 'For one or ten, I said before,
> This is the rice, and there's no more.
> Agreeing, ten you chose to pay,
> So take your bargain, and away.'
> The jest no joke the good man feels,
> And to the judge the trick reveals,
> To whom the storekeeper is bold
> To say he's done as he was told.
> Raman ordains, 'A month must glide,
> Ere I this matter can decide.
> Be it till then your equal doom

Your meals to eat in the same room.
You, plaintiff, the boil'd grain receive,
And just a half to this man give.'
  Then privately he shows his plan:
'You take a bellyful, my man;
And break a grain of rice in two,
And give him half of it to chew.'
  Two meals of half a grain suffice
The hungry seller of the rice
So far that loudly he complains,
And access to the judge obtains.
Raman the other calls, and, 'Why,'
He asks, 'your mess-mate's food deny?'
Says he 'I duly dealt the meat,
One half the grain: he would not eat.'
The storekeeper begins to' explain,—
'He pinches off just half one grain,
And tells me all my dinner's there:
How can I live upon such fare?'
The buyer, 'Tit for tat,' replies;
'He in a basket show'd some rice;
'Whatever price you pay,' said he,
'This is the article you see;'
I ten pagodas paid; behold,
'T was but the sample that he sold!
So I the letter keep, and deal
With him by contract at each meal.'
  The judge now to the culprit turns,
Who with long face his sentence learns.
'According to the country-price,
His ten pagodas' worth of rice
Supply to him, or be agreed
A month on his half-rice to feed.'
  Consenting, as compell'd by law,
The seller verifies the saw,—
'By meanness meanness is made void,
And trick by counter-trick destroy'd.' (1873)

EDWARD JEWITT ROBINSON[160]

## 7. Court of justice in the jungle

On the evening of the 6th, having made my usual rounds, I retired to rest, after placing my chronometer and its chain in a heavy steel box of English make, which I pushed under my bed, not going to sleep, however, without first verifying the state of my rifle and revolvers, which were within reach. Towards midnight a slight noise awakened me; but, as nothing seemed to be moving either in the tent or outside, I dozed off again. An hour later I was startled out of my sleep by a noise apparently proceeding from the head of my bed. I sprang to my arms, but the tent, lighted by a small lamp, presented nothing unusual. I then went out with my gun, took a turn round the camp, and returned to my little bed, laughing at my own fears. As soon as it was daylight I had the chowkeydars summoned, and they assured me they had remarked nothing extraordinary during the night. Quite reassured, I made my preparations to go as usual to my laboratory, when I soon discovered that a box containing stereotype plates was missing, and at the same time ascertained the disappearance of the steel box. Forthwith all my servants in great excitement set about searching in the neighbourhood of the camp: and after an hour's hunting they brought me back the box broken open by blows from a pickaxe, and bereft of its contents. This was a heavy loss to me. Besides a valuable watch and a thousand rupees in silver, it contained a very fine collection of diamonds and jewels presented to me by various rajahs; and, moreover, bills of exchange on the bankers at Bhopal for a very large amount. I found myself completely plundered.

I sent word in haste to the Bhopal magistrate of the district, who arrived the same day at Sanchi, with a strong escort of scribes and gendarmes. His first act was to put the chowkeydars in irons, and to seize all the population of the two hamlets, men, women, and children. These unfortunate people were all penned into an enclosure of stakes and cords to await their examination. The next day an express sent from Bhopal informed me that the Government of the Begum declared itself responsible for the crime, and would indemnify me for my losses.

A judge from the capital came to preside at the court. The villagers were examined one after another, but denied all participation in the robbery. At last a poor child, eight years old, frightened at the terrible whip of the sepoys, pointed out four of our chowkeydars as the guilty parties. These wretched men, when brought before the tribunal, allowed themselves to be lacerated by the whip rather than confess; nevertheless, the proofs were overwhelming. One of them had been placed by me at the very spot where the thief had effected an entrance into the tent by cutting the canvas with his knife, while another had been seen by one of my servants during the night on the spot where the strong box had been found; but nothing could wrest a confession from him.

Some days afterwards the bills of exchange, of the value of which the thieves were ignorant, were found near the village; and the Begum's Government indemnified me for my loss; but nothing could replace for me the memorials to which I attach so great a value. (1875)

LOUIS ROUSSELET[161]

## 8. *The Indian judge*

A cloud was on the Judge's brow,
   The day we walked in Aitwar-Pet;
I knew not then, but since I know
   What held his earnest features set:

That great cause in the Suddur Court!
   To-morrow judgment should be given;
And in my old friend's troubled thought
   Conscience and prejudice had striven;—

Nay, nay! No juster Judge on bench!
   But justice in this cause of 'Wheatstone's'
Was hard to do. I could not wrench
   His sombre eyes from Poona's street-stones.

Silent we threaded Moti-chouk,
   Paced silent past the Dharma-sala;
At last, half petulant, I spoke;
   'Here is our Sanskrit School—Pat-shala!'

'See! Listening to their grey Gooroo,
   The Brahman boys read Hindu cases;
Justinian and the Code for you,
   Manu for them! What solemn faces

'Range, in dark ring, around the book
    Wherefrom the grim Acharya preaches!'
He paused, and, with a wistful look,
    Said: 'Might one know what Manu teaches?'

So drew we nigh the School, and paid
    Due salutations; while the Master—
Proud to be marked by Sahebs—made
    The strong shlokes roll, fuller and faster.

'*Na vismayeta tapasa*
    *Vadedishtwa cha nanritan*
*Na parikirttay et datwa*
    *Nartti pyapavaded vipran*

'*Namutra hi sahayartham*
    *Pita mata cha tishtatas*
*Na jnatir na putradaram*
    *Tishtati dharma kevalas.*

All down to *Kasaririnam*
    Gravely the Shastri chants the verses,
Rocking his head; while, after him,
    The turbaned class each line rehearses.

'What is the lesson?' asked my friend,
    With low salaam, reply was given:
'Manu's Fourth Chapter—nigh the end—
    At Shloke two hundred thirty-seven.'

Then, turning to the brightest-eyed
    Of those brown pupils round him seated,
'Gunput,' the Shastri said, with pride,
    'If it shall please my lords, can read it.'

We nodded; and the Brahman lad—
    At such great charge shy, but delighted—
In what soft English speech he had
    The Devanagiri recited:

'Be not too proud of good deeds wrought!—
    When thou art come from prayer, speak truly!—
Even if he.wrongeth thee in aught
    Respect thy Gooroo! Give alms duly;

'But let none wist! Live, day to day,
　By little and by little swelling
Thy tale of duty done—the way
　The wise ant-people build their dwelling;

'Not harming any living thing:
　That thou mayst have—at time of dying—
A Hand to hold thee, and to bring
　Thy footsteps safe; and, so relying,

'Pass to the farther world. For none
　Save Justice brings there! Father, mother,
Will not be nigh; nor wife, nor son,
　Nor friends, nor kin; nor any other

'Save only Justice! All alone
　Each entereth here, and each one leaveth
This world, alone; and every one
　The fruit of all his deeds receiveth

'Alone—alone; bad deeds and good!
　That day when kinsmen, sadly turning,
Forsake thee, like to clay or wood,
　A fragment fitted for the burning.

'But Justice shall not quit thee then,
　If thou hast served her; therefore never
Cease serving; that she hold thee, when
　The darkness falls which falls forever;

'Which hath no road, nor ray to guide.
　But Justice knows the road; the midnight
Is noon to her. Man at her side
　Goes through the gloom safe to the hid light.

'And he who loved her more than all,
　Who purged by sorrow his offences,
Shall shine in realms celestial
　With glory, quit of sins and senses.'

●　●　●　●　●

What made my friend so softly lay
　His hand on Gunput's naked shoulder

With gentle words of praise, and say—
   His eyes grown happier and bolder—

'I too have been at school! Accept
   Thanks, Gooroo! for these words imparted.'
And when we turned away he kept
   Silence no more, but smiled, light-hearted.

And, next day, in his Indian court,
   That summing-up he did declaim us—
Straight in the teeth of what was thought—
   Which made 'His Honour' feared and famous. (1886)

EDWIN ARNOLD[162]

## 9.   *The humour of justice*

I do not think that there has been any time in my service when I have found my work light except, perhaps, when, many years ago, I was Excise Commissioner of the Central Provinces, before that office was amalgamated with several other miscellaneous departments, and before Berar came under the Central Provinces administration; but though our work has generally been quite sufficient for each day, it has been varied work; and as a great deal of it had to be done outside the office, in the town or among the villages, it has been both interesting and healthy. There have also been incidents occurring every now and again which have been of a more or less humorous character and have relieved the monotony of our work. Many such incidents crowd on my memory now. But I shall only relate a few of them. The homely character of our life in the Central Provinces led to many private little jests which were pleasant at the time, but would seem almost silly if set down in print. I shall therefore confine myself to a few incidents more or less connected with work.

On one occasion, when I was a District Magistrate, I exposed myself to severe censure from the European ladies of the station on account of the version which got about of a decision in my court. I was reported to have judicially ruled that, according to the law prevailing in India, a husband had a right to beat his wife, and that she had no remedy in such a case. It will be understood that this was not a very popular decision with the ladies. The facts of the case were a little interesting. There had been a long-standing feud between two small Zamindars (or landowners) in a certain village; and they had been in the habit for some time of taking all manner of means to annoy one another. At last one of them got an opportunity of which he promptly availed himself. His rival Ramparshad was heard speaking in strong terms to his wife in the verandah of their house; and the sound of a slap was heard. Gangaparshad either heard the quarrel or was told of it; and he got hold of a friend to take a document to Ramparshad's wife on which she was asked to make a mark, and was informed that by doing so she would receive considerable benefit. Trusting to the friendliness of Gangaparshad's messenger she made a mark.

The document stated that Ramparshad very frequently assaulted her, entered in detail into an exaggerated recital of the events of the quarrel above referred to, and ended by asking the protection of the Magistrate. There is no doubt that Gangaparshad thought that Ramparshad would suffer very much in dignity by this attack on his character, and by the necessity for having his wife called as a witness in court; and Gangaparshad being a relative of the lady was able to appear as her friend and quasi guardian in the case. A very careful inquiry on the spot showed the triviality of the incident, and the enmity which lay at the bottom of the complaint.

The case came up for hearing, and Ramparshad was advised by his counsel to allow his wife to appear, closely veiled, as a witness for the prosecution. She admitted that her husband had spoken roughly to her and had given her a slap in a fit of temper for which she proceeded to make an elaborate apology. In cross-examination by the accused she spoke of the excellent terms on which she lived with her husband, and I allowed villagers to appear to corroborate her evidence. I was entitled under the law to compel Gangaparshed to make compensation to Ramparshad for a frivolous and vexatious complaint; and I did so. The effect was not satisfactory. It did not indeed make Gangaparshad more friendly to his rival; but it made him a little more cautious in his conduct. It is very curious how much we see even in very serious cases of the use of the courts for purpose of private enmity. Cases have been well known in which even a charge of murder has been trumped up by a man against his enemy.

Another matter which, though very serious, has its more or less humorous side, is the practice of trial by jury, as we not infrequently find it in India. Every country has experience of the difficulty of persuading men to find a verdict against the accused in certain cases where political or faction feeling is involved; and this, of course, is found in India as elsewhere. There is, however, a case peculiar to

India which is of very common occurrence, that is, the difficulty of persuading jurors or assessors to find a verdict against a Brahman, especially in cases involving capital punishment. Assessors differ from jurors in that their verdict has not the weight of that of the jury. Assessors are there to advise the Judge, not to decide with any finality even questions of fact, and in the more backward tracts we have much more of trial with assessors than trial by jury.

As a young officer, I was once called on to inquire into a case of murder and to prosecute it before the Court of Session. It was as clear a case as ever had been. The murder was cruel, and the eye-witnesses were beyond suspicion. There were two assessors, and both of them returned a verdict of 'not guilty.' The Judge differing from the assessors sentenced the Brahman accused to death, and he paid the penalty. Some time afterwards, one of the assessors came to visit me. He was a fairly influential landowner, and himself a Brahman, well educated in the vernacular, but without knowledge of English. I asked him how he could find a verdict so contrary to the evidence, and he frankly said to me in the most friendly way, 'I could not possibly find a verdict which would lead to the death of a Brahman. You know that it is grievous sin for any Hindu to cause the death of a Brahman; and it does not matter whether you do it with your own hand or indirectly by the hand of another.' 'But,' I said, 'it is a serious thing for you to betray the trust which is reposed in you by the Government on behalf of the public; and you cannot help regarding this as most blameworthy failure of duty.'

He replied with some emotion, 'It is you really who are to blame. You are not ignorant of our views in this matter. Why, then, should you put us in a position where we might be called upon, as I was on that occasion, to choose between the sin of saying what I believed to be untrue, and the infinitely awful sin of causing the death of a Brahman?' The strong feeling with which my old friend spoke to me on the subject made a great impression on my mind, and I have often thought that we do not know, or at all events do not fully consider, what grievous injury we inflict on the people of India by forcing on them customs and duties which are altogether inconsistent with their traditions and beliefs.

I remember another case in which an Honorary Magistrate tried a Hindu belonging to a religious order for habitually receiving stolen property. As in this country so in India, the receiver of stolen property ought to be severely dealt with because of the demoralising effect of his occupation on the community. The evidence was clear and conclusive, and the Magistrate felt himself bound to convict; but there is a provision of the law whereby the period of police custody after conviction is included in the period of imprisonment. The worthy Magistrate therefore set himself to calculate how long it would take to march the prisoner, from one police station to another, to the head-quarters of the District where the jail was situated. He calculated that it would take a week; and he sentenced the sacred receiver to a week's imprisonment. I well remember how he could not conceal from me afterwards his disappointment that he had forgotten that there was an indirect road to head-quarters which included a considerable stretch of newly made railway line; and the prisoner arrived at the jail in time to undergo three days' imprisonment. The washing off of the sacred ashes and filth which he had, perhaps for years, allowed to accumulate, was a terrible blow to the criminal; and he very vigorously cursed the magistrate.

Another curious case may be recorded. When I was Commissioner of Chhattisgarh I had appellate jurisdiction over certain civil courts. In one of these subordinate courts a certain plaintiff had brought a suit against a debtor. The debtor's plea was that he had certainly incurred the debt, but that he had also repaid it; and he challenged the plaintiff to make an oath to the effect that he had not been paid. The law allows a case to be decided in this way with the consent of parties. The party agreeing must take an oath which he regards as most certainly binding upon him, and the sanctity of which, as respects him, the opposite party is also prepared to admit. The parties in this case agreed that the plaintiff should take his oath with his hand on the tail of the sacred cow at the great temple of the goddess Samlai in Sambalpur—an oath of great solemnity in these parts. The plaintiff took the oath and declared that he had not been paid; and decree was passed accordingly in his favour. That night the plaintiff died; and the ground of appeal to me was that the gods had manifested their displeasure at the false affirmation by taking the plaintiff's life, and that therefore the decree ought to be reversed. I have very little doubt that the plaintiff's oath was false; but I was, of course, unable to alter the decision; for the law makes such an oath, when taken by consent of parties, final in the case. (1911)

ANDREW HENDERSON LEITH FRASER[163]

# 8. Administration

## 1. The Civil Service

For a considerable number of years after the East-India Company had acquired large territorial possessions in India, the gentlemen sent out to fill the various civil offices of the government were selected without any peculiar references to qualification. A writership was considered a provision for life, if not a source of large ultimate fortune; for if the salary was not liberal, the opportunities of gain, by means of trade and other less honourable proceedings, were numerous; while a knowledge of languages and of official business would, it was considered, be acquired in due course of time. The evil working of this loose system, however, at all times partially obvious, was the more apparent as the demand for talent augmented, and rigid integrity and an independence of native connection became a *sine qua non* of good government. It was then that the Company began to devise plans of home education, for parties aspiring to serve them in the civil departments abroad. Character, connections, and a certain stock of knowledge, were declared the essential concomitants of a writership, though merely preparative to other qualifications, of which the candidate was to possess himself in India. This declaration was a material step towards the improvement of the service; but it was not until the year 1809, when the college of Haileybury, in Hertford, was founded, that the education of the future civilian resolved itself into a system, the adherence to which has since been uniform. A few years ago some exceptions to a collegiate education were made in favour of young men who had earned much distinction at some of the other great public schools or colleges, and who were honoured with presentations of Indian appointments by Presidents of the Board of Control, or Chairmen of the Direction, anxious to promote individual merit; but at present *all* the civil officers in the service of the East-India Company are obliged to receive instruction at the Haileybury College, the nomination to which is dependent upon the ... regulations and preparatory instructions. (1845)

JOACHIM HAYWARD STOCQUELER[164]

## 2. Punjab administration

The principal difficulty in the Punjab administration has been in getting good executive officers of districts, for the reduced scale of pay which modern economy prescribes is not sufficient to tempt men within several years of a corresponding grade in the provinces to run the risk of health, and undergo the hardships and labour which must be required of them in a new territory. And as the duties involved teaching ignorant establishments, it was for the most part only from the north-west provinces that men sufficiently acquainted with the language, the people, and the system to be introduced could be drawn. To find men young enough to accept the pay, and yet efficient enough for the duties, was not easy; and the exposure and labour being so great, the consumption from sickness and consequent change of officers was large, and created further difficulties. Hence much was thrown on the superior officers, and their duties have been very severe; yet have things been wonderfully well managed. A good system has been introduced, and the administration goes on quietly and well. . . .

The country having had the benefit of our previous experience, the best systems have been introduced, while all vexatious native taxes have been at once swept away, transit duties abolished, and the plain of the Indus opened to free and unrestricted commerce. Especial encouragement has been given to a manly and industrious agricultural population, and altogether the condition of the people has been made so good, and they are so well satisfied, that the perfect quiet and facility of administration which we have hitherto experienced in the Punjab (cis-the Indus) is likely long to continue. (1852)

GEORGE CAMPBELL[165]

# 9. Police and Army

## 1. The soldiers of Golconda

The King of *Golconda* pays above Five hundred thousand Soldiers; and that makes the Riches of the *Omras,* because he who has Pay for a thousand Men, entertains but Five hundred, and so do the rest proportionably. He allows a Trooper (who ought to be either a *Mogul* or *Persian*) ten *Chequins* a month, and for that pay, he ought to keep two Horses and four or five Servants. A Foot-Soldier (of these nations) hath five *Chequins,* and ought to entertain two Servants, and carry a Musket. He gives not the *Indians* (his own subjects) above two or three Roupies a month, and these carry only the Lance and Pike. Seeing the late King gave his Soliders better Pay than this do's, he was far better served: He entertained always a strong Army, and the number of Men he payed was always compleat. By that means he easily hindered the *Great Mogul* from attempting any thing against him, and was not tributary to him as his Son is. (1666)

JEAN DE THEVENOT[166]

## 2. Respecting the police

If the Sepoys, Picdars, or any other people belonging to the Nabob, have any cause of complaint against the soldiers, Sepoys, or any other person of the garrison, they will address themselves to Colonel Campbell, who will make them be punished by his laws, according as the case requires. On the other hand, if the soldiers, sepoys, or any other people of the garrison, have any cause of complaint against the Sepoys, Picdars, or any of the people belonging to the Nabob, they will address themselves to the Commanding Officer of the Prince, who will likewise make them be punished according as they deserve. Any person taking revenge at his own hand, will be punished by order of his own officer. (1783)

A BRITISH OFFICER[167]

## 3. Mendicant  soldiers

By a statute of Elizabeth it was made a capital offence, felony without benefit of clergy, for soldiers or sailors to beg on the high roads without a pass; and I suppose this statute arose from their frequently robbing on the highways in the character of beggars. There must at that time have been an immense number of soldiers in the transition state in England; men who disdained the labours of peaceful life, or had by long habit become unfitted for them. Religious mendicity has hitherto been the great safety valve through which the unquiet transition spirit has found vent under our strong and settled government. A Hindoo of any caste may become a religious mendicant of the two great monastic orders of Gosaens, who are disciples of Sewa, and Byragies, who are disciples of Vishnoo; and any Mahomedan may become a Fakeer—and Gosaens, Byragies, and Fakeers, can always secure or extort food from the communities they visit.

Still, however, there is enough of this unquiet transition spirit left to give anxiety to a settled government; for the moment insurrection breaks out at any point, from whatever cause, to that point thousands are found flocking from north, east, west, and south, with their arms and their horses, if they happen to have any, in the hope of finding service either under the local authorities or the insurgents themselves; as the troubled winds of heaven rush to the point where the pressure of the atmosphere has been diminished. (c. 1833)

WILLIAM HENRY SLEEMAN[168]

## 4. On the native army

There are few subjects on which a young man, on his first arrival in India, is more prone to entertain erroneous notions, than concerning the native soldiery. On all sides he hears philippics against the *natives* of India, who are represented as possessing almost every bad quality; while, on the other hand, he is overwhelmed by the laudatory expressions adopted whenever the sepoys are mentioned; whose sense of honour, gratitude, and devotion to us; whose bravery, patience in undergoing fatigue and privations; honesty, and various other good qualities, are described as being beyond all praise. Many a young man has consequently made the mistake to suppose that the sepoys were from a foreign territory, totally unconnected with India: no one would ever have imagined that men, of whom such totally opposite characters were given, could be of the same country and race. I confess that at first I fell into this mistake, but at length I made the discovery that the sepoys were the common peasantry of India; and that those who were spoken of as 'the natives,' from whose character that of the whole population was' described, were a few of the refuse of the country, who attended the English as menial servants.

Many of the military officers, when reminded of their inconsistency, endeavour to explain it by asserting, what they really believe, that the sepoys are from the middling and better classes of the people. This, however, is a complete mistake: the majority of the native infantry belong to the poorer classes of cultivators; some, chiefly the Muhammedans, are inhabitants of towns; these sometimes possess gardens or small fields near the town, and live by selling the produce: they are, for the most part, descendants of the old soldiery of the native princes: and there are a few of a miscellaneous description whom it would be difficult to class.

The whole of these are the very same description of people who serve as policemen, or even as common watchmen (chokedars) to individuals. Notwithstanding what is so often said about the preference shown by certain classes for a military life, there are very few of any description who would not rather stay at home if they could; although, if from want of means to do this, obliged to go to service, undoubtedly there are large classes who prefer the army to any other. In spite of the high pay and privileges which our native soldiery enjoy, there are few men who, if they possessed an income equal to three or even two and a half rupees per month, would ever leave home to enter the army; but when the income is less than that, then one or more members of the family set out to seek service. A party of six or seven, or more, from the same village or neighbourhood, is often made, and the first step usually is, to offer themselves as soldiers; then as policemen or revenue officers, and such as are unsuccessful in all these departments, take the situation of chuprassee, or watchmen to individuals. Some will choose one of the other situations, when they can obtain it near their own houses, in preference to the army. These observations apply nearly to all the native soldiery, with this addition that the same class of town-bred Muhammedans who enlist in the army, will also enter the service of individuals as table-attendants, grooms, or other capacity. Many of these servants have brothers, or other near relations, in the army;

and there is scarcely a policeman, chuprassee, or private watchman, who has not also. So completely erroneous is the notion that our native soldiery are drawn from the middling and better classes of the people. The regular cavalry are, on the whole, composed of a description of men inferior to those who form the infantry of the line: the artillery, horse and foot, may rank with these two as to the sort of men of which they are composed; and the only branch of our army which contains a better description of men than those above mentioned, is the local or irregular horse.

It is true that many men are to be found in the army who are entitled to pensions, or who now have it in their power, if they pleased, to retire on a very comfortable income: they have become accustomed to the service, like their comrades, have acquired expensive habits, look forward to promotion, and a still higher income—various reasons may be assigned: there are also some who have a natural wish for distinction, instead of remaining clodhoppers all their lives; but the majority of the natives of any class would certainly not leave home for any service, if they could live there with but very moderate comfort.

Much of the praise which is bestowed on the sepoys is, indirectly, flattery to ourselves. They are so faithful to *us*; they will endure so much in *our* service; and other expressions of a similar nature are made use of, thereby intimating that *we* had so treated them as to produce the feeling of gratitude (which, however, *the natives* do not possess). Instances are quoted, such as the attack on Warren Hastings by Chait Singh at Benares; the retreat of Colonel Monson; the disturbance at Barelly, where an attempt was made, by the fanatics who headed the mob, to excite the religious feelings of the troops against their officers; and various others, all tending to show how much the sepoys will do for *us,* and what an excellent class of men they are while *the natives* are everything that is degraded and bad. It is surprising that the absurdity of it never strikes those who are constantly talking in this style; for surely a good many of the military officers must know of what class of people the native army is composed.

But the above circumstances, which we endeavour to turn to the account of our vanity, are in truth only characteristic of one peculiar feature in the character of the natives—the narrow circle to which they confine their feelings and affections. Patriotism in its proper sense, *i.e.* a love of one's country (not according to Johnson's definition, which probably is a much truer one according to modern practice than the other), is a sentiment unknown to any native of India: he has a strong attachment to his own home and village, but so far from extending it beyond that immediate sphere, he probably may be at feud with half the neighbouring hamlets: and so far is this indifference carried towards any thing but what is immediately connected with himself, that if it were the purpose of Government to ravage, with fire and sword, any particular district, it might be done just as effectually with soldiers raised in that province, as with regiments composed of foreigners. When it came to the point, each man would be anxious to save his own particular village. but he would most likely have no sympathy for its neighbour. It is this feeling which makes the native ready to engage in any service of which the pay and treatment are good. They are, in short, complete Captain Dalgettys.

Their attachment, if it may be called such, to the British Government, arises from the high pay, higher than can be obtained in any other service; the privileges they enjoy; the circumstance that our Government is in appearance more stable than any native sovereignty; and the greater regularity with which pay is issued. The following is the rate of pay received by the respective grades in the native infantry and foot artillery in the Bengal presidency. That of the cavalry, and horse artillery, and sappers and miners, is higher.

| Rank | Rupees pay per month |
|---|---|
| Subadar or native captain | 67 |
| Jemadar, ditto lieutenant | 24 |
| Havildar, ditto serjeant | 14 |
| Naik, ditto corporal | 12 |
| Private sepoy | 7 |
| Drummer | 11 |

In addition to which they receive some articles of clothing: certain regimental staff appointments are open to them: their letters are transmitted free of postage: facilities are afforded them in preferring suits in courts, beyond what are granted to other suitors: and it is also ordered that any cause in which a sepoy is concerned is to be heard in preference to others, without reference to its place on the file. They have also a pension when worn out. The pay of a native infantry private, compared with the income of the agricultural classes, the wages of labourers, and of menial servants, is equivalent to paying an English soldier of the same rank about sixty pounds sterling per annum; besides the clothing and privileges above enumerated; of which, however, those regarding suits in court would be little valued in England, although of some importance here. Could we afford to pay our army at home at this rate, there would be little difficulty in recruiting, even in the most desperate wars. The native has, besides, the almost certain prospect, if he only live long, of rising to the rank of commissioned officer; and in the interim, the staff situations are open to him. There is, on the whole, little campaigning and less fighting; and notwithstanding the outcry that has been made, of late years, about the heavy duty which falls upon the sepoys, consequent upon the reduction of their numbers, their labour is not half so great as that of a peasant, police-officer, or some descriptions of servants.

There is no service in India for the lower classes so good as that of the native army in the British employ; the usual pay of an infantry private, in those of the native chiefs, is five rupees per month; and there is no regular pension, although an individual sometimes obtains one. It is no wonder then, that we have found so little difficulty in raising recruits.

There is no more striking contrast, than the behaviour of the British Government towards its native army, and the principles on which the rest of the population have been governed. While the latter, as a whole, have been subject to every species of extortion and oppression, and to a virtual denial of justice; the army is cherished in every possible way. The fact is, that Government have all along been aware that our tenor of India is that of the sword, and that as long as the native army should remain staunch, the whole at large might be tyrannized over to any extent. This is the secret of the high pay and privileges of the native soldiers, and the leniency with which their faults are treated. Should they plunder the villagers in marching the country, redress is almost out of the question, except by a process so tedious that the cure would be worse than the original evil: sometimes, indeed, the most gross outrages and wanton attacks on harmless villagers, or townspeople, in which several of the latter are killed or wounded, are hushed up with a mock inquiry, and passed over for fear of annoying the soldiery—a strong proof that Government are well aware of our real position in India, and how we are detested by the people; and that even the army has

not that attachment to us which formerly existed; which will be
presently alluded to. (1835)

FREDERICK JOHN SHORE[169]

## 5.  *The Goorkhas*

Colonel Y. had us out early in the morning to see his little Ghoorka
regiment manoeuvre. Most of the men are about five feet
six, with little hands and feet in proportion. All the mountaineers are verv small creatures, but they make excellent little soldiers; and the Ghoorkhas beat our troops at this spot twenty-five
years ago, and killed almost all the officers sent against them. Now
they are our subjects they fight equally well for us, and were heard
to say at Bhurtpore that they really thought some of our soldiers
were nearly equal to themselves. They look like little black dolls.
They are quite unlike natives. There is a regular fool attached to
the regiment, who had stuck a quantity of wild flowers in his helme ,
and came up and saluted G. with a large drawn sword in a most
ridiculous manner. (1838)

EMILY EDEN[170]

## 6.  *Police abuses*

The European magistrate of a district has perhaps a million of
people to look after. The native officers next under him are the
Thanadars of the different subdivisions of the district, containing
each many towns and villages, with a population of perhaps one
hundred thousand people. These officers have no grade to look
forward to; and get a salary of *twenty-five rupees a month each!*

They cannot possibly do their duties unless they keep each a
couple of horses or ponies, with servants to attend to them, indeed
they are told so by every magistrate who cares about the peace of his
district. The people, seeing how much we expect from the
Thanadar, and how little we give him, submit to his demands for
contribution without a murmur; and consider almost any demand
venial from a man so employed and so paid. They are confounded at
our inconsistency; and say, where they dare to speak their
minds—'We see you giving high salaries, and high prospects of
advancement to men who have nothing on earth to do but to collect

your revenues and to decide our disputes about pounds, shillings, and pence, which we used to decide much better among ourselves when we had no other court but that of our elders to appeal to; while those who are to protect life and property, to keep peace over the land, and enable the industrious to work in security, maintain their families and pay the government revenue, are left without any prospect whatever of rising, and almost without any pay at all.'

There is really nothing in our rule in India which strikes the people so much as this glaring inconsistency, the evil effects of which are so great and so manifest. The only way to remedy the evil is, to give to the police what the other branches of the public service already enjoy,—a feeling of security in the tenure of office; a higher rate of salary; and above all a gradation of rank which shall afford a prospect of rising to those who discharge their duties ably and honestly. For this purpose all that is required is, the interposition of an officer between the Thanadar and the magistrate, in the same manner' as the Sudder Ameen is now interposed between the Moonsiff and the judge. On an average there are perhaps twelve Thanas, or police subdivisions in each district; and one such officer to every four Thanas would be sufficient for all purposes. The Governor-general who shall confer this boon on the people of India, will assuredly be hailed as one of their greatest benefactors. I should, I believe, speak within bounds when I say, that the Thanadars throughout the country, give, at present, more than all the money which they receive in avowed salaries from government, as a share of indirect perquisites to the native officers of the magistrate's court, who have to send their reports to them, and communicate their orders, and prepare the cases of the prisoners they may send in, for commitment to the sessions courts. Were they not to do so, few of them would be in office a month. The intermediate officers here proposed, would obviate all this, they would be to the magistrate at once the *tapis* of prince Hosain, and the *telescope* of prince Alee,—media that would enable them to be everywhere, and see everything! (1844)

WILLIAM HENRY SLEEMAN[171]

## 7. Rajput rebels

### On the Sardah, 1858

Where the mighty cliffs are frowning

Far o'er the torrents fall,
And the pine and the oak stand crowning
    The ridges of high Nepaul,

Sat twenty Rajput rebels,
    Haggard and pale and thin,
Lazily chucking the pebbles
    Into the foaming lynn.

Their eyes were sunken and weary
    With a sort of listless woe
They looked from their desolate eyrie
    Over the plains below.

They turned from the mountain breezes
    And shivered with cold and damp,
They had brought up some choice diseases
    From the deadly jungle swamp.

Two had wounds from a sabre
    And one from an Enfield ball,
But no one cared for his neighbour,
    There was sickness or wounds in all

The Rajput leader rose then
    Stiffly and slow from the ground,
He looked at the camp of his foes then,
    And he looked at his brethren round;

And he said: 'From my country driven
    'With the last of my hunted band,
'My home to another given
    'On a foreign soil I stand.

'They have burnt every roof in the village
    'They have slain the best of my kin,
'They have ruined and burnt and pillaged
    'And yet we had done no sin;

'Our clans were heady and rude,
    'Our robbers many and tall,
'But our fighting never shed English blood,
    'Nor harried an English hall.

'The king took tithe if he might;
  'He was paid by a knave or a fool;
'For we held our lands on a firmer right
  'Than is given by parchment rule;

'Our fathers of old had cleared it
  'From the jungle with axe and sword,
'Our ancient rights had endeared it
  'To him who was chief and lord.

'My father's curse with my father's land,
  'Their curse on the smooth pale face
'On the crafty head and the iron hand
  'Of the treacherous English race.

'From the banks of Ganges holy,
  'From the towers of fair Lucknow,
'They have driven us surely and slowly,
  'They have crushed us blow on blow.

'As our fathers fought, we fight;
  'But a sword and a matchlock gun,
 'Gainst the serried line of bayonets bright
  'A thousand moving like one!

    \*        \*        \*
    \*        \*        \*

'When the army has slain its fill,
  'When they bid the hangman cease;
'They will beckon us down from the desert hill
  'To go to our homes in peace.

'To plough with a heavy heart,
  'And, of half our fields bereft,
 ' 'Gainst the usurer's oath, and the lawyer's art
  'To battle that some be left.

'At the sight of an English face
  'Loyally bow the head,
'And cringe like slaves to the surly race
  'For pay and a morsel of bread;

'Toil like an ox or a mule

'To pay the stranger his fee—
'Our sons may brook the Feringhee's rule,
'There is no more life for me! (1858)

ALFRED C. LYALL[172]

# 10. Education

## 1. The great sangharma of Nalanda

The priests, to the number of several thousands, are men of the highest ability and talent. Their distinction is very great at the present time, and there are many hundreds whose fame has rapidly spread through distant regions. Their conduct is pure and unblamable. They follow in sincerity the precepts of the moral law. The rules of this convent are severe, and all the priests are bound to observe them. The countries of India respect them and follow them. The day is not sufficient for asking and answering profound questions. From morning till night they engage in discussion; the old and the young mutually help one another. Those who cannot discuss questions out of the *Tripitaka* are little esteemed, and are obliged to hide themselves for shame. Learned men from different cities, on this account, who desire to acquire quickly a renown in discussion, come here in multitudes to settle their doubts, and then the streams (*of their wisdom*) spread far and wide. For this reason some persons usurp the name (*of Nalanda students*), and in going to and fro receive honour in consequence. If men of other quarters desire to enter and take part in the discussions, the keeper of the gate proposes some hard questions; many are unable to answer, and retire. One must have studied deeply both old and new (*books*) before getting admission. Those students, therefore, who come here as strangers, have to show their ability by hard discussion; those who fail compared with those who succeed are as seven or eight to ten. The other two or three of moderate talent, when they come to discuss in the assembly, are to be humbled, and to forfeit their renown. (A.D. 629–645)

HIUEN TSIANG[173]

## 2. The Hindus and writing

The tongue communicates the thought of the speaker to the hearer.

Its action has therefore, as it were, a momentary life only, and it would have been impossible to deliver by oral tradition the accounts of the events of the past to later generations, more particularly if they are separated from them by long periods of time. This has become possible only by a new discovery of the human mind, by the art of writing, which spreads news over space as the winds spread, and over time as the spirits of the deceased spread. Praise therefore be unto Him who has arranged creation and created everything for the best!

The Hindus are not in the habit of writing on hides, like the Greeks in ancient times. Socrates, on being asked why he did not compose books, gave this reply: 'I do not transfer knowledge from the living hearts of men to the *dead* hides of sheep.' ...

The Hindus have in the south of their country a slender tree like the date and cocoa-nut palms, bearing edible fruits and leaves of the length of one yard, and as broad as three fingers one put beside the other. They call these leaves *tari (tala* or *tar-Borassus flabellijormis),* and write on them. They bind a book of these leaves together by a cord on which they are arranged, the cord going through all the leaves by a hole in the middle of each.

In central and northern India people use the bark of the *tuz* tree, one kind of which is used as a cover for bows. It is called *bhurja.* They take a piece one yard long and as broad as the outstretched fingers of the hand, or somewhat less, and prepare it in various ways. They oil and polish it so as to make it hard and smooth, and then they write on it. The proper order of the single leaves is marked by numbers. The whole book is wrapped up in a piece of cloth and fastened between two tablets of the same size. Such a book is called *puthi* (cf. *pusta, pustaka*). Their letters, and whatever else they have to write, they write on the bark of the *tuz* tree. ...

The Hindus write from the left to the right like the Greeks. They do not write on the basis of a line, above which the heads of the letters rise whilst their tails go down below, as in Arabic writing. On the contrary, their ground-line is above, a straight line above every single character, and from this line the letter hangs down and is written under it. Any sign *above* the line is nothing but a grammatical mark to denote the pronunciation of the character above which it stands.

The most generally known alphabet is called *Siddhamatrika,* which is by some considered as originating from Kashmir, for the

people of Kashmir use it. But it is also used in Varanasi. This town
and Kashmir are the high schools of Hindu sciences. The same
writing is used in Madhyadesa, i.e. the middle country, the country
all around Kanauj, which is also called Aryavarta. . . .

They use black tablets for the children in the schools, and write
upon them along the long side, not the broad side, writing with a
white material from the left to the right. One would think that the
author of the following verses had meant the Hindus:

'How many a writer uses paper as black as charcoal,
Whilst his pen writes on it with white colour
By writing he places a bright day in a dark night,
Weaving like a weaver, but without adding a woof.'

(c. A.D. 1100)

ALBERUNI[174]

## 3. Muslim education

They [Muslims] learn, through the medium of the Arabic
and Persian languages, what young men in our colleges learn
through those of the Greek and Latin—that is, grammar, rhetoric,
and logic. After his seven years of study, the young Mahomedan
binds his turban upon a head almost as well filled with the things
which appertain to these three branches of knowledge, as the young
man raw from Oxford—he will talk as fluently about Socrates and
Aristotle, Plato and Hippocrates, Galen and Avicenna, *alias*
Socrate, Aristotalees, Aflaton, Bocrate, Jaleenoos, and Booalee
Sehna; and what is much to his advantage in India, the languages in
which he has learnt what he knows are those which he most requires
through life. He therefore thinks himself as well fitted to fill the high
offices which are now filled exclusively by Europeans, and naturally
enough wishes the establishments of that power would open them to
him. On the faculties and operations of the human mind on man's
passions and affections, and his duties in all relations of life, the
works of Imam Mahomed Ghuzallee and Nirseerooddeen Jansee,
hardly yield to those of Plato and Aristotle, or to those of any other
authors who have ever written on the same subjects in any country.
These works, the Aheaololoom, epitomised into the Keemeeai
Saadul, and the Akhlaki Naseree, with the didactic poems of Sadee,
are the great 'Pierian spring' of moral instruction, from which the
Mahomedan delights to 'drink deep' from infancy to old age, and a

better spring it would be difficult to find in the works of any other three men. (1830's)

WILLIAM HENRY SLEEMAN[175]

## 4.  On education, for Indians

Among some persons who are favourable in a general way to the establishment of schools, there still prevails the strange fallacy that we may venture to teach the natives truth on subjects of science, history, etc., but that we must use their own religious books in our schools, and, in fact, teach nothing but falsehood on matters connected with religion. Such arguers forget, or do not know, that what is physical science with us is religious doctrine with the Hindoos. We cannot teach them the most common known fact,—such, for instance, as that the earth is suspended in space, instead of being perched upon an elephant, or that an eclipse is caused by a shadow instead of a snake,—without overturning two or three dozen of their religious tenets: therefore, if we are to teach them nothing that is contrary to their own notions of religion, we must just leave them where they are on all other subjects: which procedure, or rather non-procedure, I believe few persons are quite prepared to advocate.

The expense of Government national education is, I conceive, greatly over-calculated, or rather, over-estimated, for it is probably not calculated at all. A valuable and comprehensive Government general education might be given at a very moderate outlay, by the following plan.

Let there be four schools at Madras—one of which should be considered the central or model school; one, at the principal station of every Zillah; and one in every Talook: all, of course, free, unless it should be thought desirable to establish some payment at the Presidency central school, which might be rendered and considered superior to the rest, and would be chiefly attended by boys of the higher and richer classes. At the Presidency and station schools English should be taught, and a good substantial education given. In the Talook schools English would be unnecessary, but education should be carried on in the native languages to whatever extent the books published in those languages render possible. The Madras schools should be under the superintendence and direction of a Board of Education; and the provincial schools under that of the principal European residents at their respective stations. There should be a certain number of books authorized by Government, and a fixed general plan, upon which all the schools should be conducted; but it appears to me expedient not to lay unnecessary restrictions upon the European superintendents' occasionally introducing additional books, or trifling modifications of the system, according to their judgment. If they be too much fettered and restricted, they will naturally take less interest in the work, and their superintendence will be proportionably inefficient. (1836–9)

JULIA CHARLOTTE MAITLAND[176]

## 5. *Schools for girls: Bombay*

A native gentleman, one of those who originated the schools, told me that he was hooted in the streets for what he was doing, and especially by women, as it was supposed that this was a plot to prevent the marriage of their daughters. But, in spite of all this, they succeeded, as men who are thoroughly in earnest always will succeed; and now in Bombay there are many Hindoo and Parsee female schools, which lack only female teachers to make them the finest agents in the world for the social regeneration of the upper classes, and, through the upper classes, the lower, of India. There is some difficulty in accomplishing this object; but enlightened Bombay gentlemen in England have been, in conjunction with Miss Carpenter, endeavouring to accomplish this most important object with the assistance of the Indian Secretary of State. In January last (1868), a memorial, signed by about thirty Hindoos and Parsees resident in England, submitted to the Secretary of State for India the 'favourable consideration of the subject of the establishment of Female Normal Training Schools at Bombay and Ahmedabad.' In this memorial it is said: 'Female education in India is surrounded with great and many difficulties; and it is a matter of congratulation and much credit to the people of Bombay and the Northern Division, that they have not only spontaneously accepted it as necessary and important, but have actually established and supported schools for the past seventeen years, so that there are now sixty-three schools in the Northern Division, giving instruction to 2,300 girls, and thirteen schools in Bombay, teaching about 1,600 girls. To these will be added another school in Bombay, under the bequest of 40,000 rupees by the late Goculdass Teffall. Considering how great must and will be the influence of the millions of mothers of India for

the stability of the British rule, as well as for the regeneration of
the country, it is of great importance that when spontaneous efforts
are made by the natives themselves of any part of India, Government ought to come forward to show their high appreciation of such
efforts, by giving every encouragement in their power, so as to
induce a desire in other parts of India to do likewise. Taking into
account how much the natives of the Presidency of Bombay have
done in the cause of education generally, as well as of female
education, and the effects of four successive commercial crises, it is
a great hardship to be at present so exacting with them.' And there
was, doubtless, much truth in this complaint. The Government of
India had not sanctioned the prayer of the Bombay memorialists,
and the proposals which had emanated from the Bombay Government, 'because half of the expenses had not been offered to be
contributed by the memorialists.' But no community in the world,
perhaps, has done more to promote great educational and other
beneficient institutions and undertakings than the Parsee community of Bombay; and they may conscientiously defend themselves
against any accusation of not putting their own shoulders to the
wheel. The assertion, indeed, in the memorial is only faintly expressed; and, therefore, one of the memorialists, a highly intelligent
Parsee gentleman resident in London, Dadabhai Naorojee, addressed a letter to the Secretary of State for India, in which he said:
'Government have paid for imperial funds, for schools for native
girls for the year 1865-66, about 29,000 rupees for the Bengal
Presidency; 35,000 rupees for the North-Western Provinces,
33,000 rupees for the Punjab, and 5,000 rupees for the Madras
Presidency, in 1866-67; while for the Bombay Presidency, for the
same period, 341 rupees, or almost nothing.' And he contrasted the
small amount contributed by Government with the large private
contributions of the community, showing that Bombay had sub-
scribed more than any of the other Presidencies towards the promotion of female education, and had existing endowments for the
purpose, amounting to between £30,000 and £40,000. (1867)

JOHN WILLIAM KAYE[177]


## 6. A School in Allahabad

On our way, we entered with Mr. C——into a little school, the
master of which was a Mussulman, and had been an old servant of

the family. About twenty children were seated on the floor round
the professor, who was making them sing the Ourdhoo alphabet in
chorus; and each child had a slate before him, which served for the
practice of the difficult art of Persian and Nagari writing. The
schoolroom was in the verandah itself of the master's habitation,
overlooking a small yard where the children play. (1875)

LOUIS ROUSSELET[178]

## 7. *The students*

Yesterday I learnt . . . a few facts about the budget of the students of Allahabad: Rs. 5/- college fees for each month, Re. 17-
stationery and library charges per month, Rs. 2/- per month for
lodging, Rs. 2/- for service, Rs. 4/- for cooking, Rs. 8/- for board.
The total comes to Rs. 22/- per month. A student spends Rs. 10/-
per year on clothes. He pays 4 annas to the washerman for 20
articles of clothing. Small pieces not counted. It is necessary for a
student to spend about Rs. 30/- per month. It is understandable why
they are dissatisfied: at the conclusion of his studies a student may
reckon on securing a position with a salary of Rs. 30/-. (1880)

IVAN PAVLOVICH MINAYEFF[179]

# 11. Commerce

## 1. A form of taxation

It is obligatory with them [Indians] every day to give alms as much as possible. They do not let money become a year or even a month old, for this would be a draft on an unknown future, of which a man does not know whether he reaches it or not.

With regard to that which he earns by the crops or from the cattle, he is bound first to pay to the ruler of the country the tax which attaches to the soil or the pasture-ground. Further, he pays him one-sixth of the income in recognition of the protection which he affords to the subjects, their property, and their families. The same obligation rests also on the common people, but they will always lie and cheat in the declarations about their property. Further, trading businesses, too, pay a tribute for the same reason. Only the Brahmans are exempt from all these taxes.

As to the way in which the remainder of the income, after the taxes have been deducted, is to be employed, there are different opinions. Some destine one-ninth of it for alms. For they divide it into three parts. One of them is kept in reserve to guarantee the heart against anxiety. The second is spent on trade to bring profit, and one-third of the third portion (*i.e.* one-ninth of the whole) is spent on alms, whilst the two other thirds are spent according to the same rule.

Others divide this income into four portions One-fourth is destined for common expenses, the second for liberal works of a noble mind, the third for alms, and the fourth for being kept in reserve, i.e. not more of it than the common expenses for three years. If the quarter which is to be reserved exceeds this amount, only this amount is reserved, whilst the remainder is spent as alms.

Usury or taking percentages is forbidden. The sin which a man commits thereby corresponds to the amount by which the percentages have increased the capital stock. Only to the Sudra is it allowed to take percentages, as long as his profit is not more than one-fiftieth of the capital (*i.e.* he is not to take more than two per cent). (*c.* A.D. 1000)

ALBERUNI[180]

## 2. *The beginnings of English trade*

The third of October, Hoja Nassan the Governour of Surat, and the Governours brother of Cambaya, sent a Mogoll unto me with a present of refreshing, and in their names offered to doe me all the kindnesse they could, but the Portugals, hee said, were the cause they could not doe what they would, but for their part they desired to trade with us, which they see no way possible to effect, so long as we should ride there, and the Portugall Armado by us, and therefore they would counsell me to goe for Goga, a better place, where wee should ride nearer the shore with our ships, where the Armado could not hinder our landing; and likewise it was nearer Cambaya, where there were more Merchants, and greater and better store of merchandize for our turnes: having to this effect delivered his message, hee was desirous to know what I determined to doe, whether I would stay heere, or goe thither: I answered, as yet I had received no answere from the shore, save a letter of small import, and till I knew what was become of our country-men and goods formerly left in the Countrey, I could not resolve him; and therefore I desired him to be a meanes, that some one of our people might come abord to conferre with me, and Pilots to conduct us thither, and then would I quickely resolve them what I would doe: in the meane while I could say nothing, I gave him and his Interpreter a small reward, and dispeeded them.

The fift, a Bramyney, or Priest of the Bannians, which came with the Mogoll for an Interpreter, came in a Boate of the Towne with a letter from Nicholas Bangham, and Captaine Hawkins letter from Agra, dated in April last, relating the manner of his favouring and dis-favouring by the Great Mogoll, his ficklenesse in granting us Trade, and afterward disallowing the same, giving the Portugals Firmaes against us, contradicting thereby what formerly hee had granted to us and our Nation. (1611)

HENRY MIDDLETON[181]

## 3. *Adventures of medieval trade*

Their trading is by Banian Brokers, who are subtile and deceitful both to the buyer and seller, if not prevented. In their Weights each Citie differeth from other. The Commodities are infinite: the chiefe, Indicoes of two sorts, Checques the courser, and Lahor the finer; Cloth made of Cotton-wooll, as Callicoes white and coloured, contayning fourteene yards the Booke, from two to one hundred Mamudies the piece, Pintados, Chints and Chadors, Shashes and Girdles, Cannakens, Treckanees, Serrabaffs, Aleiaes, Patollas, Sellas, Quilts, Carpets; Greene Ginger, Suckets, Lignum Aloes, Opium, Salarmoniacke and abundance of other Drugs. Commodities vendible are Knives, Glasses, Pictures and such like toyes; English cloth; China wares, Silke and Porcelane; all manner of Spices. The Guzerats lade their great ships of nine, twelve or fifteene hundred tunnes at Goga, and steale out unknowne to the Portugals.

Chiefe Cities for Trade on the River Sinde or Indus, are Tatta, (on a River which fals into it) Duilsinde, Multan, Lahore. At Duilsinde the Expedition in her former Voyage had delivered Sir Robert Sherley the Persian Ambassadour, of whom I thought good to adde this (which I learned by inquiry of some of his Followers to Agra) as an appendix to that relation in my former journall. Being weary of Duilsinde by the Governours evill intreatie and suffering the Portugals to molest him, seeking also to cut him off, for which purpose twelve Portugals came from Ormus; Hee sought libertie to goe to Tatta, but the Governour not permitting (as was thought of evill purpose) hee went without leave, and was by the way to passe a River, where none durst carrie him or his, being prohibited on paine of death by the said Governour. They therefore made rafts of boords and Timbers, on which the Ambassadour shipped himselfe with Nazerbeg one of his Followers to helpe him over: and were 1.o sooner put off, but twentie or thirtie Horsemen came from the Governour in great haste to stay them. Thus were they brought backe, men swimming to the raft, which Nazerbeg was not able to guide against the tyde, and they narrowly escaped drowning. His Followers disdaining this rude dealing, one Master John Ward shot off his Pistoll in their faces, and was instantly slaine by another shot, and the rest carryed away Prisoners to Duilsinde, being pillaged by the way of the Souldiers. After some time of imprisonment, the Governour permitted their departure to Tatta, where they were friendly entertained of the Governour being a Persian. Sir Thomas Powell, and Master Francis Bub, were then dead before in Duilsinde. Hee remayned at Tatta till fit opportunitie for Agra, the way long and in danger of Theeves: whither hee went in company of a great man which had a strong Convoy, for whom hee waited also two moneths.

The Ladie Powell in this space was delivered of a Sonne, but shee and it together with Master Michael Powell, Brother to Sir Thomas, lost their lives in this tedious expectation, in Boats, for that great man aforesaid. At his comming to Agra the Mogoll gave him favourable entertainment, and upon his complaint sent for the Banian Governour of Duilsinde, to answere at the Court, promising him his owne revenge, if hee would stay. But hee hasting to the Persian, after many Presents from the Mogoll, with a Convoy and necessaries for his journey, departed for Persia, not having one Englishman with him. Master Richard Barber his Apothecarie returned to Surat, and John Heriot dyed at Agra. There remayned with him of his old Followers only his Ladie, and her Woman, two Persians, the old Armenian and the Chircassian: His Dutch Jeweller came from Agra to Surat, with Master Edwards. (1615)

WALTER PAYTON[182]

## 4. *Exports*

On the other hand, I do not calculate upon any extension of the total value of the exports to Great Britain during the five years of our inquiry; because I consider, that the price of indigo will constantly be declining, and that the quantity sent home will not advance, except perhaps for the two next ensuing seasons, to recruit the present reduced stock at home: for the increase of the home consumption of Britain may barely cover the deficit in such part of the total export, as is remitted merely in depot for the continental demand, which will every day be supplied more directly. Assuming the present crop at 1000,000 *maunds,* I allow 70,000 for British consumption.

On Raw-silk, I admit an augmentation of five per cent; on Sugar and Cotton, of ten per cent, calculating the export of the latter to revive in the second year of the five. I have already explained my motives for believing both these articles capable of bearing the competition of the West-Indies and America, to a certain extent, provided that shipping freights continue moderate; and I hope to see the exports of both increase in the full ratio assigned them. The

West-Indian interest cannot surely be strong enough in the national councils, to add a third protecting duty to the last imposition on Asiatic sugars, even if it shall prevail to protract the unjust and impolitic operation of existing regulations of finance. Liberal men of all parties, on the principles of humanity, as well as of political economy, warmly protest against a system of legislative partiality, which gives an artificial value to slavery, and cramps the consumption of the parent state, and sacrifices her capital, for the benefit of a class of speculators, that have little merit to plead, and little benefit to offer in return.

The present exports of Saltpetre, can scarcely be maintained, without war in some part of Europe. Taking all chances, however, I value them rather boldly at the fixed rate of 250,000 *maunds,* which perhaps I have priced too highly at Rs. 5, since I understand it may now be brought at 4½, and is likely to be yet cheaper. Silk Piece-goods, for re-export to our colonies and other parts, I assume at 150,000 pieces, or 10½ *lakhs,* without increase, since our own manufactures are interfering with them, though less perhaps than with Cotton articles. The latter I suppose to decrease 5 per cent; and I take them at the low valuation in quantity 200,000 pieces, because the Company have discontinued their orders. Lack, of all sorts, I suppose to be stationary in the home demand, allowing a small extension to its introduction on the Continent. Spices, and other Asiatic re-exports from Calcutta, I also take at the fixed amount of about 12 *lakhs,* allowing for the continually increasing freedom of trade, and of direct intercouse between the places of consumption and production. But upon the item of Sundries, valued at 11 *lakhs,* must be allowed an advance of 10 per cent, on account of the new commodities it may possibly embrace. Thus, adding the invoice charges, computed at only 6 per cent, instead of 7 (the assumed percentage charge upon the whole export trade), we have, for the total export invoices to Great Britain, 330 *lakhs* for the first, and nearly the same for the succeeding four years; which exceeds our first year's import invoices by 172 *l.*, and our last by only 130 *l.*; a sum in both cases unequal to the actual demands of remittance on the Company's and private account. (1822)

G.A. PRINSEP[183]

## 5. *Merchants of India*

There is no class of men more interested in the stability of our rule in

India than this of the respectable merchants; nor is there any upon whom the welfare of our government, and that of the people, more depend. Frugal, first, upon principle, that they may not in their expenditure encroach upon their capitals, they become so by habit; and when they advance in life they lay out their accumulated wealth in the formation of those works which shall secure for them, from generation to generation, the blessings of the people of the towns in which they have resided, and those of the country around. It would not be too much to say, that one-half of the great works which embellish and enrich the face of India, in tanks, groves, wells, temples, etc., have been formed by this class of the people solely with the view of securing the blessings of mankind by contributing to their happiness in solid and permanent works. (1830's)

WILLIAM HENRY SLEEMAN[184]

## 6. *Lal-Chittee ka bazaar*

At noon we passed a long, straggling, and thoroughly Bengalee wigwam, which the natives called Lal-Chittee-ka-Bazaar. The houses were all formed simply of mats, thatch, palmyra leaves, and bamboos, but the inhabitants were swarming, like bees, on the shore, and all wore a busy and a thriving air. The hamlet was backed up by a thick curtain of cocoa-trees, palmyras, and plantains, and a long line of timber-stacks indicated the chief staple of its commerce. Hundreds of boats lay along the shore freighted with wood and grain; many of the larger craft, fine teak-built vessels, were Birmese; and their crews, with their coarse flat features, and massive muscular limbs, contrasted strongly with the light, supple, and graceful figures of the Bengalees. We afterwards met one of these huge boats coming up the river. It stood at least ten feet out of the water, and was propelled by forty long oars, pulled by men in a standing position. They kept time with the greatest precision, though the measure, two short strokes succeeded by two long ones, appeared rather difficult. The rowers were in full chorus as we passed them.

The nameless creek, on which this bazaar is established, is, I should judge, at least as wide as the Thames at Windsor; and a hundred such streams intersect the Great Delta of the Ganges, rendering roads almost useless. (1832)

GODFREY CHARLES MUNDY[185]

## 7. *Kashmiri shawls*

Under the Mogul emperors Cashmere found work for 30,000 shawl looms. In the time of the Afghaun kings the number decreased to 18,000; there are now no more than 6000 employed. English imitations have not had much effect among the Asiatic nations; at first their pretty patterns and brilliant colours took the fancy of some, but their singular inferiority of softness and warmth compared with the genuine shawl, soon caused the counterfeit articles to be neglected. A camel load of them was lately put up at an outcry in Delhi, when scarcely a native would bid for one. The average value of shawls exported from Cashmere amounts annually to 1,800,000 rupees. Runjeet Singh takes two-thirds in kind as part of the gross revenue of the province, which is about 2,500,000 rupees a year. His highness is said to sell three-fourths of what he thus receives, and to keep the remainder for his own court. Of the rest, disposed of by him and left for sale in the valley, seven hundred thousand rupees' worth go to Bombay and Western India, thence to Hindostan, chiefly Oude; fifty thousand each, to Calcutta, Caubul, Herat, and Balk, whence some pass on to neighbouring countries. (1839)

J.W. MASSIE[186]

## 8. *Cotton*

Speaking of the character of the cotton crop of the Punjab, a correspondent of an Indian paper says:—'In April last (1855), I brought to England a small quantity of cotton (the raw material) grown from *acclimated* American cotton seed in a district on the banks of the river Jhelum; this specimen I had shown to several cotton spinners in Manchester. They pronounced it to be the finest specimen of cotton they had seen grown in India, even directly from American seed, and to be worth from 6¼d. to 6½d. per lb.

'Along the banks of our Punjaub rivers lie tracts of land admirably situated for the growth of cotton. It only requires steady encouragement on the part of the local Government, trouble and perseverance on the part of the district officer. to cover those lands with cotton of the finest quality.

'The cotton that could thus be grown might, with ease and at trifling cost, be conveyed in country boats (until we have, as we ought to have, steamers on those rivers) down the Indus to Kurrachee, and there shipped for England.

'Kurrachee is a port of great importance; but, like many things of great importance, not heeded or taken advantage of. *The one article, cotton, if properly cultivated in the Punjaub and in Scinde, would afford export freight for a vast number of ships visiting Kurrachee, while Government stores for the Punjaub, private property and merchandize would afford endless import freight, to say nothing of the great number of passengers who would avail themselves of that route.'*

According to a Scinde paper—'And one located on the banks of the river Indus might observe fleets of boats coming down the river in the winter months, all laden with cotton.' The cotton brought to Scinde and shipped at Sukkur comes across the Jaysulmere Desert from Rajpootana, and is either consumed in Scinde or exported to Afghanistan.

'The Cotton Wool of Cutch, which adjoins the province of Scinde, whose last year's exports to Bombay amounted to upwards of one-sixth the produce of the Bombay Presidency, will probably eventually be imported into Kurrachee as being tne nearest market.

'Two hydraulic presses, adapted for the compression of any description of produce, have lately been imported from England, so that we have now the means of packing at Kurrachee, which will afford increased facilities to direct exportation.' (1856)

W.P. ANDREW[187]

# 12. Customs and Folklore

## 1. Some Indian characteristics

The Indians all live frugally, especially when in camp. They dislike a great undisciplined multitude, and consequently they observe good order. Theft is of very rare occurrence. Megasthenes says that those who were in the camp of Sandrakottos, wherein lay 400,000 men, found that the thefts reported on any one day did not exceed the value of two hundred drachmæ, and this among a people who have no written laws, but are ignorant of writing, and must therefore in all the business of life trust to memory. They live, nevertheless, happily enough, being simple in their manners and frugal. They never drink wine except at sacrifices. Their beverage is a liquor composed from rice instead of barley, and their food is principally a rice-pottage. The simplicity of their laws and their contracts is proved by the fact that they seldom go to law. They have no suits about pledges or deposits, nor 'o they require either seals or witnesses, but make their deposits and confide in each other. Their houses and property they generally leave unguarded. These things indicate that they possess good, sober sense; but other things they do which one cannot approve: for instance, that they eat always alone, and that they have no fixed hours when meals are to be taken by all in common, but each one eats when he feels inclined. The contrary custom would be better for the ends of social and civil life. (3rd century B.C.)

MEGASTHENES [188]

## 2. Forms of politeness

There are nine methods of showing outward respect—(1) by selecting words of soothing character in making requests; (2) by bowing the head to show respect; (3) by raising the hands and bowing; (4) by joining the hands and bowing low; (5) by bending the knee; (6) by a prostration; (7) by a prostration on hands and knees; (8) by touching the ground with the five circles; (9) by stretching the five parts of the body on the ground.

Of these nine methods the most respectful is to make one prostration on the ground and then to kneel and laud the virtues of the one
addressed. When at a distance it is usual to bow low; when near,
then it is customary to kiss the feet and rub the ankles *(of the person
addressed)*.

Whenever orders are received at the hands of a superior, the
person lifts the skirts of his robes and makes a prostration. The
superior or honourable person who is thus reverenced must speak
gently *(to the inferior)*, either touching his head or patting his back,
and addressing him with good words of direction or advice to show
his affection. (A.D. 629–645)

HIUEN TSIANG[189]

## 3.　Some Hindu customs

We shall now speak of certain strange manners and customs of the
Hindus. The strangeness of a thing evidently rests on the fact that it
occurs but rarely, and that we seldom have the opportunity of
witnessing it. If such strangeness reaches a high degree, the thing
becomes a curiosity, or even something like a miracle, which is no
longer in accordance with the ordinary laws of nature, and which
seems chimerical as long as it has not been witnessed. Many Hindu
customs differ from those of our country of our time to such a
degree as to appear to us simply monstrous. One might almost think
that they had intentionally changed them into the opposite, for our
customs do not resemble theirs, but are the very reverse; and if ever
a custom of theirs resembles one of ours, it has certainly just the
opposite meaning.

They do not cut any of the hair of the body. Originally they went
naked in consequence of the heat, and by not cutting the hair of the
head they intended to prevent sunstroke.

They divide the moustache into single plaits in order to preserve
it. As regards their not cutting the hair of the genitals, they try to
make people believe that the cutting of it incites to lust and increases carnal desire. Therefore such of them as feel a strong desire
for cohabitation never cut the hair of the genitals.

They let the nails grow long, glorying in their idleness, since they
do not use them for any business or work, but only, while living a
dolce for niente life, they scratch their heads with them and examine
the hair for lice.

The Hindus eat singly, one by one, on a tablecloth of dung. They do not make use of the remainder of a meal, and the plates from which they have eaten are thrown away if they are earthen.

They have red teeth in consequence of chewing arecanuts with betel-leaves and chalk.

They drink wine before having eaten anything, then they take their meal. They sip the stall of cows, but they do not eat their meat.

They beat the cymbals with a stick.

They use turbans for trousers. Those who want little dress are content to dress in a rag of two fingers' breadth, which they bind over their loins with two cords; but those who like much dress, wear trousers lined with so much cotton as would suffice to make a number of counterpanes and saddle-rugs. These trousers have no (visible) openings, and they are so huge that the feet are not visible. The string by which the trousers are fastened is at the back. (c. A.D. 1000)

ALBERUNI[190]

## 4. On meat eating

As matters stand thus, it is allowed to kill animals by means of strangulation, but only certain animals, others being excluded. The meat of such animals, the killing of which is allowed, is forbidden in case they die a sudden death. Animals the killing of which is allowed are sheep, goats, gazelles, hares, rhinoceroses *(gandha)*, the buffaloes, fish, water and land birds, as sparrows, ring-doves, francolins, doves, peacocks and other animals which are not loathsome to man nor noxious.

That which is forbidden are cows, horses, mules, asses, camels, elephants, tame poultry, crows, parrots, nightingales, all kinds of eggs and wine. (c. A.D. 1000 )

ALBERUNI[191]

## 5. Hindu Manners

The first error of these Hindus is to believe that they are the only people in the world who have any polite manners; and the same is the case with cleanliness and orderliness in business. They think all other nations, and above all Europeans, are barbarous, despicable, filthy, and devoid of order.

The civilities they pay to each other are as follows, divisible into five categories. In the first they raise the hands to the head and prostrate themselves on the ground; this is the form in which they adore God, and salute their spiritual leaders, the *Sannyasis,* who are their monks, and they also employ it for kings, princes, and the great. Although this is practised by nearly every caste, it is not observed by the Brahmans; they prostrate themselves only before God, their teachers, who are always Brahmans, and their monks, also invariably of their own caste.

The second manner of salutation is to lift the hands to the head. It is in this fashion that they salute ordinary persons, governors, generals, and ministers of kings and princes. The third manner is to raise the hands only as high as the stomach; and this is the course adopted by equals and friends, followed by an embrace. The fourth manner is to display the two hands with the palms joined. This is done by the learned and by monks before princes and the great, when those persons make use to them of one of the three methods above described. Finally, the fifth and last mode of salutation is to display the palm of the right hand raised on high; this is how superiors act to inferiors.

Brahmans salute kings in the second manner only; and to it the latter respond in the same form. But what is delightful is to see a Brahman on a visit to another man, for without the slightest salutation he seats himself, and in the conversation the host accords him the title of lordship or excellency, and often that of highness. When he takes his leave he goes off most solemnly without being any more polite on going away than on entering. (1653–1708)

NICCOLAO MANUCCI[192]

## 6. *Superstition: a tale*

Of a point called Seeam-Ke-Teeba, on the opposite side of the river, the following strange tale is related. It is the haunt of a deity, who is by no means fond of company, and is so much feared, that none will ascend it. A man, it is said, while gathering the dwarf bamboo, found himself close to the dreaded spot, and espied a large feast set out, and many persons busily employed in nautching and amusing themselves. He was interrogated as to his intentions and wants and having told what brought him there, he was asked to partake of the feast, and having eaten some rice he was desired to retire, and by no means ever to relate what he had seen: that if he kept silent, such food would always be at his command, were he to live a thousand years; but, on the contrary, if he should be indiscreet, he should die. Having reached his village, the fool told what he had seen, and dropped down dead. (1815)

JAMES BAILLIE FRASER[193]

## 7. Human sacrifices

The Mahadeo sand-stone hills, which in the Sathpore range overlook the Nerbudda to the south, rise to between four and five thousand feet above the level of the sea; and in one of the highest parts a fair was formerly, and is, perhaps, still held for the enjoyment of those who assemble to witness the self-devotion of a few young men, who offer themselves as a sacrifice, to fulfil the vows of their mothers! When a woman is without children she makes votive offerings to all the gods who can, she thinks, assist her; and promises of still greater in case they should grant what she wants. Smaller promises being found of no avail, she at last promises her first-born, if a male, to the god of destruction, Mahadeo. If she gets a son she conceals from him her vows till he has attained the age of puberty; she then communicates it to him, and enjoins him to fulfil it. He believes it to be his paramount duty to obey his mother's call; and from that moment he considers himself as devoted to the god. Without breathing to any living soul a syllable of what she has told him, he puts on the habit of a pilgrim or religious mendicant—visits all the celebrated temples dedicated to this god in different parts of India; and at the annual fair on the Mahadeo hills, throws himself from a perpendicular height of four or five hundred feet, and is dashed to pieces upon the rocks below! If the youth does not feel himself quite prepared for the sacrifice on the first visit, he spends another year in pilgrimages, and returns to fulfil his mother's vow at the next fair. Some have, I believe, been known to postpone the sacrifice to a third fair; but the interval is always spent in painful pilgrimages to the celebrated temples of the god. (c. 1830)

WILLIAM HENRY SLEEMAN[194]

## 8  The Coorg lullaby

Juwa, juwa, baby dear!
When the baby's mother comes,
She will give her darling milk.

Juwa, juwa, baby dear!
When the baby's father comes,
He will bring a cocoanut.

Juwa, juwa, baby dear!
When the baby's brother comes,
He will bring a little bird.

Juwa, juwa, baby dear!
When the baby's sister comes,
She will bring a dish of rice. (1872)

CHARLES E. GOVER[195]

# 13. Means of Travelling

## 1. Of the modes of travelling

The Indians are in person slender and tall, and of much lighter weight than other men. The animals used by the common sort for riding on are camels and horses and asses, while the wealthy use elephants, — for it is the elephant which in India carries royalty. The conveyance which ranks next in honour is the chariot and four; the camel ranks third; while to be drawn by a single horse is considered no distinction at all. (2nd century A.D.)

ARRIAN [196]

## 2. Public inns and transport

In this Kingdome there are no Innes to entertaine Strangers, onely in great Townes and Cities are faire houses built for their receit, which they call Sarray, not inhabited, where any Passengers may have roome freely, but must bring with him his Bedding, his Cooke, and other necessaries wherein to dresse his meate, which are usually carried on Camels, or else in Carts drawne with Oxen, wherein they have Tents to pitch when they meete with no Sarrays.

The inferiour sort of people ride on Oxen, Horses, Mules, Camels, or Dromedaries; the women like the men, or else in slight Coaches with two Wheeles, covered on the top, and backe, but the fore-part and sides open unlesse they carrie women. They will conveniently hold two persons, beside the Driver, they are drawne by Oxen, one yoake in a Coach, suted for colour, but many of them are white, not very large: they are guided with Cords, which goe through the parting of their Nostrils, and so twixt their Hornes into the Coach-mens hand. They dresse and keepe them clothed as their Horses. They are naturally nimble, to which use makes them so fitting to performe that labour, as that they will goe twentie miles a day, or more with good speed. The better sort ride on Elephants, or else are carried upon mens shoulders alone, in a slight thing they call a Palankee, which is like a Couch, or standing Pallat, but covered with a Cannopie. (1616)

EDWARD TERRY[197]

## 3. A list of an establishment

As it may perhaps amuse those who have not been in India, I annex a list of our establishment for the march.

Two palankeens
Twenty-four bearers.
One sirdah, or head bearer, and his assistant.
Two elephants with their drivers, and two attendants. One of these carried a tent.
One gig.
Eight horses.
Eight grooms.
Eight grass cutters for the horses. Here it may not be amiss to mention, that the horses do not eat hay as in England, but the fibrous roots of grass well beaten, which requires a man for each horse to cut and prepare. These roots, and grain, (a kind of vetch), constitute the food of a horse in India.
One coachman.
Six clashies, or men to pitch tents.
Three tents, with two poles in each, and double walls: the space between the walls a passage of about five feet all round. These tents are twenty feet between the poles, about sixteen feet wide, and five-and-twenty feet high. Some of them have boarded floors and glass doors; but this is only in a standing encampment. They are lined throughout with chintz, carpeted, and have branch lights for candles fixed against the poles.
Twenty coolies—(people from the bazaar, at so much per diem, to carry furniture for the tents, which is all transported upon their heads.)
One washerman and his family
One baker and his assistant.
One khansomer, or house steward.
Two footmen, or waiters.
Two tailors.
One masalgie, to clean knives and carry the lanthorn, go of errands, etc.
Two women servants.
One cook and assistant.
One sweeper to each tent.
Seventy sheep.

Thirty-five goats
Two shepherds.
Nine camels.
Three camel drivers.
Fourteen bullocks.
Five Waggons.
Seven drivers.
Twenty-four fowls, forty ducks, twelve geese, twelve rabbits, twelve turkeys.
    Two men to take care of the poultry.
Besides the families of all these servants, with their horses, bullocks, and attendants, which may be computed upon an average of three to one.

As it is customary for every individual to draw water for himself from the wells, each of them are supplied with a brass pot, called a *lota*: it contains about a quart, and is shaped like two-thirds of a globe, with a rim round the top. Round this they tie a strong whip-cord, about the common depth of a well; and when travelling, each man fastens his *lota* round his waist; for they are much too cleanly to drink after one another.

Link-boys and guides are procured at every village; so indeed are coolies, should more be required on the journey. These are relieved at the next village by others, and so on. It is also customary to apply to the head man of that village to furnish a guard for the night, which guard is paid and discharged in the morning, except a robbery is perpetrated during the night, and then (unless by *dakoity,* as they are called) the man who furnishes the guard is answerable. He also presents a kid, or a couple of fowls to you, on your arrival. (1804–14)

A. DEARE[198]

## 4. A hackree

The natives of the torrid zone are not fond of exercise; walking is by no means considered as a pleasing recreation; they like to ride a good horse, with gentle paces, or to take the air in a hackree, a sort of chariot drawn by white oxen; it is seldom hung on springs, and consists of a conical dome, supported by four pillars, covered with broad cloth, and curtains in front and on each side, to open at pleasure. Officers of government, and men of rank are carried in a

palankeen, or more properly a palkee, an Asiatic luxury, as yet
unknown in Europe. (1812)

JAMES FORBES[199]

## 5. Dak journey

[1] set out on my first Dak journey. I had twelve bearers, the road
between this place [Chuckeepoor, near Benares] and Seidpoor
lying through fields and broken country, a double number beings, as
I was assured, necessary, particularly as it was not certain that I
should find a relief on this side Benares, a distance of 24 English
miles. I had my clothes and writing-desk in two petarrahs, (a sort of
wicker box), which one man carried slung on a bamboo across his
shoulders, my mate-bearer to run with me, and besides light re-
freshments. I was told to take my pistols. Such is the usual style in
which Dak journeys are made in India; and it may serve as an
additional proof of the redundant population and cheapness of
labour, that this number of bearers are obtained for such severe and
unpleasant work, at about 12s for the stage, varying from six to ten
miles. The men set out across the meadows at a good round trot of
about four miles an hour, grunting like paviours in England, a
custom which, like paviours, they imagine eases them under their
burthen. (1824)

REGINALD HEBER[200]

## 6. Travelling by 'dawk'

The manner in which I travelled on the occasion of my going back to
Vellore was by posting, on 'running dawk,' as it is termed; which
means, travelling by relays of bearers, stationed at certain stages,
where they change. When any one wishes to travel in this way, an
application is made to the Post-office authorities for the relays of
bearers being posted along the route he intends going; but , before
this arrangement can be made, the traveller is obliged to pay a
deposit of a certain sum, according to the distance, and to state
whether he is likely to be detained on the road. The deposit is
demanded purposely to avoid these detentions, the amount being
forefeited, in addition to the regulated hire, should any take place.

The requisite sum being paid down, a day is fixed upon by the
'Jack-in-office' for the traveller's starting, a certain time being
absolutely required for the posting of the bearers, which done, the

'Travelling Dak', drawn by Bishop Reginald Heber

bearers for the first stage **are** sent to his residence, and these men prepare the palankeen in their own manner, by lashing and binding, and a variety of other preliminaries, too numerous for me to detail.

A set of bearers consists of twelve men, including the *'pudda-bhuee,'* or head-bearer; besides these, there is a fellow for carrying the *'massaul,'* or torch, as also another for the *'cavary baskets,'* or *'pettarahs,'* which are a couple of baskets, or light tin boxes, generally painted green, slung on a bamboo, containing eating and drinking requisites of the journey. The whole set have a man of their own to convey their food and cooking utensils.

These poor fellows run for upwards of thirty miles, with scarcely any rest, at the rate of four miles an hour, taking little or no sustenance all the time! When arrived at the end of their stage, they put down their load, and walk off, though some of them are apt to be troublesome, by begging a present, and it is generally customary to give them a rupee or so.

The new set are not long in making their appearance. They lift up the palkee, and trudge off without saying a word to the traveller; but they can never make a start without a great noise and wrangling among themselves, which it is almost useless to attempt to check; and in this manner they proceed, running along till they come to the end of their stage, quitting the palankeen like their predecessors. (*c.* 1840)

ALBERT HERVEY[201]

## 7. *Songs of palanquin bearers*

I ought to mention the chant of the palanquin-bearers; though they keep to the same sing-song tune, yet they generally invent the words as they go along. I will give a sample, as well as I could make it out of what my bearers sang the other night; I have tried to render their words as nearly as I could into English, so as to preserve the metre. The poetry must be improved. A palkee means a palanquin: it is the Hindustanee word, though one also generally used in conversation. Each line is sung in a different voice; in the following, for instance, the first line would be sung in the usual voice, the second very high, the third in a sort of gruff tone:

Oh, what a heavy bag!
No; it's an elephant:
He is an awful weight.
Let's throw his palkee down—

> Let's set him in the mud—
> Let's leave him to his fate.
> No, for he'll be angry then;
> Ay, and he will beat us then
>     With a thick stick.
> Then let's make haste and get along,
>     Jump along quick.

And then, suiting the action to the word, off they set in a nasty jog-trot which rattled every bone in my body, keeping chorus all the time of 'jump along quick, jump along quick,' until they were obliged to stop for laughing. The second sample is from the men who carried Mrs. Acland, and is in quite a different metre. I must tell you that 'cubbadar' means 'take care,' and 'baba' (pronounced 'barba') means 'young lady':

| 1 | 2 | 3 |
|---|---|---|
| She's not heavy, | Trim the torches, | Carry her gently, |
| Cubbadar! | Cubbadar! | Cubbadar! |
| Little baba, | For the road's rough, | Little baba, |
| Cubbadar! | Cubbadar! | Cubbadar! |
| Carry her swiftly, | Here the bridge is, | Sing so cheerily, |
| Cubbadar! | Cubbadar! | Cubbadar! |
| Pretty baba, | Pass it swiftly, | Pretty baba, |
| Cubbadar! | Cubbadar! | Cubbadar! |
| Cubbadar! | Cubbadar! | Cubbadar! |
| Cubbadar! | Cubbadar! | Cubbadar! (1842) |

T. ACLAND[202]

## 8.   Travelling arrangements

When we feel inclined to start we send forward an order to the principal man at the next place, say twelve or fifteen miles distant, to build one room, about thirty feet square, in a shady place, for ourselves; for the walls we use cocoa-nut and palm leaves, bound together with bamboos, and the ceiling is made of the same material with a few pieces of matting to keep out the sun. The evening before we start we send on a cart with some of our chairs, tables, and other necessaries and provisions, which it would be very awkward to forget, under charge of some of our followers: we have about one hundred and twenty of them with us.

Then, in the morning, we get up at five: we have a bit of toast, an egg, and a cup of coffee or a glass of sherry; give orders for the tents

'Our Stage Coaching,' drawn by Captain G. F. Atkinson

to be struck and everything to be brought on as quickly as possible, and then we mount our horses; a groom runs by the side, and a little way behind come our palanquins and tonjons.

We are also attended by men carrying our guns and powder, by many other servants, and about half the inhabitants of the last village through which we passed. If we feel tired we get into our tonjons; if the sun is too hot we call for our palanquins. Every now and then we see five or six peacocks feeding in a rice-field, or we come to a place where there are plain tracks of deer. Then we give our horses to the grooms, and creep along gently with our heads down and our guns in our hands, whilst my wife either watches the sport or trots gently on. At last we arrive at our encamping-place; there we find our leafy house ready, and similar ones provided for the servants and horses; eat a hearty breakfast, at which we some-times substitute beer for tea, and by the time that is over the tents are arrived. (1845)

T. ACLAND[203]

## 9. Dak 'tats'

Soon after leaving the bridge of boats, our coachman pulled up, and commenced changing horses. Well, thought I, if this is the length of stage, we shall do well. Too soon, however, I discovered the object of this humanity. Our first steed was the 'show' horse, with which to start from the Station. Our next, and the ones following, over a journey of forty-six miles—how shall I describe them? Wretched, half-starved tats*, with every good principle they ever inherited destroyed; rendered vicious by a lifetime of starvation and ill-treatment; scarcely able to drag *themselves* along, much less a heavy, well-laden vehicle— no wonder that, with instinctive know-ledge, they put their shoulders to the wheel (*i.e.* backed) instead of to the collar, and resolutely declined to proceed. At length, goaded by the lashes of a coachman on one side, and by the thrusts and blows from a syce on the other, assisted by a steady push at the wheels from some half-dozen attendant nature-clad 'grooms,' our poor beast leaped off, to pull up again so soon as the first impulse was over; and only to be set in motion once more by a renewal of the humane treatment first adopted, or by the coachman or syce, or both, running alongside and plying it with blows thick and fast the while. Willingly would I have walked the whole way had such been

possible:—as it was, I essayed one stage, but was obliged to give in.
On remonstrating vigorously with the coachman, to whom I felt
much inclined to apply a little of the same discipline wherewith he
had treated his unfortunate horse, he said (commencing with the
usual native reply—'*Hum kea kurrega?*—What can I do?')— 'The
horses have had no food (corn) for two months, the sircar not having
given us any money.' (1866)

*A tat is a country-bred pony.

F.F. WYMAN[204]

## 10. *The Caravan*

I had fixed the departure of our caravan for the 19th inst., and at the
appointed hour the camels, grouped in the courtyard of the bungalow, were waiting to be laden. The two on which we were to ride
were smartly caparisoned with housings of silk and a profusion of
tassels; but all these ornaments were in honour of the ceremony of
departure, and would disappear when we were once on the road.
Our party consisted of our four servants, two saniwallahs, and seven
camel-drivers. All were armed with sabres and guns, and each
imagined it extremely probable that he would shortly be called
upon to make use of them. I assembled them all before the steps of
the bungalow, and made them a brief speech, assuring them that the
country we were about to traverse was perfectly safe, and that,
moreover, being well armed, we should have nothing to fear from
the Bheels. I appointed a leader of the caravan; and, having consulted the itinerary I had drawn up, I ordered him to encamp that
same night at the village of Rajpoor, fifteen miles to the north-east
of Ahmedabad. As for our two selves, I had decided that we should
pass one more night beneath the hospitable roof of the bungalow,
and only join our camp next morning.

Our baggage was soon laden, amid the terrible cries of the camels,
and I saw the little band set off, surrounded by friends and relatives
who were going to escort them as far as the gates of the city. Some
officers came to pass the evening with us, and kept us up till
midnight. At four o'clock I was awoke by my saniwallah, who
came to warn me that it was time to be starting. I, in turn, woke
Schaumburg, and in a few minutes we were ready. The sani, or
riding-camel, squatted at the door, waiting for me: I threw some
coverings over the saddle to make it more comfortable, and took my

'Manner of Travelling in Palankeen in India', drawn by James Forbes

place on the hind seat; my driver bestrode that in front, and the camel sprang to his feet. The saddle used for camel-riding, as no doubt most of my readers are aware, is double, so that the two riders find themselves fitted close to one another. The position of the one who is behind is not the most agreeable on account of this proximity; but I had chosen it, to accustom myself a little to the motion of the camel before I attempted to guide it myself. I remained for half an hour without being able to find my equilibrium, violently jolted and clinging to the back of the camel; my companion, however, suffered equally with myself. At the end of this time I felt more at my ease, and was able to take some notice of the road we were travelling. Ahmedabad was already far off, and the daybreak lighted up an immense plain covered with bare fields and dotted with groups of trees denoting the sites of the villages. (1875)

LOUIS ROUSSELET[205]

# 14. Languages

## 1. The Malabar language

The *Malabars* write upon the leaves of the wild palm-trees with iron pencils; their letters are very antient, and distinguished into, (1) *Short or running letters;* (2) *Long ones;* (3) *Vowels;* (4) *Consonants;* (5) *Dipthongs;* (6) *Letters used only in the beginning of a word;* (7) *Such as are used only in the middle;* and (8) *Such as are used only in the end;* ... And seeing that the *Malabar* letters have hitherto not appeared in publick print, either in *Holland* or *Germany*, it will not be amiss to alledge the reasons thereof, and to shew that this language is no less worth our care now-a-days, than the *Hebrew, Chaldean, Arabian, Persian, Samaritan*, and other languages.

The main reason why the *Malabar* language has remained so long unknown to us, is, because that country was not conquered by the *Dutch* company till in the years 1661, 1662, 1663, from the *Portuguese;* and it is not their custom to send any ministers into those places, where they are not sovereign masters.'Tis true, I assisted at the sieges of *Coulang, Cranganor, Cochin*, etc. and, 1658 at the sieges of *Tutecoryn, Manaar, Jafnapatnam,* and *Negapatan;* but was immediately after ordered to Psephina in the kingdom of Jafnapatnam, where I had the oversight over twenty-four churches. During the space of near four years, that I staid here alone, I was sensible what obstacle the ignorance of the native language was to my good intentions; for though many of the Christians here were well enough versed in the *Dutch* and *Portuguese* languages, yet some belonging to the more remote churches, who had been but slenderly instructed in the principles of the Christian religion by the *Roman* missionaries, were strangely at a loss till I got a good interpreter, who being well skilled, both in his mother-tongue, the *Malabar*, and the *Portuguese* languages, did me great services for eight years together. (1671)

PHILIP BALDAEUS[20]

## 2. *Hindoostanee, the useful language in India*

The language which in my proposition I have specified by the name of Hindoostanee, is also frequently denominated Hindee, Oordoo, and Rekhtu. It is compounded of the Arabic, Persian and Sunskrit, or B,hak,ha, which last appears to have been in former ages the current language of Hindoostan.

Owing in some measure to the intercourse of the merchants of Arabia with this country, but more particularly to the frequent invasions of *it by* the Moosulmans, and their ultimate settlement in it, a considerable number of Arabic and Persian words became engrafted on the original language of the natives, and out of this mixture arose a new language, the Hindoostanee, like a modern superstructure on an ancient foundation.

By degrees it assumed its present appearance and estimation; and the court of Dihlee made choice of it, as the medium in all affairs depending on colloquial intercourse. Hence its influence gradually spread abroad so widely, that it became universally used in the courts of the Moosulman princes. Many of the native inhabitants also grew familiarized to it, and used it in all concerns, the validity of which did not depend upon written documents.

As the intercourse and communication of the Moosulmans with the natives of India was greater or less, according to certain circumstances and situations, the Hindoostanee naturally varied considerably, with respect to the prevalence of one or other of the languages composing it. This circumstance will sanction a division of it into three distinct dialects, namely: the pristine, or country; the middle, or familiar; and the learned, or court dialect; each of which are respectively useful in different districts, situations and families.

In the first, or pristine dialect, there is a smaller admixture of foreign words; hence this is more nearly related to the original dialects of the country.

In the second, or familiar dialect, the number of foreign words bear nearly an equal proportion to the original ones.

In the third, or court dialect, Arabic and Persian words are by far the most numerous.

It is unnecessary for me to explain the various moral and physical causes, which have rendered the Hindoostanee less prevalent in some parts of India than in others, since they must be evident to every reflecting mind. This circumstance, however, by no means invalidates my proposition; for although I can grant that particular dialects are spoken by the inhabitants of several districts and provinces of India, yet I assert, that no one of them, taken individually is so generally useful and necessary as the Hindoostanee. Nor will my assertion appear too bold when it be considered that however extensive a country may be, and how numerous soever the dialects spoken in it, still the language of its court and metropolis will always be most generally known and understood, and must of consequence be that most worthy of attention and cultivation by foreigners.

I shall now advert to a few arguments, which I trust will be convincing and satisfactory proofs of the truth of my proposition.

In the whole of the vast country of Hindoostan, scarce any Moosulman will be found, who does not understand and speak the Hindoostanee.

Every Hindoo also, of any distinction, or who has the least connection either with the Moosulman or the British government, is, according to his situation, acquainted, more or less, with this language.

It is moreover the general medium by which many persons of various foreign nations settled in Hindoostan, communicate their wants and ideas to each other. Of the truth of this indeed we ourselves are an evidence, as are the Portugueze, Dutch, French, Danes, Arabs, Turks, Greeks, Armenians, Georgians, Persians, Moghuls, and Chinese.

In almost all the armies of India this appears to be the universally used language; even though many of the individuals composing them, be better acquainted with the dialects peculiar to their respective districts.

Nearly from Cape Comorin to Kabool, a country about 2000 miles in length, and 1400 in breadth within the Ganges, few persons will be found in any large villages or towns, which have ever been conquered or much frequented by Moosulmans, who are not sufficiently conversant in the Hindoostanee: and in many places beyond the Ganges, this language is current and familiar.

An accurate knowledge of the customs, and manners, of a nation, depends principally on an acquaintance with its colloquial language; and in no country perhaps, is this knowledge more essential or a more desirable object of attainment than in Hindoostan, the inhabitants of which differ so widely in religion, laws, customs and prejudices.

When the conquerors and rulers of a country are unacquainted with the current speech of their subjects, the natural consequences must evidently be injustice on the one part, and disaffection on the other.

Although in the popular language of any country, there may be a deficiency of books of science, still that language is the most proper and necessary for conducting the affairs of civil government and commerce, of military, as well as judicial concerns. I may here observe, that many centuries have not elapsed since the learning, laws, and religion of our own country were preserved and studied in a foreign language; that language however has been superseded by the English, a sufficient proof that the current language of the country was deemed most worthy of cultivation and study.

Although the Hindoostanee language does not boast of very many prose compositions, or works of science, yet how many elegant tales and beautiful poems have been composed in it! How universally are commercial and military concerns, and even political correspondence of the highest consequence, connected with it and carried on it! And in this place, I may observe, that the instructions of the learned natives, and all their disputations and arguments on subjects of literature, are conducted in it; and that in every case, where a native of this country wishes either to compose or to dictate any thing to be written, he constantly arranges his ideas, and explains his meaning, in the Hindoostanee.

Lastly, a correct and general knowledge of this language greatly facilitates the acquisition of many others, and is the only means by which we can effectually prevent injustice and imposition.

If the assertions which I have here made be founded on truth, what argument can be brought to invalidate my proposition? The conclusion from the premises is this, that to the merchant, the traveller, the civil and military officer, the philosopher and physician; in short, to every one who carries on concerns of any moment in India, the Hindoostanee language is more generally necessary and advantageous than any other; and on this account, it ought to be the most cultivated and esteemed. (1802)

W.B. BAYLEY[206][a]


## 3.  Sanskrit

The language which Sir W. Jones conjectures might have been the

primeval language of Upper India, the Hindee, upon the basis of
which Hindustani has been formed, is not known to me to possess
any literature, and the dialect derived from it is obviously destitute
of any *classical* literature. From a certain analogy which he forms on
the subject of the language of conquerors, he is almost induced to
conjecture that the Sanscrit was introduced by conquerors, in some
very remote age, from other kingdoms. I do not adopt either his
theory or analogy, though I differ, with the greatest deference,from
so high an authority. As a language, the Sanscrit possesses a perfect
construction, and is as copious as the Latin and Greek, with many
grammatical intricacies. The roots of its verbs and forms of its
grammar bear a strong affinity to these languages. The characters of
its alphabet, reputed to have been taught by the divinity, and
therefore designated *Devanagaree,* have been adopted for the languages of more than twenty kingdoms and states, with certain
variations; and Sir W. Jones believed that the square Chaldaic
letters in which most Hebrew books are copied were originally the
same; while the Ethiopic and Phœnician bear a close relation to the
Devanagaree. An enthusiasm in literature may surely be carried to
as great an excess as fanaticism has ever gone in religion. Speaking
of a commentary on a philosophical *Shastra,* Sir W. Jones says, 'I am
confident in asserting, that until an accurate translation of it shall
appear in some European language, the general history of
philosophy must remain incomplete, for I perfectly agree with those
who are of opinion that one correct version of any celebrated
Hindoo book would be of greater value than all the dissertations or
essays that could be composed on the same subject.' To complete
the climax I may just add another sentence: 'So I can venture to
affirm, without meaning to pluck a leaf from the never-fading
laurels of our immortal Newton, that the whole of his theology, and
part of his philosophy, may be found in the Vedas, and even in the
works of the Sufis.'

One should think this is bold enough! We may however remark,
that this theology and philosophy were possessed of a wonderful
self-secreting power. It has been bottled up in hermetical recepta-
cles, without the power of expansion, and its influence upon those
who were the *hidden ones* has been the reverse of productive and
useful. Is this the nature of such philosophy? Will such a germ
produce no fruit? Will an ointment so odorous and rich diffuse no
perfume? Or is it all so etherealized that it evaporates so soon as the

precious vial is opened? I cannot avoid declaring that my inquiries have led to a far different estimate. I have held most familiar, frequent, and studious intercourse with Brahmins of no ordinary acquirements and sagacity, who still adhered to the practices of their own creed. I have closely and repeatedly interrogated my own moonshees, or pundits, and sought to ascertain, not what was contained in the Shastras, but what was most commonly believed by the would-be-wise among the people,—what they understood was taught in the Puranas and the more sacred Vedas. I did meet with something which partook of the character of a mythological, metaphysical jargon, a sort of abstract, pantheistic mysticism, which might more properly be deemed the puerilities of philosophy, falsely so called. Sir W. Jones confesses that 'one original treatise on medicine, considered as a science, in any language of Asia,' does not exist. However, he exults in 'the ample field presented by *six* philosophical Shastras. for a development of the metaphysics and logic of the Brahmins,' besides the works of the heterodox philosophers. I believe, however, that the instruction most valuable to be found in the Sanscrit belongs to grammar and the derivation of languages, which shoot out from it as from a parent stem. The poetical and religious fire which blazes out in some of the poems, as Sir W. Jones describes it, has entirely escaped my observation. (1839)

J.W. MASSIE[207]

## 4. The language of Sind

The language of Sinde, both oral and written, differs very much from that of the rest of India, but the princes and people are so ignorant, that very few Mahometans are able to write it. The characters are called Khada-wadi, and are found in the letters of the merchants. Compared with most of the alphabets of Hindostan, that of Sinde is very poor: there are but two characters which designate vowels, and these are only used as initials. Hence the written language is used merely in letter writing, and the few books in Sinde are written in Persian characters. The pronunciation of the Belooches is so uncouth that the Sindians say they learnt it from their goats, when they were herdsmen in the mountains of Kelat! (1845)

LEOPOLD VON ORLICH [208]

## 5.  *Moonshees*

A proper moonshee will know, that the adopting of a [standard] course is of no use whatever, and will set his pupil on the right track of discovering that which he so ardently desires, viz, a proper idea of the *idiom* of the language, without a knowledge of which, all the fagging in the world will be of no avail. No European can, in my opinion, teach an oriental language, whatever his own capabilities may be.

The next difficulty to be overcome is to know the way in which these sable-browed teachers are to be dealt with, when once admitted into the service of a student. There is an old saying about too much familiarity breeding contempt. In nothing is this saying more verified than in the intercourse of Europeans with natives generally, and in nothing more so than in the daily dealings of the pupil with his teacher.

These men are the most insinuating rascals under the Indian sun! Their very address gives rise to a degree of familiarity on the part of the student, who imperceptibly finds himself on terms of intimacy with his employer, who allows him to do just as he likes; he comes to give lessons, or he does not come at all; he talks and laughs, instead of teaching, and wastes time which ought to be spent in the occupation for which he is paid; the student, careless about progress, and too glad, probably, to chat and amuse himself, instead of learning, encourages the teacher, and there the two sit for hours together in perfect idleness.

The progress which a man makes depends greatly on himself; there is a regular rule laid down for gaining a knowledge of, and mastering the eastern languages. The alphabet being acquired, the putting together of letters, so as to form words of one, or two, or three syllables, should then follow; after that, the finding out their meanings, and then learning them by heart; again, those words should be thrown into easy sentences, and rendered into English; the same sentences should be committed to memory, and re-translated into the original.

Again, the reading of easy sentences, in the rough character, in order to acquire a knowledge and practice of the hand-writing (which is of the utmost importance), and the conversing in familiar language with the moonshee, putting down all words looked out in the dictionary; all these preliminaries facilitate the labours of the

'Our Moonshee', drawn by Captain G. F. Atkinson

beginner. After this, the grammar may be brought into action, so as to give the student a helping hand in his translations from the English, and assist him materially in the idiom. He may then commence the 'Stories of the Parrot'; after which, he must read the *Bagh-wu-bahar,* or *Chur-Dur-wesh* (the Adventures of the four Durweshes), and from that to the *Ikh wauool-suffa,* and then the *Gool-i-bukawullee,* and *Goolistan.* (1850)

ALBERT HERVEY[209]

## 6. A conversation

Today I went to the Bhutia bustee and the temple [in Darjeeling]. The temple is neither big nor interesting. Upstairs the Lama has many pictures. I bought two from him for Rs. 20. The arrangement inside the temple is not in any way different from that of an inner chamber in Southern-Buddhist temples. The images are different and this row of 'wheels of prayer' (Dharma Chakra) is quite unknown to the south.

I did not enter into a discussion with the Lama. We had to explain ourselves in Hindustani i.e. in a language little known to either participant in the conversation. But when the talk turned to books, it very soon became comprehensible.

I came up from there after a very long time, and all the while constantly halting and labouring in Hindustani and in ethnological observations: met a Gurung who, it transpired, did not know the Gurung language. I had Limbus, Lepchas, Bhutanese and Tibetans as interlocutors. I also came across a lama; some lamas wear caftans or cassocks of a white colour, others of a red or rather of the colour of Bordeaux. (1886)

IVAN PAVLOVICH MINAYEFF[210]

# 15. The Occupations

## A. PROFESSIONS

### 1. Spice sellers

In Goa and on the Sea coasts there are many Bramenes, which commonly doe maintayne themselves with selling of Spices and other Apothecarie ware, but it is not so cleane as others, but full of garbish and dust. They are very subtile in writing and casting accounts, whereby they make other simple Indians beleeve what they will. (1583)

JOHN HUIGHEN VAN LINSCHOTEN[211]

### 2. Indian painters

I have often admired the beauty, softness, and delicacy of their paintings and miniatures, and was particularly struck with the exploits of *Ekbar,* painted on a shield by a celebrated artist, who is said to have been seven years in completing the picture. I thought it a wonderful performance. The *Indian* painters are chiefly deficient in just proportions, and in the expression of the face; but these defects would soon be corrected if they possessed good masters, and were instructed in the rules of art.

Want of genius, therefore, is not the reason why works of superior art are not exhibited in the capital. If the artists and manufacturers were encouraged, the useful and fine arts would flourish; but these unhappy men are contemned, treated with harshness, and inadequately remunerated for their labour. The rich will have every article at a cheap rate. When an *Omrah* or *Mansebdar* requires the services of an artisan, he sends to the *bazar* for him, employing force, if necessary, to make the poor man work; and after the task is finished, the unfeeling lord pays, not according to the value of the labour, but agreeably to his own standard of fair remuneration; the artisan having reason to congratulate himself if the *korrah* has not been given in part payment. How then can it be expected that any spirit of emulation should animate the artist or manufacturer? Instead of contending for a superiority of reputation, his only anxiety is to finish his work, and to earn the pittance that shall supply him with a piece of bread. The artists, therefore, who arrive at any eminence in their art are those only who are in the service of the King or of some powerful *Omrah,* and who work exclusively for their patron. (1656–68)

FRANCOIS BERNIER[212]

## 3.  *A butcher*

The *Moors* are only bound to abstain from Unclean Beasts, and load their Tables with Fish and Fowl, and other Fare. And it is only among them that the Butchers kill the Meat, and sell it to strangers; for the *Indians* will scarce look upon a mangled Carkass. A Butcher with them is little less than a Murtherer, but of all Vocations that is the most odious with them. (1689)

J. OVINGTON [213]

## 4.  *A fruit merchant*

We had at the same time a much more welcome visitor in the person of a fruit merchant from the Punjab, with an assortment of pears, apples, grapes, apricots, etc. who having before experienced the protection of a Mahratta camp, has wisely taken up his quarters, this time, in ours. The fruits are packed in small round boxes between layers of cotton, and are generally brought in a very good state of preservation. (1809)

THOMAS DUER BROUGHTON[214]

## 5.  *Religious employments*

The Malabar brahmins, like those in other parts of India, form two distinct classes, engaged in different pursuits: both are held sacred by the other castes: one has the absolute and entire management of every thing relating to religion: occupied by no secular concerns, they spend their days under the sacred groves of their temples in superstitious ceremonies, and listless indolence, or study the sacred volumes, treatises on astrology, medicine, and fabulous legends; they inculcate benevolence to man, and kindness to the animal creation, and are reverenced by the inferior tribes, who swear by their heads, and treat them with filial affection. (1812)

JAMES FORBES[215]

## 6.  *The village barber*

Every village in India is a society complete in itself, containing, generally, all the various Trades requisite for the comfort and convenience of the whole community; as the blacksmith, washer-man, carpenter, and last, not least, the barber. The plate represents this official in the act of shaving a fat Baboo; they are seated before a cottage, covered, as all are at a particular season, with the Kudhoo. The castor-oil plant is growing at the side of the hut. A Toolsee Chourah of a more simple character is at the door, where there is also a bamboo frame for pigeons. On the left of the picture is a plantain-tree, with its beautiful bright green leaves and pendant fruit.

A Jhamp and Ghura are placed against the tree; on the right is a little girl rather smartly dressed, with a brass Lotah under her arm. One of those little urchins with large heads and distended stomachs, for which India is unrivalled, is holding unwilling parley with a gigantic southern Cock, who seems more than half inclined to share the rice with his youthful neighbour. (1842)

WILLIAM TAYLOR [216]

## 7.  *A moonshee*

The word Moonshee means an amanuensis, or secretary; though in India it is used to signify a teacher of Persian, or of the Mussulman portion of Hindustani; for this language is a compound one; having Hindi (the original language of the country) for its basis, upon which Persian, Arabic, and Turkish words were subsequently grafted by the Mahometan invaders; the whole together constituting Hindùs-tani. A Moonshee is a Mussulman, and teaches only that portion of the mixture, which was introduced by his own people. A Pundit, who is a learned Brahmin, instructs in Hindi; so that to the student both are necessary as guides to assist him in mastering the current language of India. Both are attached to a native regiment; the Sepoys, (or native soldiers), of which are composed of Mussulmen

'The Village Barber', drawn by William Taylor

and Hindoos. Moonshees are revered by the one, for their attainments, and position in society: Pundits, because they are Brahmins,
by the others. So, in judicial matters, both are in attendance to
administer oaths to the witnesses, in accordance with their respective creeds. (1848)

CHARLES RICHARD FRANCIS[217]

### 8. Confectioners

Returning to the Fort, we have to traverse, throughout its entire
length, the Maidan or Esplanade, in order to reach the Indian town,
called by the Europeans Black Town. On entering its huge bazaars
for the first time, one is immediately deafened by the din that
prevails, and half suffocated by the smells that impregnate the atmosphere. A heavy perfume of 'ghee' and grease, which is exhaled
from numerous shops belonging to the poorer class of confection-
ers, turns the stomach of all who, for the first time, experience it. In
spite of this source of discomfort, the visitor cannot help admiring
those famous bazaars. A world of people and races, of perfectly
distinct types and costumes, are crowded together in the streets of
this capital, which supplies the products of Europe to two-thirds of
India. (1875)

LOUIS ROUSSELET [218]

### 9. Tom, the barber

In India it is not good form to shave yourself. You ought to respect
the religious prejudices and social institutions of the people. If
everyone shaved himself, how would the Barber's stomach be
filled? The pious feeling which prompts this question lies deep in the
heart of Hindoo society. We do not understand it. How can we, with
our cold-blooded creed of demand and supply, free trade and
competition, fair field and no favour? In this ancient land, whose
social system is not a deformed growth, but a finished structure,
nothing has been left to chance, least of all a man's beard; for
cleanliness and godliness not being neighbours here, a beard well
matted with ashes and grease is the outward and visible sign of
sanctity. And so, in the golden age, when men did everything that is
wise and right, there was established a caste whose office it was to
remove that sign from secular chins. How impious and revolutio-

nary then must it be for a man who is not a barber to tamper with his own beard, thus taking the bread out of the mouths of barbers born, and blaspheming the wisdom of the ancient founders of civilization! It is true that, during the barber's strike a few years ago, the Brahmins, even of orthodox Poona, consecrated a few of their own number to the use of the razor. But desperate diseases demand desperate remedies. When the barbers struck, Nature did not strike. Beards grew as before, and threatened to change the whole face of society. In view of such an appalling crisis who would say anything was unlawful? Besides, British rule is surely undermining the very foundations of society, and I doubt if you could find a Brahmin to-day under fifty years of age whose heart is not more or less corroded by the spirit of change. Your young University man is simply honey-combed: he can scarcely conceal his mind from his own mother or wife.

But I must return to the Barber. The natives call him *hujjam*. He has been bred so true for a score or so of centuries that shaving must be an instinct with him now. His right hand is as delicate an organ as a foxhound's nose. I believe that, when inebriated, he goes on shaving, just as a toad deprived of its brain will walk and eat and scratch its nose. If you put a jagged piece of tin into the hand of a baby *hujjam*, he will scrape his little sister's face with it. In India, as you know, every caste has its own 'points', and you can distinguish a Barber as easily as a *dhobie* or a Dorking hen. He is a seek, fair-complexioned man, dressed in white, with an ample red turban, somewhat oval in shape, like a sugared almond. He wears large gold earrings in the upper part of his ears, and has a sort of false stomach, which, at a distance, gives him an aldermanic figure, but proves, on a nearer view, to be made of leather, and to have many compartments, filled with razors, scissors, soap, brush, comb, mirror, tweezers, earpicks, and other instruments of a more or less surgical character; for he is, indeed, a surgeon and especially an aurist and narist. When he takes a Hindoo head into his charge, he does not confine himself to the chin or scalp, but renovates it all over. The happy patient enjoys the operation, sitting proudly in a public place. When a Barber devotes himself to European heads he rises in the social scale. If he has any real talent for his profession, he soon rises to the rank and title of Tom, and may eventually be presented with a small hot-water jug, bearing an inscription to the effect that it is a token of the respect and esteem in which he was held by the officers of the –th Regiment at the station of Daree-nai-hona. This is equivalent to a C.I.E., but is earned by merit. In truth, Tom is a great institution. He opens the day along with tea and hot toast and the *Daree-nai-hona Chronicle,* but we throw aside the *Chronicle.* It is all very well if you want to know which band will play at the band-stand this evening, and the leading columns are occasionally excruciatingly good, when a literary corporal of the Fusiliers discusses the political horizon, or unmasks the *Herald,* pointing out with the most pungent sarcasm how 'our virtuous contemporary puts his hands in his breeches pockets, like a crocodile, and sheds tears;' but during the parade season the corporal writes little, and articles by the regular staff, upon the height to which cantonment hedges should be allowed to grow, are apt to be dull. For news we depend on Tom. He appears reticent at first, but be patient. Let him put the soap on, and then tap him gently.

'Well, Tom, what news this morning?'

'No news, sar.' After a long pause, 'Commissioner Saheb coming to-morrow.'

'To-morrow? No, he is not coming for three weeks.'

'To-morrow coming, Not telling anybody; quietly coming.'

'Why?'

'God knows.' After another pause, 'Nana Shett give Mamletdar 500 rupee for not send his son to prison. Then Nana Shett's brother he fight with Nana Shett, so he write letter to Commissioner and tell him you come quietly and make inquire.'

'The Mamletdar has been taking bribes, has he?'

'Everybody taking. Fouzdar take 200 rupee, Dipooty take 500 rupee.'

'What! Does the Deputy Collector take bribes?'

'God knows. Black man very bad. All black man same like bad.'

'Then are you not a black man?'

Tom smiles pleasantly and makes a fresh start.

'Colonel Saheb's madam got baby?'

'Is it a boy or a girl?'

'Girl, sar. Colonel Saheb very angry.'

'Why?'

'He say, " I want boy. Why always girl coming?" Get very angry. Beat butler with stick.'

Yes, Tom is a great institution. Who can estimate how much we owe to him for the circulation of that lively interest in one another's well-being which characterises the little station? Tom comes, like the Pundit, in the morning, but he is different from the Pundit and we welcome him. He is not a shadow of the black examination-cloud which lowers over us. There is no flavour of grammars and dictionaries about him. Even if he finds you still in bed, conscience gets no support from him. He does not awaken you, but slips in with noiseless tread, lifts the mosquito curtains, proceeds with his duty and departs, leaving no token but a gentle dream about the cat which came and licked your cheeks and chin with its soft, warm tongue, and scratched you playfully with its claws, while a cold frog, embracing your nose, looked on and smiled a froggy smile. The barber's hand *is* cold and clammy. *Chacun a son gout.* I do not like him. I grow my beard, and Tom looks at me as the Chaplain regards dissenters. (*c.* 1889).

E.H. AITKIN[219]

## 10. *The Miscellaneous wallahs*

I have yielded to the claim of the *doodwallah* to be reckoned among the *nowkers*. His right is more than doubtful, and I will yield no further. Nevertheless, there is a cluster of petty dependents, a nebula of minor satellites, which have us for the focus of their orbit, and which cannot be left out of a comprehensive account of our system. Whence, for example, is that raucus stridulation which sets every tooth on edge and sends a rheumatic shiver up my spine? 'It is only the *Kalai-wallah,*' says the boy, and points to a muscular black man, very nearly in the garb of a Grecian athlete, standing with both feet in one of my largest cooking pots. He grasps a post with both hands, and swings his whole frame fiercely from side to side with a circular motion, like the balance wheel of a watch. He seems to have a rough cloth and sand under his feet, so I suppose this is only his energetic way of scouring the pot preparatory to tinning it, for the *Kalaiwallah* is the 'tin-man,' whose beneficent office it is to avert death by verdigris and salts of copper from you and your family. His assistant, a semi-nude, fleshless youth, has already ex-temporized a furnace of clay in the ground hard by, and is working a huge pair of clumsy bellows. Around him are all manner of copper kitchen utensils, *handies,* or *deckshies,* kettles, frying-pans and what not, and there are also on the ground some rings of *kalai*, commonly called tin; but pure tin is an expensive metal, and I do not think it is any part of the *Kalai-wallah*'s care to see that you are not poisoned with lead. One notable peculiarity there is in this *Kalai-wallah*, or tin-man, which deserves record, namely, that he pays no *dustooree* to any man. I take it as sufficient evidence of this fact that, though even the *matie* could tell you that the pots ought to be tinned once a month, neither the butler nor the cook ever seems to remember when the day comes round. This is a matter which you must see to personally. Contrast with this the case of the *Nalbund,* the clink of whose hammer in the early morning tells that the 15th of the month has dawned. His portable anvil is already in the ground, and he is hammering the shoes into shape after a fashion; but he is not very particular about this, for if the shoe does not fit the hoof he can always cut the hoof to fit the shoe. This is an advantage which the maker of shoes for human feet does not enjoy, though I have heard of very fashionable ladies who secretly have one toe amputated that the rest may more easily be squeezed into that curious pointed thing, which, by some mysterious process of mind, is regarded as an elegant shoe. But this is by the way. To return to the *Nalbund.* His work is guaranteed to last one calendar month, and your faithful *ghorawallah,* who remembers nothing else, and scarcely knows the day of the week, bears in mind the exact date on which the horse has to be shod next, and if the careless *Nalbund* does not appear, promptly goes in search of him. Does not this speak volumes for the efficiency of that venerable and wonderful institution *dustooree* by which the interests of all classes are cemented together and the wheels of the social system are oiled? The shoeing of the bullock is generally a distinct profession, I believe, from the shoeing of the horse, and is not considered such a high art. The poor *byle* is thrown, and, his feet being tied together, the assistant holds his nose to the ground, while the master nails a small slip of bad iron to each half of the hoof. I often stop on my way to contemplate this spectacle, which beautifully illustrates that cold patience, or natural thick-skinnedness, which fits the *byle* so admirably for his lot in this land. He is yoked to a creaking cart and prodded with a sharp nail to make him go, his female ancestry reviled to the third generation, his belly tickled with the driver's toes, and his tail twisted till the joints crack, but he plods patiently on till he feels disposed to stop, and then lies down and takes with an even mind such cudgelling as the enraged driver can inflict. At last a fire of straw is lighted under him, and then he gets up and goes on. He never grows restive or frets, as a horse would, and so he does not wear out. This is the reason why bullocks are used throughout India for all agricultural purposes. The horse does not suit the genius of the people. I wish horses in India could do without shoes. In sandy districts, like Guzerat, they can, and are much better unshod; but in the stony Deccan some protection is absolutely necessary; and the poor beast is often at the mercy of the village bullock *Nalbund*. It carries my thoughts to the days of our forefathers, when the blacksmith was also the dentist.

The *Nalbund* leads naturally to the *Ghasswallah,* or grass-man, whose sign is a mountain of green stuff, which comes nodding in at the back gate every day upon four emaciated legs. A small pony's nose protrudes from the front, with a muzzle on, for in such matters the spirit of the law of Moses is not current in this country. The mild Hindoo does muzzle the mouth of the ox that treadeth out the corn. His religion forbids him to take life, and he obeys, but he steers as near to that sin as he can, without actually committing it, and vitality is seen here at a lower ebb, perhaps, than in any other country under the sun. The grassman maintains just so much flesh on the bones of his beast as will suffice to hold them together under their burden, and this can be done without lucerne grass, so poor Tantalus toddles about, burried under a pile of sweet-scented, fresh, green herbage, ministering to the sleek aristocracy of his own kind, and returns to gnaw his daily allowance of *kurbee*. There is, however, one allevia-tion of his lot for which he may well be thankful, and that is that his burden so encompasses him about that the stick of his driver cannot get at any part of him. I believe the *Ghasswallah* is an institution peculiar to our presidency—this kind of *Ghasswallah,* I mean, who is properly a farmer, owning large well-irrigated fields of lucerne grass. Hay is supplied by another kind of *Ghasswallah,* who does not keep a pony, but brings the daily allowance on his head. That allowance is five *polees* for each horse. A *polee* is a bundle of grass about as thick as a tree, and as long as a bit of string. This hay merchant does a large business, and used to send in a monthly bill to each of his constitutents in due form. thus:  [see page 287]

As the monsoon draws to a close and the weather begins to get colder, a man in a tight brown suit and leather belt, with an unmis-takable flavour of sport about him presents himself at the door. This is the *shikaree* come with *khubber* of *ishnap,* and quail, and duck,

| To Hurree Ganesh, | *January* |
| Mr. Esmith, Esquire | Dr. |
| To supplying grass to one horse | Rs. 700 |
| To supplying grass to 1/2 horse | Rs. 380 |

Total:                                    Rs. 1080
E.E. & contents received
The 1/2 horse was a cow.

and in fact of anything you like up to bison and tiger. But we must dismiss him today. He would require a chapter to himself, and would take me over ground quite outside of my present scope. What a *loocha* he is!

What shall I say of the *Roteewallah* and the *Jooteewallah,* who comes round so regularly to keep your boots and shoes in disrepair, and of all the vociferous tribe of *borahs?* There is the *Kupprawallah,* and the *Boxwallah,* and the *Ready—made—clothes-wallah'* ('readee made cloes, mem sa-ab! dressin' gown, badee, petticoat, drars, chamees, everything, mem sa-ab, very che-eap!') and the *Chowchowwallah* and the *Maiwawallah* or fruit man, with his pleasant basket of pomeloes and oranges, plantains, red and white, custard apples, guavas, figs, grapes, and pineapples, and those suspicious-looking old iron scales, hanging by greasy, knotted strings. Each of these good people, it seems, lives in this hard world for no other end but to supply my wants. One of them is positive that he supplied my father with the necessaries of life before I was born. He is by appearance about eighteen years of age, but this presents no difficulty, for if it was not he who ministered to my parent, it was his father, and so he has not only a personal, but a hereditary claim on me. He is a *Workboxwallah,* and is yearning to show his regard for me by presenting me with a lady's sandalwood dressing-case in return for the trifling sum of thirty-five rupees. The *Sindworkwallah,* who has a similar esteem for me, scorns the thought of wishing to sell, but if I would just look at some of his beautiful things, he could go away happy. When they are all spread upon the ground, then it occurs to him that I have it in my power to make him lucky for the day by buying a fancy smoking-cap, which, by-the-by, he brought expressly for me. But this subject always makes me sad, for there is no disguising the fact that the *borah* is fast passing away for ever, and with him all the glowing morning tints of that life which we used to live when India was still

India. But let that regret pass. One *wallah* remains, who presents himself at your door, not monthly, or weekly, but every day, and often twice a day, and not at the back verandah, but at the front, walking confidently up to the very easy-chair on which we stretch our lordly limbs And I may safely say that, of all who claim directly or indirectly to have eaten our sal , there is not a man for whom we have, one and all of us, a kindlier feeling. You may argue that he is only a public servant, and has really far less claim on us than any of the others; never mind—

'I pray thee, peace. I will be flesh and blood.'

The English mail is in, and we feel, and will feel, towards that red-liveried man as Noah felt towards the dove with the olive branch in her mouth. And when Christmas comes round, howsoever we may harden ourselves against others, scarcely one of us, I know, will grudge a rupee to the *tapalwallah. (c.* 1889)

E.H. AITKIN[220]


# B.   INDUSTRIES

## 1. Wine in India

In India wine is made of the substance of the tree which bears the *Cocos*, called palm. because it is like the true palm, and it is of two sorts. *Sura* is that kind which is got raw, dropping of itself into vessels set to receive it. The other, called *araca*, is distilled by fire from this *Sura*, and is very strong. Into this they throw dried grapes, which takes off its roughness and sweetens it; and it improves with age, which is not the case with that made of dried grapes and water.

Other wine is made of another palm called *nipa* growing in watery places. This is distilled like the last, but is softer and sweeter, transparent as pure water, and said to be very wholesome. A great deal of it is made and shipped in Pegu, Tanasarim, Malaca, and the Phelipines or Manilla. That of Tanasarim is much the best of all. (1587)

PEDRO TEIXEIRA[221]


## 2. English factories

The Factories which I could heare of setled for the Company in the East-Indies are these: Bantam (wherein were George Barkley

Chiefe, John Jordan, George Ball, Ralph Copendale, with divers others both Factors and Attendants) Jacatra, Surat, Amadavas, Agra and Azmiro, Brampore, Calecut, Masulipatan, Petapoli, Patania, Siam, Beniarmasse, Socodania, Macasser, Achen, Jambe, Tecoo, Ferando in Japan, Japar, Banda. (1616)

WALTER PAYTON[222]

## 3. Dutch factory, Agra

The *Dutch* have a factory in *Agra*, in which they generally keep four or five persons. Formerly they carried on a good trade in that city by the sale of broad-cloths, large and small looking-glasses, plain laces, gold and silver laces, and iron wares; likewise by the purchase of *anil* or *Indigo*, gathered in the neighbourhood of *Agra*, particularly at *Bianes*, two days' journey from the city, whither they go once every year, having a house in the place. The *Dutch* used also to make extensive purchases of cloths not only at *Jelapour*, but at *Laknau*, a seven or eight days' journey from *Agra*, where they also have a house, and despatch a few factors every season. It seems, however, that the trade of this people is not now very lucrative, owing probably to the competition of the *Armenians*, or to the great distance between *Agra* and *Sourate*. Accidents continually befall their caravans, which, to avoid the bad roads and mountains in the direct road through *Goualeor* and *Brampour*, travel by way ot *Ahmed-abad*, over the territories of different *Rajas*. But whatever may be the discouragements, I do not believe the *Dutch* will follow the example of the *English*, and abandon their factory at Agra; because they still dispose ot their spices to great advantage, and find it useful to have confidential persons near the court always ready to prefer a complaint against any governor, or other officer, who may have committed an act of injustice or tyranny in any of the *Dutch* establishments in *Bengale*, or at *Patna, Sourate*, or *Ahmed-abad*. (1656–68)

FRANCOIS BERNIER[223]

## 4. French factories

If [the loss of] this factory, which had only a junior merchant and a clerk in charge of it, caused so much stir in the country to the dishonour of our nation, we must expect even more disastrous results from the abandonment of the factory at Tellicherry. It had been established with much trouble, due to opposition by the Dutch, who moved heaven and earth to prevent it. But, in spite of this, we succeeded, owing to the might and help of the King of Cananor [Cannanore] and other neighbouring princes who had invited us there and gave us every possible assistance. We found that our first post established at Baillepatan [Baliapatam] was too inconvenient on account of its distance from the sea; so, as a further token of their protection and friendship, they gave us Tellicherry, which is much more advantageous for obtaining merchandise, for accommodation, and for easy access by ships, as I have mentioned fully in describing the place in my first Journal. I had seen the beginning of this factory and the expenses entailed in making suitable houses and storerooms all in a fine enclosure and situated on the best part of the coast. I was, therefore, so moved on learning of the orders which the Surat directors were sending to dissolve and abandon this factory, that I could not restrain myself from showing my resentment to the director Gueston. I impressed upon him the harm and dishonour that this order would cause to the company and to our nation. I said so many things in trying to prevent this action that he was obliged to tell me that he was doing nothing on his own responsibility, but on the orders he had received from the Directors of General Chamber at Paris to stop all trade in India and to reduce the Company's business to two or three factories. I admit that I have seldom been more surprised, and I could not imagine what aim or design the French directors could have in sending this order to close down factories, which had been opened so quickly and inexpensively in contrast with the trouble, expense, and time, devoted by the other European nations, in order to get places for their trade in this country. (1972-4)

ABBE CARRE[224]

## 5. *Golgutt, the English factory at Hughley*

Golgutt, an English factory, subordinate under Calcutta, is seated in the city of Hugly on the banks of the river, it here forming itself into a cove, being deep water, ships riding 16 and 18 fathom not a stones cast off shore. Being landed and ascended the bank, you enter the factory through a large gate beautified and adorned with pillars and cornishes in the chanam (plaster) work, and on the top of all is the flag-staff, fixed into the brickwork, whereon they hoist St George's flag. Being entered the gate, you come into a small courtyard, on the right hand being a row of apartments, and on the left, a viranda for the guard. You ascend into the house by steps, having under it two square cellars with staircases to descend. The hall is indifferent large. Besides two indifferent apartments with chimneys, there are other rooms and closets in the house, the whole consisting but of one story.

Behind the house is a garden, in which grows nothing but weeds. In the middle is an ugly well, and at one corner upon the wall is built a round sort of a business, like a sentry box but much larger. You ascend it by a narrow chanam staircase, which have no rails or fence to keep you from tumbling into the garden; and when entered, you see nothing worth observation having a door but never a window, tho' it yields an excellent echo, it being contrived, as I have been informed, as a magazine for powder.

At the end of the garden are the ruins of several apartments, the roofs being fallen in, and indeed all the outhouses are in the like condition, of which there are several. You may ascend to the top of the factory by an old wooden staircase which is well terras'd, with seats all round and a small oblong place included by its self, from whence you have a prospect of the river. To conclude, it is an old, ugly, ill contrived edifice wherein is not the least spark of beauty, form, or order to be seen, being seated in a dull melancholy hole enough to give on the Hippocondra by once seeing it. The Company have no factor at present that is resident here, being left in the charge of a molly and two or three punes, tho' in truth it is hardly worth looking after. (1712)

JOHN BURNELL[225]

## 6. Manufacturers of Surat

The inhabitants of Surat are generally merchants or manufacturers: after the Mahrattas conquered Guzerat, the weavers of keemcabs, and other rich stuffs, the embroiderers, jewellers, painters, and inlayers of ivory, ebony, and sandal-wood, meeting with no encouragement from the Mahratta government, emigrated from Ahmedabad to Surat, and other flourishing cities in the western districts of Hindostan, where they have resumed their employments with great success.

Surat is also a considerable market for shawls, one of the most delicate fabrics yet brought from the loom: they are not indeed manufactured at Surat, nor in any of the southern provinces, being chiefly the produce of Cachemire, that 'paradise of nations,' where Acber, and many of the imperial princes retired from the cares of government: encircled by their favourite courtiers, and in the bosom of their family, they enjoyed in that mild climate the picturesque scenery of the surrounding mountains,. and the rural beauties of the delicious valley, watered by the celebrated Hydaspes, and refreshed by many other streams from its lofty boundaries. The shawls manufactured in Cachemire, from the delicate silky wool of a goat peculiar to Thibet, are an elegant article of luxury, too well known in Europe, to need a particular description: this manufacture is not confined to Cachemire, but all others are deemed of an inferior quality: their prime cost is from twenty to five hundred rupees a shawl, according to the size, texture, and pattern: some, perhaps, may be more valuable. (1812)

JAMES FORBES[226]

## 7.  Paper manufactory

We mounted Captain Sydenham's horses, though I was still suffering from my accident, and went on about a mile and a half to the village of Karguswarrah, or Paper Town, so called from a large manufactory of that article being established in it, in consequence of the advantageous vicinity of some large tanks of spring water. Paper is made in India, though leaves are still used for writing upon. The houses are of hewn stone, badly joined, and not half inhabited. (1817–18)

LT. COL. FITZCLARENCE[227]

## 8.  Pestle and mortar sugar mills

On the 13th we came on the Burwa Saugor, over a road winding amongst small ridges and conical hills, none of them much elevated or very steep; the whole being a bed of brown syenite, generally exposed to the surface in a decomposing state, intersected by veins and beds of quartz rocks, and here and there a narrow and shallow bed of dark basalt. One of these beds of basalt was converted into grey syenite by a large granular mixture of white quartz and

'The Sugar Mills at Belaspore', drawn by Major Parlby

feldspar, with the black hornblende. From this rock the people form
their sugar-mills, which are made like a pestle and mortar, the
mortar being cut out of the hornblende rock, and the pestle out of
wood, thus:

We saw a great many of these mortars during the march, that
could not have been in use for the last half-dozen centuries, but they
are precisely the same as those still used all over India. The driver
sits upon the end of the horizontal beam to which the bullocks are
yoked; and in cold mornings it is very common to see him with a pair
of good hot embers at his buttocks, resting upon a little projection
made behind him to the beam for the purpose of sustaining it. I am
disposed to think that the most productive parts of the surface of
Bundelcund, like that of some of the districts of the Nerbudda
territories which repose upon the back of the sandstone of the
Vindhya chain, is fast flowing off to the sea through the great rivers,
which seem by degrees to extend the channels, of their tributary
streams into every man's field, to drain away its substance by
degrees, for the benefit of those who may in some future age occupy
the islands of their delta. I have often seen a valuable estate reduced
in value to almost nothing, in a few years, by some new *antennoe,* if I
may so call them, thrown out from the tributary streams of great
rivers into their richest and deepest soils. Declivities are formed, the
soil gets nothing from the cultivator but the mechanical aid of the
plough, and the more its surface is ploughed and cross-ploughed,
the more of its substance is washed away towards the Bay of Bengal
in the Ganges, or the Gulf of Cambay in the Nerbudda. In the
districts of the Nerbudda, we often see these black hornblende
mortars, in which sugar-canes were once pressed by a happy
peasantry, now standing upon a bare and barren surface of sandstone rock, twenty feet above the present surface of the culturable
lands of the country. There are evident signs of the surface on which
they now stand having been that on which they were last worked.
The people get more juice from their small straw-coloured canes in
these pestle and mortar mills, than they can from those with cylindrical rollers in the present rude state of the mechanical arts all over
India; and the straw-coloured cane is the only kind that yields good
sugar. The large purple canes yield a watery and very inferior juice;
and are generally, and almost universally, sold in the markets as a
fruit. The straw-coloured canes, from being crowded under a very
slovenly system, with little manure and less weeding, degenerate

into a mere reed. The Otaheitie cane, which was introduced into India by me in 1827, has spread over the Nerbudda, and many other territories; but that that will degenerate in the same manner, under the same slovenly system of tillage, is too probable. (1836)

WILLIAM HENRY SLEEMAN[228]

## 9. Kimkhwab manufactory

On my return to my budjerow, a number of native merchants were in waiting, hoping to dispose of their goods to the strangers; they had boxes full of Benares turbans, shawls, gold and silver dresses, kimkhwab, and cloth of gold. This place is famous for its embroidery in gold, and for its tissues of gold and silver. I purchased some to make a native dress for myself, and also some very stiff ribbon, worked in silk and gold, on which are the names of all the Hindoo deities; the Hindoos wear them round their necks; they are holy, and called juneoo. (1850)

FANNY PARKES[229]

## 10. Ivory and silk manufacturers

Provisions are very cheap here. Berhampore is noted for its ivory and silk manufacturers, specimens of which were brought on board for sale. It is likewise one of the coal depots for the river steamers, as well as one of the principal stations for embarking goods. The coal depots are Mirzapore, Benares, Ghazepore, Dinapore, Bar, Monghyr, Colgong, Rajmahal, Berhampore, and Kutwa. There is a great deal of communication between this place and Calcutta, which is only 161 miles distant by the river route, the intercourse being now carried on with great regularity and speed. (1854)

W.W.W. HUMBLEY[230]

## 11. Indigo factory, Allahabad

Our host's residence was a perfect type of the English planter's dwelling in India. It was a large and very low brick-walled house, supporting an immense pyramidal roof formed of a thick covering of maize thatching. Its exterior, which was of extreme simplicity, conveyed no notion of the elegance and comfort of the interior, which was composed of four handsome bedrooms, each with its own verandah and bath-room, opening on to a large, richly furnished, square sitting-room. A kitchen garden, in which the principal European vegetables are grown, surrounded the house, separating it from the work-buildings which constitute the factory. It was in this edifice, which we visited immediately on our arrival, that the indigo-producing plant was submitted to the different processes of its preparation. Unfortunately the harvest takes place only after the rainy season, so we were unable to witness this interesting manufacture. Our host, however, furnished us with so many details, that our regret was greatly diminished.

'It is the young shoots of the humble plant you see around you,' he said, 'which provide us with the precious material for dyeing, and not the flowers, as is commonly supposed. The gathering of these shoots is a very delicate operation. When they have arrived at a proper degree of maturity, they must be speedily removed; and each cutting must be executed with rapidity, and during the night, for the sun would wither the branches, and deprive them of their properties. We therefore require a great many hands; all the villages on my estate are placed in requisition. The workmen are all dispersed in the fields at midnight; and in the morning the produce of the harvest is deposited in these stone troughs, which have been previously filled with water. Then is the time for the sun to perform its part. Under the influence of its rays the substances undergo a species of fermentation; the water becomes coloured with variegated tinges, and rapidly turns blue. After a space of about forty-eight hours, the liquid is drawn off from the smallest troughs; it now emits a slightly ammonial smell, and the colour is almost black. It is allowed to evaporate again, and is then placed in metal vats heated by steam, in which, when the evaporation has ceased, a deposit of pure indigo is formed. It only remains to dry this deposit, pack it, and send it to the market at Calcutta.'

The situation of this indigo plantation is one of the most westerly in India; but after this point, going on towards the east, vast districts are to be found in which this material forms almost the sole product manufactured. Tirhout, Upper Behar, and Bengal are almost entirely in the hands of the indigo planters.

These details were quite new to me. There exist, therefore, in India, besides the soldiers, public functionaries, and tradesmen, real planters established on the soil and cultivating its riches. Their number, it is true, must be comparatively limited; but the mere superintendence of these field works implies an acclimatisation I had not thought the English capable of. And yet the planter's life in these parts has charms of which Europeans generally have little idea. For a man inured to the heat of this climate, what finer existence could there be than this of reigning lord over these vast fields and over these mild and timid people? While on the one hand he enjoys all the comforts of civilisation, he has on the other all the advantages of a life in the jungles. The railways are at his disposal; the forests are his hunting-preserves; and, if he is kind and indulgent, he is sure to be loved and respected by the population. (1875)

LOUIS ROUSSELET[231]

# 16. Medicine

## 1. Sicknesses and disease

The sicknesses and diseases in Goa, and throughout India, which are common, come most with the changing of the times and the weather, as it is said before: there raigneth a sicknesse called Mordexiin, which stealeth upon men, and handleth them in such sort, that it weakneth a man, and maketh him cast out all that he hath in his body, and many times his life withall. This sicknesse is very common and killeth many a man, whereof they hardly or never escape. The bloudy Fluxe is there likewise very common and dangerous, as the Plague with us. They have many continuall Fevers, which are burning Agues, and consume mens bodies with extreme heate, whereby within foure or five dayes they are either whole or dead. This sicknesse is common and very dangerous, and hath no remedie for the Portugals but letting bloud: but the Indians and Heathens doe cure themselves with herbes, as Sanders, and other such like ointments, wherewith they ease themselves. The sicknesse consumeth many Portugals every yeere, some because they have little to eate, and lesse to drinke of any meate or drinke that is nourishing, and use much company of women, because that Land is naturall to provoke them thereunto, as also the most part of the Souldiers by such meanes have their living and their maintenance, which oftentimes costeth them both life and limme, for although men were of Iron or Steele, the unchaste life of a woman, with her unsatiable lusts were able to grind him to powder, and sweepe him away like dust, which costeth many a mans life, as the Kings Hospitall can well beare witnesse, wherein they lodge, whensoever they are sicke, where every yeere at the least there entered five hundred live men, and never come forth till they are dead, and they are onely Portugals, for no other sicke person may lodge therein, I meane such as are called white men, for the other Indians have a Hospitall by themselves. In this Hospitall they are very well looked unto by the Jesuites, and Gentlemen; whereof every moneth one of the best is chosen and appointed, who personally is there by them, and giveth the sicke persons whatsoever they will desire, and sometimes spend more by foure or five hundred Duckets of their owne purses, then the Kings allowance reacheth unto.

But returning to our matter of sicknesse, Pockes and Piles, with other secret diseases, they are in those Countries very common, and not hidden or concealed, for they thinke it no shame, more then to have any other disease. They heale them with the root China: there are some that have had them at the least three or foure times, and are not any thing at all shunned or disliked for the same, but dare both boast and bragge thereof. It is not any thing perilous for the body, insomuch that they had rather have them, and feare them lesse then any of the foresaid diseases. The Plague hath never beene in India, neither is it knowne unto the Indians, but poisoning, witchcraft, and such like, whereby some lose their healths, and some their lives, is their daily exercise, and very common with them. (1583)

JOHN HUIGHEN VAN LINSCHOTEN[232]

## 2. Medicinal stones

... There is a stone of the porcupine, which grows in his belly, of such excellent virtue that only such as have tried it can believe it without a doubt. Whereof I am a good witness, having seen its effect at different times and in various places, and especially in the city of Cochin in the year 1590 and 1591. The Governor there used up two such stones in the service of the poor, working wonders against a disease more dangerous and violent than the plague, which lasted for two whole years and carried people off in four or five hours. This was a choleraic complaint, which the Indians call *morxy,* and the Portuguese *mordexim.* An infusion of this stone in water is effective in all maladies, and may be safely given in all, except to pregnant women in whose case some inconvenience may result from its extreme bitterness. (1590–1)

PEDRO TEIXEIRA[233]

## 3. Hindu medicine

The Hindoos reckon upon 3 humors in mans body, *viz.,* By (*bai,* air), Pitt (*pit,* bile), Cuff (*kaf,* phlegm), which they know by the pulse upon the right hand, lying one finger neare the bottome of the thumb upon the pulse upon the wrist, and that is for Cuff; another

'Barbarous Ceremony in Honour of Mariatale, Goddess of the Smallpox', drawn by Charles Gold

finger by it nearer the arme and that is for Pitt; and another nearer the arme and that is for By. So that if the pulse under the last finger named beate high, then is the body full of By; if under the other, then of Pitt; if under the other, then of Cuff. If all the 3 beat high, then is the body inclining to a fever; if low and even, then is little nature (vital power) in a man; if indifferent high and even, then in good health, if have good stomach (digestion).

When the By abounds, the Belly, Armes and Feet swell, and sometimes have paines in them. If Pitt abounds, then the Belly, Armes, feet and eyes are hot, and a man is thirsty. If Cuff abounds, the boddy and limbs are weak and have no stomack, if any—ill digestion proceeds from it, also much sweat.

The By rules the body from 2 Gurries (*ghari,* an hour of 24 minutes) before Sunrise and rules till 1 Purr (*pahar,* watch of 8 *ghari*) 3 Gurries; then Pitt rules till night; then Cuff till By begins againe.

I have met with some Doctors who call that By which here above is called Cuff, and that Cuff which above is called By, so no certainty which is true. (1668–72)

JOHN MARSHALL[234]

## 4. The treatment of small-pox

The skill of their physical people is very mean. Mr. *Thomas* and I once employed one of the black doctors to procure us a list of such medicines as they used in their practice. Instead oi this, he brought with him a number of leaves, plants, barks, roots of trees, etc. which, he told us, they generally made use of in decoctions; and that their common method of practice was, if one root, leaf, or herb failed, to put in others of different sorts. In fevers, he added, they used pepper, and such-like inflammatory substances. We enquired whether they had any written accounts of their method of practice; he told us they had, and brought us a large book, made up of a number of leaves of the *Palmita* tree, such as they keep their accounts upon, part of which we afterwards got translated by a black *Conucopola* or clerk. It was written in the high *Eastern* stile, and began with giving great praises to the Almighty for the wonderful formation of man: it then went on with observing that this formed man was divided into two or three hundred thousand parts; ten thousand of which were made up of veins; ten thousand of nerves;

seventeen thousand of blood; a certain number of bones, choler, lymph, etc. And all this was laid down without form or order, either of history, disease or treatment. We found this to be all the written account they have of physic; which they never study, but, like the other castes, the son of a doctor is a doctor also, and so he will continue to be from generation to generation.

The custom of inoculating for the *Small-pox* among the natives, though not common in other parts of the *East Indies,* is frequent in *Bengal;* and the manner of performing the operation is in many respects singular, and different from that now practised in *England.* They take, as Mr. *Thomas* and I were informed, some matter from the pock of a person who has the disease in a favourable way, and put it into a phial or gallipot. They then dip the point of a needle in this matter, and with it prick the person intended to be inoculated several times in a circle, on the fleshy part of the arm. If he be a grown person, they prick him in both arms. After the blood is wiped away, they rub some more matter on the part, and order the patient to bathe in cold water three times a day, and to live on the most cooling things he can possibly procure, such as water-melons, cucumbers, rice, water, etc. As soon however as the fever comes on, which happens about the fifth or seventh day, the patient is ordered to leave off bathing and the cool diet, and to live on milk and sugar: the fever generally lasts three days and then goes quite off. On the second day after the pock has appeared, they wash the whole body with cold water, which fills the pustules; and this they do for the three succeeding days, two or three times each day, continuing the same regimen of milk and sugar for diet. When the pock is drying off, they sprinkle the patient with rose-water; or when this cannot be had with the juice of *Suttamullie, Suctapot, Culmee,* and root of green *Turmeric.* If the pock be very thick, they give the patient *Joan-seeds* to chew, and frequently tie *Bang*-leaves (which is a kind of hemp) on the parts most affected. It is a common practice among the *Portuguese,* and some of the *Indians* on the *Malabar* coast, when the pock is fairly turned, to lay on wood and cow-dung ashes very thick, which they think imbibe the matter, and make the scab fall off the more easily. They leave it to nature to disengage herself from this compound of ashes and pustulary discharge. Their hopes of a cure from this method, seem to be founded on the supposed antiputrescent and absorbent quality of the ashes. I refer it to better judges to determine whether this practice be rational or not; however, in general the patients recover from this loathsome disorder. (1755–7)

EDWARD IVES[235]

## 5. *Diseases produced by Devils*

These diseases are numerous, as they not only enabled the practitioner to account for various and unusal forms of diseases, which they did not understand, but also afforded a favourable opportunity for the brahmans to reap a rich harvest from the ignorant people. I have before given a full account of these devils, from its forming such a curious chapter of the history of medicine. Infants are supposed to be liable to be affected by nine kinds of spirits or devils, which may assume various forms at will. They are produced from the mother, or the nurse having committed certain improprieties, by which the devil enters their bodies, in order to amuse himself. When a devil distresses an infant. it becomes depressed in spirits, and starts from fear. The eyes of the child swell, he cries, his fingers are contracted, and at other times he tears his body and clothes with his nails, and bites with his teeth, both himself and nurse. The child turns his face to one side, and moves about his eyes; grinds his teeth together, makes a noise like a person who cannot speak from the severity of the disease, and he frequently yawns. His eyelids and eyebrows are in cont nual movement, and the two foreteeth and lips remain shut, and foam proceeds from the mouth. The child becomes thinner, cannot sleep, his eyes swell, has frequent motions, and an unnatural noise proceeds from the throat. The smell of the body resembles that of blood, or flesh; and the child will not take his usual food. These are the usual symptoms indicating the presence of a devil. (1845)

T. A. WISE[236]

## 6. *Ravages of cholera*

In due time the force arrived within view of Kolapur, a town of considerable extent, situated on a plain with the two important hill-forts of Pangarh and Panallagarh some six miles distant. The encampment was made in the vicinity of the town, on a slight rise of the ground having a hard gravelly soil covered with scanty grass, and to all appearance as healthy a spot as could be desired; the escort of the Commissioner on its flank, and only divided from the main body by a small rocky nulla. We, the escort, had, however, a large tank in our front. I am thus particular in describing the ground, inasmuch that it renders unaccountable our exemption from the dreadful epidemic that followed. That very evening two cases of the worst type of cholera were reported, and the third day the troops shifted ground, having, during that period, in a force of five thousand men, and probably double that number of followers, lost by this scourge at the rate of one hundred and fifty men a day; nor did the pestilence finally disappear till tne force left the place. But the most singular thing is that both the escort, two hundred and fifty strong, and the town in their close vicinity, were completely exempt from a single case of the disease. (1881)

T.G. FRASER[237]

## 7. Enteric fever

...Typhoid fever prevailed in the artillery barracks at St. Thomas' Mount, near Madras, 'local nuisances were abundant in the shape of foul drains and cesspools in the neighbourhood of barracks and hospitals.' As for the old privies of the Secunderabad barracks—I quote from the official report of Superintending-Surgeon Cole—'They were positively pestiferous, the buildings and their neighbourhood were sodden and saturated with the foul imbibitions of a long series of years, and emitted most offensive odours.' When this description was written, the regiment then in barracks was suffering from a non-malarious fever of a continued type, and extremely fatal, and Mr. Cole was of opinion that the disease was propagated by a direct contagium from the morbid alvine discharges. I pray you to note this significant fact. The 17th Lancers occupied these barracks after these dreadful latrines were abolished and the dry-earth system substituted, and the result was that the regiment, with an average strength of 576, in three years lost only 37 men from all causes; a death-rate which, at the period in question, was a mere flea-bite when compared with the mortality of previous years in the same barracks, such, for example, as that which the Royal Scots suffered, when in one year, out of a strength of 1098 men, the regiment lost 104 men from dysentery alone. (1886)

WILLIAM CAMPBELL MACLEAN[238]

## 8. A Rajput nurse

'Whose tomb have they builded, Vittoo? under this tamarind tree,
With its door of the rose-veined marble, and white dome, stately to
   see;
Was he holy Brahman, or Yogi, or Chief of the Rajput line,
Whose urn rests here by the river, in the shade of the beautiful
   shrine?'

'May it please you,' quoth Vittoo, salaaming, 'Protector of all the
   poor!
It was not for holy Brahman they carved that delicate door;
Nor for Yogi, nor Rajput Rana, built they this gem of our land;
But to tell of a Rajput woman, as long as the stones should stand.

'Her name was Moti*, the pearl-name; 'twas far in the ancient
   times,
But her moon-like face and her teeth of pearl are sung of still in our
   rhymes;
And because she was young, and comely, and of good repute, and
   had laid
A babe in the arms of her husband, the Palace-Nurse she was made.

'For the sweet chief-queen of the Rana in Jeypore city had died,
   Leaving a motherless infant, the heir to that race of pride;
The heir of the peacock-banner, of the five-coloured flag, of the
   throne
Which traces its record of glory from days when it ruled alone;

'From times when, forth from the sunlight, the first of our kings
   came down
And had the Earth for his footstool, and wore the Stars for his
   crown,
As all good Rajputs have told us; so Moti was proud and true,
With the Prince of the land on her bosom, and her own brown baby
   too.

*Commonly known as 'Panna', she was the nurse of Udai Singh, the Rana of Mewar
   (1529–72). Her name has become proverbial in Rajasthan for devotion to her
   royal ward.

'And the Rajput women will have it (I know not, myself, of these
    things)
As the two babes lay on her bosom, her lord's and the Jeypore
    King's,
So loyal was the blood of her body, so fast the faith of her heart,
It passed to her new-born infant, who took of her trust its part

'He would not suck of the breast-milk till the Prince had drunken his
    fill;
He would not sleep to the cradle-song till the Prince was lulled and
    still;
And he lay at night with his small arms clasped round the Rana's
    child,
As if those hands like the rose-leaf could guard him from treason
    wild.

'For treason was wild in the country, and villainous men had sought
The life of the heir of the Gadi, to the Palace in secret brought;
With bribes to the base, and with knife-thrusts for the faithful, they
    made their way
Through the line of the guards, and the gateways, to the hall where
    the women lay.

'There Moti, the foster-mother, sate singing the children to rest,
Her baby at play on her crossed knees, and the King's son held to
    her breast:
And the dark slave-maidens round her beat low on the cymbal-skin,
Keeping the time of her soft song—when, Saheb!—there hurried in

'A breathless watcher, who whispered, with horror in eyes and face:
"Oh! Moti! men come to murder my Lord the Prince in this place!
They have bought the help of the gate-guards, or slaughtered them
    unawares,
Hark! that is the noise of their tulwars, the clatter upon the stairs!"

'For one breath she caught her baby from her lap to her heart; and
    let
The King's child sink from her bosom, with lips still clinging and
    wet;
Then tore from the Prince his head-cloth, and the putta of pearls
from his waist,

And bound the belt on her infant, and the cap on his brows, in haste;

'And laid her own dear offspring, her flesh and blood, on the floor,
With the girdle of pearls around him, and the cap that the King's son
    wore;
While close to her heart, which was breaking, she folded the Rajah's
    joy,
And—even as the murderers lifted the purdah—she fled with his
    boy.

'But there (so they deemed) in his jewels, lay the Chota Rana, the
    Heir,
"The cow with two calves has escaped us,' cried one, 'it is right and
    fair
She should save her own butcha; no matter! the edge of the dagger
    ends.
This spark of Lord Raghoba's sun-light; stab thrice and four times,
    O friends!"

'And the Rajput women will have it (I know not if this can be so)
That Moti's son in the putta and golden cap cooed low
When the sharp blades met in his small heart, with never one moan
    or wince,
But died with a babe's light laughter, because he died for his Prince.

'Thereby did that Rajput mother preserve the line of our kings.'
'Oh! Vittoo,' I said, 'but they gave her much gold and beautiful
    things,
And garments, and land for her people, and a home in the palace!
    May be
She had grown to love that Princeling even more than the child on
    her knee.'

'May it please the Presence!' quoth Vittoo, 'it seemeth not so! they
    gave
The gold and the garments and jewels, as much as the proudest
    would have;
But the same night deep in her bosom she buried a knife, and
    smiled,
Saying this, 'I have saved my Rana! I must go to suckle my child!'
    (1886)

EDWIN ARNOLD[239]

# 17. Astronomy and Astrology

## 1. Hindu astrology

Our fellow-believers in these [Muslim] countries are not acquainted with the Hindu methods of astrology and have never had an opportunity of studying an Indian book on the subject. In consequence, they imagine that Hindu astrology is the same as theirs and relate all sorts of things as being of Indian origin of which we have not found a single trace with the Hindus themselves. As in the preceding part of this our book we have given something of everything, we shall also give as much of their astrological doctrine as will enable the reader to discuss questions of a similar nature with them. If we were to give an exhaustive representation of the subject, this task would detain us very long, even if we limited ourselves to delineate only the leading principles and avoided all details.

First, the reader must know that in most of their prognostics they simply rely on means like auguring from the flight of birds and physiognomy, that they do not—as they ought to do—draw conclusions, regarding the affairs of the sublunary world, from the seconds (*sic*) of the stars; which are the events of the celestial sphere'.

Regarding the number seven as that of the planets there is no difference between us and them. They call them *graha*. Some of them are throughout lucky, viz. Jupiter, Venus and the Moon, which are called *saumyagraha*. Other three are throughout unlucky, viz. Saturn, Mars, and the Sun, which are called *Kruragraha*. Among the latter, they also count the dragon's head though in reality it is not a star. The nature of one planet is variable and depends upon the nature of that planet with which it is combined, whether it be lucky or unlucky. This is Mercury However, alone by itself, it is lucky. (*c.* 1000 A.D.)

## 2. *Astrologers and royalty*

Dara was also possessed with the craze of putting faith in astrologers, of whom he entertained a considerable number. The chief of them was called Bavani Das (Bhawani Das), who had a great liking and affection for me, because he enjoyed drinking my wine. This man had placed his head in danger by a paper, in which he declared that without the slightest doubt the said prince [Dara] would become king. I asked him in familiar conversation how he could have had the audacity to sign such a paper, and what excuse he had ready to produce if it did not happen accordingly. The astrologer laughed long and heartily at my question, and said to me that if the said prince should come to be king, he would accord to him the greatest credit; if not, the prince would be sufficiently busied in saving his own life, and not likely to have time to seek that of an astrologer.

During the time that this prince [Shah Shuja] governed the kingdom of Bengalla [Bengal], where he held his principal court in the city of Regemal [Rajmahal], there happened, a few years before the rebellion in the Mogul kingdom, an extraordinary case, about which he wrote to king Shahjahan. At eight o'clock in the day there appeared near the said city, in a plain a league and a half broad, a great number of cobra snakes, large and small. They covered the field and moved from west to east until four o'clock in the afternoon; they looked like ripples in the ocean. In the greatest fright, the inhabitants of the villages climbed upon the tops of their houses and upon trees. They beheld moving in the midst of the said cobras one of great size, which carried on its head another smaller one, entirely white. They pursued their way without harming anyone, many remaining behind in the suburbs of the city and in the villages, and through losing their companions they died. Hearing of this event, Shahjahan asked his astrologers what it meant. They replied that the wickedness of the empire was taking its departure, and that he would survive for many prosperous years.

The prince Shah Shuja also consulted his astrologers, and they told him that before much time had passed there would arise a rebellion in the empire, and that he would become emperor. The little cobra carried upon the head of the large one was, they said, the king of the cobras, who had come to the end of his reign, and was thus compelled to leave his old abode. This event caused considerable fear to all people, and it was spoken of in many directions. Both Mahomedans and Christians assured me that it was as the astrologers had divined, and that it must happen as they had said. But in saying that Shah Shuja must become king they went too far. All the same, this may have been the reason for Shah Shuja rising in rebellion against his father. (1653–1708)

NICCOLAO MANNUCCI[241]

## 3. Astronomy

In regard to astronomy, the *Gentiles* have their tables, according to which they foretell eclipses, not perhaps with the minute exactness of *European* astronomers, but still with great accuracy. They reason, however, in the same ridiculous way on the lunar as on the solar eclipse, believing that the obscuration is caused by a black, filthy, and mischievous *deuta*, named *Rach*, who takes possession of the moon and fills her with infection. They also maintain, much on the same ground, that the moon is four hundred thousand coses, that is, above firty thousand leagues, higher than the sun; that she is a luminous body, and that we receive from her a certain vital liquid secretion, which collects principally in the brain, and, descending thence as from its source into all the members of the body, enables them to exercise their respective functions. They believe likewise that the sun, moon, and stars are all so many *deutas;* that the darkness of night is caused by the sun retiring behind the *Someire,* an imaginary mountain placed in the centre of the earth, in form like an inverted sugar loaf, and an altitude of I know not how many thousand leagues: so that they never enjoy the light of day but when the sun leaves the back of this mountain. (1656–68)

FRANCOIS BERNIER[242]

## 4. Benares observatory

From thence we proceeded to the observatory, so renowned throughout India, and the subject of much discussion in Europe. We ascended by a flight of steps to an open terrace, where several astronomical instruments, formed of stone, are in perfect preservation. The principal object is a large semicircle graduated, seemingly intended for a dial.

I pass over Mr. Cruso's further remarks on the observatory at Benares, which so far from ascribing to remote antiquity, he did not consider to have been erected more than a century. The following remark in the Edinburgh Review on Mr. Bentley's treatise on the Hindoo systems of astronomy should not be omitted. That 'the consideration of the facts ascertained therein, and of many more which it would be easy to produce, ought to keep our curiosity alive to the remains of science in the east. Their extent and accuracy are so considerable—their origin and genealogy so completely unknown—they are united with so much extravagance and superstition, and so totally separated from any general stock of knowledge, that we cannot but consider them as forming altogether the most enigmatical monument of antiquity that is to be found on the face of the earth.' A great degree of scepticism on this subject ought most carefully to be preserved, until the industry and learning of the Asiatic Society, to which we have already so great obligations, shall furnish us with a more complete catalogue and description of the remains of oriental science. We may then decide, whether the east has only borrowed from the west, or whether it be true, as Lucian says, that it was in India that philosophy first alighted on the earth. (1812)

JAMES FORBES[243]

## 5. Disobliging astrologers

The Guicowar was exceedingly superstitious. For several days we postponed our hunting-parties because the astrologers had not been able to fix on a suitable day to commence them. Every morning the venerable pundits, adjusting their spectacles, arranged themselves in a circle, and made a pretence of consulting certain tables of copper covered with cabalistic signs. At the end of an hour, one of them would approach us, shaking his head, and announce to the king, with a melancholy air, that the omens were not favourable. What their intentions were in acting thus I could not comprehend, and the pleasantry seemed to me to be carried a little too far. Happily, the king at last showed himself so greatly annoyed, and manifested so keen a desire to follow my advice and leave the astrologers to con over their conjuring-books, that permission was given us next day. (1875)

LOUIS ROUSSELET[244]

# 18. Flora and Fauna

## A. IRRIGATION, FORESTS AND AGRICULTURE

### 1. The fruits of Calicut

I found in Calicut a kind of fruit which is called *ciccara* [jack-fruit]
Its stem is like that of a large pear tree. The fruit is two or two and a
half *palmi* long and is as thick as a man's thigh. This fruit grows on
the trunk of the tree, that is to say, under the boughs, and partly on
the middle of the stem. The colour of the said fruit is green, and it is
formed like the pine, but the work is more minute. When it begins to
ripen, the skin becomes black and appears rotten. This fruit is
gathered in the month of December, and when it is eaten it seems as
though you were eating musk melons, and it appears to resemble a
very ripe Persian quince. It appears also, as though you were eating
a preparation of honey, and it also has the taste of a sweet orange.
Within the said fruit there are some pellicles like the pomegranate.
And within the said pellicles there is another fruit which, if placed
on the embers of the fire and then eaten, you would say that they
were most excellent chestnuts. So that this appears to me to be the
best and the most excellent fruit I ever ate. Another fruit is also
found here, which is called *amba* [amb, amba, mango], the stem of
which is called *manga* [manga, mango]. This tree is like a pear
tree, and bears like the pear. This *amba* is made like one of our
walnuts in the month of August, and has that form; and when it is
ripe it is yellow and shining. This fruit has a stone within like a dry
almond, and is much better than the Damascus plum. A preserve is
made of this fruit, such as we make of olives, but they are much
superior. Another fruit is found here resembling a melon, and it has
similar divisions, and when it is cut, three or four grains, which look
like grapes or sour cherries, are found inside. The tree which bears
this fruit is of the height of a quince tree, and forms its leaves in the
same manner. This fruit is called *corcopal* [papau]; it is extremely
good for eating, and excellent as a medicine. I also found there

another fruit, which is exactly like the medlar, but it is white, like an apple. I do not remember by what name it was called. Again, I saw another kind of fruit which resembled a pumpkin in colour, is two spans in length, and has more than three fingers of pulp, and is much better than a gourd [*zuccha*] for confections, and it is a very curious thing, and it is called *comolanga* [melon], and grows on the ground like melons. This country also produces another very singular fruit, which fruit is called *malapolanda* [plantain, banana]. The tree which bears this fruit is as high as a man or a little more, and it produces four or five leaves which are branches and leaves. Each of these covers a man against rain and sun. In the middle of this it throws out a certain branch which produces flowers in the same manner as the stalk of a bean, and afterwards it produces some fruits which are half a *palmo* and a *palmo* in length and they are as thick as the staff of a spear. And when they wish to gather the said fruit they do not wait until it is ripe, because it ripens in the house. One branch will produce two hundred or thereabouts of these fruits, and they all touch one against the other. Of these fruits there are found three sorts. The first sort is called *cianchapalon;* these are very restorative things to eat. Their colour is somewhat yellow, and the bark is very thin. The second sort is called *cadelapalon,* and they are much superior to the others. The third sort are bitter. The two kinds above mentioned are good like our figs, but superior. The tree of this fruit produces once and then no more. The said tree always has at its stem fifty or sixty shoots [*figlioli*], and the owners remove these shoots by the hand and transplant them, and at the end of a year they produce their fruit. And if the said branches are too green when they cut them, they put a little lime upon the said fruits to make them ripen quickly. You must know that a very large quantity of such fruits is found at all times of the year, and twenty are given for a *quattrino*. In like manner, roses and most singular flowers are found here on all the days of the year. (1502–8)

LUDOVICO DI VARTHEMA[245]

## 2.  The Coco tree

In the whole world there is not a tree more profitable and of more goodnesse then this tree is, neither doe men reape so much benefit of any other tree as they doe of this, there is not any part of it but serveth for some use, and none of it is worthy to be burnt. With the timber of this tree they make Ships without the mixture of any other tree, and with the leaves thereof they make Sayles, and with the fruit thereof, which bee a kinde of Nuts, they make Wine, and of the wine they make Sugar and Placetto, which Wine they gather in the spring of the yeere; out of the middle of the tree where continually there goeth or runneth out white liquor unto water, in that time of the yeere they put a vessell under every tree, and every evening and morning they take it away full, and then distilling it with fire it maketh a very strong liquor: and then they put it into Buts, with a quantity of Zibiboo, white or blacke and in short time it is made a perfect Wine. After this they make of the Nuts great store of Oyle: of the tree they make great quantitie of boords and quarters for buildings. Of the barke of this tree they make Cables, Ropes, and other furniture for ships, and, as they say, these Ropes be better then they that are made of Hempe. They make of the Bowes, Bedsteds, after the Indies fashion, and Scavasches for merchandise. The leaves they cut very small, and weave them, and so make Sayles of them, for all manner of shipping, or else very fine Mats. And then the first rinde of the Nut they stampe, and make thereof perfect Ockam to calke ships, great and small: and of the hard barke thereof they make Spoones and other vessels for meate, in such wise that there is no part thereof throwne away, or cast to the fire. When these Mats be greene they are full of an excellent sweet water to drinke: and if a man bee thirsty, with the liquor of one of the Mats he may satisfie himselfe: and as this Nut ripeneth, the liquor thereof turneth all to kernell. (1563)

CAESAR FREDERICK[246]

## 3. Rice

The Rice is sowed upon low ground, which in Winter time is covered with water, wherewith those Canariins doe maintaine themselves: these bring Hennes, Fruit, Milke, Egges, and other such like wares into the Towne to sell. They dwell in little straw Houses, the Doores whereof are so low, that men must creepe in and out, their houshold-stuff is a Mat upon the ground to sleepe upon, and a Pit or hole in the ground to beat their Rice in, with a Pot or two to seeth it in, and so they live and gaine so much as it is a wonder. (1583-9)

JOHN HUIGHEN VAN LINSCHOTEN[247]

## 4. *Fruits of Goa*

### i. *Jamboes*

Jambo trees, which then blossomed, when (and) then I thincke few trees More beautifull to the Eye, the flower of a good bignesse, fine forme and of an excellent vermillion Dye, very thicke sett, growing on the stalkes and biggest bowes, not at the very end of the sprigges as trees Doe bear with us. This fruit is ordinarily now served att our table, in forme like an apple or peare, of a whitish coullour with a Dash of red as some of our apples. It smelles betweene a violett and a rose; of a Pleasaunt tast, though somwhat Flashy (insipid) or waterish.

### ii. *Cajooraes: of a straunge propertye*

Cajoora trees, whose blossome casteth a Most Fragrant smell into the ayre, the Fruit somwhatt harsh in tast and strong, although it hath this property, thatt I thincke none elce (hath) the like, *viz.* thatt wheras the seedes or Kernells of other fruittes grow within them, the Kernell of this growes quite withoutt it at the very end, resembling a French beane, though much bigger, and beeing roasted, eateth like a Chestnutt.

### iii. *Jackes*

Jacke trees, whose Fruitte groweth on the very body, stemme, or biggest braunches of the tree. There bee some thatt Wey Near 40 pound waight, and in my opinion is the biggest Fruit thatt groweth on trees, as I thincke the Cocotree beares the biggest Nutte.

### iv. *Coconutts: its wonderfull benefit and use*

Cocotrees have onely stemme and No braunches or boughes att all, with a great bush att the very toppe. It is in many places much commended for the great benefitt itt affoards to Mans use, and not undese(r)ved, For to my Knowlidg it affoardes Meat, Drink and lodging, Oyle, Wyne, Milk, Sugar, etts., and good Cordage Made of the outtward rinde of the Nutte, which in Clusters grow outt att the toppe on a sprigge, as Doe allsoe the Papaes in a Manner, the tree Differing in leaves and height. (1634–8)

PETER MUNDY[248]

## 5. Growth and collection of opium

The poppy flowers in the end of January and beginning of February, and the capsules are sliced in February and March with a little instrument like a saw, made of three iron plates with jagged edges, tied together. The cultivation is very carefully conducted, nor are there any very apparent means of improving this branch of commerce and revenue. During the N.W., or dry winds, the best opium is procured, the worst during the moist, or E. and N.E., when the drug imbibes moisture, and a watery bad solution of opium collects in cavities of its substance, and is called Passewa, according to the absence of which the opium is generally prized.

At the end of March the opium jars arrive at the stores by water and by land, and continue accumulating for some weeks. Every jar is labelled and stowed in a proper place, separately tested with extreme accuracy, and valued. When the whole quantity has been received, the contents of all the jars are thrown into great vats, occupying a very large building, whence the mass is distributed, to be made up into balls for the markets. This operation is carried on in a long paved room, where every man is ticketed, and many overseers are stationed to see that the work is properly conducted. Each workman sits on a stool, with a double stage and a tray before him. On the top stage is a tin basin, containing opium sufficient for three balls; in the lower another basin, holding water: in the tray stands a brass hemispherical cup, in which the ball is worked. To the man's right hand is another tray, with two compartments, one containing thin pancakes of poppy petals pressed together, the other a cupful of sticky opium-water, made from refuse opium. The man takes the brass cup, and places a pancake at the bottom, smears it with opium-water, and with many plies of the pancakes makes a coat for the opium. Of this he takes about one-third of the mass before him, puts it inside the petals, and agglutinates many other coats over it: the balls are then again weighed, and reduced or increased to a certain weight if necessary. At the day's end, each man takes his work to a rack with numbered compartments, and deposits it in that which answers to his own number, thence the balls, (each being put in a clay cup) are carried to an enormous drying-room, where they are exposed in tiers, and constantly examined and turned, to prevent their being attacked by weevils, which are very prevalent during moist winds, little boys creeping along the racks all day long for this purpose. When dry, the balls are packed in two layers of six each in chests, with the stalks, dried leaves, and capsules of the plant, and sent down to Calcutta. A little opium is prepared of very fine quality for the Government Hospitals, and some for general sale in India; but the proportion is trifling, and such is made up into square cakes. A good workman will prepare from thirty to fifty balls a day, the total produce being 10,000 to 12,000 a day; during one working season 1,353,000 balls are manufactured for the Chinese market alone. (1848)

JOSEPH DALTON HOOKER[249]

## 6. Mode of irrigation

In my walk this morning I passed through some fields of grain, and observed the mode of irrigation, which was to divide the land into very small square plots, separated by banked-up channels, or troughs filled from the water-skins carried on bullocks from the nearest tank, so that the operation is slow and laborious, and it's only on the banks of streams that there is any soil capable of cultivation, the high lands being all volcanic rock. (1857–9)

MRS. LEOPOLD PAGET[250]

## 7. Forest conservancy

In connexion with the clearing of forests for coffee-cultivation, it is imperative that due attention should be paid to the preservation of valuable timber, and the conservancy of the belts of wood near the sources and along the upper courses of streams, so as to ensure the usual supplies of water, and to retain a due amount of moisture in the atmosphere. For the superintendence of these important measures, together with other duties, Dr. Cleghorn has been placed at the head of a Forest Conservancy Department in the Madras Presidency. He strongly urges that the high wooded mountain-tops over-hanging the low country should not be allowed to be cleared for coffee-cultivation, lest the supplies of water should be injured. 'The courses of rivulets,' he says, 'should be overshadowed with trees, and the hills should therefore be left clothed for a distance of half their height from the top, leaving half the slopes and all the valleys for cultivation. Immense tracts of virgin forest in the valleys of the Koondah hills are eminently suited for coffee-cultivation.

The clearing should only be allowed from 2500 to 4500 feet, this being the extreme range within which coffee planted on a large scale is found to thrive.'

There are still thousands of acres of uncleared forests, at suitable elevation, well adapted for the growth of coffee, in the cultivation of which the English capitalist would make large and rapid profits; yet it is not many years since the first coffee-plants were introduced into these hills. Coffee now forms an important item in the exports from the Madras Presidency. There is every reason to hope that the bark from quinine-yielding chinchona-trees may also become one of the valuable products of the hills; and in the following chapter I propose to give an account of the selection of the sites for the first experimental plantations. (1862)

CLEMENTS ROBERT MARKHAM[251]

## 8. A forest

Having descended at least 5,000 feet since leaving Mount Singaleelah, we were now below the region of cloud, and the forest, though dense as ever, wore a totally different aspect. Our senses, too, under altered feelings, were suddenly kindled to the fair and gentle beauty of the scene; 'for lo! the winter is past, the flowers appear on the earth, and the time of singing of birds is come.'

None of the trees at this elevation are deciduous, and a lap of soft and living green lies stretched above and around us. From the loftiest tree, with its graceful parasite and glorious orchids, to the ferns and mosses we tread beneath our feet, there is no sign of the 'sere and yellow leaf.' Does Nature never decay in this fair Eden? Is it one perpetual burst of undying spring, as on the first Sabbath of the world's history, when God rested from His labours, and 'behold, everything was very good'?

The plaintive and soothing note of the kokra now greets us, and the forest is tuneful with the joyous melody of other birds; the river too becomes once more a foaming torrent, lashing itself into spray as it plunges over boulders of gneiss, whilst here and there, forming deep green pools, it sleeps to the music of its own lullaby. Following its banks for another hour, we came upon evidences of man's existence in traps to catch fish; and beneath these traps, which are long fences of bamboo spanning the river, were singular conical baskets, which Tendook informed me were placed there to catch edible frogs.

The woods now began to be alive with sunshine, as golden arrows pierced the leafy canopy; and soon emerging upon the open, we found ourselves again in the haunts of men, and amongst gentle acclivities planted with millet and buckwheat, all aglow with wild flowers, and higher up smiling patches of Indian corn, still shimmering in the mellow sunlight. (1875)

NINA ELIZABETH MAZUCHELLI[252]

## 9. The Wainaad forest

We took the road leading north from Ooty to the Segor ghaut and Mysore, and as soon as we were well out of the town it began to rain. For nearly two hours we plodded along through a steady down-pour that completely drenched everything save my two packs, which I had covered with my waterproof blankets. Just at dark we reached the Kulhutty bungalow, wet, cold, tired, and hungry, and only eight miles from Ootacamund. But we soon had a good fire blazing on the hearth, a steaming pot of chocolate on the table, and dry clothes on ourselves.

As if to atone for our miserable drenching, the next morning broke clear and sunny, and we lost no time in starting on our way down the pass. Four miles from the Kalhutty bungalow we reached the Segor bungalow, a mere hovel at the foot of the ghaut, elevation twenty-seven hundred and ninety feet. From thence the road lay through a generally level country, thinly covered with low bushes and short, scrubby trees. Quartz rocks were quite abundant along the road, and in one ledge I found a bed of Muscovite mica, which furnished several fine specimens. Six miles from Segor we reached the village of Musnigoorie, which stands on a smooth bed of reddish porphyrite, through which run long, narrow, vertical veins of quartz, several of which extend lengthwise along the middle of the street.

After leaving Musnigoorie the jungle grows denser and higher, until it soon becomes a genuine forest, and the road is both hilly and rocky. Late in the evening we crossed the Moyar River and halted for the night at the Tippecadu traveller's bungalow, twenty-two miles from Ooty. The next morning the ponies, which had been turned out to graze, were missing, and it was not until 4 P.M. that they were found. To occupy the time, I took my rifle and strolled out into the forest along the river, which I found in places to be composed chiefly of the common bamboo *(Bambusa arundinacea),* which here grows in scattering clumps to a height of forty to sixty feet. While I was walking alone, lost in admiration of the first bamboo forest I had ever seen, a large animal suddenly leaped to the ground from a tree a few paces in front of me, flourished a long tail in mid-air, and rushed away through the grass. From the length of its tail I thought it was a young leopard, and immediately gave chase, when the animal ran up a tree. and in another moment my rifle brought down a fine old gray monkey, the Madras langur *(Semnopithecus leucoprimnuns).* The report started a whole troop of the same species which had been feeding quietly in an adjoining tree, and away they went at a great rate, galloping through the tree-tops a little faster than I could run on the ground below. But one of the monkeys could not resist the temptation to stop and have a look at me, a very common habit with monkeys generally, and a moment later he, too, was tumbling to the ground. The largest monkey of this species which I obtained in the Wainaad measured as follows: length of head and body 23 inches, tail 37. I also shot a Malabar squirrel *(S. Malabaricus),* one of the handsomest of all the *Sciuridæ,* and also one of the largest. (1885)

WILLIAM T. HORNADAY[253]

## 10. Water for irrigation

There are three special methods of obtaining a supply of water for irrigation purposes, *viz.,* by means of wells, storage tanks, and canals derived from the rivers of the country—any or all of which may be combined. Canal methods may be divided into several classes. First, there are simple 'inundation' canals, consisting of water-channels, artificial or semi-artificial, unprovided with any means of regulating and controlling the supply at the head—which lead water away from the rivers, and are filled only when the latter are in flood, being incapable of drawing off water at other times. Secondly, there are canals which may be called 'periodic.' These are derived from rivers having a changeable and uncertain supply. In order to prevent the water running to waste, some kind of temporary or permanent dam is constructed across the river bed, to intercept, store up, and divert the water into the canal, either during the rainy season only, or more constantly, as the supply in the river admits. Lastly, there are those which are called constant or 'perennial' canals. These draw their supply from rivers which at all times of the year run with a sufficient volume to supply the canals, without previous storage, and are supplied with dams or weirs, and necessary works at the head for raising and regulating the supply of water as required. (1894)

G. W. MACGEORGE[254]

# B. ZOOLOGY AND ANIMAL HUSBANDRY

## 1. Ants that dig for gold

They get the gold from ants. These creatures are larger than foxes, but are in other respects like the ants of our own country. They dig holes in the earth like other ants. The heap which they throw up consists of gold the purest and brightest in all the world. The mounds are piled up close to each other in regular order like hillocks of gold dust, whereby all the plain is made effulgent. It is difficult, therefore, to look towards the sun, and many who have attempted to do this have thereby destroyed their eyesight. The people who are next neighbours to the ants, with a view to plunder these heaps, cross the intervening desert, which is of no great extent, mounted on wagons to which they have yoked their swiftest horses. They arrive at noon, a time when the ants have gone underground, and at once seizing the booty make off at full speed. The ants on learning what has been done, pursue the fugitives, and overtaking them fight with them till they conquer or die, for of all animals they are the most courageous. It hence appears that they understand the worth of gold, and that they will sacrifice their lives rather than part with it. (3rd century B.C.)

MEGASTHENES[255]

## 2. Domestic animals

... They have a beast very large, having a smooth thicke skinne without haire, called a Buffelo, which give good Milke: the flesh of them is like Beefe, but not so wholsome. They have no want of Venison of divers kinds, as red Deare, fallow Deare, Elkes, and Antelops; but no where imparked: the whole Kingdome is as it were a Forrest, for a man can travell no way but he shall see them, and (except it bee within a small distance of the King) they are every mans Game. To these they have great stores of Hares, and further to furnish out their feasts, varietie of Fish and Fowle; it were as infinite as needlesse to relate particulars. To write of their Geese, Duckes, Pigeons, Partridges, Quailes, Peacockes, and many other singular good Fowle, all which are bought at such easie rates, as that I have seene a good Mutton sold for the value of one shilling, foure couple of Hennes at the same price, one Hare for the value of a penie, three Partridges for as little, and so in proportion all the rest. There are no Capons amongst them but men.

The Beeves of that Countrey differ from ours, in that they have each of them a great Bunch of grisselly flesh which growes upon the meeting of their shoulders. Their Sheepe exceed ours in great bob-tayles, which cut off are very ponderous, their wooll is generally very course, but the flesh of them both is altogether as good as ours. (1616)

EDWARD TERRY[256]

## 3. Wild elephants

On the 27th [August], after having marched two hours, we came to a large village, where we saw the two elephants which had been captured. Each of these wild elephants was between two tame ones, and around the wild ones there were six men with fire-darts, who spoke to the animals when feeding them, saying in their language, 'Take that and eat it.' They were small wisps of hay, pieces of black Sugar, or rice cooked in water, and pounded peppercorns. When the wild elephant would not do what was ordered, the men told the tame elephants to beat him; this they immediately did, one striking him on the fore head and head with his trunk, and if he made as though to revenge himself, the other struck him from his side, so that the poor elephant knew not where to turn; this educated him to obey.

As I have insensibly drifted into a history of elephants, I shall add here some other remarks which I have made on the nature of these animals. Although the elephant does not approach the female after having been captured. it happens nevertheless that he becomes in season sometimes. One day when Shah Jahan was out hunting upon his elephant with one of his sons, who sat with him in order to fan him, the elephant became so much in heat that the driver, not being able to control it any longer, told the King that in order to arrest the rage of the elephant, which might crush them among the trees, it was necessary that one of the three who was on the elephant should offer

himself up, and that with all his heart he sacrificed his life for the
King and for his son, begging his majesty to take care of the three
children whom he was leaving. Having said so, he threw himself
under the elephant, and immediately the animal took him with his
trunk, and having crushed him under his feet, became mild and
tractable as before. The King, for this wonderful escape, gave
200,000 rupees to the poor, and promoted at court each of the sons
of the man who had so generously given his life for the safety of his
Prince. (1666)

JEAN BAPTISTE TAVERNIER[257]

## 4.  A tigress and her cubs

The number of cubs usually borne by a tigress is not I believe
perfectly ascertained: such as have been killed in a state of preg-
nancy have varied extremely, from one to five. Two may, however,
from all I have been able to discover, be considered as their usual
progeny, of which one generally becomes a favourite, to the destruction of the residue. While stationed in the Ramghur district,
some people, who had been cutting grass in a jungle about half a mile
distant from the cantonments, found four cubs, which the mother
had left, no doubt while questing for prey. I purchased two; they
were but a few days old, not having then opened their eyes. They
were about the size of a cat, but roared most vociferously, especially
at night; on which account I had them kept in a small hut just by my
stable, which was about an hundred and fifty yards from my
*bungalow,* or house. During the second night my servants were
alarmed by the mother, who, having been attracted by the howlings
of the little miscreants, and to which she gave responses in the most
awful strains, had resorted to the spot. As it would have been no
difficult matter for the tigress to have forced her way into the place,
which no doubt she would have soon done, the people deemed it
most prudent to put the cubs out; in consequence all was soon quiet,
and at day light the mottled animals were not to be seen. (1819)

THOMAS WILLIAMSON[258]

## 5.  The fish of Bengal

Except in wanting teeth, the *Ilisha* has the most strong resemblance
to the *Shad (Clupea alosa),* and there is reason to suspect that the

Indian and Latin names may be radically the same. The *Ilisha* frequents the bay of Bengal and the large salt water estuaries of the Ganges, and in the rainy season ascends the larger rivers to spawn. I have seen it as high as Agra and Kanpur, but so high up it is very rare. At Patna on the Ganges, and Goyalpara on the Brahmaputra, it is pretty common, but rather poor and exhausted. About Calcutta and Dhaka it is in the utmost abundance and perfection, and is the richest and highest-flavoured fish that I know, having a taste of both the salmon and herring; but, owing to innumerable small bones, it is difficult to eat, and it is heavy of digestion. Its common size is about a foot and a half in length, but it is occasionally twice that dimension. ...

The fish is ... of a green *colour,* with a gloss of gold changing to purple, and below silver. In young fishes there is generally a row of four or five black spots on each shoulder; but in large individuals some of these generally, and often all of them, disappear. The fins are diaphanous; that of the tail is edged with black. (1822)

FRANCIS HAMILTON[259]

## 6. *Hospital for animals*

At Broach is one of those remarkable institutions which have made a good deal of noise in Europe as instances of Hindoo benevolence to inferior animals. I mean hospitals for sick and infirm beasts, birds, and insects. I was not able to visit it, but Mr. Corsellis described it as a very dirty and neglected place, which, though it has considerable endowments in land, only serves to enrich the Brahmins who manage it. They have really animals of several different kinds there, not only those which are accounted sacred by the Hindoos, as monkeys, peacocks, etc. but horses, dogs, and cats, and they have also, in little boxes, an assortment of lice and fleas. It is not true, however, that they feed those pensioners on the flesh of beggars hired for the purpose. The Brahmins say that insects, as well as the other inmates of their infirmary, are fed with vegetables only, such as rice etc. How the insects thrive I did not hear, but the old horses and dogs, nay the peacocks and apes are allowed to starve, and the only creatures said to be in any tolerable plight are some milch cows, which may be kept from other motives than charity. (1824–5)

REGINALD HEBER[260]

'A Hospital for Sick Animals', from P. Della Valle's *Reizen*

## 7. The Indian cobra

The Moors know nothing about snakes, not troubling themselves about any branch of zoology unconnected with sport; while the veneration of the Hindus being concentrated in the typical *nagam* they know little about any other snake. Snake-charmers and jugglers tell a lot of nonsense; and low Indians wishing to show off their intelligence before master, find little trouble in evolving from their inner consciousness a name for any snake pointed out to them. They have perceived that it is a point of honour with most Englishmen to have a name ready for every strange beast, and they humour this weakness by having a name ready for every snake, and also a wonderful account of the deadly effects produced by its bite or by a blow of its tail. ...

A cobra standing at bay can be readily captured; put the end of a stick gently across his head and bear it down to the ground by a firm and gradual pressure; he will not resist; then place the stick horizontally across his neck and take him up. You must not dawdle about this; sharp is the word in dealing with snakes, and they have as much respect for firm and kind treatment as contempt for timidity and irresolution. When, however, an active snake carries on a running fight, the only way to capture him is to give him a tap across the back sufficiently hard to take the go out of him without injuring him. If you wish to capture your specimen alive, err rather on the side of mercy and see how gentle a blow will suffice to put him *hors de combat*. Even if you want the snake for the museum and not for the menagerie, it is still important to secure him with as little injury as possible.

The juggler or snake-exhibitor keeps his snakes in flat baskets of just sufficient size to hold a cobra when coiled up. However convenient this basket may be for portability and exhibition purposes, it is not suitable for other snakes than the cobra, and it is only admissible as a temporary lodging. The best habitation for snakes would doubtless be a verandah fenced to a sufficient height with wire gauze; it might be divided into compartments in order to separate snakes of ophiophagous habits from the rest of the community, and be provided with water and shrubs sufficiently to gratify the desire for coolness and shade. Such a serpentarium would enable interesting observations to be made on the habits of snakes. The floor should be strewn with sand; it would not often require renewal owing to the inoffensive nature of the uric acid excreta of snakes. (1874)

EDWARD NICHOLSON[261]

## 8. The grey peacock-pheasant

It is in the dense hill forests of the Indo-Burmese region that the Grey Peacock-Pheasant has its home.

Its furthest limits northwards and westwards, so far as I yet know, are the Baxa Duars and the outer slopes of the Bhutanese Himalayas. Eastwards it is far from rare, in suitable localities in the Eastern Duars, the northern portions of Goalpara, Kamrup, and Darrang, and possibly, but I have no certain information on the subject, further east. South of the Brahmaputra it occurs in the Garo, Khasia, and Naga Hills, in Sylhet, Cachar, Hill Tipperah, Chittagong, Arakan, Pegu and Tenasserim, as far south as Tavoy, and perhaps some distance further, but not according to our present information, so far down as Mergui town .

I know so little of this bird that I have asked friends who know more for some little information in regard to it, and writing from North-east Cachar, Mr. Inglis remarks:

'Although anything but rare here, this bird is but seldom seen, owing to its shy and retiring habits. It affects thick jungle with an open bottom, and it is especially fond of hilly lands where bamboos and young trees predominate.

'About the beginning of the year, the male begins to call in the early morning and late in the afternoon; perched on the bough of a tree, or on the top of a stump, about eight or ten feet from the ground, he emits his loud call-note about every half minute. This call is often kept up for an hour or two at a time, and can be heard on a quiet morning a very long way off. Then is the time to stalk him, but it requires a large amount of patience and perseverance to do it successfully, as you have only the sound to guide you, and after approaching within about one hundred yards of your game, it is unsafe to proceed except during the calls; thus you can only advance a few yards per minute.' (1879)

ALLAN HUME[262]

## 9. The Gangetic crocodile

The Indian gavial inhabits all the large rivers of Northern India, the

Ganges up to Hurdwar, nine hundred and eighty-three feet above the sea, the Jumna, Sardah, Indus, Brahmapootra and their tributaries, but does not occur anywhere in Southern India, nor Burmah. Another species of gavial, called by Dr. Gray, *Tomistoma schlegelli*, is found in Borneo, but nowhere else so far as we know at present. The mugger *(Crocodilus bombifrons)*, inhabits all India from the foot of the Himalayas where the water is often frozen, almost to Cape Comorin. I saw only one small specimen of this species in the Jumna, and as it lay upon a sand-bar close beside some gavials, the points of difference between the two were very striking. I observed it long and carefully with a powerful field-glass, and fully satisfied myself as to its identity. The gavial looked smooth and yellow, whereas the little mugger had a very rugose appearance, and in color was of a dirty gray. When he left the water he deliberately walked out upon the sand, and when I finally fired at him he sprang up on his feet, and ran across the bar into the water, in doing which he more nearly resembled a huge iguana than a crocodile. I examined the spot directly afterward, and besides the tracks left by his feet there was only a broken mark where the tip of his tail had touched the sand as he ran. Out of perhaps four hundred and fifty to five hundred gavials, crocodiles, and alligators which I have watched getting from the land into the water, only four have stood up on their legs and run. This mugger was one, and another was a Mississippi alligator, which I afterward killed, and found to be in a very emaciated condition, owing to the fact that nearly half of its upper jaw had been bitten off, and it had apparently experienced great difficulty in capturing its prey. (1885)

WILLIAM T. HORNADAY[263]

## 10. The hunting leopard

The hunting-leopard *(Felis jubata)* is quite distinct from the common leopard *(Felis pardus)*, or panther, as it is as often called, and by the hill-men 'cheetooa.' The former animal is more slightly made, lighter in colour, and its markings are black spots—not rings, as they are on the skin of the latter—and its claws are not so retractile as those of the panther. I have never heard of its being found in the Himalayas. The snow-leopard or ounce *(Felis uncia)*, which is only found on the higher ranges near the snow, differs from both the above in having paler, softer, and longer pile, with its black

markings less distinctly defined. Another kind—the clouded
leopard *(Felis diardi)*—a very beautiful animal, which is I believe,
found only on the more eastern Himalayan ranges, is about similar
in size to the common leopard. Its black markings are more blotchy
and irregular, and the ground colour of its skin is darker and of a
more greyish hue.

It may here be worth mentioning that I once, in the mountains,
came suddenly upon a leopard in full chase after a large sandy-
coloured wild cat. A feline animal hunting one of its own species I
coinsidered rather singular. Possibly its intentions were more
amorous than deadly. (1889)

DONALD MACINTYRE[264]

## 11. A monster fish

Those who have fished both for salmon and mahseer will doubtless
agree with me in thinking that they are nearly on a par as far as sport
is concerned. In its habits the mahseer much resembles the salmon,
except that it never migrates to the sea, but in appearance it is very
different. The mahseer *(Barbus Tor)* of Himalayan rivers, which is
said to belong to the carp family, is a beautiful fish both in form and
colour, but in flavour it does not approach the salmon. Yet its firm
white flesh is by no means to be despised for the table. On the back
its hue is a dark olive-green, shaded off, on the sides of a well-
conditioned fish, into a golden orange, which merges into pale pink
and silvery white below. It has rather large toothless jaws lined with
a very tough membrane, so it requires to be struck pretty hard to be
properly hooked. When I say *struck,* I mean that after the fish has
hooked itself, as it will do by its own weight, a good pull, without a
jerk, is necessary to drive home the barb into its leathern jaws.
Owing to this toughness of mouth, a mahseer when fixed is seldom
lost unless it breaks the tackle. This a big fish often will do in its first
plunge, when it sometimes has a way of lashing its tail over the line.
That crisis being safely over, if your tackle is trustworthy, landing
your fish is usually only a matter of time and patience. Its strong
teeth are set far back in its gullet, and the stoutest tackle has a poor
chance if it gorges your lure beyond them. It cannot be easily
clipped, as its large round scales are so hard that the sharpest gaff
will glance off them. When running a mahseer after it has been fairly
hooked, I have never known it leap from the water, and I think it
rarely does so, but its long and rapid rushes quite equal if they do not

surpass those of any salmon of a similar size. As regards its weight, I
am well within the mark when I state that the mahseer reaches
nearly, if not quite, 100 lb. The largest mahseer I ever heard of as
having been taken with a trolling bait, was 93 lb.; and with fly, one
that turned the scale of 62 lb. But such monsters as these are very
seldom landed with the rod. (1889)

DONALD MACINTYRE[265]

## 12. *Poisonous snakes*

Besides the cobra, there is only one poisonous kind of snake at all
common here, and that is a prettily-marked little reptile called
*Echis carinata,* about a foot in length, with a most cantankerous
temper and an abusive tongue. There are two others to be met with
sometimes, the chainviper *(Daboia elegans)*, which is in appearance
and temper just an enlarged edition of *Echis,* and a slender inoffensive species, with whitish rings on a dark ground, which also must be
content to go by its scientific name of *Bungarus arcuatus,* for want of
another. There are names in plenty, such as carpet-snake, whip-
snake, krait, foorsa; but they are applied promiscuously to any sort
of snake, real or imaginary, and are therefore of no use. The fact is
that in real life, as distinguished from romance, snakes are so
seldom seen that no one who does not make a study of them can
know one from another. Still, you may easily learn to recognise a
cobra or an *Echis* when you see it, and for the rest it is useful to keep
in mind that the whole tribe of slender, whip-like, green, brown, and
yellow snakes are as harmless as lambs a month old, notwithstanding anything your butler says to the contrary. Next to his own
religion, there is nothing an average native knows less about than
nature, and domestic servants are generally below the average. Yet
natives in all their ignorance are comparatively free from the
European's superstitious antipathy to the serpent race. The cobra,
indeed, is regarded by natives of the better classes with a kind of
veneration. When a Hindoo observes that a large cobra regularly
haunts his garden, so far from treating it in a hostile spirit, he will, if
piously disposed, propitiate it with an offering of milk.

Firmly believing myself that all the larger snakes, and cobras
especially, do man invaluable service by devouring field-rats, I am
unable to tread my feelings underfoot, and let unbridled reason run
away with me so completely as to let them off when I meet them. A

man who is caught lurking about your premises with a concealed dagger need not talk of his past services to the State. I slay a poisonous snake when and where I find it, and if there is any doubt about its being poisonous, I slay it to settle the matter. In my walks abroad I generally carry a strong, supple, walking cane. This is the prime weapon for encountering snakes. Armed with it, you may rout and slaughter the hottest-tempered cobra in Hindustan. Let it rear itself up and spread its spectacled head-gear and bluster as it will, but one rap on the side of its head will bring it to reason, and another about the middle of the body will bring it to its end. Without a stick you can do nothing. Twice have I fled before an angry cobra, having unwisely attacked it with stones. The cobra, though of a peaceable disposition in the main, is hasty in his temper...

But of all the things in this earth that bite or sting, the palm belongs to the biscobra, a creature whose very name seems to indicate that it is twice as bad as the cobra. Though known by the terror of its name to natives and Europeans alike, it has never been described in the proceedings of any learned society, nor has it yet received a scientific name. In fact, it occupies much the same place in science as the sea-serpent, and accurate information regarding it is still a desideratum. The awful deadliness of its bite admits of no question, being supported by countless authentic instances; our own old *ghorawalla* was killed by one. The points on which evidence is required are—first, whether there is any such animal as the biscobra; second, whether, if it does exist, it is a snake with legs or a lizard without them. By inquiry among natives I have learned a few remarkable facts about it, as, for instance, that it has eight legs, and is a hybrid between a cobra and that gigantic lizard commonly miscalled an iguana; but last year a brood of them suddenly appeared in Dustypore, and I saw several. The first was killed by some of the bravest of my own men with stones, for it can spring four feet, and no one may approach it without hazard of life. Even when dead it is exceedingly dangerous, but, with my usual hardihood, I examined it. It was nine inches long, and in appearance like a pretty brownish lizard spotted with yellow. It has no trace of poison-fangs, but I was assured that an animal so deadly could dispense with these. If it simply spits at a man his fate is sealed, for, excepting a few cunning Bengalees, no one knows any *muntra,* or charm, which has power against it. Afterwards one appeared in my own garden, and I made an attempt to capture it alive with my butterfly-net, my devoted butler's hair turning grey as he watched me from a great distance; but the biscobra got off into a hole. It escaped me once or twice again, and then, finding I was bent on catching it, it gradually changed colour, like a chameleon, and grew larger at the same time, until in a few weeks it had developed into an unmistakable iguana. Some people would jump to the conclusion that it was a young iguana to begin with. My butler would endure the thumbscrew sooner. (c. 1890)

E.H. AITKIN [266]

## 13. A Durbar in Bombay

Just at that time when all is stillest and sleepiest, I hold a *levee,* for a house is like the shadow of a great rock in a weary land, and to its blessed shelter, as the sun grows fiercer and fiercer, all the neighbourhood 'foregathers.' The choicest place, of course, is that moist spot at the back of the house, under the pomegranate-trees, where the bath-water runs out into the ground. The fowls have taken possession of that, and are fitting themselves into little hollows scraped in the cool damp earth. The next best place is the broad verandah, with the elephant-creeper oppressing the trellis. Here long before noon the birds begin to come to-gether. Up among the rafters first I generally detect a social lark sitting solitary and speechless; then down among the roots of the creeper, hopping idly about, turning over a dead leaf here and there, and talking to one another in querulous falsettos, come a dozen dingy-brown 'rat-birds,' feeble folk, which keep in flocks, because they have not back-bone enough to do anything singly. They are just miniatures of the 'Seven Brothers,' only there are no differences of opinion among them. A little later on, two or three well-breakfasted *mynas* drop in and assume comfortable digestive attitudes. The *myna* is the most proper of birds, respectable as Littimer himself. In his sober snuff-brown suit and yellow beak, he is neither foppish nor slovenly, and his behaviour is stamped with self-respect and good breeding. Nevertheless, he is eaten up with self-admiration, and, when he thinks nobody is looking, behaves like a fool, attitudinizing and conversing with himself like Malvolio. But in public he is decorum itself. He sets his face, too, like a flint, against every form of vice, and is the abhorrence of the mungoose, the wild cat, and all the criminal classes.

On one of the beams of the roof is a meek turtle-dove that coos patiently, so that his spouse may hear him as she sits upon her two white eggs in (of all places for a nest!) the prickly pear hedge. Their nest, consisting of three short twigs and a long one, was first built on one of the rafters but it was dissipated by that painted iniquity, the squirrel, out and out the most shameless ruffian that haunts the house. See him lying flat on his belly upon the stone step, crunching a crust of bread, stolen of course. This is tiffin. For breakfast he had a dozen or two of the tender shoots of the convolvulus which I have been pruning and watering to make it grow. And his conscience does not trouble him! He should die the death if I could make up my mind what manner of death would best befit his crimes. Of all my guests there is not one more dainty, or more modest (with so much to be vain of), than the hoopoe, which sits unostentatiously in a corner, with even its gorgeous crest folded decently down. Every minute or two it trots out to one of those cup-shaped little hollows in the dust, where the ant-lion lies in wait. Once a poor ant slips over the treacherous edge of that crater, it has as much chance of coming out again as Empedocles from Etna. It may struggle to keep its footing on the slippery bank, but the unseen monster below jerks up showers of sand, and soon sand and ant go rolling down together, where the out-stretched grey jaws lie waiting in the dust. The hoopoe knows exactly what is there, pokes its long beak down into the funnel, fumbles about for a moment, and pulls out the slayer of ants, to be swallowed like a pill.

Along with the birds a pretty green lizard used to come every forenoon, shikarring ants and other insects, but it was breakfasted on yesterday by that sinister-looking butcher-bird which now stands on the floor of the verandah, with legs straddled, like Apollyon in the Valley of Humiliation, and mouth agape, gasping from the heat. With his pale grey mantle, snow-white breast, and black 'points,' the butcher-bird would be handsome, but for his villainous eyebrows and generally assassinous aspect. Nothing living comes amiss to him, from the sparrow, if he can surprise it, down to the large fussy black ant, which comes hurrying along, to catch the train or something, with its tail cocked over its head, till it is suddenly arrested and introduced into that *atram ingluviem* where a dozen of its fellow-citizens have gone before it. *Cremes aux fourmis* must be as good as the Frenchman thought it. Now, wherever this bird comes, comes also a smaller bird, with the same white breast, the same shaggy black eyebrows, and the same brigand look, and it stands close by and shrieks and hisses and heaps opprobrious epithets on the other. This is a cousin of the bird it vilifies. *Lanius* is the surname of both; the Christian name of the big one is *Lahtora*, and of the other *Hardwickii*. (It was named after one General Hardwicke, poor man! but he did nothing wrong.) And as the little one hisses out its impotent rage, it cocks the stump of a tail which was once long and flowing as that which adorns the objects of its wrath. Short as the stump is, thereby hangs a tale, and I happen to know it.

One Sunday morning, not long ago, Hardwickii was busy murdering some small creature at the foot of a tree, when Lahtora spied him, and came gliding gently down, and, before he was aware of any danger, he was knocked over on his back, with those sharp claws imbedded in his snowy breast, and that murderous beak hammering his head. He hit back most pluckily, and shrieked piteously. *Arcades ambo,* thought I, and declined to interfere. Still, my appearance on the scene created a diversion in the little butcher's favour. and with a desperate struggle he freed himself and was off. but, like Tam o' Shanter's mare, without his tail. *Hinc illae lachrimae!* At the sight of his oppressor the bitter memory of that morning comes upon him, and, as he glances back at the place where the tail should be, he can no longer contain his feelings. The 'poor dumb animals' can give each other a bit of their minds, like their betters, and to me their fierce or tender little passions, their loves and hates, their envies and jealousies, and their small vanities, beget a sense of fellow-feeling which makes their presence society.

The touch of Nature which makes the whole world kin is infirmity. A man without a weakness is insupportable company, and so is a man who does not feel the heat. There is a large grey ring-dove that sits in the blazing sun all through the hottest hours of the day, and says *coo-coo, coo, coo-coo, coo,* until the melancholy, sweet monotony of that sound is as thoroughly mixed up in the cells of my brain with $110^0$ in the shade as physic in my infantile memories with the peppermint lozenges which used to 'put away the taste.' But as for those creatures which confess the heat, and come into the house and gasp, I feel drawn to them. I should like to offer them cooling drinks. Not that all my midday guests are equally welcome: I could dispense, for instance, with the grey-ringed bee which has just reconnoitred my ear for the third time, and guesses it

is a key-hole—she is away just now, but only I fancy, for clay to stop
it up with. There are others also to which I would give their *conge* if
they would take it. But good, bad, or indifferent, they give us their
company whether we want it or not; and from any point of view it is
strange that Europeans in India know so little, see so little, care so
little about all the intense life that surrounds them. The boy who was
the most ardent of bug-hunters, or the most enthusiastic of bird-
nesters, in England, where one shilling will buy nearly all that is
known, or can be known, about birds or butterflies, maintains in this
country, aided by Messrs. B. and S., an unequal strife with the
insupportableness of an *ennui*-smitten life. Why, if he would stir up
for one day the embers of the old flame, he could not quench it again
with such a prairie of fuel around him. I am not speaking of Bombay
people, with their clubs and gymkhanas and other devices for oiling
the wheels of existence, but of the dreary up-country exile, whose
life is a blank, a moral Sahara, a catechism of the Nihilist creed.
What such a one needs is a hobby. Every hobby is good, a sign of
good and an influence for good. Any hobby will draw out the mind;
but the one I plead for touches the soul too, keeps the milk of human
kindness from souring, puts a gentle poetry into the prosiest life.
That all my own finer feelings have not long since withered up in this
land of separation from 'the old familiar faces,' I attribute partly to a
pair of rabbits. All rabbits are idiotic things, but these come in and
sit up meekly and beg a crust of bread, and even a perennial fare of
village *moorgee* cannot induce me to issue the order for their
execution and conversion into pie. But, if such considerations cannot lead, the struggle for existence should drive a man in this
country to learn the ways of his border tribes. (*c.* 1890)

E.H. AITKIN[267]

## 14. Bears

Bears were plentiful in that land (Deogarh jungles)—black bears
that, when they rose on their hind-legs, stood about six feet in
height, powerful but clumsy beasts, that ordinarily employed their
strength harmlessly enough. Now and again one of these would
attack a man and maul his face and head with its cruel nails. One
bear in my district was rumoured to be carnivorous; but, as a rule,
these bears were strictly vegetarian, and lived upon the wild figs (the
fruit of the *Ficus indicus)* and other products of the forest: and if

they did not live in amity with man, their inclination was, I fancy, to preserve peaceable relations with him and other animals, by the simple device of having nothing to do with them. But perhaps by way of exceptions to a general rule, several of the Deoghurites wore on their heads and faces the scars of bear-wounds that they would carry to their grave or funeral pyre. (1895)

EDWARD BRADDON[268]

# 19. The Arts

## A. PAINTINGS

### 1. The Muslim and Hindu styles

I cannot look back at the various scenes through which I passed in these excursions, without almost involuntarily indulging a train of reflections relative to the state of the arts, under this, as well as under the Hindoo government. The amazing monuments which are still to be found in India, prove the Mussulman conquerors, to have been well acquainted with the principles of architecture, and at least to have had a taste for grand composition; in painting, on the contrary, they have only exercised themselves in miniature, many of which are highly beautiful in composition and in delicacy of colour; their attempts in this art have also been confined to water-colours and they have laboured under a further disadvantage the religion of Mahommed prohibiting all resemblances of animated nature. Whether the Arabs have ever transgressed the law in this point, I know not; but probably, on account of the remoteness of India from the original seat of the religion of Mahommed, it may have lost much of its rigour, and may, therefore, have left the princes of India at more liberty to indulge themselves in this elegant art. . . .

The paintings of the Hindoos, as they are, like their sculpture, chiefly applied to represent the objects of their religious worship, are certainly not so perfect as the Moorish pictures, which are all portraits. A constant study of simple nature, it is well known, will produce a resemblance which is sometimes astonishing, and which the painter of ideal objects never can arrive at. (1780–3)

WILLIAM HODGES[269]

### 2. Ragmala paintings

Happily, the inexhaustible fountain of Hindu mythological imagi-nation provides a group of subjects which invite the freest play of fancy, and give unlimited opportunities for artistic treatment. During the eighteenth century, the class of material alluded to, the symbolism connected with the 'musical modes,' was exploited by numerous artists, whose works were eagerly collected by Warren Hastings and his contemporaries and brought by them to Europe, where they now enrich various libraries, museums, and private collections. The works in question, known as Ragmalas, or 'Garlands of Musical Modes,' are characterized by singular tenderness of sentiment, and present examples of some of the best pictorial work ever produced in India. Such praise applies, of course, only to specimens of the highest class. The collections include much rubbish.

Before proceeding to describe and reproduce a few select typical examples, an attempt must be made to give some notion of the strange manner in which Hindu thought associates music with painting. Even with the help of such exposition as I am able to offer, on the authority of Sir William Jones, who had some practical knowledge of both arts, it is not easy for the European mind to discover any real bond of union between a given picture and the sounds which it is supposed to symbolize. Personally, I am wholly unable to trace the connexion, and can discuss the paintings simply with reference to their aesthetic value as expressions of Hindu sentiment, imagination, and observation of nature. I do not know anybody who could explain why a particular design was appropriated to certain music. The association of the various musical modes with the seasons—a subject sufficiently obscure in itself—does not help me much to realize the ideas underlying the pictorial symbolism, and I cannot judge how far any selected work is to be commended for its significance as a suggestion to the eye of certain musical combinations of sounds. To some extent the general nature of the subject appropriate to the illustration of each 'musical mode' was fixed by rule or tradition, but the treatment allowed free scope to the exercise of each individual artist's fancy and skill. The *Ragmala* illustrations are of special interest because of their freedom from the fetters of immutable rules, bondage to which has been the chief support of the common belief that India possesses no fine art. (1911)

VINCENT A. SMITH[270]

## 3. Paintings on cotton

A remarkable set of twenty-four large paintings on cotton, in Mongol style, preserved in the Indian Section of the Victoria and Albert Museum, South Kensington, seems to have been produced in Kashmir about the middle of the sixteenth century before Akbar took measures to encourage painting after the Persian manner. These cotton paintings, bought in Kashmir for low prices by Sir Purdon Clarke, are said to have been illustrations of a manuscript book of stories which has not been preserved or identified. . . .The rocky scenery found in all, or almost all, the pictures is connected with Kashmir in one case by the introduction of black bears, and with India in two cases by the insertion of banyan-trees. These works may be conjectured to have been executed in Kashmir between A.D. 1540 and 1551, when that country was ably ruled by Babar's cousin, Haidar Mirza Dughlat, the accomplished author of the *Tarikh-i-Rashidi.* (1911)

VINCENT A SMITH[271]

## B. DRESS FASHION AND COSTUMES

## 1. Some characteristics

The dress worn by the Indians is made of cotton, as Nearchos tells us,—cotton produced from those trees of which mention has already been made. But this cotton is either of a brighter white colour than any cotton found elsewhere, or the darkness of the Indian complexion makes their apparel look so much the whiter. They wear an under-garment of cotton which reaches below the knee halfway down to the ankles, and also an upper garment which they throw partly over their shoulders, and partly twist in folds round their head. The Indians wear also earrings of ivory, but only such of them do this as are very wealthy, for all Indians do not wear them. Their beards, Nearchos tells us, they dye of one hue and another, according to taste. Some dye their white beards to make them look as white as possible, but others dye them blue; while some again prefer a red tint, some a purple, and others a rank green. Such Indians, he also says, as are thought anything of, use parasols as a screen from the heat. They wear shoes made of white leather, and these are elaborately trimmed, while the soles are variegated, and made of great thickness, to make the wearer seem so much the taller. (3rd century B.C.)

ARRIAN[272]

## 2. Indian dress

[In] India ... .everyone goes naked; the women go bareheaded and with breasts uncovered, their hair plaited into one braid. Many women are with child, they bear children every year, and have many children. The men and women are all black. Wherever I went I was followed by many people who wondered at me, a white man.

And their prince wears a dhoti upon his head and another about his loins; their boyars wear a dhoti round their shoulders and another about their loins; their princesses wrap a dhoti round their shoulders and another round their loins. As for the servants of the prince and the boyars, they wear a dhoti wound about their loins, and carry shield and sword in their hands, while others have spears or knives or sabres, or bow and arrows. And all are naked and barefoot, and strong. And the women go bareheaded and with breasts uncovered; as for the little boys and girls, they go naked till the age of seven, and do not hide their shame. (1466-72)

AFANASY NIKITIN[273]

## 3. Fashions

With respect to their fashions of dress, I may say that the great nobles wear nothing more than the following: They bind their hair with a scarf of very fine gold stuff that they call *romals (rumali)*. Then they tie round their waist a piece of white cloth (as is the usual practice in India); it is about four cubits in length, and has a red border. It comes down to their knees. Above this they wear a white wrapper; but it is to be noted that the manner of putting this on varies in each caste. Some among them wear gold or silver rings on the toes. The children of these last carry from birth to seven years of age little bells on their legs, either of gold or silver, and a little chain of the same metal round the waist. As for the rest, they are no more covered than when they were brought into the world.

Some great lords wear a sort of turban on their heads, and put on a gown of white cloth that they call a *cabaye (qaba)*, and underneath it very tight drawers; on their feet they have shoes of velvet or red leather. These they remove when they enter a house or speak to a person of quality, for it is a great piece of bad manners in this country to speak to such a person with your shoes on and your head uncovered. The monks, called *Sannyasis,* are excepted, also ascetics, called Tavagi *(tapasa)*, and Brahmans, and all castes up to about the age of eighteen. This last exception is because up to that age they neither allow their hair to grow nor bind on the scarf of gold, of which I spoke above; they only leave on the middle of the head a little tail of hair.

The above is the apparel of the princes and the richest nobility. As for the soldiers, labourers, and other ordinary people, they have no more than a cloth bound round their head, and a little string round their middle, attached to which is a morsel of cloth, a span wide and a cubit in length, about the size of one of our ordinary napkins. With this cloth they cover the parts of the body that natural modesty requires to be concealed. Lastly, they have another cloth, somewhat of the same size, bound round the body, which serves in the daytime as a garment and at night as a bed, their mattress being identical with the damp earth. A stone or a piece of wood serves as bolster. Thus what would be looked on in Europe as a severe penance is in this country the ordinary habit. There are some so badly provided that they content themselves with the piece of cloth spoken of above as used to cover the private parts. In this equipment they hold themselves fully dressed and fit to talk to anyone, wherever it might be.

Having spoken of men's dress, the next thing is to say a little about that of women. It is very indifferent, and little can be said about it. From the age of twelve and upwards almost all of them allow their hair to grow long; up to that age they wear only a small tail of hair on the top of the head, like that of the little boys. They do not bind anything on, nor do they make the hair into tresses, but make it into a roll on one side of the head. All have their ears pierced, but not in the European way, for the holes are so large that the ears droop almost to the shoulders. In these holes they wear their ornaments, each according to her degree or her wealth. The custom of having the ears pierced is in this country common to men and women. (1653-1708)

NICCOLAO MANUCCI[274]

## 4. *Fancy beards, dress and turbans*

The higher classes of these men wear their beards long, and bushy up to the eyes, and are extremely fanciful in the colour of them, sometimes tinging them with lilac, pink, light blue, yellow, and even scarlet. I saw one man whose beard was white, edged with purple. Mahometans in general only wear mustachios. The dresses of the Sieks we saw, were made of silk, wadded with cotton, reaching to their feet; the sleeves entirely obscuring the hands, and edged with a broad gold or silver lace all round the skirts. These dresses are made to fit the shape; the skirt to wrap across the front, and fasten by strings on one side; their throat being always exposed. Over this, they wear a long shawl, bound tight round the waist; a turban on their heads: and in cold weather, when they go out of doors, two square shawls, one plain, the other sprigged, envelope turban, face, and shoulders, leaving the smallest possible aperture, just that they may see their way: shawl socks, and shoes trimmed up at the points, either embroidered on scarlet or yellow cloth, or made of scarlet or yellow leather. Mussulmen are fond of gay colours, and have not the same objection to wearing any thing made of leather as the Hindoos have. (1809)

A. DEARE[275]

## 5. *Dress and manners of the men at Serran*

The dress and manners of the men have varied little since we entered Bischur; or, at least, any slight difference that may be traced is not of a nature to call for a description. That they are more open, more free, and more respectable and independent in their carriage, may be felt; but it is not easy to explain the causes of the impression thus given. The dress of the women has undergone more alteration: the handkerchief which used to cover the head is here discarded, and its place is occupied by a woolen cap resembling that of the men; the crown of which is sometimes crimson, sometimes plain black. The hair is not now suffered to hang down the back in a long thick tail, but this tail is carefully rolled up behind the head, and fixed there; so that the end, in its formidable tassels of red wool and hair, appears behind each ear, and is tied up with much red wool and flowers. A string of flowers is hung from the side of each bonnet, by both the sexes. Instead of a courtee, or coat, like that of the men, the women wear, besides the petticoat, a blanket that folds partly round the body, and partly comes up around the shoulders and across the breast, where it is fastened by a large copper or brass broach: in other instances, the blanket only comes over one shoulder, somewhat like the Scots plaid. On the whole, the dress is more fanciful and becoming; and there is much more use made of a striped stuff, resembling the tartan of the highlands, than I have before observed. The women are certainly improved in looks. I have seen several that might be considered as handsome and fair, with something of a good complexion: indeed, I think that both the sexes may be fairly pronounced more comely and personable to the northward than they are further south. (1820)

JAMES BAILLIE FRASER[276]

### 6. *North Indian costume*

Our approach to the Mohammedan countries became evident daily, and showed itself in nothing more than the costume of the women, many of whom we now met veiled. One girl whom we saw on the road had a canopy of red cloth erected over her on horseback, which had a ludicrous appearance. It seemed to be a framework of wood, but as the cloth concealed every thing as well as the countenance of the fair lady, I did not discover the contrivance. The costume of the unveiled portion of the sex had likewise undergone a change; and they wore wide blue trowsers, tightly tied at the ankle, which taper down, and have a graceful appearance. A web of cloth sixty yards long is sometimes used in a single pair, for one fold falls upon the other. (1831)

ALEXANDER BURNESS[277]

### 7. *Costs*

The commonest articles of dress in Calcutta are at least three times as dear as they are in England. I bought a silk hat which would have cost five shillings at home, and paid fourteen rupees for it here; and some ribbon, which would have been threepence a-yard in England, cost a rupee and a half here. Then on the other hand many things are cheaper. (1843)

T. ACLAND[278]

## C. THEATRE

### 1. *Classical drama*

I never saw any Indian theatricals on a larger scale; but on these occasions I have at times heard some very humorous and witty dialogues, but never witnessed a representation that offended piety, morality, or delicacy. That some of their dramatic writings merit very high encomium, we may judge from the beautiful play of Sacontala, translated by Sir William Jones. Nothing can be more innocent, or illustrative of the simplicity of ancient Hindoo manners. The stage ought every where to be a school for virtue. Addison justly remarks, that theatrical entertainments were invented for the accomplishment and refinement of human nature; and the Athenian and Roman plays were written with such a regard to morality, that Socrates used often to frequent the one, and Cicero the other.

In the preface to Sacontala, Sir William Jones observes, that 'by whomsoever or in whatever age the entertainment of dramatic poetry was invented, it is very certain, that it was carried to great perfection in its kind when Vicramaditya, who reigned in the first century before Christ, gave encouragement to poets, philologers, and mathematicians, at a time when the Britons were as unlettered and unpolished as the army of Hanumat. Nine men of genius, commonly called the Nine Gems, attended his court, and were splendidly supported by his bounty. Calidas, the author of Sacontala, and the Shakespeare of India, is unanimously allowed to have been one of them. Some of his contemporaries, and other Hindoo poets even to our own times, have composed so many tragedies, comedies, farces, and musical pieces, that the Indian theatre would fill as many volumes as that of any nation in ancient or modern Europe. They are all in verse where the dialogue is elevated, and in prose where it is familiar: the men of rank and learning are represented speaking pure Sanscrit, and the women Pracrit; which is little more than the language of the brahmins melted down by a delicate articulation to the softness of Italian; while the low personae of the drama speak the vulgar dialects of the several provinces, which they are supposed to inhabit'. (1812)

JAMES FORBES[279]

## 2. Amateur theatre

In the evening, I attended an amateur play at the Station Theatre: and here I was as much delighted as I had been at the review. The house is a long quadrangular, rat-trap-like building, in which those who might have the good fortune to sit in the rear, would certainly hear no single word from the stage. This evil, however, may very possibly be less felt here than it would be elsewhere; for, judging by the 'beggarly account of empty benches,' exhibited upon the occasion in question, there can be little competition for the best seats. A more unfortunate display of bad management never was made upon any stage.

Many of the scenes had been designed and painted by a masterhand, Captain Luard, formerly of the 16th Lancers; but their effect and stage-delusion were utterly destroyed by bad selections, and most clumsy shifting. At the change of a scene, you might behold the respective wings of two separate running-scenes thrust forward to meet each other; a palace, or saloon, and the interior of a dungeon, very possibly presented as moieties of the same picture; then, upon the mistake being discovered, one of the wings would probably be withdrawn, and another wrong one would take its place; then a forestslip would be run in as a wall for a chapel, or a sea-piece would make its appearance in place of a boudoir, a round table with a green-baize cloth upon it with his Majesty's state-room, or a gilt chair in a cottage.

The acting, if such it could be called, was equally execrable. Who the manager might have been, I know not, but the characters were badly cast, ridiculously dressed, and, to a man, without the remotest conception of stage-knowledge or stage-address. Grouping was lost sight of altogether; no personage had any determinate walk or position on the stage; every man did that which was right in his own eyes, and the certain consequence was, that they were continually in one another's way, and played *against* instead of *to* one another. Fixed *entrees* and *exits* were out of the question: you might see the heroine, expecting her lover, look off the stage upon the O.P. (Opposite Prompter) side, exclaiming, 'Ah, here he comes!' when in blunders the hero P.S. (Prompter Side), just behind his mistress. Again, black servants in their ordinary garbs might be seen walking coolly across the stage during the performance, or acting the part of stage-waiters; with an infinity of the like bad management, displaying fully to the audience all the arcana and trickery of the stage. (1831–6)

THOMAS BACON[280]

## 3. *Puppet plays*

More amusing than Indian conjuring or the nautch is the *kutpootli*, or puppet-play, that in Northern India is the especial treat of European children, and the frequent joy of the adult native. It is true that the comedy played by the *kutpootli* dolls is mainly a procession of rajahs, who enter two and two (after the manner of Noah's beasts), and range themselves silent and motionless in durbar; but there is an undercurrent of farce which gives some life to the affair, and much delight to British children. A wayfarer is robbed by a thief and bullied by a policeman; a sweeper and his wife are prominent upon the scene in the prologue, and as comic as circumstances will permit; and although the farce of these minor characters had for me no particular meaning, it is quite possible that the initiated saw in it something of a distinctly edifying and satirical character.

Sometimes this oriental Punch and Judy travesty was elaborated for older audiences by the addition of a ludicrous caricature of the Anglo-Indian. This uncomplimentary rendering of the white man's peculiarities was given, not by dolls, but by the men attached to the show. Dressed in odds and ends of cast-off European clothing, and wearing masks designed to represent the European countenance, these dismal mimes presented their view of the average Briton's demeanour. As far as I can remember, the Britannic character thus portrayed was singularly circumscribed. The sahib in mask and scarecrow apparel was a creature of three emotions and no moral. He got drunk, he said d——n frequently, and he thumped his native attendant. (1845)

EDWARD BRADDON[281]


## 4.  Theatre in South India

In the course of conversation one day with a friend, hearing that there are companies of Hindu theatrical performers who go about the country acting at the houses of the wealthier natives, we were anxious to see them exhibit; and after some inquiry learnt that a band, fourteen in number, were then in Bangalore, and we engaged them to perform before us. These actors came from either Tanjore or Madura; the women's parts are taken by youths and young boys. It seems worthy of note that all the personages in the drama whom they intend to represent as spiritual beings, or possessed of divine power, have their faces painted *white*. By some means these dark coloured natives made themselves look as fair as ourselves; their hands, not being considered important, were suffered to retain their ordinary colour.

The representation took place in the evening and the *dramatis personae* were as follows:

1. *Kamsu*, or *Kamsudu*, maternal uncle of Krishna.
2. *Devakidevi*, the mother of Krishna.
3. *Yesoda*, his foster-mother.
4. *Krishna*, the eighth incarnation of Vishnu.
5. *Mayasakti*, the spiritual being born to Yesoda, and substituted by Vasudeva (husband of Devakidevi) for his son Krishna.
6. *Gollabhamula*, wives of Krishna (five in number).
7. *Putana*, a witch disguised as a nurse, and deputed by Kamsudu to kill Krishna, whilst he is a child.
8. *Bhutaki*, a giantess, also sent by Kamsudu, who tries to carry off Krishna.
9. *Gollamusulaveshalu*, are people disguised as aged shepherds. Krishna lived with them many years.

When acted before a native audience, the play is sometimes prolonged for days, performers and spectators both retiring at intervals for the needful refreshment and repose. In our case only a portion was given; the time it occupied in representation was about three hours. The scene opens just before the birth of Krishna. It having been foretold to his uncle Kamsudu, King of Mathura (the modern Muttra), that he would be killed by the eighth child of his sister, Devakidevi, he takes precautions, as he believes, to prevent this, and tells the nurse, who is about to attend upon her, to let him know when the child is born, that he may kill it. It so happens that Devakidevi's eighth child, Krishna, or the eighth incarnation of Vishnu and Mayasakti, the child of his foster-mother, Yesoda, are both born about the same time. Vasudeva, Krishna's father, goes to see Yesoda, taking his child with him; he changes the children, and returns home. Kamsudu then comes to Vasudeva's house, and not knowing that the babes have been changed, seizes Mayasakti with the intention of murdering her; this he cannot do, for she is a spiritual being. The next scene is laid at Yesoda's house; the real Krishna is there; the fairy Putana, disguised as a nurse, and a giantess also come to him, both have been deputed by Kamsudu to try and kill him, but Krishna strangles them both through his divine power. Failing in these attempts, Kamsudu orders his warriors to make search for all young children throughout his dominions, and slay every male child. Krishna, after this, is represented as being placed with some shepherds, and he is seen going to the houses of the milkmaids to beg for butter. He next appears with five wives who also go about with him, and they all dance and sing together. Some years are supposed to have expired between this scene and the next, which is laid at Mathura, where Kamsudu resides. Krishna goes thither, accompanied by his brother, and Kamsudu, hearing of his nephew's arrival, hides himself; but Krishna finds him, and touches him on the forehead, on which he instantly expires. Vasudeva, Krishna's father, is then by his son's influence declared King of Mathura.

One of the most striking parts of the whole exhibition was the funereal dirge, which was sung, and the dance which was afterwards executed over the corpse of the witch, Putana, by some youths disguised as women. Their movements were remarkably graceful, and the music wild and melancholy; it ended by the sounds dying away in the distance as the body was removed by the attendants. (1881)

MRS. J.C. MURRAY-AYNSLEY[282]

## D. JEWELLERY AND PRECIOUS STONES

### 1. Diamond mine, Raichur[1]

At Raichur diamonds are mined—old and new ones; one *pochka*[2] of diamond is sold at five rubles, and if very good, at 10 rubles; one *pochka* of new diamond, however, is worth only five *kanis*[3], one of blackish colour, from four to six *kanis,* and a white diamond, one *tanga.*[4] Diamonds are mined in a rocky mountain, which is sold at 2,000 gold pounds a cubit if the diamonds are new, or at 10,000 gold pounds if they are old. (1466–72)

AFANASY NIKITIN[283]

[1]A town to the South-west of Hyderabad.
[2]An old Russian weight for precious stones, about 10 carats.
[3]A small coin, 1/64 of a *tanga*.
[4]A silver coin varying locally in weight and value.

### 2. The order how they fish for pearles

The Sea that lyeth betweene the Coast which descendeth from Cape Comori, to the low land of Chilao, and the Iland Zeilan, they call The fishing of Pearles, which fishing they make every yeere, begin-

ning in March or Aprill, and it lasteth fiftie dayes, but they doe not
fish every yeere in one place, but one yeere in one place, and
another yeere in another place of the same Sea. When the time of
this fishing draweth neere, then they send very good Divers, that
goe to discover where the greatest heapes of Oysters bee under
water, and right against that place where greatest store of Oysters
be, there they make or plant a Village with houses and a Bazaro, all
of stone, which standeth as long as the fishing time lasteth, and it is
furnished with all things necessarie, and now and then it is neere
unto places that are inhabited, and other times farre off, according
to the place where they fish. The Fishermen are all Christians of the
Countrey, and who so will may goe to fishing, paying a certaine
dutie to the King of Portugall, and to the Churches of the Friers of
Saint Paul, which are in that Coast. All the while that they are
fishing, there are three or foure Fusts armed to defend the Fishermen from Rovers. It was my chance to bee there one time in my
passage, and I saw the order that they used in fishing, which is this.
There are three or foure Barkes that make consort together, which
are like to our little Pilot boates, an a little lesse, there goe seven or
eight men in a Boat: and I have seene in a morning a great number
of them goe out, and anker in fifteene or eighteene fathom of water,
which is the ordinarie depth of all that Coast. When they are at
anker, they cast a rope into the Sea, and at the end of the rope, they
make fast a great stone, and then there is readie a man that hath his
nose and his eares well stopped, and annointed with Oyle, and a
basket about his necke, or under his left arme, then hee goeth
downe by the rope to the bottome of the Sea, and as fast as he can he
filleth the basket, and when it is full, hee shaketh the rope, and his
fellowes that are in the Barke hale him up with the Basket: and in
such wise they goe one by one untill they have laden their Barke with
Oysters, and at evening they come to the Village, and then every
companie maketh their mount or heape of Oysters one distant from
another, in such wise that you shall see a great long row of mounts or
heapes of Oysters, and they are not touched untill such time as the
fishing be ended, and at the end of the fishing every companie sitteth
round about their mount or heape of Oysters, and fall to opening of
them, which they may easily doe because they be dead, drie and
brittle: and if every oyster had pearles in them it would bee a very
good purchase, but there are very many that have no pearles in
them: when the fishing is ended, then they see whether it bee a good

gathering or a bad: there are certaine expert in the Pearles, whom they call Chitini, which set and make the price of Pearles according to their carracts, beautie, and goodnesse, making foure sorts of them. The first sort be the round Pearles, and they be called Aja of Portugall, because the Portugals doe buy them. The second sort which are not round, are called Aja of Bengala. The third sort which are not so good as the second they call Aja of Canara, that is to say, The Kingdome of Bezeneger. The fourth and last sort, which are the least and worst sort, are called Aja of Cambaia. Thus the price being set, there are Merchants of every Countrey which are readie with their money in their hands, so that in few dayes all is bought up at the prises set according to the goodnesse and carracts of the Pearles. (1567)

CAESAR FREDERICK[284]

## 3. A large pearl

On the following day they all three came to see me, one after the other, and they wished to get from me amongst other things a grand bouquet of nine large pearl-shaped pearls, of which the largest was thirty carats and the least sixteen, with another single pear-shaped pearl of fifty five carats. As for the bouquet the King took it; but with regard to the pearl, seeing that, not withstanding all that they could say, I was unwilling to sell them anything, they so managed that before I had shown my jewels to the King, Zafar Khan, uncle of the King, saw it, after which he did not wish to return it saying that he would pay me as highly for it as the King, asking me not to mention it; for in fact he desired to present it to the King.

After the King had selected from among my jewels those which he desired, Zafar Khan bought several pieces from me, and at the same time purchased the great pearl. Some days afterwards he caused my payment to be made according to what had been agreed upon, with the exception of the pearl, upon which he desired me to rebate, 10,000—rupees. The two Persians and the Banian had maliciously informed him that on my arrival they might, if they had wished, have had the pearl for 8,000 or 10,000 less than I had sold it to him— for; this was wholly untrue, and Zafar Khan having told me that if I would not accept the money which he offered me I might take it back, I took him at his word, assuring him that during his life he would never see it again. (1640-1)

JEAN BAPTISTE TAVERNIER[285]

## 4. *Various stones*

The *Granate* resembles in colour to the coral. There are two sorts, the *Indian* and *Spanish;* the last are very red and bright; those found in *Ethiopia,* are scarce to be distinguished from the hyacinth, except that their lustre is somewhat less than that of the hyacinth.

The stone call'd *Olbos de Gatos,* i.e. *Catseyes,* by the *Portugueses,* is in much greater esteem among the Indians than the *Portugueses;* who are of opinion, that if you rub linen cloth with them, it will be fire-proof: but this I have found contrary to truth by my own experience.

The *Hematites*, or blood-stone, has got its name from its dark-red colour, and its virtue in quenching of blood. It is found in *New-Spain,* and reputed by them a kind of *Jaspir;* the *Indians* make beads of them, and wear them about their necks: they also lay them in water, and afterwards hold them close in their hands, and look upon this as an excellent remedy to stop the superfluous monthly times of the women, or any other flux of blood. This stone is also found in *Ceylon* and *Cambaja* where it is call'd *Silakenea.*

The *Nephritis,* or *Kidney-stone,* has got its name from the word neqgos, i.e. a kidney, because it is worn by the Indians agains the pain of the kidneys, and therefore in great esteem among them. It is found in *New-Spain;* and the greener it is, the better it is.

The naturalists tell us, that the stag, when tormented in his bowels by certain poisonous worms, runs up to the neck in water, at which time the slimy tears which adhere to the corners of his eyes are coagulated to the bigness of a wallnut, which thence have got the name of *Hart-stones;* which taken in wine, are looked upon as a sovereign antidote against all manner of poisons and infections. (1671)

PHILIP BALDAEUS[286]

## 5. *Of stately mansions, new and old*

> There stately mansions new and old
> Flame with Barbaric gems and gold;
> There shine, with pride, the regal stores,
> Of ivory roofs, and cedrine floors;
> There diadems of price unknown
> Blaze with each all-attracting stone:

Firm diamonds, like fix'd honour true,
Some pink, and some of yellow hue;
Some black, yet not the less esteem'd,
The rest like tranquil Jumna gleam'd,
When in her bed the Gopia lave
Betray'd by the pellucid wave.
Like raging fire the ruby glow'd
Or soft, but radiant water show'd
Pure amethysts, in richest ore
Oft found, a purple vesture wore;
Sapphires, like yon ethereal plain;
Emeralds, like peipal fresh with rain;
Gay topazes, translucent gold;
Pale chrysolites of softer mould;
Fam'd beryls, like the surge marine,
Light azure mix'd with modest green;
Refracted every varying dye,
Bright as yon bow that girds the sky.
Here opals, which all hues unite,
Display their many-tinctur'd light;
With turquoises divinely blue,
(Though doubts arise where first they grew,)
Whether chaste elephantine bone,
By minerals  ing'd or native stone)
And pearls unblemish'd, such as deck
*Bhawanee's* wrist, or *Lecshmy's* neck. (1803)

                                    ENCHANTED FRUIT[287]

## 6.  *Some Magnificent jewels*

I saw a valuable assortment of precious stones at Cambay, belonging to a Persian nobleman, intended for sale; among them was a
diamond of the first water, shaped like a prism, weighing an
hundred and seventeen carats, and estimated at twenty-five
thousand pounds. The proprietor informed me of a diamond then in
the royal treasury at Ispahan, which weighed two hundred and
sixty-four carats, and was valued at four hundred and twenty
thousand pounds. This is probably the same stone mentioned by
Tavernier, at that time in possession of the Mogul emperor, which
weighed two hundred and seventy-nine carats, and its value was
estimated at half a million sterling. The variation in the weight and

price in a gem of such magnitude, may be easily allowed between a Persian and European traveller. This imperial diamond is a brilliant of beautiful shape, called by way of eminence *Kooi Toor,* 'the Hill of Lustre,' alluding to Mount Sinai, in Arabia, where GOD appeared in glory to Moses. Another diamond of a flat surface, nearly as valuable as the former, is denominated *Doriainoor,* 'the Ocean of Lustre.' These magnificent jewels formed part of Nadir Shah's plunder at Delhi in 1739; when the riches he carried off exceeded seventy millions sterling. The most superb article of this imperial spoil was the *Tucht-Taoos,* or peacock-throne, in which the expanded tail of the peacock, in its natural size, was imitated in jewellery, composed of the most costly diamonds, rubies, emeralds, sapphires, topazes, and amethysts, producing a wonderful effect. This throne was valued at ten crore of rupees, upwards of twelve millions sterling. After the assassination of Nadir Shah this plunder was transported into various countries, and since the late revolutions in Persia has been more widely dispersed.

Jewels have been always held in high estimation; sacred and profane writers extol their beauty and value; the Romans, under their luxurious emperors, carried this extravagant superfluity to the utmost prodigality. Diamonds with them do not appear to have been in so much request as pearls, of which they possessed some immensely valuable: one, presented by Julius Caesar to Servilia, the mother of Brutus, cost him forty-eight thousand pounds sterling. The celebrated pearl ear-rings of Cleopatra were valued at one hundred and sixty thousand pounds.

In the oppressed and impoverished city of Cambay, at the time I last saw it, there was no demand for jewels, nor any other valuable commodity; they were generally sent to Surat, Bombay, or China, where they found a ready sale. The magnificent prismatic diamond I have just mentioned, was lost in a dreadful storm a few months afterwards at Surat bar, where the ship in which it was freighted, with a number of other vessels, foundered at their anchors. (1812)

JAMES FORBES[288]

## 7.  *Muslim ornaments*

The dopatta is so transparent it hides not; it merely veils the form, adding beauty to the beautiful, by its soft and cloudlike folds. The jewellery sparkles beneath it; and the outline of its drapery is continually changing according to the movements or coquetry of the wearer. Such was the attire of the Princess! Her head was covered with pearls and precious stones, most gracefully arranged: from the throat to the waist was a succession of strings of large pearls and precious stones; her arms and hands were covered with armlets, bracelets, and rings innumerable. Her delicate and uncovered feet were each decorated with two large circular anklets composed of gold and precious stones, and golden rings were on her toes. In her nose she wore a n'hut, a large thin gold ring, on which was strung two large pearls, with a ruby between them. A nose-ring is a love token, and is always presented by the bridegroom to the bride. No single woman is allowed to wear one. (1835)

FANNY PARKES[289]

## E.  INDIAN COOKING

### 1.  Modes of eating

Princes and kings eat in the following manner: They are seated on the ground on a piece of fine cloth. Then the house or the room in which they are to eat is rubbed over with a solution of cowdung. As the palaces of kings have floors made of a cement which looks like fine marble, there they do nothing more than throw down some cowdung mixed in water, and then wipe the floor with a piece of cloth. The floor then looks like a looking glass. Without all this ceremonial of cleansing with the dung of this animal, as above described, no person of quality sits down to eat. These preparations finished, they bring a great platter of enamelled gold, which is placed on the ground in front of the diners, but without allowing it to touch the cloth on which they are seated. After this some small gold dishes are placed around, and the food is brought from the kitchen in bowls or vessels of silver, fashioned in the shape of cooking-pots. First of all, from these bowls they place rice cooked without salt or other condiment in the large dish, and on this they put some stew. If the whole cannot be contained in the large dish, they put the remainder in the small dishes round about it.

Then the rajah takes whatever pleases him, throwing it with his hand into a plate of rice, where he mixes it and rolls it into balls, which he throws into his mouth with the right hand. The left hand is not allowed to touch any food. All is swallowed without mastication. This fashion they consider very cleanly, and that there is no better way of satisfying oneself; and they say that Europeans eat rice like pigs. Then, before finishing the meal, they send as much as they think sufficient to their wives. For in this country these never eat with their husbands, even though those waiting on the king be eunuchs, children, or women.

The way of eating among the other castes who are not kings is as follows: Monks, ascetics, Brahmans, and the learned before eating wash their hands and bodies. Then they put upon their foreheads, stomach, shoulders, knees and sides a little ashes mixed in water. This ash is either of a white earth they call *naman (namam)*, or of sandal, according to their caste or the faith they follow. Next they enter the house, finding its floors all rubbed over with cowdung, in the way I have spoken of. They bind round their body a piece of cloth, and sit down with their legs crossed, or upon a small mat of about one cubit in length. Before them is placed the large leaf of certain trees, or smaller leaves of other trees stitched together, not with needle and thread, but with rushes. Upon this leaf is put first of all a pinch of salt and two drops of butter, with which they anoint or rub the leaf. This ceremony completed, they deposit on this platter some rice cooked in water without salt, followed by a little vegetables and some green stuff. When this is eaten, they throw upon the rice left on the said leaf a little sour curds or some whey. When all this food has been swallowed, they rise from the place and move to a courtyard or garden, if there is one in the house where they live. If there is not, they go into the street, and there bathe their hands, mouth and feet. They do not return to their dwellings till the leaves they have eaten from have been removed, and the ground has been rubbed over afresh in the way already mentioned. For they say that if they did so their bodies would be as polluted as the house.

Since neither Brahmans, ascetics, monks, nor the learned eat any meat or fish in this country (eggs, being here included under the head of meat, are also avoided), I think it as well here to state the food and manner of eating of the other castes. None of those I have hitherto spoken of ever eat cow's flesh. To do so is a very low thing, a defilement, and sinful beyond all imagination. But they eat all the other meats consumed in Europe, and, in addition thereto, rats and lizards. As for shell-fish, these also are classed among the most impure of things, and are not used except by the pariahs. However, almost all the castes eat of the other kinds of meat, and judge it to be most delicious fare.

The food of these people is usually placed on a little cooked rice, and it consists generally of a portion of dry and salted fish. For goats, sheep, chicken, rats, and lizards, are only for the nobility, and if other men eat of these, it is solely at their festivals and at marriages. Their plate is a leaf, as described above, or a small plate of copper, out of which the whole family eats, one after the other.

Although these people hold it an abomination to eat of the cow, they believe, however, that it is a venerable thing, and one worthy of all praise, to drink that animal's urine, and to smother their faces with it. It is in pursuance of this opinion that the most noble and the most gallant among them rise betimes in the morning, and holding a cow's tail, worship the spot covered thereby. The reason they give is that this is Lakshmi, mother of their god, Vishnu, and goddess of prosperity. Their worship over, they hold out their two hands and receive the cow's urine, of which they take a drink. Then, turning the tail into a sort of holy-water sprinkler, they immerse it in the said liquid, and with it they daub their faces. When this ceremonial is over, they declare they have been made holy.

To obtain plenary indulgence for all their sins, they say it is necessary to obtain a beverage composed of milk, butter cowdung and cow's urine. With this medicament not only is all sin driven away, but all infamy. In this the Brahmans intervene, for it is they alone who can secure this 'jubilee'. It is obligatory when marrying for the first time, when women arrive at puberty, and on any unlucky day. Even the cleverest men, those who look down on the rest of the world, have their houses rubbed with cowdung before they eat, and then, without other ceremony, have their food brought, and eat it.

There is another class of persons called Nostiguer (?Nastika), who not only may not be looked upon when eating, but may not hear the sound of any human voice while so occupied. So far is this carried that, when eating, they cause a copper vessel to be beaten hard at their door. Men of this caste do not allow their beard to be touched either by the razor or by scissors, but it is dragged out, hair by hair, with a small pincers. The first time that the pulling out of the hair of the head and beard is begun, if the patient betrays no sign of pain, he is accepted as a firm disciple; if, on the contrary, he weeps, cries, or makes faces, they say he is too tender, and thereby unworthy to be admitted into the confraternity.

These men are not the only ones who may not be seen eating, for other castes may not look at Brahmans who are eating. In regard to this these Hindus have a rather amusing habit. The Brahmans, according to their view, are the noblest family of all mankind, and the one most venerated, not merely as superiors, but as gods. Other castes cannot wait on them or fetch them water, nor cook for them. They must wait upon each other for these two purposes, or do it each for himself. With all that, however, they may carry water and cook for the other castes, which appears a moral contradiction, for if it dishonours them to be served by others, how can they be servants to others?

When Brahmans cook for another caste they act as follows: after having cooked the food, they bring it in brass or copper vessels to the house where it is to be eaten—that is, of the man who has given the order. Not being a Brahman, he cannot enter the kitchen, nor inspect the pots in which the food is being cooked. The food having been brought, it is laid out upon leaves, or on copper or brass vessels made like dishes. Having helped the food, the Brahmans do the waiting until the end of the repast. Then they and the master and his guests, if any, come out, and the Brahmans throw water over the eaters' hands and feet; but they do not clear away what has not been eaten, for that would be a dishonour and a disgrace beyond repair. To remove the unused food it is necessary to have another man who is not a Brahman, and if there is none such, he who has eaten must himself remove the leavings, along with the leaf or dish from which he has eaten, and afterwards cleanse the house in the way already described.

As to their mode of eating, it is as follows: they all eat with the right hand, and may not touch anything with the left, not even the plate or leaf from which they have eaten, or the spoon with which they sup a concoction by way of wine, which is some water boiled with pepper. But a vessel of cold water they lift with the left hand, at the same time never putting the vessel to the mouth. They hold their mouth open and raised to catch the liquid they pour into it. In fine, the greatest piece of refinement in this country is considered to be eating in a clean and orderly way, but this is carried out in no other manner than that described above. Yet, being so very different from that practised by Europeans and Mahomedans, it forms the ground for their strong contempt for these latter. (1653–1708)

NICCOLAO MANUCCI[290]

## 2. *Reception at dinner*

From the ramparts of a small mud-fort, in which live the softer part of nature's journey-work, the Commander-in-Chief and his party were saluted with the roar of cannon. Outside the fort is a good brick house, surrounded by a capital garden. Here are extensive indigo works, and other mercantile speculations, all of which from constant superintendence, are in the best possible order. Skinner invited his Excellency to breakfast and dinner; at both of these banquets, the viands in quality and quantity would have done honour to a baronial feast. The Hindoostani cookery was in the best taste and style, and captivated all palates. Several sets of nautch women had arrived from Delhi; these and his own band of kulamets (men singers) entertained us during our repasts. After dinner, some acting gentry, or rather buffoons, made their appearance, and caused us to laugh by their most ludicrous representation of the capture of Bhurtpore, and our plundering it, with such vivacity as even to cut the hair off the heads of the people. To sum up all the feasting, Colonel Skinner fed 'the whole general camp, pioneers and all.' There were 5000 to whom were distributed flour, butter, and sweetmeats; each received ample for two days' consumption. This princely mode of entertaining is peculiar to, and worthy the best days of Hindoostan. (1828)

EDWARD C. ARCHER[291]

## 3. *The Bowurchee-khanah*

The *Bawurchee-khanah*—cook-house, or kitchen—if it merit such a name — first claims attention, and what a mass of novelty is here!—Where is the dresser?—Where the stove?—the oven?—the copper?—'and echo answers where?' I'm almost ashamed of introducing to you their substitutes. Here, however, are the fire places, sometimes a dozen in a row, contained in a brick and plaster building,—being, in short, but an improvement upon the common *chool'has. These* are nothing more than thick vessels of clay, formed by plastering that material over small earthenware gumblas. They are used by the natives of the country, who either buy them ready sundried and portable, or, when travelling, may be seen rough shaping them of clay upon the banks of the river, where the boat is made fast for the night,—the period of the people's second meal.

The front row of the fire niches—generally used for charcoal only—have attached to them grated bottoms, to which the square apertures beneath form the cinder holes. The hinder row, as well the larger chool'has near the ground that are intended for wood fires—for no *coals* are used—have no gratings, but are simply hollowed out of the brick work. The little eminences, or mounds, you will at once perceive, form the hobs or supports for the cooking vessels. The large arch on the right is used merely as a receptacle for wood, an immense bundle of which, unless, as is usually the case, laid up in monthly stores, is brought with the marketing for the day.

The elevated portion of roof that you may observe on the outside of the building, presenting about a dozen rectangular openings on either side is the chimney; one broad slip of the ceiling, the full breadth of the room, being left open beneath for the purpose.

The cooking utensils—that is the Asiatic portion of them, (for English kettles, pots and pans are also in requisition,) . . . In some families, they are nearly all of earthenware, and in others, though similar in shape, all of copper. The former, which are unglazed, have consequently to be frequently changed, and are sold at the trifling prices of from three to nine pice (about 3d). The copper, unlike the metalware of England, is re-tinned, both inside and out. every three or four weeks,—an operation, as conducted here, the most simple you can imagine.

Men, whose business it is, go round to their regular houses, and mustering the pots and pans in some waste part of the compound, they light a charcoal fire, making a communication into the midst of it by means of a little clay or mud tunnel. To the outer opening of this they apply the mouth (for want of a nosle) of a most primitive pair of bellows, being nothing more than a large leathern bag, one entire side of it left open, serving for valve, and which, by aid of bamboo laths sown to and strengthening the lips, is of course opened and closed by hand. The vessels being well scrubbed with mud or ashes, and cleaned, are placed on the fire, when the bellows are brought into requisition and the vessels soon thoroughly heated. A powder of calcined sal-ammoniac is then spread over with a handful of cotton,—the tin applied in little dabs—rapidly rubbed on with the powdered cotton, and the whole operation concluded in the space of a few minutes.

And now you will ask how we roast.—I might, if I desired to avoid the question, inform you with some anxiety that we have amongst us a few English kitchen ranges, but I must honestly confess my fear that we could not muster many more than a sufficiency of them to roast the joints of a Herefordshire ox or an Airedale heifer.

Probably, however, the introduction of all the goods, chattels and fixtures of an English kitchen would do but little towards an anglicizing of the cook-room, unless there were also introduced the intelligent moveables—the English servants, who could use them. In short, until kitchens and servants become marvellously altered, there will be but little temptation, I imagine for ladies to visit and inspect their bawurchee-khanas. I do not mean by this that there are *no* ladies who evince so much of the spirit of housewifery as to overcome the obstacles of long established custom—disinclination, and a heated atmosphere, and the greater credit is therefore due to them,—but that it is neither general nor systematic,—and until it becomes so,—until sufficient courage be summoned to set on foot a drilling and reformation, I need hardly say that little improvements will or can take place —Of the climate you have some conception;—the kitchens are probably situated fifty or sixty yards from the house,—whilst the servants, generally speaking, wedded to old customs. and in their habits partaking literally of the character of the scripture Pharisees, who made clean 'the outside of the cup and of the platter' but left within all uncleanness, are unable to appreciate English notions of nicety, though they generally well know how, in the presence of their lord or mistress, to 'assume a virtue if they have it not.' 'Those who consult their health' says Dr. M'Cosh 'will do wisely in making occasional visits to their cookrooms';—fair advice,—for which, however, many unphilosophical persons are content to substitute the 'somewhat musty' adage, that 'what the eye seeth not—' you know the rest.

Referring once more to the fire-places, I may state, that the introduction of coal as an article of fuel for my purpose has been a very recent event indeed. It was first discovered in Burdwan in 1804, but little more than talked of for twelve years afterwards. It has since been found in various parts of India, but only of late, when the increasing demands of steam navigation have given an impetus to enquiry and speculation, has it fairly been brought into use. Indeed it was not until the year 1837 that a committee 'for investigating the coal and mineral resources of India' sent in the Report of their Secretary, Dr. McClelland, to Government, when about forty different sites of coal existing on the continent of India were enumerated.

Were coal, therefore, even cheaper than it is,—about nine annas the maund, which is about eighteen-pence per hundred weight,— or were wood dearer than it is,—from four to five maunds for the roopee—say six-pence half-penny per hundred weight, and equally adapted with the last for the Indian fire-places, we could not expect its immediate adoption for domestic purposes. At present its consumption rests with our steamers, foundries, and mills,—objects of considerably greater importance than all the operations of the gastronomist.

With this apologetic digression I beg to introduce the cause of it,—the very antipodes to every thing that is English,—neat, or apparently cleanly,— . . .

. . .The fire, which is of charcoal, is kindled within the centre of a heap of ashes, and that the meat, which is probably wrapped in paper to prevent its drying or burning, is cooked but a small degree in advance of the fire, whilst a dish is placed beneath the cooking article, and almost in the burning embers, to receive the drippings. The spit is generally turned by hand, for Roasting Jacks are more rare even than stoves.

For the other culinary operations English frying-pan, and grid-iron are called in to their respective offices; whilst a couple of frying handees, the one filled with fire, forming a lid to the other, generally supply the place of oven for home-made tarts and patties. For larger baked dishes, unless the cook-room contain an oven, which, though not common, is far from rare, the services of the baker are available.

Such and so furnished then is the interior of an Indian cook-house,—that is—lest I even yet appear to generalize—the *majority* of cook-houses. (1849)

AN ARTIST IN INDIA[292]

## 4. *Domingo, the cook*

Do not remember who was the author of the observation that a great nation in a state of decay betakes itself to the fine arts. Perhaps no one has made the observation yet. It is certainly among the records of my brain, but I may possibly have put it there myself. If so, I make it now, for the possibilities of originality are getting scarce and will soon disappear from the face of the earth as completely as the mastodon. The present application of the saying is to the people of Goa, who, while they carry through the world pat-

ronymics which breathe of conquest and discovery, devote their
energies rather to the violin and the art of cookery. The caviller
may object to the application of the words 'fine art' to culinary
operations, but the objection rests on superficial thought. A deeper
view will show that art is in the artist, not in his subject or his
materials. Perusal of the Codes of the Financial Department
showed me many years ago that the retrenchment of my pay and
allowances could be elevated to a fine art by devotion of spirit,
combined with a fine sense of law. And to Domingo the preparation
of dinner is indeed a fine art. Trammel his genius, confine him within
the limits of what is commonly called a 'plain dinner.' and he cannot
cook. He stews his meat before putting it into a pie, he thickens his
custard with flour instead of eggs, he roasts a leg of mutton by
boiling it first and doing 'littlee brown' afterwards; in short, what
does he not do? It is true of all his race. How loathsome were
Pedro's mutton chops, and Camilo could not ooil potatoes decently
for a dinner of less than four courses. But let him loose on a *burra
khana,* give him *carte blanche* as to sauces and essences and spicery,
and all his latent faculties and concealed accomplishments unfold
themselves like a lotus flower in the morning. No one could have
suspected that the shame-faced little man harboured such resources. If he has not always the subtlest perception of the harmonies of flavours, what a mastery he shows of strong effects and
striking contrasts, what manual dexterity, what rapidity and certainty in all his operations! And the marvel increases when we
consider the simplicity of his implements and materials. His studio is
fitted with half a dozen small fireplaces, and furnished with an
assortment of copper pots, a chopper, two tin spoons—but he can
do without these,—a ladle made of half a cocoanut shell at the end
of a stick, and a slab of stone with a stone roller on it; also a rickety
table, a very gloomy and ominous looking table, whose undulating
surface is chopped and hacked and scarred, begrimed, besmeared,
smoked, oiled, stained with juices of many substances. On this table
he minces meat, chops onions, rolls pastry and sleeps; a very useful
table. In the midst of these he bustles about, putting his face at
intervals into one of his fires and blowing through a short bamboo
tube, which is his bellows, such a potent blast that for a moment his
whole head is enveloped in a cloud of ashes and cinders, which also
descend copiously on the half-made tart and the *souffle* and the
custard. Then he takes up an egg, gives it three smart raps with the

nail of his forefinger, and in half a second the yoke is in one vessel and the white in another. The fingers of his left hand are his strainer. Every second or third egg he tosses aside, having detected, as it passed through the said strainer that age had rendered it unsuitable for his purposes; sometimes he does not detect this. From eggs he proceeds to onions, then he is taking the stones out of raisins, or shelling peas. There is a standard English cookery book which commences most of its instructions with the formula, 'wash your hands carefully, using a nail brush.' Domingo does not observe this ceremony, but he often wipes his fingers upon his pantaloons. It occurs to me, however, that I do not wisely pursue this theme; for the mysteries of Domingo's craft are no fit subject for the gratification of an irreverent curiosity. Those words of the poet,

> What ignorance is bliss,
> 'Tis folly to be wise.

have no truer application. You will reap the bliss when you sit down to the savoury result.

Though Domingo is naturally shy, and does not make a display of his attainments, he is a man of education, and is quite prepared, if you wish it, to write out his *menu*. Here is a sample:

*Soup.*
Salary Soup.

*Fis.*
Heel fish fry.

*Madish.*
Russel Pups. Wormsil mole.

*Joint.*
Roast Bastard.

*Toast.*
Anchovy Poshteg.

*Puddin.*
Billimunj. Ispunj roli.

I must take this opportunity to record a true story of a *menu*, though it does not properly pertain to Domingo, but an ingenious Ramaswamy, of Madras. This man's master liked everything very proper, and insisted on a written *menu* at every meal. One morning Ramaswamy was much embarrassed, for the principal dish at breakfast was to be devilled turkey. 'Devil very bad word,' he said to himself; 'how can write?' At last he solved the difficulty, and the dish appeared as 'D——d turkey.'

Our surprise at Domingo's attainments is no doubt due very much to the humble attire in which we are accustomed to see him, his working dress being a *quondam* white cotton jacket and a pair of blue checked pantaloons of a strong material made in jails, or two pairs, the sound parts of one being arranged to underlie the holes in the other. When once we have seen the gentleman dressed for church on a festival day, with the beaver which has descended to him from his illustrious grandfather's benevolent master respectfully held in his hand, and his well brushed hair shining with a bountiful allowance of cocoanut ointment, surprise ceases. He is indeed a much respected member of society, and enjoys the esteem of his club, where he sometimes takes chambers when out of employment. By his fellow servants, too, he is recognised as a professional man, and called The Maistrie, but, like ourselves, he is an exile, and, like some of us, he is separated from his wife and children, so his thoughts run much upon furlough and ultimate retirement, and he adopts a humble style of life with the object of saving money. In this object he succeeds most remarkably. Little as we know of the home life of our Hindoo servants, we know almost less about that of Domingo, for he rarely has his family with him. Is he a fond husband and an indulgent father? I fancy he is when his better nature is uppermost, but I am bound to confess that the cardinal vice of his character is cruelty, not the passive cruelty of the pure Asiatic, but that ferocious cruelty which generally marks an infusion of European blood. The infusion in him has filtered through so many generations that it must be very weak indeed, but it shows itself. When I see an emaciated crow with the point of its beak chopped off, so that it cannot pick up its food, or another with a tin pot fastened with wire to its bleeding nose, I know whose handiwork is there. Domingo suffers grievously from the depredations of crows, and when his chance comes he enjoys a savage retribution. Some allowance must be made for the hardening influence of his profession; familiarity with murder makes him callous. When he executes a *moorgee* he does it in the way of sport, and sits, like an ancient Roman, *verso pollice,* enjoying the spectacle of its dying struggles.

According to his lights Domingo is a religious man; that is to say, he wears a necklace of red beads, eats fish on Fridays, observes festivals and holidays, and gives pretty liberally to the church under pressure. So he maintains a placid condition of conscience while his monthly remittance to Goa exceeds the amount of his salary. He rises early on Sunday morning to go to confession, and I would give something to have the place, just one day, of the good father to whom he unbosoms himself. But perhaps I am wrong. I daresay he believes he has nothing to confess.

One story more to teach us to judge charitably of Domingo. A lady was inveighing to a friend against the whole race of Indian cooks as dirty, disorderly, and dishonest. She had managed to secure the services of a Chinese cook, and was much pleased with the contrast. Her friend did not altogether agree with her, and was sceptical about the immaculate Chinaman. 'Put it to the test,' said the lady; 'just let us pay a visit to your kitchen, and then come and see mine.' So they went together. What need to describe the *Bobberjee-Khana*? They glanced round, and hurried out, for it was too horrible to be endured long. When they went to the Chinaman's kitchen, the contrast was indeed striking. The pots and pans shone like silver; the table was positively sweet; everything was in its proper place, and Chang himself, sitting on his box, was washing his feet in the soup tureen! (*c.* 1889)

E.H. AITKIN[293]


# F. MUSIC

## 1. *Musical modes of the Hindus*

The most valuable work, that I have seen, and perhaps the most valuable that exists, on the subject of *Indian* musick, is named *Ragavibodha,* or *The Doctrine of Musical Modes;* and it ought here to be mentioned very particularly, because none of the *Pandits,* in our provinces, nor any of those from *Casi* or *Cashmir,* to whom I have shown it, appear to have known that it was extant; and it may be considered as a treasure in the history of the art, which the zeal of Colonel Polier has brought into light, and perhaps has preserved from destruction. He had purchased, among other curiosities, a volume containing a number of separate essays on musick in prose and verse, and in a great variety of idioms: besides tracts in *Arabick, Hindi,* and *Persian,* it included a short essay in *Latin* by ALSTEDIUS;

with an interlineary *Persian* translation, in which the passages quoted from Lucretius and Virgil made a singular appearance: but the brightest gem in the string was the *Ragavibodha,* which the Colonel permitted my *Nagari* writer to transcribe, and the transcript was diligently collated with the original by my *Pandit* and myself. If seems a very ancient composition, but is less old unquestionably than the *Tatnacara* by Sarnga Deva which is more than once mentioned in it, and a copy of which Mr. Burrow procured in his journey to *Heridwar:* the name of the author was So'ma, and he appears to have been a practical musician as well as a great scholar and an elegant poet; for the whole book, without excepting the strains noted in letters, which fill the fifth and last chapter of it, consists of masterly couplets in the melodious metre called *A'rya*; the *first, third* and *fourth* chapters explain the doctrine of musical sounds, their division and succession, the variations of scales by temperament, and the enumeration of modes on a system totally different from those, which will presently be mentioned; and the *second* chapter contains a minute description of different *Vinas* with rules for playing on them. This book alone would enable me, were I master of my time, to compose a treatise on the musick of *India,* with assistance, in the practical part, from an *European* professor and a native player on the *Vina*; but I have leisure only to present you with an essay, and even that, I am conscious, must be very superficial: it may be sometimes, but, I trust, not often erroneous; and I have spared no pains to secure myself from error.

In the literature of the *Hindus* all nature is animated and personified; every fine art is declared to have been revealed from heaven; and all knowledge, divine and human, is traced to its source in the *Vedas*; among which the *Samaveda* was intended to be *sung,* whence the reader or singer of it is called *Udgatri* or *Samaga*: in Colonel Polier's copy of it the strains are noted in figures, which it may not be impossible to decypher. On account of this distinction, say the *Brahmens,* the *supreme preserving power,* in the form of Crishna, having enumerated in the *Gita* various orders of beings, to the chief of which he compares himself, pronounces, that *among the* Vedas *he was 'the* Saman.' From that *Veda* was accordingly derived the *Upaveda* of the *Gandharbas*, or musicians in Indra's heaven; so that the divine art was communicated to our species by Brahma himself or by his *active power* Sereswati, the Goddess of Speech; and their mythological son Na'red, who was in truth an ancient lawgiver and astronomer, invented the *Vina,* called also *Cach'hapi,* or *Testudo*: a very remarkable fact which may be added to the other proofs of a resemblance between that *Indian* God, and the MERCURY of the *Latians.* Among inspired mortals the first musician is believed to have been the sage BHERAT, who the inventor, they say, of *Natacs,* or dramas, represented with songs and dances, and author of a musical system, which bears his name. If we can rely on MIRZAKHAN, there are four principal *Matas,* or systems, the first of which is ascribed to ISWARA, or OSIRIS; the second to BHERAI; the third to HANUMAT, or PA VAN, the PAN of *India,* supposed to be the son of PAVANA, the regent of air; and the fourth to CALLINATH, a *Rishi,* or *Indian* philosopher, eminently skilled in musick, theoretical and practical: all four are mentioned by SOMA; and it is the *third* of them, which must be very ancient, and seems to have been extremely popular, that I propose to explain after a few introductory remarks; but I may here observe with SOMA, who exhibits a system of his own, and with the author of the *Narayan,* who mentions a great many others, that almost every kingdom and province had a peculiar style of melody, and very different names for the modes, as well as a different arrangement and enumeration of them. (1784)

WILLIAM JONES[294]

## 2. Instrumental music in Ladakh

The Lamas (of Ladakh) then sat down in rows from east to west, from the door to the shrine, upon cushions of felt, or low wooden benches. One of them had a sort of reading-desk before him, with the leaves of a book, from which he read, and was followed by the rest in the recitation. They then began a performance of instrumental music, almost each man being provided with some instrument. The majority had small flat drums, but I noticed also two horns or cornets of copper, two large cymbals, two haut boys, two trumpets, and a bell. The haut boys were made of wood with silver mouthpieces, and shifting seeds. The trumpets were of copper, eight or ten feet long, and made with three joints, like those of a telescope. The open end was about five inches in diameter, the mouth-piece small. The tone was clear and deep, and might be heard to a great distance, but it requires long practices to blow the instrument properly. Nothing could be harsher than the sounds emitted by unpractised players. In the temple the trumpet rested on the ground: when used in processions a young Lama assists in carrying it. The drum was not above five inches deep, and about twenty in breadth. It was suspended by a ring on one side of a cord sketched across the chamber, and, being selected by the player with his left hand, was beaten by him with a crooked metallic rod, capped with leather on the striking end. The recitations or chants alternated with the music though monotonous, was not unpleasing, and the strength and spirit of the singers and players were kept up by copious libations of tea and chang. (1819–25)

WILLIAM MOORCROFT[295]

## 3. Music, musicians and instruments

... the Hindoos, like the Greeks and Arabs, sing only in unisons; though in the native concerts I have sometimes distinguished a third or a fifth struck upon the final note. But this is mere instinct; the human ear naturally conceives these harmonic intervals, and this is so true that I have heard bands of Mozambique negroes, whose music is strictly that of nature, sing in three parts, and their ear led them instinctively to the common chord, and the chord of the dominant seventh. The Hindoos pretend to musical science, and are, therefore, disposed to reject that which Nature teaches them. The consequence is, that when they light unconsciously upon and sound a harmonic interval, with its fundamental note, it breaks the monotony of their unisons, and they consider it a blemish. ...

Captain Luard exhibits among his groups of Indian figures a band of itinerant musicians, such as are commonly engaged by wealthy natives at their entertainments, for the niggard remuneration of a few pice—a small copper coin, in value about the third of our penny. In these bands there is occasionally a mixture of Hindoo and Mohammedan performers, which is a symptom that the inveterate prejudices of caste are fast subsiding throughout India. This union of interest, indeed, among the votaries of Mohammed and of Brahma, can only take place where those prejudices are despised, which is now by no means unfrequently the case among the lowest of the four civil divisions of the Hindoo population.

These bands of native performers are commonly seated upon a coarse rug in the veranda of the house where they exercise their skill for the amusement of the lord of the mansion and his guests. Usually there is a vocal performer, who beats time with the fingers of his right hand on the palm of his left, while he is accompanied by his companions on their respective instruments.

In Captain Luard's group one is represented playing upon a sort of trilateral guitar, an instrument certainly not common among Hindoo musicians, as it is neither enumerated by Ward nor by the author to whose works I have before alluded. Another is playing on a serinda, the common violin of Hindostan; while a third performs upon two drums, one of which he strikes with the fingers of his left hand, and rubs the other with those of his right, as Europeans occasionally play the tambourine. (1838)

JOHN HOBART COUNTER[296]

## 4. Specimens of Assamese music

Assam is so intersected by rivers, that the Assamese prefer moving about in their little canoes to travelling by land; and Dooms or Nudeals (watermen) seem greatly to enjoy themselves on these boat trips, for they are always singing songs as they paddle along. A facetious friend has felicitously given me the following version of one of these boat songs universally sung throughout the province:—

### ASSAMESE BOAT SONG

"Keep the boithas cheerly going;
Rough and fierce the river's flowing,
     Ram bol, Hurry bol, Hurry bol Aee.

"See! the sun is fast declining,
To the moon his charge resigning,
     Ram bol, Hurry bol, Hurry bol Aee.

"Pull away, boys, nothing fearing,
Though the rapids we are nearing,
     Ram bol, Hurry bol, Hurry bol Aee.

"In the well-plied oar confiding,
Safely o'er them we are gliding,
     Ram bol, Hurry bol, Hurry bol Aee.

"Keep her clear that granite block there,
See, she nears the sunken rock there,

# ASSAMESE BOAT SONG

# SONG

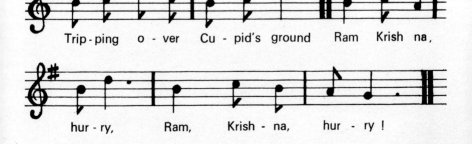

Ram bol, Hurry bol, Hurry bol Aee.

"Now the threatened danger's over
Nothing from her course shall move her,
   Ram bol, Hurry bol, Hurry bol Aee.

"Soon we'll make the ghat, my hearties!
Spend the night in jovial parties,
   Ram bol, Hurry bol, Hurry bol Aee."

  For the amusement of my fair readers. I have also
added other specimens of Assamese harmony.

## AN ASSAMESE AIR

"Shades of night are falling fast—pull away, eh, hey;
All our toil will soon be past—pull away, eh, hey.

"Round Thamlya's point we steer—pull away, eh, hey;
See the Puckah Ghat appear—pull away, eh, hey.

"Strike together for your lives—pull away, eh, hey,
Towards our sweethearts and our wives—pull away, eh, hey.

"First we smoke the fragrant weed—pull away, eh, hey,
Morpheus then will slumbers speed—pull away, eh, hey.

"We must work if we would live—pull away, eh, hey;
Sahib will our backshish give—pull away, ey, hey."

## SONG

"Come and join this merry round,
Tripping over Cupid's ground,
   Ram, Krishna, Hurry.

"Dance and sing we all night long,
This shall be the only song,
   Ram, Krishna, Hurry.

"Love and music all the theme,
Till the ruddy morning beam,
   Ram,  Krishna, Hurry.

"Let the ruddy morn arrive,
It shall but our song revive,
   Ram, Krishna, Hurry.

"Aided by the solar ray,
Blithe we'll sing throughout the day,
   Ram, Krishna, Hurry.

"Let the shadow upwards tend;
Let the weary sun descend;
Still our song shall find no end!
Ram, Krishna, Hurry."(1850)

JOHN BUTLER[297]

## AN ASSAMESE AIR

Shades of night are fal - ling fast,
pull a - way, he - ey,
pull a - way, he - ey.

# 20 Architecture and Monuments

## 1.  Towns and buildings

The towns and villages have inner gates;[1] the walls are wide and
high; the streets and lanes are tortuous, and the roads winding.
The thoroughfares are dirty and the stalls arranged on both sides of
the road with appropriate signs. Butchers, fishers, dancers, executioners, and scavengers, and so on, have their abodes without
the city. In coming and going these persons are bound to keep on the
left side of the road till they arrive at their homes. Their houses are
surrounded by low walls and form the suburbs. The earth being soft
and muddy, the walls of the towns are mostly built of brick or tiles.
The towers on the walls are constructed of wood or bamboo; the
houses have balconies and belvederes, which are made of wood, with
a coating of lime or mortar and covered with tiles. The different
buildings have the same form as those in China: rushes, or dry
branches, or tiles, or boards are used for covering them. The walls
are covered with lime and mud, mixed with cow's dung for purity.
At different seasons they scatter flowers about. Such are some of
their different customs. (629–645 A.D.)

HIUEN TSIANG[298]

## 2.  Housing

The buildings are all base, of mudde, one story high, except in
Surat, where are some stone houses, but I know not by what policie,
the King seekes the ruine of all the ancient Cities which were
bravely built, and now lye desolate and ruined. His owne houses are
of stone, both in good forme and faire, but his great men build not

[1] Such is the meaning generally assigned to the symbols *leu yen*. I [Samuel Beal]
do not understand the translation given by Julien; the texts perhaps are different.

for want of inheritance, but as farre as I have yet seene, live in Tents, or houses worse then a Cottager; yet where the King affects, as at Agra, because it is a City erected by him, the buildings are (as is reported) faire and of carved stone. (1615)

THOMAS ROE[299]

### 3. Tippoo's fortress

This stupendous fortress, situated nineteen miles nearly west by south from Bangalore, enjoys such advantages from nature, as to need little assistance from art; though art seems to have neglected nothing to render it absolutely impregnable. It is a vast mountain of rock, supposed to rise above half a mile in perpendicular height, from a base of eight or ten miles in circumference.

Completely surrounded by walls, and defended by cross walls and barriers wherever it was deemed accessible, it has the farther advantage of being divided above by a vast chasm, separating it into two hills; each of which having it's own defences, two distinct citadels are formed, capable of being maintained independent of the lower works. Beside all this, added to the rocky hills and natural forest thickened with clumps of planted bamboos, which constitute no easily surmountable barricade, the pestiferous atmosphere threatens with inevitable destruction the hardiest troops, should they lie long before it. Hence it's significant appellation of Savendroog, or the Rock of Death. So confident indeed was Tippoo Sultan in it's strength, that he was highly pleased when he heard the British troops had run their heads against the tremendous Gurdun Sheko, a name he had himself given it, implying the Neck of Majesty; and his courtiers even congratulated him on the event, as on a victory. (1794)

MR. HOME[300]

### 4. Jama Masjid, Delhi

We had now only to view the *Jumna Musjeed,* or principal place of Mahometan worship in this city; for which purpose some of the party set forward immediately after breakfast. This stands in the middle of the city. The ascent to it is by a number of large, handsome, stone steps, on three sides of an immense square area, out of three principal streets. To this area you pass, one either side,

'Eastern Gate of the Jumma Masjid at Delhi', drawn by William Daniell

through a double gateway, having apartments over it crowned by a parapet of cupolas. The area is arcaded on three sides—the fourth is the *musjeed,* or chapel, at one corner of which a saint is interred within an enclosure or skreen of marble net-work, covered by a superb canopy: near this no person is permitted to approach with shoes on. The large area is paved all over with white marble, having a square reservoir of water in the centre. This *musjeed* is surmounted by three marble domes, with gilt ornaments of a spiral form on the tops of each, and is supported at either end by a handsome minaret of granite three stories high, each story having a balcony round it with marble net-work railing, and on the top of each a dome, open all round, supported upon pillars of granite. A spiral staircase leads to the top. The ascent to the *musjeed* from the area was by seven steps of granite, to a terrace of marble twenty feet broad, on which it stood, extending the whole length of the front. (1804–14)

A. DEARE[301]

## 5. The great cave at Carli

I am told that we are now at least six thousand feet above the level of the sea, and the greatest part of that height we have ascended to-day. We left Compowli in the dark at five o'clock, and reached the foot of the ghaut at sunrise. The ascent was so steep and rugged, that I soon left my palankeen, and with one of my companions walked up the mountain. It is impossible to describe the exquisite beauty of the landscape. High mountains and bold projecting rocks, overhang deep woods of trees unknown to Europeans. Flowering shrubs of most delicious perfumes, and creeping-plants of every various hue, form natural bowers as they hang from tree to tree, and now shewing, now concealing the distant ocean, delight the eye at every step; while here and there an opening like a lawn, with herds of antelopes, makes you forget that the tiger prowls through the of antelopes, that makes you forget that the tiger prowls through the overhanging forest, and that the serpent lurks beneath the many-coloured bower.

At Condowli, a pretty village just above the ghaut, the hamauls stopped to bathe and drink, and to claim the fee for coming up the mountain, which is a sheep; it costs from one to two rupees, and is divided between the twelve hamauls, who belong to one palankeen, for very few Hindoos abstain entirely from animal food, although none eat of the cow or of the hog. Here I got into my palankeen, and went on to the foot of the hill where the cave of Carli is situated. As it was near twelve o'clock when we reached the village below the cave, we heartily wished that we had ordered our breakfast to await us there, for we had half a mile to climb up a rugged rock on foot, in the eye of the mid-day sun of India; and having tasted nothing since dinner yesterday, we were so exhausted when we reached it, that we could hardly raise our eyes to observe the wonders of the cavern.

When at length we looked round, we almost fancied ourselves in a Gothic cathedral. Instead of the low flat roof of the cave of Elephanta, this rises to an astonishing height, with a highly coved roof, supported by twenty-one pillars on each side, and terminating in a semicircle. Opposite to the entrance is a large temple (if I may call it so,) not hollowed, with a dome, on which is fixed a huge teak umbrella, as a mark of respect. Without the pillars there is a kind of aisle on each side of about six feet wide; the length of the cave is forty paces, and its breadth is fourteen. Here are no sculptures within the cavern except on the capitals of the pillars. The columns are mostly hexagons, though the number of angles varies; the bases are formed like compressed cushions; the capitals resemble an inverted flower, or a bell, on the top of which are two elephants, with two riders on each; and on several of the columns there are inscriptions in a character not hitherto decyphered. There is a very curious circumstance in this cavern, which is, that the roof is ribbed with teak wood, cut to fit the cove exactly, and supported by teeth in the timber fitting to corresponding holes in the rock; I imagine this to be a precaution against the destruction of this beautiful work by the monsoon rains. The cave of Carli is really one of the most magnificent chambers I ever saw, both as to proportion and work-manship. It is situated near the top of a wooded mountain, com-manding one of the finest prospects in the world; its reservoirs cut, like itself, out of the living rock, overflow with the purest water, and the country around it is fertile enough to supply every thing in abundance for human subsistence. The cave is a temple, and on each side there are corridores, with cells proper for the residence of priests and their families. But the most laboured part of the work is the portico of the temple. One-third of its height is filled up by a variety of figures, one of which, in a dancing posture, is remarkable for gracefulness of design, and the ends are occupied to the same height by gigantic elephants; above these is a cornice of reeds, bound together by fillets at equal distances, and the space over it is filled by small arched niches, finshed with the same cornice. The centre is occupied by a horse-shoe arch, with a pointed moulding above, and below there is a square door of entrance to the cave. To protect the portico from the injuries of the weather, a rude screen was left at the entrance, part of which has fallen in; before it there is an enormous pillar, crowned with three animals, and now overgrown with moss and grass. (17 December 1809)

MARIA GRAHAM[302]

## 6. The Gate, Akbar's mausoleum, Sikandra

This magnificent Gate (of the Mausoleum of the Emperor Akbar, at Secundra) is built of reddish free-stone, and the ornamental part inlaid with stones of various colours. The minars are of white marble, executed with great neatness; originally they were crowned with turrets, which have been destroyed by lightning. The Mausoleum within the garden, composed of the same materials, has a striking and grand effect; at the top of which, on the terrace, is placed the body of the Emperor, enclosed in a white marble tomb, elegantly ornamented.

Secundra is nine miles from Agra, and about one hundred and twenty eight southward of Delhi. (1812)

THOMAS AND WILLIAM DANIELL[303]

## 7. The temple of Barolli

We now come to the grand temple itself, which is fifty-eight feet in height, and in the ancient form peculiar to the temples of Siva. The body of the edifice, in which is the sanctum of the god, and over which rises its pyramidal *sikr*, is a square of only twenty-one feet, but the addition of the domed vestibule *(munduf)* and portico makes it forty-four by twenty-one. An outline of this by Ghassi, a native artist (who labours at Oodipoor tor the same daily pay as a tailor, carpenter, or other artizan), will give a tolerably good notion of its appearance, though none of its beauty. The whole is covered with mythological sculpture, without as well as within, emblematic of the 'great god' *(Mahadeo),* who is the giver, as well as the destroyer, of life. In a niche outside, to the south, he is armed against the Dytes (Titans), the *roond-mala,* or skull-chaplet, reaching to his knees, and in seven of his arms are offensive weapons. His cap is the frustrum of a cone, composed of snakes interlaced, with a fillet of skulls: the *cupra* is in his hand, and the victims are scattered around. On his right is one of the maids of slaughter *(Jogini)* drunk with blood, the cup still at her lip, and her countenance expressive of vacuity; while below, on the left is a female personification of Death, mere skin and bone: a sickle *(koorpi)* in her right hand, its knob a death's head, completes this group of the attributes of destruction.

To the west is Mahadeo under another form, a beautiful and animated statue, the expression mild, as when he went forth to entice the mountain-nymph, Mera, to his embrace. His tiara is a blaze of finely-executed ornaments, and his snake-wreath, which hangs round him as a garland, has a clasp of two heads of Schesnag (the serpent-king), while Nanda below is listening with placidity to the sound of the *dumroo*. His *cupra,* and *karg,* or skull-cap, and sword, which he is in the attitude of using, are the only accompaniments denoting the god of blood.

The northern compartment is a picture, disgustingly faithful, of death and its attributes, vulgarly known as *Bhooka Mata,* or the personification of famine, lank and bare; her necklace, like her lord's, of skulls. Close by are two mortals in the last stage of existence, so correctly represented as to excite an unpleasant surprise. The outline, I may say, is anatomically correct. The mouth is half open and distorted, and although the eye is closed in death, an expression of mental anguish seems still to linger upon the features. A beast of prey is approaching the dead body; while, by way of contrast, a male figure, in all the vigour of youth and health, lies prostrate at her feet.

Such is a faint description of the sculptured niches on each of the external faces of the *mindra,* whence the spire rises, simple and solid. In order, however, to be distinctly understood, I shall give some slight iconographic details. First, is the *mindra* or *cella,* in which is the statue of the god; then the *munduf,* or, in architectural nomenclature, the *pronaos;* and third, the portico, with which we shall begin, though it transcends all description.

Like all temples dedicated to Bal-Siva, the vivifier, or 'sun-god,' it faces the east. The portico projects several feet beyond the *munduf,* and has four superb columns in front, of which the outline by Ghassi conveys but a very imperfect idea. Flat fluted pilasters are placed on

'Akbar's Tomb, Secundra', drawn by W. Purser

either side of the entrance to the *munduf,* serving as a support to the internal *torun,* or triumphal arch, and a single column intervenes on each side between the pilasters and the columns in front. The proportions are perfect; and though the difference of diameter between the superior and inferior portions of the shaft is less than the Grecian standard, there is no want of elegance of effect, whilst it gives an idea of more grandeur. The frieze is one mass of sculptured figures, generally of human beings, male and female, in pairs; the horned monster termed *Gras,* separating the different pairs. The internal *torun* or triumphal arch, which is invariably attached to all ancient temples of the sun-god, is of that peculiar curvature formed by the junction of two arcs of a circle from different centres, a form of arch well known in Gothic and Saracenic architecture, but which is an essential characteristic of the most ancient Hindu temples. The head of a *gras* crowns its apex, and on the outline is a concatenation of figures armed with daggers, apparently ascending the arch to strike the monster. The roof of the *munduf (pronaos)* . . .cannot be described: its various parts must be examined with microscopic nicety in order to enter into detail. In the whole of the ornaments there is an exact harmony which I have seen no where else; even the miniature elephants are in the finest proportions, and exquisitely carved.

. . . The engraving falls short of the drawing of the ingenious Ghassi, my native artist, who again is but a humble imitator of the original. Of the exterior I shall not attempt further description: it is a grand, a wonderful effort of the *silpi* (architect) one series rising above and surpassing the other, from the base to the urn which surmounts the pinnacle.

The *sanctum* contains the symbol of the god, whose local appellation is *Rori Barolli,* a corruption of *Bal-rori,* from the circumstance of Balnat'h, the sun-god, being here typified by an orbicular stone termed *rori,* formed by attrition in the *choolis* or whirlpools of the Chumbul, near which the temple stands, and to which phenomena it probably owed its foundation. This symbolic *rori* is not fixed, but lies in a groove in the internal ring of the *Yoni*; and so nicely is it poised, that with a very moderate impulse it will continue revolving while the votary recites a tolerably long hymn to the object of his adoration. The old ascetic, who had long been one of the zealots of Barolli, amongst his other wonders gravely told me, that with the momentum given by his little finger, in former days, he could make it keep on its course much longer than now with the application of all his strength. (1832)

JAMES TOD[304]

## 8. *Humayun's tomb*

In the midst of the ruins of Old Delhi, about four or five miles from the south entrance, or Agra-gate, of the present city, the tomb of Humaioon is situated. This melancholy but picturesque scene of desolation is well described in Hamilton's East India Gazetteer, in the following words. 'The ruins of Old Delhi cover the plain for an extent of nearly eight miles (diameter) to the south of the modern Shahjehanabad, and connects that city with the village of Cuttub, exhibiting throughout this great tract one of the most striking scenes of desolation to be met with throughout the whole world. Some of the gates, caravanseras, and mosques of the ancient city, are still tolerably entire, but the objects most worthy of attention are the two splendid mausoleums of the Emperor Humaioon, and Sefdar Jung; and smaller but not less elegant sepultures of Khaneh Azim, the Emperor Mahomet Shah, and Jahanara Begum, daughter of Shah Jehan; the fort of Shere Shah, the temporary reviver of the Patan dynasty; and the curious remains of old forts and other buildings, ascribed to the Emperor Feroze Shah.'

'Humaioon's Tomb,' says Bishop Heber, 'is a noble building of granite, inlaid with marble, in a very chaste and simple style of Gothic architecture. It is surrounded by a large garden with terraces and fountains, all now gone to decay, except one of the latter, which enables the poor people, who live in the outbuildings of the tomb, to cultivate a little wheat. The garden itself is surrounded by an embattled wall, with towers, four gateways, and a cloister within, all the way round. In the centre of the square is a platform of about 20 feet high, and I should apprehend 200 feet square, supported also by cloisters, and ascended by four great flights of granite steps. Above, rises the tomb, also a square with a great dome of white marble in its centre. The apartments within are a circular room, about as big as the Ratcliffe Library, in the centre of which lies, under a small raised slab, the unfortunate prince to whose memory this fine building is raised. In the angles are smaller apartments, where other branches of his family are interred. From the top of the building I was surprised to see that we had still ruins on every side;

'Tomb of Humaioon, Delhi', drawn by Captain R. Elliot

and that, more particularly to the westward, and where old Indraput stood, the desolation apparently extended to a range of barren hills, seven or eight miles off.' (1833)

ROBERT ELLIOT[305]

## 9.  Gwalior fort

We were all glad that we did not miss Gwalior fort. The carriage took us to the commencement of the old town, where we found the elephants, and on them proceeded to the entrance of, and part of the way up, the flight of steps which leads to the fort itself. We might have gone the whole way on the elephants, but preferred walking. The approach is perhaps the finest part of it  The staircase, as it may be called, is carried up the side of the rock, and is overhung by the great battlemented walls of the castle towering over it in all their feudal grandeur. The walls are curiously ornamented with glazed tiles of various colours, placed in patterns representing trees, etc. Two or three turns in the road add to the strength of the defences, before reaching the gateway, which leads into the interior, and is a genuine Hindoo archway, or rather is not an archway, properly so called, at all, for the Hindoos knew nothing of the principle of the arch, but built their gateways by laying one stone upon another. ... Even their circular domes, of which there are specimens at Gyah, Bindrabund and here also, are built on the same principle. (1852)

FRANCIS EGERTON[306]

## 10.  The caves of Ellora

The Ellora caves are of three kinds, and belong to three different periods. Some are Buddhist; some are Brahminical; and there is besides a group of Jain caves belonging to a later epoch. The remote antiquity of their birth, once an article of European faith, has been proved to be a delusion. But, after all, the investigations of modern Orientalists, though they may have assisted to explode some errors, have added but little to our knowledge of material facts. There is still space for speculation and conjecture as why and how these mighty excavations were made, and why, after such an enormous expenditure of labour, these temples and monasteries, which erst resounded with the worship of the gods, and were swarming with

human life, have become silent and deserted. There is a tradition
that the Eeloo Rajah caused the works to be commenced as a
thank-offering, after being cured of a loathsome disorder by immer-
sion in a neighbouring tank; and the alleged date of this event
corresponds with our later knowledge of the date of the first series,
or Buddhist caves. It is supposed that the emulation of the Brahmins
was fired by the success of the great efforts of their rivals, and that
they resolved to equal, if not to excel them. But how such a prodigious amount of human labour was got together, whether it was
voluntary labour freely given for love of the gods, or whether it was
forced labour, or paid labour; whether, indeed, the workmen were
enthusiasts, or serfs, or hirelings, we do not know, neither do we
know whether the work was executed by the contemporaneous
labour of vast multitudes, or of smaller numbers of men ranging
over a larger number of years—though there is much to favour the
latter hypothesis. If the former is to be sustained, we may wonder
how such a vast congeries of people was fed. Then again, we are
driven into mazes of speculation when we think how it came to pass
that stupendous works of this kind, the leading object and the
prevailing sentiment of which are their durability, should, after the
lapse of a few centuries, have become merely 'monuments of an
unaccomplished purpose.' There is, however, in this direction, one
rational conjecture. They were desecrated by the Mahomedans. It is
stated that in the time of Aurungzebe, kine were slaughtered in the
temples, and other acts of sacrilege committed. But, whatsoever the
history of this great Indian Ichabod, these holy places, to which ruin
is denied, are little more than melancholoy deserts. A few fakirs find
shelter, at times, in their recesses, and every now and then a
Brahmin from a distance, moved as much perhaps by curiosity as by
spiritual zeal, comes to make his orisons there. But it is little more
than a great desolation.

It was, doubtless, a grand conception thus to bring together in a
vast massive whole the work of God and the labour of man. It must
not, however, be supposed that these excavations present the original idea of a Hindoo temple, as it first suggested itself to the minds of
the priests. For there is evidence in them that they are imitations of
edifices constructed of mixed materials brought together and joined
together by human hands. Neither form can be said to have preceded the other; for beasts burrowed and birds built. But it is a
remarkable proof either of the slavery of imitation, or of a strong

'Ruins South Side of Old Delhi', drawn by T. Boys

superstitious desire to preserve a pre-existing type of sacred architecture, that in some of these temples beams and rafters of wood are simulated by rock-cut devices. These servile copies remain, whilst the original conceptions have been obliterated by the hand of time. Mr. [James] Fergusson, whose authority it is always a pleasure to quote, observes, that they are the only architectural remains which 'serve to illustrate the Arts in History of the period to which they belong. The structural monuments erected during the early centuries of our era are scarce and widely scattered over the whole area of the country, and few, even of these, are in the state in which they were first executed; whereas one of the great merits of cave architecture is that it remains unchanged and unchangeable during the whole period of its existence.' And, again, with reference to the imitation of constructive art, of which I have spoken, the same erudite writer observes: 'One of the most interesting points brought out by the study of the caves, is the fact, that the earliest are mere petrifactions of wooden buildings. The mortices, the tenons, and every form of wooden construction, is repeated in the rock in the earliest caves; and frequently even the woodwork still remains as if placed there to support the mountains, instead of being merely intended to recall the structure of the metal-covered or boarded roof, from which it was copied.' . . .

It is necessary that, in describing such works, the writer should be careful with respect to the words which he employs. The Kylas temple is not like the majority of the rock-cut temples and monasteries, an excavation in the side of a rocky mountain, which has externally a beginning, but no ending, and is architecturally only a great interior. The mind which conceived the idea of the Kylas, was bent on excelling these old types, and to present to the eye a perfect edifice with external walls; but all hewn out of a single stone—a grand monolithic temple. So the outer rock was cut into, leaving an open space—a court-yard as it were—around the contemplated temples, which was to be carved out of the immense block which was thus left open on all sides to the hands of the carvers. The labour of this far exceeded all other labours, and the Brahmins rejoiced in a victory over their rivals.

The architectural design of this temple evidently came from Southern India, and, perhaps too, some of the work. 'Lanka' signifies the island which we know as Ceylon; and the sculptures of the great Kylas temple represent an episode of Hindoo scriptural

history, the scene of which is the southern extremity of the Indian
Peninsula and the island at its foot. The legend is, that a famous
giant, of more than Titanic power, named Ravana, carried off Seeta,
the betrothed wife of Rama—or the incarnate Vishnu—to his kingdom in Ceylon. Rama, then calling in Hunooman, the monkey-god,
to his aid, set out for Southern India, resolute to rescue his bride and
to avenge his wrongs. But, having reached the foot of the Peninsula,
the allies were brought up by the water, which impeded their further
progress. In this strait, literal and metaphorical, the allies bethought
themselves of improvising a bridge, by casting huge rocks into the
water. So the monkey-god and his army of monkeys went back to
the regions of the north, and brought thence, from the mountain-
ranges, immense masses, which they cast into the sea, and thus
forming an isthmus, passed over to Ceylon. There they attacked
Ravana in his stronghold, and restored Seeta to her lawful lord. And
the bridge which the monkeys built remains to this day, and is
known by the name of 'Adam's Bridge.'

This story is carved out with elaborate minuteness of detail, in
eight or nine tiers of bas-relief—grotesque as a whole, but not
without some touches of beauty in its parts. The artist or artists who
carved them out with such patient care, were not wanting in imagination; and as illustrations of the great epic of the Ramayana, they
have a characteristic vigour, which is not even in an artistic sense to
be despised. 'But it is not,' says Mr. Fergusson, 'the art of these
sculptures which makes the Kylas so wonderful, so much as their
quantity and variety; for after you have examined all those of the
temple itself, with its porches, and those of the stone bridges that
connect one part with the other, there is still the cloister, and above
the beautiful temple of Lanka and others cut in the rock on the sides
of the pit, which make up together an exhibition of human labour
and perseverence seldom surpassed.' (1867)

JOHN WILLIAM KAYE[307]


## 11. The effect of soft music at Taj

Over all this richness and beauty rises the magnificent dome, which
is so constructed as to contain an *echo* more pure, and prolonged,
and harmonious than any other in the world, so far as known. A
competent judge has declared, 'Of all the complicated music ever
heard on earth, that of a flute played gently in the vault below,

'The Taj Mahal at Agra', drawn by William Daniell

where the remains of the Emperor and his consort repose, as the sound rises to the dome amid a hundred arched alcoves around, and descends in heavenly reverberations upon those who sit or recline on the cenotaphs above, is perhaps the finest to an inartificial ear. We feel as if it were from heaven; and breathed by angels. It is to the ear what the building itself is to the eye; but unhappily it cannot, like the building, live in our recollections. All that we can in after life remember is, that it was heavenly and produced heavenly emotions.' An enthusiast thus more glowingly describes it: 'Now take your seat upon the marble pavement beside the upper tombs, and send your companion to the vault underneath to run slowly over the notes of his flute or guitar. Was ever melody like this? It haunts the air above and around. It distills in showers upon the polished marble. It condenses into the mild shadows, and sublimes into the softened, hallowed light of the dome. It rises, it falls; it swims mockingly, meltingly around. It is the very element with which sweet dreams are builded. It is the melancholy echo of the past—it is the bright, delicate harping of the future. It is the atmosphere breathed by Ariel, and playing around the fountain of Chindara. It is the spirit of the Taj, the voice of inspired love, which called into being this peerless wonder of the world, and elaborated its symmetry and composed its harmony, and, eddying around its young minarets and domes blended them without a line into the azure of immensity.' (1873)

WILLIAM BUTLER[308]

# 21. Wild Life and Sport

## 1. Wild beasts

The largest tigers are found among the Prasii, being nearly twice the size of the lion, and so strong that a tame tiger led by four men having seized a mule by the hinder leg overpowered it and dragged it to him. The monkeys are larger than the largest dogs; they are white except in the face, which is black, though the contrary is observed elsewhere. Their tails are more than two cubits in length. They are very tame, and not of a malicious disposition: so that they neither attack man nor steal. Stones are dug up which are of the colour of frankincense, and sweeter than figs or honey. In some parts of the country there are serpents two cubits long which have membranous wings like bats. They fly about by night, when they let fall drops of urine or sweat, which blister the skin of persons not on their guard, with putrid sores. There are also winged scorpions of an extraordinary size. Ebony grows there. There are also dogs of great strength and courage, which will not let go their hold till water is poured into their nostrils: they bite so eagerly that the eyes of some become distorted, and the eyes of others fall out. Both a lion and a bull were held fast by a dog. The bull was seized by the muzzle, and died before the dog could be taken off. (3rd Century B.C.)

MEGASTHENES [309]

## 2. Tiger-shooting

When the king desires to go out hunting, the huntsmen are warned. These men see to the finding of the tigers, and send out into the jungle asses, cows, sheep, and goats to prevent the tigers changing their haunts. The king goes out on his tallest elephant, and the other princes likewise on elephants acquainted with the requirements of this sort of fight. They sit in uncovered howdahs, each one with his matchlock. Then they encircle the jungle with high nets, leaving

'A Battle Between a Buffalo and a Tiger', drawn by Samuel Howitt

only one opening, through which the king and the huntsmen enter. Around the net, on the outside, stand a number of soldiers who cannot wound the tiger when it comes near the net, nor can the tiger injure them, for in no manner can it break the net and get out.

The order in which the king moves is as follows: In front go the buffaloes, sometimes more than one hundred in number, all in a row. On each one is mounted a man with his legs guarded by leather, and having a broadsword in one hand and holding with the other the reins, which are passed through the buffalo's nostrils. Behind them comes the king on an elephant, and after the king the princes and the men in highest favour.

When they get into the jungle where the tigers are, the buffaloes advance slowly in the formation of a half-moon, until the tigers are in sight. After locating the tigers by sight and smell a circle is formed, leaving them in the centre. In this way the tigers, finding themselves caught, search for an exit. Unable to get away, each one makes its spring in the direction that it sees best. When this spring takes place the man who is mounted on top jumps off with agility, and the buffaloes seize the tigers on their horns with great dexterity, and, shaking their heads tear them to pieces. If any one of the tigers escapes the horns, or refuses to stir from its place, the king fires his gun and kills it, or gives an order to kill it. (1650's)

NICCOLAO MANUCCI[310]

## 3. Nawaub Vizir Asop-ul-Dowlah's method of sporting

This prince took the field at all seasons of the year, but more frequently in the months of March, April, and May: at these times the best sport was expected, the covers being thin, and the animals of the forest in the greatest abundance, where cover and water could be found together, or near to each other. The excursion was talked of, and preparations made during many preceding months. All the court, great part of his army, and *seraglio,* accompanied him; a guard only being left for the protection of his capital. About ten thousand cavalry, nearly the same number of infantry, thirty or forty pieces of artillery, and from seven to eight hundred elephants, attended. The number of bullocks, camels, carts etc. for the tents and baggage, were innumerable. For himself, his women, ministers, European gentlemen of his suite, and visitors, double sets of tents were sent off, of large dimensions. Some with extensive enclosures,

made of cloth and bamboos, about seven feet high, forming a kind
of wall round each tent, of a hundred yards or more in circumference. ...

. When any game was sprung or started, those near it commenced
firing; sometimes a line of firing was kept up, resembling a *feu de
joie,* at a poor diminutive quail, and whenever the bird fell, should
his Highness have fired, a general shout of approbation followed
*Wah! Wah!* the Vizier killed it! Should a jackall or fox be seen, the
grey-hounds were slipped, and the fortunate keeper whose dog
caught it, brought the animal to his Highness with great exultation,
and received half a rupee, a rupee, and, on extraordinary occasions,
a gold *Mohur,* (value two pounds,) in proportion to the amusement
the sport afforded. The same took place, when a poor dove, curlew,
or any other bird was sprung, not considered game for the gun, but
likely to afford more sport with the hawks, which were loosened
after it, and the fortunate keeper whose bird caught it, received a
reward in like manner. (1800)

DANIEL JOHNSON[311]

## 4. The Indian game of Chess

If evidence be required to prove that chess was invented by the
*Hindus,* we may be satisfied with the testimony of the *Persians;* who,
though as much inclined as other nations to appropriate the ingenious inventions of a foreign people, unanimously agree, that the
game was imported from the west of *India,* together with the charming fables of VISHNUSARMAN. in the sixth century of our era: it seems
to have been immemorially known in *Hindustan* by the name of
*Chaturanga,* that is, the four *anga's,* or *members,* of an army, which
are said in the *Amaracosha* to be *hastyas warat' hapadatam,* or
*elephants, horses, chariots,* and *foot-soldiers*; and, in this sense, the
word is frequently used by Epick poets in their descriptions of real
armies. By a natural corruption of the pure *Sanscrit* word, it was
changed by the old *Persians* into *Chatrang,* but the *Arabs,* who soon
after took possession of their country, had neither the initial nor
final letter of that word in their alphabet, and consequently altered
it further into *Shatranj,* which found its way presently into the
modern *Persian*, and at length into the dialects of *India.* ... This
game is also called *Chaturanga,* but more frequently *Chaturaji,* or
the *four Kings,* since it is played by four persons representing as
many princes, two allied armies combating on each side: the de-

'Playing Chess While Smoking the Hooka', drawn by Charles Gold

scription is taken from the *Bhawishya Puran,* in which
YUDHISTHIR is represented conversing with VYASA, who explains
at the king's request the form of the fictitious warfare and the
principal rules of it: 'having marked *eight* squares on all sides, says
the Sage, place the *red* army to the east, the *green* to the south, the
*yellow* to the west, and the *black* to the north: let the *elephant* stand
on the left of the *king;* next to him, the *horse;* then, the *boat;* and,
before them all, four *foot-soldiers*; but the *boat* must be placed in
the angle of the board.' From this passage it clearly appears, that
an army, with its four *anga's*, must be placed on each side of
the board, since an *elephant* could not stand, in any other position,
on the *left* hand of each *king;* and RADHACANT informed me, that
the board consisted, like ours, of *sixty-four* squares, half of them
occupied by the forces, and half, vacant: he added, that this game is
mentioned in the oldest law-books, and that it was invented by the
wife of RAVAN, king of *Lanca,* in order to amuse him with an image
of war, while his metropolis was closely besieged by RAMA in the
second age of the world. ...I cannot agree with my friend
RADHACANT, that a ship is properly introduced in this imaginary
warfare instead of a *chariot,* in which the old *Indian* warriors
constantly fought; for, though the *king* might be supposed to fit in a
*car,* so that the four *anga's* would be complete, and though it may
often be necessary in a real campaign to pass rivers or lakes, yet no
river is marked on the *Indian,* as it is on the *Chinese,* chess-board,
and the intermixture of ships with horses, elephants, and infantry
embattled on a plain, is an absurdity not to be defended. The use of
*dice* may, perhaps, be justified in a representation of war, in which
*fortune* has unquestionably a great share, but it seems to exclude
chess from the rank, which has been assigned to it, among the
sciences, and to give the game before us the appearance of *whist,*
except that pieces are used openly, instead of cards which are held
concealed: nevertheless we find, that the moves in the game described by VYASA were to a certain degree regulated by *chance;* for
he proceeds to tell his royal pupil, that, 'if *cinque* be thrown, the *king*
or a *pawn* must be moved; if *quatre,* the *elephant*; if *trois,* the *horse*;
and if *deux,* the *boat.*'

He then proceeds to the moves: 'the *king* passes freely on all
sides but over one square only; and with the same limitation, the
*pawn* moves, but he advances straight forward, and kills his enemy
through an angle; the *elephant* marches in all directions, as far as his
driver pleases; the *horse* runs obliquely, traversing three squares;

and the *ship* goes over two squares diagonally.' The elephant, we find, has the powers of our *queen,* as we are pleased to call the *minister,* or *general,* of the *Persians,* and the *ship* has the motion of the piece, to which we give the unaccountable appellation of *bishop,* but with a restriction, which must greatly lessen his value.

The bard next exhibits a few general rules and superficial directions for the conduct of the game: 'the *pawns* and the *ship* both kill and may be voluntarily killed; while the *king, the elephant,* and the *horse* may slay the foe, but cannot expose themselves to be slain. Let each player preserve his own forces with extreme care, securing his *king* above all, and not sacrificing a superior, to keep an inferior, piece.' Here the commentator on the *Puran* observes, that, the *horse,* who has the choice of *eight* moves from any central position, must be preferred to the *ship,* who has only the choice of *four*; but this argument would not have equal weight in the common game, where the *bishop* and *tower* command a whole line, and where a knight is always of less value than a tower in action, or the bishop of that side on which the attack is begun. 'It is by the overbearing power of the *elephant,* that the king fights boldly; let the whole army, therefore, be abandoned, in order to secure the *elephant:* the king must never place one elephant before another, according to the rule of GOTAMA. unless he be compelled by want of room, for he would thus commit a dangerous fault; and, if he can slay one of two hostile elephants, he must destroy that on his left hand." The last rule is extremely obscure; but, as GOTAMA was an illustrious lawyer and philosopher, he would not have condescended to leave directions for the game of *Chaturanga*, if it had not been held in great estimation by the ancient sages of *India.* (1810)

WILLIAM JONES[312]

## 5. The hog-deer at bay

I have often seen hog-deer taken by means of nets stretched across grass plains and *jow* jungles, but never, except in one instance, did I know that springes were in use among the natives, especially for this purpose. All who witnessed it seemed to consider the circumstance as perfectly unprecedented. The method was very simple, and where hog-deer abound, it may, I conceive, be frequently successful. A line of considerable strength, and about a hundred yards long, was stretched in the same manner as is usual in fixing nets . . .along the line, at the distance of about a foot or fifteen inches, loops, or springes of horse hair, were hanging. The line was raised by means of several short sticks, which sustained it to such a level as occasioned the springes to be hid in the grass at about a foot from the ground. This being done, all the people who could be collected were formed into a line, which moved on towards the snares. Many hogs, hog-deer, etc. were roused, and passed under the rope. One doe, however, happened to be less fortunate than the others, and was, to her great astonishment, brought up short by a noose, through which her head had passed.

The operator was a stranger, and came from some very remote quarter. He was not wanting in encomiums on his own abilities, and laid great stress on the originality of the contrivance, claiming the entire merit of invention to himself. He was much displeased at my asserting that every poacher in England was acquainted with that very common trick of setting springes, and in a most contemptuous manner insinuated, that our country was held in detestation, as harbouring infidels and outcasts: and that were he to visit it, he might find my assertion to be unfounded. But a rupee or two put the adventurer into good humour, and we parted with the appearance of reconciliation; though no doubt he never forgot, nor forgave my unintentional derogation of his ingenuity. Certainly his device could not be held in comparison with a net, in regard to certainty; but for cheapness and ease of conveyance it was absolutely preferable.

In hunting hog-deer, greyhounds are very serviceable; they not only keep the game to its utmost speed, but prevent it from squatting, as hog-deer, especially the does, are very apt to do. The buck is extremely fierce when closely pursued, and rarely fails to make an obstinate defence. I have been several times in considerable danger from their sudden charges. They have an ugly trick of stopping short until the horse may have passed, when they rush at his hind quarters with amazing impetuosity. If there be two persons in company, this affords a favourable opportunity for delivering a spear; but this branch of sporting does not require such support from colleagues as hog-hunting, whence many follow hog-deer without adverting to the difficulties that may eventually present themselves to a single person; and of which the bucks rarely fail to take every advantage.

Sometimes a doe will make a little show of resistance; but they, for the most part, succumb with resignation to their fate; lying down when exhausted with fatigue, and allowing the hunter to dismount to tie their legs with his handkerchief, or whatever may present itself

for that purpose. In this manner they are frequently taken home
alive. (1819)

THOMAS WILLIAMSON[313]

## 6. *A Mhow song for the Malwa Meltonians*

Mount, mount, ye Meltonians, our Huntsman's away
To the plain, with his dogs and his gallows old Grey,
And see o'er yon hill-top the whipper-in goes,
I know him right well by the tip of his nose.

Chorus.

Come along, come along, for the dogs are laid on,
May we find and we'll kill, I'll bet fifty to one;
Yet if foxes be wanting our fun need not flag,
If it comes to the worst we can *dig at a Drag*.

Chorus.

They've hit it, they have found, I was certain they would—
A gallant grey fox. can the scent be but good—
Breast high, by the gods! and I thought 'twould be so,
Yoicks to Tippoo and Vickee—my eyes! how they go.

Chorus.

Over rocks, over nullahs, thro' bramble and bush,
Delighted we ride with a pull and a push—
A *pull*, for the wind of your Nag, on the rein,
And a jolly gay *push* just to breathe him again.

Chorus.

See our Huntsman, how fearless he follows the pack,
With the boys of the Hermitage close at his back,
While the Tinkers seem careful of crowding each other
Down, down goes a Snob, and whack! there goes another.

Chorus.

Now the pack view the Varmint, and fleeter they rush,
While Reynard strives harder to save his grey brush;
But what *spoon* is that, who so bellows and flogs?
Hold hard, and be d—d, don't ride over the dogs.

Chorus.

He turns and he doubles—but doubles in vain;
Not a yard, not a foot, on his foes can he gain;

Close on hand is his earth, and he'll gain it—he will,
Fling at him, dash at him, dogs, whoo-opp, *what a kill!*
Chorus.

Now off with your heeltaps and up on your feet,
May our sport be the better the oftener we meet,
And may Friendship its bonds of good-fellowship throw
Round the Malwa Meltonians, wherever they go!
Chorus. (1827)

ORIENTAL SPORTING MAGAZINE[314]

## 7. *Bear fighting (Dharwar)*

Major R——, an officer in the Madras service, who was lately
stationed here, had gone out lately to a jungle at some distance from
the cantonments, to look for a bear, of which there are great
numbers in this neighbourhood. I may here mention that those
which have been killed here have always been found unusually large
and savage, and in several instances have commenced the attack
without being previously molested. After beating a nullah for some
time without success, he was suddenly attacked by an enormous
bear, which rushed from a thick patch of jungle a few paces from
him.

He had just time to raise his rifle and to fire, before the bear was
aboard of him: he missed, the beaters bolted, and the only resistance he could make was to charge with the muzzle of his rifle
against the bear's breast as he reared at him. This he did with so
much force as to wrench up the elevation rib from the barrels (it was
a seven-barrelled rifle), and a quantity of the animal's hair was
afterwards found sticking to it. The bear directly seized him by the
arm and he was left without bottle-holder or second to mill a bruie,
who was not likely to fight fair, at least according to the rules of
modern pugilism.

The major is a man of immense strength, and hits with the
impetus of a sledge-hammer: with one hand he battered Bruin
between the eyes, and with his feet kept up a most vigorous can-
nonade against his bread basket. The bear constantly shifted his
hold from one arm to the other, but the iron knuckles of his
antagonist prevented him from retaining his grip long enough to
break the bones, and at last both fell together, Bruin uppermost.
The gallant resistance which the major had hitherto made was now

getting more feeble; he felt the hot breath of the bear blowing on his
face, as his grey muzzle was thrust forward endeavouring to seize
him by the head, which he defended as well as he could by repeated
blows on the brute's nose. In the scuffle they had both rolled to the
edge of the raome, and the final act of the tragedy seemed approaching, when the major gathered himself up for one last effort, hit right
and left at his friend's head, and at the same moment drawing his
knees to his chin, kicked out with such strength, that he fairly canted
the bear into the nullah, and had the satisfaction of seeing him roll to
the bottom. Upon rising and shaking himself after so extraordinary
an engagement, Major R—— found that he had escaped with much
less damage than he expected: his arms were terribly torn, but he
was able to walk some distance to his palankeen, and is now perfectly recovered. (1831)

ORIENTAL SPORTING MAGAZINE[315]

## 8. *Hog hunting in Guzerat*

A small party of only four, without wagrees, and with but little
knowledge of a country much of which never before was hunted, left
Hursole a few days ago on a *voyage* of discovery, and I now send you
the result.

Pomal is a small village surrounded by beautiful large trees, and,
what is better, has a fine bheer of grass within a short distance, as
also some small jungles of stunted baubul trees. In these shades
dwelt for many years, in peace and security, our friends the grun-
ters; hoary age had grizzled their visages, yet had not taken a whit
from their sturdiness or keenness of tush. But life is uncertain, and
the old boar, when roused by the cries of the beaters, dreamt not
danger was nigh, or that life depended on the swiftness of those
limbs that hitherto had but led him to scenes of joy.

'Hold back, he breaks, let him go!' was the cry as the hoary
patriarch slowly emerged from the grass, whilst a grunt expressed
his dissatisfaction at being roused from his morning slumber. His
object evidently was to gain a jungle about half a mile ahead, but not
caring to heat him, he trotted leisurely along.

The intensity of feeling at such a moment as this becomes truly
painful; the heart throbs in the throat, and the hand all but refuses to
hold the rein, and this agitation as powerfully affects your horse; his
eye kindles, a slight tremor shakes his body, and his restlessness

shows how eager he is to commence operations.

The word was given, the heel dashed in, and then, too late indeed, the brute cast his sluggard eye behind, and sniffing danger, increased his pace; but he died an easy death, conquered by his own fat.

One run varies but little from another, and there is a sameness in all accounts of fox and hog-hunting, that is alone to be overcome by such pens as Nimrod's. I will not attempt that in which I know I shall fail. Why were we not all born, as asserted by a French philosopher, with equal talents? I might then have been enabled to have furnished you with matter for ten pages, and your readers with amusement for ten minutes.

We killed this day four hog, and two at the same place on the succeeding day.

Corsar is a wretched place on the banks of a river whose name I cannot recollect; the bheer near it is large, but its waving tops smile over deep and hidden nullahs. The sport was good the first day, four being killed; the next, however, was a blank. (1831)

ORIENTAL SPORTING MAGAZINE[316]

## 9. *Encounter with a hyena and a ghorawallah race*

About a month ago, while Captain G., of this station, was out one morning with his greyhounds in search of a fox, he came suddenly upon a large hyena, who was quietly taking his repose in the bed of a lindy nullah. The dogs four in number, were immediately slipped at the animal, who set off for the adjacent hills as if the devil was after him. The dogs, however, had the speed, and soon brought him to bay. Whilst he was in this predicament the gallant captain came up; he had only a short thick stick in his hand, which belonged to his dog boy. No sooner, however, did the animal perceive the approach of another enemy, than he charged openmouthed at Captain G.'s horse's legs. Fortunately for the latter, at that critical moment, one of the dogs laid hold of the hyena's tail, and on his turning his head to chastise the dog for his impudence, he got a tremendous blow on his head from the captain, which stunned him a little, and forced him to take refuge under a bush; but there, after gallantly standing for some time the attacks of the dogs, the volleys of stones flying about his ears and head from the dog boy, and receiving a few more blows from the Captain, he breathed his last. When he was brought into the cantonments I saw him, and he was certainly a very fine animal. The dogs, before they saw him, had killed a hare, which being taken into consideration, I think shows they performed their duty for that morning very well. By-the-by, I must tell you that not many weeks ago we had a ghorawallah race here for a purse of 10 rupees. The distance half a mile. The man who came in second to get 2 rupees. There were six competitors for the prize. The racecourse was thronged with natives of all descriptions to see the race, it being quite a novelty to them. The men started well, but ere they had finished a quarter of a mile only three seemed inclined to contest the prize. They continued in this way until within 100 yards of the winning post, when one dashed forward and kept the lead, winning by about 15 yards. Time, 3m. 15s. (1832)

TIM TAFY[317]

## 10. Indian wrestling

The men whom I accompanied on these excursions were mostly Gwalas, and the Kishengunj Gwala, besides being almost invariably a *lattial* and very frequently a dacoit, was as much at home in the water as the hippopotamus or the human frog, or any other amphibious creature.

Those Gwalas were by no means effeminate, as are the Bengalis generally, and they were sportsmen in a way. Some of them were accomplished quarter-staff players, and could have shaped fairly well, I fancy, in a bout with Little John or Friar Tuck; some were also wrestlers of the first class, who would have shaped fairly well against their rivals of Cornwall or the North Country; and those who were expert in these arts were as greedily enlisted in the service of rajas and other magnates of large revenues as were the giants of Europe for the Gargantuan corps of Frederick William of Prussia.

And those employers also engaged the services of up-country *pulwans*, men of the Sepoy class drawn mostly from Oudh and the North-West Provinces, who did little or nothing with the quarter-staff of the Gwala, but much in wrestling. The services of these men consisted only, in fact, of wrestling and constant training for the arena; and their most arduous duty was the struggle with a dietary scale of awful character and dimensions. Vast quantities of milk, a bilious sweet concocted of curd and sugar, and other uninviting food, had to be consumed daily, so that the *pulwan* should put on flesh; and all day long, when not engaged in demoralising his interior economy, he had to exercise himself violently with Indian clubs and other calisthenics, so that some portions of the constantly superadded flesh should be solidified into muscle. I have seen these *pulwans*—men celebrated through more than one province—enter the wrestling-ring in a condition that seemed to suggest expediency of tapping for dropsy rather than promise of athletic feats, and those corpulent gladiators have, amidst the cheers of an admiring crowd, amply sustained their reputation.

Indian wrestling differs *toto cœlo* from that of England; there is more of art and less of mere brute force in it. When I was a learner of this science there were 360 *penches* or dodges to be acquired, and to-day there may possibly be more. Even then the practised English wrestler who knew nothing of those many *penches* would, I fancy, have had the worst of an encounter with one of those trained *pulwans:* as likely as not he would have been put down on his back before he had come to grips with his antagonist, or thought the tussle had commenced.

As a sport pursued by the natives of India generally, wrestling occupies a pre-eminent position. Second in the public estimation comes another display of the amphitheatre and survival of the gladiatorial time—the contest between two picked men armed with quarter-staff, or sword or shield. Then, *longo intervallo,* comes kite-flying, the sport whereof consists in cutting through the string of one kite with the string of another, the victory going to him whose string holds out and kite remains. This game is, I think, more in vogue in Northern India than elsewhere. In the towns thereaway scores of kite-duels are to be sometimes witnessed waging at once, and the uninitiated globe-trotter might assume that these aerial toys were being flown by the youth of the place whose inexpert hands permitted much unpremeditated fouling; but that impression would be wholly incorrect, those kites being flown by sportive men, and fouling being an essential feature of the game. (1850's–70's)

EDWARD BRADDON[318]

## 11. A fine buck-ibex

After several hours' clambering over broken ground, scarped rocks, and deep gullies, without seeing any indication of animal life, except a few butterflies, Naga called our attention to something moving along the scarped edge of a high ridge of cliff which frowned like a wall high above our heads, and with the aid of my field-glass I discerned a fine buck-ibex, evidently the sentinel of a herd, poised on a pinnacle of rock nearly half-a-mile distant. As his head was turned towards us, and he seemed to be watching our movements, I took it for granted that our presence was discovered, so I told Googooloo, Naga, and Hassan, to remain quiet where they were, whilst B——, Chineah, and myself, made a detour so as to circumvent him.

After intense labour we clambered up the face of the cliff, having frequently to crawl along ledges of rock, overhanging precipices down which we dare not look, and with a good deal of manoeuvring managed to get above our wary quarry, who was still apparently intently observing the movement of our party below, whilst, seven others, confident in his watchfulness, were carelessly browsing on the short crisp herbage close by. By dodging from crag to crag, after some intensely-exciting stalking, we crept behind an isolated boulder of rock about a hundred and twenty paces to leeward of the herd, who were still grazing unconscious of danger; and, as the nature of the ground was such that we could not hope to steal any nearer without great fear of discovery, we prepared for immediate offensive action. Having taken the precaution of putting fresh caps on our rifles, B—— aimed at a fine buck that was carelessly receiving the caresses of a couple of does, whilst I took the sentinel, and firing almost simultaneously both fell to our shots. I wounded a doe with my second barrel, but it got away with a broken leg; B——, however, was more fortunate, for he stopped a second doe with a ball through the spine, and killed a young buck with the second gun as it was bounding along a ledge of rocks at least four hundred paces distant. 'Well done, indeed, Ned!' I exclaimed, rather taken aback with this splendid display of marksmanship; 'that was a shot I envy you tor having made, as I have rarely seen a bounding deer bagged at such a distance, notwithstanding I have hunted with the crack sportsman of the day. It would have gladdened old Walter's heart to see one of his pupils do such credit to his "bringings up." (1850's)

H. A. LEVESON[319]

## 12. A hard-lived beast

Next morning, 21st May, we again visited the thicket in which we had last evening left the tiger, and walked most carefully through

'Bringing Home the Jaat Man-eater in Triumph', drawn by William Rice

the whole cover, but still, strange to say, could find no blood. We
next, by chance, intending to hunt for him from a cover some
distance off, passed by the small ravine where the men had set fire to
the high grass. Here we came upon the tiger's fresh prints, and,
following them, soon found plenty of blood. We took these prints
easily as far as a ravine named 'Neereea Kal,' about two miles off,
and beat this long cover in two drives, but no tiger appeared. We
then agreed to go back through this ravine and carefully examine
every part of it, expecting to find this tiger dead. We had gone thus
through the thickest part of the cover, when suddenly one of my
men and myself saw the tiger lying down close in front of us,
apparently dead.

At this time we were rather scattered and walking carelessly over
what seemed not the most likely spot to find the tiger in. Little was
gathering 'corinda' berries to eat, while Forbes, before being
aware of his danger, strolled on within four yards of the tiger, when
the brute's ear was observed to move. The alarm was quickly, but
silently, given to the rest of our men following behind us. With all
the guns and beaters we climbed up a steep bank overlooking the
thicket in which the tiger was hiding, and then fired a volley into him
quite close, from some high rocks on which we were standing
directly over the beast. Up jumped the tiger, and with loud roars he
endeavoured to get out of the small cover; but was quickly rolled
over for good by our guns. This brute still seemed quite fresh and
active, although, on skinning him, which we at once proceeded to
do, no less than twelve of yesterday's bullets were found in his body.
These we knew by the marks he had made in licking them with his
tongue clearing off the hair round each shot-hole. A tiger's tongue is
remarkably rough and covered with innumerable stout short points
of hard flesh, resembling thorns, closely packed together, and lying
backwards. With these he easily scrapes off every atom of flesh
adhering to the bones of his prey.

This tiger measured eleven feet six inches long, and was extremely stout. At the time we found him, he was lying with his body
half in some water to allay the pain of his wounds. Over head was a
beautiful 'oleander' bush in full blossom. These pretty pink and
white flowers are very common in all the jungles about this part of
the country. Forbes had rather a narrow escape, had he not been
warned in time by my man, of stepping on this crouching tiger.
(1853)

WILLIAM RICE[320]

## 13.  A fine old stag

About an hour after starting, still following the same ridge upwards, I had made a momentary halt to recover breath, for it was hard work, when one of my men gave a low 'hist,' and held up his hand; a dead silence followed, then we distinctly heard, far down below, something moving about among the dead oak leaves. It was impossible to catch a glimpse of the animal whatever it was on account of the density of the foliage. '*Bhaloo*' (a bear) said the paharies, and I thought it very likely to be the case; but how to get down was the difficulty. The animal appeared to be directly below us; but if we descended, which was no easy matter, just at the spot, by the face of the open slope, we certainly should be discovered; so at length we determined to retrace our steps for a few hundred yards to where the descent was less steep.

We got down without much difficulty and commenced carefully advancing up the gorge; and presently, to my delight, on turning a corner, came right upon a fine old stag. He stood staring at us, offering a splendid chance. I was rather above him, and just as he turned round to make off, hit him behind the shoulder with a heavy bullet; he stumbled forward, fell over, and while he was attemping to regain his legs, my second shot dropped him dead. He was a noble brute; I brought his stuffed head to England. (1868)

J. H. BALDWIN[321]

## 14.  A huge elephant

I remember one day when snipe-shooting with a brother officer, on the margin of the Lowqua jheel, in the Tezpore district, we came across a very large 'tusker.' This jheel or lake was surrounded by heavy jungle, and nearer the water by dense masses of reeds and tall grass; but there was a narrow strip of swampy ground on the very margin of the lake, covered with short rushes; and here in the cold season snipe were to be found, though not in great abundance. There was just room for a couple of guns to walk abreast, with two men between us. The gun next the water got nearly all the shooting, but every now and then we changed places. We had just landed from a 'dugout,' or a log of timber, generally from the mango tree, hollowed out into a canoe, had advanced only about fifty yards, and hardly commenced operations, when a crackling in the jungle close at hand brought us to a halt, and soon to a retrograde movement in

the direction of our boat.

There were only wild animals, such as rhinoceri, elephants, and buffalo in that neighbourhood, and not a village within many miles. It was evident that some big brute was approaching the water: we had only our shot guns, so that the best thing to do was to retreat and get out of his way. We therefore scrambled into the canoe again, and in a few minutes a huge elephant came out of the grass, probably either to drink or bathe; but on seeing us he pricked up his ears and came to a halt. We asked the boatmen if he was a wild elephant, or one that had escaped from Nowgong, a station six or seven miles off. They replied that the beast was undoubtedly a wild one, and that they had often seen him before near this very spot. He stood swinging his trunk and eyeing us, as we imagined, in any but a friendly way, but presently turned round and walked slowly back again into the reeds. He might have been, and probably was, a harmless beast enough, but we did not begin our snipe-shooting again till we had paddled a good quarter of a mile from the place where we had viewed our friend. He was one of the largest elephants that I have ever seen. Not far from this same *jheel,* I fired at and wounded most severely a 'rogue' elephant. (1868)

J.H. BALDWIN[322]

## 15. Leopard shooting

The distant yells of t' e beaters soon warned me that the sport had commenced. Some little time passed when I saw my signalman raise both arms, a sign from the beaters that the two leopards were afoot. I was expecting their speedy appearance when an extra storm of yells, and an interchange of abuse amongst the men, followed by a sudden silence, told me that the leopards had broken back, I only hoped without accident. The men ran back to head them, and they recommenced at the original place and beat up merrily. Presently I heard a rustling in the dry leaves, and saw one leopard sneaking down the sandy ravine. It came on very cautiously and hesitatingly, and I amused myself by watching it. Though full grown it was a small animal (few if any leopards exceed five and a half feet in length), and I felt rather ashamed of being in a tree to shoot such a creature. I would have met it on foot with pleasure. It looked as if half inclined to turn back, but each yell of the men appeared to call to its mind some act of spoilation for which it feared retribution, and to make it dread a return more than an advance. On it came, and when directly

under me I dropped it dead with a bullet through the neck. It never moved, but lay prone as it fell, with one paw before it in the attitude of advancing. I telegraphed 'dead,' and the beaters came on with redoubled cries.

Soon the male leopard approached with slow and stealthy step down the bed of the ravine. He looked very pretty to a sportsman's eye, grinning with mingled fear and anger at being disturbed in his early sleep. His belly almost touched the ground as he crept along. Fortunately the wind was from him to me, so he did not scent his dead spouse, nor did he even observe her as she lay. He seemed to have thoughts of leaving the bed of the ravine before he reached me, and drawing his head level with the bank he peered cautiously through the garden to see if the coast were clear in the line of his meditated departure. He gave me a rather difficult shot, but I rolled him over. He got up and rushed up the bank, but I tumbled him over again into the ravine. He now cantered back, but I caught my empty rifle between my knees and siezed the spare one, and just as he was getting out of sight I killed him with a lucky shot in the ear. (1870)

G.P. SANDERSON [323]

## 16. The tigress

I was sitting in my tent one afternoon, when a hillman burst rudely upon me, almost speechless with emotion, yet stuttering that his brother had been killed by the tiger. In answer to hurried questions, he had not seen the beast, his brother was cutting bamboos about twenty yards away, he had heard a blow and a groan and a dragging through the leaves; the forest was extremely dense, and the affair was not five minutes old: he could lead us to the spot. In less than that time we two, with an orderly carrying a spare gun, had set out, and ten minutes later had reached the scene. On the swaying bamboos there was blood as far as a man might reach; on the ground was a billhook and torn pieces of cotton cloth; a sinister-looking trail led towards the higher ground above. It was easy to follow, with its fresh blood and fresh footmarks, and we hurried along for about two hundred yards till we entered the bed of a dry watercourse where there was even less need for tracking. Judging from the marks, the tigress was evidently just ahead of us, when our way was barred by a wall of dry rock, a waterfall in the rainy season. This was about eight feet high, and my companions pushed me up and handed the rifle.

The man lay some twenty yards farther on, probably abandoned at the sound of our pursuing steps; he had no face, his skull had been flattened on his neck by a blow from above, and he had been gripped in the loins when carried away; the eight-foot obstacle had apparently been negotiated at a bound, for there was no mark of dragging up the face of the rock.

The tigress, I thought, was certain to return, and I proposed to go back to camp and bring the necessary materials to fix up a seat in an adjoining tree; the brother followed wailing and weeping, but immediately on his arrival, collecting friends from the neighbouring bamboo-cutters' huts, he set out to retrieve and burn his brother's corpse. They were a party of twenty or more, making a sufficient uproar to communicate to the tigress the fear they themselves felt. The next day I wrote to the officer commanding a Gurkha regiment at Dehra Dun, for the loan of a non-commissioned officer and ten or twelve men to try their luck; and fortune was with them even on their arrival at Chila, opposite Hardwar, a few days later, for almost simultaneously came a report that a woman had been killed some miles from the camp, and they at once started in pursuit. They formed, with the neighbouring villagers, a wide circle in the forest, and advanced towards the spot where the corpse was supposed to be lying, and soon in the centre of this ring of rifles and bayonets the tigress leapt on to a rock to determine her line of retreat. She fell with her back broken by a lucky shot fired by the son of the 'havildar,' a lad of about fifteen years old, and the little Gurkhas, closing in, soon despatched her. They brought down a tigress of under eight feet long in the prime of life, and vouched for her identity by some poor bones taken from her stomach; but I only looked at the pad of the right fore-paw, and paid the reward with a thankful heart. (1880)

SAINTHILL EARDLEY-WILMOT[324]

## 17. The rhinoceri

Passing before me at a distance of only a few yards, but quite invisible, Rhino received from my rifle two shots, the first causing it to turn fiercely upon my elephant, when the second struck it in the shoulder, bringing it down upon its knees, but only for a second or two. Before I could exchange the discharged muzzle-loader rifle for a loaded one, Rhino was off again, making for the deep 'nullah' on the left, towards which we all turned, and being on that flank, it was my luck to view it as it showed on the bank before plunging down with another ball in the neck, which laid it dead in the water below. The sides of the stream being almost perpendicular, we had no little trouble in getting down to cut off the head and shields. This proved to be a young but full-grown cow, with a slender horn of moderate length.

We had killed three and wounded at least as many more that day, and might altogether have roused from first to last ten or a dozen small and great, though some were never once sighted in that dense covert. Turning homewards we gained the tents about sunset, picking up on our way half-a-dozen marsh and hog-deer for our hungry camp followers.

Having seen so many rhinoceri that day, we devoted the next to the same pursuit, but killed only one, although at one time we had seemingly half-a-dozen ahead of us. The previous day's firing had driven many of them farther away towards the foot of the Garo hills without having had any effect upon other game, of which we met with great numbers, without finding a single tiger in these, its well-known haunts; nevertheless we enjoyed a good day's sport, and made a large bag both in weight and numbers, viz., a rhinoceros, five buffaloes (unsought), nine marsh and seven hog-deer, two peacocks, a floriken, five brace of 'kyah' partridge, and a pink-headed duck. The scenery near the foot of the hills was wild in the extreme, and in the eyes of a sportsman lovely beyond compare; but the jungles were so extensive and dense that our line of eighteen elephants was lost in it, and had we not carried on some of them flags of white cloth on bamboo poles to regulate our movements in wheeling, and to dress the line, we should sometimes have inevitably lost each other, or got astray, particularly in beating round morasses. (1886)

EDWARD B. BAKER[325]

## 18. The two rams

After a longish pull we reached the top of the mountain opposite the camp, and here Saibra met us with the welcome news that he had seen a large flock of napoo feeding on the eastern side. The ground here consists of precipitous rocks at the top, with the usual steep stone slopes below. Advancing cautiously we soon made out a flock of about thirty napoo far below us; some were feeding on the scanty herbage, whilst others slept or rested on their sides, with their legs stretched out at full length. Amongst them were four or five good rams, but it was out of the question to fire at them from where I was, as they were some four hundred yards away, and directly below me. Accordingly, taking advantage of a ridge of rocks that ran vertically down the hillside, we clambered down, and having reached a point that we judged must be almost opposite to them, we peeped over. At that moment the wind changed, and blew from us straight towards them; in an instant they were all in full flight. It is incredible with what alacrity these animals, apparently stretched out fast asleep one moment, will be galloping away with the rest of the flock a second afterwards. I ought not to have fired, but I was anxious to get a head, so putting up my sight for three hundred yards (they were far below me and going straight away), so as to be well ahead of the animal I aimed at, I fired right and left at two rams which were bringing up the rear of the flock. Both bullets told, one ram separating from the rest, while the other went on slowly, and evidently in distress. It was a lucky shot, but scarcely, I am afraid, to be commended as a sporting one. (1894)

F.E.S. ADAIR[326]

# 22. Literature

## 1. Translations of literary works

By the desire of the Literary Society of Bombay, I have the honour of laying before you, for the information of the Asiatick Society, some suggestions which appear to us likely to contribute to the progress of knowledge, and to the honour of our national character. The proposition which we are about to make, arose in a great measure from an act of your learned Society: on that account, as well as on every other, you are entitled to be consulted regarding it, to decide on its reasonableness, and if you approve it, to take the lead in its execution. We observe that you patronize the projected translation of the *Ramayan* by Mr. Carey and his friends:— the choice does honour to your discernment. As an example of the taste, a monument of the genius, and a picture of the manners, as well as a record of the mythology and poetical history of the heroic ages of India, it will undoubtedly lay open more of this country to the learned of Europe, than they could discover from many volumes of ingenious dissertations. The Iliad and Odyssey are as valuable to the philosopher as to the man of taste; their display of manners is as interesting to the one, as their transcendent beauties are delightful to the other; but the most ingenious essay on the origin of the *Pelasqi* is not quite so interesting, though we are far from denying to such inquiries their proper rank amongst the most elegant amusements of curiosity and leisure. Works so voluminous, and likely at first to find so few purchasers as the translation of the Ramayan, require patronage, which is an encumbrance and a restraint on compositions addressed to the general taste of an enlightened nation. We have no doubt that your patronage will procure to these meritorious translators such pecuniary assistance as may protect them from suffering by their useful labours.

Permit us to observe, that something more seems to be required. It is well known that Mr. Wilkins, a distinguished member of your

Society, has long had ready for the press a complete translation of the *Mahabharat;* but no private individual of moderate fortune can ever hazard the publication of so immense a work; no bookseller can with common prudence undertake it; so that without extraordinary assistance this noble work must remain obscure and useless in the closet of the translator. Nor is this all:— many individuals are now qualified and well disposed to undertake translations from the Sanscrit, if they were assured of the means of publication without loss, and of moderate remuneration where their circumstances required it. On the other hand, it cannot be doubted, that in an opulent and liberal community, there are many perfectly ready to supply those small contributions which would be sufficient for such a purpose; but the indigent scholar does not know whence he is to receive, and the generous patron does not know where he ought to bestow. We wish to see a common centre, to which both may be directed; and we beg leave to suggest, that the Asiatick Society may, in a public address to the British inhabitants of India, propose a general subscription to create a fund for defraying the necessary expenses of publishing translations of such Sanscrit works as shall most seem to deserve an English version, and for affording a reasonable recompense to the translators where their situation makes it necessary. It is proposed that the money when collected should be vested in a body, of whom your Society would naturally furnish the majority, who would be trustees of the fund and judges of the works to be translated, of the qualifications of those who are appointed to translate, and of the merit of their versions. If the principle were approved, the detailed regulations would be easily arranged.

It is premature, and might be presumptuous in us to point out the publications to which such a fund might be more especially destined; it is however obvious that the first place is, on every principle, due to the two great epic poems of which we have spoken. The impression made by *Sacontala* in every country of Europe would be sufficient, if other arguments were wanting, to point our attention to the drama. The celebrated dramatic pieces of India are said not to be very numerous, and it would not be difficult to realize the wish of the French missionary, who in the *Lettres Edifiantes* expresses a hope of presenting his country with a Sanscrit Theatre. We shall not speak of a grammar and dictionary of that language, because we understand that they are in great forwardness, and may soon be expected from learned members of your Society:— we shall not presume to decide whether the *Vedas* ought to form part of the plan, because we cannot estimate the difficulties which seem to attend the translation of these books. The province of history appears to be absolutely vacant in Hindu literature; but among the innumerable treatises on speculative philosophy and ethics, some might be chosen very interesting to European philosophers: not perhaps for any new certain knowledge which they might afford on these subjects, but for the light which they must throw on the history of opinion, and for a conformity not only in morals,— which would not be extraordinary, because, notwithstanding the difference of dress and exterior, the moralists of all ages and nations have in general agreed; but in the devious and eccentric speculations of the metaphysicians, which seem to fluctuate more with the intellectual and moral peculiarities of the individual, and which therefore more excite our wonder, when we find them agree in distant times and places. (1806)

JAMES MACKINTOSH[326a]

## 2. Prakrit poetry

The rules of prosody are contained in Sutras, or brief aphorisms, the reputed author of which is Pingalanaga, a fabulous being, represented by mythologists in the shape of a serpent; and the same who, under the title of Patanjali, is the supposed author of the Mahabhashya, or great commentary on grammar, and also of the text of the Yoga Sastra; and to whom likewise the text or the commentary of the Jyotisha annexed to the Vedas appears to be attributed. The aphorisms of Pingalacharya, as he is sometimes called, on the prosody of Sanskrit (exclusive of the rules in Prakrit likewise ascribed to him), are collected into eight books, the first of which allots names, or rather literal marks, to feet consisting of one, two, or three syllables. The second book teaches the manner in which passages of the Vedas are measured. The third explains the variations in the subdivision of the couplet and stanza. The fourth treats of profane poetry, and especially of verses, in which the number of syllables, or their quantity, is not uniform. The fifth, sixth and seventh, exhibit metres of that sort which has been called monoschematic, or uniform, because the same feet recur invariably in the same places. The eighth and last book serves as an appendix to the whole, and contains rules for computing all the possible combinations of long and short syllables in verses of any length.

This author cites earlier writers on prosody, whose works appear to have been lost: such as Saitava, Kraushtika, Tandin, and other ancient sages, Yaska, Kasyapa, etc.

Pingala's text has been interpreted by various commentators; and, among others, by Halayudha Bhatta, author of an excellent gloss entitled *Mrita Sanjivini*. It is the work on which I have chiefly relied. A more modern commentary, or rather a paraphrase in verse, by Narayana Bhatta Tara, under the title of *Vrittokti Ratna*, presents the singularity of being interpreted throughout in a double sense, by the author himself, in a further gloss entitled *Pariksha*.

The Agni Purana is quoted for a complete system of prosody, founded apparently on Pingala's aphorisms; but which serves to correct or to supply the text in many places; and which is accordingly used for that purpose by commentators. Original treatises likewise have been composed by various authors; and, among others, by the celebrated poet Kalidasa. In a short treatise entitled *Sruta Bodha*, this poet teaches the laws of versification in the very metre to which they relate; and has thus united the example with the precept. The same mode has been also practised by many other writers on prosody; and in particular, by Pingala's commentator Narayana Bhatta; and by the author of the Vritta Ratnakara and Vritta Darpana.

Kalidasa's *Sruta Bodha* exhibits only the most common sorts of metre, and is founded on Pingala's Prakrit rules of prosody; as has been remarked by one of the commentators on the *Vritta Ratnakara*.

The rules generally cited under the title of Prakrit Pingala, have been explained in a metrical paraphrase, teaching the construction of each species of metre in a stanza of the same measure, and subjoining select examples. This Prakrit paraphrase, entitled *Pingala Vritti*, is quoted under the name of Hammira, who is celebrated in more than one passage given as examples of metre, and who probably patronized the author. It has been imitated in a modern Sanskrit treatise on Prakrit prosody, entitled *Vritta Muktavali*: and has been copiously explained in a Sanskrit commentary named *Pringala Prakasa*.

Though relative to Prakrit prosody, the rules are applicable, for

the most part, to Sanskrit prosody also: since the laws of
versification in both languages are nearly the same. (1808)

H.T. COLEBROOKE[327]

## 3.   *Ganesh, the patron of literature*

Work-perfecting Guneshu! Salamut.
Ganesh!—Ganesh!
Two-mothered! One-toothed!
Portly-paunched! Elephant-faced Guneshu!
Salam!!
Moon-crowned! Triple—eyed!
Thou who in all affairs claimest precedence in adoration!
Calamity-averting Ganesh!
Salam!!
Thou who art invoked on the commencement of a journey,
the writing of a book,
Salam!!
Oh! Ganesh, 'put not thine ears to sleep!'
'Encourage me, and then behold my bravery;
Call me your own fox, then will you see me perform
the exploits of a lion!'
'What fear need he have of the waves of the sea,
who has Noah for a pilot?'
First-born of Mahadeo and Parvuti!
God of Prudence and Policy!
Patron of Literature!
Salam!!
May it be said,
'Ah! she writes like Ganesh!' (1822)

FANNY PARKES[328]

## 4. *Theatre of the Hindus*

The *Nataka* or the Play par excellence, comprises all the elements of
a dramatic composition, and its construction, therefore, is fully
explained in the original systems, before any notice is taken of the
inferior varieties. This method is perhaps the most logical, and
obviates the necessity of some repetition; but in an inquiry of the
present description, the first point to determine appears to be, what

the dramatic amusements of the Hindus really were, before we examine their constituent parts.

Specimens of the *Nataka* are not wanting to illustrate its technical description, and we can therefore follow the original authorities with entire confidence. It is declared to be the most perfect kind of dramatic composition. The subject should always be celebrated and important. According to the *Sahitya Derpana,* the story should be selected from mythological or historical record alone; but the *Dasa Rupaka* asserts, that it may be also fictitious or mixed, or partly resting on tradition, and partly the creation of the author. The practice of the early writers seems to have sanctioned the latter rule, and although they adopted their plots from sacred poems or *Puranas,* they considered themselves at liberty to vary the incidents as they pleased. Modern bards have been more scrupulous. The restriction imposed upon the selection of the subject is the same as that to which the French theatre so long submitted, from whose tragic code all newly invented topics were excluded, in supposed imitation of the Greek theatre, in which however the *Flower of Agathon,* founded altogether upon fiction, was an early and popular production.

Like the Greek tragedy, however, the *Nataka* is to represent worthy or exalted personages only, and the hero must be a monarch, as Dushyanta; a demigod, as Rama; or a divinity, as Khrishna. The action, or more properly the passion, should be but one, as love or heroism. The plot should be simple, the incidents consistent; the business should spring direct from the story as a plant from its seed, and should be free from episodical and prolix interruptions. The time should not be protracted, and the duration of an act, according to the elder authority, should not exceed one day; but the *Sahitya Derpana* extends it to a few days, or even to one year. When the action cannot be comprised within these limits, the less important events may be thrown into narrative, or may be supposed to pass between the Acts; or they may be communicated to the audience by one of the actors, who holds the character of an interpreter, and explains to the persons of the assembly whatever they may require to know, or what is not conveyed to them by the representation; a rather awkward contrivance to supply the deficiencies of the piece, but one that would sometimes be useful to insinuate the plot into the audiences of more polished communities. The diction of a *Nataka* should be perspicuous and polished. The piece should consist of not fewer than five Acts, and not more than ten.

In many of these characteristics, the *Nataka* presents an obvious analogy to the tragedy of the Greeks, which was, 'the imitation of a solemn and perfect action, of adequate importance, told in pleasing language, exhibiting the several elements of dramatic composition in its different parts, represented through the instrumentality of agents, not by narration, and purifying the affections of human nature by the influence of pity and terror.' In the expansion of this definition in the 'Poetics,' there are many points of affinity, and particularly in the selection of persons and subjects; but there are also differences, some of which merit to be noticed.

With regard to the Unities, we have that of action fully recognised, and a simplicity of business is enjoined quite in the spirit of the Greek drama. The unity of place is not noticed, as might have been expected from the probable absence of all scenic embellishment. It was impossible to transport the substantial decorations of the Grecian stage from place to place, and therefore the scene was the same throughout; but where every thing was left to the imagination, one site was as easily conceivable as another, and the scene might be fancied, one while a garden, and another while a palace, as well as it could be imagined to be either. The unity of time is curiously modified, conformably to a principle which may satisfy the most fastidious; and 'the time required for the fable elapses invariably between the acts.' In practice there is generally less latitude than the rule indicates, and the duration of an act is very commonly that of the representation, or at most 'one course of the sun,' the night elapsing in the interval. In one piece, the *Uttara Rama Cheritra,* indeed, we have a more extensive period, and twelve years are supposed to pass between the first and second acts. This was the unavoidable consequence of the subject of the play, and affords an analogy to the license of the Romantic drama.

Another important difference from the Classical drama, and from that of most countries, is the total absence of the distinction between Tragedy and Comedy. The Hindu plays confine themselves neither to the 'crimes nor to the absurdities of mankind;' neither 'to the momentous changes, nor lighter vicissitudes of life;' neither 'to the terrors of distress nor the gaieties of prosperity.' In this respect they may be classed with much of the Spanish and English drama, to which, as Schlegel observes, 'the terms Tragedy and Comedy are wholly inapplicable, in the sense in which they were employed by the Ancients.' They are invariably of a mingled web and blend 'seriousness and sorrow with levity and laughter.' (1827)

HORACE HAYMAN WILSON[329]

## 5. On Kalidasa

Of the history of KALIDASA, to whom by general assent the KUMARA SAMBHAVA, or BIRTH OF THE WAR-GOD, is attributed, we know but little with any certainty; we can only gather from a memorial-verse which enumerates their names, that he was one of the 'Nine Precious Stones' that shone at the Court of VIKRAMADITYA, King of OUJEIN, in the half century immediately preceding the Christian era. As the examination of arguments for and against the correctness of this date is not likely to interest general readers, I must request them to rest satisfied with the belief that about the time when VIRGIL and HORACE were shedding an undying lustre upon the reign of AUGUSTUS, our poet KALIDASA lived, loved, and sang, giving and taking honour, at the polished court of the no less munificent patron of Sanskrit literature, at the period of its highest perfection.

Little as we know of Indian poetry, here and there an English reader may be found, who is not entirely unacquainted with the name or works of the author of the beautiful drams of SAKONTALA and THE HERO AND THE NYMPH, the former of which has long enjoyed an European celebrity in the translation of SIR WILLIAM JONES, and the latter is one of the most charming of PROFESSOR WILSON'S specimens of the Hindu Theatre; here and there even in England may be found a lover of the graceful, tender, picturesque, and fanciful, who knows something, and would gladly know more, of the sweet poet of the CLOUD MESSENGER, and THE SEASONS; whilst in Germany he has been deeply studied in the original, and enthusiastically admired in translation,—not the Orientalist merely, but the poet, the critic, the natural philosopher,—a GOETHE, a SCHLEGEL, a HUMBOLDT, having agreed, on account of this tenderness of feeling and his rich creative imagination, to set KALIDASA very high among the glorious company of the Sons of Song. (1853)

RALPH T.H. GRIFFITH[330]

## 6. Sakoontala

It may be remarked that in every Sanskrit play the women and
inferior characters speak a kind of provincial Sanskrit or *patois*,
called Prakrit—bearing the same relation to Sanskrit that Italian
bears to Latin, or that the spoken Latin of the age of Cicero bore
to the highly polished Latin in which he delivered his Orations.
Even the heroine of the drama is made to speak in the vulgar dialect.
The hero, on the other hand, and all the higher male characters,
speak in Sanskrit; and, as if to invest them with still greater dignity,
half of what they say is in verse. Indeed the prose part of their
speeches is often very commonplace, being only introductory to the
lofty sentiment of the poetry that follows. Thus, if the whole composition be compared to a web, the prose will correspond to the
warp, or that part which is extended lengthwise in the loom, while
the metrical portion will answer to the cross-threads which constitute the woof. The original verses are written in a great variety of
Sanskrit metres. For example, the first thirty-four verses of the
Sakoontala exhibit eleven different varieties of metre. No metrical
system in English could give any idea of the almost infinite resources
of the Sanskrit in this respect. Blank verse has therefore been more
in unison with the character of our own dramatic writings, and
rhyming stanzas have only been admitted when the subject-matter
seemed to call for such a change. Perhaps the chief consideration
that induced me to adopt this mode of metrical translation [of
Sakoontala] was, that the free and unfettered character of the verse
enabled me to preserve more of the freshness and vigour of the
original. If the poetical ideas of Kalidasa have not been expressed in
language as musical as his own. I have at least done my best to avoid
diluting them by paraphrastic circumlocutions or additions. If the
English verses are prosaic, I have the satisfaction of knowing that by
resisting the allurements of rhyme. I have done all in my power to
avoid substituting a fictitious and meagre poem of my own for the
grand, yet simple and chaste creation of Kalidasa ...

The poetical merit of Kalidasa's Sakoontala is so universally
admitted that any remarks on this head would be superfluous. I will
merely observe that, in the opinion of the learned natives, the
Fourth Act, which describes the departure of Sakoontala from the
hermitage, contains the most obvious beauties; and that no one can
read this act, nor indeed any act of the play, without being struck

with the richness and elevation of its author's genius, the exuberance and glow of his fancy, his ardent love of the beautiful, his deep sympathy with Nature and Nature's loveliest scenes, his profound knowledge of the human heart, his delicate appreciation of its most refined feelings, his familiarity with its conflicting sentiments and emotions. But in proportion to the acknowledged excellence of Kalidasa's composition, and in proportion to my own increasing admiration of its beauties, is the diffidence I feel lest I may have failed to infuse any of the poetry of the original into the present version. Translation of poetry must, at the best, resemble the process of pouring a highly volatile and evanescent spirit from one receptacle into another. The original fluid will always suffer a certain amount of waste and evaporation ...

Kalidasa's Sakoontala seems to have been acted at the commencement of the summer-season—a period peculiarly sacred to Kama-deva, the Indian God of Love. We are told that it was enacted before an audience 'consisting chiefly of men of education and discernment.' As the greater part of every play was written in Sanskrit, (which, although spoken in some portion of India at a remote period, was certainly not the vernacular language of the country at the time when the Hindu dramas were performed), few spectators would be present who were not of the learned and educated classes. This circumstance is in accordance with the constitution of Hindu society, whereby the productions of literature, as well as the offices of State, were reserved for the privileged castes.

Every play opens with a prologue, or, more correctly, an introduction, designed to prepare the way for the entrance of the dramatis personæ. The prologue commences with a benediction or prayer (pronounced by a Brahman, or if the stage-manager happened to be of the Brahmanical caste, by the manager himself), in which the poet invokes the favour of the national diety in behalf of the audience. The blessing is generally followed by a dialogue between the manager and one or two of the actors, in which an account is given of the author of the drama, a complimentary tribute is paid to the critical acumen of the spectators, and such a reference is made to past occurences or present circumstances as may be necessary for the elucidation of the plot. At the conclusion of the prologue, the manager, by some abrupt exclamation, adroitly introduces one of the dramatic personages, and the real performance commences.

The play, being thus opened, is carried forward in scenes and acts; each scene being marked by the entrance of one character and the exit of another, as in the French drama. The dramatis personæ were divided into three classes—the inferior characters *(nicha),* who were said to speak Prakrit, in a monotonous unemphatic tone of voice *(anudattoktya);* the middling *(madhyama),* and the superior *(pradhana),* who were said to speak Sanskrit with accent, emphasis, and expression *(udattoktya).* In general, the stage is never left vacant till the end of an act, nor does any change of locality take place till then. The commencement of a new act is often marked, like the commencement of the piece, by an introductory monologue or dialogue, spoken by one or more of the dramatis personæ, and called Vishkambha or Pravesaka. In this scene allusion is frequently made to events supposed to have occurred in the interval of the acts, and the audience is the better prepared to take up the thread of the story, which is then skilfully carried on to the concluding scene. The piece closes, as it began, with a prayer for national plenty and prosperity, addressed to the favourite deity, and spoken by one of the principal personages of the drama.

Although, in the conduct of the plot, and the delineation of character, the Hindu dramatists show considerable skill, yet they do not appear to have been remarkable for much fertility of invention. Love, according to Hindu notions, is the subject of most of their dramas. The hero, who is generally a king, and already the husband of a wife or wives (for a wife or two more or less is no encumbrance in Indian plays), is suddenly smitten with the charms of a lovely woman, sometimes a nymph, or, as in the case of Sakoontala, the daughter of a nymph by a mortal father. The heroine is required to be equally impressible, and the first tender glance from the hero's eye reaches her heart. With true feminine delicacy, however, she locks the secret of her passion in her own breast, and by her coyness and reserve keeps her lover for a long period in the agonies of suspense. The hero, being reduced to a proper state of desperation, is harassed by other difficulties. Either the celestial nature of the nymph is in the way of their union, or he doubts the legality of the match, or he fears his own unworthiness, or he is hampered by the angry jealousy of a previous wife. In short, doubts, obstacles and delays make great havoc of both hero and heroine. They give way to melancholy, indulge in amorous rhapsodies, and become very emaciated. So far, it must be confessed, the story is decidedly dull, and its pathos, notwithstanding the occasional grandeur and beauty of the imagery, often verges on the ridiculous. But, by way of relief, an element of life is generally introduced in the character of the Vidushaka, or Jester, who is the constant companion of the hero; and in the young maidens, who are the confidential friends of the heroine, and soon become possessed of her secret. By a curious regulation, the Jester is always a Brahman, and, therefore, of a caste superior to the king himself; yet his business is to excite mirth by being ridiculous in person, age, and attire. He is represented as grey-haired, hump-backed, lame and hideously ugly. In fact, he is a species of buffoon, who is allowed full liberty of speech, being himself a universal butt. His attempts at wit, which are rarely very successful, and his allusions to the pleasures of the table, of which he is a confessed votary, are absurdly contrasted with the sententious solemnity of the despairing hero, crossed in the prosecution of his love-suit. His clumsy interference in the intrigues of his friend, only serves to augment his difficulties, and occasions many an awkward dilemma. On the other hand, the shrewdness of the heroine's confidantes never seems to fail them under the most trying circumstances; while their sly jokes and innuendos, their love of fun, their girlish sympathy with the progress of the love-affair, their warm affection for their friend, heighten the interest of the plot, and contribute not a little to vary its monotony. (1855)

MONIER WILLIAMS[330] [a]

## 7. Vernacular Literature

As far as my information goes, the earliest vernacular literature of Hindustan is the bardic chronicles of Rajputana. The first bard of whom we have any certain information was the well-known Chand Bardai, who celebrated, towards the end of the twelfth century, the fortunes of Prithwi Raj, the Chauhan, of Dilli, in the famous *Prithi Raj Ray'sa.* Contemporary with him was the bard Jagnayak who attended the court of Prithwi Raj's great rival. Paramardi of Mahoba, and who was probably the author of the *Alha Khand,* a work equally famous in Hindustan with the Prithi Raj Ray'sa, but which has had the misfortune of being preserved by oral tradition instead of in manuscript.

Turning aside from these bardic historians we may now revert to the growth of vernacular literature in the Gangetic valley, coincident with the rise of the Vaishnava religion at the commencement of

the 15th century. Ramanand, the popularizer of the worship of
Rama, flourished about the year 1400; and even greater than he was
his famous disciple Kabir, who succeeded in founding a still existing
sect, which united the salient points of Muhammadanism and Hinduism. Here we first touch upon that marvellous catholicity of
sentiment of which the key-note was struck by Ramanand, which is
visible in the doctrines of all his successors, and which reached its
truest height in the lofty teaching of Tulsi Das two centuries later.
The worship of the deified prince of Audh, and the loving adoration
of Sita, the perfect wife and the perfect mother, have developed
naturally into a doctrine of eclecticism in its best form—a doctrine
which, while teaching the infinite vileness of mankind before the
Infinitely Good, yet sees good in everything that He has created,
and condemns no religion and no system of philosophy as utterly
bad that inculcates, Thou shalt love the Lord thy God with all thy
heart, and with all thy soul, and with all thy strength, and with all thy
mind; and thy neighbour as thyself.

Far different has been the fate of that other great branch of the
Vaishnava religion which is founded on mystic interpretations of
the love which Krishna bore to Radha. Beautiful in itself, paralleled,
also by the teaching of many Christian doctors, and rendered more
beautiful by the magic poetry of Mira Bai (fl 1420) in the west, and
of Bidyapat'i Thakur (fl 1400) in the east, its passionate adoration,
whose inner meaning was too esoteric for the spirits of the common
herd of disciples, in many cases degenerated into a poetry worthy of
only the baser sorts of Tantrik Siva worshippers. But at its best the
Krishna cult is wanting in the nobler elements of the teaching of
Ramanand. Its essence is almost selfish—a soul-absorbing, nay
all-absorbing, individual love cast at the feet of Him who is Love
itself. It teaches the first and great commandment of the Christian
law, but the second, which is like unto it—Thou shalt love thy
neighbour as thyself—it omits.

Leaving these two sects aside for a moment, we must pause at one
remarkable man, who in some respects was an offshoot from the
Rajput bards, while on the other hand his writings bear strong
marks of the influence of Kabir's teaching. Malik Muhammad (fl
1540) studied under both Musalman and Hindu doctors, and wrote
in the purest vernacular of his time, the fine philosophic epic entitled the *Padmawat*. This work, while telling in vivid languáge the
story of Ratan Sen's quest for the fair Padmawat, of Alaud-din's

siege of the virgin city of Chitaur, of Ratan's bravery, and of Padmawat's wifely devotion which culminated in the terrible sacrifice of all in the doomed city that was true and fair, to save it from the lust of the conqueror, is also an allegory describing the search of the soul for true wisdom, and the trials and temptations which assail it in its course. Malik Muhammad's ideal is high, and throughout the work of the Musalman ascetic there run veins of the broadest charity and of sympathy with those higher spirits among his Hindu fellow-countrymen who were groping in the dark for that light of which so many of them obtained glimpses. . .

It was in Braj, the country of the cowpens and the scene of the childhood of Krishna and of his early amours with the herdmaidens of Gokula, that the Krishna cult naturally took its strongest root; and during the 16th century it was the home of a school of poets devoted to the worship of that god founded by the great apostle Ballabhacharj and his son Bitthal Nath. Of their eight principal disciples, grouped under the name of the *Ashta Chhap,* Krishn Das and Sur Das were the ones most celebrated. The latter is considered by his fellow-countrymen to share with Tulsi Das the throne of absolute perfection in the art of poesy; but European critics will be inclined to award the latter poet alone the supreme crown, and to relegate the blind bard of Agra to a lower, though still an honourable, place. One more poet of this group may here by noticed for his fame as a singer. I allude to Tan Sen, who besides being an author was chief court-singer to the Emperor Akbar. The principal native authority for the Krishna poets of the 16th century is the enigmatical *Bhakt Mala* of Nabha Das, with its various commentaries.

While the successors of Ballabhacharj were filling Braj with their music, the not distant Mughal Court at Dilli had collected a group of state poets, some of whom were of no mean reputation. Todar Mall, who besides being a great finance minister was the immediate cause of the acceptance of the Urdu language, Birbal, Akbar's friend and author of many witty impromptus, Abdur Rahim Khankhana, and Man Singh of Amer, were more famous as the patrons of authors than as vernacular writers themselves; but Narhari, Hari Nath, Karan, and Gang, are justly celebrated as poets of a high rank.

Thulsi Das (fl. 1600, d. 1624), the greatest poet of the deeds of Ram, occupies a position amongst these authors peculiar to himself. Far different from the founders of the Braj school, who were surrounded by numerous imitators and successors, he lived in

Banaras, unapproachable and alone in his niche in the Temple of Fame. Disciples he had in plenty,—to-day they are numbered by millions,—but imitators, none. Looking back along the vista of centuries we see his noble figure standing in its own pure light as the guide and saviour of Hindustan. His influence has never ceased—nay, it has increased and is still increasing; and when we reflect on the fate of Tantra-ridden Bengal or on the wanton orgies which are carried out under the name of Krishna worship, we can justly appreciate the work of the man who first in India since Budha's time taught man's duty to his neighbour and succeeded in getting his teaching accepted. His great work is at the present day the one Bible of a hundred millions of people; and fortunate has it been for them that they had this guide. .

This Augustan age was not only a period of the erotic poetry of Sur Das and of the nature-poetry of Tulsi, but was also signalized by the first attempts to systematize the art of poetry itself. The young growth had shown a tendency to shoot forth too luxuriantly, and even Malik Muhammad wrote verses which were quaintly unmusical. Sur Das and Tulsi Das possessed the strength of giants, and were far beyond their contemporaries in polish and in a sense of proportion; but the works of the other early writers of this period jarred upon the senses of scholars brought up in the strictly classical schools of Sanskrit philology. So after one or two earlier attempts by minor authors, such as the poet Khem, Kesab Das (fl. 1580) stepped forward and settled for ever the cannons of poetic criticism. A romantic story connects him with the poetess Par'bin Rai, and it is said that it was for her sake that he composed his great work the *Kabi-priya*. Seventy years later, in the middle of the seventeenth century, Chintamani Tripathi and his brothers amplified and developed the rules laid down by him. This group of critical poets is fitly closed at the end of the 17th century by Kalidas Tribedi, the author of the *Hajara*, the first great anthology of extracts from the works of the Augustan age of Hindustan.

The latter half of this period, that is to say the 17th century, saw the rise of some remarkable religious sects, which gave birth to a considerable body of literature. The principal reformers who may be mentioned were Dadu (fl. 1600), founder of the Dadu Panthi sect; Pran Nath (fl. 1650), founder of the Pran'nathis; and Gobind Singh (fl. 1698), the founder of the militant Sikh religion and compiler of the *Granth*, or holy book of that sect. (1888)

GEORGE A. GRIERSON[330] [b]

# 23. Geography

## A. HARBOURS AND COASTS

### 1. Bombay harbour

The river, on which Panwell is situated, is in the dry season only an
inlet of the sea, and navigable to that place at high water; we were
therefore obliged to consult the tide. It turned at eight, and we set
off with it, under a salute of fifteen guns from the fort. The
Governor's Aides-de-camp, and Major Green, attended me to the
water side. The balloon boat, from its drawing less water, was
preferred to the yacht; it had a cabin, and held us very well. The
harbour improved in beauty as we advanced. The islands are, in
general, covered with wood; but Butcher's Island is clear, except at
the northern side, where several buildings are erected close to an
old Mahratta fort. Among the lofty hills, which formed a back
ground to the scene, Funnel Hill was most conspicuous from the
singularity of its shape; the summit has all the appearance of a vast
pillar, elevated in the centre of a flat, on the top of a rock. The whole
range of hills is singular in its appearance, and continually afforded
subjects for Mr. Salt's pencil. We passed between the islands of
Salsette and Elephanta, where the bay begins to contract in its
dimensions. The sea breeze here overtook us. The entrance to the
river Pan is defended by a small fort, which was built by the English,
and formed into a depot during the old Mahratta war: it is now
nearly in ruins. The river was full; the trees being actually half
covered by the water. The paddy fields presented a cheering prospect by their healthy state, and even the mountains were covered
with verdure, except where their smooth surface was broken by
rocky pinnacles rising to a great height. The clouds floated around
them, and occasionally, in part, concealed them from our view,
which greatly improved the scene. High cultivation and picturesque
scenery have no where in India been so perfectly united. (1802–6)

GEORGE, VISCOUNT VALENTIA[331]

## 2.  The Malabar coast

At length, after being disappointed by many deceitful appearance of imaginary shores, and when reduced to our last cask of water, the man at the mast-head saw land, and the coast of Malabar was soon discerned through the telescopes on deck: the powers of language fail to express the joy which thrilled in our hearts at this happy prospect; those only who have been in a similar situation can conceive it: favoured by a gentle breeze, we gradually approached the cocoa-nut groves, which seemed to rise from the ocean, on the low sandy shore, near the Dutch settlement of Cochin, where we anchored in the evening. The ship was soon surrounded by boats, laden with cattle, poultry, fruit, and vegetables: this was indeed a most grateful visit to us all: but especially to our poor invalids; who were immediately brought upon deck to enjoy the refreshing gales from the land, and partake of our delicious fare. The town of Cochin is pleasantly situated near the road, at the entrance of a broad river, surrounded by the low lands and cocoa-nut trees just mentioned; beyond them are woody hills, and majestic mountains, forming a noble boundary to the landscape. (1812)

JAMES FORBES[332]

## 3.  The coast of Orissa

Juggurnaut is one of the euphonious titles of the preserving deity, Vishnu, and signifies 'supreme in the world.' The temple stands in the ancient town of Poori, or Pursottem, upon the coast of Orissa, which is of all other coasts the most sterile in appearance, being a mere succession of sand-hills, without a single blade of vegetation to refresh the eye. The city itself is not visible from the sea, but on the N.E. side of the temple is a small collection of white bungalows, which form the European station, and these from their very low walls and high conical roofs appear half-buried in the sandy beach: they, however, enjoy the luxury of the same sea breeze as is found so grateful at Madras. The surf along this coast is quite as tremendous as at Madras, and *massulah* boats of a similar construction are used for landing. (1831–6)

THOMAS BACON[333]

'Approach of the Monsoon, Bombay Harbour', drawn by William Daniell

## 4.  *Landing at Madras*

Everybody has heard or read of the famous Madras surf,—that tremendous barrier which guards the shores of the coast, so replete with danger to the uninitiated; and those dreadful sharks which swarm outside ready to pounce upon any unfortunate victim who may fall into the water. Everybody knows this surf now-a-days; I will not therefore attempt its description, nor will I trouble the reader with aught about the Massulah boats or catamarans. Both are also too well known to require comment, or remark; suffice it to say that the latter are just as well adapted to the purposes of crossing the surf, as the surf is just the kind of hot water for such strangely-constructed boats to float upon.

To new comers, however, the whole is worthy of remark, and no doubt matter of surprise. It frequently happens that griffins in landing are liable to be imposed upon by the men who pull them on shore. In crossing the surf some degree of skill is necessary to strand the boats in safety, and the boatmen usually demand a present for a job, for which they are already well paid, and which they have no right whatsoever to ask or expect; but griffins are *so* kind and *so* liberal, and these boatmen are *such* acute judges of physiognomy, that they can tell at a glance, whether there is a probability of success or not. If refused, they sometimes bring their boats broad-side on to the surf; the consequence is a good ducking, if not an upset altogether into the briny element;—this is by way of revenge. But such rascality is now-a-days seldom practised. The person who most deserves a present, if any, is the poor man, *'catamaran jack,'* who follows each boat in his frail bark, ready to pick up any body in case of an upset; and I have invariably given these poor fellows half a rupee (one shilling), as a present, merely for being ready, in case of necessity.

I remember an instance of a boat crossing the surf without the attendance of one of these men. The surf was very high—the boat was upset; the crew all escaped by swimming; but one poor old soldier, going as a passenger to one of the ships, not being able to swim, was seen to sink, and rose no more: he must either have been drowned or carried off by a ground shark. Accidents seldom or ever occur now-a-days. The boatmen are paid by government, and held in proper check, by the master attendant of the port, who keeps a strict watch over them, punishing instances of neglect or misconduct most severely.

But to proceed. We crossed the dreaded surf and landed in safety. Passengers are either carried out of the way of the water in a chair or on the backs of the boatmen. Upon gaining a footing, I was instantly surrounded by a multitude of naked looking savages, all jabbering away broken English and Malabar, asking me to take a palankeen, and some actually seized hold of me, and were about to lift me into one; however, I asked the sergeant, who was with me, for his cane, which being obtained, I laid about me right and left, and soon cleared myself of the crowd. (1833–42)

ALBERT HERVEY[334]

## 5. *Dangerous surf*

We reached Gopalpur on the afternoon of the 1st of June. A flagstaff and a few white houses distinguish an otherwise monotonous coast-line, but to ensure vessels making no mistake as to the locality its name is painted in letters 3 feet high on a large signboard which runs along the roof of the Steamer Company's office, as if the port were a sort of marine Clapham junction instead of being the *ultima Thule* of the Madras presidency and of India. The landing through the much-dreaded surf had now to be faced. The horses that we brought with us and our luggage left the ship in advance, and all landed safely with the exception of one cargo-boat which was overturned in the surf and several very necessary articles of apparel found their last resting place at the bottom of the sea. We ourselves landed in a large surf boat, and the question arose whether we might not have to swim for it. 'Can you swim, Mr. Archdeacon,' asked the Governor; 'no' was the ominous reply, but though thus in the hands of Providence, we felt that, under the circumstances, we were probably fairly secure. And under the charge of the head boatman, who boasted that this was the fourth Governor he had successfully guided through their dangers, we got through the breakers in safety. (1889)

J.D. REES[335]

## B. CITIES

### 1. *Palibothra (Patna)*

At the meeting of this river (Ganges) and another is situated Palibothra, a city eighty stadia in length and fifteen in breadth. It is

'Illumination of the Surf at Madras', *Illustrated London News*, 8 June 1872

of the shape of a parallelogram, and is girded with a wooden wall, pierced with loopholes for the discharge of arrows. It has a ditch in front for defence and for receiving the sewage of the city. The people in whose country this city is situated is the most distinguished in all India, and is called the Prasii. The king, in addition to his family name, must adopt the surname of Palibothros, as Sandrakottos, for instance, did, to whom Megasthenes was sent on an embassy. (c. 3rd. Century B.C.)

MEGASTHENES[336]

## 2.   Magadha and the city of Patna

Crossing the river, and proceeding towards the south one yojana, we arrive at Magadha, and the town of Pa-lin-fou (Patna). This is the town in which king Asoka reigned. In the middle of the city is the royal palace, the different parts of which he commissioned the genii (demons) to construct. The massive stones of which the walls are made, the doorways and the sculptured towers, are no human work. The ruins of this palace still exist. The younger brother of king Asoka having arrived at the dignity of a Rahat, was in the habit of residing in the hill Khi-chi-kiu (Gridhrakuta), finding his chief delight in silent contemplation. . .

In this city (i.e. of Patalipoutra or Patna) once lived a certain Brahman, called Lo-tai-sz-pi-mi, of large mind and extensive knowledge, and attached to the Great Vehicle. There was nothing with which he was unacquainted, and he lived apart occupied in silent meditation. The King of the country honoured and respected him, as his religious superior (Guru). If he went to salute him he did not dare to sit down in his presence. If the King, from a feeling of affectionate esteem, took him by the hand, the Brahman immediately washed himself from head to foot. For something like fifty years the whole country looked up to this man and placed its confidence on him alone. He mightily extended the influence of the Law of Buddha, so that the heretics were unable to obtain any advantage at all over the priesthood.

By the side of the tower of king Asoka is built a Sangharama belonging to the Greater Vehicle, very imposing and elegant. There is also a Temple belonging to the Little Vehicle. Together they contain about six or seven hundred priests, all of them exceedingly well conducted. In the College attached to the temple one may see eminent Shamans from every quarter of the world, and whatever scholars there are who seek for instruction, they all flock to this temple. The Brahman teacher (of whom we have just spoken) is also called Manjusri. The great Shamans of the country, and all the Bikshus attached to the Great Vehicle, universally esteem and reverence him; moreover he resides in this Sangharama. Of all the kingdoms of mid-India, the towns of this country are especially large. The people are rich and prosperous and virtuous. . . . King Asoka having destroyed seven (of the original) pagodas, constructed 84,000 others. The very first which he built is the great tower which stands about three li to south of this city. In front of this pagoda is an impression of Buddha's foot, (over which) they have raised a chapel, the gate of which faces the north. To the south of the tower is a stone pillar, about a chang and a half in girth (eighteen feet), and three chang or so in height (thirty-five feet). On the surface of this pillar is an inscription to the following effect, 'King Asoka presented the whole of Jambudwipa to the priests of the Four Quarters, and redeemed it again with money, and this he did four times.' Three or four hundred paces to the north of the pagoda is the spot where Asoka was born (or resided). On this spot he raised the city of Ni-lai, and in the midst of it erected a stone pillar also about thirty-five feet in height, on the top of which he placed the figure of a lion, and also engraved an historical record on the front of the pillar, giving an account of the successive events connected with the city of Ni-lai, with corresponding year, day, and month. (A.D. 400)

FAH HIAN[337]

## 3. Delhi

The city of Delhi is made up now of four neighbouring and contiguous towns. One of them is Delhi proper, the old city built by the infidels and captured in the year 1188. The second is called Siri, known also as the Abode of the Caliphate; this was the town given by the Sultan to Ghiyath ad-Din, the grandson of the' Abbasid Caliph Mustansir, when he came to his court. The third is called Tughlaq Abad, after its founder, the Sultan Tughlaq, the father of the Sultan of India to whose court we came. The reason why he built it was that one day he said to a former Sultan 'O master of the world, it were fitting that a city should be built here.' The Sultan replied to him in jest 'When you are Sultan, build it.' It came about by the decree of God that he became Sultan, so he built it and called it by his own name. The fourth is called Jahan Panah, and is set apart for the residence of the reigning Sultan Muhammad Shah. He was the founder of it, and it was his intention to unite these four towns within a single wall, but after building part of it he gave up the rest because of the expense required for its construction. (1325–54)

IBN BATTUTA[338]

## 4. Bidar

. . . Bidar is the capital of Moslem Hindustan. It is a large city, and many people live in it. The Sultan is young—only 20 years old—and those who govern are princes and boyars of Khorassan; those who fight in wars are Khorassanis too.

In that city there lives Malik-at-Tujjar the Khorassani, a boyar who has an army 200,000 strong. Melik Khan has 100,000 and Farkhad Khan 20,000. And many Khans have an army of 10,000 each. The Sultan goes to war with an army of 300,000. The land is very populous; the countrymen are very poor, but the boyars are rich and live in luxury; they are carried in silver litters, preceded by as many as 20 horses in golden harness and followed by 300 horse, 500 foot, 10 trumpeters, 10 drummers, and 10 pipers. And the Sultan goes forth with his mother and wife to amuse himself, and is accompanied by 10,000 horse and 50,000 foot. And there also go forth 200 elephants in gilt armour. And the Sultan is preceded by 100 trumpeters, 100 dancers, and 300 spare horses in golden harness, and followed by 100 monkeys and 100 *gaurikas* or hand-maidens.

The Sultan's palace has seven gates, with a hundred guards and a hundred *kafir* scribes at each gate; some of them register those coming in and others, those going out; but strangers are barred from the palace. And the palace is very beautiful, with fretwork and gilt all over it, and its everystone is fretted and very beautifully painted in gold; and inside the palace there are sundry vessels. (1466–72)

AFANASY NIKITIN[339]

## 5. Canonor

Canonor is a fine and large city, in which the King of Portugal has a very strong castle. The king of this city is a great friend of the King of Portugal, although he is a pagan. This Canonor is the port at which the horses which come from Persia disembark. And you must know that every horse pays twenty-five ducats for customs duty, and then they proceed on the mainland towards Narsinga. There are many Moorish merchants in this city. No grain nor grapes grow here, nor any productions like ours, excepting cucumbers and melons. Bread is not eaten here, that is to say, by the natives of the country, but they eat rice, fish, flesh, and the nuts of the country. At the proper time we will speak of their religion and customs, for they live after the manner of those of Calicut. Here we begin to find a few spices, such as pepper, ginger, cardamums, mirabolans, and a little cassia. This place is not surrounded by a wall. The houses are very poor. Here also are found fruits different from ours, and which are also far superior to ours. I will make the comparison when the proper time comes. The country is well adapted for war, as it is full of hollow places artificially made. The king of this place has 50,000 Naeri (Nairs), that is, gentlemen who fight with swords, shields, lances and bows, and with artillery. And yet they go naked and unshod, with a cloth around them, without anything on their heads, excepting when they go to war, when they wear a turban of a red colour passed twice round the head, and they all have them tied in the same manner. They do not use here either horses, mules, camels, or asses. Elephants are sometimes used, but not for battle. At the proper time we will speak of the vigour exerted by the King of Canonor against the Portuguese. There is much traffic in this place, to which two hundred ships come every year from different countries. (1502–8)

LUDOVICO DI VARTHEMA[340]

## 6.   *Agra and Fatehpur Sikri*

From thence we went to Agra, passing many Rivers, which by reason of the raine were so swollen, that we waded and swamme of-tentimes for our lives. Agra is a very great Citie and populous, built with stone, having faire and large streets, with a faire River running by it, which falleth into the Gulfe of Bengala. It hath a faire Castle and strong, with a very faire Ditch. Here bee many Moores and Gentiles, the King is called Zelabdim Echebar: the people for the most part call him The great Mogor. From thence we went for

Fatepore, which is the place where the King kept his Court. The
Towne is greater then Agra, but the houses and streets bee not so
faire. Here dwell many people both Moores and Gentiles. The King
hath in Agra and Fatep'ore, as they doe credibly report, one
thousand Elephants, thirtie thousand Horses, one thousand and
foure hundred tame Deere, eight hundred Concubines: such store
of Ounces, Tygres, Buffles, Cockes and Hawkes, that is very strange
to see. He keepeth a great Court, which they call Dericcan. Agra
and Fatepore are two very great Cities, either of them much greater
than London, and very populous. Betweene Agra and Fatepore are
twelve miles, and all the way is a Market of victuals and other things,
as full as though a man were still in a Towne, and so many people as
if a man were in a Market. They have many fine Carts, and many of
them carved and gilded with Gold, with two wheeles which bee
drawne with two little Bulls about the bignesse of our great Dogs in
England, and they will runne with any Horse, and carrie two or
three men in one of these Carts: they are covered with Silke or very
fine cloth, and bee used here as our Coaches bee in England. Hither
is great resort of Merchants from Persia, and out of India, and very
much Merchandize of Silke and Cloth, and of precious Stones, both
Rubies, Diamants, and Pearles. The King is apparelled in a white
Cabie made like a Shirt tyed with strings on the one side, and a little
cloth on his head, coloured often-times with red and yellow. None
come into his house but his Eunuches which keepe his women.
(1583–91)

RALPH FITCH[341]

## 7. Surat

The city of *Suratte* did (pursuant to their ancient records) pay a
yearly tribute of two millions *Mamoidys,* or one million of livres, or
four hundred thousand crowns, to their king *Achabaar*, one *Ganna
Ganna* being then their governor, who had eighteen hundred villages under his jurisdiction. All about *Suratte* are abundance of very
pleasant and stately summer-seats, and magnificent burying-places,
(a thing much in request among the *Moors,*) besides several large
cisterns, or rather ponds, faced with freestone. Among the rest one
deserves particularly to be taken notice of, as having no less than an
hundred angles of twenty-eight yards each, with stone steps to lead
you down into the cistern; in the midst of which stands the tomb of
the founder.

About an hour and a half to the north from the mouth of the river of *Suratte*, (named *Tap-gyly*) is a road, where ships may ride at anchor near a ridge of sand-banks, which, together with part of the continent, breaks the force of the winds. The road, commonly called *Chom Suhali*, or *Sualicom*, lies at twenty-one degrees fifty minutes north latitude, extending from north-east to north, and again south-west to south: the entrance of it is but narrow, and at high water not above seven, but at low water scarce five fathoms deep, with a hard sandy bottom: the north-north-east, and south-south-west winds make here the highest tides. The harbour of *Suhali* is not above a musket-shot broad: the south-south-west winds make this road unsafe, the landshelves lying then almost dry. The *English* settled their factory there 1609, and the *Dutch* 1616, who carry their merchandizes upon waggons drawn by oxen from the said road four leagues to the city.

It is to the settlements of those two nations *Suratte* owes its chief increase in trade, many rich merchants and artisans having been drawn thither since that time, who send their commodities thence by the *Red Sea* to *Arabia, Aden, Mocha, Hideda, Juda, Mecca, Chihiry, Catziny, Doffer* and *Souakin,* (in *Ethiopia*) consisting in fine and coarse *Indian, Gusuratte, Decan*, and *Bengale* stuffs and cloths, callicoes, indigo, sugar, gums, ginger, tobacco, wheat, rice, butter, and other provisions, in which this country abounds. Besides that, two or three of the king's ships trade into these parts, and transport certain precious commodities belonging to some peculiar merchants and persons of the first rank: these are generally obliged to the company, for furnishing them with some able seamen and constables, (the *Moors* being but ill versed in these things;) especially while they were at enmity with the *Danes*. (1671)

PHILIP BALDAEUS[342]

## 8. *Jodhpur*

The sand, since we crossed the Looni, had become gradually heavier, and was quite fatiguing as we approached the capital of 'the region of death;' but the Marwarries and the camels appeared to move through it as briskly as our men would on the plains of the Ganges.... The fort is erected on a mole projecting from a low range of hills, so as to be almost isolated, while, being higher than the surrounding objects, it is not commanded. This table-ridge (mountain we can scarcely term it, since its most elevated portion is not more than three hundred feet in height) is a curious feature in these regions of uninterrupted aridity. It is about twenty-five miles in length, and, as far as I could determine from a bird's-eye view and from report, between two and three in breadth, the capital being placed on the highest part at the southern extremity, and may be said to be detached from it. The northern point, which is the highest, and on which the palace is built, is less than three hundred feet. Every where it is scarped, but especially at this point, against which the batteries of the League were directed in 1806, at least a hundred and twenty feet of perpendicular height. Strong walls and numerous round and square towers encircle the crest of the hill, encompassing a space of great extent, as may be judged from the dimensions of the base, said to be four miles in circuit. Seven barriers are thrown across the circuitous ascent, each having immense portals and their separate guards. There are two small lakes under the walls: the *Ranni Talab,* or 'Queen's Lake,' to the east; and the *Golab Sagur,* or 'Rose-water Sea,' to the south, from which the garrison draws up water in buckets. There is also inside a *coond,* or reservoir, about ninety feet in depth, excavated from the rock, which can be filled from these tanks; and there are likewise wells within, but the water is brackish. Within are many splendid edifices, and the Raja's residence is a succession of palaces, each prince since the founder having left memorials of his architectural taste. The city to the eastward of the citadel is encompassed by a strong wall, three coss, or nearly six miles, in extent, on which a hundred and one bastions or towers are distributed, on the rampart are mounted several *raiklas* or swivels. There are seven gates to the capital, each bearing the name of the city to which it leads. The streets are very regular, and adorned with many handsome edifices of free-stone, of which the ridge is composed. The number of families some years ago were stated to be 20,000 probably 80,000 souls, an estimate far too great for the present day. The *Golab Sagur* is the favourite lounge of the inhabitants, who recreate amongst its gardens; and, strange to say, the most incomparable pomegranates (*anar*) are produced in it, far superior even to those of Cabul, which they resemble in the peculiarity of being *be-dana*, 'without grain:' rather a misnomer for a fruit, the characteristic of which is its granulations; but this is in

contradistinction to those of India, which are all grain and little
pulp. The *anars* of the *Kagli-ca-bagh,* or 'Ravens' Garden,' are sent
to the most remote parts, as presents. Their beautiful ruby tint
affords an abundant resource for metaphor to the Rajpoot bard,
who describes it as 'sparkling in the ambrosial cup.' (1829)

JAMES TOD[343]

## 9. *Lucknow*

'The city of Lucknow,' says a distinguished modern writer, 'built on
the right of the river Goomtee, and extending for four miles along
its banks, lies about fifty miles to the north-east of Cawnpore. All
the principal buildings including the Inam-barrah, the king's palace,
and the adjoining gardens, are between the city and the river bank.
Here also is the Residency, a large walled enclosure, comprising not
only the palace of the Resident, but other houses and out-houses as
well as underground buildings, or vaults on a large scale. It is
situated on a higher ground than the rest of the town, which it may
be said to command. Near this; and higher up the river, almost on its
bank, is a strong castellated building called the Muchee-Bawn, very
well adapted for defence against native troops. To the south, and
covering an immense space, lies the town, intersected by a canal,
which falls into the Goomtee close to the Martiniere, about three
miles south-east of the Residency, a little to the south of this is the
Dil-Koosha, a hunting-box or palace, within an enclosed park. To
the north-east of the Residency and on the left bank of the Goomtee
is the cantonment, communicating with the right bank by means of
two bridges, one of stone near the Muchee-Bawn, the other of iron
close to the Residency. Recrossing the right bank we come to the
space between the Residency and the Martiniere. This is filled up
principally by native palaces, amongst which the Motee-Mehal,
Shah-munzil, Secundra-bagh, and Furukh-buksh-ka-kotee, are the
most conspicuous —many of the buildings here indicated are to be
seen in Mr. Simpson's drawing. The view here given was taken from
the 'Tower of the Residency.' 'It looks,' says the artist, 'over the
ground by which the relief and taking of Lucknow were accomplished. All the points of that memorable struggle can be made out as
far as the Martiniere and Dil-Koosha. The Kaiserbugh, and Chattur
Munzil, Dilaram, Motee Mehal, Thirty-second Mess-house, Shah
Nujief, Kadam Russool, etc. are distinctly visible. Within the

'Lucknow', drawn by William Simpson

entrenchments are the Banqueting Hall, Dr. Fayrer's house, and the crumbling walls of the Residency itself. Through the nearest arched window in the foreground came the ball which killed Sir Henry Lawrence.' The picture has thus a deep historical interest apart from its topographical importance. (1867)

JOHN WILLIAM KAYE[344]

## 10. Delhi monuments

March 12

The walk to Tughlakabad is nearly four miles over a perfectly uninteresting flat; corn for the most part, but sometimes quite bare and without any view right or left, before or behind, but the fort ahead and the needle Minar back. Stopped to sketch the tomb and fort, which have a certain grandeur; but it is folly to speak of them as equal to Baalbek or Karnak, as I have heard some folk do. Tughlak's tomb is a massive, small fort in itself, and not un-Egyptian in its leaning walls. The wind is cold, and I didn't wait long, but came to the fort, and have drawn there till II at two views, each very remarkable, and characteristic of the eternal squash and harry this land has been devoted to. The fort is simply a vast mass of ruin, such as I have already seen many; but the city walls are in many parts perfect, being built among rock buttresses and bases, the area enclosing a bald space of ruin, with no sign of life but two small patches of huts. On the west side all is green corn, at times water, for the Jumna is close by, and old Tughlak's tomb stands finely off the great plain. On the east, the broad stretch of the river is imposing, the grimness of the dark gray and red fortress walls and the hopeless bareness of most of the scene very striking. We are going to break-fast on the step outside, though the wind and the dust are not agreeable; so we move on to the shade of a mimosa, which, small as it is, has this virtue and interest, that it is full of birds, namely: one roller, six bee-eaters, 23 turtledoves and II Alexandrien parrots, for the foliage is so thin you may count all the party. Breakfast at 12.30 as usual on bread and cold mutton, eggs, sherry and soda water, little and good. Diversion afterwards from kites and crows intriguing about bones and scraps of bread. Lying in the meagre shade of this tree is, after all, far from unpleasant; the kite's shrill, tremulous fifing, and the parrots converse-familiar, and the cool breeze. I discourse with Giorgio about India and we perceive that its sham cyclopaean ruins are not equal to those of Samos or Norba; as for its fruit and fish, those we had disposed of before. I still hoping to get another drawing, but there was no effect whatever of light and shade, and the whole tiresome four miles were slowly paced over, the afternoon unmarked by an incident but this, firstly a great gathering of huge vultures, over sixty in number, round a dead horse, lying in a hollow among young mimosa bushes; such a scuffling and tearing and community of filth. Secondly, a very large jackal suddenly leaped into the midst of that society and put them all to flight; not even the great condor-like black vultures were able to face him, as he bounced and leaped and bit their throats and legs, and bullied the cowardly lot inconceivably. So they all flapped away, and then stood quietly gazing at the Lord of the Feast.

March 13

Got two feeble memoranda of the Cutub and went on then to Saftar Jung's tomb, by no means a grand or simple edifice but over be-ornamented. In the garden are some good trees, very like walnut, and I drew the building, combined with some adjacent moskinesses and tomb-like heaps of ruin till it was time for breakfast. The noise from the multitude of pigeons here is wondrous, and parrots abound; air delightful and the sun not too hot. It is past 1 arabic. I am really getting too tired of this noise of innumerable doves. This garden is full of oranges and citron bushes, quite neglected and wild, but if cared for, the whole place might be made a sort of paradise. As we left, a lot of naked children ran after the carriage, screaming 'Baksheesh', as in Egyptian days. Promising an extra rupee to the driver for this extra work, to the Raj Ghat, where I made three slight reminders of those exquisite palaces, but must go back to work there on larger drawings. When the river comes fully up to the palace walls the effect must be truly beautiful; even now the pools of water, and the black buffaloes contrasting with the pale colours of the architecture are a sight. To the post office, but disgusted at finding NO LETTERS!

March 14

The particularly desolate sphere of the. Delhi suburbs and neighbourhood or surroundings only comes home to one after much going about the place; the endless heaps of ruin; the countless tombs; the small amount, at least apparently, of population. Before leaving the Delhi gate, one or two views about the fort seemed worth drawing in the very early morning light; and, besides, there

were lots of clouds, with a general hazy dimness making near things
seem far. At the Shere Shah fort, I could willingly have stopped to
draw, but didn't; it is very grim, and grandly gray against the early
sun. The crowd of tombs all about Humayun's passes belief. We
arrived at the garden 7.15, when I set to work immediately, and
drew hard for four and a half hours on end. Happily, there was
neither wind nor sun in any violent extreme, but a very pleasant
calm over everything except the turtle-doves, which are hereabouts
in myriads and ever loudly discoursing. At noon breakfast occurred
on the terrace, in a shady nook of those marble 'alls and windless,
for only just round the corner the wind was like iced knives.
Eggs, cold lamb, bread, sherry and soda water, all in small quantities—experience showing that the less a man eats at mid-day
the better. Quiet moments are rare nowaday. Yet one may not use
them as in former times by comparing them with those long past.
Early life is becoming remote though ever clearly remembered (not
as little Milly L. said—'I have lived too long to remember a far back
ago'), and as nearly all with whom quiet moments used to be passed
are either gone or changed, to think back is merely sadness, and
mere sadness is what one can't afford to entertain here in India.
Therefore I finish my moralizing, shut my note-book, and give
myself up to observing the astute, but absurd, hooded crows, who
abruptly arose at the sound of a soda water cork and fled the scene.
Went on again to Hindu Rao's house on the ridge, where, spite of a
hot sun, I got what I wanted in granite rocks and foreground. Dinner
is really good here, viz. a good soup, then a 'side dish' which one
don't eat, a capital dish of roast mutton, followed by indifferent
curry, and excellent Cheshire cheese. I don't know if I am wrong in
drinking so much beer, but I certainly do drink two bottles sometimes, and yet, so far, I am thankful to say I am in far better health
than I have known for years. About midnight Giorgio called and
woke me, as a heap of people were knocking at the door, and had
lights. Open and a telegram, but it was for one Captain Bissett, so I
eschewed book and bearer in a rage, and could not sleep again for a
long time. (1874)

EDWARD LEAR[345]

## 11. Gaya

Gaya is a little country town, and, allowing for the differences attendant upon its Indian site, may be said to bear the characteristics typical of so many small towns in Germany and the rest of Europe. There is no hotel, but as elsewhere where a hotel is wanting, a Dak Bungalow or Rest House, kept up by the Government. In it every traveller may lay claim to one night's quarters at least, at the rate of one rupee per bed. There is generally a cook on the premises who, according to tariff, provides tiffin for 1½ rupees, and dinner with two meat courses for two rupees. We ordered dinner for the evening, took possession of a room, and soon after got into the most miserable of country carts, to have ourselves jolted along a fine broad road, through wooded fields, to Buddha-Gaya, a distance of about one hour and a half. The place consists of a cluster of houses by the wayside; to the left of the road lies a monastery of Brahman *Sadhus,* while to the right lies a great temple of Buddha in a hollow, care having been taken to prevent the debris of ages raising the level of the soil. This is surely the spot where the sublime one sat under a fig tree in that great night in which he received his Buddahood, for Buddha lived long enough to point out the exact spot to his numerous disciples. ... In Buddha-Gaya, as everywhere else in India, there was not a single Buddhist to be found, with whom we might have exchanged impressions. (1893)

PAUL DEUSSEN[346]

## C. VILLAGES

### 1. *Mountain villages*

The Paharee, or mountaineer, is not so incommoded; indeed the persons of both sexes are overrun with them; the coarse blanket covering they wear encourages the generation of these vile insects, and the irritation they produce on the skin seems to be agreeable to them in this cold climate: when it becomes excessive, they immerse their clothing in hot water, destroying myriads, and restoring their own rest.

The habitations of these people are always in villages; a single insulated house is never seen, or very rarely. These villages consist of from five to twenty houses, some even larger are met with. They frequently form a picturesque object at a distance, crowning some height, and hanging over some glen, or intermingled with wood on the uprising face of a hill: every one according to its size has one or

'Village of Kursalee', drawn by G. F. White

more lofty towers overlooking the village; these are, as has been heretofore observed, temples; some are very large and high, and are commonly ornamented with much art, and frequently with some taste.

All the inhabitants of this region, as well as those near the plains, are Hindoos. Their features for the most part, although gradually altered by the climate, as we leave the low country, and also perhaps by country customs, and possibly by the remaining mixture of an ancient indigenous race, still retain traces that point to the chief original stock in the plains.

Their language, their religion, and the general tone of their customs and prejudices tend to confirm this. Their language for a considerable way into the h'lls is corrupted dialect of true Hindostanee, in which Shanscrit and Hindoo words predominate; but the farther we penetrated to the north, the more corrupt it became, till it was so mixed with foreign tongues as to be unintelligible by a low countryman.

They worship the chief Hindoo deities, adore and protect the cow, and blindly follow and practise most of the rites of Hindooism; but they are Hindoos in a sorely degraded and truly ignorant state, mingling the wild superstitions and blind adorations of that religion with the utmost grossness of character, and a total deficiency of acquaintance with even their legendary origin; and they adhere to the chief manners and customs of Hindoos, only because they were adopted by their fathers before them; nor does there seem to be a Brahmin among them of more enlightened mind, or in any degree more intelligent than the rest.

In every village, and on each way-side, there are temples to different Hindoo divinities; some to Mahadeo, or Seeva, under innumerable names; some to Gonesh, others to Bhowannee, or to Calee; but there is an infinite variety of deities of their own, to whom they pay much adoration, and their temples are found on every hill, at every turn and remarkable place on the road. These are the Genii Loci, and their symbols and memorials are numerous and various; there is not a Teeba, or pinnacle of a hill, that is not topped with a heap of stones; a single pillar, or a small hut, to which the Paharee turns with mysterious solemnity, and prostrating himself, prays to the spirit of the place, and to every one of these are strange tales and curious legends attached. . .

The internal regulation of their villages and small communities perfectly resembles the patriarchal form of their more important governments. In every village there is a man to whom they pay great deference, and to whom they refer all disputes; who, in short, is their chief, and who goes by the name of the Seana: he always possesses much influence, and when any requisition is to be made from a village, the Seana is the person to apply to. He also makes the collection of tribute for government, frequently is an officer under it, and I believe is always looked to, as in some measure answerable for the conduct of his villagers. (1815)

JAMES BAILLIE FRASER[347]

## 2.   A haunted village

While I was in charge of the district of Nursingpore, in the valley of the Nerbudda, in 1823, a cultivator of the village of Bedoo, about twelve miles distant from my court, was one day engaged in the cultivation of his field on the border of the village of Burkhara, which was supposed to be haunted by the spirit of an old proprietor, whose temper was so forward and violent that the lands could hardly be let for anything; for hardly any man would venture to cultivate them lest he might unintentionally incur his ghostship's displeasure. The poor cultivator, after begging his pardon in secret, ventured to drive his plough a few yards beyond the proper line of his boundary, and thus to add half an acre of the lands of Burkhara to his own little tenement, which was situated in Bedoo. That very night his only son was bitten by a snake, and his two bullocks were seized with the murrain. In terror he went off to the village temple, confessed his sin, and vowed not only to restore the half acre of land to the village of Burkhara, but to build a very handsome shrine upon the spot as a perpetual sign of his repentance. The boy and the bullocks all three recovered, and the shrine was built; and is, I believe, still to be seen as the boundary mark!

The fact was, that the village stood upon an elevated piece of ground rising out of a moist plain, and a colony of snakes had taken up their abode in it. The bites of these snakes had, on many occasions, proved fatal; and such accidents were all attributed to the anger of a spirit which was supposed to haunt the village. At one time, under the former government, no one would take a lease of the village on any terms; and it had become almost entirely deserted, though the soil was the finest in the whole district. With a

view to remove the whole prejudices of the people, the governor,
Goroba Pundit, took the lease himself at the rent of one thousand
rupees a year; and in the month of June went from his residence,
twelve miles, with ten of his own ploughs, to superintend the commencement of so *perilous* an undertaking  On reaching the middle
of the village, situated on the top of the little hill, he alighted from
his horse, sat down upon a carpet that had been spread for him
under a large and beautiful banyan tree, and began to refresh
himself with a pipe before going to work in the fields. As he quaffed
his hookah, and railed at the follies of men 'whose absurd superstitions had made them desert so beautiful a village with so noble a
tree in its centre', his eyes fell upon an enormous black snake which
had coiled round one of its branches immediately over his head, and
seemed as if resolved at once to pounce down and punish him for his
blasphemy! He gave his pipe to his attendant, mounted his horse,
from which the saddle had not yet been taken, and never pulled rein
till he got home. Nothing could never induce him to visit this village
again, though he was afterwards employed under me as a native
collector; and he has often told me, that he verily believed this was
the spirit of the old landlord that he had unhappily neglected to
propitiate before taking possession! (1823)

WILLIAM HENRY SLEEMAN[348]

### 3.   Cleanliness of villages under the French

As long as the revenue is collected, the condition of the miserable
peasantry, and of their villages, is of secondary consideration. Were
the inhabitants to be improved in mind, as well as in body, all other
improvements would necessarily follow. Let the civil authorities be
made to look to the comforts of the inhabitants in their respective
districts; let their towns and villages be cleaned, their houses and
huts repaired, or better constructed; and let the head-men of each
be made to look more after their duty than they do; and, it is more
than probable that there would not be the misery which, every one
knows, now exists to such a fearful extent; and the whole country
would be, altogether, in a more flourishing state. The towns and
villages would be more healthy, and the inhabitants more comfortable.

How is it that cholera is so frequent a visitor amongst our native
hamlets and towns? Because of the filthy state in which they gener-

ally are found, and because of the poverty of the inhabitants.
People say that this epidemic is in the air; no doubt such is the case,
because, if the ground is charged with filth and dirt, it stands to
reason that the air becomes impregnated with noxious exhalations;
and, if the inhabitants are so pinched with want, as to have nothing
to eat, it is not matter of surprise that they are unable, from weakness of stamina, to wrestle with a disease which the inhaling of an
unhealthy atmosphere brings on.

But we seldom hear of cholera, or any other epidemic, breaking
out in the villages of the French territories. Let the traveller visit any
of them, and he will see how neat and clean they are; let him look
at the *'paysans,'* and he will observe them to be much better clad,
and stouter than our ryots generally are. And, why is the difference? Because the poor people are not so heavily taxed by the
revenue collector, and they have, consequently, more to live upon. I
think if we were to take a leaf out of the Frenchman's book, it would
be a good thing for the country, as well as for the inhabitants.
(1833–42)

ALBERT HERVEY[349]

# D.  LANDSCAPES

## 1.  View between Natan and Taka-Ca-Munda

On proceeding from Natan towards Serinagur, the road still con-
tinues to ascend, and from a point of great elevation this view was
taken. The eye is here on a level with the tops of most of the
surrounding mountains; the forms of which are more pointed and
irregular than those passed before, and resemble the tumultuous
agitation of the ocean, roused by a tempest. The general aspect of
the whole is dreary and vast; vegetation is scanty; the scattered trees
that here and there occur, seem to be embellishments misplaced and
inappropriate; although, if trees are admissible, it could certainly be
no other than misshapen blights like these.

But the circumstance which. from this point of view, chiefly raises
our astonishment is, the appearance of a prodigious range of still
more distant mountains, proudly rising above all that we have
hitherto considered as most grand and magnificent, and which,
clothed in a robe of everlasting snow, seem by their etherial hue to
belong to a region elevated into the clouds, and partaking of their

'View Between Natań and Taka-Ca-Munda', drawn by William Daniell

nature; having nothing in common with terrestrial forms. It would be in vain to attempt, by any description, to convey an idea of these sublime effects, which perhaps even the finest art can but faintly imitate. These mountains are supposed to be a branch of the Emodus, or Imaus, of the ancients; and, so great is their height, they are sometimes seen in the province of Bahar, and even in Bengal. (1814)

THOMAS AND WILLIAM DANIELL[350]

## 2. Waterfall of Pappanassum

The Fall of Pappanassum is on the river Tumrabunni, a considerable stream in the district of Tinnyvelly. A few miles below the fall, that river passes the fort of Palamcotta, and thence proceeds in an easterly course towards the sea, into which it is received in the gulph of Manapar.

This magnificent cataract is held by the Hindoos in great veneration, and is accordingly visited by innumerable devotees. The only approach to it is by a single path on the right-hand side of the valley, whence, though near to the fall, it cannot be seen, owing to the interposition of a large mass of rock that projects into the water. The path is continued up the face of the rock by means of a flight of steps; and at the summit a gate is so placed, that all visitors must of necessity pass through it, but which nevertheless readily opens to all who are provided with a small fee for the bramins that guard the sacred portal.

Nothing can be more grand and impressive than when, on first throwing open the gate, this extraordinary scene bursts upon the sight. It would be difficult for those who have never seen a vast river precipitated down a rocky steep of considerable elevation, to form an adequate idea of such a spectacle, accompanied by a noise so tremendous, that, comparatively, all other sounds are but whispers. Upon the minds of Hindoos, who attach ideas of a religious nature to these objects, such scenes must operate with great effect, and powerfully stimulate their piety. Indeed their prostrations, and other anticks of enthusiasm, on first beholding this tremendous object, are evident proofs of the intensity of their feelings. (1814)

THOMAS AND WILLIAM DANIELL[351]

### 3. An evening walk in Bengal

Our task is done! on Gunga's breast
The sun is sinking down to rest;
And, moored beneath the tamarind bough,
Our bark has found its harbour now.
With furled sail, and painted side,
Behold the tiny frigate ride.
Upon her deck, 'mid charcoal gleams,
The Moslems' savoury supper steams,
While all apart, beneath the wood,
The Hindoo cooks his simpler food.
Come walk with me the jungle through;
If yonder hunter told us true,
Far off, in desert dank and rude,
The tyger holds his solitude;
Nor (taught by recent harm to shun
The thunders of the English gun)
A dreadful guest but rarely seen,
Returns to scare the village green.
Come boldly on! no venom'd snake
Can shelter in so cool a brake.
Child of the sun! he loves to lie
'Midst Nature's embers, parch'd and dry,
Where o'er some tower in ruin laid,
The peepul spreads its haunted shade;
Or round a tomb his scales to wreathe,
Fit warder in the gate of Death!
Come on! Yet pause! behold us now
Beneath the bamboo's arched bough,
Where, gemming oft that sacred gloom,
Glows the geranium's scarlet bloom,
And winds our path through many a bower
Of fragrant tree and giant flower;
The ceiba's crimson pomp display'd
O'er the broad plaintain's humbler shade,
And dusk anana's prickly blade;
While o'er the brake, so wild and fair,
The betel waves his crest in air.
With pendant train and rushing wings,

Aloft the gorgeous peacock springs;
And he, the bird of hundred dyes,
Whose plumes the dames of Ava prize.
So rich a shade, so green a sod,
Our English fairies never trod!
Yet who in Indian bow'r has stood,
But thought on England's 'good green wood?'
And bless'd, beneath the palmy shade,
Her hazel and her hawthorn glade,
And breath'd a prayer, (how oft in vain!)
To gaze upon her oaks again?
A truce to thought, the jackall's cry
Resounds like sylvan revelry;
And through the trees, yon failing ray
Will scantly serve to guide our way.
Yet mark! as fade the upper skies,
Each thicket opes ten thousand eyes.
Before, beside us, and above,
The fire-fly lights his lamp of love,
Retreating, chacing, sinking, soaring,
The darkness of the copse exploring;
While to this cooler air confest,
The broad Dhatura bares her breast,
Of fragrant scent and virgin white,
A pearl around the locks of night!
Still as we pass in softened hum,
Along the breezy alleys come
The village song, the horn, the drum.
Still as we pass, from bush and briar,
The shrill cigala strikes his lyre;
And, what is she whose liquid strain
Thrills through yon copse of sugar-cane?
I know that soul-entrancing swell!
It is—it must be—Philomel!
Enough, enough, the rustling trees
Announce a shower upon the breeze,—
The flashes of the summer sky
Assume a deeper, ruddier dye;
Yon lamp that trembles on the stream,
From forth our cabin sheds its beam;

And we must early sleep, to find
Betimes the morning's healthy wind.
But oh! with thankful hearts confess
Ev'n here there may be happiness;
And He, the bounteous Sire, has given
His peace on earth—his hope of heaven! (1824)

REGINALD HEBER[352]

## 4.  *Morning, near Bombay*

It is generally admitted that the earlier portion of the day is most
favourable to the contemplation of the grandeur of mountain scenery; and this remark applied with peculiar force to the scenery of the
Ghauts in India, when the daylight bursts suddenly upon a wonder-
ous scene of gigantic pinnacles, apprently floating in an ocean of
white mist, which, rising in successive rolling masses and dissipating
under the increasing influence of the sun, gradually developes the
connecting range of mountains and the wide-spread plain below,
studded with forests and cocoa-nut groves. In the neighbourhood of
rivers and marshes the mist is more dense, and often lingers till
noonday in picturesque wreaths along the mountain-side, or en-
velopes its fantastic peaks, investing the scene with a poetical and
picturesque effect, which the excessive brightness of the atmosphere might otherwise destroy. . . .

The singular form of these mountains and their almost insulated
position give them the appearance, when first discovered at day-
break, of gigantic Gothic cathedrals; and some of their pinnacles are
surmounted with those forts, in the impregnability of which the
natives of India had, through so many ages, placed reliance, until
British intrepidity has shewn them their error. (1827)

ROBERT MELVILLE GRINDLAY[353]

## 5.  *Scenery near Hyderabad  (Sind)*

The scenery near the capital of Sinde is varied and beautiful: the
sides of the river are lined with lofty trees; and there is a background
of hill to relieve the eye from the monotony which presents itself in
the dusty arid plains of the Delta. The Indus is larger, too, than in
most places lower down, being about 830 yards wide; there is a
sand-bank in the middle, but it is hidden by the stream. The island

on which Hyderabad stands is barren, from the rocky and hilly nature of the soil, but even the arable parts are poorly cultivated. (1830)

ALEXANDER BURNES[354]

## 6. Superb landscape

We are now in the very heart of Mewar, plains extending as far as the eye can reach. ... The prospect from this ground is superb: the Oodipoor hills in the distance; those of Poorh and Goorlah, with their cupolas, on our right; the fantastic peak of Burruk rising insulated from the plain. We are now approaching a place of rest, which we all much require; though I fear Cary's will be one of perpetuity. Saw a beautiful Mirage *(See-kote)* this morning, the certain harbinger of the cold season. The ridge of Poorh underwent a thousand transformations, and the pinnacle of Burruk was crowned with a multitude of spires. There is not a more delightful relaxation than to watch the changes of these evanescent objects, emblems of our own ephemeral condition. (1832)

JAMES TOD[355]

## 7. Panoramic view of the Dhoon

The houses at Mussoori, though small, are very commodious, and are built something in the style of English cottages. They are stuck about the sides of the mountains, like gulls' nests on a cliff, there being scarcely ten square yards of level ground to be found in the place, except such as has been carved out of the rocky steeps. The position of the place is exquisitely romantic, and the view from it grand beyond description. A verbal outline of the most formal kind is all I dare attempt.

Upon the left, that is, eastward of the place, lies that magnificent extent of mountains through which the sacred Ganges forces a broken and disturbed course, fading, as they recede from the eye, in all the endless tints of mountain-scenery, from the rich autumnal browns, in the foreground and middle-distance, to the palest azure and aerial grey; along the foot of these a narrow stream of water is seen, creeping in beautiful contortions over the surface of the level country, until it is lost in the distance, where the earth and sky are blended into one. This last expression will hardly be intelligible to those who have not witnessed what the words are intended to convey. To the beholder thus exalted above the level of the plains, no positive horizon is visible, the landscape, as it recedes in distance, being gradually obscured until it vanishes entirely from the sight, mingling imperceptibly with the sky, as the intervening body of atmosphere increases. Thus, when the sun's rays happen to be strongly reflected from any distant stream of water, so as to catch the eye of a person stationed on the mountains, the course of the river may be distinctly traced, like a silver thread running into the sky, beyond the distance at which all the rest of the landscape vanished: a phenomenon which, though easily explained, is at first sight startling, as it is strange to those living in the level country.

[ In ] the centre . . .is an expanse of distant lands well-nigh endless, embracing many towns and villages, rich in stupendous forests, and intersected with patches of cultivation, through which streams and roads are seen winding in all directions. Upon the right, far, far in the distance, the Jumna runs meandering through a succession of undulating lands, thickly studded with trees, in a serpentine and fantastic course, the nearest extremity of which is shut out by the abrupt and precipitous outline of mountains in the neighbourhood of Budrajh. When the day is tolerably clear, the Sivalic ridge of hills is seen stretching itself directly across the champaign country, from the Ganges to the Jumna. At times, over the summits of these hills, a fresh extent of plain is again visible, mingling with the sky. It has been stated to me by those upon whose word I can depend, that during the month of November, when the atmosphere is clearest, the white houses at Moozaffirnuggur have been distinctly seen, with the assistance of strong glasses: this is a distance of eighty-two miles. (1831–6)

THOMAS BACON[356]

# E. THE HIMALAYA AND OTHER MOUNTAINS

## 1. *View of the Aravulli*

It was nearly noon when I cleared the pass of Seetla Mata, and as the bluff head of Mount Aboo opened upon me, my heart beat with joy as, with the Sage of Syracuse, I exclaimed, *Eureeka!* Half an hour more brought me to my tents at Beejipoor,—thermometer 98°, barometer 28° 60', shewing a difference of about five hundred feet in elevation between the plains of Mewar and those of Marwar, skirting the Aravulli on either side, the desert being the most elevated. At 3 P.M., the barometer was 28⁰ 50', and thermometer 102⁰,—the rains collecting in the west, and the hot winds blowing a sirocco over the desert. I lamented my folly in throwing away my refrigerators, as I looked back from the arid sand, on which my tent was pitched, to those lofty and delightful regions I had quitted. The prospect was indeed magnificent, and infinitely more imposing than any part of the gradual ascent from Mewar. Here I had a full view of the precipitous face of the noble Aravulli; its towering and ever-varied pinnacles of gneiss, its dark indented recesses, lined with forest and underwood, through which stole many a crystal rivulet from its alpine cradle, to refresh the inhabitants of Maroost'huli. But the heat had been unusually great, and little rain having fallen this year, some of these Naiads had altogether abandoned their sandy beds. Had public duty permitted, I should have started at least a fortnight earlier; for the clouds of the *chootabursat,* or introductory monsoon, are congregating fast, and I fear may frustrate much of my design. Already am I compelled to forego one object, which induced a preference of this route to that through the Bhil forest, *viz.* the temple of Rayn-poorji, in the Sadri Nal, one of those clefts in the ribs of the Aravulli, accessible only to foot-passengers; and although within view, I dare not attempt it, being in the direction diametrically opposed to that in which the many objects of my journey lay. (1822)

JAMES TOD[357]

## 2. The ghats

The range of mountains which extend from the 9th to the 22nd degree of north altitude from Cape Comorin, the southern extremity of the peninsula of India, to the river Tapty, is known by the name of *Ghaut,* which signifies a pass, indicating the passes or descents from the elevated table-land above to the low tracts of Canara, Malabar. and the Concan on the western side, and descending less abruptly on the east.

This celebrated ridge does not terminate in a point, or promontory, when it approaches the Tapty, but, departing from its meridional course, bends eastward, in a wavy line, parallel to the river, and is afterwards lost among the hills in the neighbourhood of

*Burhanpour.* In its course along the Tapty it forms several passes or descents towards the river; whence the country into which the passes descend was originally named Candeish, or the low country. It would appear that the ridge abates of its great height, after passing the parallel of *Basseen,* northward; for Mr. FARMER, in his way from *Poonah* towards *Naderbar,* observed, that the passes had all a descent northward, forming, as it were, a series of steps, until he landed in Candeish.

The country inclosed by this bend of the Ghauts is named Baglana, or Bocklana, and extends the whole way from the Tapty river to *Poonah*. It is mountainous of course, and contains in it many strong fortresses. Among these were *Rairee* and *Jeneaghur*, the strongholds of Sevagee in the last century. . .

The following description, by Lord VALENTIA, of one of the more southern Ghauts may be considered as conveying a correct idea of their general character:

'At three in the morning I began to descend the celebrated Ghaut. The road has been formed, with great labour, out of a bed of loose rock, over which the torrents in winter had run with such force as to wash away all the softer parts, and in several places to leave single rocks, of four or five feet diameter, standing in the centre of the road, not above two feet asunder. To get the palanquin over these was a tedious and difficult business: however, it escaped uninjured. The boys were obliged to use sticks with iron spikes at the end, to prevent themselves being thrown forward by the weight of the palanquin, though I walked the whole way, not only to relieve them, but to admire the sublimity of the scene. We had entered a forest of the largest trees of the East, several of which were one hundred feet in the stem before a single branch extended: yet the descent was so steep that I was frequently on a level with their tops, at so small a distance as to be able to distinguish them by the gleam of the numerous torches that accompanied me, but which were insufficient to enlighten the impenetrable canopy of foliage that for miles concealed the face of heaven, or the deep gloom of the abyss into which we seemed descending. In the daytime the scene could not have been half so awful or magnificent. PURNEAH had continued his attentions to us by an endeavour to repair the worst part of the road; had nothing been done to it, I know not how we should have passed it. General WELLESLEY made the road perfectly good; but the descent was so steep, and the torrents so violent, that

'View from the Top of the Bore Ghaut', drawn by William Westall

one rainy season reduced it to the state in which I found it. Our descent was impeded by meeting with numerous droves of oxen, which were ascending the Ghaut, loaded with salt, having carried down grain to *Mangalore*. Towards day I came to a turn in the road, where an opening shewed me the lofty mountains I had been descending, covered with forests to nearly their summits. We had passed several rivulets; here they had joined and formed a small stream. I was now able to perceive the rich vegetation around me, and which immediately struck me with surprise, from its resemblance to that of Ceylon. The branches of the loftiest trees were covered by the parasitical tribe; the *epidendrons* and *felices* were various and beautiful; but the most conspicuous was the *dracontium pertusum*, which perfectly covered the gigantic stem of the *ficus Bengalensis* with its leaves. The *laurus cassia* was amongst the underwood; and the side of the road was beautified by several species of *justicia*.'

'I frequently stopped to wander a little from the road to collect seeds, in which I was very successful. I passed a small village in the centre of this immense forest, where the inhabitants were thrashing their grain, in a truly patriarchal manner, on a floor of hard earth: the grain was trodden by oxen, which, according to the Mosaical law, were left unmuzzled.'

ROBERT MELVILLE GRINDLAY[358]

## 3. *Impact of the Himalaya*

Look at the outline of the highest range of the Himalaya, and picture to yourself its grandeur and its beauty, which are not to be fully enjoyed in the society of others, in the midst of the gaiety of a party. Seek the highest point of the lone mountains, and the shade of the deep forests, whose beautiful foliage is varied by majestic pines, ever-green oaks, and brilliant rhododendrons. In solitude gaze on the magnificence of such a scene:
'Look through nature up to nature's God:'
'Commune with thine own heart, and be still.' Let none be near to break the reverie: look on those mountains of eternal snow,—the rose-tints linger on them, the white clouds roll below, and their peaks are sharply set upon a sky of the brightest, clearest and deepest blue. The rushing wing of the black eagle—that 'winged and cloud-cleaving minister, whose happy flight is highest into heaven,'—may

be heard above. The golden eagle may be seen below, poised on his wing of might, or swooping over a precipice, while his keen eye pierces downward, seeking his prey, into the depths of the narrow valley between the mountains. The sweet notes of the Hill birds are around you; and the gay butterflies, enamoured of the wild flowers, hover over their blossoms.

Who may describe the solitary loveliness, the speaking quietude, that wraps these forest scenes? Who may tell how beautiful they are? Who that loves solitude does not enjoy the

'—dewy morn, and od'rous noon, and even
With sunset, and its gorgeous ministers?'

Who can look unmoved on the coronets of snow that crown the eternal Himalaya? Who can gaze without delight on the aerial mountains that pour down the Ganga and Yamuna from their snow-formed caves?

'My altars are the mountains and the ocean,
Earth, air, stars,—all that springs from the great Whole,
Who hath produced and will receive the soul.'
'I love snow, and all the forms
Of the radiant frost;
I love waves, and winds, and storms,
Every thing almost
Which is nature's, and may be
Untainted by man's misery.'

There, indulge in solemn vision and bright silver dream, while 'every sight and sound from the vast earth and ambient air' sends to your heart its choicest impulses: gaze on those rocks and pinnacles of snow, where never foot of common mortal trod, which the departing rose-tints leave in colder grandeur, and enjoy those solemn feelings of natural piety with which the spirit of solitude imbues the soul.

'Are not the mountains, waves, and skies, a part
Of me and my soul, as I of them?
Is not the love of these deep in my heart
With a pure passion?'

'On accuse l'enthousiasme d'etre passager; l'existence sera trop heureuse si l'on pouvait retenir des emotions si belle; mais c'est parcequ'elles se dissipent aisement qu'il faut s'occuper de les conserver.'

'Mont Blanc is the monarch of mountains,

They crown'd· him long ago,
On a throne of rocks, in a robe of clouds,
With a diadem of snow.' (1838)

FANNY PARKES[359]

## 4. Contrasts in Himalayan Vegetation

There is a great difference between the vegetation of Dorjiling
[Darjeeling] and that of similar elevations near Choongtam
situated far within the Himalaya: this is owing to the steepness and
dryness of the latter locality, where there is an absence of dense
forest, which is replaced by a number of social grasses clothing the
mountain sides, many new and beautiful kinds of rhododendrons,
and a variety of European genera, which, (as I have elsewhere
noticed) are either wholly absent from the damper ranges of Dorjiling, or found there several thousand feet higher up. On the hill
above Choongtam village, I gathered, at 5,000 to 6,000 feet,
*Rhododendron arboreum* and *Dalhousiæ,* which do not generally
grow at Dorjiling below 7,500 feet. The yew appears at 7,000 feet;
whilst, on the outer ranges (as on Tonglo), it is only found at 9,500
to 10,000 feet; and whereas on Tonglo it forms an immense tall tree,
with long sparse branches and slender drooping twigs, growing
amongst gigantic magnolias and oaks, at Choongtam it is small and
rigid, and much resembling in appearance our churchyard yew. At
8,000 feet the *Abies Brunoniana* is found; a tree quite unknown
further south; but neither the larch nor the *Abies Smithiana*
(Khutrow) accompanied it, they being confined to still more northern regions. (1849)

JOSEPH DALTON HOOKER[360]

## 5. The Western Himalaya

The Western Himalayas may be divided into three regions.

*1st.* The lower or Sewalik region, comprehending the lesser
ranges which border the plains of India, and differ but little from the
latter in climate and natural productions. This region extends to an
elevation of about 3,000 feet above the level of the sea.

*2nd.* The middle or forest region embraces the highly-cultivated
and forest tracts, where nature wears the garb of the temperate
zone.

*3rd.* The upper or snowy region, comprising the table-lands and mountains of Thibet, Ladakh, etc., extending from the stunted birch at 8,000 to 9,000 feet above the sea-level to the limits of perpetual snow. The fauna and flora of this region are distinct from the foregoing, inasmuch as its animals seldom descend to the lower zones unless driven by the rigors of winter, and its plants present an arctic facies. The geological features vary much, from the upper and mid tertiary beds of the lower hills to the secondary and azoic rocks of the middle and upper regions. But what gives a most characteristic appearance to each of these belts is their flora. Although perhaps not so well defined as that of the Andes, still the tropical, temperate, and arctic forms preserve their position with marked regularity. Thus the naturalist from Kalka, at the foot of the Sewalik range, on his journey by the hill-road to Simla, can trace without difficulty the gradual botanical changes, from the stunted palm-tree to the gnarled oak, on to the stately pine, and thence to the lichen and rhododendron. The journey through the mountains to Simla and other hill-stations is usually performed by a litter, sedan-chair, or on horseback. The stages are easy, and there is tolerably good accommodation at the various halting-places. So marked are the gradations of climate, and so rapid, that from the torrid heat of the plains, and 90° Fahrenheit in the shade, one may be easily transported in forty-eight hours to a temperature below zero. The scenery of the lower ranges is exceedingly striking and beautiful. I felt as if suddenly conveyed to the temperate zone, and more especially when the stately cheer-pines, wild roses, jessamines, violets and dandelion met my view; but, however, there was an admixture of stranger plants and trees peculiar to the region, then quite unknown to me, such as the coral-tree with its gorgeous red flowers, and oaks with laurel-shaped leaves.

The mountains forming the lesser ranges which border on the plains of India present in general great broken chains running for the most part parallel and from east to west, separated by broad valleys called khuds; in the interior this regularity is less observable, and the mountains, instead of rounded summits, have a bold and well-defined outline. (1867)

ANDREW LEITH ADAMS[361]

## 6. *Mahadeo hills*

In the eyes of the Hindu inhabitants of the neighbouring plains, the whole of the range of hills which culminated in the Puchmurree plateau is sacred to their deity Siva, called Mahadeo, or the Great God; and the hills themselves are called by his name, the Mahadeos. A conception of awe and mystery had always been associated with their lofty peaks, embosomed among which lies one of the most sacred shrines of the god, to which at least one pilgrimage was a necessity in the life of every devout Hindu. But excepting at the appointed season for this pilgrimage, no dweller of the plains would venture at the time of which I am writing, to set his foot on the holy soil of Mahadeo's hills; and, as we approached its neighbourhood, gloomy looks began to gather on the faces of my followers, whose fears had been acted on by the conversation of the people they had met. The road to the top was represented as impassable from natural difficulties; and guarded by wild beasts, goblins, and fell disease.

I halted a day at Jhilpa, the last village on the plains, to make arrangements for the ascent, and procure guides; and on the 22nd packed my small tent and a few necessaries on a pony, and with two attendants started up the hill on foot. For the first ten miles or so the pathway led up an easy and regular ascent over shelving rocks and scanty soil, whereon grew a thin forest of the commoner sorts of trees, Salei (*Boswellia thurifera*), Dhaora (*Conocarpus latifolia*), and Saj (*Pentaptera glabra*), being the most numerous species; the grass and vegetation on these slopes had begun already to assume the yellow tinge of the dry season. Such a prospect as this, which is typical of vast tracts in the jungles of Central India, is sadly disappointing to him who looks for the luxuriant tropical forest of low-lying equatorial regions. Forests like those of southern Africa and the littoral countries of Asia, with their close array of giant trunks, dense canopy of vegetation, impenetrable underwood, gorgeous flowers, and mighty tangled creepers—

'From branch to branch close wreaths of bondage throwing'
are unknown in these central regions of India; and their character is rarely approached save in some occasional low moist valley, where the axe of the woodcutter has not penetrated, and the stagnation of some stream has united with the heat of a close valley in giving to the vegetation a more truly tropical character. Indeed, but for the

preponderance of yellows where rich reds and browns should be, and the rare appearance of a palm or other eastern form, most of these low forest tracts might be taken after December for a late autumn scene in a temperate climate. Nothing is more striking than the absence of brilliant flowers, which contrary to popular idea are far more characteristic of temperate than of tropical regions. The Palas (*Butea superba*) is almost the only tree in our forests which possesses really bright colouring.

When an elevation of about 2,000 feet (above the sea) had been attained,the character of the scenery began to change. Vertical scarps of the red sandstone which forms the higher plateau began to rise into view at every turn of the path, which now plunged into narrow and gloomy glens, following the boulder-strewn bed of a small stream. The dried and yellow grasses and naked tree stems of the lower slope gave place to a green vegetation thickly covering the soil, and in places almost meeting overhead. The moist banks of the stream were covered with ferns and mosses, and the clear sparkle of the little brooks appeared singularly refreshing after our long walk up-hill in the heat of a sultry and lowering day. The baggage-pony found considerable difficulty in scrambling over the boulders that now began to block the road; and we relieved him by putting about half of his load on the two guides. After scrambling thus along the sides and bottoms of ravines for some miles, steadily rising at the same time, we suddenly emerged through a narrow pass, and from under the spreading aisle of a large banyan tree (from which this pass gets its name of the Burghat), on to an open glade, covered with short green grass, and studded with magnificent trees, which I found was the commencement of the plateau of Puchmurree. (1871)

J. FORSYTH[362]

## 7. Kanchenjunga

From Rangoon we steamed to Calcutta, and thence took rail to Darjeeling, where we remained a month, enjoying for the second fortnight of that time an almost unclouded view of the sublime Himalayan range. I shall never forget my first sight of Kinchinjunga, the highest mountain, after Mount Everest, in the known world. The monsoon clouds, which had hitherto shut out the mighty mountains, had begun to break and scatter, and we were told that the snowy range would now become visible. The great valley lying north of Darjeeling, also the near mountains, about twelve thousand feet above sea-level, which formed the back-ground, was still occupied by floating, changing cloud masses; and I pitched my eye high enough, as I thought, to see the wished-for peaks beyond, when a rift in the clouds should give the opportunity. For some time I watched, and saw many a dark, dim mass unveiled for a second or so behind the changing clouds; but not what I desired. At last I happened to look up very much higher, and, with a feeling of awe and astonishment, I then saw a dazzling snow-peak rise, vast and majestic, above the mantling clouds, where I should never have thought of looking for anything of earthly mould. As the clouds cleared away, swept by a strong east wind, the thronging peaks and rounded buttresses of this 'roof of the world' came in view, all wrapped in eternal snow, and unvisited, since their creation, by aught of mortal frame. No living thing, bird, insect, or even grass or moss, could ever have reached the unchanging summit of Kinchinjunga: the snows which we this day viewed with wondering eyes have been lying there, in their pale beauty, for tens of centuries. At that tremendous height (Kinchinjunga is not far short of twenty-nine thousand feet), no storms, no rains, can ever come to wash away the snow: fall it may, from time to time, in small degree, to be gradually replaced by condensed vapour; but on the smoother and less precipitous slopes the frozen masses must remain unchanged for ever. (1882)

E.F. BURTON[363]

## 8. The sacred Himalaya

When contemplating the sublime grandeur of those majestic snow-crowned peaks, standing there as they have done for unknown time, and, for aught we know, as they will do for countless ages, un-changed in their wan solemnity, it seemed to me that nowhere could a place in which to hold communion with the great Creator of the universe have been more fitly chosen than there, among His own mighty and wonderful works. What is the basilica of St Peter at Rome, with its vast and perfect proportions and gorgeous interior; or the Duomo at Milan, with its forest of elaborately wrought pinnacles: or the mosque of Sta Sophia at Istamboul, with its precious marbles, jasper, and porphyry, its huge cupola and graceful minarets; or our own St Paul's Cathedral, with its more solemn style of architecture; or any other grand fane fashioned by human art,—when compared with the awful magnitude and natural beauty of the creations around this hallowed spot? For hallowed it may certainly be termed as every place which is dedicated by any creed whatsoever to the service of the one Supreme Being whom all acknowledge ought to be. Yet, sad to say, there are some—let us hope they are few—who ignore the sanctity of a Hindoo place of pilgrimage, and who preach nothing but damnation for the lame, the blind, and the poor infirm old devotee who, to show his faith in the tenets of a religion in which he has been brought up to believe, and to whom they have been rendered venerable by the observances of ages, trudges his weary way from the uttermost parts of Hindustan, often barefooted and enduring the most cruel hardships, all in the earnest hope of being able to wash away his sins in the, to him, holy hotspring at Badrinath. Surely this faithful, though in many respects misguided, pilgrim may, through the infinite mercy of the Almighty, hope for salvation as much as the uncharitable individual, calling himself a Christian, who presumes to condemn him as a 'heathen.' Does such an one ever think, when fulfilling his mission to make converts to a better religion, that many professing it have but the form and little of the real unselfish religious feeling which is so fully manifested by many a poor Hindoo?

Some such thoughts as these filled my mind whilst I sat enraptured with the glorious scene before me. Not a sound was there to disturb my reverie but the wild call of the moonal pheasant echoing among the neighbouring crags, as I watched the cold grey shade creeping slowly on, gradually darkening each successive sunlit mountain tier, until it stole over the highest peaks of eternal snow, leaving them weird-looking and unearthly in their stern frozen dignity, their pallid lineaments each moment growing more dim in the deepening gloom.

The chilly night wind that came whispering through the pine-trees, wafting an alluring odour from the culinary department, and a voice at my elbow murmuring 'Khana tyar' (dinner is ready), soon recalled me from the ideal to the real; and I was very hungry. (1889)

DONALD MACINTYRE[364]

# F. RIVERS AND BRIDGES

## 1. *An awful bridge*

We passed Jum-ka-gurh, an old house or fort, built on a projecting
rock on the opposite side of the river, which formerly was a place of
considerable sanctity, where religious people performed one of the
many customary ablutions, as preparatory purifications in the way
to Gungotree. Just below it the Jum-ke-Gad, h empties itself to the
river: somewhat further on we passed the small poor village of
Innoo, where were some of the largest peaches I ever saw, either in
India or at home. The path still leads along the river bank, occasionally on rice grounds; at times through thick tangled, but small
jungle. to Goaree-ke-Gad, h, about two miles from Innoo, which
we crossed with some difficulty, being deep and rapid, and went on
to Reene-ke-Gad, h, a large and headlong torrent, much swelled by
the rains.

This k, hola, which we reckon to be about nine miles from Incolla,
is that over which the zemindars had been sent to throw a bridge;
but we were detained a full hour till it was ready, and a most frail
fabric it was when finished, consisting of two small round sticks,
extending from the one bank to a large rock in the middle; and from
thence to the other side, three still smaller tied together, formed the
whole machine, on which a wild mountain stream was to be crossed
by fifty or sixty persons, many of them heavily laden.

By care, however, we succeeded, though it bent and shook till
nearly touching the stream, with the exception of one unfortunate
cooley, who missed his step from the reaction of the timber, and fell
into the furious water. In a moment he was carried away to the
junction of the nullah with the river, about 150 yards below, where
his head appeared for an instant, and his load floating beside him;
but the foaming current of the Bhagiruttee, here tumbling over
large rocks with a mighty roar, seized him, and hurried him along
with its tremendous torrent. (1815)

JAMES BAILLIE FRASER[365]

## 2. *A jhoola*

A communication is here kept up across the Sutlej by means of that
singular and dangerous kind of bridge (if it may be so called) which

in the hills is termed a jhoola. At some convenient spot, where the river is rather narrow and the rocks on either side overhang the stream, a stout beam of wood is fixed horizontally upon or behind two strong stakes, that are driven into the banks on each side of the water; and round these beams ropes are strained, extending from the one to the other across the river, and they are hauled tight, and kept in their place by a sort of windlass. The rope used in forming this bridge is generally from two to three inches in circumference, and at least nine or ten times crossed to make it secure. This collection of ropes is traversed by a block of wood hollowed into a semicircular groove large enough to slide easily along it, and around this block ropes are suspended, forming a loop, in which passengers seat themselves, clasping its upper parts with their hands to keep themselves steady; a line fixed to the wooden block at each end, and extending to each bank, serves to haul it, and the passenger attached to it, from one side of the river to the other. (1815)

JAMES BAILLIE FRASER [366]

## 3. Bridge of boats

Marched to Nowbutgunge, thirteen miles on the left bank of the Ganges: employed in getting all ready for crossing the river: the banks full of quick-sands and holes: the weather threatening rain, which at night came down 'con spirito,' and greatly added to the previous difficulties in crossing: the Oude thieves very busy in endeavouring to make us remember them. One of our party had ample cause to admire their *handicraft* in the abstraction of some considerable property.

Crossed the Ganges to Nanamow: the operation of transporting a large camp over a river is a work of infinite trouble, and generally of loss. The banks on one side or the other are precipitous; quick-sands abound, or else deep mud; and the native boats are ill adapted for ferries, being the common boats used for the transport of mer-chandize: They are large, cumbrous, and unwieldy, high at the sides, and square at each end. Notwithstanding the inconvenience is daily seen and felt, the Government take no steps to remedy the evil. A bridge of boats at the large stations would not cost a very great sum, and it could be available at any intermediate point, at a few days' warning: the original cost and the subsequent charge when in use would, I am assured by good judges, be quickly covered by a small

'Grass Rope Bridge at Teree-Gurwall', drawn by David Cox

toll on passengers, cattle, and goods. The convenience and comtort, to say nothing of the means of obviating loss and damage to horses and other animals, would be acknowledged. Any person would gladly pay a few rupees to have a valuable horse taken over with safety and celerity. The cavalry of the army are numerous, and one would suppose valuable enough to cause some little expense being incurred in their safe transport, even if the exigencies of service, though only probable, did not demand it, or the intercourse of commerce did not point out the manifest advantages, and the sure return for any reasonable outlay. In the present instance the King, as we were in his dominions, fitted up eight platform boats for carriages and cattle, and as many were prepared by our own commissariat. (1827)

EDWARD C. ARCHER[367]

## 4. *Legend of the Nerbudda river*

The legend is, that the Nerbudda which flows west into the gulf of Cambay was wooed and won in the usual way by the Sohun river, which rises from the same table land of Omurkuntuk, and flows east into the Ganges and Bay of Bengal. All the previous ceremonies having been performed, the Sohun came with due 'pomp and circumstance to fetch his bride, in the procession called the *Burraet,* up to which time the bride and bridegroom are supposed never to have seen each other, unless perchance they may have met in infancy. Her majesty the Nerbudda became exceedingly impatient to know what sort of a personage her destinies were to be linked to, while his majesty the Sohun advanced at a slow and stately pace. At last the Queen sent Jhola, the daughter of the barber, to take a close view of him, and to return and make a faithful and particular report of his person. His majesty was captivated with the little Jhola, the barber's daughter, at first sight; and she 'nothing loath,' yielded to his caresses. Some say that she actually pretended to be Queen herself; and that his majesty was no further in fault, than in mistaking the humble handmaid for her noble mistress; but, be that is it may, her majesty no sooner heard of the good understanding between them, than she rushed forward, and with one foot sent the Sohun rolling back to the east whence he came, and with the other kicked little Jhola sprawling after him: for, said the high priest, who told us the story, 'you see what a towering passion she was likely to have been in under such indignities, from the furious manner in which she cuts her way through the marble rocks beneath us, and casts huge masses right and left as she goes along, as if they were really so many cocoa-nuts!' 'And was she,' asked I, 'to have flown eastward with him, or was he to have flown westward with her?' 'She was to have accompanied him eastward,' said the high priest; 'but her majesty, after this indignity, declared, that she would not go a single pace in the same direction with such wretches, and would flow west, though all the other rivers in India might flow east: and west she flows accordingly a virgin queen!' I asked some of the Hindoos about us why they called her *Mother Nerbudda,* if she was really never married. 'Her majesty,' said they with great respect, 'would really never consent to be married after the indignity she suffered from her affianced bridegroom the Sohun; and we call her mother because she blesses us all and we are anxious to accost her by the name which we consider to be at once the most respectful and endearing.' Any Englishman can easily conceive a poet in his highest 'calenture of the brain,' addressing the ocean as 'a steed that knows his rider,' and patting the crested billow as his flowing mane: but he must come to India to understand how every individual of a whole community of many millions can address a fine river as a living being—a sovereign princess, who hears and understands all they say, and exercises a kind of local superintendence over their affairs, without a single temple in which her image is worshipped, or a single priest to profit by the delusion. As in the case of the Ganges, it is the river itself to whom they address themselves, and not to any deity residing in it, or presiding over it—the stream itself is the deity which fills their imaginations, and receives their homage. (1844)

WILLIAM HENRY SLEEMAN[368]

## 5. Cane bridge

In the gorge of the Rungeet the heat was intolerable, though the thermometer did not rise above 95°. The mountains leave but a narrow gorge between them, here and there bordered by a belt of strong soil, supporting a towering crop of long cane-like grasses and tall trees. The troubled river, about eighty yards across, rages along over a gravelly bed. Crossing the Rungmo, where it falls into the Rungeet, we came upon a group of natives drinking fermented

Murwa liquor under a rock; I had a good deal of difficulty in getting my people past, and more in inducing one of the topers to take the place of a Ghorka (Nepalese) of our party who was ill with fever. Soon afterwards, at a most wild and beautiful spot, I saw, for the first time, one of the most characteristic of Himalayan objects of art, *a cane bridge*. All the spurs, round the bases of which the river flowed, were steep and rocky, their flanks clothed with the richest tropical forest, their crests tipped with pines. On the river's edge, the Banana, *Pandanus,* and *Bauhinia,* were frequent, and Figs prevailed. One of the latter (of an exceedingly beautiful species) projected over the stream, growing out of a mass of rock, its roots interlaced and grasping at every available support, while its branches, loaded with deep glossy foliage, hung over the water. This tree formed one pier for the canes; that on the opposite bank was constructed of strong piles, propped with large stones; and between them swung the bridge, about eighty yards long, ever rocking over the torrent (forty feet below). The lightness and extreme simplicity of its structure were very remarkable. Two parallel canes, on the same horizontal plane, were stretched across the stream; from them others hung in loops, and along the loops were laid one or two bamboo stems for flooring; cross pieces below this flooring, hung from the two upper canes, which they thus served to keep apart. The traveller grasps one of the canes in either hand, and walks along the loose bamboos laid on the swinging loops; the motion is great, and the rattling of the loose dry bamboos is neither a musical sound, nor one calculated to inspire confidence; the whole structure seeming as if about to break down. With shoes it is not easy to walk; and even with bare feet it is often difficult, there being frequently but one bamboo, which, if the fastening is loose, tilts up, leaving the pedestrian suspended over the torrent by the slender canes. When properly and strongly made, with good fastenings, and a floor of bamboos laid *transversely,* these bridges are easy to cross. The canes are procured from a species of *Calamus;* they are as thick as the finger, and twenty or thirty yards long, knotted together, and the other pieces are fastened to them by strips of the same plant. A Lepcha, carrying one hundred and forty pounds on his back, crosses without hesitation, slowly but steadily, and with perfect confidence.

A deep broad pool below the bridge was made available for a ferry: the boat was a triangular raft of bamboo stems, with a stage on the top, and it was secured on the opposite side of the stream, having

a cane reaching across to that on which we were. A stout Lepcha
leapt into the boiling flood and boldly swam across, holding on by
the cane, without which he would have been carried away. He
unfastened the raft, and we drew it over by the cane, and, seated on
the stage up to our knees in water, we were pulled across, the raft
bobbing up and down over the rippling stream. (1848)

JOSEPH DALTON HOOKER[369]

## 6. Floating bridge across the Goomti

As we were sitting over pipes and cigars, after dinner, a disconsolate
young artillery officer and an aide de-camp come into us from the
adjoining Head-Quarters camp, and asked 'where the bridge is?'
They have to bring down some guns to the river, and can not find
their way. Thus the secret is known. The engineers are at work on
the Goomtee, throwing a floating bridge across, and these guns are
going down to defend it. The night is fine, clear moonlight. Who will
come and have a look at the bridge? It is near 10 o'clock—late for
camp, and so only some four or five of us start off with the artillery.
It is not very easy to find the way, for the wood is thick, and the
moonlight falls fitfully and uncertainly through the dense branches,
but at last we emerge on the meadows, which lie between Bibliapore
and the river, and we see its waters like a strip of mirror in one bend,
as it whirls through the dark plain. At one place there is a black,
ant-heap-like body, which resolves itself, as we approach close, into
a body of sappers, some carts laden with empty porter casks, and
native drivers and coolies. They are close to the river, which is here
about forty yards broad, with deep banks on both sides. Not a very
silent party, for there is a row of voices and creaking of cart-wheels,
which could be heard a mile away. Already the men have cut down
the bank and made a rough roadway to the water's edge, and the
first raft of casks is in the stream. (1858–9)

WILLIAM HOWARD RUSSELL[370]

## 7. The cow's mouth: a source of the Ganges

Among the many 'physical errors of Hindooism,' is one to the effect
that the great rivers of India issue out of the mouth of some familiar
animal of supernatural power and proportion; and in accordance
with this superstition it is beleived that the source of the holy river,

the Ganges, is to be sought in the mouth of that sacred animal, the
Cow. The source of the Ganges is, therefore, known to the Hindoo
as the 'Cow's Mouth.' The stream, which is here some 13,000 feet
above the level of the sea, issues in a very slender current from the
glacier, 'which,' says the artist, 'is seen lying in the hollow of the
valley covered with earth and stones, which, as it melts, are precipitated below in great masses.' The Hindoos make pilgrimages to the
source of the sacred river, but seldom reach this extreme point.
They commonly stop short at a temple some twenty miles below the
Cow's Mouth; and there they may be seen—of many tribes and
from many places—some having come, weary and footsore,
perhaps from the uttermost parts of India, begging their bread by
the way, and sustained by the thought of the holiness of the act in the
eyes of the Almighty, and the increased veneration with which they
will be regarded, on their return, by their fellow men.

There is nothing more strongly implanted in the mind of an
orthodox Hindoo than the holiness of the water of the Ganges. He is
sworn upon the Gunga-pauni, as an imprecation of the most awe-
inspiring character, and he can assoil himself by extreme unction
from this sacred source without the aid of a priest. Thousands are
carried to the banks of the Ganges to die there, not without some
knowledge of the fact that impatient relatives may be minded to
expedite the coming of the last hour of the sick man by putting some
Gangetic clay into his mouth. Thousands, too, from the inland
districts, make long journeys to the banks of the river to carry
thence bottles full of the holy water. In the great City of
Benares—the 'Sacred City of the Hindoos,' 'Devotees and pilgrims,' writes the Rev. Mr. Sherring, 'separately or in crowds, are
entering or departing from the place constantly throughout the
year, especially on the occasion of a great festival. Many carry back
with them the sacred water of the Ganges, in small bottles, hermeti-
cally sealed, placed in baskets hanging from the extremity of poles
which they bear upon their shoulders. The poor deluded sensualist,
whose life has been passed in abominable courses; or the covetous
*mahajun*, or native banker, who has made himself rich by a long
course of grinding extortion; or the fanatical devotee, more simple
than a babe, yet sometimes guilty of the foulest crimes, still comes of
old, from the remotest corners of India, as the sands of time are
slowly ebbing away, and fearful lest the last golden grains should
escape before his long journey is ended, makes desperate efforts to

hold on his course, till at length, arriving at the sacred city, and
touching its hallowed soil, his anxious spirit becomes suddenly calm,
a strange sense of relief comes over him, and he is at once cheered
and comforted with a treacherous lie, that his sins are forgiven and
his soul is saved.' (1867)

JOHN WILLIAM KAYE[371]

## G. THE MONSOON AND RAIN

### 1. The monsoon

On the 15th of October (183   ?) the flag-staff was struck as a signal
for all vessels to leave the roads, lest they should be overtaken by
the monsoon. On that very morning some premonitory symptoms
of the approaching 'war of elements' had appeared; small fleecy
clouds were perceived at intervals to rise from the horizon and to
dissipate in a thin and almost imperceptible vapour over the deep
blue of the still bright sky. There was a slight haze upon the distant
waters, which seemed gradually to thicken, although not to a density sufficient to refract the rays of the sun, which still flooded the
broad sea with one unvarying mass of glowing light. There was a
sensation of suffocating heat in the atmosphere, which at the same
moment seemed to oppress the lungs and depress the spirits. Towards the afternoon, the aspect of the sky began to change; the
horizon gathered blackness, and the sun, which had risen so
brightly, had evidently culminated in glory, to go down in darkness,
and to have his splendour veiled from human sight by a long,
gloomy period of storm and turbulence. Masses of heavy clouds
appeared to rise from the sea, black and portentous, accompanied
by sudden gusts of wind, that shortly died away, being succeeded by
an intense, death-like stillness, as if the air were in a state of utter
stagnation, and its vital properties arrested. It seemed no longer to
circulate, until again agitated by the brief but mighty gusts which
swept fiercely along, like the giant heralds of the storm. Meanwhile
the lower circle of the heavens looked a deep brassy red, from the
partial reflection of the sunbeams upon the thick clouds, which had
now everywhere overspread it. The sun had long passed the meri-
dian, and his rays were slanting upon the gathering billows, when
those black and threatening ministers of the tempest rose rapidly
towards the zenith.

The dim horizon lowering vapours shroud.
And blot the sun yet struggling through a cloud,
Through the wide atmosphere, condensed with haze,
His glowing orb emits a sanguine blaze.

About four o'clock the whole sky was overspread, and the deep gloom of twilight was cast over the town and sea. The atmosphere was condensed almost to the thickness of a mist, which was increased by the thin spray scattered over the land from the sea, by the violence of the increasing gales. The rain now began to fall in sheeted masses, and the wind to howl more continuously, which, mingling with the roaring of the surf, produced a tumultuous union of sounds, perfectly deafening.

As the house which we occupied overlooked the beach, we could behold the setting in of the monsoon in all its grand and terrific sublimity. The wind, with a force which nothing could resist, bent the tufted heads of the tall, slim cocoanut trees almost to the earth, flinging the light sand into the air in eddying vortices, until the rain had either so increased its gravity, or beaten it into a mass, as to prevent the wind from raising it. The pale lightning streamed from the clouds in broad sheets of flame, which appeared to encircle the heavens as if every element had been converted into fire, and the world was on the eve of a general conflagration, whilst the peal, which instantly followed, was like the explosion of a gunpowder-magazine, or the discharge of artillery in the gorge of a mountain, where the repercussion of surrounding hills multiplies with terrific energy its deep and astounding echoes. The heavens seemed to be one vast reservoir of flame, which was propelled from its voluminous bed by some invisible but omnipotent agency, and threatened to fling its fiery ruin upon every thing around. In some parts, however, of the pitchy vapour by which the skies were by this time completely overspread, the lightning was seen only occasionally to glimmer in faint streaks of light, as if struggling, but unable, to escape from its prison, igniting, but too weak to burst, the impervious bosoms of those capacious magazines in which it was at once engendered and pent up. So heavy and continuous was the rain that scarcely any thing, save those vivid bursts of light which nothing could arrest or resist, was perceptible through it. The thunder was so painfully loud, that it frequently caused the ear to throb; it seemed as if mines were momentarily springing in the heavens, and I could almost fancy that one of the sublimest fictions of heathen fable was realized

at this moment before me, and that I was hearing an assault of the
Titans. The surf was raised by the wind and scattered in thin billows
of foam over the esplanade, which was completely powdered with
the white feathery spray. It extended several hundred yards from
the beach; fish, upwards of three inches long, were found upon the
flat roofs of houses in the town during the prevalence of the monsoon, either blown from the sea by the violence of the gales, or taken
up in the water-spouts, which are very prevalent in this tempestuous
season. When these burst, whatever they contain is frequently
borne by the sweeping blast to a considerable distance overland,
and deposited in the most uncongenial situations, so that now,
during the violence of these tropical storms, fish are found alive on
the tops of houses; nor is this any longer a matter of surprise to the
established resident in India, who sees every year a repetition of this
singular phenomenon.

I have mentioned the intense loudness of the thunder, but between its pauses, as the hurricane increased, the roaring of the surf
was scarcely less loud, so that there was an unceasing uproar, which
to those who lived near the beach was most distressing, though the
sublimity of the scene fully compensated for any annoyances which
were induced by this fierce collision of the elements. During the
extreme violence of the storm, the heat was occasionally almost
beyond endurance, particularly after the first day or two, when the
wind would at intervals entirely subside, so that not a breath of air
could be felt, and the punka afforded but a partial relief to that
distressing sensation which is caused by the oppressive stillness of
the air, so well known in India whilst the monsoon prevails. This was
not our only inconvenience; insects of all kinds crept along the
walls, and the most disagreeable reptiles crawled over our floors.
Legions of ants, cockroaches, and lizards, were forced from their
dark recesses by the torrents, and absolutely invaded us. Scorpions,
toads, centipedes, and even snakes, made free entrance into our
apartments, as if they had been Hindoo lazar-houses for the recep-
tion of wandering and homeless reptiles. The toads, centipedes, and
snakes, we could manage to destroy, but the scorpions, lizards, ants,
and cockroaches, defied us by their numbers and maintained a
complete though not undisturbed possession of our chambers.

Day after day the same scene was repeated with somewhat less
violence, though at intervals the might of the hurricane was truly
appalling; but, during its occasional pauses, visits were paid and

returned as usual, while those accustomed to the sight seemed almost to forget that there was any thing in these mighty jarrings of inanimate nature beyond its ordinary conflicts. There are no doubt many parts of the world where, during the presence of hurricanes, the wind is more impetuous than during these periodical visitations in India; but in none, I will venture to say, does the rain pour in such a mighty deluge, and in no place can the thunder and lightning be more terrific. (c. 1820–34)

JOHN HOBART CAUNTER[372]

## 2. The monsoon at Dum Dum, Calcutta

During the season of the monsoon, Dum Dum, and the whole neighbourhood, are so completely inundated, that a small *dingi* may be paddled from the cantonment to the salt-water lakes, or to the Sundurbunds, and thence into the open ocean, which is distant something more than one hundred miles. This may appear very strange, and the more so from the vicinity of the Ganges, whose channel might be expected to carry off the flood, as it does not here overflow its banks; but when the profusion of a tropical rain is recollected, and its continuance, the fact is not so surprising.

At Dum Dum, in 1831, the heavens did not cease, during a space of one hundred and forty hours, to pour down without intermission a deluge of water, as if the flood gates had been a second time opened for destruction. Still the station is not an unhealthy one, that is, not more so than most parts of the lower provinces of the Bengal presidency, and many persons have found its situation more favourable to their health than most other places. Among horses, however, there has more than once been a strange epidemic, by which vast numbers have fallen victims to an inscrutable disease, which leaves no traces of its work upon the carcase, and which affords no time for attempts at remedy; it has been attributed to exhalation, wet fodder, etc. all equally unsatisfactory; for were it any of these, how comes it that, at other times, during the rainy season, the troop horses have been in excellent order, and the hospital stables occupied only by *bursautti* cases and common casualties. This, however, has been very rare, and, generally speaking, Dum Dum is not reckoned an unhealthy situation for cattle. (1831)

THOMAS BACON[373]

## 3. The monsoon along the Madras coast

In consequence of the exposed state of the roadsted, the monsoon, or rather the effect of it, is felt much more at Madras than anywhere along the coast, thereby rendering it very dangerous for shipping lying at anchor, or indeed coming in. It is considered to be so hazardous, that the flag-staff is struck during its prevalence, as a signal for all vessels to leave the anchorage, giving timely warning that it is not safe to remain there longer than is absolutely necessary. All the smaller country craft invariably quit, and nothing is to be seen in the roads at such a period, save the larger vessels and of these only a very few.

The communication from shore with ships in the roads is very hazardous, owing to the surf which rolls upon the beach with terrific violence, causing its roar to be heard for several miles inland. It not unfrequently occurs that ships and other vessels are cast away, and many lives lost. The sacrifice of valuable cargoes is oftentimes truly lamentable, and I cannot better sum up my remarks than by saying that the monsoon may be looked upon by many as a dreadful calamity, which not only blasts their prospects, but ruins them, perhaps, past redemption.

I myself witnessed a truly distressing circumstance of the above description, during the monsoon, when a very beautiful ship was completely lost, and the fortunes of the commander blighted for ever. She had come into Madras, laden with teak-timber, on account of government, from the Tenasserim provinces, and was waiting for the weather to moderate, previously to landing her cargo. The day after her arrival, it blew a dreadful gale, so much so that all the different vessels, large and small, slipped or cut their cables and stood out to sea, but the Th—— held her ground beautifully, and weathered the gale, which blew with unabated fury for the whole of that night.

The day following there was a lull, and the captain determined on shifting his berth and bringing her close in shore, so as to be able to float out and land his timber in safety. He was advised by many seafaring men at Madras to remain where he was, as her anchor had good holding-ground, and there was no necessity for his landing his timber in such a hurry. One old gentleman, in particular, who was an intimate friend of Captain B——'s (Mr. D——, well known at Madras, but now no more), declared to him that he would not value

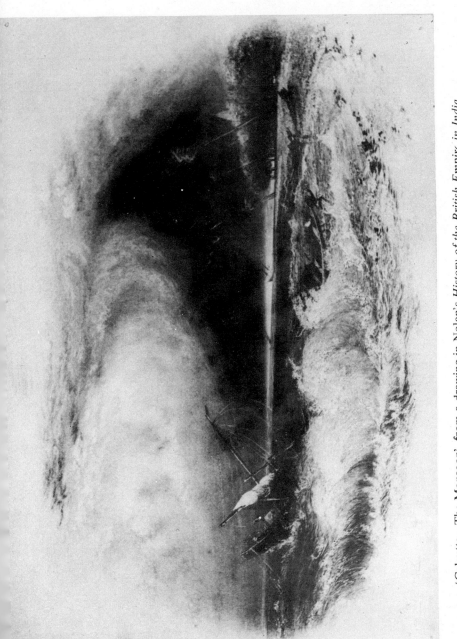

'Calcutta—The Monsoon', from a drawing in Nolan's *History of the British Empire in India*

his ship at a brass farthing, if he moved her from her anchorage.

However, in spite of all the advice he had received, he shifted his ship's berth and coming close in shore, commenced landing his timber. So secure did he consider his vessel to be, and so certain that there would be no rough weather, that he actually slept on shore that night, leaving the ship in charge of his chief officer. It blew a perfect hurricane during that awful night, and the sea rose tremendously high, and beat right into the buildings on the beach.

Towards morning, the hapless ship was discovered to be dragging her anchor, and drifting fast in shore. The mate saw the danger in which his ship was placed. To put sail upon her and stand out to sea was impossible, for the gale blew right on to the land. He therefore let down another anchor, in the hopes of bringing her up; but such was the violence of the sea, and the consequent strain upon the cables, that in a very short time the chain of the last snapped like whip-cord, and the vessel came rapidly and struck the shore. I never can forget this truly appalling sight. A huge vessel, as she was, carried by the force of the mighty waves, as easily as a piece of cork, and dashed on to the beach, within twenty yards of the high road.

The agony of mind which the unfortunate captain suffered must have been intense. I saw him standing on the beach, evidently under great anxiety, without being able to avert the destruction of perhaps all he possessed in the world, and no doubt reproaching himself for his obstinacy in not having taken the advice of his friends for the safety of his ship. Shortly after she grounded, ropes and hawsers were passed on shore, and the whole crew, including officers, were landed in safety. The surf made a clean breach over her, from stem to stern, dashing the spray into the very houses, and drenching the thousands, who congregated to see the spectacle, to the skin. She was so strongly, and so well put together, that she lay on the shore for several months after, and was eventually taken to pieces by degrees.

The captain was from that time a broken-hearted man. He quitted Madras soon after, and went to Rangoon, where he died, without relations or friends to cheer his last moments, which must have been embittered by the thoughts that his misfortunes were attributable to his own obstinate determination, on the occasion above related; for had he either gone out to sea with the other ships or had he not shifted his berth, which his vessel had so nobly held during the previous gales, all might have been well.

I remember several other disastrous shipwrecks taking place along the coast, during that truly terrific monsoon. At Coringa, a place up the north-eastern coast, there was a large ship blown high and dry out of the water into the garden of one of the houses! The occupant of the mansion awaking one morning, saw his bed-room window wide open and something intruding, which he could not at all understand, but which, after due examination, proved to be the jib-boom end of the said ship, it was just as well she had not come further, else, I think, the sleep of the tenant of the house would have been disturbed in a manner that would not have conduced much to his comfort.

Up the river Hooghly, and in the neighbourhood of Calcutta, a huge East Indiaman, of eight hundred or a thousand tons, was lifted out of the water and landed in the middle of a rice-field, several hundred yards from the banks of the river. No one who has not witnessed the terrific effects of a monsoon storm in the east, can conceive the mischief it causes. Suffice it to say, that such visitations are in themselves appalling, and attended with most ruinous consequences from the which it is almost impossible to recover. (1833–42)

ALBERT HERVEY[374]

## 4. A downpour

About half way we were overtaken by one of the heaviest showers of rain I ever saw; it threatened us from neither side, but began to descend from an apparently small bed of clouds directly over our heads, which seemed to spread out on every side as the rain fell, and fill the whole vault of heaven with one dark and dense mass. The wind changed frequently; and in less than half an hour the whole surface of the country over which we were travelling was under water. This dense mass of clouds passed off in about two hours to the east; but twice, when the sun opened and beamed divinely upon us in a cloudless sky to the west, the wind changed suddenly round, and rushed back angrily from the east, to fill up the space which had been quickly rarified by the genial heat of its rays, till we were again enveloped in darkness, and began to despair of reaching any human habitation before night. Some hail fell among the rain, but not large enough to hurt any one. The thunder was loud and often startling to the strongest nerves; and the lightning vivid and almost incessant.

We managed to keep the road because it was merely a beaten pathway below the common level of the country, and we could trace it by the greater depth of the water, and the absence of all shrubs and grass. All roads in India soon become water-courses—they are nowhere metalled; and, being left for four or five months every year without rain their soil is reduced to powder by friction, and carried off by the winds over the surrounding country. I was on horseback, but my wife and child were secure in a good palankeen that sheltered them from the rain. The bearers were obliged to move with great caution and slowly, and I sent on every person I could spare that they might *keep moving,* for the cold blast blowing over their thin and wet clothes seemed intolerable to those who were idle. My child's playmate, Gholab, a lad of about ten years of age, resolutely kept by the side of the palankeen, trotting through the water with his teeth chattering as if he had been in an ague. The rain at last ceased, and the sky in the west cleared up beautifully about half an hour before sunset. (1844)

WILLIAM HENRY SLEEMAN [375]

## H. STORMS & HURRICANES

### 1. A river storm

After procuring some necessary supplies by means of a small wherry from *Allahabad,* we proceeded next day as usual; but no village being in sight at the hour for *legowing,* our boats were made fast to a sand-bank in the middle of the river. Our voyage to-day was by no means agreeable; for the river was bounded on either side by high, and almost perpendicular banks. The wind blew strong from the eastward during the night, which being against the stream, caused a heavy swell, and annoyed us not a little; in fact, we were obliged to quit the position we had taken, and not without great difficulty gained the opposite shore. The river shortly after assumed the appearance of a sea, for which our boats were by no means calculated. Unfortunately for us, it soon increased to a gale of wind; during which, one of our baggage boats was upset, and the *budgerow* broke from her moorings, drifting with considerable rapidity towards a place in the Nawaab's country inhabited by thieves, whose chief support is from the plunder of boats, which they have a most ingenious mode of attacking without being seen.

Accustomed to swimming and diving from their infancy, the water may almost be termed their natural element. When they perceive boats *legowed* for the night, and that the crews are retired to rest, they cover their heads with earthen pots, having two holes bored through them for eyes, and slipping into the river, float silently round until an opportunity offers of climbing upon deck, when making themselves masters of all property that is moveable, without disturbing any one, they swim off with it securely. So expert are they at this occupation, that a gentleman has frequently missed his writing desk in the morning, without the smallest appearance of any one having been there.

The next morning was cloudy, with a drizzling rain; but the wind proved fair and we let go our anchorage. The river however winds so considerably here, that a fair wind one half hour is contrary the next, so that we made but little progress. The banks were still high, almost inaccessible: on their summits we observed several large villages. The weather had now become cool and pleasant. (1809)

A. DEARE[376]

## 2. *Violent hurricane at Madras*

By the great kindness of Providence, the expedition sailed on the evening of the 30th of April; for on the 1st of May, the dawn was ushered in by an exceedingly heavy fall of rain, which continued without intermission until five o'clock the next morning. The wind, which was at first moderate, gradually rose, and at ten A.M., on the 2nd, had increased to a perfect hurricane, which continued with unabated fury for seventeen hours; the last six, indeed, seldom equalled in any part of the world: during which, houses were upset, doors and windows blown off their hinges, trees torn up by the roots, and streams were running with great force in every direction. The sea forcing it's way into both rivers, swept all before it; two bridges could not be discovered for two days afterwards, and the Marmelong one, having it's centre arch carried away, was impassable for a considerable time. The house I was living in, with an old friend, Lieutenant-colonel Charles Trotter, was nearly dismantled, and we had taken shelter in the last room, when it abated.

After this faint outline of the damage sustained on shore, I know not what words can picture the horrors of the scene in the roads. Of all the ships, brigs, cutters, ketches, donies, etc. only one solitary brig escaped, by putting out to sea, at the commencement of the storm. Many foundered at their anchors, for the surface rose as far out as nine fathoms, others were literally torn to pieces, and the rest dashed against the shore, in all directions. The whole beach was covered with wrecks, from St. Thome to the Custom House, a distance of nearly three miles; and so thickly were the fragments strewed, that it was with difficulty we could find our way through them, as soon as the storm was over; yet, wonderful to relate, the hand of the Almighty was most singularly extended over the crews of His Majesty's fine frigate *Daver* and stone-ship *Chichester*, and several other English ships which were totally lost; only two Europeans losing their lives, of hundreds exposed to the most imminent peril, and I believe, only a few hundred natives perished, of thousands, whose floating habitations were buried in the waters. One small English brig totally dismasted, being of more than ordinary strength in her hull, was washed high and dry upon the shore, with her crew snug on board, cutting a most ludicrous figure in the sands: but the most extraordinary sight witnessed that evening, was a small French cartel brig, which returned to the roads, with her colours flying from her only remaining topmast, and thus, while at war with that nation, the French flag was flying alone triumphant in those roads, that had contained at least one hundred English the day before. These are the wonderful ways of Providence; and poor silly man, forgetting both his terrors and his promises the moment they are over, considers them as mere matters of course. (1811)

JAMES WELSH[377]

## 3. *Mountain storms*

In the mountainous regions of Boutan the accommodation for travellers is very uncertain. Occasionally is found in the passes erected for that purpose, a small empty hut, which affords a welcome shelter from the violent storms that frequently take place in those alpine solitudes. Sometimes the clouds appear suddenly to roll towards one common centre, and condensing into a thick mist, involve every object, investing the whole landscape with a general hue of sickly grey, rendering the air damp and chilly, and adding greatly to the natural difficulties of the route. Upon these occasions the Bouteas invariably maintain a profound silence, in order that their voices may not disturb the elements; for they gravely assert

that even so slight a concussion of the air as that produced by the
voice in ordinary conversation would open the gathered reservoirs
above, and cause them immediately to void their stores in torrents
of rain.

The violence of the storms which so often occur in these hills can
scarcely be imagined by those who have never witnessed them; they
far exceed anything ever seen in the more mountainous districts of
Europe. The thunder rolls down the precipices and is reverberated
from hill to hill with a loudness and continuity perfectly appalling.
The lightning absolutely seems to fill the valleys, wrapping every
object in a sheet of flame, the flashes being so successive that there is
scarcely time to draw breath between the intervals. The hot sul-
phurous smell—the smoking ground fired in places by the electric
blaze—the singed shrubs, with occasionally the riven and charred
trunks of huge trees quivering like grim and blackened skeletons,
form a union of objects which the eye cannot meet without terror.

The quantity of rain poured from the clouds is so prodigious, that,
in an almost inconceivably short space of time, from the side of
every mountain within the tempest's range, cataracts are seen pouring into the valleys beneath, dashing from rock to rock, or from
ledge to ledge, foaming, sparkling, and hissing with a turbulence
which drowns every other sound but that produced by the awful
crashings of the thunder above. The wind, rushing in terrific eddies
down the slopes of the hills, tears away in its impetuous progress the
smaller growth, laying them in many places perfectly bare, uproot-
ing trees, and hurling huge masses of rock into the ravines below,
through which the congregated waters are forcing their way, interrupted by these and other impediments.

If the traveller should not obtain shelter during these fierce
conflicts of the elements, his peril must become imminent, for the
wind would most probably sweep him from the path and send him to
his grave amid the foaming waters. These mountain storms are
generally accompanied by whirlwinds which nothing can resist;
even horses are borne away in the mighty vortex, being elevated
many feet into the air and dashed over the mountain's brow. The
natives take shelter, on these occasions, in nooks under the projec-
tions of the hills; but even here they are exposed to great danger, as
the superincumbent masses occasionally give way, sweeping them
down the precipice to certain destruction.

It sometimes happens that whole villages are destroyed by those dreadful hurricanes, some of the lesser cones of the hills being dislocated and cast into the valleys, involving houses and inhabitants in one common ruin. An event of this kind happened a few years before Captain Turner's visit to Boutan. One night, during the frightful climax of one of those mountain storms, nine houses were dashed from the brow of a hill upon which they had been erected but a few years previously, and their unhappy inmates, whilst reposing in imagined security, were buried beneath the ruins: none remained alive to tell the tale of signal disaster. Unawed, however, by so terrible a warning, another village was subsequently built in the same locality: nor does the slightest apprehension appear to be entertained of the recurrence of a similar accident. (1838)

HOBART CAUNTER [378]

## 4. Marching after a storm

Heavy storms of wind and rain during the night have prevented marching this morning, but at twelve, the rain having held up, and the tents being dry, we got under way, and accomplished the march of thirteen long miles by four o'clock. There is no material difficulty in the route, except the number of times we crossed the streams— fifteen or sixteen times in all: in fact the whole road seemed to be water. Two camels slipped in the worst and deepest ford, near the end, and were drowned; but with this exception I heard of no casualties. (1839)

HENRY EDWARD FANE[379]

# 24. History

## A. ANCIENT

### 1. Asoka the king

Formerly, when King Asoka was a lad, when he was playing on the road, he encountered Sakya Buddha going begging. The little boy, rejoiced to have the opportunity, immediately presented him with a handful of earth, as an offering. Buddha received it, and on his return sprinkled it on the ground on which he took his exercise. In return for this act of charity the lad became an iron-wheel king, and ruled over Jambudwipa. On assuming the iron wheel (*i.e.* when he became a universal monarch) he was on a certain occasion going through Jambudwipa in the administration of justice, at which time he saw one of the places of torment for the punishment of wicked men, situated between two mountains, and surrounded by an iron wall. He immediately asked his attendant ministers, 'What is this place?' To this they replied and said, 'This is the place where Jemma, the infernal king, inflicts punishment on wicked men for their crimes.' The king then began to reflect and said, 'The Demon King, in the exercise of his function, requires to have a place of punishment for wicked men. Why should not I, who rule these men (on earth), have a place of punishment likewise for the guilty?' On this he asked his ministers, 'Who is there that I can appoint to make for me a Hell, and to exercise authority therein for the punishment of wicked men?' In reply they said, 'None but a very wicked man can fulfil such an office.' The king forthwith dispatched his ministers to go in every direction to seek for such a man. In the course of their search they saw, by the side of a running stream, a lusty great fellow of a black colour, with red hair and light eyes, with feet like talons, and a mouth like that of a fish. When he whistled to the birds and beasts they came to him, and when they approached he mercilessly shot them through, so that none escaped. Having caught this man, he was brought before the king. The king then gave him these secret orders, 'You must enclose a square space with high walls, and with this enclosure plant every kind of flower and fruit (tree), and make beautiful lakes and alcoves, and arrange every-thing with such taste as to cause men to be anxious to look within the enclosure. Then, having made a wide gate, the moment a man enters within the precincts, seize him at once, and subject him to every kind of infernal torture. And whatever you do, let no one (who has once entered) ever go out again. And I strictly enjoin you, that if I even should enter the enclosure, that you torture me also and spare not. Now then, I appoint and constitute you Lord of this place of Torment!' It happened that a certain Bikshu, as he was going his rounds begging for food, entered the gate. The Infernal Keeper seeing him (seized his person) and made preparations to put him to torture. The Bikshu, being very much frightened, suppliantly begged for a moment's respite, that he might, at least, partake of his mid-day meal. It so happened that just at this moment another man entered the place, on which the keeper directly seized him, and, putting him in a stone mortar, began to pound his body to atoms, till a red froth formed on the surface of the mass. The Bikshu having witnessed this spectacle, began to reflect on the impermanency, the sorrow, the vanity of bodily existence, that it is like a bubble and froth of the sea, and so he arrived at the condition of a Rahat. This having transpired, the Infernal Keeper laid hold of him and thrust him into a cauldron of boiling water. The heart of the Biskshu and his countenance were full of joy. The fire was extinguished and the water became cold, whilst in the middle of it there sprung up a Lotus, on the top of which the Bikshu took his seat. The keeper (on witnessing this) forthwith proceeded to the king and said, 'A won-derful miracle has occurred in the place of Torture—would that your Majesty would come and see it.' The king said, 'I dare not come, in consideration of my former agreement with you.' The keeper replied, 'This matter is one of great moment: it is only right you should come; let us consider your former agreement changed.' The king then directly followed him and entered the prison; on which the Bikshu, for his sake, delivered a religious discourse, so that the king believed and was converted (obtained deliverance). (A.D. 400)

FAH-HIAN[380]

## 2. *Ujjain and Vaisali*

The king of Ujiyana (U-shi-yen), down the stream going out for an excursion, observed a yellow-cloud-covered box floating on the water and coming towards him. He took it and opened it, and there saw a thousand boys; being well nourished, when they came to perfect stature, they were of great strength. Relying on these, he extended his kingdom in every direction and encouraged by the victories of his troops, he was on the point of extending his conquests to this country (*i.e.*, Vaisali). Brahmadatta-raja hearing of it, was much alarmed; fearing his army was not able to contend successfully with the invaders, he was at a loss what to do. At this time the deer-footed girl, knowing in her heart that these were her sons, addressed the king thus: 'Now that these youthful warriors are approaching the frontier, from the highest to the lowest there is an absence of courage (*heart*). Your feeble wife by her thought is able to conquer those redoubtable champions.' The king not yet believing her, remained overwhelmed with fear. Then the deer-girl, mounting the city wall, waited the arrival of the warriors. The thousand youths having surrounded the city with their soldiers, the deer-girl said to them 'Do not be rebellious! I am your mother; you are my sons.' The thousand youths replied, 'What extravagant words are these!' The deer-girl then pressing both her breasts, a thousand jets of milk flowed out therefrom, and by divine direction fell into their mouths. Then they laid aside their armour, broke their ranks, and returned to their tribe and family. The two countries mutually rejoiced, and the people rested in peace.

Not far from this spot is a *stupa*. This is where Tathagata walked for exercise, and left the traces thereof. In teaching (*or,* pointing to the traces) he addressed the congregation thus: 'In ancient days, in this place, I returned to my family on seeing my mother. If you would know them, those thousand youths are the same as the thousand Buddhas of this Bhadra-kalpa.' (A.D. 629)

HIUEN TSIANG[381]

# B. MEDIEVAL

## 1. Akbar prepares for war

When all was in readiness for the campaign, the priests approached the King [Akber] and declared themselves eager to share his journeys and his labours, if it so pleased him. He thanked them, and said that he had already seen ample proof of their good-will toward

him, but that his opinion was that men of religion, devoted to peace
and literary ease and divine meditations, should not be dragged
away from their pleasant pursuits. Hence he had laid upon his
mother the charge of their kindly and hospitable treatment. He
begged them to accept his decision without demur, and to pray for
him. The priests replied that this was continually upon their hearts,
and that they would gladly obey his orders, though they were greatly
attached to him and desired to be with him. The next day he
happened to meet the teacher of his son in the school-room, and
said to him, 'Make your preparations, Father, for a journey; for you
are going with me.' Forthwith he ordered all necessary transport
and provision to be immediately supplied.

The King, as was the way with him, declared that he was going
hunting, and ordered his royal pavilion to be set up four miles away
from the city. The following were the arrangements for the government of the empire in his absence:— His mother remained at
Fatehepurum with his youngest son Danialus. Agiscocanus was
made the viceroy of Gangaris, and Cutubdicanus of Gedrosia. The
King's mother was to be superior to both of these, and was to have
charge of the province of Indicum or Delinum. Ten thousand
cavalry were left as a garrison in Gedrosia and twelve thousand with
the King's mother. He gave Agiscocanus twenty thousand for conducting the war in Gangaris, and as auxiliaries four or five generals,
with five or six thousand cavalry (or at the least four thousand)
besides infantry and labourers. He left a suitable garrison in the
principal cities. He took his eldest and second sons with him and the
priest who was the latter's tutor. He left his infant daughter with her
grandmother at Fatehepurum. He took with him a few of his principal wives, and his older daughters. He gave instructions for a great
quantity of gold and silver and of other stores to be carried along
with him, by means of elephants and camels. On the day of his
departure his mother set out with him, and spent two days in camp
with her son, in his immense white pavilion. The priests likewise
accompanied their companion to the camp, where they also spent
two days with him.

The King ordered the camp to be made in the traditional Mongol
style. The ancient custom is that the royal pavilion (which they call
the Pexqhanaae, or 'chief house') should be placed in a pleasant
open space, if such can be found. On the right are the tents of the
King's eldest son and his attendant nobles; these are placed next to

the royal pavilion. On the left are those of the second son and his attendants. In the second line are placed tents of the other royal princes (if they are present) and of their attendants. If there are no princes in camp, the most important nobles (whether they owe their importance to high position or to the King's kindness and favour) have their quarters to the right and left in the second line, next to the King's pavilion. Behind these come the rest of the troops in tents clustered as closely as possible round their own officers. To avoid crowding and confusion they are divided into messes, each with its own location. A separate bazaar is established for the King and each of the princes and the great nobles, near the tent of the general who is in attendance on each. Those of the King and the princes are very large and very well-stocked, not only with stores of grain and other provisions, but also with all sorts of merchandise, so that these bazaars seem to belong to some wealthy city instead of to a camp. They are always made on one plan, so that anyone who has spent a few days in camp knows his way about the bazaars as well as he does about the streets of his own city. These bazaars are called Urdu. During the advance for a campaign the artillery is grouped together in front of the camp, opposite the entrance to the royal quarters, in the broadest part of the open ground. The King had with him twenty-eight field guns, which would have been useless, however, for siege-purposes, as the largest of these guns was not as big as a hemisphere (to adopt the common military term). In this same spot a flaming torch is each night erected on the top of a tall mast, to act as a guide to stragglers. If any tumult arises in the camp, everyone immediately rushes to this torch, as though it were the heart and head of the whole camp. During the return from a campaign the artillery is collected in the rear, behind the royal quarters. The King uses two pavilions, identical in size and appearance, which are employed for alternate marches, one being carried on ahead, while he occupies the other. These pavilions have curtains instead of walls, which divide the entrance-apartment from the rest of the tent. The area they cover is very great. The King has also a roofed building, like an ordinary house, with steps up to the roof. Such is the style and arrangement of the Mongol camp.

Zelaldinus ordered Xamansurus to accompany him, in order that the latter might not increase the queen-mother's cares by attempting to destroy the empire with a revolution. (1581)

FATHER ANTONIO MONSERRATE.[381a]

## 2. Mhamood Shaw*

Mhamood Shaw, to celebrate his escape from this danger, held a magnificent festival of forty days, and went in solemn procession through the city, the streets of which were adorned on the occasion. As he regarded the royal tower as auspicious, he erected upon it a splendid pavilion, in which, when finished, he spent most of his time in a continued round of voluptuous amusements. To the affairs of government he paid no attention; leaving them entirely to the direction of his favourites. Musicians and dancers flocked to his court from Lahore, Dhely, Persia, and Khorassan; as also story tellers, reciters of the Shaw Nammeh, and all other ministers of pleasure. The people, copying the example of the prince, studied nothing but dissipation; reverend sages pawned their decent robes at the wine cellars, and holy teachers, quitting their cells, retired to the taverns, and presided over the cask. The governors of provinces, seeing the court thus employed, acted independently; so that the royal officers only who joined their views were allowed to hold their posts, and those who refused to wink at their encroachments, were expelled with disgrace. In a short time, except the province of Telingana and the districts adjacent to Ahmedabad, no parts of the kingdom properly remained in possession of the sultan. The ter-ruffdars, however, except Mallek Ahmed Beheree, openly acknowledged the royal authority; but their submission was only shewn in this point; If the sultan, at the desire of his minister Casim Bereed, took the field, and they saw advantage to themselves in the expedition, they accompanied the royal standard, but with a force and splendour, before which the sultan's sunk to wretchedness of appearance; and upon a return, they quitted him on the route for their several countries, without even the ceremony of asking leave. That they might not undergo the mortification of standing in the royal presence, or performing the customary obeisance to the sultan, they evaded visiting the court. Mallek Ahmed Beheree never accompanied the royal standard at all, but assumed independance; founded the city of Ahmednuggur; and taking upon himself the honours of majesty, sent ambassadors to Eusuff Adil Khan and Fatteh Oolla Ummad al Moolk, to prevail upon them to copy his example, and read the khootbah in their own name. It was accord-

---

*Sultan Mahmud Shah Bahmani (1482–1518), ruler of the Deccan.

ingly resolved by all three, to avow their claims to royalty.
(1589)

MOHAMMED KASIM FERISHTA[382]

### 3. Dara's army

The Governor whom he had left in the castle of *Ahmed-Abad,*
alarmed by the menaces, or allured by the promises of
*Aureng-Zebe,* had basely deserted the cause of his master; and sent
a letter to *Dara* by which he desired him not to advance nearer to the
city, whose gates were shut, and whose inhabitants were armed to
oppose his entrance. I had now been three days with *Dara,* whom I
met on the road by the strangest chance imaginable; and being
destitute of any medical attendant, he compelled me to accompany
him in the capacity of physician. The day preceding that on which he
received the Governor's communication, he expressed his fear lest I
should be murdered by the *Koullys,* and insisted upon my passing
the night in the *Karavanserrak,* where he then was. The cords of the
*kanates*, or screens, which concealed his wife and women (for he was
without even a tent) were fastened to the wheels of the carriage,
wherein I reposed. This may appear almost incredible to those who
know how extremely jealous the great men of *Hindoustan* are of
their wives, and I mention the circumstance as a proof of the low
condition to which the fortunes of the Prince were induced. It was at
break of day that the Governor's message was delivered, and the
shrieks of the females drew tears from every eye. We were all
overwhelmed with confusion and dismay, gazing in speechless horror at each other, at a loss what plan to recommend, and ignorant of
the fate which perhaps awaited us from hour to hour. We observed
*Dara* stepping out, more dead than alive, speaking now to one, then
to another; stopping and consulting even the commonest soldier.
He saw consternation depicted in every countenance, and felt assured that he should be left without a single follower; but what was
to become of him? whither must he go? to delay his departure was to
accelerate his ruin.

During the time that I remained in this Prince's retinue, we
marched, nearly without intermission, day and night; and so insupportable was the heat, and so suffocating the dust, that of the three
large oxen of *Guzarate* which drew my carriage, one had died, another was in a dying state, and the third was unable to proceed from

fatigue. *Dara* felt anxious to retain me in his service, especially as one of his wives had a bad wound in her leg; yet neither his threats nor entreaties could procure for me a single horse, ox, or camel; so totally destitute of power and influence had he become! I remained behind, therefore, because of the absolute impossibility of continuing the journey, and could not but weep when I beheld the Prince depart with a force diminished to four or five hundred horsemen. There were also a couple of elephants laden, it was said, with gold and silver. *Dara*, I understood, intended to take the road to *Tatta-bakar*, and under all circumstances this was not perhaps an unwise selection. There was indeed only a choice of appalling difficulties, and I could not cherish the hope that the Prince would succeed in crossing the sandy desert which separated him from that Fort. In fact, nearly the whole of the men, and many of the women, did perish; some dying of thirst, hunger, or fatigue, while others were killed by the hands of the merciless *Koullys*. Happy would it have been for Dara had he not himself survived this perilous march! but he struggled through every obstacle, and reached the territory of the *Raja Katche*.

The *Raja* received him with the utmost hospitality, promising to place the whole of his army at *Dara's* disposal, provided that Prince gave his daughter in marriage to his son. But the intrigues of *Jesseingue* were as successful with this *Raja* as they had been with *Jessomeseingue;* a change in his conduct was very soon perceptible, and *Dara*, having reason to apprehend that the barbarian had a design against his life, departed without a moment's hesitation for *Tata-bakar*.

I should, I fear, only tire my readers were I to enter upon a long narration of my own adventures with *Messieurs* and *Koullys,* or robbers; relating how I moved their compassion, and by what means I preserved the little money which was about my person. I made a grand display of my professional skill; and my two servants, who experienced the same terror as myself, declared I was the most eminent physician in the world, and that *Dara's* soldiers had used me extremely ill, depriving me of everything valuable. It was fortunate for me that we succeeded in creating in these people an interest in my favour: for after detaining me seven or eight days, they attached a bullock to my carriage, and conducted me within view of the minarets of *Ahmed-Abad*. In this city I met with an *Omrah* who was proceeding to *Delhi*, and I travelled under his protection. On the road our eyes were too often offended with the sight of dead men, elephants, oxen, horses, and camels; the wrecks of poor *Dara's* army. (1656–68)

FRANCOIS BERNIER[383]

## 4. The English confined at Surat

AUGUST the 27th 1691. All the *English* in the Factory of *Suratt* were under a close confinement from the *Moors* Governour of the City, and surrounded with a Guard of Horse and Foot. Nor were the *French* or *Dutch* permitted to pass without the Walls. The occasion of it was a Report spread abroad, that a Rich *Moor*-ship belonging to one *Abdel Gheford,* was taken by *Hat-men,* that is, in their Dialect, *Europeans*; and therefore 'till Restitution is made by them of nine Lacks of Roupies, which exceeds the value of 100000 £ Sterling, no liberty must be granted. The Ship was in her Passage from *Mocha* to *Suratt*, and tho' the *Indians* were averse from Fighting, or hazarding their Lives for four Roupies a Month, yet the *Turks,* who had a valuable Cargo of Goods on Board, behav'd themselves with redoubted Valour, 'till after the loss of some of their Lives, they were overpower'd by Men, and forc'd to surrender.

The Accusation run against all the *Europeans,* because the Pirate shew'd both *English, French,* and *Dutch* Colours, and a Restitution was expected from them all; especially too, because the *Moor*-ship which was taken, sailed from *Suratt* River with all their several Passes.

Our Honourable President *Bartholomew Harris* made his Defence to the Governour after this manner. That for the certainty of the Fact, tho it might be disputable, because our grand Accuser *Abdel Gheford* had been found formerly faulty in such a case, wherein he suborn'd a Multitude of Sailers, who afterwards confest his Bribery and their Perjury; yet admitting it true, he thought it unreasonable for us to be charg'd any more with the payment of Money taken by the *Pirates* at Sea, than the *Mogul* is for Robberies at Land. However thus far he will ingage his Honour for satisfaction of the Piracy, if it can be fairly prov'd, that the Ship belong'd to his Master, the *East-India* Company.

The Old Governour finding the *Mogul's* Customs begin to sink, by reason of the Embargo, which was as well upon our Ships, as our selves; and knowing that the Advancement of them was the great Instrument of his Promotion; and unable to remonstrate any thing material to our Presidents Reasons, directs a Letter to *Aureng-Zebe* to this effect. That since the late Wars the *English* Merchants at *Suratt* have traded fairly, and liv'd peaceably; that much of the Money due to the Merchants upon the Accounts of the Wars was already paid, and the rest would follow; and that for the Pirates at Sea, they were neither Authoriz'd by the Company, nor were they within the reach of their Command: All which things might justly plead the Innocence of the *English,* excuse their payment of any Money, and give them therefore a Release. But the exasperated *Turks,* and the violent *Abdel-Gheford* prevail'd for a closer Confinement of us, not only to the Walls of the Factory, but our very Chambers, had not the vigilant Industry of our President opportunely repealed that severe Decree. Our Enemies, likewise, incessantly urg'd the Governour to menace and disturb our President, that he might be thereby wrought upon to their Designs. To which the sage Governour mildly reply'd, That he knew Mr. *Harris* too well, to value any Threatnings which were Injurious to the Company's Interest or Honour; and that tho' he suffer'd much, he would endure much more, rather than yield to an unjust Compliance.

The inraged *Turks* finding their Machines would not work, and that they could get no ground upon us this way, began now to threaten our Lives, because the loss of our Liberty did not appease them, so much that the Governour as he formerly set a Guard upon us to shut us in, now increases it to keep our Enemies out.

In the mean time, the Providence of God so contriv'd for our Innocence, that the *Turks* began to clash among themselves, and heated with some private Dissentions, became their own Accusers. For some of them came to *Dungevora,* a famous *Persy* Merchant, and Friend to the *English,* and inform'd him that all their Allegations against us were built upon Falsehood and Malice, and their Charge was all a contriv'd Design, in as much as they were all satisfied in their own Minds, that the *Pyrates* were *Danes,* and not *English.* But this they durst not discover to the Governour, for fear of a publick Examination, which if they submitted to, their lives would be exposed to the Fury of the rest of the Confederates. Neither durst we encourage them with any Present of Money to proceed in their Depositions, lest we should find it a Stratagem of theirs, thereby to insnare us.

*November* the *Ist.* arriv'd a Pattamar or *Courrier,* from our Fakeel, or Solliciter at Court, acquainting us that the *Mogul* had News from the *Danes* themselves, of their taking and plundering the *Moor*-ship, and that they resolv'd upon a continued Enmity to the Moors,' till their Demands were fully satisfied for the Injuries which they formerly sustain'd from them. The Letter was directed to *Isa Cooly*, Principal of the *Armenian* Merchants at Court, who by making a noise, which is the method for obtaining Audience, was called upon by the *Mogul,* to read his Letter upon a publick Court day.

This brought down the *Mogul's* Letters to the Governour, requiring a speedy Respect and Civility to the *English,* with a permission and Encouragement of Trade. But the Pishcashes or Presents expected by the *Nabobs* and *Omrahs* retarded our Inlargement for some time notwithstanding. For the strong Contest and Application which was made for the Government of *Suratt,* which was then said to be dispos'd of, put a stop to the Emperours more absolute determinations. The *Mogul's* Resolution of continuing the present Governour, frustrated all the Court Interests for themselves, which mov'd *Salabet Chan,* a Bosom Favourite, to wave the Solicitations he had begun for his son, and end them for the Governour. For he design'd to send his son to *Suratt,* Invested with the Command of the City, and the Messenger of this welcom News to us, which would render him thereupon more acceptable to the *English* Nation, and would be apt to gain him some costly Present from us at his Entrance upon his Authority.

Therefore *December* the *2nd.* in the Evening, word was brought by the Brokers to our President, of a *Cosset's* Arrival with Letters from Court to the *Vacinavish*, injoyning our immediate Release; and the day following the *Chocadars* or Souldiers, were remov'd from before our Gates. (1689)

J. OVINGTON[384]

## C. MODERN

### 1. Insurrection in Benares

In January, 1799, my friend Sir Willaim Dunkin once more embarked for England, taking a final leave of the East. By this departure I ceased to received the salary and emoluments of Judge's Clerk. During the last two years he remained in Bengal the Macnaghtens and he resided together in the house which Mr Justice Hyde occupied until his decease, a very spacious one most delightfully situated upon the Esplanade, commanding an extensive prospect down the river with Fort William directly in front.

At this period an insurrection of the most alarming nature broke out in the City of Benares and the vicinity thereof, excited and fomented by a young man named Vizier Ally, who from his earliest infancy had been brought up in the midst of European gentlemen, by all of whom he had constantly been cherished and noticed in the kindest and most affectionate manner. This youth when a child had been adopted by the Nabob Azaphat Dowlah, from which circumstance he had buoyed himself up with the expectation of succeeding to the Musnud upon the death of that Prince. Being disappointed in those vain and unfounded hopes, he thenceforward betrayed, whenever opportunities occured of so doing, a disposition excessively hostile to the British interests, entering into private treaties and engagements with several of the Native princes who were avowedly enemies to Europeans in general, but especially so to the East India Company and their servants, both civil and military. So open and so loud was this Vizier Ally in his declarations of vengeance against the English, but more particularly against Mr. John Lumsden, the Company's Resident at the Durbar of Lucknow, and Mr. George Frederick Cherry, the Chief of Benares, as to draw the attention of certain persons sincerely attached to the British Government to his proceedings, through whose medium, backed by different Agents himself employed, Mr. Lumsden soon ascertained that some desperate steps were likely to be resorted to, and that he and Mr. Cherry were the two grand objects whom Vizier Ally wished to sacrifice, from his entertaining an idea that they had been the chief instruments in preventing his succession to Azaphat Dowlah.

Mr. Lumsden, upon getting this information, directly dispatched a confidential person to Benares to communicate the same to Mr. Cherry and put him upon his guard against the machinations of Vizier Ally and his supporters, a few days after which, from still further accounts that Mr. Lumsden received from Native Agents he had employed, he had reason to apprehend an attempt upon the life of Mr. Cherry was meditated, whereupon he instantly sent off a special messenger to Mr. Cherry to tell him what was on foot, and the channel through which the intelligence had reached him, which he had every reason to believe was but too well founded, under

which circumstances he strongly recommended him to prohibit
Vizier Ally from entering the City of Benares without his (Mr.
Cherry's) special permission, or at any rate not to permit him to be
attended by any person bearing arms. Mr. Lumsden, still further by
the most powerful language advised Mr. Cherry to discontinue the
custom of receiving Vizier Ally at his house as he had long been in
the habit of doing, and to direct his principal native officers to watch
his proceedings very closely. To all these cautionary messages and
recommendations Mr. Cherry replied that he would undoubtedly
be upon his guard, although he must add that he was not under the
least apprehension of any violent or hostile measure being pursued
by Vizier Ally, whose general conduct and behaviour he was very
well acquainted with, and knew how every hour was occupied
throughout the day; that he, Vizier Ally, usually spent two hours
daily with him, and appeared as amicably disposed as ever towards
him personally, notwithstanding he had often complained of the
injustice with which he had been treated by the British Government. He added that he received the most authentic accounts of all
his, Vizier Ally's, political measures, and had no reason to think any
violence was in contemplation.

Again Mr. Lumsden, in the utmost alarm, sent down his head
assistant to Mr. Cherry to inform him his life was aimed at, beseeching him not to admit Vizier Ally within his doors until he heard
further from Lucknow, as he (Mr. Lumsden) was about to adopt
measures that he trusted would render futile all the treacherous
schemes of the base and unprincipled Vizier Ally, and his numerous
host of associates. Mr. Cherry repeated that he should not be
unmindful of his own safety, but that he was confident the alarm
was unfounded, and that the representations of what Vizier Ally
was doing had been greatly exaggerated to him (Mr. Lumsden). In
short, the conduct of this excellent man (Mr. Cherry) seemed like
infatuation, for notwithstanding he received hourly information
that considerable parties of armed men, both cavalry and infantry,
were assembling in every direction round the City with the most
unqualified symptoms of hostility, yet did he not take a single
precautionary measure, not even to the putting on an additional
sentry in the avenues leading to his mansion. So far from anything of
that sort, upon Vizier Ally's sending a chubdar with his best compliments and that he would breakfast with him the following morning, Mr. Cherry, without a moment's pause, returned for answer

that he should be happy to see him.

Vizier Ally accordingly went at seven O'clock in the morning to Mr. Cherry's. Upon entering the apartment where Mr. Cherry was, ready to receive him, he with apparently the greatest cordiality, went through the usual ceremony of embrace and complimentary speeches, shewing not the least agitation or slightest symptom of animosity or resentment.

Breakfast being immediately called for, Mr. Cherry and his malignant guest sat down at the table. Having taken their tea, during which they conversed upon common topics with the utmost good-humour, Vizier Ally's hookah bedah brought in his hookah, when the villian rose from his seat, as if to meet the hookah, instantly drew his scimitar, and with it made a blow at Mr. Cherry that brought him to the ground; a band of armed ruffians at the same moment rushed in, put every servant to death, and following the example of their base master began cutting and slashing poor Mr. Cherry in the most inhuman manner so that his life was soon put an end to.

While this bloody scene was performing above stairs, the insurgents were not idle below, every sepoy of the usual guard, and every domestic of Mr. Cherry's that they met with were inhumanly butchered. Vizier Ally then headed his myrmidons in the street, directing them without loss of time to put to death every European throughout the City and every individual belonging to them, to accomplish which bloody purpose he, with about fifty chosen followers, proceeded to the house of Mr. Samuel Davis, the gentleman next in rank to Mr. Cherry, on their way to whose residence they unhappily met Captain Conway, a gentleman then upon a visit to Mr. Cherry, and Mr. Graham, Mr. Cherry's assistant, who were returning home from their morning ride; both of whom they put to death, but while so doing, some person ran to Mr. Davis's to give him notice of the intended attack. The career of the assassins was further delayed by encountering three other Englishmen whom they also slew. This afforded Mr. Davis time sufficient to convey his wife and children to the top of the house, the only approach to which was by a very small spiral staircase which he had only just erected, as a means to getting to the top of the building in order to enjoy a grand and extensive prospect from there.

Scarcely had the mother and her family reached their doubtful place of security when the house was surrounded and attacked in several directions by some hundreds of Vizier Ally's followers. Mr. Davis, while conducting his wife and children to the top of the house, had seized upon a hog spear that by chance was placed in a corner, which weapon, through the blessing of providence, and the wonderful resolution and presence of mind of Mr. Davis, proved the salvation of his own and every one of his family's lives, indeed in all probability of the lives, too, of every European throughout the City of Benares.

Vizier Ally's people, having ransacked every part of the house in search of the owner, destroying the furniture and every article they met with, at last ascended the above-mentioned spiral staircase, which from its construction would admit only one at a time, and from its being circular those who were a few steps down could not see what was going forward above. Of this Mr. Davis availed himself, spearing each man as he appeared, one after another falling back mortally wounded so that the assailants, finding their comrades thus slaughtered, first paused and finally retreated to the foot of the staircase, where they entered upon a consultation as to what should next be done: during which debate Mr. Treves, Mr. Aguilar, and other English gentlemen being apprized of the murders already committed, mounted their fleetest horses and galloped off to the Cavalry Cantonments distant only a few miles from Benares, for assistance which was promptly afforded. A Troop of Dragoons were instantly sent off to the City followed with all possible dispatch by two Regiments of Cavalry, of which Vizier Ally's people hearing, they suddenly and rapidly retreated, closely pursued by the Light Dragoons, who, as they overtook cut them up without mercy. Vizier Ally, being mounted upon a remarkably fleet horse, effected his escape into the Rohilla country, the Rajah of which for a considerable time granted him shelter and protection, but was at last induced from motives of policy to surrender him into the hands of the British Government under an express and positive stipulation however, that he should not be put to death, which engagement has been most faithfully adhered to.

Vizier Ally, upon being delivered up to the English, was immediately conveyed to the Presidency, where he was lodged in one of the bomb proofs under the ramparts of Fort William, thentofore used as a magazine for keeping military stores in, and where he was kept a close and solitary prisoner, no person whatsoever being allowed access to him except the officer of the guard placed round

his prison, and occasionally a Magistrate of Calcutta who visited
him in order to report to the Governor-General the state he was in.
In that dismal and forlorn situation the treacherous wretch still
remains equally unpitied and unlamented. (1799)

WILLIAM HICKEY[385]

## 2. *An imprisoned prince*

Although I had ceased to have anything to do with the Sheriff's
office, yet Moiz-oo-Deen, Tipoo Sultaun's son, still continued
almost daily to send messengers to my house to request I would call
upon him, which summons I obeyed as frequently as possible. These
visits were, however, rendered exceedingly unpleasant to me, from
his extreme agitation when I did call and especially as the time of my
departure, of which he heard, drew nearer; he constantly wept and
lamented most bitterly, saying, 'When you are gone I shall not have
a single friend in the universe, not a human creature who will bestow
a thought upon me, or care what becomes of me. When you may
last, my only refuge forsake me, what can I do? Nothing but lay
myself prostrate on the earth and die.'

The last time I saw this unfortunate Prince he was in utter despair;
he threw himself upon the floor, clung to and embraced my feet,
most earnestly beseeching that I would take him with me to England, where he would serve me as the humblest of my slaves. In vain
did I assure him that however well disposed I might feel to comply
with every wish of his, yet was it impracticable to accomplish that of
taking him out of the country, as the Governor-General and Council never would permit him to go to Europe. Upon my saying which
he seemed very indignant, exclaiming with great vehemence, 'And
why not? Why am I thus cruelly treated? Will nothing short of my
life satisfy the East India Company? After murdering my father,
seizing his dominions, and imprisoning in a strange land every
branch of his wretched family, am I alone doomed to a more severe
punishment than any other, to drag on a miserable existence in a
loathsome prison, and this under an infamous pretence, which the
members of Government well know to be wholly unfounded and
false? I thought the new Governor, Lord Minto, had the character
of being a humane, benevolent man who would in mercy have pitied
and relieved me from my unmerited sufferings. I was assured that he
would do so, but I find it was delusive assurance. Oh, Sir! Speak to

him, represent my hard case to him, and in my name beseech him to
grant me permission to attend you wherever you may go. My wants
are few, a little rice and water daily will suffice, I will work for you as
well as I can: do all that I am directed to do: I will be your slave!'
During this speech he became agitated almost to suffocation, and I
was at last obliged to call up Mr. Gordon, the Gaoler, to hold him
whilst I left his apartment, promising however that I would see him
in a day or two, but I never did call afterwards, as I was conscious it
could be of no use and would only occasion him a renewal of his
distress and lamentations. (1808)

WILLIAM HICKEY[386]

## 3. British power in Central India

It appears of essential importance that the great change which has
taken place in the British Empire in the East should be fully understood. We have been reluctantly compelled, by events far beyond
our power to control, to assume the duties of Lord Paramount of
that great Continent; and it is now confessed by all, that our domin-
ion can rest upon no secure basis but the general tranquillity of
India.

Our present condition is one of apparent repose, but full of
danger. With the means we had at our command, the work of force
was comparatively easy: the liberality of our Government gave
grace to conquest, and men were for the moment satisfied to be at
the feet of generous and humane conquerors. Wearied with a state
of continued warfare and anarchy, the loss even of power was
hardly regretted: halcyon days were anticipated, and men pros-
trated themselves in hopes of elevation. All these impressions,
made by the combined effects of power, humanity, and fortune,
were improved to the utmost by the character of our first measures.
The agents of Government were generally individuals who had
acquired a name in the scene in which they were employed: they
were unfettered by rules, and their acts were adapted to soothe the
passions, and accord with the habits and prejudices, of those whom
they had to conciliate or to reduce to obedience. But there are many
causes which operate to make a period like this, one of short
duration; and the change to a colder system of policy, and the
introduction of our laws and regulations into countries immediately
dependent upon us, naturally excite agitation and alarm. It is the
hour in which men awake from a dream. Disgust and discontent

succeed to terror and admiration; and the princes, the chiefs, and all
who had enjoyed rank or influence, see nothing but a system doom-
ing them to immediate decline and ultimate annihilation. (1823)

JOHN MALCOLM[387]

## 4.  The British as mediators in Cutch

In spite of the absence of those bonds of unity, and those symbolic
evidences of supremacy, analogous to the incidents of European
feudal polity, between the Raos and the aristocracy of Cutch, there
existed a division of the country which, with proper management,
might have broken up the power of the aristocracy, and left the
authority in the hands of its princes. The crown domain surpassed
that of the whole body, and it engrossed the commercial revenues of
several cities and towns. With the means this afforded, it could
always command the services of a portion of the feudatories; for
there are, and ever have been, adverse parties and rival principles at
every court; and I was informed of instances wherein the entire
*bhyad* united to punish acts committed by one of their own body,
which were held derogatory to their prince. With such influence, it
was not difficult to call out the *kher,* or entire feudal array; and
when the country was menaced by foreign invasion, the Jharejas
have stood their ground against aggression. But the fashion, of late
years, of introducing bands of Arabs, Sindies, or Rohillas among the
retainers of these princes, has often produced great jealousy and
heart-burning in their nobles, whilst these mercenaries were the
cause of no small embarrassment to their employers. They were
always ready to do their masters' bidding; but that mutual forbearance, that kind of politic balance, when there was no foreign interference, was lost. The fate of the last Rao, Bharmul, illustrates these
deviations from ancient usage. His naturally intemperate disposition was aggravated by a love of strong drink; and, with these
hireling foreigners at his command, he set at nought the ancient
limitations of his power, for which he substituted his own will. But
he had to deal with those who well knew their rights, and, rather
than surrender them, they invited the British as mediators, which
interference ended in an intimate alliance, and was followed by its
invariable concomitant, a BRITISH SUBSIDIARY FORCE! Rao
Bharmul's intemperance increased to a state of madness, and he
was deposed, confined, and his son Rao Desil put upon the *gadi.*

Being an infant, a council of regency was formed, composed of some
of the principal Jhareja chiefs, and the old civil officers, one of
whom, my informant, Ruttunji, is entirely devoted to English interests. Moreover, the British Resident is considered as the head of
the regency. As far as I could learn or observe, matters seemed to go
on very smoothly; tranquillity was universal, and every one enjoyed
the fruits of his industry, or his patrimony; nor is there any likelihood of this state of things being disturbed, so long as Rao Desil is a
minor. The future will depend on his personal disposition, and the
use that is made of the interim. The chiefs, while they preferred
surrendering their independence to a foreign power, to seeing it
wrested from them by their sovereign, have secured, by the guarantee of that power, the integrity of the r possessions; and the little
obedience they formerly acknowledged is now virtually annulled,
though the mediator will be perpetually tormented by appeals from
each, and most probably hated by both parties. (1833)

JAMES TOD[388]

## 5. Siege of the Lucknow Residency, 1857

The 2nd of July was the most eventful day during the siege, for a sad
calamity overtook us. After arranging for the posting of the Mutchi
Bhowan force, and placing some field-pieces in position, Sir Henry
Lawrence, who was exhausted with work and heat, lay down on a
couch in the room through which the round-shot had passed the day
before. An 8-inch shell from the ill-starred howitzer lost at Chinhut
came in through the window and exploded, filling the room with
smoke, flame, and *debris*. Captain Wilson, D.A.G., and Mr. George
Lawrence were with him; Wilson, with one knee on the couch, was
reading a memo to Sir Henry. He was knocked down, and then Sir
Henry's voice was heard saying he had been wounded. A native
servant who was in the room had his foot carried off by a fragment of
the shell, Wilson was bruised, but George Lawrence was unhurt.
They summoned assistance, carried Sir Henry into the drawing-
room, and laid him on a table, supporting him with pillows. Meanwhile George Lawrence had run over to my house, not more than
150 yards away. I went and found Sir Henry Lawrence lying as
above described, with several officers about him. I saw he was
seriously injured, for he was pale, his voice was low, he was semi-
collapsed, and was talking in a hurried and excited manner. He

begged me to tell him how long he had to live. On examining the
wound I found that the muscles and integuments of the hip were
lacerated, the upper part of the thigh-bone being comminuted. In
his enfeebled and exhausted condition I knew that so serious a
wound must soon prove fatal, and said I thought he might live
forty-eight hours. I did what was possible to arrest hae-
morrhage,—there was not much,—to alleviate pain and relieve
the condition of shock. It was a very trying time. The Residency was
already much injured by heavy shot and shell, the room we were in
was knocked almost to pieces, while round-shot were striking the
house frequently: the whole force of the enemy's fire seemed to
be concentrated on it. Fearing that more might be killed, we
carried him as carefully and tenderly as we could to my house, and
laid him on a bed in the deep front veranda. The fire was not so
heavy on my house at that moment, and we placed him where there
was shelter. His bed was soon surrounded by his sorrowing friends.
The enemy must have found out what had happened, for he was
scarcely there when a most fiendish fire was rained upon my
house, and both round-shot and musketry came fast and furiously.
The principal officers were soon about him, and knowing he was
dying, he directed Colonel Inglis to assume command of the troops,
and Major Banks the commissioner of Lucknow, to succeed him in
the duties of chief commissioner. He was perfectly clear and collected, though much exhausted, and gave full instructions as to what
he wished to be done. He most earnestly adjured us never to
surrender or treat with the enemy, and to do everything possible to
protect the women and children, to economise provisions and defend the Residency to the last or until relief should arrive. He took
leave of us all in the most affecting manner, spoke most humbly of
himself and all that he had done, and expressed a desire that the
only epitaph on his tomb should be, 'Here lies Henry Lawrence,
who tried to do his duty.' He reproached himself for what he called
his shortcomings, but said he had endeavoured to do his best.
Partridge and I examined the wound thoroughly under chloroform,
and found it so grave, extending into the pelvis, that nothing could
be done but try to relieve pain and sustain the failing strength. He
remained sensible for a long time, and was closely watched by his
nephew, George Lawrence, with the chaplain (Mr. Harris) and
some of the ladies. We removed him to the inner room after a time,
as the veranda became more and more exposed to fire. I was with

him constantly and at the last, doing what I could with chloroform and otherwise to relieve him. He ultimately became unconscious from exhaustion and died on the morning of the 4th, and was buried the same evening in the Residency churchyard, in the grave with the other dead of that day. The death of our excellent Chief threw a great gloom over all. A letter of mine to Colonel Wilson, published in Edwardes and Merivale's 'Life of Sir Henry Lawrence.' gives fuller details of all the circumstances attending his death. Mrs. Harris, the wife of the chaplain, says in her diary: 'About twelve I was obliged to ask J. to have the body carried outside, so he called some soldiers to help carry the bed into the veranda. When they came in, one of the men lifted the sheet off poor Sir Henry's face and kissed him.' Major Banks says that Sir Henry's last communications delivered to him after his wound were chiefly these: 'Reserve fire; check all wall-firing; carefully register ammunition for guns and small arms in store; carefully register daily expenditure as far as possible; spare the precious health of the Europeans in every way from shot and sun; organise working-parties for night labour; in-trench, intench, intrench; erect traverses, cut off the enemy's fire; turn every horse out of the garrison except enough for four guns, but keep Sir Henry Lawrence's horse, it is a gift to his nephew, George Lawrence; use the State prisoners as a means for getting in supplies, by gentle means if possible, or by threats; enrol every servant as a *bildar*, or carrier of earth; pay liberally—double, quadruple; turn out every native who won't work, save menials who have more than abundant labour; write daily to Allahabad or Agra. Sir Henry Lawrence's servants to receive one year's pay; they are to work for any other gentleman who wants them, or they may leave, if they prefer to do so.'

'A hurricane of shot, gingal, and musketry all day and all night', says Wilson; 'probably not less than 10,000 men fired into our position. The balls fell in showers, and hardly any place was safe.' My house got its full share. The bullets found their way everywhere, and people were hit in places that seemed safe. The ladies were giving out rags and old linen to make bandages. Mr. Harris read prayers to the ladies and to all whose duties allowed them to attend. This night the ladies and children slept in the *tyekhana*. (1857)

JOSEPH FAYRER[389]

## 6. Badminton

Hardly a shot from the gate we stormed,
    Under the Moree battlement's shade;
Close to the glacis out game was formed,
    There had the fight been, and there we played.

Lightly the demoiselles littered and leapt,
    Merrily capered the players all;
North, was the garden where Nicholson slept,
    South, was the sweep of a battered wall.

Near me a Musalman, civil and mild,
    Watched as the shuttlecocks rose and fell;
And he said, as he counted his beads and smiled,
    God smite their souls to the depths of hell. (1876)

ALFRED LYALL[390]

## 7. The British in India

I spent two days in Baroda. I occupied the same historic room where an attempt was made to poison the British Resident.

Drove round the city; saw everything in Baroda which merits special attention i.e. the palace, the famous hawat (?), where Ameena Aiya was going to have a meeting with Mulhar Rao, saw the stalls for elephants, arena for gladiators, golden and silver guns of the Gaekwars and the buildings which were being constructed, for instance, the new palace of Gaekwad, and the High School.

But the most interesting thing in Baroda was the Dewan Sir Mahadava Rao.

I visited him and talked with him for a sufficiently long time; we discussed many subjects and incidentally the social position of the British in relation to the natives. He observed that the existing relationship of the British with the natives was extremely beneficial to India. The British are keeping themselves aloof from the natives and are not striking roots in India. The natives in consequence are preserving their originality. His words meant: thank God, the British are keeping aloof; thank God, the Indian climate is unbearable to Europeans, else they would have occupied the whole of India and would have turned India into Australia. But now it is not difficult to drive out the British. Indians send up their prayers to the sun not for nothing; the sun has done a great service to them.

One of the interlocutors observed in this connection that the British intended to occupy Kashmir. 'Yes', said Sir M.R. 'There is a saying that in a lesser State it is easy to find something not to one's liking and then to annex or to seize it.'

Sir M.R. observed that British rule was nevertheless necessary for India; it was uniting India. Drive out the Britishers and Indians will scatter themselves in different directions and begin to antagonise one another. Internecine feuds will ruin India.

He considers the Afghan war to be unjustified. The sooner it is ended, the better. His sympathies are with the Liberal Ministry.

He does not apprehend evil influence on the natives; educated people understand very well why troops should be recalled, but the *badmashes* of the bazar, notwithstanding their dissatisfaction against the British Government, do not have any political importance; they do not have leaders and are not dangerous for the British Government.

This morning I took a drive round Ahmedabad; saw Jumma Musjid and Rowza.

In the opinion of Buler, Muslims do not have any political importance in India, British Government have committed a great political blunder in introducing teaching of English language in schools. (1880)

IVAN PAVLOVICH MINAYEFF[391]

# Notices on Sources

1  Samuel Purchas. *Hakluytus posthumus; or, Purchas his pilgrims.* 20 vols. Glasgow: James MacLehose and Sons, 1905–7. v. 11, p. 298.

2  Ibid. v. 2, pp. 70–1.

3  William Hodges. *Travels in India.* London: The Author, 1793. pp. 4–5.

4  James Bryce. *A sketch of the state of British India.* Edinburgh: George Ramsay & Co., 1810. pp. 1–3.

5  Maria Graham. *Letters on India.* London: Longman, Hurst, etc., 1814, pp. 5–7.

6  Thomas Bacon. *First impressions.* 2 vols. London: W. H. Allen, 1837. v. 1, pp. 95–6.

7  Julia Charlotte Maitland. *Letters from Madras.* London: John Murray, 1843. pp. 220–1.

8  J. W. Massie. *Continental India.* London: Thomas Ward, 1839. pp. 213–14.

9  Mark Twain. *The complete works of Mark Twain. v. 14: Following the equator.* New York: Harper & Brothers, 1925, Pt. 2, p. 223.

10  Flora Annie Steel. *India.* London: Adams and Charles Black, 1912. pp. 205–8.

11  Walter Del Mar. *India of today.* London: Adams and Charles Black, 1905. pp. 6–7.

12  William H. Hart. *Everyday life in Bengal and other Indian sketches.* London: Charles H. Kelly, 1906. pp. 1–8.

13  T. W. Holderness. *People and problems of India.* London: Williams & Norgate, 1911, pp. 7–8.

14  John Fortesque. *Narrative of the visit to India.* London: Macmillan & Co., 1912. pp. 1–2.

15  Samuel John Thomson. *The silent India.* Edinburgh: William Black wood, 1913. pp. v–vi.

16  John Marshall. *John Marshall in India.* London: Oxford University Press, 1927. pp. 186–8.

17  William Jones. *Dissertations and miscellaneous pieces relating to the history and antiquities, the arts, sciences and literature of Asia.* London: G. Nicol, 1792. p. 108.

18  James R. Ballantyne. *Christianity contrasted with Hindu philosophy.* London: James Madden, 1859. pp. xv–xviii.

19  Monier Williams. *Indian wisdom.* 3rd. ed. London: W. H. Allen & Co., 1876. pp. 102–4.

20  Alfred Comyn Lyall. *Verses written in India.* (publisher unknown), 1889. pp. 14–15.

21  Edward Carpenter. *A visit to a gnani.* London: George Allen & Unwin, 1920. pp. 3–5.

22   John McKenzie. *The religious quest of India: Hindu ethics.* London: Oxford University Press, 1922. pp. 205–7.

23   Edward C. Sachu, ed. *Alberuni's India.* 2 vols. in one. Delhi: S. Chand & Co, 1964 reprint. v. 1, p. 121.

24   Afanasy Nikitin. *Afanasy Nikitin's voyage beyond the three seas, 1466–72.* Moscow, 1960. pp. 114–15.

25   Edward Farley Oaten. *A sketch of Anglo-Indian literagure.* London: Kegan Paul, Trench, Trubner, 1908. pp. 28–9.

26   James Forbes. *Oriental memoirs.* 4 vols. London: White, Cochrane & Co., 1813. v. 1., pp. 61–2.

27   Ibid., v. 2, pp. 510–11.

28   Massie, op. cit., pp. 429–31.

29   William Henry Sleeman. *Rambles and recollections of an Indian official.* 2 vols. London: J. Hatchard & Son, 1844. v. 1, pp. 12–15.

30   Mark Twain, op. cit., p. 165.

31   Steel, op. cit., pp. 62–9.

32   J. Horton Ryley. *Ralph Fitch, England's pioneer to India and Burma.* London: T. Fisher Unwin, 1899. pp. 103–6.

33   Godfrey Charles Mundy. *Pen and pencil sketches.* 2 vols. London: John Murray, 1832. v. 2, pp. 246–9.

34   Fanny Parkes. *Wanderings of a pilgrim* . . .2 vols. London: Pelham Richardson, 1850. v. 1, p. 260.

35   Frank Elias. *The gorgeous East.* London: Adam & Charles Black, 1913. pp. 61–3.

36   Fah-Hian and Sung-Yun. *Travels of Fah-Hian and Sung-Yun, Buddhist pilgrims from China to India.* Tr. by Samuel Beal, London: Reprinted by Susil Gupta, 1964. pp. 8–12.

37   Edwin Arnold. *India revisited.* London: Trubner, 1886. pp. 247–8.

38   E. F. Knight. *Where three empires meet.* London: Longmans, 1897. pp. 206–8.

39   R. W. Frazer. *Indian thought—past and present.* London: T. Fisher Unwin, 1915. pp. 156–9.

40   James Tod. *Annals and antiquities of Rajasthan.* 2 vols. London: Smith, Elder, 1829–32. v. 1, pp. 780–1.

41   Joseph Dalton Hooker. *Himalayan journals.* 2 vols. London: John Murray, 1854. v. 1, pp. 18–19.

42   H. T. Colebrooke. *Miscellaneous essays.* Edited by E. B. Cowell. 2. vols. London: Trubner & Co., 1873. v. 1, pp. 404–5.

43   J. Ovington. *A voyage to Surat in the year 1689.* London: Oxford University Press, 1929. pp. 144–6.

44   F. E. Penny. *Southern India.* London: Adam & Charles Black, 1914. pp. 53–6.

45   Father Antonio Monserrate. *The commentary of Father Monserrate, S. J. on his journey to the court of Akbar.* Tr. from original Latin by J. S. Hoyland. London: Oxford University Press, 1922. pp. 62–7.

46   Purchas, op. cit., v. 1, pp. 362–3.

47 George, Viscount Valentia. *Voyages and travels to India* . . ., 3 vols. London: William Miller, 1809. v. 1, p. 243.

48 Forbes, op. cit., v. 1, pp. 406–7.

49 Bacon, op. cit. v. 2, p. 34.

50 Joseph Wolff. *Travels and adventures of Rev. Joseph Wolff.* 2 vols. London: Saunders, Otley & Co., 1861. v. 2, pp. 224–7.

51 Albert Hervey. *Ten years in India.* 3 vols. London: William Shoberl, 1850. v. 1, p. 105.

52 G. C. Dyson. *From a Punjaub pomegranate grove.* London: Mills & Bonn, 1913. pp. 144–51.

53 Hiuen Tsiang. *Chinese accounts of India.* Tr. from the Chinese of Hiuen Tsiang by Samuel Beal. v vols. Reprinted. Calcutta: Susil Gupta, 1957–58. v. 2, pp. 190–1.

54 Purchas, op. cit., v. 11, p. 395.

55a Ludovico Di Varthema. *The itinerary of Ludovico Di Varthema of Bologna from 1502–1508.* Tr. by Richard Carnac Temple. London: The Argonaut Press, 1928. p. 46.

55 Monserrate, op. cit., pp. 196–7, 201–2.

56 Donald Campbell. *Narrative of the extraordinary adventures and sufferings* . . . .London: T. N. Longman, etc., 1801. p. 248.

57 Maria Grahm. *Journal of a residence in India.* Edinburgh: Constable, 1812 pp. 201–02.

58 Lt. Col. Fitzclarence. *Journal of a route across India* . . .London: John Murray, 1819. pp. 187–90.

59 Bacon, op. cit. v. 2, pp. 51–3.

60 Emily Eden. *Up the country.* London: Oxford University Press, 1937. pp. 205–6.

61 Eliza Ruhamah Scidmore. *Winter India.* London: T. Fisher Unwin, 1903. pp. 202–3.

62 J. W. McCrindle. *Ancient India as described by Megasthenese and Arrian.* London: Trubner & Co., 1877. p. 70.

63 Varthema ,op. cit., pp. 57–8.

64 Forbes, op. cit., v. 4, pp. 305–6.

65 W. W. Hunter. *The annals of rural Bengal.* London: Smith, Elder & Co., 1868. pp. 137–40.

66 An Ex-Civilian. *Life in the mofussil; or, the civilian in lower Bengal.* London: C. Kegan Paul & Co., 1878. v. 2, pp. 155–6.

67 Mark Twain, op. cit., v. 2, p. 187.

68 Andrew H. L. Fraser. *Among Indian rajahs and ryots.* London: Seeley & Co., 1911. pp. 78–80.

69 Bacon, op. cit., v. 2, pp. 133–4.

70 William Knighton. *Tropical sketches.* 2 vols. London: Hurstad & Blackettl 1855. v. 1, pp. 236–40.

71 G. O. Trevelyan. *The competition wallah.* London: Macmillan & Co., 1864. pp. 195–96.

72 A Retired Chaplain. *Episodes in the life of an Indian chaplain.* London: Sampson Low, etc., 1882. pp. 262–4.

73  Niccolao Manucci. *Storia do Mogor; or, Mogul India.* Tr. by William Irvine. London: John Murray, 1907. v. 1, pp. 63–4.

74  Ovington, op. cit., pp. 262–4.

75  Edward Ives. *A voyage from England to India.* London: Edward and Charles Dilly, 1773. pp. 32–3.

76  Valentia, op. cit., v. 2, pp. 187–9.

77  Maria Graham, op. cit., pp. 216–22.

78  Williams, op. cit., pp. 287–8.

79  Thomas Twining. *Travels in India.* London: James R. Osgood, 1893. pp. 463–7.

80  Godfrey Charles Mundy, op. cit., pp. 41–3.

81  Massie, op. cit., v. 2, pp. 151–4.

82  W. W. W. Humbley. *Journal of a cavalry officer.* London: Longman, Brown, Green & Longmans, 1854. pp. 354–5.

83  William Henry Sleeman. *A journey through the kingdom of Oudh.* 2 vols. London: Richard Bentley, 1858. v. 2, pp. 84–6.

84  F. Schurr. *The Experiences of a landholder and indigo planter in Eastern Bengal.* Aberdeen: John Smith, 1859. pp. 43–4.

85  Fraser, op. cit., pp. 185–6.

86  Hooker, op. cit., v. 1, pp. 128–32.

87  James Forsyth. *The highlands of Central India.* London: Champan & Hall, 1872. pp. 6–9.

88  Louis Rousselet. *India and its native princes.* Ed. by Lt. Col. Buckle. London: Chapman & Hall, 1875. pp. 543–5.

89  Donald Macintyre. *Hindu koh: wanderings and wild sport on and beyond Himalayas.* London: William Blackwood, 1889. pp. 74–5.

90  Ethel St. Clair Grimwood. *My three years in Manipur and escape from the recent mutiny.* London: Richard Bentley, 1891. pp. 14–16.

91  Ives, op. cit., pp. 47–8.

92  Reginald Heber. *Narrative of a journey through the Upper Provinces of India from Calcutta to Bombay, 1824–25.* 3rd. ed. 3 vols. London: John Murray, 1828. v. 2, p. 225.

93  *Anglo-Indian domestic sketch: A letter from on artist in India, to his mother in England.* Calcutta: Thacker, 1849. pp. 78–88.

94  Christina S. Bremner. *A month in a Dandi: A woman's wanderings in northern India.* London: Simpkin, Marshall, etc., 1891. pp. 52–3.

95  Ovington, op. cit., pp. 210–13.

96  Forbes, op. cit., v. 2, pp. 465–7.

97  James Tod. *Travels in western India.* London: Smith, Elder, 1829–32. pp. 383–5.

98 .  Godfrey Charles Mundy, *op. cit.,* v. 2, pp. 237–8.

99  William Butler. *The land of the Veda.* 5th ed. New York: Nelson and Phillips, 1873. pp. 192–7.

100  John David Rees. *Narrative of a tour in India made by His Excellency Lord Connemara.* London: Kegan Paul, Trench, Trubner, 1892. pp. 244–5.

101 T. G. Fraser. *Record of sport and military life in Western India.* London: W. H. Allen, 1881. pp. 34–5.

102 Edward Braddon. *Thirty years of shikar.* Edinburgh: William Blackwood, 1895. pp. 338–9.

103 E. F. Burton. *Reminiscenes of sport in India.* London: W. H. Allen, 1885. pp. 15–16.

104 Mark Twain, op. cit., v. 2, p. 226.

105 Edward Moor. *Hindu pantheon.* London: J. Johnson, 1810. pp. 352–3.

105a Literary Society of Bombay. *Transactions.* London: Longman, Hurst, Rees, Orme, and Brown, 1819. pp. 161–2, 177–80.

106 Rousselet, op. cit., pp. 396–7.

107 John Malcolm. *A memoir of central India, including Malwa, and adjoining provinces* ...London: Bentley, 1823. 2 vols. v. 1, 427–32, 461–2.

108 Maria Grahm, *Journal of a residence in India, op. cit.,* pp. 134–5.

109 Braddon, op. cit., pp. 334–6.

110 Rousselet, op. cit., pp. 438–40.

111 Arnold, op. cit., pp. 82–4.

111a Monserrate, op. cit., p. 175.

112 Maria Graham. *Journal of a residence in India,* op. cit. p. 134.

113 Heber, op. cit., p. 134.

114 Sleeman: *Rambles and recollections, op. cit., v. 1, pp. 1–2.*

115 Acland, op. cit., pp. 49–50.

116 Parkes, op. cit., v. 1, pp. 426–7.

117 John William Kaye. *India: ancient and modern.* London: Day and Son, 1867. p. 100.

118 Charles E. Gover. *The folksongs of southern India.* London: Trubner & Co., 1872. p. 269.

119 Rousselet, op. cit., pp. 28–9.

120 Purchas, op. cit., v. 10, p. 173.

121 Ibid., v. 9, p. 43.

122 Ovington, pp. cit., p. 191.

123 A Deare. *A tour through the upper provinces of Hindostan.* London: C. &. J. Rivington, 1823. pp. 164–9.

124 Sleeman: *Rambles and recollections, op. cit., v. 1, pp. 50–1.*

125 Parkes, op. cit., v. 1. pp. 420–6.

126 Heber, op. cit., v. 2, p. 433.

127 Tod, *Annals and antiquities of Rajasthan,* op. cit., v. 2, pp. 623–4.

128 Parkes, op. cit., pp. 428–9.

129 Sleeman: *Rambles and recollections,* op. cit., v. 2, pp. 239–41.

130 Francois Bernier. *Travels in the Mogul empire.* London: Oxford University Press, 1916. pp. 248–9.

131 Charles Richard Francis. *Sketches of native life in India.* London: Meldola, Calin & Co., 1848. pp. 4–5.

132 F. F. Wyman. *From Calcutta to the snowy range.* London: Tinsley, 1866. pp. 187–8.

133    Kaye, op. cit., p. 79.
134    Hiuen Tsiang, op. cit., v. 2, pp. 141–2.
135    Purchas, op. cit., v. 9, pp. 37–38.
136    Manucci, op. cit., v. 3, pp. 71–3.
137    Henry George Briggs. *The cities of Gujarashtra* . . .Bombay: The Author, n.d. pp. 127–31.
138    Thomas Duer Broughton. *Letters written in a Mahratta camp during the year 1809*. Westminster: Archibald Constable, 1892. pp. 24–5.
139    Hervey, op. cit., v. 2, pp. 108–10.
140    Bremner, op. cit., pp. 192–94, 198–200, 201–03.
141    Acland, op. cit., p. 27.
142    Bremner, op. cit., pp. 194–95.
143    Forbes, op. cit. v. 1, pp. 392–93.
144    Bacon, op. cit. v. 2, pp. 181–82.
145    Emily Eden. op. cit., p. 275.
146    W. H. Sleeman: *Ramaseeana; or a vocabulary of the peculiar language used by the Thugs*. Calcutta: Military Orphan Press, 1836. pp. 330–2.
147    A. H. E. Boileau. *Miscellaneous writings in prose and verse*. Calcutta: W. Thacker & Co., 1845. pp. 204–6.
148    Sleeman: *Ramaseeana, or a vocabulary of the peculiar language used by the Thugs*. Calcutta: Military orphan Press, 1836. pp. 107–10.
149    Sleeman: *Rambles and recollections,* op. cit., v. 1, pp. 304–5.
150    Mark Twain, op. cit., pt. 2, pp. 122–4.
151    William Crooke. *Things Indian*. London: John Murray, 1906. pp. 473–7.
151a   Manucci, op. cit. v. 2, pp. 5–6.
152    Sleeman: *Rambles and recollections*, v. 2., pp. 114–16.
153    Frederic J. Mouat. *Prison system of India*. National Association of the Promotion of Social Sciences, 1872. pp. 13–19.
154    Rousselet, op. cit., pp. 113–14.
155    Rees, op. cit., pp. 334–5.
155a   Monserrate, op. cit., pp. 209–10.
156    Purchas, op. cit., v. 9, pp. 47–8.
157    Forbes, op. cit., v. 2, pp. 316–20.
158    James Baillie Fraser. *Journal of a tour through* . . .London: Rodwell & Martiny, 1820. p. 335.
159    Tod: *Travels in western India*, op. cit., pp. 66–7.
160    Edward Jewitt Robinson, *Tamil wisdom*. London: Wesleyan Conference Office, 1873. pp. 138–41.
161    Rousselet, op. cit.. p. 418.
162    Arnold: *India revisited*, op. cit., pp. 86–8.
163    A. H. L. Fraser, op. cit., pp. 339–43.
164    Joachin Hayward Stocqueler. *The handbook of India*. 2nd ed. London: W. H. Allen, 1845. pp. 88–9.

165     George Campbell. *Modern India: a sketch of the system of civil government*. London: John Murray, 1852. pp. 253–4.

166     Jean de Thevenot. *The travels of Monsieur de Thevenot into the Levant*. 3 parts. London: Printed by H. Clark, 1687, Pt. 3, pp. 100–1.

167     *An account of the gallant defence made at Mangalore in the East Indies* ...London: C. Bathurst, 1786. pp. 107–8.

168     Sleeman: *Rambles and recollections*, op. cit. v. 2, pp. 90–1.

169     Frederick John Shore. *Notes on Indian affairs*. 2 vols. London: John W. Parker, 1837. v. 2, pp. 414–20.

170     Eden, op. cit., pp. 112–13.

171     Sleeman: *Rambles and recollections,* op. cit., v. 2, pp. 451–4.

172     Lyall, op. cit., pp. 11–13.

173     Hiuen Tsiang, op cit., v. 3, pp. 385.

174     Sachu; op. cit., v. 1, pp. 170–1, 172–3, 182.

175     Sleeman: *Rambles and recollections,* op. cit., v. 2, pp. 283–4.

176     Maitland, op. cit., pp. 257–9.

177     Kaye, op. cit., pp. 22–3.

178     Rousselet, op. cit.; pp. 523.

179     Ivan Pavlovich Minayeff. *Travels in and diaries of India and Burma*. Tr. by Hirendranath Sanyal. Calcutta: Eastern Trading Co., n.d. pp. 83.

180     Sachu; op. cit., v. 2, pp. 149–50.

181     Purchas, op. cit., v. 3, pp. 174–75.

182     Ibid., v. 4, pp. 296–7.

183     G. A. Prinsep. *Remarks on the external commerce and exchanges of Bengal with appendix of accounts and estimates*. London: Kingsbury, Parbury & Allen, 1823. pp. 33–5.

184     Sleeman: *Rambles and recollections*, op. cit., v. 2, pp. 143.

185     Mundy, op. cit., v. 2, pp. 206–7.

186     Massie, op. cit., v. 1, pp. 206–8.

187     W. P. Andrew. *The Indus and its provinces*. London: W. H. Allen, 1858. pp. 174–6.

188     McCrindle, op. cit., pp. 69–70.

189     Hiuen Tsiang, op. cit., v. 2, pp. 140–1.

190     Sachu, op. cit., pp. 179–80.

191     Ibid. v. 2, pp. 151–2.

192     Manucci, op. cit., v. 3, pp. 37–8.

193     James Baillie Fraser, op. cit., pp. 500–1.

194     Sleeman: *Rambles and recollections*, op. cit., pp. 132–3.

195     Gover, op. cit., pp. 146.

196     McCrindle, op. cit., pp. 221–2.

197     Purchas, op. cit., v. 9, pp. 33.

198     Deare, op. cit., pp. 239–41.

199     Forbes, op. cit., v. 1, p. 80.

200     Heber, op. cit., v. 1, p. 359.

201     Hervey, op. cit., v. 2, pp. 209–11.

202      Acland, op. cit., pp. 40–1.

203      Ibid., pp. 146–47.

204      Wyman, op. cit., pp. 88–9.

205      Rousselet, op. cit., pp. 130–1.

206      Philip Baldaeus. *A true and exact description of the most celebrated East India coasts of Málabar and Coromandel, etc.* Amesterdam: Henry Lintot and John Oborn, 1672. v. 3, p. 598.

206a      *Essays by the students of the College of Fort William in Bengal to which are added the theses pronounced at the public disputations in the oriental languages on the 6th February, 1802.* Calcutta: Printed at the Honorable Company's Press, 1802. pp. 220–8.

207      Massie, op. cit., v. 1, pp. 268–70.

208      Leopold von Orlich. *Travels in India, including Sinde and the Punjab*, 2 vols. London: Longman, Brown, Green & Longmans, 1845. v. 1, p. 97.

209      Hervey, op. cit., v. 2, pp. 202–4.

210      Minayeff, op. cit., p. 200.

211      Purchas, op. cit. v. 10, p. 256.

212      Bernier, op. cit., pp. 254–6.

213      Ovington, op. cit., p. 144.

214      Broughton, op. cit., p. 45.

215      Forbes, op. cit., v. 1, p. 375.

216      William Taylor. *Sketches illustrating the manners and customs of the Indians and Anglo-Indians.* London: Thomas McLean, 1842. plate 6.

217      Francis, op. cit., p. 12.

218      Rousselet, op cit., p. 8.

219      E. H. Aitkin. *Behind the bungalow.* 14th ed. London: W. Thacker, 1932. pp. 130–5.

220      Ibid., pp. 150–59.

221      Pedro Teixeira. *Travels of Pedro Teixeira.* Tr. and annoted by William F. Sinclair. London: The Hakluyt Society, 1902. (Hakluyt Society, 2nd ser., v. 9) p: 198.

222      Purchas, op. cit., v. 4, p. 305.

223      Bernier, op. cit., pp. 292–3.

224      Abbe Carre. *The travels of Abbe Carre in India and Near East.* Tr. by Lady Fawcett and edited by Sir Chalres Fawcett. London: The Hakluyt Society, 1947. v. 1, pp. 153–5.

225      John Burnell. *Bombay in the days of Queen Anne. With an intro.* and notes by Samuel T. Sheppard. London: The Hakluyt Society, 1933. (The Hakluyt Society, 2nd ser. no. 72) pp. 151–2.

226      Forbes, op. cit., v. 1, pp. 257–8.

227      Fitzclarence, op. cit., p. 191.

228      Sleeman: *Rambles and recollections, op. cit.*, v. 1, pp. 267–9.

229      Parkes, op. cit., v. 2, p. 62.

230      Humbley, op. cit., p. 437.

231      Rousselet, op. cit., pp. 524–6.

232    Purchas, op. cit., v. 10, pp. 253–54.
233    Teixeira, op. cit., pp. 231–2.
234    Marshall. op. cit., pp. 319–20.
235    Ives, op. cit., pp. 53–4.
236    T. A. Wise. *Commentary on the Hindu system of medicine*. Calcutta: Thacker & Co., 1845. pp. 430–1.
237    T. G. Fraser, op. cit., pp. 34–5.
238    William Campbell Maclean. *Diseases of tropical climates*. London: Macmillan & Co., 1886. pp. 78–9.
239    Arnold: *India revisited*, op. cit., pp. 137–40.
240    Sachu, op. cit., pp. 211–12.
241    Manucci, op. cit., v. 1, pp. 224, 228–9.
242    Bernier, op. cit., pp. 339–40.
243    Forbes, op. cit., v. 4, pp. 87–8.
244    Rousselet, op. cit., p. 105.
245    Varthema, op. cit., pp. 64–5.
246    Purchas, op. cit., v. 10, pp. 91–92.
247    Ibid., p. 262
248    Peter Mundy. *The travels of Peter Mundy in Europe and Asia*. Ed. by Sir Richard Carnac. London: The Hakluyt Society, 1919. v. 3, pt. 1, pp. 56–8.
249    Hooker, op. cit., v. 1, pp. 83–4.
250    Leopold Paget. *Camp and cantonment*. London: Longman, Green, Longman & Green, 1865, p. 101.
251    Clements Robert Markham. *Travels in Peru and India*. London: John Murray, 1862. pp. 377–8.
252    Nina Elizabeth Mazuchelli. *The Indian Alps*. London: Longman, Green, 1876. pp. 479–81.
253    William T. Hornaday. *Two years in the jungle*. London: Kegan Paul, 1885. pp. 106–7.
254    G. W. MacGeorge. *Ways and works in India*. Westminster: Archibald Constale & Co., 1894. p. 109.
255    McCrindle, op. cit., p. 217.
256    Purchas, op. cit., v. 9, pp. 17–18.
257    Jean Baptiste Tavernier. *Travels in India*. Tr. by V. Ball. 2 vols. London: Macmillan & Co., 1889. v. 1, pp. 275–6.
258    Thomas Williamson. *Oriental field sports*. 2 vols. 2nd ed. London: H. R. Young, 1819. v. 2, pp. 50–1.
259    Francis Hamilton. *An account of the fishes found in the river Ganges and its branches*. 2 vols. London: Constable, 1822. p. 244.
260    Heber, op. cit., v. 3, p. 67.
261    Edward Nicholson. *Indian snakes*. Madras: Higginbotham & Co., 1874. pp. 132, 135–6.
262    Allan Hume and C. H. T. Marshall. *Game birds of India, Burmah and Ceylon*. 3 vols. Calcutta: The Author, 1888–91. v. 1, pp. 105–6.
263    Hornady, op. cit., p. 55.

264 Macintyre, op. cit., pp. 118–19.

265 Ibid., pp. 28–29.

266 E. H. Aitkin. *The tribes of my frontier.* 4th ed. Calcutta: Thacker, Spink, 1890. pp. 196–8, 204–6.

267 Ibid., pp. 2–10.

268 Braddon, op. cit., pp. 195–6.

269 Hodges, op. cit., pp. 151–2, 53.

270 Vincent A. Smith. *A history of fine art in India and Ceylon.* Oxford: The Clarendon Press, 1911. pp. 330–1.

271 Ibid., p. 454.

272 McCrindle, op. cit., pp. 219–20.

273 Nikiton, op. cit., p. 112.

274 Manucci, op. cit., v. 3, pp. 38–40.

275 Deare, op. cit., pp. 183–4.

276 James Baillie Fraser, op. cit., pp. 348–9.

277 Alexander Burnes. *Travels into Bokhara.* 3 vols. London: John Murray, 1834. v. 1, p. 61.

278 Acland, op. cit., p. 31.

279 Forbes, op. cit., v. 2, pp. 477–8.

280 Bacon, op. cit., v. 1, pp. 322–4.

281 Braddon, op. cit., pp. 339–40.

282 J. C. Murray-Aynseley. *Our tour in Southern India.* London: F. V. White, 1883. pp. 159–62.

283 Nikitin, op. cit., p. 116.

284 Purchas, op. cit., v. 10, pp. 105–6.

285 Tavernier, op. cit., v. 1, pp. 137–8.

286 Baldaus, op. cit., v. 3, p. 593.

287 Forbes, op. cit., v. 3, p. 111.

288 Ibid., pp. 84–5.

289 Parkes, op. cit., v. 1, pp. 384–5.

290 Manucci, op. cit., v. 3, pp. 41–6.

291 Edward C. Archer. *Tours in Upper India and in parts of the Himalayan mountains.* 2 vols. London: Richard Bentley, 1833. v. 1, pp. 101–2.

292 Anglo-Indian domestic sketch, op. cit., pp. 24–8.

293 Aitkin: *Behind the bungalow*, op. cit., pp. 46–52.

294 *Asiatic Researches; or, transactions of the society instituted in Bengal for inquiry into the history and antiquities, and the art, sciences and literature of Asia.* 6 vols. London: J. Swell, 1801, v. 1, pp. 66–8.

295 William Moorcroft and George Trebeck. *Travels in the Himalayan provinces of Hindustan* ...2 vols. London: John Murray, 1841. pp. 13–14.

296 John Hobart Caunter. *The oriental annual.* London: Edward Bull, 1834. pp. 61, 66–7.

297 John Butler. *Travels and adventures in the province of Assam.* London: Smith, Elder, 1855. pp. 220–3.

298     Hiuen Tsiang, op. cit., v. 2, pp. 132–3.
299     Purchas, op. cit., v. 4, p. 443.
300     Home. *Select views in Mysore.* London: Bowler, 1794. p. 9.
301     Deare, op. cit., pp. 172–3.
302     Graham: *Journal of a residence in India,* op. cit., pp. 63–65.
303     Thomas and William Daniell. *Oriental scenery.* London: The Author, 1814, v. 1, plate 9.
304     Tod: *Annals and antiquities,* op. cit., pp. 706–8.
305     Robert Elliot. *Views in the East.* 2 vols. London: H. Fisher, Son & Co., 1833. v. 1, n.p.
306     Francis Egerton. *Journal of a winter's tour in India.* 2 vols. London: John Murray, 1852. v. 2, pp. 136–8.
307     Kaye, op. cit., pp. 2–3, 3–4.
308     Butler, op. cit., pp. 139–40.
309     McCrindle, op. cit., p. 56.
310     Manucci, op. cit., v. 1, pp. 191–2.
311     Daniel Johnson. *Sketches of Indian field sports.* 2nd ed. London: Robert Jennings, 1827. pp. 148–9, 153–4.
312     William Jones. *The works of Sir William Jones.* Comp. by Lord Teignmouth. London: John Stockdale, etc., 1807. v. 4, pp. 323–4, 324–6, 327–9.
313     Williamson, op. cit., v. 2, pp. 230–2.
314     *Oriental Sporting Magazine* from June 1828 to June 1833. London: Henry S. King & Co., 1873. v. 1, pp. 397–8.
315     Ibid., v. 2, pp. 107–8.
316     Ibid., p. 174.
317     Ibid., p. 333.
318     Braddon, op. cit., pp. 61–4.
319     H. A. Leveson. *The hunting grounds of the old world.* 2nd ed. London: Saunders, Otley & Co., 1860. pp. 243–4.
320     William Rice. *Tiger shooting in India.* London: Smith, Elder & Co., 1857. pp. 180–1.
321     J. H. Baldwin. *The large and small game of Bengal and the North Western Provinces of India.* 2nd. ed. London: Kegan Paul, Trench, 1883. pp. 159–60.
322     Ibid., pp. 140–1.
323     G. P. Sanderson. *Thirteen years among the wild beasts of India.* 2nd ed. London: W. H. Allen & Co., 1879. pp. 357–8.
324     Sainthill Eardley-Wilmont. *Forest life and sport in India.* London: Edward Arnold, 1910. pp. 66–68.
325     Edward B Baker. *Sport in Bengal.* London: Ledger, Smith & Co., 1887. pp. 254–5.
326     F. E. S. Adair. *A summer in High Asia.* London: W. Thacker & Co., 1899. pp. 147–9.
326a    Literary Society of Bombay., op. cit., pp. 309–11.
327     Colebrooke, op. cit., pp. 58–60.
328     Parkes, op. cit., v. 1, p. v.

329     Horace Hayman Wilson. *Select specimens of the theatre of the Hindus.* 2 vols. 2nd. ed. London: Parbury Allen & Co., 1835. pp. xxiii-xxvi.

330     Ralph T. H. Griffith. *The birth of the war god.* 2nd. ed. London: Trubner & Co., 1879. pp. vii-viii.

330a     Monier Williams, tr. *Sakoontala; or, The lost ring—an Indian drama, translated into English prose and verse from the Sanskrit of Kalidasa.* Hertford: Stephen Austin, 1855. pp. xii-xiii, xiv-xv, xvi-xx.

330b     George A. Grierson. *The modern vernacular literature of Hindustan.* Calcutta: Asiatic Society, 1889. pp. xvi, xvii-xviii, xix-xx, xx-xxi.

331     Valentia, op. cit., v. 2, pp. 107–8

332     Forbes, op. cit., v. 1, pp. 12–13.

333     Bacon, op. cit., v. 1, p. 174.

334     Hervey, op. cit., v. 1, pp. 27–9.

335     Rees, op. cit., p. 177.

336     McCrindle, op. cit., pp. 66–7.

337     Fah Hian and Sung-Yun, op. cit., pp. 103–4, 104–6, 107–9.

338     Ibn Batuta. *Travels in Asia and Africa, 1325–54.* Tr. by H. A. R. Gibb. London: George Routledge & Sons, 1929. pp. 194–5.

339     Nikitin, op. cit., pp. 112–13.

340     Varthema, op. cit., pp. 50–1.

341     Purchas, op. cit., v. 10, pp. 173–4.

342     Baldaeus, op. cit., v. 3, p. 520.

343     Tod: *Annals and antiquities.* op. cit., v. 1, pp. 709–10.

344     Kaye, op. cit., p. 38.

345     Edward Lear. *Indian journal.* Ed. by Ray Murphy. London: Jarrolds, 1953. pp. 99–101.

346     Paul Deussen. *My Indian reminiscences.* Tr. by A. King. Madras: G. A. Nateson, 1893. pp. 167–8.

347     James Baillie Fraser, op. cit., pp. 214–15. 217–18.

348     Sleeman: *Rambles and Recollections,* op. cit., v. 1, pp. 288–90.

349     Hervey, op. cit., v. 2, pp. 282–3.

350     Daniell, op. cit., v. 2, plate 21.

351     Ibid., plate 2.

352     Heber, op. cit., v. 1, pp. 245–7.

353     Robert Melville Grindlay. *Scenery, costumes and architecture.* 3 parts. London: Smith, Elder & Co., 1826. part 3, n.p.

354     Burnes, op. cit., v. 3, p. 49.

355     Tod: *Annals and antiquities,* op. cit., p. 682.

356     Bacon, op. cit., v. 2, pp. 99–101.

357     Tod: *Travels in Western India,* op. cit., pp. 50–1.

358     Grindlay, op. cit., n.p.

359     Parkes, op. cit., v. 2, pp. 272–4.

360     Hooker, op. cit., v. 2, pp. 24–5.

361     Andrew Leith Adams. *Wanderings of an naturalist in India.* Edinburgh: Edmonston, 1867. pp. 62–3.

363     Forsyth, op. cit., pp. 81–4.
363     Burton, op. cit., pp. 415–16.
364     Macintyre, op. cit., pp. 456–8.
365     James Baillie Fraser, op. cit., pp. 492–3.
366     Ibid., p. 260.
367     Archer, op. cit., v. 1, pp. 40–2.
368     Sleeman: *Rambles and recollections*, op. cit., v. 1, pp. 18–20.
369     Hooker, op. cit., v. 1, pp. 148–50.
370     William Howard Russell. *My diary in India.* 2 vols. London: Routledge, Warne and Routledge, 1860. v. 1, pp. 269–70.
371     Kaye, op. cit., p. 27
372     Chaunter, op. cit., pp. 6–10.
373     Bacon, op. cit., v. 1, pp. 159–61.
374     Hervey, op. cit., v. 3, pp. 117–22.
375     Sleeman: *Rambles and recollections*, op. cit., v. 2, pp. 12–14.
376     Deare, op. cit., pp. 227–9.
377     James Welsh. *Military reminiscences.* 2nd ed. 2 vols. London: Smith, Elder, 1830. v. 2, pp. 1–3.
378     Caunter, op. cit., pp. 227–9.
379     Henry Edward Fane. *Five years in India.* 2 vols. London: Henry Colburn, 1842. v. 2, pp. 72–78.
380     Fah-Hian and Sung-Yun, op. cit., pp. 127–30
381     Hiuen Tsiang, op. cit., v. 3, pp. 312–13.
381     Monserrate, op. cit., pp. 74–77.
382     Mohammed Kasim Ferishta. *Ferishta's history of the Dekkan from the first Mahummedan conquests.* Tr. by J. Scott. 2 vols. Shrewsbury: J. Scott, 1794. v. 1, pp. 187–9.
383     Bernier, op. cit., pp. 89–92.
384     Ovington, op. cit., pp. 239–42.
385     William Hickey. *Memoirs of William Hickey.* Edited by Alfred Spencer. 4 vols. London: Hurst & Blackett, 1925. v. 4, pp. 212–17.
396     Ibid., v. 4, pp. 378–9.
387     Malcolm. op. cit. v. 2, pp. 264–5.
388     Tod: *Travels in Western India*, op. cit., pp. 490–1.
389     Joseph Fayrer. *Recollections of my life.* Edinburgh: William Blackwood & Sons, 1900. pp. 164–7.
390     Lyall, op. cit., pp. 21–22.
391     Minayeff, op. cit., pp. 98–100.

# INDEX